12 February 2005

# RUSSIAN ORTHODOXY
## ON THE EVE
## OF REVOLUTION

The Frank S. and Elizabeth D. Brewer
Prize of the American Society of Church History

# RUSSIAN ORTHODOXY
# ON THE EVE
# OF REVOLUTION

## VERA SHEVZOV

OXFORD
UNIVERSITY PRESS

2004

# OXFORD
UNIVERSITY PRESS

Oxford   New York
Auckland   Bangkok   Buenos Aires   Cape Town   Chennai
Dar es Salaam   Delhi   Hong Kong   Istanbul   Karachi   Kolkata
Kuala Lumpur   Madrid   Melbourne   Mexico City   Mumbai   Nairobi
São Paulo   Shanghai   Taipei   Tokyo   Toronto

Copyright © 2004 by Oxford University Press, Inc.

Published by Oxford University Press, Inc.
198 Madison Avenue, New York, New York 10016

www.oup.com

Oxford is a registered trademark of Oxford University Press

Library of Congress Cataloging-in-Publication Data
Shevzov, Vera.
Russian Orthodoxy on the eve of revolution / Vera Shevzov.
p.   cm.
Includes bibliographical references and index.
ISBN 0-19-515465-7
1.  Russkaia pravoslavnaia tserkov'—History.   2.  Russia—Church history—1801–1917.
3.  Laity—Russkaia pravoslavnaia tserkov'—History.   I. Title.
BX491.S54 2003
281.9'47'09041—dc21   2002042510

1 3 5 7 9 8 6 4 2

Printed in the United States of America
on acid-free paper

For my husband and children—John, Nina, and Anya—

and my parents—Nina and Theodore

‹—➤◉⊂—›

# ACKNOWLEDGMENTS

Like many of the icons I write about, books, too, have their stories. The story of this book is a long one that began in 1988, when, during my years in graduate school at Yale University, I spent a year and a half at the St. Petersburg (then Leningrad) Theological Academy. Since then, I have met many people who have assisted and encouraged me in my efforts and thereby contributed to this book's making. I am pleased finally to move my gratitude from the transient field of oral history to the more permanent written word.

When I began working on this project, Gregory Freeze encouraged me to take on a local study. Considering that it was still before the fall of the Soviet Union, his proposal was challenging. It was difficult enough for foreign scholars to get themselves settled in Moscow or St. Petersburg in order to work in central archives, to which they did not always receive full access. The bureaucratic maze through which one would have to pass to get to the provinces for any lengthy stay seemed too complicated to take on. The time I spent at the Leningrad Theological Academy did much to further the biblio-graphical and archival work that made my future research more productive. I thank the St. Petersburg Theological Academy, and Fr. Michael Roshak, for making my stay possible. I thank Metropolitan Kiril (Gundiaev) and the office of External Affairs of the Moscow Patriarchate, as well as the former dean of the Academy, Fr. Vladimir Sorokin, for accommodating me. The late deacon Andrei Chizhov and Fr. Markell Vetrov facilitated travel and permissions. I am also grateful to Alexander Anatol'ievich Alexeev, who aided me in obtain-ing archival access in the years when such access was still a problem. Thanks to him, I was able not only to work in archives in St. Petersburg but also to make my first trip to a provincial archive, namely, the one in Kursk. Although that archive turned out not to house the types of sources that I was seeking, I was grateful for the opportunity to meet several wonderful people in Kursk and to witness Orthodoxy as it was being lived at the grassroots. I thank the bishop of Kursk, Iuvenalii, for the hospitality he extended during that trip.

Things changed considerably in the two years that passed from my stay at the Theological Academy to the year of research on a grant from the Interna-tional Research and Exchanges Board in 1991–92. In particular, the failed coup against Mikhail Gorbachev in August 1991 paved the way for a more open society, one in which access to archives became less complicated and less guarded. Serafima Igorevna Varekova at the Russian State Historical Archive and Valentina Petrovna Ivanova of the Russian Museum of Ethnography, which houses the invaluable Tenishev archive, facilitated my research in these two archives. In terms of regional work, I had decided to focus my research on the diocese of Vologda, since its archival holdings were reputedly very good and indeed turned out to be so. B. V. Ananich of the St. Petersburg branch of the Institute of History provided crucial assistance with living arrangements in Vologda. I am also grateful to the staff of the State Archive of the Vologda Region. They accommodated me in every way possible. In Vologda itself, I could not have managed without the aid of V. A. Sablin of the Vologda Pedagogical Institute. Not only did he introduce me to Vologda and its surrounding areas but he also made my trip to Totma possible. I went there to read the diaries of a peasant, A. A. Zamaraev. Although those diaries have subsequently been published, there was a beauty in reading them in the original and in the place where A. A. wrote. I very much enjoyed the company of the staff at the Totma Regional Museum whose daily teas were a welcome break.

While the initial task of focusing on a single diocese was helpful in narrowing my source base, it became apparent to me that many of the themes and issues I was investigating reached beyond not only geographical confines but also immediate historical concerns. In particular, the topic of "popular" or "lived" Orthodoxy as I had come to understand it was really more about the Church itself and what it meant to belong to it. This was in many ways a new topic. It called for rethinking the material I had already read and for finding other sources that could further illuminate the story of the workings of that phenomenon called "church."

I embarked on several more years of research before writing the book. Serafima Igorevna at the Russian State Historical Archive assisted me in ordering copies of materials from which I could work while continuing to teach. Similarly, Olga Anatol'evna Rodionova has been instrumental in helping me with bibliographic work. At the eleventh hour, several museums and archives have helped to provide photographs. In particular, I thank Ludmila Borisovna Uritskaya from the Russian Museum of Ethnography, the staff at the Central State Archive of Cine- and Photo-Documents, the staff of the Office of Internal Book Exchange at the Russian National Library in St. Petersburg, the director of the Russian State Historical Archive in St. Petersburg, Aleksandr Rostislavovich Sokolov, and Tat'iana Aleksandrovna Kulakova, the director of Vologda's regional archive. I also thank Olga Anatol'evna Poliakova from the Kolomenskoe State Museum Reserve and Maria A. Aleksandrova from the Tretyakov Gallery. In the United States, the staff at St. Anne's Shrine in Sturbridge, Massachusetts, Gary Hollingsworth of Hollingsworth Fine Arts, and Dr. Robin Jones graciously provided photographs of icons of the Mother of God from their private collections. I also thank the staff of the Prints and Photographs Division of the Library of Congress for helping me to secure photographs from the Prokudin-Gorskii Collection.

As anyone who has spent any length of time in Russia knows, it is almost impossible to survive there on one's own. Several friends offered encouragement and help in priceless ways. Nataliia Gorelova, Sergei Zimin, Fr. Boris Pivovarov, and Olga Anatol'ieva Rodionova saw me through many difficult moments and spent time discussing my work as well. Fr. Nikolai Chemodanov, Nikolai Stepanov (now bishop Tikhon of Arkhangelsk), and Sergei Popov (now bishop Ioann of Belgorod) often creatively challenged my thinking about the phenomenon called "church." Irina Mol'skaia and Feliks Solomonik graciously shared their home with me when, during my year of research, my housing arrangements suddenly fell through. Ivan Steblin-Kamensky went out of his way to facilitate my access to the Tenishev archive at a time when access was not easy to obtain.

Mentors and colleagues here in the United States, too, have provided much appreciated support and cheer. Paul Bushkovitch, Jaroslav Pelikan, and Mark Steinberg have seen the project from its earliest stages and have offered helpful advice, often on short notice. Kosara Gavrilovic read and commented on an early draft. Paul Valliere offered invaluable comments on the book's introduction and its first chapter.

The study of Orthodoxy has been developing at a steady pace among historians of Russia. Although I have changed paths by working more in religious studies than in history per se, I am grateful for the continued collegiality of Chris Chulos, Eugene Clay, Robert Geraci, Nadieszda Kizenko, and Laurie Manchester, who were neighbors and friends during the 1991–92 IREX trip and who themselves have worked on significant aspects of Russian Orthodoxy. I have also benefited from conversations or correspondence over the years with Stephen Batalden, Heather Coleman, Nikolaos Chrissides, Laura Engelstein, Gregory Freeze, David Goldfrank, Valerie Kivelson, Eve Levin, Brenda Meehan, Roy Robson, Jennifer Spock, Olga Tsapina, William Wagner, and Christine Worobec. I extend special gratitude to Laurie Manchester not only as a constructive critic but also as a supportive and dear friend.

I also am very grateful to many people at Smith College, my intellectual home. From the members of my department to the administration, I have found only unwavering support and generosity. In particular, I would like to thank John Connolly, first dean of the faculty, then provost, and finally acting president, for regularly responding to research needs, ranging from the allocation of more resources for interlibrary loan materials to funds for research assistance and microfilming costs. I also thank the various members of the Committee on Faculty Compensation and Development, who through the years granted various forms of financial assistance for the completion of this project. The interlibrary loan staff at Smith, especially Christina Ryan and Naomi Sturtevant, have worked very hard at processing my steady flow of requests over the past years. Dick Fish and Eric Parham have helped with photographs. Mary Bellino and Ekaterina Ites helped in preparing the manuscript for publication. My colleagues Joan Afferica, Dennis Hudson, Justina Gregory, Carol Zaleski, and Lois Dubin have provided the moral support which such a project often needs. In particular, I am grateful to Carol Zaleski for looking at the manuscript and suggesting I turn to Oxford. At Oxford, I thank Cynthia Read, executive editor for Religion, for her enthusiasm for this project, and her assistant, Theo Calderara, for answering numerous questions along the way.

Various institutions outside of Smith also provided funding for research and the writing of the book. I thank the Joint Committee on the Soviet Union and its Successor States of the Social Science Research Council and the American Council of Learned Societies, the National Endowment for the Humanities, and the International Research and Exchanges Board for their generous support.

Finally, none of this could have been accomplished without the sustained love of my family. My parents, Fr. Theodore and Nina Shevzov, went beyond the call of any duty as parents in helping me complete this project. My mother in particular has essentially dedicated the past eight years of her life to helping me raise my two girls, Nina and Anya. Nina and Anya have been a source of joy throughout and I regret I will never be able to make up for the long work days and absent weekends. My husband, Dr. John Zebrun, whom I met while a student at St. Vladimir's Seminary, has been an informed critic from the start. Though a physician with his own career and concerns, he proved unwavering in his support. Not only has he listened to countless icon stories and parish-related anecdotes from prerevolutionary Russia over the past ten years but, through lively discussion, he has greatly contributed to my intellectual processing of them. Moreover, each draft along the way was subjected to his critical eye. It is to these ever-patient and caring members of my home community that I dedicate this book.

An early version of chapter 3 was previously published as "Chapels and the Ecclesial World of Prerevolutionary Russian Peasants," in *Slavic Review* 55 (fall 1996): 508–613. Parts of that article are reprinted here with permission from the American Association for the Advancement of Slavic Studies, which holds the copyright. Portions of chapter 4 appeared as "Icons, Laity, and Authority in the Russian Orthodox Church, 1861–1917," in *Russian Review* 58 (January 1999): 26–48; and as "Icons, Miracles, and Orthodox Communal Identity in Late Imperial Russia," in *Church History: Studies in Christianity and Culture* 69: 3 (September 2000): 610–31. I thank both journals for permission to reprint these materials.

Grateful acknowledgment is made for permission to reprint the following illustrations.

Figure 2.1: The Tretyakov Gallery, Moscow
Figure 2.2: The Russian Museum of Ethnography, St. Petersburg
Figure 2.3: Prokudin-Gorskii Collection, Library of Congress

Figure 2.4: Frank and Frances Carpenter Collection, Library of
    Congress
Figure 3.1: Prokudin-Gorskii Collection, Library of Congress
Figure 3.2: Prokudin-Gorskii Collection, Library of Congress
Figure 3.3: The Russian Museum of Ethnography, St. Petersburg
Figure 3.4: The Russian Museum of Ethnography, St. Petersburg
Figure 3.5: The Russian Museum of Ethnography, St. Petersburg
Figure 3.6: Vologda State Regional Archive
Figure 3.7: The Russian National Library, St. Petersburg
Figure 3.8: The Russian Museum of Ethnography, St. Petersburg
Figure 4.1: Central State Archive of Cine-, Photo-, and Phono-
    Documents, St. Petersburg
Figure 5.1: The Russian State Historical Archive, St. Petersburg
Figure 5.2: Private collection of Robin R. Jones, M.D
Figure 5.5: The Russian Museum of Ethnography, St. Petersburg
Figure 5.6: Tretyakov Gallery, Moscow
Figure 5.7: The Russian State Historical Archive
Figure 6.2: Private collection of Robin R. Jones, M.D
Figure 6.3: The St. Anne Shrine Icon Museum, Sturbridge, Mass.
Figure 6.4: The Russian State Historical Archive
Figure 6.5: Central State Archive of Cine-, Photo-, and Phono-
    Documents, St. Petersburg
Figure 6.6: Collection of the Kolomenskoe State Museum-Preserve
Figure 6.7: Private collection of Gary Hollingsworth, Hollingsworth
    Fine Arts, Orlando, Fl.
Figure 6.8: Tretyakov Gallery, Moscow
Figure 6.9: The Russian State Historical Archive.

# CONTENTS

## CONCLUSION

## NOTES

## BIBLIOGRAPHY

## INDEX

# RUSSIAN ORTHODOXY
## ON THE EVE
## OF REVOLUTION

# Introduction

The body is one and has many members, and all
the members of the body, though many, are one body.

—1 Corinthians 12:12

This book is about sacred community, and how it "worked" (or sometimes did not) in Russian Orthodoxy before the fateful historic events of 1917.

The matter of community has been central to Christianity from its very inception. As the Russian Orthodox theologian and historian Georges Florovsky has noted about the early Christian experience, "to be a Christian meant just to belong to the community. Nobody could be a Christian by himself, as an isolated individual, but only together with 'the brethren,' in a togetherness with them."[1] Despite its significance, the issue of community in Christianity—its nature and patterns—was the subject of relatively little systematic reflection until modern times. The communal aspect of Christianity was, as Yves Congar put it, a reality that was "lived" rather than theologized and dogmatized.[2] When the subject arose, it usually did so in the context of crisis. Christian thinking about the nature of the Christian community—its purpose and vision, the character and meaning of the relationships among its members, and its organizational forms—intensified when the normative ways of that communal life were challenged socially, politically, or philosophically. So it was in the mid–first century when the apostle Paul wrote to the Christian communities in Corinth and Philippi. So it was again in the second and third centuries when Irenaeus of Lyons and Cyprian of Carthage faced the fallout from the challenges of gnosticism and persecutions, and again thereafter during the course of the medieval and early modern periods.

The sixteenth-century Reformation marked a watershed in the history of Christian thinking about community. Before that time, Christian thinkers were preoccupied mainly with the identity of Christ and theological anthropology, but in the modern age they turned their attention to the nature and definition of communal Christian identity.[3] In particular, Martin Luther's emphasis on the teaching of the "priesthood of all believers" unleashed what some scholars have termed "the emancipation of lay persons."[4] Despite his own rethinking of the matter in light of the Peasants' Revolt in 1525, Luther's protest against the division of clergy and laity into "spiritual" and "secular" classes within the Christian community echoed long after his death. This protest, combined with post-Enlightenment developments in democratic social and political thinking, drew further attention to the definition and role of the lay person in the Christian community and, perhaps more significantly, to believers' own sense of belonging to the "body of Christ." Such developments constituted a challenge that struck at the heart of the issue of religious authority—an issue that both Protestants and Catholics would have to confront (or choose to avoid) throughout the nineteenth century, and that contributed to the unprecedented interest among Western Christian thinkers in the late nineteenth and early twentieth centuries in the nature of the Church.[5]

Eastern Orthodox Christianity, especially as it had taken root in Russia, had not remained untouched by these trends. An example of the kinds of concerns on the minds of some Russian laity can be seen in a letter sent in September 1917 by a group of believers to the members of the historic All-Russian Church Council, or *Sobor*, that was meeting in Moscow at this time (1917–18). In that letter, the believers spoke of themselves as "a union of enthusiastic supporters of the Holy faith" and offered a bold array of suggestions for church reform. They also complained that the hierarchy of the Orthodox Church in Russia had assigned to lay believers a passive role as "silent observers." But people, they argued, could not remain passive with respect to religious questions. "Religion is tied to devotional attachment, and without that attachment, the life of the community is impossible."[6]

These sentiments, which were related to notions of hierarchy, the individual, and community, were expressed in a critical year in Russia's history: 1917. This year marked both a culmination and a beginning of political and social upheaval that dramatically altered the nation's cultural contours. In a relatively short time the home of the largest Christian culture of modern times became an officially atheistic state.[7] On the eve of that violent turnaround, Orthodox churchmen perceived a complete "ecclesiastical collapse" in their midst.[8] In response, they took upon themselves the task of reconceptualizing the institutional framework of Orthodoxy based on a fresh reading of their corporate past. In the process, they became embroiled in heated debates over the principles that governed and defined the Orthodox community's internal life and organization—debates that in many ways were analogous to those of the Reformation and later Vatican II. Associated with the modernization that Russia was experiencing, these debates focused in large measure on the issues of lay authority in the religious life and government of the Church.

This historical moment marked a crescendo in the evolution of Orthodox Christianity in Russia. Many Orthodox Christians both in Russia and abroad continue even today to direct their gaze back to these times in deciding how to proceed in a rapidly changing world. In many ways, the period that culminated in the All-Russian Church Council of 1917 can be said to extend back roughly to 1861, when the majority of the people who constituted the Orthodox laity in Russia—the peasantry—were freed from the bonds of serfdom to direct their lives more or less on their own. With respect to the organization of their religious lives, the emancipation benefited serfs of landowners most directly, as the establishment of local parish life was no longer dependent on the disposition of the landowner. State and appanage serfs, who had become subject to less control in their day-to-day lives, were also boosted by the Great Reforms of the 1860s into a new social and political standing. Moreover, 1861–1917 was a period of intensified schooling efforts by both church and state, in which formal religious education played a part. That development, which affected both the peasantry and other social groups, combined with the heightened emphasis on the sermon in parish churches, the wider availability of devotional literature, and the establishment of rural libraries, increased the exposure of common believers to formal explications of their faith.[9]

Religious education probably had a significant impact on the sacred community. Education tended to move faith from being a matter of passive acceptance to one of conscious acceptance or rejection. In this sense, even modest educational developments undoubtedly furthered the process of religious diversification among ordinary Russians well before a 1905 law on the freedom of conscience gave official permission to act on such choices. Growing literacy and a significant increase in the availability of devotional literature fostered some degree of spiritual and religious independence, since a local cleric was no longer as necessary for the reading and interpretation of texts. Moreover, devotional literature was in large part oriented to the individual. Collections of saints' lives and guides to spiritual development, as well as booklets about the responsibilities of a Christian and the obstacles on the path toward salvation, rarely explicitly stressed the importance of the community in the Christian way. Finally, recognition of education would have made at least some churchmen more inclined to view members of their flock not merely as peasants or simply as a mass of people but as self-conscious and informed laity. From this perspective, it is not surprising that the question of the role and function of laity in the Orthodox community emerged as one of the pressing questions on the eve of the 1917 revolutions.

The social and political climate in Russia in the late nineteenth and early twentieth centuries precipitated Orthodoxy's own confrontation with "modernism." The period of history that has been termed "modern" (the beginning and ending of which are debated by historians themselves) has posed several challenges to Christianity that are in many ways connected by the issue of religious authority. In the Catholic world, reactions to these challenges are evident in several papal documents, including the 1864 *Syllabus of Errors* (*Quanta Cura*) and a 1907 papal encyclical (*Pascendi dominici gregis*) on the teachings of the "modernists." Both of these were attempts by the Vatican to shield Christianity and the Christian community from what they perceived as the threats of modernity. Among the areas that figured prominently in these documents were conceptions of the Church, the Magisterium, and the liberty of believers.[10]

Critical times in the life of a sacred community often prove revealing to those who study the dynamics of such communities. The strain in a religious community caused by larger historical movements tends to expose the seams of that community and thus affords a special opportunity to examine how it is shaped and constituted from within. This book takes as its task the examination of the religious infrastructure and communal dynamics of Orthodoxy—as it was lived and practiced in Russia in the decades preceding 1917—that affected belivers' sense of belonging. It was, after all, on this sense of belonging that the existence and fate of the community depended.

Several longstanding interests with respect to religion and to the history of Russian Orthodoxy converged to lead me to this study. One was a general curiosity about the workings of sacred communities. In particular, apart from their institutions, by what mechanisms and images do persons who claim to belong to a particular religious tradition express and maintain a sense of collective identity in any given historical period? I was also keenly interested in those historical moments when Christians focused on their collective identity. What events and broader social or cultural movements helped induce such moments, and what were their effects on the collective religious life of Christians? These broad questions were channeled by a specific, historical interest in the fate of Orthodox Christianity in the modern period, namely in its Russian manifestation. The result was a study of Orthodoxy in Russia on the eve of the 1917 revolutions, and an excursion into the archival and published sources that could tell me about Orthodoxy as it was then lived.

The question of what approach to take in studying this topic is, from a researcher's standpoint, a difficult one, both practically and conceptually. Practically speaking, the researcher is faced with a statistic of more than eighty million "official" Orthodox Christians in European Russia at this time, constituting some 85 percent of the population.[11] Most of these individuals belonged to the peasantry, although merchants, townspeople, and nobility figured prominently as well. Given the vast territory of European Russia, and the wide variety of persons included under a term like "laity," how does one go about meaningfully exploring and speaking about sacred community and in particular the patterns of its life and the people's sense of identity as Orthodox believers?

Conceptually, the study of community in Christianity inevitably leads the researcher to the term *church*. This word ultimately derived from the Greek term *kyriakon*, which meant "belonging to the Lord" and was applied to the place of worship. It is also, however, the English word used to translate the Greek word *ekklesia* (gathering, calling forth), the term early Christians used to describe themselves as a special community. The term *ekklesia* in the Septuagint was a translation of the Hebrew term that referred to the People of God—Israel—assembled in the presence of God.[12] Given the two basic meanings carried by the single English word "church"—a building and a gathering—

and the centuries of church institutional and liturgical developments that have passed, the notion of "church" has been recognized even by professional church historians in recent times as a "protean concept" whose field of study is difficult to delineate and define.[13] One scholar maintains that church history "includes everything, even, in its widest sense, the Scriptures themselves":[14] that is, it encompasses anything that could fit under the broad heading of the "history of Christianity"—liturgical rituals, iconography, music, dogma, and the lives of saints, as well as the piety of the faithful. In this broad view, the study of "church" and the study of what academically is understood by the term "religion" are inseparably intertwined.

Prior studies of church and religion within the context of Christianity in general and Orthodoxy in Russia in particular have usually proceeded along one of three basic lines. The first approach is that of traditional church history, which as a field has concerned itself primarily with episcopal activity, ecclesiastical and related state bureaucracies, and the institutional means by which sacred doctrines have been passed on to the unordained masses.[15] This has been the case especially among clerical authors since late antiquity, when ordained clergy increasingly became identified with the "sacred" while "the people" were relegated to the profane.[16] A limitation of this approach is that the thoughts and activities of lay believers have rarely figured as a prominent part of that history, which has often been written by male members of the ecclesiastical establishment. In the second half of the twentieth century, historians of the Orthodox Church became an increasingly diverse group, as was also the case with respect to historians of Protestant and Catholic churches. Confessional affiliation is no longer a given.[17] Nevertheless, the tendency to equate the study of church largely with institutional structures and with clergy and monastics has continued.[18]

The second approach is that of ecclesiology, which is a special field of theology. Drawing on scriptural as well as patristic sources, ecclesiology involves an intellectual and spiritual reflection on the nature of the Christian community, its structure and life.[19] One strength of the ecclesiological approach is that it attempts to articulate a coherent intellectual vision of the sacred community that is supposedly (or ideally) endorsed by all of its members. This vision typically includes and even embraces the laity. A weakness here, however, is that "the people" usually figure into the vision only in their idealized forms and in the roles that theologians assign them. In this approach, too, the people have generally remained voiceless.[20]

More recently, a third (and initially more secular) approach has been developed by academic social and cultural historians interested in the buried voices and practices of the common folk. While historians working in this discipline of "popular religion" have often successfully recovered the voices of the people, they have also often conceptually left these people outside the parameters of the Church to which many of them professed to belong. Studies of the general religiosity of the common folk have also tended to reinforce the notion of "church" as an entity associated with the religious "elite" or the "virtuosi." One of the byproducts of this approach has been a way of thinking that presents "the Church" and "the people" as coexisting but often opposing religious subcultures, with the Church—"the official"—on one side and whatever constitutes "the popular" on the other.[21] Until the fall of communism, this had been the case among many scholars of Orthodox Christianity in Russia as well. A strong ethnographic tradition was often combined with a methodology influenced by Marxist-Leninist principles and resulted in the study of a peasant or popular (*narodnoe*) Orthodoxy that was treated as if it had little connection to the institutional church or was a lesser form of an "official" Orthodoxy.[22]

While each of the aforementioned approaches had heuristic value in the early stages of this project, none of them would prove adequate in and of itself for the study of community and identity in Russian Orthodoxy. In the end, this complex subject matter required a more synthetic approach. Accordingly, this book is primarily concerned with the active interface between the ecclesiastical institution, the theological vision (or visions) of the community, and the so-called popular forms of devotion. My approach is to look precisely at the interplay of these three facets of the Church's existence, with an eye to convergence as well as to tensions within the Orthodox community in prerevolutionary Russia. As such, the book at times joins the work of scholars who, in following the contours of "lived religion," move beyond simple dichotomies with respect to the workings of religious cultures.[23]

When I first embarked on this study, I focused primarily on the religious beliefs and practices of "the people" and pursued this subject initially on a local level by conducting research in the regional archives of the northern diocese of Vologda. This exercise soon provided me with valuable insights. In contrast to the view that the "Holy Synod was as distant from the Russian village as the Winter Palace," I found that it was in fact much closer than one might think.[24] Orthodox lay people, especially peasant laity, were passionate about the matters they considered holy and sought assertively to manage these as they deemed fit. They actively engaged the ecclesiastical system in several ways, one of which was by boldly drafting letters and petitions to the diocesan chancery as well as to the Holy Synod. In this wealth of writings we can find their views on various aspects of ecclesial life and on their own place in that life. This book is based in large part on the reading of hundreds of such letters.

Another serendipitous finding in the local archives was that most petitions tended to cluster thematically around certain centers of religious life. Although these centers were certainly popular among large numbers of believers, they were hardly exclusive expressions of some sort of self-contained peasant Orthodoxy, a notion the data soon led me to dismiss. Identifying these major foci of religious life—local in manifestation yet universal in scope—and exploring the dynamics and tensions associated with them ultimately provided an organizational key to this project.

In light of this finding, I have chosen to organize this book around a series of sacred centers in the lives of Orthodox Christians in prerevolutionary

Russia. The book begins with an immersion in the conceptual world of Orthodoxy at that time; it takes the reader to the heart of an escalating and heated controversy among clergy and lay intellectuals who sought to identify the organizational center of church life and to define its communal order. While acknowledging the influence that political factors had on these debates, as well as the debates' deep roots in Russia's secular and religious intellectual history, I do not examine these aspects of the debates at length. I also do not present a detailed chronology of the various developments in institutional church life during this time. Indeed, each of these subjects would require a monograph of its own. Instead, my goal is to introduce readers to the competing strands of thought about church, community, and laity that existed in the late nineteenth and early twentieth centuries. Orthodox churchmen in the early twentieth century were experiencing a crisis in corporate self-understanding that continued all the way up to the All-Russian Council of 1917–18 and beyond. Neither before nor since have the very organizing principles governing ecclesial life been discussed so widely or so ardently in Orthodox circles. In the arena of theology, any resolutions of the conflicts involved could have had profound effects on the future of Russian Orthodoxy and the organization of its communal life. In addition, the various competing images of church, community, and laity presented in chapter 1 often informed and influenced that ecclesial culture in which communal worship as well as church conflict occurred during the years between 1861 and 1917.

Chapters 2 through 6 turn to those spaces, places, times, and images around which Orthodox believers frequently ordered their religious lives— parish churches, chapels, feast days, miracle-working icons, and Mary, the Birth-Giver of God (*Bogoroditsa*)—in order to explore how Orthodox communal identity was fostered and sustained. Each of these chapters pauses at a type of sacred center a point or focus around which communal attachment and conceptualization took place. In so doing, the chapters proceed along two lines. First, they trace the plexus of stories, teachings, beliefs, and, occasionally, rituals that were associated with these centers. Such cultural associations provided individual believers, both lay and clerical, with a common pool of religious narratives and historical reference points that semantically enriched their communal lives. Second, the chapters also consider the order and organizational trends of church community life and look at the complex working relations between clergy and laity. What was the nature of the tensions and contestations that arose around these centers and what understandings of church did they reveal?

This approach to the study of collective Orthodox identity demands a certain qualification of frequently used terms and notions in the study of religious cultures. First, although the study focuses on "the people," it does so in terms of self-designated believing Orthodox Christians rather than an undifferentiated Russian "folk" or "people" (*narod*). The peasantry in Russia was a religiously heterogeneous group. Different peasants identified with different faith communities, and some with none at all. Moreover, the sacred centers that I discuss were not associated exclusively with any particular class. They served as symbolic markers of sacred community for countless believers, regardless of social and economic background. In order accurately to study community in Orthodoxy, the lines of inquiry must be drawn so as to include the voices and actions of "common folk" and "elite" alike who, as *believers*, often thought about and expressed their collective Orthodox identity in similar ways. By thinking specifically about the laity (*miriane*)—persons who volitionally and actively participated in church life and who at the same time were considered part of the flock by clergy—instead of "the people" at large, we can avoid the perennial questions concerning the religiosity of the "Russian people" and turn our attention instead to the practices and beliefs of those who considered themselves Orthodox and were regarded by ecclesiastical officials as such.

Second, the notion of "church" in this study takes on a more nuanced meaning than historians have usually granted it. In academic circles the term "church" has generally been reserved for events, activities, and opinions of members of the ecclesiastical establishment—bishops, monastics, and pastors. Like the notion of "nation," however, the notion of "church" was (and is) a complex phenomenon that cannot be objectively defined solely by its empirical bureaucratic structures or by the beliefs and imaginings of its policymakers.[25] In this study, I use the term "church," as the translation of the Greek term *ekklesia*, to denote the Christian community. Accordingly, I often use the phrase "ecclesial community" alternatively for "church." "Community" here denotes the body of faithful, constituted by both clergy and laity, that was rooted in a specific locale yet also extended to the diocesan bishop and even to the ecclesiastical officials in the chancery office of the Holy Synod in St. Petersburg. It is a term that carries simultaneously local, regional, and national connotations. The adjective "ecclesial" as used in this study carries the connotation of the community's sense of itself as unique and sacred.

When I began work on this topic more than a decade ago, researching the subject of community and corporate Orthodox identity in prerevolutionary Russia might have seemed like an inquiry into a "museum" religion. Its relevance for the broader public became evident briefly during the millennial celebrations of the Baptism of Rus' in 1988, when both non-Orthodox Russians and foreigners displayed a heightened interest in a tradition that had been buried, marginalized, and misconstrued by an officially atheistic state— and yet had managed to survive. Since then, the rapid political changes that have overtaken Russia and eastern Europe have pushed the subject into bold relief. While working on the project in its final stages, I could not help but take note of various headlines from Russia's religious and secular press: "The Synod against a Council," "The Laying of the Foundation of a Church in Honor of the Icon of the Mother of God Named 'She Who Reigns'," "The Blessing of the Foundation of a Chapel on the Anniversary of the Chernobyl Disaster," "The Importance of Processions," "In Ivanovo More Than One Thousand Icons Streaming Myrrh," and "The Land of the Mother of God."[26]

These headlines demonstrate that despite the pressures of the past century, the "instinctive realism" of Orthodox collective identity remains alive and well.[27] Many of the same dynamics and tensions I describe in this book continue to characterize Orthodoxy and still await their resolution or further evolution. I hope this book helps readers to appreciate these dynamics in history and in the present, along with the challenges they pose for the future development of Orthodoxy in Russia.

# I

‹•┄═◉╺═┄•›

# The People of God

## Competing Images of Community and Laity

A political revolution is taking place in our midst, and,
perhaps, we are on the verge of a religious reformation.

—A. CHIRETSKII, "O tserkovnoi reforme," 1906

At the outset of the twentieth century, the Orthodox Church in Russia
found itself in the midst of rapid social and political changes that
challenged its very identity. In particular, the new laws of 17 April
1905 and 17 October 1906, which established religious tolerance and granted
Old Believers and "sectarian" communities the rights of self-government and
property ownership, set the reality of an openly religiously pluralistic society
before the institutional Church. These laws created problems typical of those
that modernization was posing for Orthodoxy, bringing forth calls for church
reform and worsening an already growing internal division within church
ranks on two fronts.

On one front, Orthodoxy faced growing fissures in its relationship with
the state. Many Orthodox churchmen felt that the state, in issuing the laws,
had "completely ignored the special role of the Orthodox Church . . . which
until this time had been considered a spiritual-organic force of Russian nationality and the characteristic feature of the Russian State."[1] In response to this
perceived disregard of the ancient alliance between the Orthodox Church and
the state, bishops, priests, and Orthodox intellectuals heatedly debated the
very nature of that relationship and its organic relevance to Orthodoxy as a
whole.[2] Given that one's official status as Orthodox was tied to and often
determined by state ascription, the very existence of these debates indicated
that some of the age-old ways of thinking about Orthodox identity were
being challenged.

On a second front, and more significantly for my purposes, churchmen
were being forced to think more locally and to pay attention to their growing
isolation and marginalization in an increasingly fragmented society. "The
terrifying moment has arrived," wrote one priest, "when our flock has turned

from us, does not listen to our voice, chooses for themselves new leaders, guides, and teachers."[3] From the Orthodox pastor's perspective, the prospect of an openly religiously pluralistic society could only worsen the predicament of the Church. In part, churchmen attributed the religious and cultural fragmentation to the strong inroads being made in Russian society by the modern Western notion of individual autonomy. As Evdokim, bishop of Volokolamsk and dean of Moscow's Theological Academy, wrote in 1905, "one of the most characteristic traits of our time is that the individual [lichnost'], previously strongly suppressed, now unreservedly strives forward in his or her development and self-expression."[4] This interest in individuality seemed to correlate with a modern phenomenon that churchmen termed a "churchless Christianity" (beztserkovnoe khristianstvo), or "modernized Christianity": a vision of Christianity in which the larger ecclesiastical order—and community itself—was no longer considered central in the economy of salvation.[5] Having encountered such trends, churchmen became acutely aware that the institutional Church in its current state in Russia could not meet the challenges being posed by modernity. Consequently, they became engaged in heated debates over both the means by which the Church could reestablish its relevance as a community, and the nature of that relevance, in a world in which it was at best relativized and, at worst, seen as an obstacle that had to be overcome to reap the fruits of "progress."

These debates became more intense in the wake of the events of 1905 and signaled a crisis in modern Russian Orthodox ecclesial identity. Clergy and educated lay believers alike began to reconsider and assess the working principles and boundaries of their own ecclesial community, especially as they were reflected in the main legislation governing the institutional life of the Russian Orthodox Church; often they found no consensus. As one Orthodox publicist wrote, "the contemporary church-consciousness is unclear and undefined."[6] The very meaning of church, the conceptualization of its character and life, and the internal principles by which it should be ordered—these were the fundamental issues being radically questioned and reexamined.

Comparable in some ways to the internal debates over church organization in Roman Catholicism during the councils of Trent (1545–63) and Vatican II (1962–65), the controversies over reform within the Russian Church in the early twentieth century embraced all levels of ecclesial life—relationship to the state, higher church administration, diocesan administration, and more local parish organization. While at times perhaps seemingly bureaucratic in tone, these debates within Russian Orthodoxy's establishment would certainly have defined the character of any future reform within Orthodoxy had not the revolution intervened.

Although politically charged and not without social implications, these debates were set apart from other political and social discourse by religious sensibilities and theological criticism that not only determined their scope and direction but also informed the discussion of even seemingly mundane issues. As the priest Dimitrii Silin wrote in 1905, "just as a writer continually worries about the precision of his word choice for conveying the meaning of things, so the Church, in creating forms and in organizing its life, is concerned with these forms as being a precise reflection of its spirit."[7] Deliberations over ecclesiastical organizational forms arose because of varying perceptions of the Christian "group experience." While the differing parties in the debates would have agreed that the religious dimension of human life found expression and possibly even fulfillment in ecclesial communality,[8] they could not agree on the character of that life.

Discussions about communal identity were not new to Russian Orthodoxy. In the past, Orthodox thinkers had spoken of ecclesial identity mainly in reference to the alien or competing "other." In particular, they defined corporate boundaries primarily with respect to three fronts: other Eastern Christian churches, Western Christian churches (especially Roman Catholicism), and the Old Believers who emerged from the seventeenth-century schism within Russian Orthodoxy's own ranks. The debates that arose in the period 1905–17, however, were of a different quality. They were inwardly focused, with attention given to Roman Catholics, Protestants, Old Believers, and others only insofar as such comparisons helped demarcate the Orthodox community in the new sociopolitical environment.

Moreover, the debates captured the interest of an unprecedented range of people that included members of the ecclesiastical academy as well as religious intellectuals and the secular press. Taking place in the context of the political liberation movement, news about ecclesiastical reform, the Slavophile general A. A. Kireev noted, "sounded like thunder from a cloudless sky"[9] and caught the attention of all those who considered ecclesiastical reforms essential to Russia's religious, social, and political future.[10] It is revealing in this respect that the general discussions during the first meeting of the St. Petersburg Religio-Philosophical Society—a group composed of some of Russia's leading intellectuals and churchmen—in 1903 were focused on the definition of "church."[11]

Another intriguing feature of these debates was that the different ecclesial visions that publicly emerged during the period 1905–17 crossed social and ecclesiastical class lines. Bishops often espoused some of the more liberal visions, while conservative counterparts were often found among the laity.[12] Similarly, some of the most conservative periodicals were secular (*Russkii Vestnik, Moskovskie Vedomosti*), while some ecclesiastical journals (*Bogoslovskii Vestnik, Tserkovnyi Vestnik*) were accused of preaching "republican ideas and desiring to bring the totally foreign spirit of life, which had expressed itself during the French Revolution, into the Church."[13] The apparent classlessness of these debates indicates that the fundamental categories of this discourse transcended purely socioeconomic and political concerns.

Finally, the scope of this ecclesiological dialogue was without precedent, running the gamut from peasant to patriarch. In the past, discussion among state and ecclesiastical officials about the Church focused primarily on clerical interests and institutional and administrative matters. The Orthodox establishment generally had not viewed lay persons and their role in the local parish community as essentially related to the understanding of Orthodox ecclesial identity. In part because of Peter the Great's reorganization of the ecclesiastical apparatus in the eighteenth century, laity in particular, especially from the legislative point of view, had come to be considered incidental to the structure and workings of the Church.[14] Now, with official ecclesiastical questioning of the existing system of church government that had been put in place largely by Peter, the topics of the local faith community (the parish) and the laity emerged at every level of the broader debates about church reform and, for a substantial constituency, took precedence. "Without the correct organization of the parish," A. A. Kireev wrote in 1905, "the [future] patriarch and synod will be rootless, and without any influence on the life of laity."[15] Some considered the parish not only the most pressing religious issue but also the most urgent social and political one, ranking it in significance alongside the emancipation of the serfs a half-century earlier.[16]

This chapter looks at these debates, especially as they pertained to the laity and to the parish, since it was at the local level that most believers would experience and come to form their own understanding of "church." The task here is to identify the various competing modes of thinking about church and community that were already present in the mid–nineteenth century but that began to coalesce and surface with a vigor in 1905. Whether these different modes of thought were something new to Orthodoxy or simply expressions of internal tendencies already present within the Byzantine tradition that Russia had inherited remains to be debated. Whatever the case, these differing views on the Church continued to be expressed—although sometimes in a more subdued fashion by those frightened by unfolding political events—right through the historical meeting of the 1917–18 All-Russian Church Council.

The chapter begins with a brief discussion of the legislation that lay at the basis of the institutional structure of the Orthodox Church during this period, namely the *Spiritual Regulation* of Peter the Great. It then considers the problems in the understanding of parish and laity in church administrative circles that rose to the surface in the period following the emancipation of Russia's serfs in 1861. Following this brief review, I turn to tensions emerging in the theological realm, tensions epitomized by the contrast between the thought of the eminent churchman, the metropolitan of Moscow, Makarii, and the thought of the layman and Slavophile A. S. Khomiakov. Given this background, we can better appreciate the dissonance between the ecclesial models that later intensified in 1905, as represented by the competing views of two Orthodox canon lawyers, A. A. Papkov and I. S. Berdnikov. The differing patterns of thought informing their ecclesial worldviews continued to be influential within Orthodoxy until the momentous crossroads at which Orthodoxy came to stand in Russia in 1917.

## Institutional Thinking about Laity and Parish

Parish reform in the early twentieth century had an involved history that can be linked most immediately to the mid-nineteenth-century emancipation of the serfs and the reign of Alexander II. In their debates on church reform in the early twentieth century, however, many clergy and educated laymen traced the roots of the problems being debated much farther back in history, to the ecclesiastical reforms of Peter the Great and even to Byzantium. If Orthodoxy was to remain viable in the face of "modernism," many clergy and theologians believed that they had to address the negative fallout from the church reforms of Peter the Great. They attributed the weakness of the Church in large part to structural defects and bureaucratic stress that the Petrine reforms had introduced into the institutional order of the Orthodox Church.[17] Some even went so far as to blame the Petrine system for the lack of uniformity in nineteenth-century Russian Orthodox theology.[18]

Although Petrine religious reforms included a broad array of legislation enacted over his years as ruler, at the heart of these reforms stood the *Spiritual Regulation*. Instituted in 1721, the *Spiritual Regulation* and its Supplement remained at the foundation of the institutional culture of the Orthodox Church in Russia until 1917.[19] Peter the Great's reason for instituting the reforms was clear: to bring order to the ecclesiastical realm as part of his broader efforts to modernize the state. Peter reorganized the ecclesiastical apparatus not primarily from the standpoint of a believer but mainly from that of a statesman who worried about revenue and potentially competing sources of authority.[20] Informed by the experience of his own father, Tsar Alexei Mikhailovich, with Patriarch Nikon, whose decisions had helped create a major schism in the Orthodox Church in the mid–seventeenth century, Peter was aware of the potential political threat of a single ecclesiastical leader at the helm of the Church. As the *Spiritual Regulation* said, "the common people do not understand how spiritual authority is distinguishable from the autocratic . . . they imagine that such an administrator is a second Sovereign, a power equal to that of the Autocrat, or even greater than he."[21] One of the purposes of the *Regulation* and the reorganization of church life it entailed was to prevent any such "misunderstandings" in the future.

In order to remove the threat of competition in the figure of the patriarch, Peter instituted a collegial (*sobornyi*) way of governing the clergy. The central ruling body of the Orthodox Church eventually was called the "Most Holy Governing Synod." Whether Peter's version of the collegial principle could be considered compatible with ancient Orthodox canonical formulations or viewed as foreign to Orthodoxy was something that churchmen in the early twentieth century actively discussed. Whatever the case, it is clear that Peter in his reform efforts was not concerned with Orthodox ecclesiology proper and seemed to show little regard for the notion that the Church might have its own principles of internal order.

Although, as Gregory Freeze has argued, the Church never became a mere department of state and should be understood as having operated "parallel to, not inside the state apparatus,"[22] from Peter's perspective the Church did represent another domain within his state that needed efficient ordering. In this sense, as John Meyendorff has noted, the ecclesiastical reforms of Peter the Great effectively did away with the legal recognition of a faith community distinct or separate from that of the state. Orthodoxy was understood not so much in terms of community or "church" but in terms of "a body of beliefs shared by the emperor's subjects."[23]

Following the reign of Peter, Russia's rulers continued, in greater or lesser degree, to concern themselves with aspects of church life. State-initiated regulations during the eighteenth century made themselves felt in internal, even sacred, aspects of ecclesial life. Toward the goal of a proper ordering of the state, which included a populace of good Orthodox standing, state officials often took an interest in ensuring that church life was properly observed. In this vein, for instance, a 1774 directive delegated to local civil officials the responsibility of making sure that people attended church on Sundays and major feast days, thereby blurring the boundaries between civil and purely ecclesial life.[24] A similar blurring of boundaries was evident in civil legislation mandating annual confession and Communion.[25]

In terms of the ecclesial body, the *Spiritual Regulation* was concerned mostly with clergy. For Peter, the realm of the Church signified primarily the clergy; these comprised another service rank, comparable to the military, whose worth he judged according to his perception of their usefulness to society. Ecclesiastical administration, or the "spiritual domain" (*dukhovnoe vedomstvo*), was understood almost exclusively in terms of clergy. From Peter's point of view, as members of the state, the service of lay people (*miriane*) lay elsewhere.

Since the notion of a well-ordered church meant a well-ordered and well-maintained clergy, the late eighteenth and early nineteenth centuries saw periodic state preoccupation with the question of how to support the clergy financially. It gradually became clear to state officials that, given the enserfment of much of Russia's rural population, parishioners themselves could not always provide such support. State efforts to enhance the material well-being of the clergy resulted in less attention being paid to laity in church-related legislation. By the time Russia's laws were codified during the reign of Nicholas I in the first half of the nineteenth century, the laity as such factored little into what these laws construed as the local ecclesial establishment. For instance, church lands, which had in many cases been donated by parishioners for use by their clergy, were by law placed under the direct management of parish clergy. In instances where a particular parish church had been closed, or was to be attached to another nearby parish, the land and other property would not be returned to parishioners but would become the property of the parish to which it was assigned. Perhaps most important, nowhere in Russia's legal code was the parish as a collective body of believers that included clergy and laity recognized as a juridical entity (*iuridicheskoe litso*) that held the right, for instance, to purchase and sell property. These rulings, which were meant to provide support for an impoverished clergy, inadvertently resulted in a minimization of the role of lay people in the management of their parish life.

The subject of laity, however, was not entirely ignored in the *Spiritual Regulation*. Thoughts about the laity were integrated into the *Regulation* but only insofar as "they were concerned with religious instruction."[26] The section of the *Regulation* dealing with the laity was somewhat ambiguous. This is not surprising, given the profile of its author, Bishop Feofan Prokopovich (1681–1736). Feofan had been trained in the Kievan Academy, the curriculum of which was heavily influenced by Roman Catholic, Jesuit teachings. Feofan had also spent time studying in Rome and in order to do so had converted to Catholicism. Later, however, he looked back on this training with disdain and found himself more comfortable in the theological world of seventeenth-century Protestants. The *Regulation* reflects this variegated influence with respect to its treatment of the laity.

On the one hand, Feofan (and Peter, with whom Feofan usually agreed) directly opposed the view of the laity that, to a large extent, had come to characterize medieval Western as well as Byzantine Christianity. Generally speaking, in the Byzantine and medieval views, laity (except for lay monastics and the emperor) had come to be identified with the things of "this world"—with the profane—in contrast to the ordained members of the Church. This understanding of laity differed from the earlier biblical notion of the "People of God," a phrase that referred to all members of the Christian community, irrespective of their specific ecclesial vocation. The *Spiritual Regulation* sought to fend off the idea that laity were somehow inferior to the clergy by reiterating the well-known Protestant appeal to the scriptural principle of the "priesthood of all believers" (1 Cor. 12:12–13; 1 Pet. 2:9).[27]

On the other hand, Feofan also fell back on the classical Roman Catholic teaching that the clergy were those who taught and the laity were those who were taught. It is noteworthy in this context that the *Regulation* seemed to refer to laity (*miriane*) and "the people" (*narod*) interchangeably, betraying a lack of conceptual discrimination between the two. A similar blending of these two notions was common among churchmen in the nineteenth and early twentieth centuries and often resulted in thinking of laity, especially if they were peasants, in terms of the "dark masses." Certain publicists became aware of the confusion in the mid-nineteenth century and its potential implications for discussions about the parish and lay involvement in it. It would become an especially poignant problem in debates concerning ownership of church property.

When speaking about the laity, the *Regulation* had little to say about any governing roles of laity in ecclesial life; the notable exception was the assumed lay role in appointing a parish priest. Instead, the *Regulation* included what at first reading might appear to be a motley list of expectations insofar as the laity were submitted to "spiritual administration."[28] This included the obligations to listen to Orthodox instruction, not to defend schismatics, not to construct private churches in their homes, and not to accept vagrant priests or to baptize infants in private homes. The ruling mentioning annual participation in confession and Communion was based mostly on the desire to check dissent: participation in the Eucharist was looked on as a sign of belonging to the Orthodox faith, as opposed to any sectarian or Old Believer group (an association that suggested potential political trouble). The *Regulation* also included a reminder to civil administrators and landowners that they, too, as Orthodox laymen, were subject to the council of bishops. Such a seemingly random group of prescriptions was formed with a single, paramount concern: to contain Orthodox believers and the manifestations of Orthodoxy itself in a manageable sphere of governance.

The *Regulation* also dealt with another issue related to the topic of church community: superstition. Superstition was a pejorative term that in its classical usage often implied "bad" or "false" religion.[29] The terms spoke to the matter of authenticity with respect to ways of belonging to the faith. Peter's plan to ensure that "everything was done properly and according to Christian law" included the idea of ridding the Church of those practices that to him appeared superstitious.[30] This aspect of the *Regulation* was not aimed only at the lower classes or discussed solely with respect to the simple folk, as is sometimes assumed. It is clear that whatever Peter and Feofan understood by the term *superstition*, they considered it an affliction that could potentially affect Orthodox believers of any ecclesiastical or social standing: cleric or layman, nobleman or peasant. The subject of superstition was raised in the first section of the *Regulation* under the heading of "Common Matters" and revisited in subsequent sections dealing with various ecclesiastical ranks: bishops, monks, priests, and lay people.

The issue of superstition in the *Regulation* was complex and held potentially profound ecclesial implications. Vaguely described as "that which is superfluous, not essential to salvation . . . beguiling the simple, and like snow-drifts, hindering passage along the right path of truth," superstition was thought of as something knowingly fabricated and subsequently "accepted [by others] as real through ignorance." The trouble with superstition, according to the *Regulation*, was twofold. First, it was a sin, in that those who recounted such fabrications were associating God's name with a lie, which was considered tantamount to taking God's name in vain. Second, perpetrators of superstition, in their acts of fabrication, manifested a kind of coarse fearlessness, a trait that potentially was too closely linked with resistance to authority.[31] The *Regulation*, however, did not address those cases in which the originator of the story of a miracle sincerely believed the miraculous event to be true.

With regard to superstition, the *Regulation* seemed to conflate two types of rituals and practices. First, it criticized those practices that were often seen, even by nineteenth-century clergy, as lingering pagan customs, such as the celebration of Fridays.[32] Such phenomena were usually associated with the peasantry. Of more concern in the *Regulation* was the potential for abuses related to prayers, rituals, and beliefs that traditionally had been very much part of Orthodox ecclesial life, such as *akathistoi* hymns, the celebration of various feast days, and the veneration of miracle-working icons.[33] Though seemingly suspicious of these practices, the *Regulation* did not in theory deny their validity. It did not, for instance, categorically deny the existence of miracle-working icons and thus did not go as far as Protestant criticism of Roman Catholicism, let alone as far as the radical thinking of the French Enlightenment that applied the term *superstition* to all traditional religions. Instead, the *Regulation's* preoccupation with what it calls "false miracles" and with rituals based on fabrications paralleled the concerns of Catholic church-men during the Council of Trent who, as one historian has noted, sought "to prevent their flock from crying miracle too easily."[34] A major issue associated with superstition as it was discussed in the *Regulation* was that of religious authority and the prerogative to discern what events or experiences were authentically revelatory and therefore "of the community." Though the Holy Synod was charged with investigating reported miracles and ascertaining their truth, how this assigned task fit into a traditional Orthodox understanding of miracles and Orthodox church life was not addressed in the *Regulation* and was apparently left to churchmen themselves to interpret and decide.[35]

Despite the potential for broad interpretation among churchmen when it came to the notion of superstition, the willful propagation of superstitions was a civil crime in imperial Russia. Although by the nineteenth and early twen-tieth centuries the penalties for the spreading of superstitions were no longer as severe as they had been in the eighteenth century (and often not even pursued by secular courts), the very act itself remained a civil crime, and its report usually sparked an investigation, at least on the diocesan level. Accord-ingly, superstition remained a subject of concern in late nineteenth- and early twentieth-century pastoral handbooks. In these handbooks, the relevant parts of the *Regulation* were often quoted.

While the parish unit as such received little direct attention in the *Spiritual Regulation*, the bureaucratization of ecclesiastical life that the *Regulation* initi-ated did affect the way the parish or local ecclesial community came to be perceived during the eighteenth and early nineteenth centuries. Peter had directed that central and diocesan ecclesiastical administrative organs be ar-ranged according to bureaucratic principles similar to those that governed Russia's civil administration. In eventually falling victim to an "organizational revolution," the parish was divested of some of its more secular functions.[36] Tasks such as the drawing up of legal documents fell to newly established civil agencies. Although, as Gregory Freeze has shown, its role as a local adminis-trative unit with a broad social and administrative purview may have de-creased, the parish retained at least two significant functions. First, it served as the place where births, deaths, and marriages were registered. Second, Russia's emperors continued to view the parish church as a forum for the proclamation of important decrees.

In addition, the size of parishes grew significantly since the number of people who constituted the parish rose as a result of state and ecclesiastical efforts to diminish the number of "superfluous" parishes by setting a minimum number of households required to constitute a parish. As a result, the typical pattern of the geographic parameters of the local natural community being coextensive with those of the parish community disappeared. The rural parish was now often comprised of numerous villages and became much more socially diverse.[37] Finally, by the late eighteenth century, church bureaucratization had led to diocesan incursions into functions that traditionally had involved the laity, such as the management of certain parish finances and the selection of their priests. (In areas where the laity were predominantly landowners' serfs, these functions had often been surrendered even earlier, albeit to the landowner). The extent to which bureaucratization affected the conception of the parish as a viable unit composed of active lay members alongside the clerical ones would eventually be subject to debate.

In the mid–nineteenth century, state and church officials revisited the parish in their respective reform efforts. First, in the context of plans for the emancipation of the serfs in the mid–nineteenth century, government officials became interested in the parish as a purely social and territorial unit. At that time the Editing Commission on Peasant Affairs was faced with the question of territorial and administrative organization of peasant communities in anticipation of the emancipation. The Commission retained the village commune as the basic unit of peasant organization but superimposed on it a new territorial-administrative unit, the township. Many of the Commission's members, however, opposed the imposition of a newly created territorial unit and instead favored the use of the parish unit, which was a familiar construct in peasant life.[38] They believed that the parish could serve as a center around which schools, hospitals, and charity organizations could be formed. The parish as a civil administrative unit was also politically attractive since, by definition, it included all social groups and therefore could be used as a convenient context for socially integrating the rural population.[39] While in the end state officials found it impractical to limit local administrative units to parishes because of the disparity in their sizes, legislation governing peasant life nevertheless eventually in theory linked formation of the township with the parish unit.[40]

Interest in the parish as a purely civil and social administrative unit continued to surface in governmental spheres throughout the late nineteenth century. For instance, in the 1880s various zemstvo organizations took an active interest in the parish as a practical administrative unit through which the demands of local charity work could be met.[41] In December 1880, members of the Moscow provincial zemstvo assembly petitioned the Ministry of Internal Affairs to assign to parishes the permanent function of overseeing local charity work. At the same time, they set out those conditions that would have to be met for parishes to carry out such work effectively. In particular, they advocated granting the parish more legal autonomy, especially with respect to electing its own clergy, as well as acquiring and owning property. The Holy Synod, the central governing body of the Orthodox Church, was not very open to such proposals, in large part because the Synod understood the parish primarily as a unit that belonged to the ecclesial and not the civil community. Therefore, it saw the zemstvo's program as arising from outside the boundaries and interests of the Church proper. Denying the proposal, the Synod responded that the Church's organization was based on a set of religious considerations that were not taken into account by other state agencies.[42]

In addition to the attention it received from government officials and peasant-reform activists, the parish also enjoyed the attention of ecclesiastical circles. The Church responded to a general call for *glasnost'* during the reign of Alexander II with its own series of ecclesiastical Great Reforms, which proposed fundamental changes to various aspects of the Church, including its administration, clergy, and educational institutions.[43] Church reforms at this time, however, were still focused predominantly on the plight of Russia's parish clergy, indicating the common association between the notions of church and clergy.[44] Many believed that the renewal of Orthodox religious life in Russia depended on the improvement of the lot of the clergy. Except for reference to the laity as subjects to be educated so that they might become more sensitive to the plight of their pastors, the topic of the laity remained secondary in institutional discourse. The social, financial, educational, and administrative problems regarding Russia's clergy to a large extent dominated the discussion in Russia's Orthodox establishment.[45]

The extensive preoccupation with the clerical issue was reflected in the name of the main synodal committee charged with parish reform issues, "The Special Commission on Affairs of Orthodox Clergy." Indeed, the commission's parish reform initiative of 1869 was anything but lay-friendly. Effectively considering the parish community as a dispensable unit, it either closed smaller parishes or attached them to larger ones in order to maximize the number of parishioners in remaining parishes so as to provide a greater income to the ministering parish priests, a measure that had been taken in the eighteenth century as well.[46]

We can appreciate the elusiveness of the very concepts of Church and parish as they were related to the local faith community in the general culture of the late imperial period when we note the lack of any single systematized set of legislation or bylaws delineating official parish identity. In order to understand just the legal aspects of local church or parish life, both from the Church's and the state's points of view, one would have to review fifteen to twenty different bodies of legislation, in addition to some forty more synodal decrees between the years 1865 and 1902.[47] The scattered nature of such legislation was symptomatic of the lack of clarity of thought regarding the parish experience that existed at the time. Moreover, churchmen had little in the way of historical texts to draw on in their thinking about the parish, since both canon law and Byzantine legal codes failed to define it.

The hazy understanding of community with respect to contemporary thinking about "church" can also be seen in the manner in which Russia's laws used the words "church" (*tserkov'*) and "parish" (*prikhod*). *Tserkov'*—which was in part derived from the Greek word *kyriakon*, meaning "belonging to the Lord"—was an ambiguous word in the Russian language. It was used to translate both the Greek term *ekklesia* (gathering, calling forth) and *naos* (temple). Hence this single word, as in the English language, was used to mean both the universal community of Christians, as referred to in the Nicene-Constantinopolitan Creed, and to the church building or temple as such.

The word for parish (*prikhod*) in Russian did not convey the same notion as its Greek counterpart, *paroikia*, which meant those living near or beside one another. The Greek term also referred to "resident aliens," and in this sense the term was often used biblically to describe, for example, the Israelites in Egypt: foreigners temporarily residing in a strange land. This sense of the term was also picked up by early Christians to refer to their own local congregations of believers. Christians saw their lives in somewhat mystical terms, as a community of earthly sojourners whose true homeland was in heaven and who awaited the heavenly eternity.[48] The notion of parish thus originally referred more to a state or condition than a locality. Later in the first century the term came to designate an individual local Christian community. Originally, the Church as *ekklesia* had also been understood as *paroikia*. The Russian word *prikhod*, however, in no way conveyed the early Christian meaning of *paroikia*. Rather, it described persons coming together or arriving at a destination and in that sense conveyed the notion of community, or *obshchina*.

To add further to the muddle, the primary legislation defining the system of diocesan administration in the nineteenth century, the "Regulations Governing Ecclesiastical Consistories," treated the notions of church and parish as separate categories. The church (*tserkov'*), understood as the temple together with the local ecclesiastical establishment, was the active subject; the parish in turn was understood simply as a particular number of men and women attached to the church, though not an essential part of it.[49] There was a category of nonparish churches, suggesting that the gathering of lay faithful was superfluous to the notion of church when understood in this way. In contrast, the clergy were considered essential to the church's functioning, and therefore they were categorized separately from the parish, or *prikhod*, which was understood as including only laity. Consequently, the Church, in its local manifestation, consisted of a temple, blessed by a bishop and constructed with his blessing, the clergy, who serviced that temple and fulfilled the religious needs of believers, and a church elder, whom parishioners (or a town council in the case of nonparish churches) chose to help manage parish finances. As the canon lawyer N. Zaozerskii noted, the believers themselves were basically incidental to its definition. There could be a church without a parish but no parish without a church.[50]

Laws governing local church property reflected the same understanding. Technically, property belonged to the church, meaning the church building, and not to the persons who comprised the parish community.[51] While local clergy and the church elder immediately managed this property, ultimately it fell under the supervision of diocesan authorities and the Holy Synod.[52] No new properties, for instance, including those willed or donated by laity, could be acquired or liquidated without direct permission from higher church authorities.[53] Similarly, all earnings and donations over 100 rubles had to be reported to the diocese.[54] Legally, the local faith community enjoyed no ownership or direct management of its church's property.[55]

The only place where the laity were legally granted any collective self-expression as part of the sacred community was in the regulations concerning the church elder and parish guardians.[56] The church elder functioned as an unpaid liaison between parishioners and parish clergy.[57] Parishioners elected him once every three years and entrusted him to work with the clergy to collect, safeguard, and properly spend church funds.[58] These elections took place following a Divine Liturgy, on the initiative of the parish priest. Male members of the parish who were over the age of twenty-five and who had the right to participate in village, town, or gentry assemblies could participate in these parish assemblies. An elected church elder might also appoint parishioners as aides, and, beginning in 1890, the parish assembly elected two other parishioners to oversee the counting of collected donations.[59]

A similar assembly was recognized for the purposes of electing parish guardians. The parish guardianship (popechitel'stvo, from the Russian word meaning "caretaker") was introduced by ecclesiastical authorities during the parish reforms in the 1860s. Its introduction marked what some churchmen would later come to see as a turning point in thinking about the local ecclesial community.[60] While they were formed with the hope of "encouraging and inspiring parish independence and independent lay activity,"[61] these voluntary lay organizations received official sanction in large part because church officials believed they might improve the material well-being of clergy. The notion of independent lay activity was still considered largely in the context of that improvement. The guardianships were composed of an elected chairman and anywhere from two to fifty members; their established duties included not only maintenance of church properties, charity work, and the education of children in the parish but also the financial support of parish clergy. The chairman of the parish guardianship had the right to call parish assemblies, but only for the purpose of discussing and gaining parish approval for guardianship projects.

While at first glance elders and guardians seemed to function, at least to some extent, as voices of the local faith community, in neither case was there any guarantee that the community's interests would prevail. In the instance of the church elder, both parish clergy and diocesan authorities could reject the candidate chosen by the laity.[62] The guardians, in turn, were by legal definition not an integral part of the sacred ecclesial unit. According to the 1864 Rule, they were a voluntary, purely social organization, not an ecclesiastical one. Characteristically, civil officials were among the guardianship's required members.[63] Although they concerned themselves with church-related affairs, legally they had no access to church funds and had to find their own sources of funding for their causes. Technically speaking, they were legally segregated from the Church proper, thereby perpetuating the notion that lay involvement was extrinsic to the "essential" activity of the Church.[64]

Such vague and ambiguous formulations regarding church and parish in ecclesiastical legislation, combined with the reform emphasis on the well-being of the clergy, however genuinely motivated, reinforced the tendency among believers to equate the word "church" with clergy. This tendency elicited a heated reaction in the press, long before 1905, especially among Orthodox lay intellectuals. Writing in 1873, D. F. Samarin, the brother of the well-known Slavophile Iurii Samarin, for example, noted that the 1869 parish reform stirred educated laity to begin considering "the rights" of the parish community to self-determination as well as to question the working relationship between clergy and laity implied in the legislation.[65] In 1864 the publicist and Slavophile I. S. Aksakov had questioned the essence of the reform effort with its emphasis on the welfare of parish clergy. Was this effort a matter of "the clergy for the parish or the parish for the clergy?"[66] Contending that such constant preoccupation with clergy misrepresented the true interests of the Church, he called for a reformulation of the working vision of the parish as a community that included both clergy and laity. He did so in language that foreshadowed the reform debates that erupted within the ecclesiastical establishment in 1905.[67]

Many parish clergy also came to the realization that their plight was inseparable from that of their flock. Taking a relatively empathic attitude toward the people (*narod*) and a self-critical approach toward their own role in furthering parish improvements, many parish priests began to pay growing attention to the structure and organization of the local faith community, especially with respect to educational and charitable activities, which they saw as matters of sacred concern.[68] Although his pastoral career unfolded mostly in and around St. Petersburg, the activities of the priest A. V. Gumilevskii (1830–69) most vividly manifested this shifting clerical outlook. The son of a village deacon, Gumilevskii became noted for his preaching and his approach to pastor-flock relations. His attempts to understand and fulfill the needs of his parishioners brought the acclaim of his contemporaries, who saw him as a "true pioneer in the awakening of church life."[69] Among his numerous other activities in the 1860s, Gumilevskii was remembered mostly for founding St. Petersburg's first confraternity. "As the first open experiment in Christian social work in Russia," it proved to be the inspiration behind most of St. Petersburg's later parish-related charity work.[70] For this reason Gumilevskii was said to be the "first to awaken the dozing hierarchy in his attempt to direct clergy to practical pastoral work."[71]

Gumilevskii's views on the Church, as well as those of like-minded colleagues, were expressed in the journal *Spirit of a Christian*, of which he was one of the editors. A sounding board for the new generation of Russia's parish clergy in the 1860s, the journal was inspired by social changes in ecclesial life brought about by the emancipation of serfs. The editors steered away from theological discussions and focused instead on the formulation of a "simplified Orthodoxy" for the people, as well as on the practical application of Orthodoxy in terms of social work. Thus the journal's socioreligious scope of interest and application extended beyond St. Petersburg's city limits into the villages, thereby bonding urban and rural priests in mutual concerns with respect to "the people."[72]

In striking contrast to the spirit of the *Spiritual Regulation*, Gumilevskii's approach proceeded from the belief that the Russian people shared a collective consciousness that latently retained many ancient Christian principles. In order to help the people recall the knowledge of these principles, he composed talks or discussions about ecclesial life that he hoped would activate those dormant memories. In doing so, he attempted to instill in the common laity a consciousness of the parish and to associate their religious feelings and experiences with a larger whole. He also attempted to instill in his listeners the spirit of the early church, as opposed to the "spirit of Byzantium." He sought to develop the early Christian ideal of brotherhood in which active care for one another bonded together members of the local parish community. Finally, he stressed the social in contrast to the more ascetic and mystical teachings of Orthodoxy. Yet despite such pastoral activism, discussions about the laity in *Spirit of a Christian* retained paternalistic overtones that placed laity in the position of being taught and transformed rather than being comembers, as some similar discussions would some forty years later.

During the reign of Alexander III (1881–94), both church and state officials effectively recoiled from those initiatives taken during the reign of Alexander II to modify laws governing parish life.[73] Most institutional thought about the Church and reform efforts at this time remained focused on the well-being of the clergy. This was thanks in large part to K. P. Pobedonostsev, the ober-procurator of the Holy Synod in the final critical decades of the nineteenth century, who was neither a theologian nor a religious visionary.[74] Pobedonostsev's views were significant in that, by virtue of the office he occupied, they shaped official Orthodox policy. Firmly entrenched in the Petrine ecclesiastical system, Pobedonostsev was not interested in any notion of the Church as its own community of believers, independent of the state. He fully endorsed the Petrine system of ecclesiastical administration. Those who were critical of the system, he claimed, "were not familiar with the current state of ecclesiastical administration or with the moral or social conditions within which church life takes place." The weaknesses in the current administration, in his eyes, stemmed not so much from Peter but from the rulers of Russia who came after him and were "foreign to Russia and the Russian faith." Yet by the nineteenth century, Pobedonostsev maintained, such obstacles had passed and nothing blocked the Church from exerting its influence in society and among the people.[75] To a large extent, Pobedonostsev was the embodiment of everything that many church officials were to react against by 1905. For him, even the suggestion of distinguishing between church and state order would mean "losing something of Orthodox 'churchness.' "[76] The state was Pobedonostsev's main concern, and its shadow usually fell across any of his discussions of religious or ecclesiastical issues. Though predisposed to the faith of the Russian people, he never discussed the people as active, thinking, constructive members of the ecclesial community.[77] In his view, just as in matters of the state, where the theory of the sovereignty of the people was "the falsest of political principles," so in the ecclesial realm the idea of laity actively participating in church governance was not acceptable.

⊷⊜⊷

## Theologizing Church: The Bishop and the Layman

In the mid– and late nineteenth century, then, much of the official legislation concerning the Church tended to marginalize the parish and community, despite efforts from the civil sphere to mobilize the Church for state purposes and pastoral efforts to raise the ecclesial self-awareness of parishioners. At the same time, multiple historical factors—the cultural thaw and *glasnost'* of Alexander II's reign, greater exposure to competing philosophical and religious ideas from the West, conflicts between different schools of thought within the Russian Church itself—all contributed to enlivening the field of Orthodox theology. Yet even in the purely theological realm, we can see a struggle over the conceptualization of the ecclesial community. Two of the nineteenth century's best-known theological authors—the instructor in dogmatics and later bishop of Moscow Makarii Bulgakov (1816–82) and the lay theologian, Slavophile, and landowner Aleksei Khomiakov (1804–60)—represented competing ways of envisioning the Church as a whole. Their visions subsequently informed the way early twentieth-century Orthodox churchmen and theologians thought about the laity and the local ecclesial community.[78]

Makarii, who might be seen as an academic theologian par excellence and whose dogmatic texts continued to be used in the late imperial period, portrayed the Church as a community that transcended the historical present and included within its ranks those rational and free beings—including deceased ancestors and the angelic ranks—who confessed Christ as Savior and who were united with him. He saw the Church as a mixed community, consisting of both saints and sinners, and rejected the distinction between the visible and the invisible Church—a Reformation teaching that was espoused particularly by Calvin. Yet he considered it proper, in the spirit of Augustine, to speak of the Church in terms of its earthly and heavenly aspects. Although not separating these aspects into two strictly divided communities, Makarii maintained that for instructional purposes they could be discussed separately. In his writings, therefore, he devoted most of his attention to the earthly aspect of the Church.[79]

According to Makarii, Christ himself endowed the Church, as the transmitter of grace and the keeper of the Christian narrative, with a particular organizational structure that would most effectively allow it to fulfill its divinely ordained tasks.[80] The Church was divided into two essential "classes" (klassy): the flock and the "divinely ordained hierarchy" (consisting of bishops, priests, and deacons). Both of these classes were subordinate to episcopal councils. Christ as the common head brought unity to these diverse members. He also established a special estate (soslovie), the hierarchy, to whom he specifically granted the authority of teaching, of priestly function, and of spiritual direction. He did not grant these functions arbitrarily to all. Clergy dispensed the "things needed"; laity listened to the teachings, utilized the rituals, and obeyed the clergy. In its earthly manifestation, then, the Church was divided into those who were "subordinate" (podchinennye) and those who divinely directed (sviashchennonachal'stvuiushchie), a view of church that his detractors would attribute to a heavy Roman Catholic influence. Although Makarii's definition of the community depended on both these classes, for all practical purposes the laity, as subordinates, were relegated to the periphery of the Church's institutional life.

Makarii paid particular attention to the importance of the episcopacy. Basing his thought in selections from the writings of Ignatius of Antioch, Irenaeus of Lyons, and Cyprian of Carthage, Makarii claimed that bishops were the "braces" of the Church, on which it rested. They were "the abundant source" of all sacraments, as well as the focus of spiritual authority in every local church. Only the local and ecumenical councils, consisting exclusively of bishops, stood over them. Bishops, then, were the practical or immediate source of the Church's unity: those who were not in communion with the bishop (as determined by the bishop) were not in the Church.

Though drawing on a similar body of scriptural and patristic sources, A. S. Khomiakov's depiction of the faith community was strikingly different from Makarii's.[81] As a Slavophile, Khomiakov belonged to a core group of early nineteenth-century Russian thinkers who provided an "Orthodox-Russian orientation" in thought in counterbalance to the intense westernization that Russia had undergone during the past century.[82] He was also a theologian whose thinking about the Orthodox Church was often formulated in his polemics with Western Christian faiths. Preoccupied with the notions of the commune (obshchina) and communality (obshchinnost'), as seen in his social thought, Khomiakov concerned himself in his religious thought almost exclusively with the biblical image of the Church as a living organism. He agreed, therefore, with the classical teaching presented by Makarii that this body extended to those who came before, and even forward in time to those who will be:

Only with respect to humanity is it possible to accept the division of the Church into the visible and invisible; her unity, in contrast, is true and absolute. Those who have completed their earthly paths, those who are not created for earthly paths (such as angels) and those who have not yet begun their earthly paths, all are united in one Church— in the one grace of God.[83]

Unlike Makarii, whose concerns lay almost purely with institutional, organizational principles of church life, Khomiakov attempted to express the internal character of the church experience and to articulate the metaphysics and intuition of that communal life.[84] In doing so, he refocused attention away from institutional indicators of unity, such as the episcopacy and formal canons, to interior principles, especially to the Spirit of God, in whom all members were called equally to participate. The Church's essence, accordingly, lay "in the agreement and unity of spirit and life of all the members who acknowledge it."[85]

Concerned with the internal unifying spirit of the community, Khomiakov distinguished between the concepts of religious authority and religious "truth." He claimed that authority was an external principle, forced from without, and that it was inaccurate to apply the notion to ecclesial life. "The Church is not an authority," he wrote, "just as God is not an authority, and Christ is not an authority, since authority is something external to us." God, Christ, Church—these were all "truth" in that all were known in the believer's inner experience, and "more real than the heart that beats in his breast or the blood flowing in his veins, insofar as that believer lives a universal life of love and unity."[86]

Since the determining principle of communal life in the Church was a spiritual one, no particular group or local community, let alone a single individual, according to Khomiakov, could be acknowledged as the keeper of the whole faith, or the representative of the whole Church's sanctity.[87] In this sense, he deemphasized the role of the ecclesiastical hierarchy and the clergy in general. Strongly antipapal in his writings, Khomiakov stressed that it was not individuals or a group of individuals who preserved or guarded the faith but the Spirit of God, who lives in the totality of the ecclesial organism. It was in explicating this idea that Khomiakov disclosed his appreciation of the laity. As textual support he cited the famous 1848 "Encyclical of the Eastern Patriarchs" to Pope Pius IX—a document that Khomiakov deemed "the most significant event in church history in many centuries":

> Infallibility resides solely in the universality of the Church united by mutual love; the protection of both the constancy of dogma and purity of rite was entrusted not to any hierarchy but to the people of the Church as a whole, which is the body of Christ.[88]

This emphasis on the unifying spirit obviated the establishment of any rigid notions of hierarchical power relations within the body, as had been put forth, for example, by Makarii. Khomiakov's ecclesial vision stressed mutuality and asserted that superficial reasoning and mere logic could often be confounded by deeper principles in matters of faith. The episcopacy, though sacramentally ordained, did not intrinsically possess any monopoly over Christian teachings, as Khomiakov graphically noted when speaking about the history of the Church's councils. Why were some councils denied as heretical and others embraced as ecumenical, when outwardly nothing distinguished them? Khomiakov answered with the following well-known passage:

> Solely because their decisions were not recognized as the voice of the Church by the entire ecclesial people [*tserkovnym narodom*], by that people and within that world where, in questions of faith, there is no difference between the scholar and the unlearned, cleric and lay person, man and woman, and king and subject . . . and where . . . the heresy of a learned bishop is refuted by an illiterate shepherd, so that all might be joined in the free unity of living faith which is the manifestation of the Spirit of God.[89]

As has been noted by the well-known scholar of the Slavophiles, Peter Christoff, Khomiakov used the Russian word *obshchina*, or "commune"—the same term that denoted the Russian village community—synonymously with the term *church*. The Slavophiles had tended to idealize the Russian peasant community and felt that it had, among other things, helped to prepare the way for Russia's assimilation of Orthodox Christianity. By closely associating the Church with the notion of commune, Khomiakov meant to move away from the understanding of church primarily as a bureaucratic institution and instead to emphasize such notions as togetherness and fellowship.[90] This emphasis that Khomiakov placed on the Church as a unity of all members—clergy and laity—stood in sharp contrast to that offered not only by Makarii but also the *Spiritual Regulation* of Peter the Great.

Historically, Khomiakov's understanding of the Church with its emphasis on unity, love, and freedom became inextricably linked with the concept of *sobornost'*, although scholars have noted that Khomiakov never actually used the term *sobornost'*.[91] The word comes from the verb *sobirat'*, which means to gather or bring together. The noun *sobor*, meaning council, is the Slavonic translation of the Greek word *synaxis*, or the related *synagoge*, and conveys as well the meaning of the Greek term *ekklesia*.[92] The adjective *sobornyi* is the Slavonic rendition of the word "catholic" found in the ninth clause of the Nicene-Constantinopolitan Creed concerning the nature of the Church. Khomiakov believed that Saints Cyril and Methodius had consciously chosen the word *sobornyi* in order to convey not merely the static idea of geographic universality but the notion of active unity in plurality, a coming together of the many and the diverse into a unified whole. Khomiakov asserted that this one word, *sobornyi*, "contains a whole confession of faith."[93]

Khomiakov's understanding of the word *sobornyi*, however, did not preclude a hierarchical principle in his ecclesial vision, as his detractors later contended. V. F. Pevnitskii, professor of homiletics at the Kievan Theological Academy, for example, argued that Khomiakov's understanding of the Church diminished the significance of the episcopacy and priesthood by confounding the distinguishing features of the ecclesial organism. Khomiakov's vision, he claimed, consisted "of a single undifferentiated mass, inspired by the Spirit of God, in which each member was indistinguishable from the other."[94]

Though Khomiakov did not give a systematic presentation of the external organization of ecclesial life, he nevertheless clearly recognized the importance of external unity and saw the source of that unity manifested in the communion of the sacraments.[95] Here the hierarchy found a place within his scheme. "Ordination contains within itself," he wrote, "all the fullness of grace given by Christ to his Church. . . . If ordination ceased, all the sacraments, except for baptism, would also cease; and the human race would be torn away from grace."[96] He never denied that the earthly church community should coalesce around the bishop. The bishop and the priest, he wrote, were not servants of any local community but first and foremost servants of Christ in the universal community. "Through them, through the ages, the earthly Church adjoins its Divine Creator and through them it feels itself continually lifted to the One whose hand placed the apostle in office."[97]

Moreover, nowhere in his writings did Khomiakov equate the idea of *sobornyi* with "the will of the people," juxtaposing the hierarchical and the communal as two diametrically opposed or contending principles.[98] Though eventually some churchmen would shun the principle of *sobornost'* as introducing a democratic or parliamentarian spirit into church life, Khomiakov's own vision of ecclesial relations certainly was not democratic in the usual meaning of the word. In fact, *sobornyi*, as Khomiakov understood it, had nothing in common with secular democracies or any other form of purely human social organization, since its underlying ordering principle was a metaphysical, divine, spiritual one. Equality and unity, as he said, were not products of human determination but manifestations of the presence of God's grace.

*Sobornyi*, therefore, in Khomiakov's thought referred more to the notion of communion than to any simple idea of community as such. From a theological perspective, it would not be an exaggeration to call his notion of that term the communal counterpart of the Eastern Orthodox teaching of *theosis*, or deification. This doctrine, which developed in a monastic context, is usually associated with the personal prayer life and spiritual experience of the individual believer. According to this teaching, humans are called to a direct personal union with God, to a participation in divine life through the grace of the Holy Spirit. This communion with God, which involves a cooperation of the human will with the divine will, occurs only after a person engages in a life of continuous prayer and ascetic denial of the passions that combats self-aggrandizement, ambition for power, and divisive partisanship. The indwelling of the Holy Spirit effects a transformation of the whole person, including even the senses, such that the true nature and relational order of created beings are clearly perceived in the light of God.

Khomiakov's understanding of *sobornyi* can be read as proposing that the same "communion of the Holy Spirit" is manifested in the corporate experience and activity of the Church, and that the inner life of the Church reflects human relationality transfigured. His use of this term suggests the descent and manifestation of the very Spirit of the "divine Council," bonding humans one to another in a communion of love in their ascent together toward union with God. Ideally, in Khomiakov's view, those who participate in the ecclesial life—clergy and laity alike—are united in mind, will, and action, yet this life is ordered with a cohesive multiformity of uniquely personal operations. This heterogeneity of function, however, does not allow for unconditional subordination or for absolute power or authority of any one member, clerical or lay, *over* another.

Such a vision was discordant with certain teachings that had gained popularity in Russia. Khomiakov adamantly opposed, for example, the division of the Church into those who teach and those who are taught, insisting this was a feature of Western Christianity, both Roman Catholic and Protestant. Edification took place not solely through the word but through a person's entire way of life. "Every person," he wrote, "no matter how highly situated in the hierarchy or how hidden from view in the shadow of humble circumstances, both edifies and is edified. For God endows whom He desires with the gifts of His wisdom, without regard to person or position."[99]

Whether in the history of Orthodox thought as a whole Khomiakov's views were revolutionary, or even new, is open to debate. But in the theological context of the time his presentation was jarring. It was not even wholeheartedly accepted among his Slavophile peers. In ecclesiastical circles, his views prompted even more skepticism. P. S. Kazanskii, professor of history at the Moscow Theological Academy, for instance, referred to Khomiakov's teachings as fantastical, claiming that in order to accept such a conceptualization one would have to reject completely "our understanding of church." In 1884, P. Linitskii, professor at the Kiev Theological Academy, criticized Khomiakov's understanding of church as an organism in contrast to an institution. Linitskii maintained that in formulating his view of church in this way, Khomiakov stood closer to a Protestant than a Catholic view, and therefore failed in his attempt to articulate an authentically Orthodox ecclesiology that stood equally distinct from both. The main problem with Khomiakov's thought, Linitskii concluded, lay in the fact that he sought a distinctively Orthodox ecclesiology in the first place, instead of one that was contiguous with both Protestant and Catholic teachings.[100]

Whatever the criticisms, Khomiakov's great achievement was to recover and reanimate an understanding of church conveyed by early Christians in their use of the terms *ekklesia* and *koinonia*, the meanings of which were often obscured in its Slavonic and Russian translations of the word "church" (*tserkov'*). He reinstated the laity as essential constituents of the ecclesial body and did not ascribe any power or authority to the hierarchy independent of that body. The Church was not the building with its clergy, as suggested by Russian ecclesiastical laws, but the gathering of the People of God, which necessarily included the collective activity and experience of *both* clergy and laity. Moreover, Khomiakov tied his views on the Church to salvation, a process that at that time was usually thought of with respect to the individual. In Khomiakov's thinking it was inseparable from the body of believers as well.

Although Khomiakov wrote his principal essay, "The Church Is One," during the 1840s, it appeared in print in Russia only in the 1860s, in the progressive journal the *Orthodox Review*, during the dynamic period of social reforms under Alexander II. The appearance of his work corresponded to a general revival in Orthodox thought, and his work found kindred spirits among clergy who independently shared many of his intuitions about the notion of church. According to Khomiakov himself, the clergy who had read the treatise claimed that it "was completely Orthodox and only its format was unsuitable and doubtful."[101]

That there were members of the Orthodox establishment whose own ecclesial sensibilities reverberated with those of Khomiakov is not difficult to show. In 1866, for instance, the canon lawyer from the Kazan Theological Academy, A. S. Pavlov, delivered a lecture at Kazan University on the participation of laity in the affairs of the Church. Basing his views on a historical investigation of canon law, Pavlov came to the conclusion that laity can play any administrative or teaching role in the Church. The only ecclesial role that they could not take on was the carrying out of sacrament rituals (with the exception of baptism). For the sacraments, from the Orthodox perspective, ordination was required. He also concluded that lay participation in and management of ecclesial life historically had been directly related to the extent of the Church's protection by the state. The looser those ties, the more laity tended to be involved.[102]

It is not clear from the essay whether Pavlov had read Khomiakov. Nevertheless, his sentiments paralleled Khomiakov's own. In particular, Pavlov argued against the notion of a church whose members were easily divided into those who directed and those who were directed, into the active and the passive. Pavlov, too, emphasized the principles of love and freedom and defined the hierarchy according to the principle of service.

Despite the presence of clergy and academic theologians who shared Khomiakov's views on laity and community in the 1860s (and earlier), other members of the Orthodox establishment did not wholeheartedly embrace his thought. Until the 1890s, academic theological treatises on the Church seldom discussed or agreed with his ideas.[103] For example, the 1889 dogmatic theological textbook of Bishop Sylvester (Malevanskii), though influenced by Khomiakov, emphasized the divinely ordained status and exclusive privileges of the clergy in the Church. Contrasting Orthodoxy to Catholicism with its papal authority, he identified the "catholic voice" (*sobornyi golos*) of the Church solely with collective episcopal decisions.[104] Similarly, the priest and one-time rector of the Vologda diocesan seminary, N. Malinovskii, who even listed Khomiakov in the bibliography of standard ecclesiological texts in his 1909

*Orthodox Dogmatic Theology*, reiterated the earlier teaching of a body consisting of "unequal members" (*neravnykh*): those who teach and those who receive the teaching; those who perform rituals and those who utilize these rituals; and those who lead in the name of God and those who "with full confidence in the saving nature of their leadership submit themselves." Yet his presentation was tempered by his insistence that the relationship between the bishop and the laity did not rest on a "slavish obedience" of the latter. Rather, that relationship was to be based on a mutual faith in Christ, the true head of the Church. By virtue of this common faith, Malinovskii maintained, believers were to participate in the earthly affairs of the Church. "Faith and mutual love," he wrote, describing early Christian times, "so united pastors and the flock that neither the hierarchy without the laity nor the flock without the hierarchy wished to decide important matters concerning the Church."[105] More public theological discourse on the Church gradually began to include those who shared Khomiakov's vision, especially with regard to the lay principle in ecclesial life.[106] By the end of the nineteenth century, such sentiments were widespread and the notion of *sobornost'* had taken on a life of its own.

The growing tensions between the different ways of envisioning the Church were evident in the discussion that erupted in 1893 over a tedious article entitled "The Clergy and Society in the Contemporary Religious Movement" (*Dukhovenstvo i obshchestvo v sovremennom religioznom dvizhenii*) by Lev Tikhomirov, the one-time radical revolutionary turned conservative. While writing about the inspiration behind the religious awakening taking place among Russia's intellectuals, Tikhomirov tended to equate church with clergy and spoke of the clergy as teachers and laity as pupils. This aspect of his essay elicited a wave of heated responses, the most animated of which was that of N. P. Aksakov, a theologically trained lay publicist and administrator of the synodal chancellery.

In his article "Quench Not the Spirit" (*Dukha ne ugashaite*) Aksakov attacked Tikhomirov's essay as indicative of a level of ecclesiological ignorance that had reached epidemic proportions in Russia.[107] He questioned Tikhomirov's definition of teaching in the church community and challenged whether all lay-initiated participation in teaching activity could properly be termed "arbitrary" or "unauthorized" (*samochinstvo*). He noted the lack of any sense of communality in Tikhomirov's discussion about clergy and laity, the latter of which Tikhomirov described as isolated individuals superfluous to the Church. In the end, Aksakov claimed that Tikhomirov's views on the relationship between clergy and laity perverted the very essence of the Christian faith.

While it can be questioned whether Aksakov's attack on Tikhomirov was warranted, this incident showed the latent sensitivity that had emerged among Russia's educated believers to the lay question. One would assume that by 1905, when *sobornost'* surfaced as the single most influential principle within the reform debates, those such as Aksakov could have claimed a victory. Indeed, in 1906, Nikolai D. Kuznetsov, a legal advocate in the Moscow

District Court and one of the leading figures in the reform debates, said: "One of the main tasks of all of the anticipated reforms—and with which everyone appears in agreement—is the implementation of the principle of *sobornost'* in all spheres of church life."[108] Not all, however, would agree with him. Makarii's theology, despite being seen as the work of a "dogmatic bureaucrat" who was heavily influenced by Roman Catholic theology from his days at the Kievan Theological Academy, presented powerful traditional ecclesial images that had scriptural and patristic roots and that to many held almost irresistible political appeal.[109] Moreover, even if everyone might have agreed that *sobornost'* was a noble concept, it was unclear whether the term was uniformly understood. Khomiakov's writings on the nature of the Church emerged largely as a result of his polemics with Western Christian confessions.[110] By 1905, however, the term *sobornost'* was being applied not so much in polemics about Orthodox identity vis-à-vis Catholicism or Protestantism as in disputes about Orthodox corporate *self*-identity. In this context, its meaning was not always axiomatic or self-evident.

⋯⟾◉⟽⋯

## Debating the Base Ecclesial Unit: A. A. Papkov and I. S. Berdnikov

The lack of a uniform, official ecclesiological vision in Russian Orthodoxy became abundantly clear during the Preconciliar Commission that met between March and December 1906. The commission gathered for the purposes of evaluating the current Petrine system of church administration, planning ways to reinvigorate church life, and assessing what church reforms were needed in the rapidly changing social and political environment. This commission, consisting of twelve bishops, eight priests, seven laymen, and more than two dozen professors from theological academies, some of whom were ordained priests, was quintessentially official in its composition. Some educated members of society later criticized the work of the commission precisely because participation in it had been limited to members of the Orthodox establishment.[111]

Yet, despite its official character, it is noteworthy that this commission remained divided over the most fundamental issues. Its members differed markedly, for instance, in their reading of the Church's past. To a large extent, the commission's proceedings were an exercise in collective memory. In order to decide how best to proceed with reforms, the members attempted to recall and define the guiding principles of the Orthodox tradition not only in Russia but also in Byzantium and other traditionally Orthodox areas. Continually engaging their collective past by citing scripture, past councils, and canons in support of their various ideas, members of the commission could not agree on how to interpret this heritage.[112] They agreed even less on the meaning of current social and political events in light of Orthodoxy's own history.[113] Such fundamental discord over the interpretation of their past inevitably led to an impasse when it came to matters concerning the Petrine ordering of church life and the practical organization that church life should take in the present.[114] In reading the proceedings, one can quickly see two different ecclesiological trends at work, although variations on certain themes were evident. Two trends deserve detailed consideration, as they remain the clearest formulations of the differing ecclesial sensibilities within Orthodoxy on the eve of the revolutions of 1917.

The first of these trends conceived of parishes as the basic cells of church life that, united together, constituted the full ecclesial organism. This community-based, or "microecclesial," trend of thought maintained that the health of these parish cells determined the condition of the broader church and saw the parishes in Russia as having ceased to function properly, especially since the eighteenth century. The proponents of this approach thus advocated a fundamental restructuring of the local ecclesial system both for its own sake and for the sake of Orthodoxy as a whole.

One of the main theoreticians for this point of view was A. A. Papkov, a canon lawyer, layman, and subsequently governor in Finland.[115] For Papkov, the fundamental and irreducible unit of ecclesiology proper was the "small local church" (malen'kaia pomestnaia tserkov')—"a brotherly union of believers" that "emerged from the depths of a sense of church [tserkovnost'], and developed according to its spirit as well as to the principles characteristic only of it."[116] Papkov was concerned with the ecclesiological parameter of interpersonal relations, and specifically with the establishment of a "salvific communion" or fellowship among church members.[117] For him, the Christian community was "a family of the highest order, creating spiritual kinship among its members."[118] Papkov repeatedly stressed the idea that faith cannot be attained only intellectually. It arose not so much from solitude as from "brotherly fellowship one with another."[119]

A critical corollary of this relational principle was Papkov's affirmation of the essential equality of believers within the Church. He proposed that in [Orthodox] Christianity one finds

> a healthy and fruitful understanding of brotherhood and equality, for before God all people are equal and all people are brothers. In church or in parish assemblies . . . from the most famous to the simple folk, from the rich to the poor—all are aware of themselves and feel themselves of equal right [ravnopravnymi], and on the basis of this equality is erected an ecclesial order [blagoustroistvo] for the good of all faithful.[120]

While at the time such an affirmation might have sounded startlingly novel or suspiciously Western to some, similar ideas were not foreign to the Eastern patristic heritage.[121]

This principle of equality, however, did not mean that the ecclesial community was amorphous or undifferentiated. Papkov saw the distinction between clergy and laity as essential to church life. He envisioned the parish as an "ecclesial union consist[ing] of clergy and laity, who converge around the temple [*khram*] for the fulfillment of their Christian responsibilities and activities."[122] Papkov considered the quality and nurturing of this union to be the top priority of ecclesiastical reform efforts:

> The restoration of Christian sociability [*obshchitel'nosti*] both between pastor and flock, as well as among parishioners themselves, presents itself as the main task that should be placed at the basis of parish reform. Once this miracle-working communality [*obshchestvennost'*] appears, the parish will be resurrected as well.[123]

Papkov also proposed that the parish community was independent, not merely in a practical or legal sense but in its very being and activity. His theological justification for this belief was fourfold. First, since the small, local church was established by Christ himself, its origin and existence could not be made dependent on the will of ecclesiastical or secular authorities. Second, the ecclesial union was absolutely unique; it was "distinct from other human unions, and could not be associated with such institutions that require for their manifestation the sanction of any authorities." Third, he asserted that the Christian community (*obshchina*) "in its nature is a self-sufficient unity"; in order to flourish it must be left free and independent in the manifestation of its life, both in the religiomoral and the social sense. Finally, Papkov called on the "principles of Christian freedom" and the exhortation "not to quench the spirit" to support his assertion that subordination to episcopal authority cannot be unqualified.

With respect to this relation between the parish and the bishop, Papkov endorsed the teaching of hierarchical oversight but also affirmed the religiomoral competence of the local church. For example, after asserting that the parish must undoubtedly make itself subject to episcopal authority, Papkov proposed that the "collective conscience of the ecclesial community must always be watchful for the purity of Christian discipline." In his view, if a bishop violated Christian canons or ethics, the Christian ecclesial community had not only the right but also the responsibility to appeal his incorrect actions to the conciliar authorities, who decide all disagreements and misunderstandings.[124]

With such teachings Papkov sought not merely to obviate the entrenchment of any pernicious clericalism into local parish life but to promote the development of *sobornost'* at every level of ecclesial structure. Toward this end, he and his sympathizers focused their reform efforts on various relations within the ecclesiastical institution. They were mainly concerned with "including the laity in the fullness of church life and church interests" and incorporating them as full and equal members of the ecclesial body.[125] They thought that unless believers manifested the unifying spirit of their communal prayer outside the bounds of temple worship, the unity of spirit itself would be undermined.[126] Papkov and others sought legally to facilitate the engagement of laity in all aspects of parish affairs and to institute an independent system of self-government at the parish level. They planned to restructure the parish in such a way as to expand the scope of the popular understanding of the Church from its previous emphasis on the temple and hierarchy to include a vision of salvific communion embracing both clergy and laity.[127]

For these churchmen, *sobornost'* entailed a certain relative autonomy and independence of the local church.[128] Not surprisingly, their plan for practically implementing such an ecclesial philosophy bore little resemblance to the status quo. First, Papkov argued strongly for the recognition of the parish as a legal entity. This would allow the parish—laity together with clergy—to gain full rights to acquire and manage church property, with the stipulation that the Russian Orthodox Church at large would remain the technical owner of the property. He opposed the prevailing understanding of church property as belonging to the church, with *church* here defined as a temple building, managed by the clergy. Moreover, he argued, the fact that revenues and property belonging to the parish church had been donated most often by the laity themselves meant that they had a right to participate in managing these assets. Papkov and his supporters believed that proper relations among the body's members could develop only when lay men and women participated in all aspects of their parish life—administrative, liturgical, missionary, chari-table, and educational.[129] Among other things, this meant cultivating among laity the sense of their own community, so they would take more interest and responsibility in its affairs; it meant transforming laity from a passive group, on whom the Church acts and whom the Church produces, into conscious creators of that community.[130]

Papkov planned that laity would manage their parish affairs through the self-governing organs of the parish assembly and the parish council.[131] Accord-ing to the draft of the parish statute that Papkov and his supporters helped formulate, the parish assembly was designated primary manager of parish affairs.[132] All aspects of parish life would come under its jurisdiction, including participation of laity in the parish's liturgical life, the maintenance of the temple, education, charity work, and the moral behavior of community members.[133] Papkov personally advocated the involvement of all adult parish members, without regard to sex or social standing.[134]

The parish council, in turn, was the parish assembly's main executive organ, which directly organized and oversaw those activities of concern to the assembly, including educational, charitable, and missionary work. Papkov thought that except for the recognition of the parish priest as the council's chairman, the council's composition should not be strictly regulated and was best left to the decision of local parish assemblies.[135] In cases where the parish priest was unable to perform the function of council chairman, a lay person could be chosen in his stead.

Papkov supported neither the current legislation on parish guardians dating back to 1864 nor the Holy Synod's temporary measures on parish life issued in November 1905. The parish guardians, whose history began with the establishment of parish councils in border regions of the Russian Empire, were not parish councils. Nikolai Kuznetsov, whose vision was similar to Papkov's, noted that parish guardians technically were detached from the Church, as it was legally defined.[136] Because these guardians had no access to church funds, charity work and the work of the Church were viewed as belonging to two different spheres.[137] Papkov's supporters also maintained that the Synod's ruling of November 1905—the Church's official response to contemporary social and political pressures—did nothing to eliminate the bifurcation of clergy and laity that the rules governing diocesan administration reinforced.[138]

Finally, these thinkers believed that laity should choose their own pastor when vacancies appeared, so as to increase the likelihood of positive mutual regard between pastor and flock.[139] Moreover, Papkov proposed that should a bishop not agree to assign a particular elected candidate, he should be required to send a written response explaining why he declined to assign that candidate.[140] Papkov also advocated parishioners taking full responsibility for the financial support of their clergy, and he opposed a state-financed clergy. The community, together with the clergy, should agree on the terms of financial support. Only those parishioners who agreed to the amount each household should contribute would be held morally responsible for fulfilling their dues.

Papkov's sympathizers never denied the role of bishops or clergy in the life of the parish, let alone in the entire body of the Church. Indeed, the commission's draft of the parish statute retained the priest as chairman of both parish assembly and parish council. In both assemblies he held the deciding vote in cases of deadlock. Similarly, the local community's unity with the universal Church was defined through the bishop.[141]

Yet many who shared Papkov's views felt that a misrepresentation of the clerical vocation in the Church presented one of the main obstacles to the implementation of genuine change in the system as it stood. Papkov, for instance, denounced the stereotypic active/passive model of clergy/laity relations. Even though he did not deny the sacramental character of ordination, Papkov believed that the grace bestowed through the sacrament was passed to the entire community. Given the Orthodox teaching on grace and human cooperation, the grace received through ordination called for the active cooperation of all members of the ecclesial body for its realization.[142] Papkov, therefore, shifted the focus in ecclesiology from clergy to the entire community of laity and pastors. As one supporter of this vision of parish reform said, "it is not the parish that should nestle around the priest, but the priest who should nestle around the parish."[143]

Some of those who shared Papkov's views were inspired to do so by reasons other than theological and religious. Bishop Stefan of Mogilev, for example, was more concerned with a potential exodus of Orthodox believers to so-called sectarian groups. Amid the broader trends toward self-government and social activism, he maintained, the clerical principle would only push genuine Orthodox believers to seek fulfillment of their religious needs in different religious communities. It would be much wiser, he claimed, for clergy to give general sociopolitical aspirations ecclesial direction rather than repudiate or ignore them.[144]

Similarly, Bishop Sergii Stragorodskii, the future controversial patriarch of Russia, voiced more practical considerations in his support for broader lay participation or rights in parish administration. Without such participation, clergy would remain an isolated estate to whom laity would continue to defer responsibility, even for defending the Church against any widespread animosity that might develop toward it. With lay involvement, on the other hand, laity would perceive any direct attack or confiscation of church properties as a personal attack, involving something intimately their own.[145]

The second ecclesiological tendency that surfaced in Russia at the beginning of the twentieth century maintained that reform should begin not with the parish but with the higher church administration, be it with the establishment of a patriarch, the convening of a church council, or the reform of the Holy Synod. The main theoretician of this vision, I. S. Berdnikov, also a canon lawyer and layman, taught at the Kazan Theological Academy and the University of Kazan.[146] Proceeding from a fundamental principle of Ignatian ecclesiology—"where the bishop is present . . . there is the Catholic Church"[147]—Berdnikov advocated an episcopocentric or "macroecclesial" vision of the Church that resonated more with the notion of ordering than that of community per se. He and his supporters viewed the diocese, or *episkopiia*, not the parish, as the basic ecclesial unit and considered each priest as representative of the bishop's presence in the parish. Advocates of this view considered the idea of the parish as an independent unit foreign to the historical reality of the Orthodox Church.[148] Furthermore, they saw nothing fundamentally wrong with the existing ecclesial system. If every believer simply embarked on a quest for self-improvement, the administrative life of the Church would no longer experience stress. Therefore, they spoke more in terms of renewing rather than of reconstructing a system that had historically ceased to exist.[149]

According to an extreme version of this tendency, voiced by Dimitrii Khomiakov, the son of Alexei Khomiakov, local parish communities were seen not only as not central to the Orthodox vision of the Church but as a foreign element, historically introduced into Christianity on account of the demands of human life.[150] Church life did not demand the parish, he wrote, but simply tolerated it. Though Berdnikov never spoke in such extreme terms, he nonetheless opposed describing the parish as a cell of ecclesial life.[151] Berdnikov claimed that such an analogy was inaccurate since a cell was a self-sufficient unit for the manifestation or development of life. A parish, however, was not such a unit since it was a component of the diocese, which was its source of life. For similar reasons, Berdnikov's supporters also rejected the descriptive terms "small church" and "community" (*obshchina*) for the parish.[152]

Berdnikov's fundamental disagreement with Papkov over the position of the local faith community in church organization as a whole resulted in disagreements over other proposed reforms. For instance, Berdnikov saw no value in the idea of an autonomous parish being legally recognized as self-governing, since this status would in effect sever each parish from the diocese. Instead, Berdnikov advocated having each parish consist of two legal entities: the church building and the parish community. Citing past canons, he claimed that money and goods donated for purposes of maintaining and beautifying the church technically belonged to the Lord and therefore were most accurately designated as belonging to the church building. Laity, as donors, forfeited their rights to manage this sacred property. That responsibility belonged to ecclesiastical authorities, namely the bishop. Consequently, Berdnikov opposed any discussion of self-governing in the parish context.[153] Laity could only oversee property that they did not specifically donate to the Church but that they collected to serve other parish-related needs.

Although many who shared Berdnikov's views did not oppose lay involvement through parish meetings or parish councils, they did not support any governing roles for laity. They opposed the idea of any pastoral responsibilities being shared by laity, such as monitoring fellow parishioners' moral behavior.[154] They viewed the activity of parish councils and parish assemblies solely in terms of their consultative roles to the priest. Laity were the priest's aides and had no authority independent of him. Any lay participation, even in terms of property management, would be based not on their *right* as owners of the property but on pastoral recognition of lay zeal.[155] One Berdnikov supporter went so far as to insist that the conversion of all local funds into *parish* funds (in contradistinction to clerical and church funds) would be a form of secularization.[156] They also opposed the popular election of parish clergy but did not always oppose the then current practice of parishioners suggesting desired candidates to their bishops. Under no circumstances, however, did they believe that a bishop was accountable to the laity if he did not accede to their request.[157]

In part, this cautious view of lay participation in parish affairs emerged from practical concerns. Many, like Berdnikov, feared that once laity independently managed parish finances, nominal Christians would strive to be elected to the parish council in order to control finances and property. Distrusting the intentions of some parishioners, these thinkers maintained that the lay ecclesial vision rarely extended beyond the immediate parish. They doubted whether laity would voluntarily part with their funds to support diocesan or even nationwide church needs, such as ecclesiastical schools or missionary work. They were not even sure laity would readily financially support their parish priest. Therefore, they frequently supported a state salary for clergy. They believed that reforms should be aimed not at introducing new rights but at properly regulating lay participation to prevent abuse.[158]

Interestingly, Berdnikov also criticized the 1864 Rules governing parish guardianships, but for reasons diametrically opposed to Papkov's. Berdnikov and his supporters agreed that the guardianships were not truly ecclesial organizations because they technically stood outside episcopal jurisdiction. The concerns of Berdnikov and others, however, rested with what this guardianship status meant not for laity but for clergy. They were troubled, for instance, that the guardianship chairman by definition did not have to be the parish priest.[159] Consequently, they supported the spirit behind the Synod's latest effort to encourage the establishment of parish councils. They claimed that by emphasizing the directing role of the pastor on the parish level, the Synod's ruling of 18 November 1905 was a proper step toward reform.[160]

While those who shared Berdnikov's views voiced recognition of *sobornost'* as an ordering principle of ecclesial life, they clearly did not agree with those practical expressions or applications of *sobornost'* presented by Papkov's supporters. Although Berdnikov, too, used the Pauline bodily metaphor when speaking about the ecclesial community, he asserted that the unity of members in the Spirit in no way leveled the differences or confused the functions granted by the organism to its various members. It was according to the nature of the Church that its members did not carry out equal functions. Thus, perfect unity and communion among the members manifested themselves when each member "fulfilled exactly what was directed to him by nature, and did not deviate an iota from his position."[161] In this understanding of *sobornost'*, harmony within the Church flowed from above, from the tone set by the bishop.[162]

Like Metropolitan Makarii (Bulgakov), Berdnikov and his supporters firmly adhered to the dichotomy between teaching and learning stereotypically associated with clergy and laity, respectively.[163] For them, the episcopacy alone had been assigned the function of guarding and teaching the faith by the grace of the Holy Spirit. Therefore, they did not identify *sobornost'* with equality of ecclesial "rights." Irritated by the continual reference to *sobornost'* in the reform debates, Berdnikov asserted that it should be read solely in terms of geographic universality. Functionally, this meant that any major decisions made by the Russian Church had to be brought to the attention of and discussed with the other local Eastern Orthodox churches. F. D. Samarin, also annoyed at the continual reference to *sobornost'*, insisted that it was purely a moral idea and best not discussed in the context of legal or administrative reforms.[164]

Papkov's and Berdnikov's ideas on parish reform provide a sketch of competing ecclesiological visions that could equally be characterized as officially Orthodox in early twentieth-century Russia. In considering the broad spectrum of imaginations captured by the idea of church reform, both visions could also be categorized as centrist. Numerous variations on the themes they raised, both to the left and to the right, testified to the diverse range of ideas and opinions competing to shape official Orthodox Church policy at the time.[165] The complexity of variations can be seen in the opinions on reform held by many parish priests, in particular rural parish priests, who were conspicuously absent from the Preconciliar Commission. They, along with many of their urban counterparts, tended to look with suspicion on the work of this commission and would rather have seen issues discussed and resolved in the context of diocesan meetings.[166] They voiced their views occasionally in the religious press, especially in diocesan newspapers, and in particular during diocesan meetings.

Parish priests provided a unique perspective in the debates, occupying a position both official and local in the ecclesial system. Some of them promoted a pastor-centered vision that combined aspects of the Papkov and Berdnikov ecclesiological tendencies.[167] Many agreed with Papkov that ecclesial identity began with the parish and that the health of the Church at large depended on the well-being of local faith communities.[168] They agreed that such local sacred communal identity was not fostered by current ecclesiastical legislation. Therefore, they fervently supported the idea of legal autonomy for local parishes, some going so far as to advocate that each parish community decide its own order of liturgical services.[169] They spoke against excessive episcopal and bureaucratic intrusion into their local affairs, claiming that it only served to shackle any initiative. Feeling more burdened than honored by being the bishop's representative in the local parish, many priests called for independence from hierarchy in parish affairs.[170] They especially opposed the financial drain that the centralized ecclesiastical institutions, including both the Holy Synod and the diocese, placed on parishes.[171] Priests did not deny the episcopal vocation but rather believed that the carrying out of this vocation had been compromised, especially over the past two centuries.[172] Some of them, therefore, advocated the election of bishops by parish clergy from among parish clergy, as opposed to monastics, as a possible remedy to internal ecclesial strife.[173]

At the same time, however, many priests expressed caution with respect to the issue of lay self-determination. They criticized emphasis on lay rights without accompanying attention to lay responsibility.[174] They opposed the idea of lay election of pastors, for instance, and doubted whether granting more authority to lay persons in the ecclesial system, even in the management of parish property, would in any way remove the main obstacles to developing parish life.[175] If anything, many believed such changes would make matters worse.[176] They attributed the heightened emphasis on the lay communal element in the Church to an impulsive reaction against the Petrine bureaucratic ecclesiastical system that in the end would only hamper those improvements that to date had been made in parish life.[177]

Lay self-government and local faith communities were topics of discussion not only in church circles but also among those interested in the socioeconomic ordering of Russia's civil society. Continuing in the vein of discussions previously raised with respect to the emancipation of the serfs and to the Moscow provincial zemstvo's 1880 petition, persons such as Prince A. G. Shcherbatov, S. F. Sharapov, K. Odarchenko, and V. Ern spoke of the parish in terms of the ideal small zemstvo unit. Although at times religiously inspired, much of the discussion of the parish in this context was motivated by nationalistic sentiments. Employing the same terminology that characterized the community-based tendency discussed earlier, Prince A. Kropotkin also spoke of the parish in terms of cells. The organism in question, however, was not Christ's body but Russia.[178] Prince A. Shcherbatov similarly appropriated the concept of the parish from its original ecclesial context for political use. He spoke of the parish as the "foundation of the state" and as a "source of the Russian nationalistic spirit."[179] For such thinkers, a renewal of the Russian state depended on the vitality of local parish communities.

In this line of thought, the parish would be transformed into the main rural self-governing political unit that would be coterminous with both ecclesiastical and zemstvo administrations. Besides its purely religious functions, the parish community would also serve as the social body in which credit unions, police stations, tax collection systems, and consumer cooperatives would be established. It would also oversee and manage property, local industry, and trade.[180] As the author of an article entitled "Crime and the Parish" (*Prestupnost' i prikhod*) proposed, parish self-government would provide a balance in Russia's rural areas to the problems of the disintegration of the village communal system. "Declassed" and alienated rural inhabitants would be able to find a haven in the "fraternal unity" of an autonomous parish community.[181]

While many supporters of the parish as the small zemstvo unit clearly identified with the Orthodox faith, their discussions tended to fall outside the purview of purely ecclesial concerns. Most churchmen who in the wake of 1905 desired to see the Church freed from its bondage to the state regarded this proposal as a purely secular approach to an essentially religious matter, and rarely directly entertained such ideas in their parish reform debates.[182] As the priest Dimitrii Papov noted, such proposals only confused matters that were already complex enough in and of themselves. He believed that in their attempt to combine the spiritual and economic aspects of life, one aspect, usually the spiritual, would surely suffer.[183] This did not mean that those who did not speak of the parish in terms of a zemstvo unit were opposed to a more socially salient role for parish communities. Papkov's ecclesial vision, for instance, was clearly inspired by the idea of the parish's socially transformative role, and he himself was inspired by the broader role the parish had played in social life before the eighteenth century; he also wrote about the benefits of the small zemstvo unit.[184] Those like Papov, however, simply advocated that this work naturally emerge from within the ecclesial community rather than be artificially imposed upon it as a civil duty.

Generally, those who held either an episcopocentric or a pastor-centered view criticized thinkers such as Papkov for attempting to restructure the Orthodox ecclesial order according to congregationalist Protestant ideas that "because of a lack of hierarchical ordering" could only resort to principles that govern civil society.[185] They accused these thinkers of lacking trust in the hierarchy and attempting to introduce democratic and socialist principles into the life of the Church by establishing "parish parliaments."[186] They read Papkov's emphasis on community and on the "ecclesial people" (*tserkovnyi narod*) as excluding clergy, especially the episcopacy. Accordingly, they thought that some were equivocating in their use of the term *sobornost'*, not clearly distinguishing it from the notion of "popular rule" (*narodovlastie*). They criticized Papkov and his supporters for using the term *sobornost'* not for the purpose of expressing the Spirit of Christ but as a call to limit episcopal authority in the Church.[187]

Furthermore, they claimed that Papkov's attention to contemporary sociopolitical affairs resulted in the introduction of ideas that were foreign to the ecclesial organism itself. Antonii (Khrapovitskii), the bishop of Volhynia, for instance, compared the parish to a spiritual family and asked whether democratic principles, including the electoral principle, were proper to internal family relations.[188] The very notion of parish autonomy, Papkov's critics maintained, would lead to an ecclesial system characterized by a federation of independent communities, organized from below. Such ideas were diametrically opposed to their own understanding of church order as organized from above.[189]

Those sympathetic to Papkov, in turn, claimed that Berdnikov's vision typified Roman Catholic tendencies by reducing the Church to hierarchical structures and by speaking of the Church in a manner that divided clergy from people.[190] They criticized Berdnikov's virtual identification of the Church with clergy and parish with laity, which rendered the notion of the People of God meaningless.[191] Drawing a distinction between sacramental gifts and administrative rights, they argued that the defense of ecclesiastical authority on the grounds of institutional order was based on a misappropriation of the idea of authority. In the ecclesial context, they argued, power and authority were of a different quality, attributed not because of external power and force, as in the secular political sphere of human life, but on the basis of self-denial for the benefit of others.[192]

Furthermore, Papkov went so far as to question whether the organization of the parish as envisioned by Berdnikov could even be called "ecclesial."[193] Berdnikov's chronic distrust of lay potential and his continual efforts to minimize lay influence in the Church were unacceptable to Papkov's supporters not only theologically but practically speaking, given the contemporary demands on the Church.[194] Nikolai Kuznetsov remarked that the tendency to lower laity to the status of a tail in the ecclesial organism was an insult to Christ, the body's head, and a perversion of the very idea of the Church. Similarly, he predicted that the liberation of the Church from the state without the simultaneous reinstatement of the laity as active members in the ecclesial organism would result in a power vacuum and lead to a form of Orthodox clericalism.[195] Arguing that the lay issue was the most pressing one facing the Orthodox Church, he claimed that overlooking it could lead not only to the demise of the Church in modern Russian society but perhaps also to an internal church schism. A. A. Papkov put the matter more bluntly when he warned: "We live in difficult times . . . the people are different now. God save us if they begin striving for ecclesial rights by forcible means."[196]

## Continuing Strains

The deep-seated tensions in ecclesiological thought exposed by the Papkov-Berdnikov exchange continued to inform the debates over the long-awaited parish reform and the notion of *sobornost'* up to 1917. In 1906, the Preconciliar Commission opted against Papkov's community-based understanding of parish. This move occurred despite pockets of local initiatives among many clergy and laity to reconstruct their parishes into "autonomous, self-governing ecclesial communities."[197] Instead, the Preconciliar Commission accepted the definition proposed by the more episcopocentrically minded A. I. Almazov, another layman and professor of canon law from Novorossisk University in Odessa. Positing "spaces" between the parish, the church building, and the gathering of believers, Almazov defined the parish as an institution under the direction of the bishop that fulfilled the religious and moral needs of a group of believers who were directed by a priest and assigned to a church building for this purpose.[198]

Although the voting on most matters bearing on church reform was very close during the proceedings of the Preconciliar Commission, the weight tended to fall on the side of the episcopocentrically minded participants. Without knowledge of the internal debates among its members, it was not difficult to conclude, as indeed some publicists did, that the Commission "rejected the implementation of the broad principles of *sobornost'*."[199] During the next decade the Synod continued its preparatory work for an eventual All-Russian Church Council under the auspices of a special standing committee (*osoboe soveshchanie*) organized specifically for this purpose. The committee's stated task was to organize the results of the Preconciliar Commission. Some critics, however, saw the creation of the special committee as an attempt by central ecclesiastical authorities to regroup after the Preconciliar Commission in order to stave off any movements toward "democratization" in the Church.[200]

The parish issue stood at the forefront of the special committee's work. It continued to struggle with the parish issue and in the process gradually pulled even further away from the principles that Papkov's model had embodied.[201] When formulating their own version of a parish statute in 1907, members of the committee modified virtually all those clauses of a Papkov-inspired draft statute that hinted at parish autonomy and independence.[202] Instead of referring to the local faith community as being under the local bishop's jurisdiction, for example, they specified that the parish was "subordinate" to the bishop. They also deleted any notions of the parish as an independent ecclesial unit, claiming that such an idea introduced the federation principle into the idea of the Church.[203] The version that emerged five years later in 1911–12 was even more staunchly episcopocentric, though one of its stated goals was to attract parishioners to an active participation in parish life.[204] In this draft, the parish was defined as a "union of laity," in contrast to laity and clergy together, while the parish clergy were identified with the Church. The parish was the part of the flock that fell under the direction of the local bishop. Formal management of parish property remained with the diocesan bishop, parish priest, and church elder. As the ober-procurator of the Holy Synod, V. K. Sabler, reminded those government officials who were to review the draft statute, church property by nature belonged to God and therefore had to be managed entirely by bishops and their direct representatives.[205]

This draft too met swift criticism from more community-minded churchmen. The editors of the journal *Respite for a Christian*, for instance, commented on the draft's "Roman Catholic leaning," noting that "a single idea informs the entire draft, namely the centralization of ecclesiastical authority." Laity, they claimed, were granted no rights, only "responsibilities demanded by the Church." They were perceived as passive, uninterested bystanders who lacked any ecclesial insight. The only conclusion that they could draw from the statute was that the "Orthodox bishops have no faith in Orthodox laity, in their Christian reasoning, and in their Christian consciences."[206]

By 1916, even certain officials within the upper echelons of ecclesiastical administration voiced their criticism of the lack of movement on the front of church reform. During a review of the 1916 budget, members of a synodal committee noted that one reason for this lack of movement was that the Church had departed from that ecclesial structure that various apostolic, ecumenical, and local councils had imparted to it. The budget commission's report called for decentralizing the Church's power structure and for more local ecclesial self-government. "This principle of local self-government is so true and durable that they are trying to carry it through in various areas of state life; in the Church, however, it is lost."[207] Yet the Synod still proceeded cautiously. Although in March of that year it sent out a directive to diocesan bishops reminding them of the anticipated parish reform and urging them to take an active initiative in preparing local communities for the new legislation, by April it cited wartime unrest as a reason to postpone further action on this issue.[208]

In 1917, however, revolutionary pressures moved a newly formed Synod to change course toward the community-based line of thinking. Accordingly, on 17 June 1917 its members issued temporary parish regulations that were to remain in effect until the decrees and rulings of the anticipated All-Russian Council. Reflecting a much more lay-friendly position, these temporary regulations defined the parish as a community (*obshchina*) formed by believers around a church building for the purposes of enjoying fellowship in prayer, sacraments, and Christian teachings. With the aid of clergy they were to help each other in attaining salvation by means of a moral life and in performing Christian works of enlightenment and charity.[209] Although not dismissing the role of the episcopacy in uniting the parish to the universal Church, these regulations also actively incorporated lay people into the process of community building by giving them the responsibility of nominating candidates to serve their parish as priests. Moreover, in stark contrast to the Synod's 1912 version of a parish statute, the regulations required that diocesan bishops explain to parishioners in cases where they did not support the parishioners' candidate. They also consented to the idea that the chairperson of the church assembly would be elected from among either clergy or laity.

These temporary parish regulations, however, proved no less resistant to criticism. Local meetings of clergy in 1916 had revealed the ingrained division among parish clergy over the principles that governed the structure of community life in the Church. Clergy from the Moscow diocese, for instance, had claimed that any reforms that suppressed the hierarchical principle in ecclesial life would only destroy the parish as an ecclesial unit.[210] Not surprisingly, a priest, K. Maksimov, in response to the Synod's 1917 temporary parish regulations, wrote that "divine, sacred, ancient, and inviolable ecclesiastical law" maintained that the management of church lands belonged to the bishop and, together with him, the parish clergy. To pass this right to the laity would mean that such lands would cease being church property.[211] In the Tavrida diocese, a clergy meeting had juxtaposed their views "against the widespread view of the parish as a small church, self-governing, free and independent in its life." For them, the parish was a part of the *episkopiia*, a union of Christians assembled around their temple under the direction of the God-established hierarchy with the goals of attaining eternal salvation."[212] Yet at the same time clergy from the Tobolsk and Kursk dioceses supported the electoral principle at all levels of ecclesial life and actively cooperated with their laity in their social and political concerns.[213]

In 1917–18 the All-Russian Church Council revisited the parish issue, that "life nerve" of all of that council's work.[214] Indicative of the way churchmen were thinking, the council began its ecclesial reconstruction from the top, by addressing the issue of the reestablishment of a patriarch, rather than from the bottom, with the parish, as many churchmen had advocated. Not surprisingly, when it came to the parish, members once again found themselves polarized over the same set of issues Papkov and Berdnikov had argued about more than a decade before, namely the definition of the parish and the "Achilles heel" of parish reform: the election of pastors and the ownership and management of church property.[215] At virtually every stage, tensions surfaced between the macro- and microecclesial visions of sacred community life and over the structural organization of that life.

In a way that was reminiscent of the trends that surfaced in 1905 and 1906, these divergent modes of thinking were in part rooted in various underlying perceptions of the laity, perceptions that were easily influenced by growing revolutionary turmoil but not limited to them. Many of those who insisted on hierarchical management of church property voiced their suspicions about lay intentions when it came to sacred church items, as well as entire church buildings and cathedrals. Not distinguishing between sincere believers and those who were simply counted Orthodox by law, members of the council such as L. K. Artamonov, a general in the infantry, worried predominantly about the "armed bandits" in the countryside who "kept everyone in fear." Convinced that such groups would find their way into the parish as soon as it was declared the legal owner of church property and sell off such property for their own personal use, Artamonov and those like him sought all means to protect that property.[216]

Those who desired to see more management of church affairs at the parish level, on the other hand, tended to distinguish the laity from the *narod* and to conceive of the former as sincere believers. One layman with this perspective, the peasant A. I. Iudin from the Olonets diocese, found himself insulted by insistence on episcopal management of all church property. "It is shameful to be an Orthodox Christian if you cannot defend your church and if we will be told, 'get out of here, you drunkard, this is a matter for the bishop.' "[217] In his letter to the Council, a layman from the Riazan diocese, N. Fatov, pointed out another major problem affecting community in Orthodoxy at the dawn of the twentieth century—the definition of the parishioner. Fatov's letter at first voiced the need for an "internal cleansing" of the Church's hierarchical ranks. Fatov supported elections of priests and bishops as one means to accomplish this, but insisted on a significant condition for these elections: the parishioner had to be defined first. It was a "frustrating absurdity," he wrote, to count as parishioners all those persons who were baptized and who happened to live within a particular region around a church. Only those persons who desired to be parishioners, who regularly went to church, participated in the the sacraments, and paid dues should be so called.[218] Fatov said that without such conditions the electoral principle would not work. His conclusion was supported by reports of related problems in other dioceses.

During the meetings of the All-Russian Church Council, representatives of both macro- and microecclesial tendencies embraced the notion of *sobornost'* as the characteristic feature of their reform projects. Yet, as was already evident in the discussion about church reform in 1905–6, churchmen did not understand or use this term uniformly. While at the beginning of the twentieth century theological reflection on the notion of *sobornost'* had found more fertile ground among community-minded churchmen, now, in 1917–18, the term received more intense theological attention from the more hierarchically minded. One reason for this heightened interest was their desire to articulate a strong theological justification for the position of the patriarch in the ecclesial sacred order and to show that the notion of hierarchy was integral to the principle of *sobornost'*.

Advocates for the election of a patriarch based their theological rationale in the assertion that the trinitarian God, whose divine life was a perfect communion of three divine persons, was the eternal prototype for *sobornost'*. The unity and communion suggested by *sobornost'* did not preclude a hierarchical principle, as God the Father was the source of the Son and the Spirit.[219] Then, in their analysis of the Church, they noted that integration, subordination, and centralization were principles innate to all living organisms. The life of the human body, physiologically and chemically, depended on both mutuality and centripetalism. As a living organism, the Church, too, shared these traits. The essential indicators of *sobornost'*, in their view, included an affirmation of the individual as well as an affirmation of the hierarchical principle.[220] Moreover, since the principle of *sobornost'* affirmed those unique features of each person that distinguished them from other persons and from the whole, it could not recognize any unconditional or mechanical equality of all persons.[221] *Sobornost'* emerged when authority defined itself as service and subjects placed themselves in voluntary compliance with that which they recognized as authoritative.[222]

Those who tended toward the microecclesial vision, on the other hand, saw nothing in the nature of *sobornost'* or the Church that necessarily called for the election of a patriarch.[223] Either his presence or his absence could fit into what they envisioned as an appropriate ecclesial model. Persons of this mindset disagreed with any definition of *sobornost'* that necessarily required a patriarch—a "patriarchal *sobornost'*," as they called to it. To them such a notion of *sobornost'* only implied a latent absolutism and tendency toward bureaucratization that ran through Byzantine and Russian church history.[224] Those who shared a microecclesial vision of the sacred community supported their interpretation of *sobornost'* with a view of apostolicity that they believed could be found in the Book of Acts. Apostolicity, in their perspective, involved a close participation of all followers of Christ in the activities of the Church and the presence of an electoral principle. They put forward a metaphor used by Ignatius of Antioch to illustrate their reading of the apostolic ideal: it entailed believers forming a choir so that "in perfect harmony, they may sing in unison and with one voice" to God. Accordingly, in their minds it was of utmost importance to maintain an all-ecclesial (*vsetserkovnyi*) principle, even over a patriarchal principle. They wanted to ensure that the highest ecclesial authority would reside in an All-Russian Council comprised of both clergy and laity. In response to criticism that they were "imitating Protestants," one advocate of this way of thinking retorted that it was better to be "protestant" along with the apostles than to embark on the path to Rome and thereby "cut all ties with the unity of spirit . . . with the apostolic Church."[225]

These two ways of thinking about *sobornost'* did not abate with the onset of 1917 and continued to exist just below the appearance of unity that the council often maintained. Periodically, even in the throes of social, political, and religious upheaval, persons paused to reflect on these two ways of thinking. In 1917, B. V. Titlinov, church historian and professor at St. Petersburg's Theological Academy, for instance, wrote that despite all of the attention paid to *sobornost'* over the past decade, people were still not sure what it meant. His interest lay in tracing the historical lines of these different ways of thinking. He found the foundations of the idea in the beginnings of Christianity—in the words of Christ: "Where two or three have gathered." Titlinov maintained that the promise of divine presence was given not to individuals but to a gathering of believers. The revelation of "Truth," therefore, could best be sought in the fellowship of believers.

Despite these beginnings, *sobornost'* came to take on another meaning, Titlinov claimed, during the Byzantine period of Christian history, when bishops were torn from their representative roles within the ecclesial community and became to a large extent state bureaucrats. On account of these historical developments, the structure governing ecclesial life became such that the sacred community no longer enjoyed a "correct circulation" of life blood. "The head (i.e., the episcopacy) was sustained more by the artificial flow of energy from the side of the state then by the sap of the ecclesial body."[226]

Given that Russia inherited its ecclesial structure from Byzantium, Titlinov continued, it never knew the genuine experience of *sobornost'*, even prior to the Petrine period. Therefore, it was not surprising, he maintained, that in the current milieu of reform, those churchmen who sought a restoration of ecclesial order based on pre-Petrine principles simply adopted the Byzantine ecclesiastical model that had perpetuated the segregation of bishops from the broader ecclesial body. In this understanding, claimed Titlinov, the hierarchy enjoyed the fullness of authority, while the faithful enjoyed the fullness of obedience. This understanding of *sobornost'* inevitably found itself at odds with the view that sought to revive the latent communal currents of ecclesial life and thereby restore the "correct flow of its sap."

In 1918, during the proceedings of the All-Russian Church Council, Bishop Efrem of Selengina voiced his evaluation of the tension he saw fragmenting the ecclesial body. In his view the lines of demarcation between various readings of *sobornost'* proceeded from two different models of world order—a theocratic and a democratic one. According to the former, ecclesiastical authority was a dogmatic principle that stood alongside the Orthodox faith and the sacraments. It was even confessed in the Creed, claimed Efrem, in the notion of apostolicity. Apostolicity in his reading suggested the fullness of authority held by and passed down through the episcopacy. Since its source was "from above," from God, and not from the community of believers, the participation of the laity in ecclesial affairs took place only by episcopal fiat.

A democratic view of the world, on the other hand, found authority from below, in the will of the people. In this view the ideas of self-determination, self-government, and "all power to the people" replaced the theocratic principles of decision, direction, and "all power to God." Efrem went so far as to attribute the fall of the great archangel to a democratic disposition. This disposition, he maintained, was adopted by Protestants and was now making its way into Orthodox circles under the banner of *sobornost'*.[227] Just as Titlinov felt compelled to shed light on the historically "genuine" nature of *sobornost'*, so Efrem felt equally moved to defend his understanding of that term and to shed light on its strategic appropriation by the "ecclesiastical democrats."

The debates over reform in the period 1905–17 were monumental in the history of Orthodox thought. They signaled an intensification of collective self-consciousness that yearned for definition and clarity of ecclesiological vision. Nothing comparable in magnitude or potential impact has taken place since. The growing discourse on church, laity, and local faith communities at this time in Orthodoxy included a provocative mixture of ideas that had counterparts in the world of the European Reformation and the more contemporary world of Catholic *Aufklarung* and Catholic Romantic theologians.[228] It would later have parallels in modern Christian liberation theologies.

The divergent ecclesiological trends proved hopelessly irreconcilable, especially given that they did not fall neatly along church "class" lines. Both groups argued convincingly from a position of tradition and based their arguments on scriptural, canonical, theological, and more general historical sources. Debates over the local faith community and the role of laity in the Church at large were driven by a fundamental disagreement over the locus of manifest ecclesial identity—the episcopacy or the local church community—as well as over the definition of *sobornost'* in its practical manifestation. The fact that many churchmen still equated "laity" with some undifferentiated mass of "the people" only further complicated the debates. Participants in the debates were well aware of the extent of dissension within the Church on these issues. When it was suggested, for example, that members of the Preconciliar Commission first define the *idea* of the parish before embarking on any practical reform proposals, the bishop of Mogilev, Stefan, admitted that the commission would then get nowhere. He said that the section of the Preconciliar Commission responsible for preparing a draft parish statute deliberately avoided theoretical, theological discussions about the parish because it was evident that the range of opinions was so diverse that a consensus was out of reach.[229] More than a decade later, members of the 1917–18 All-Russian Church Council were no more uniform in their thinking on the same subject.

The continued dissension over these issues raises questions about the historical trajectory of the institutional Church in Russia in the early twentieth century.[230] As Paul Valliere has noted, the Council of 1917–18 was not a fair test of reform debates.[231] Council members were making decisions on key issues under the duress of an unstable political situation, at a time when word of arrests and shooting of clergy interrupted Council sessions and local armed skirmishes prevented members of the council from venturing out to attend its sessions. Under such conditions, it is not surprising that members began to speak of the parish as a "protective, defensive spiritual stronghold," "a moat" against various trends that were foreign to the faith.[232] Conceivably, had the processes begun by the discussions in 1905 been able to proceed without the political and social pressures brought on by the 1917 October Revolution, the Orthodox Church in Russia may have found itself divided into reformed and conservative denominations. After all, in the diaspora these ecclesiological tensions did not fade and, indeed, they contributed to later jurisdictional divisions among Russian Orthodox communities in the West.

These debates revealed a remarkable ambiguity in the notion of "center" in Orthodox thinking regarding community at a critical moment in history. Faced with the prospect and opportunity of restructuring their ecclesiastical system, Orthodox churchmen found themselves uncomfortably discordant behind a shared proclamation of *sobornost'* as the basic principle according to which such restructuring was to proceed. Debates over seemingly mundane bureaucratic matters soon revealed that much disagreement was not merely tactical or procedural, or simply colored by fears of revolution and unrest. Rather, disagreement arose from much deeper diverging theological beliefs about how the Christian community had been and should be formed and maintained. Indeed, were this study to stop at the level of bureaucratic procedures and institutional structure, it would be difficult to see how the sacred community in Orthodoxy at this critical moment in history "worked" at all.

# 2

⋅⊱═◉═⊰⋅

# Temple Dialectics
## Sacred Place and the Claim on Orthodox Identity

Sanctify those who love the beauty of Thy house;
glorify them in return by Thy divine power.

—From the Divine Liturgy of St. John Chrysostom

Caught in the tensions that surfaced in churchmen's understanding of the term "church," the church building—in Russian often referred to as a temple (*khram*)—was a symbol in flux to which theologians and ecclesiastical officials of various persuasions referred in their discourse about the normative ordering of Christian life. When considered apart from that polemical situation and observed in its lived context, we see that the processes and homiletic images that helped establish the temple as a source of Orthodox identity were no less complex and dynamic than the debates themselves. Indeed, the temple was one of those distinctive features of Russian Orthodoxy that captured Russia's nineteenth-century literary and artistic imagination. From the playwright Griboedov's claim that "We are Russians only in church" to the painter Levitan's depiction of a church as the sole resting place in the transience of human life, the church temple aroused a wide range of sentiments among educated and non-educated Russians alike (fig. 2.1).[1]

The temple played a pivotal role in the expression and formation of individual and corporate Orthodox self-understanding. It created a space where not only the hierarchical and the communal but the personal and the collective, the private and the public, the cosmological and the historical dovetailed to offer a variegated semantic arena within which believers could find the familiar and situate themselves. To fully appreciate the temple's role in fostering Orthodox identity, it should be approached from three angles. The first views the temple in terms of its material construction. Believers who lived in provincial and rural areas often exerted an inordinate amount of energy when it came to their parish church. With their meager resources, they tirelessly constructed and maintained their parish churches, both discovering

54

2.1    I. I. Levitan, *Eternal Rest*. 1894. Oil on canvas. 150 × 206 cm.
The Tretyakov Gallery, Moscow, inv. no. 1486.

meaning in and bestowing meaning on them as sacred symbols. In certain respects, data relating to construction and beautification efforts tells the story of believers' engagement in church culture. This story, however, can be compared to some extent to a silent movie in which one can follow actions but hear no dialogue. Indeed, only rarely do documents and petitions relating to the construction or maintenance of parish churches present believers' detailed reflections on the temples' significance and meaning. Instead, it is their activity itself that offers a glimpse into the manner in which the temple came to shape community in Russian Orthodoxy as it was itself being shaped and constructed.

At the same time, it is evident that the construction and maintenance of churches did not take place in a cultural vacuum. A broader religious cultural context existed that defined the temple in its own terms. Believers came to know the semantics of temple culture through sermons, popular devotional pamphlets, and periliturgical discussions. The stories and ideas therein sparked their religious imagination and often affirmed and further encouraged their temple-related efforts. The second and third parts of this chapter approach the temple through devotional literature in order to offer something of the "sound" of that spiritual culture that the temple was meant to create.

Finally, the temple was more than an inspirational architectural structure that involved notions of place and space; it also signified a gathering and community. Therefore, the last section of this chapter approaches the temple in terms of the human relations that shaped temple culture; it examines the means by which lay people participated in creating that culture and looks at how the temple was managed. The community that managed the Orthodox temple in rural nineteenth- and twentieth-century Russia did not translate as easily into idyllic representations as did the building. Competing claims to management found the temple at the center of a local ecclesial identity in flux.

⊷⊜⊶

## Constructing and Maintaining God's Abode

Between 1861 and 1917, Russia saw the construction of some thirteen thousand new parish and cemetery churches, which rose from 36,763 to 48,636 in number. Even when taking into account those churches and parishes that were located on Russia's borderlands, where missionary and state interests made Orthodox religious identity a political concern and brought state and ecclesiastical aid for the construction of these communities, we still find numerous areas where such efforts depended solely on lay initiative. A cursory glance at selected dioceses during the years 1861 and 1914 shows that even such prominent dioceses as St. Petersburg and Moscow saw significant construction activities underway (see tables 2.1, 2.2). Most activity took place in rural areas; cities and major towns tended to be saturated with church buildings, and church officials in these areas usually declined new construction projects.

The parishes that these churches marked or came to mark were anything but geographically uniform communities. Rural faith communities differed greatly from one another, with geography, climate, and socioeconomic factors all contributing to their various profiles. Such variations existed not only between dioceses but within dioceses as well. In some areas, a village might consist of more than ten thousand persons and boast several parish churches. In other areas, more than thirty or forty villages comprised a parish, some of which might be located a hundred miles from their "local" church. Church temples varied from parish to parish in size and exterior architectural style. Poorer parishes tended to construct churches out of wood; the wealthier ones usually chose stone (fig. 2.2, 2.3). Parishes especially in northern and sometimes in central Russia often had two churches—a summer and a winter one.

Recorded histories of Russia's rural churches routinely show that, except for periodic minor breaks, some sort of construction or renovation work was continually underway: the building or rebuilding of a church; the refurbishment of its interior; the construction of a bell tower or of a fence or wall around the church; the painting of an iconostasis. This activity bore testimony to believers' ardent and indefatigable devotion to the temple, since they usually initiated and funded these projects. Commenting on their devotion,

TABLE 2.1    The Number of Parish and Cemetery Churches
in Select Areas of European Russia, 1861[a]

| Diocese | Parish churches | Attached or annulled churches | Cemetery churches |
| --- | --- | --- | --- |
| Moscow | 1146 | 109 | 47 |
| Vladimir | 1034 | 22 | 38 |
| Chernigov | 969 | 47 | 46 |
| Kostroma | 948 | 8 | 31 |
| Tver | 918 | 31 | 28 |
| Kursk | 905 | — | 9 |
| Tambov | 886 | 13 | 46 |
| Iaroslavl | 836 | 19 | 20 |
| Orlov | 832 | 7 | 33 |
| Riazan | 828 | 13 | 26 |
| Tula | 819 | 14 | 25 |
| Nizhegorod | 783 | 12 | 43 |
| Voronezh | 723 | 8 | 7 |
| Vologda | 687 | 27 | 21 |
| Novgorod | 608 | 178 | 27 |
| Kaluga | 603 | 19 | 11 |
| Perm | 602 | 16 | 30 |
| Saratov | 575 | 3 | 23 |
| Simbirsk | 522 | 51 | 19 |
| Pskov | 382 | 16 | 18 |
| St. Petersburg | 252 | 16 | 17 |
| Olonets | 239 | 108 | 7 |
| Arkhangelsk | 229 | 182 | 15 |

[a]*Izvlechenie iz otcheta po vedomstvu Pravoslavnago ispovedaniia za 1861* (St. Petersburg, 1864). These figures reflect only churches whose construction was completed; they do not include those whose construction was still in process.

peasants from the village Pavlovskoe in the Penza diocese said: "We do not forget the temple of God, and in turn the Lord will not forget us."[2] The representatives of the village of Fedosino in the Novgorod diocese explained their tireless efforts in the following way: "We feel responsible, in the name of the general welfare of all the current and future population of our community, to exert all of our energy in securing that which is most valuable of all on earth—the holy temple." Believers saw the temple as holy, as the house of God.[3] Considering the effort involved in even the simplest construction projects, believers would not have expended the time and funds to see projects completed if the temple did not occupy a prominent place in their worldview. As one dean from the Vologda diocese noted, if a community decided to build a church, virtually nothing could stop them.[4]

TABLE 2.2   The Number of Parish and Cemetery Churches
in Select Areas of European Russia, 1914[a]

| Diocese | Parish churches | Attached or annulled churches | Cemetery churches |
| --- | --- | --- | --- |
| Moscow | 1228 | 114 | 40 |
| Tambov | 1155 | 30 | 50 |
| Vladmir | 1124 | 67 | 25 |
| Kursk | 1053 | 12 | 17 |
| Kostroma | 1033 | 10 | 30 |
| Chernigov | 1029 | 90 | — |
| Voronezh | 984 | 28 | 13 |
| Tver | 926 | 123 | 73 |
| Riazan | 926 | 3 | 9 |
| Nizhegorod | 893 | 24 | 65 |
| Orlov | 882 | 59 | 37 |
| Iaroslavl | 861 | — | 18 |
| Tula | 836 | 61 | 23 |
| Novgorod | 753 | 119 | 39 |
| Vologda | 748 | 89 | 33 |
| Saratov | 733 | 64 | 23 |
| Simbirsk | 703 | 136 | 16 |
| Kaluga | 615 | 59 | 9 |
| Arkhangelsk | 454 | 146 | 35 |
| Perm | 428 | 72 | 23 |
| Pskov | 377 | 67 | 27 |
| Petrograd | 301 | 166 | 38 |
| Olonets | 292 | 208 | 20 |

[a] *Vsepoddanneishii otchet oberprokurora Sv. Sinoda po vedomstvu pravoslavnago ispovedeniia* (St. Petersburg, 1915).

The process of constructing a new church and forming a new parish illustrates the demands that having a temple placed on believers. The process began with a village community petitioning the diocesan consistory for permission to embark on the construction project. The reasons they gave for their requests varied. In 1861, for instance, two peasants from the St. Basil parish (Kadnikov district) in the Vologda diocese wrote that parishioners wanted to construct a new church on the site where an icon had been found several years before. In 1863, members of the village of Shchadrino in the Viatka diocese petitioned to construct a new church because of a vow they had made before God during a fire. In 1865 members of the village of Bogoroditskoe in the Riazan diocese wrote that because their parish church was located so far away, few villagers regularly went to church. Consequently, "they were wallowing in ignorance and delusion; everyone believed however they desired." Peasants from the village of Kamennoe Zadele in the Viatka

2.2 Wooden church.
Iaroslavl province,
Malogskii district,
Koporinskaia volost',
village of Pereima.
The Russian Museum
of Ethnography,
St. Petersburg.

diocese took on the construction of a church in 1895 on the behest of their "forefathers," who had made a vow to construct a church.[5] In 1907, members of the village of Zheludkovo in the Tver diocese complained that because they could not easily reach their church year round on account of impassible roads, people frequently died without having been administered Communion or, in the case of infants, baptism.[6] Trustees from the village of Lagerei in the Kharkov diocese claimed that "nature itself" directed them to form a new parish since spring floods kept them from their assigned parish church.[7]

According to official guidelines, established during the reign of Peter the Great in the eighteenth century, a new church could be built only if a community sufficiently demonstrated a need for it. The guidelines spoke of need in terms of distance or difficulty in reaching their assigned parish church, insufficient size, or disrepair.[8] Since diocesan officials both defined "need" and determined whether in fact it existed, when believers had other reasons to construct a new church, they usually also listed one of these more conventional reasons.

**2.3** The Church of Saints Peter and Paul. Village of Pervinka. 1910. Library of Congress, Prints and Photographs Division, Prokudin-Gorskii Collection.

When the construction of a church was associated with the formation of a new parish, a community also had to offer a resolution or contract that outlined the means by which they planned to support their parish clergy. While the diocesan consistory set a minimum monetary sum for clerical support, the actual means by which communities met that sum varied from parish to parish. Each community decided on the "benefits package," which could include a combination of land, payment for requested liturgical services (baptisms, weddings), and regular annual payments in money or kind.[9] When believers could not meet the minimum salary requirement, they petitioned the state treasury, often with the support of the diocesan bishop, to allocate a supplementary state salary. By law, the community also had to provide its clergy with housing.

When the formation of a new parish was at stake, part of the petition process also included a "credit check."[10] The consistory made inquiries to local church and police authorities about any existing circumstances that might raise doubts about a community's ability to support their clergy.[11] Consistory officials were interested, for instance, in whether rural communities promptly met their other financial obligations. They also asked whether those parishes from which villages would be leaving to form a new parish would be left financially solvent. If not, the consistory usually denied the request for a new church.[12]

Finally, diocesan officials sought to insure that a church construction project and the formation of a new parish had the support of the communities involved. For example, in 1907, Tver diocesan officials at first denied the petition of the village of Zheludovko for the construction of a new church, in part because not all the families in the participating villages displayed a desire to support the project. Only when the village assembly informed the consistory that the households in question were not refusing to join the new parish, but only requested that they be exempt from any dues associated with the construction project on account of their dire financial situation, did the consistory reconsider its decision.[13]

Once diocesan officials were sure that a proposed parish could financially sustain itself, they requested an architectural plan of the proposed church. By this time in the process, communities had formed a building committee, consisting of clergy, the church elder, and elected parishioners.[14] Building committees, in turn, hired architects and engineers in order to satisfy the necessary building code and safety standards.[15]

The most time-consuming aspect of the entire process, however, was fund-raising, which was an ongoing feature of parish life. It reached its peak during the years when church construction was underway, but because churches required regular maintenance, a more tempered search for funds often continued with only periodic breaks. Weekly collections taken during the Liturgy provided the only consistent source of revenues. When a specific need arose, such as the purchase of a bell (which believers thought of as "ringing away sins") parishioners turned to more intensive fund-raising means.[16]

Such sources of funding can be divided into two categories, those internal to and those found outside the community. Members within the community contributed to the cause in terms of time, goods, and money. Parishioners often built their own brick factories both to provide themselves with bricks and to sell them for profit to go toward the building project. The preparation for construction was often a drawn-out process. For example, the ten villages that formed the St. Nicholas parish (Kadnikov district) in the Vologda diocese spent three years gathering the necessary construction materials.[17] Parishioners themselves hauled the wood and sand and provided meals for workers.[18] Poorer communities took longer to gather these materials and thus sometimes delayed construction for five, ten, or even fifteen years.[19]

Communities also introduced self-imposed collections, or "mandatory donations," for all members.[20] Many believers felt it was a sin not to give for the parish church. In addition, parishioners dedicated rents received from various properties and held special events to fund the project. For example, some communities rented out part of their communal lands and reserved the money for the project for a set number of years. They also rented trading booths on church grounds to local peasants for use on Sundays and special feast days. In the S.S. Zosima and Savvatii church in the Vologda diocese (Totma district), parishioners held an auction of donated livestock on their annual parish feast day and gave the proceeds to the maintenance of the parish church.[21]

Lack of sufficient data makes it impossible to determine the donation patterns of believers within any given parish community; nevertheless we know that donations tended to vary along gender lines. Men generally donated money. A peasant from the Kaluga diocese, for example, made coffins and sold them to poorer peasants at a reduced price and then donated the proceeds to maintain the church. Men usually responded to pledge drives in honor of a construction project. They also tended to be the ones who purchased items for the church, including icons, vestments, chalices, candle holders, censers, and curtains for the royal doors.[22] Women, on the other hand, tended to make donations in kind, which included cloth, wool, sewn and embroidered cloths for icons or table coverings, and baked goods.[23]

Two less lucrative though often critical sources of funding deserve mention. First, parishes drew on rent and interest income from land and money willed by parishioners, male and female, especially from those who had been single or childless. Persons willed property or money to the church in exchange for their commemoration during the Divine Liturgy.[24] Similarly, families often donated money or goods when a family member died as a sign of their final gift to their church; others donated money when they unexpectedly recovered from an illness.[25] Second, communities sought loans or gifts from wealthier individuals within a community.[26]

While the consistory preferred to ratify construction projects that a parish community could support on its own, many communities nonetheless depended heavily on external sources of funding. The consistory recognized two forms of outside aid. First, it processed requests for grants of wood gratis from state lands.[27] Second, and more important, the consistory routinely approved requests to allow a member of a parish community to collect donations outside the immediate parish boundaries.

This collector was an intriguing feature of temple culture in prerevolutionary Russia (fig. 2.4).[28] Frequently motivated by a personal calling, collectors wandered through towns and villages championing the sacred cause of their local communities. They could be found everywhere, wrote the ethnographer S. V. Maksimov: in the squares of Moscow and St. Petersburg, at provincial trade fairs, at village feast days, and on churches' doorsteps.[29] Collectors opened otherwise parochial projects to a broader audience, thereby blurring the boundaries that demarcated a local parish from both neighboring and distant communities. They carried with them not only their personal stories but also stories from their community, which included the tribulations connected with the construction of the temple. In return, they brought home the stories of distant donors who became accepted as the community's "own" by virtue of their gifts.

By law, each itinerant collector was required to obtain a special collection book from the diocesan consistory. These books contained a declaration of

2.4 Church collector.
Ca. 1880–1924. Frank and
Frances Carpenter Collection,
Library of Congress.

the collector's identity, the stated purpose of his collection, and a record book of the amount of donations he collected. In their petitions, parish communities specified the person of their choice and the places he planned to visit. Collectors were expected to be trustworthy members of the community and were chosen at a village or parish assembly. Their candidacy had to be approved by both the parish clergy and the local district police. No substitute collectors were permitted without sanction from diocesan authorities.[30]

Who these collectors were is difficult to determine. Often but not always male, they appear to have been people who displayed exceptional "zeal toward the holy church" and whom the community recognized as in some way different or holy.[31] Some collectors, for example, volunteered for the task in fulfillment of a personal vow they made before God. In the 1880s, the illiterate wealthy peasant Ivan Isaev from the Boitkovo parish in the Kaluga diocese had a dream that inspired him to donate all of his personal wealth to the renovation of the church. When his own funds ran out, he became an itinerant collector.[32] In 1901 the peasant Samson Luzhensk volunteered to take up a collection for the church construction project underway in the St. Nicholas parish (Nikolsk district) in the Vologda diocese. Recently healed from an ophthalmic illness, he had given a vow to collect funds for church construction as a gesture of gratitude.[33]

Communities frequently requested permission for collectors to travel not merely to other dioceses but "to various cities and towns of the Russian empire."[34] In order to approve these requests, diocesan officials first had to seek formal permission from those bishops through whose dioceses the collector proposed to journey. Bishops did not allow collectors into their dioceses as a matter of routine. In 1874, for instance, the bishop of Nizhnii Novgorod, Ioannikii (Rudnev), announced that he would temporarily curtail granting permission to outside collectors in his diocese, since inhabitants of major trading towns complained about their large numbers.[35]

The precise number of such collectors roaming Russia's rural and urban areas during any given year is difficult to determine, but evidence suggests that Ioannikii's concerns were not exaggerated. In 1880, the bishop of St. Petersburg noted that more than 350 collectors had visited the capital city annually.[36] In 1898, the bishop of Riazan reported that he granted two hundred collection books.[37] Reported figures, however, do not indicate the full magnitude of this practice. Despite attempts by diocesan officials to control the number of collectors, the practice of persons setting out "on their own" (samovol'no) to collect funds was common and often went unreported to civil and church officials.

For example, the thirty-six-year-old Viatka woman, Raisa Kropacheva, rarely had diocesan or episcopal permission for her collection activities. Born into a peasant family in the village of Bogoliubskaia, she had suffered as a child from an accidental fall from her cradle. Although her parents sought remedies to cure her, she remained disabled the rest of her life. At age twenty-two she began making frequent pilgrimages. During one of them, she was caught in a severe hailstorm and vowed to serve God by dedicating her life to the beautification of needy churches in the Viatka diocese. Although she lacked official permission, many local parish priests supported her efforts and accepted her donations. During the twelve years of her collection efforts, she donated chalices, vestments, icons, and other items to some seventeen churches.[38]

Self-appointed and diocesan-approved collectors were joined in their journeys by other collectors who had been "blessed" by their parish communities but who never went through the process of obtaining diocesan permission for their journeys. For example, in 1897 local police authorities from the Kostroma province informed the Vologda consistory that a peasant from their diocese had been found guilty of collecting donations without proper authorization. The peasant, Galaktion Stepanov Maslov, defended his activity by claiming the support of his parish priest, from whom he carried a certificate of support. When the consistory questioned the priest regarding this certificate, he admitted blessing Maslov to collect donations but only in the two neighboring parishes. Maslov had journeyed to the Kostroma province on his own initiative.[39]

Collectors sometimes set out on their journeys with only the permission of lay representatives from their parish. The guardians in the St. Nicholas parish (Velsk district) in the Vologda diocese, for instance, admitted to having issued supporting letters to twenty-eight parishioners in the 1879–80 period. They claimed that they were unaware that guardians did not enjoy the authority of granting these certificates "since they often encountered persons carrying such certificates from parish priests and monasteries."[40] Parish priests, in turn, defended their blessing of collectors, asserting that the persons themselves requested the undertaking as a service to the church.

Although itinerant collectors raised significant sums for the construction and renovation of rural parish churches, diocesan authorities endorsed the practice with some reservation. Two features of this practice in particular disturbed them. First, they looked unfavorably on the gimmicks that many collectors employed in their collection efforts. For example, during his collection for the Spaso-Sengovskii church in the Vologda diocese, the peasant Evfim Art'emev wore a piece of material that resembled an aer (the *vozduk*, a cloth that is draped over the chalice and the *diskos* during the celebration of the Divine Liturgy) on his chest and an icon around his neck.[41] Similarly, in 1891 two collectors from the Nizhnii Novgorod diocese tied a one-hundred pound bell to their sled and displayed a large icon of the Mother of God. Standing in the center of a small trading village in Vologda's Totma district, one of the men periodically rang the bell and solicited contributions for their church.[42] Diocesan officials regarded such attention-getting devices as bordering on the sacrilegious. Accordingly, laws established during the eighteenth century and reaffirmed again in the nineteenth affirmed that collectors were not to use icons, candles, or books during their collections.[43]

Second, church officials were uneasy with the large numbers of collectors, a concern also reflected in relevant ecclesiastical rulings. According to synodal directives, diocesan officials were advised to issue collection books only when a parish demonstrated a genuine need for such a collection. Synod officials feared that a proliferation of itinerant collectors would affect temple piety: people might begin to doubt the causes these collectors represented and reduce their contributions.[44]

Despite these official reservations, itinerant collectors captured the late nineteenth-century religious and cultural imagination, as reflected in their portrayal in popular devotional, literary, and ethnographic works. For instance, the populist writer M. E. Saltykov-Shchedrin, in his series of short stories entitled *Poshekhonskaia starina*, provides a "saintly" portrayal of a collector.[45] In a bittersweet account of a self-appointed collector named Satir, Saltykov describes the stark contrast between the collector's grim daily reality and the heights of the ideal for which he strives. Satir is a servant, and his fellow servants in the house usually find him alone copying prayers from books or lost deep in thought. Considering him blessed, his employers do nothing to stop him when he disappears for months at a time in order to fulfill his desire "to serve God." On several occasions, local police detain him as a "sectarian," which was a common experience for those collectors who journeyed with no official documents. Although technically an employed servant, Satir manifests his essential freedom through his unauthorized collection activity. "I am not a servant of God if I have a passport," Satir maintains at one point.[46] His life's achievement is symbolized by the bell that the local parish church was able to purchase solely on account of the funds he raised.

Parish communities also industriously found other sources to tap for their construction and renovation projects. Some communities circulated printed announcements about their construction projects describing their particular financial hardships or published such announcements in local newspapers, hoping that people would send donations.[47] Others who found themselves with exceptionally meager resources requested grants directly from the state treasury or aid from the Holy Synod, ranging from monetary support to free liturgical books. Sometimes the Synod had special funds at its disposal for such purposes. In 1914, for instance, the Synod had some 88,000 rubles for church construction and renovation projects that had been willed by a General-Lieutenant Vakuovskii-Doshchinskii. This fund aided at least twenty-five parishes that year in their projects.[48] Some communities addressed their requests for donations directly to individuals outside the parish, such as the tsar, the empress, or the well-known priest John of Kronstadt.[49] More frequently, however, parishes turned to persons who had left to make a living elsewhere, usually in St. Petersburg or Moscow, but whose religious identity remained tied to their home parish.[50]

Through personal effort and investment of resources, many rural believers unequivocally manifested their affective attachment to the temple, both individually and collectively.[51] Individuals invested in these efforts out of personal consideration, "each person zealously [donating] for his or her soul."[52] Whether to fulfill a vow in gratitude for surviving a serious illness, to make amends for one's sins before God, to win divine favor for earthly concerns, to establish the memory of deceased ancestors, or to express love and devotion toward God and one's church—every donation was a carrier of meaning that became forever enshrined in the temple.[53] Just as was the case with the building of Europe's medieval cathedrals, these seemingly disjunct individual efforts blended into a shared sacred task that bonded believers into a common saga that often lasted for decades. In this sense, temples stood as repositories of personal joys and tragedies, the subjects of which usually remained faceless but the preservation of which remained a collective duty.

⊷══◉══⊷

## The Orthodox Rubrics of Sacred Place

Whatever motivated individuals in their church construction and renovation projects, their activities were congruous with Orthodox teachings on the church building, being shaped by such teachings as well as reinforcing them. Sermons and devotional literature during this time placed tremendous emphasis on the role of the temple in Christian life. Interestingly, Orthodox writers and preachers—as their counterparts in the Christian West historically had done—drew most of their inspiration not from the New Testament but from books of the Old Testament, presenting King David and King Solomon as models of Orthodox piety.[54] Relying heavily on a reading of the Book of Psalms and the story of Solomon's temple-building, popular teaching stressed the continuity between Jerusalem's temple and Orthodox churches. Some authors even drew analogies between the fates of Russia and Israel, insofar as Russia's fate was depicted as dependent on believers' attitude toward the church building or temple.[55]

Most devotional treatises and sermons based their presentations on the biblical image of the temple as the Lord's abode and resting place. Although acknowledging that divinity could manifest itself everywhere, preachers maintained that in the temple God chose to make his presence known in a complete way.[56] The priest P. Svetlov, in a sermon delivered in 1894, compared the divine presence with light: light might be everywhere but nonetheless it is more concentrated in some places than in others. Consequently, "all the rays of divine light converge in the temple. They do so to a degree that is impossible outside the temple because of the special laws and conditions governing spiritual life."[57]

Preachers and Orthodox writers, however, were not always clear in their attempts to link biblical imagery with the New Testament story. Devotional treatises and sermons on the subject could bypass completely the Pentecost account (Acts 2:1–47) and the early Christian house-church experience.[58] When they did mention the early Christians, it was usually to "excuse" their lack of temples on account of the persecutions. They gave no sense that early Christians might have conceived of a house of worship in alternative ways.[59]

Nineteenth-century Russian Orthodox sermons and the Old Testament texts they referenced differed in that the former spoke not only of *a* temple but of temple*s* and not only about God's abode but about Christ's abode as well. Preachers' explanations of this difference, however, were not always clear. In a sermon delivered in 1908, for example, a priest explained that after the resurrection and ascension, Christ did not abandon his followers but "established here on earth . . . his eternal dwelling place. Where? In the holy Church and in holy temples."[60] In an 1862 sermon, Makarii (Bulgakov), bishop of Kharkov, moved backward in salvation history from the Jesus story. He explained that the same God who by his infinite love condescended to be circumscribed within the bounds of human nature also directed people to construct particular buildings "where he Himself promised to dwell for believers in a mysterious manner . . . forever."[61] To explain the transition in the biblical story from a single dwelling place chosen by God to numerous temples, authors frequently cited a passage from the Gospel of Mark (11:17). Here Christ, during his cleansing of the temple, is portrayed as saying, "Is it not written, 'My House shall be called a house of prayer for all the nations'?" which suggested for these authors a multiplication of temples to accommodate the diversity of the new community.[62]

Other authors pointed to the Eucharist as the crucial transitional feature between the Old and New Testament temples. The priest P. Svetlov, for instance, claimed that if the Old Testament temple was referred to as the House of God, even more does this name apply to the New Testament temple. Here "the Lord reveals His presence not in a cloud of glory or under the cover of symbols, but directly, and especially tangibly appears to us in the holy mystery of the Body and Blood of Christ."[63]

However they made the transition between the doctrine of Christ and the biblical "house of God" imagery, Orthodox writers and preachers emphasized that the temple was a place where the divine and human meet. Accordingly, just as Moses took off his shoes upon approaching the burning bush, so believers entering the temple were to shed themselves of earthly concerns.[64] Only in this way could they reorient themselves from the temporal to the eternal and allow their souls to enter into a dialogue and relationship with God.[65]

The church building, therefore, provided the space for the gaining of spiritual vision, knowledge, and enlightenment.[66] Its liturgical activity acted on humans holistically, touching and potentially transforming the mind, soul, and body. It did so, claimed the famous late nineteenth- and early twentieth-century pastor John of Kronstadt, by "sobering up" believers from the "charm" and "drunkenness" of worldly desires.[67] In this respect, the temple played a critical role in the development of a person's religious sensibilities and God-consciousness. Accordingly, Orthodox writers often stressed the importance of children's attendance in churches, since only the temple could initiate this developmental process long before a person could comprehend words about God.[68]

The church building, however, was not spoken of only in mystical terms, as a symbolic reflection of the heavenly realm. Writers and preachers also emphasized its historical dimension. By virtue of its liturgy and ritual, the temple incorporated believers into an entire sacred story of still unfolding events and called them to be active and conscious participants.[69] Again, as John of Kronstadt wrote, "the temple appears to me as sacred history in the [iconographic] faces, the marvelous words about the works of God . . . and all this for the sake of humanity, for my sake."[70] The temple domesticated the Christian master narrative and brought immediacy to the economy of salvation. The temple's meaning, consequently, emerged not only from the "holy society" of the Virgin and saints whose lives and experiences it related but also from its links to believers' deceased kin and their community's past. Writers emphasized, therefore, that the temple was not only a holy place but also a familiar (*rodnoe*) one, where collective and individual memory became inseparably intertwined.[71]

Popular devotional literature spoke about the temple's meaning for both the individual and the community. Orthodox writers and preachers did not ignore the New Testament's spiritualized reading of the temple and its association with the human soul.[72] Instead, they insisted on a direct relationship between the church building and the individual person's interior spiritual temple. Believers constructed churches, they claimed, so that in and through them they could "construct" themselves into spiritual temples.[73] Churches facilitated individuals in their development of a spiritual temple by providing a "greenhouse" for the soul.[74] As the priest I. Demkin wrote, the church building provided the means by which individuals could fashion their souls. Everything the temple offered through sight, sound, and touch—from material objects, such as church bells and candles, to prayer and sacraments—the human soul could appropriate and use to arrange and prepare itself for the indwelling of the Holy Spirit.[75] Similarly, Theophanes the Recluse explained that churches reflected the image according to which believers should model their own human nature in order to become abodes of God.[76]

Orthodox writers and preachers also stressed the importance of the temple for the gathering of the faithful, reminding their listeners again that the Russian word for church, *tserkov'*, referred to both temple and gathering. While personal prayer and repentance were critical for the Christian way, these writers maintained that the transformation of the self could not take place without participation in the corporate liturgical experience. Herein lay the reasoning behind the caveat to believers that they should not alienate themselves from the ecclesial body. Only through corporate prayer could personal prayer receive the strength and character needed to be "lifted up."[77] In this context Theophanes the Recluse compared the temple with the human heart: "The temple is for humans what the heart is for the body." It reflects any sort of movement of the body—both its strength and weakness, health or illness.[78]

In their presentation of the temple's relationship to the collective gathering and corporate prayer, Orthodox writers and preachers frequently personified the church and spoke of it as "mother," as had Christians in both East and West for centuries. The image, however, as it was presented in Russian devotional literature, was complex and is often difficult to understand. While authors used it in their discussions of the church building, it was a fluid term whose meaning related just as much to the corporate gathering. Yet the image of church as mother transcended both building and gathering and referred more to the embodiment of the prayer of the gathered faithful. Preachers spoke of the church as mother, praying with the mouths of those who pray, accompanying the faithful from birth through death into the afterlife. She watched, nurtured, and comforted them and rejoiced when seeing, in response, their care for her. The clergy were spoken of as her servants.[79] It is worthy of note that in their petitions concerning the construction of churches, rural believers also made use of intimate maternal imagery. In 1864, members of the village of Svistova in the Riazan diocese, for instance, compared the religious knowledge they gained from having a church in their village to sucking milk from a mother.[80]

Given the meanings ascribed to the temple, it is not surprising that Orthodox writers and preachers considered it an essential aspect of the Christian life. Without the temple, they maintained, there could be no salvation, since only it could facilitate the proper formation of the inner spiritual temple. Insofar as believers strove toward union and communion with God, by their nature they needed the structure and stimulus of matter. The church building provided the primary source of nourishment and healing for the human soul in its journey toward God.[81]

At the same time, however, popular devotional literature consistently emphasized that God himself in no way "needs" temples. He has the entire universe as his dwelling place and desires temples only insofar as far as humans need them. Therefore, any activity was pleasing to God only when humans themselves were actively engaged in fashioning themselves as temples of God.[82] Nevertheless, preachers often emphasized that God supported temple construction efforts and recounted stories from the lives of saints as illustrations.

The most widely told story at the time concerned the eleventh-century saints Anthony and Theodosius and the construction of the Great Church of the famous Kievan Caves Monastery, which they had founded. According to the story, four church architects from Constantinople arrived at the monastic community with a divine directive to construct a temple. In response to Anthony and Theodosius's looks of surprise, the four explained that the Mother of God had guided them to this place. Early one morning she had summoned them individually through their dreams to the church of Blacherne. There she appeared to them collectively and told them that she desired to build herself a church in Kiev. She revealed the plan of the church and then sent them to the two founders of the monastic community.[83] Though Anthony and Theodosius did not live to see the completion of the church project, they became patron saints of church construction efforts.

Despite this emphasis on the temple in devotional literature, many educated Russians criticized the common believer's propensity toward the beautification of churches. Certain churchmen, for instance, deemed parish guardianships (*popechitel'stva*) a failure because believers chose to spend the money they raised on the maintenance and beautification of church buildings rather than on support for the parish priest. Secular intellectuals in turn focused on believers' preference for church embellishment over helping the poor. Secular publicists attributed this preference to a lack of intellectual development, a blind attachment to ritual, and an inability to have a reasonable understanding of God.[84] Even some churchmen tended to agree, finding extensive attention to the church building frivolous. They also attributed it to the common person's lack of knowledge of the faith and to a lack of understanding of Christian charity work.[85]

In 1909, for instance, the bishop of Vologda, Nikon (Rozhdestvenskii), discouraged the parishioners of the Annunciation church (Totma district) from spending 200 rubles on the renovation of their church. In response to their petition, he wrote:

Our Lord Jesus Christ said, "I want mercy and not sacrifice." His holy commandment orders us: first pay back a debt and then offer a gift of sacrifice. A sacrifice is pleasing to Him (the Lord) only when the persons offering the sacrifice fulfill His commandment of love toward their neighbor. The holy Fathers said that obedience is higher than prayer and fasting and that works of Christian love are more pleasing to God than any sacrifice.[86]

The issue of giving in Orthodox culture, however, was more ambiguous from the official perspective than Nikon's words suggest. Many ecclesiastical and secular intellectuals juxtaposed two modes of giving that linguistically in Russia were not so sharply defined. The term generally used to describe donations toward church beautification—*blagotvoritel'nost'*, or "good works"— was the same term generally used to describe almsgiving and charity. To further distinguish the different kinds of good works, other words were employed: "sacrifice" (*zhertva*), which was usually associated with donations toward church embellishment, and "mercy" (*milost'*), which was usually associated with almsgiving (*milostynia*).

Many members of the secular and ecclesiastical elite wanted to redirect the understanding of good works in Orthodoxy in two ways. First, as did Nikon, they wanted good works to be understood more in terms of mercy than sacrifice. By the end of the nineteenth and the beginning of the twentieth century, ecclesiastical and secular educated circles had become interested in parish guardianships for precisely this reason. Discussion over parish reform shifted from the material well-being of clergy to the parish as a viable unit through which to serve the socioeconomic needs of the rural poor.[87] In trying to meet this goal, some ecclesiastical officials advocated removing church beautification from the list of the guardianships' tasks, and to make their primary goal charity work.[88] Second, educated laymen and church officials also hoped guardianships would reorient the widespread Orthodox understanding of charity from a primarily private act to a more organized collaborative endeavor. Many questioned the effectiveness of "penny giving," believing that it perpetuated and encouraged begging.[89]

Rural lay persons, who since the eighteenth century were conditioned to see communal caring for the poor as the responsibility of the village and not the parish community, often hampered such efforts. As a religious act, they generally saw giving as a private matter.[90] Moreover, they found support in an entire religious tradition that, though not minimizing the importance of serving the poor, encouraged church beautification as one of the best "good works" believers could offer. Referring to the gospel scene in which Christ praised the woman who poured expensive ointment on his head (Matt. 26: 10), devotional literature maintained that all forms of good works began with the church building.[91] Even the socially minded parish reformer A. A. Papkov ranked the maintenance and beautification of the church building as one of the most important ecclesial tasks.[92] Theophanes the Recluse supported this view as well, maintaining that believers were accountable not only for the care of their own and their neighbors' bodies but for the care of their souls as well. Therefore, while acknowledging the benefit of constructing schools, hospitals, and orphanages, Theophanes nonetheless highly esteemed church beautification. The construction of a church was even greater, he maintained, "because a church of God is at the same time a school, a hospital, and a place of rest [for the soul]."[93] Another writer referred to church embellishment as a form of "spiritual almsgiving."[94] Conversely, others spoke of helping the poor as another form of church decoration.[95]

In support of this position, preachers often recalled the thirteenth-century story of St. Erazm of the Kievan Caves. Having come into much wealth, the monk Erazm had donated most of his fortune to beautify churches. When he lost his fortune, he regretted the way he had spent his money, wishing he had given it to the poor instead. He fell into despair, began living a checkered life, and soon became ill. On the verge of death, he one day unexpectedly arose and explained to his surprised monastic brethren that he had had a vision of Anthony and Theodosius of the Kievan Caves. They had appeared to him saying they had prayed for God to grant him an extended period for repentance. He also had a vision of the Virgin, who announced to him: "Because you embellished my church, I will embellish you and will extol you in glory in my Son's Kingdom."[96] Such stories directly challenged elitist claims regarding the "triviality" of lay attention to the beauty and maintenance of their churches.[97] They conveyed in story form ideas that resonated with patristic teaching on the ontological character of beauty. According to this teaching, one of the names of God is Beauty, and humans are understood as by nature striving toward and desiring the beautiful.[98] Such stories, at least for some, served to transform both fund raising and donating from mundane matters into quasi-ritual sacred acts.

⋆⇒◉⇐⋆

## Laity and Liturgy in Temple Worship

Orthodox temple culture, however, was not focused solely on the building. In order for the temple to be an active carrier of meaning, and for laity to consider it "alive," it also had to be liturgically active, whether or not believers actually attended its services. How extensive was this liturgical worship, and which services did parishes typically celebrate?

While the frequency of liturgical services varied from parish to parish, the framework of services was generally the same: Matins with Divine Liturgy on Sundays and major feast days, with more frequent weekday services during the Lenten season.[99] Most priests did not have time for a fuller schedule of services, especially during the week, since during the late spring, summer, and early fall they worked or managed their land and during the late fall, winter, and early spring taught children in the villages. They served weekday Liturgies only on parishioners' requests and usually only in honor of village feast days or in memory of departed loved ones.

In addition to the schedule of services set by the Orthodox liturgical calendar, rural believers' private and communal worship included *treby*: personal and family-related services accompanying the various stages of life—birth, marriage, death. It also included an entire array of liturgical services for various occasions related to village community life—crops, weather, digging of wells, well-being of livestock, and so forth.

The schedule of services in rural parishes became fuller toward the end of the nineteenth century, in part because priests gradually came to work the land less. In addition, ecclesiastical authorities at this time began encouraging parish clergy to expand their schedule of liturgical services to include Vespers on Sundays and feast days. According to an 1886 synodal directive, priests were to supplement their vesperal services with the reading of *akathistoi* and with religious discussions in order to attract churchgoers, especially during the Lenten season.[101]

The extent of the laity's participation in the liturgical schedule varied considerably from parish to parish and depended on many factors. First, with Sunday services normally beginning at five in the morning and not ending until noon, those living at any great distance from the parish church did not participate in the Eucharistic liturgy with any regularity.[102] This factor especially affected children and the elderly. Indeed, those living at such distances considered churchgoing an adult activity that began with their wedding.[103] It was not uncommon for believers, especially peasants who had no use of a horse and carriage, to attend church on only several occasions during their lives.[104]

Second, churchgoing tended to be seasonal, with attendance being higher in the winter than in the summer when peasants worked the fields. Participation also depended in large part on the labor patterns of villagers. Attendance tended to be lower in villages where there were many migrant workers. It was difficult for migrant workers to fully readjust to the local liturgical cycle upon their return from an urban area, even if they had not been not affected there by the growing influence of Marxist ideas in the late nineteenth century. Attendance was also lower in parishes located near major trade-fair towns, which drew large crowds on Sundays and feast days.[105] In addition, poorer people attended less frequently because of a lack of proper attire. Considering the temple's space sacred, believers felt they should enter it only "in purity." This sense of purity extended to attire, and believers considered it sinful to enter a church in their work clothes.[106] Finally, peasant families rarely attended church together and instead rotated their churchgoing.[107] The question of who attended more frequently—men or women, children or the elderly—depended on location.[108]

Churchgoing, especially in less densely populated rural areas, was only one—and not always the most prominent—among many factors by which a person both developed and demonstrated a sense of belonging to the Church. What might appear from a statistical point of view to have been a sporadic attendance pattern at weekly liturgical celebrations might very well have been thought of as a regular cycle of churchgoing in the lives of individual believers. Moreover, as a symbol, an active temple had the capacity to influence and inform believers' religious sensibilities whether or not they themselves were regularly present every week at its services.

We can appreciate the general communal demand for liturgically active churches by viewing lay attitudes toward so-called attached churches—churches that were not assigned permanent clergy but were attached (*pripisany*) to a neighboring parish.[109] During the post-Emancipation period, a church generally earned this status in one of three ways. First, as a result of the 1869 parish reform, diocesan authorities assigned an attached status to numerous independent churches. By merging parishes into larger units, they hoped to provide a more secure base of material support for parish clergy.[110] Second, diocesan officials revoked or at least threatened to revoke a church's independent status when rural communities unilaterally downgraded the provisions of support for local parish clergy on which they had previously agreed. The Holy Synod began encouraging such a policy in the 1890s, and diocesan authorities resorted to its implementation, especially during the unrest of 1905. Finally, diocesan consistories assigned an attached church status to parish communities that were genuinely impoverished and could not support their own clergy.[111] Such cases appear to have become more frequent as 1917 drew nearer. Economic hardship, and an increasing inability to reach a consensus in the community for the financial support of clergy, often resulted in lengthy negotiations between rural believers and diocesan officials.

Believers usually responded with displeasure to an attached status for their parish. When petitioning for independent parish status, rural communities clearly expressed their conviction that a church temple was good only insofar as it was liturgically active. Attached churches had only a partial liturgical schedule at best, with some holding only a few liturgies per year. Rural believers claimed that such liturgical schedules did not provide "prayerful solace" and left a void that was "unbearably burdensome."[112] In addition, many believers assigned an importance to regular liturgical services in the local church that was independent of their own attendance at such services. The very *sight* of a closed church on Sundays and feast days was enough to incite many believers to complain of a "cooling" of religious sensibilities in their community and to blame diocesan authorities for alienating believers from "the Christian way."[113] After the Vladimir diocesan consistory decided to revoke the independent status of his church, one church elder wrote: "Gazing upon the closed temple, the soul is disturbed and wonders whether the temple within the Christian soul can similarly be shut and locked."[114] Not surprisingly, therefore, many rural believers never became accustomed to their attached status. Parishioners from the village of Babichev in the Kaluga diocese continued to petition vigorously for the restoration of an independent status for twenty-five years.[115]

Since believers thought a church that held infrequent liturgical celebrations was most displeasing to God and denied them what was "most essential,"[116] rural believers often went to great lengths to ensure a regular liturgical cycle for their church. When they could not sufficiently demonstrate an ability to support a priest, they sometimes sought and hired their own clergy.[117] As the peasants from the St. George church (Griazovets district) in the Vologda diocese wrote in 1874,

> we only want an independent church. If no priest wants to work and serve in our parish, then we will give our approval to the deacon. He will work. And with him it will be enough. The most important thing is that we have a service.[118]

Rural laity insisted on a liturgically active church because it also offered them a means to reaffirm their ancestral bonds.[119] An empty church was an affront to those ancestors who had maintained and frequented it. It also broke the liturgical continuity between generations. Laity whose churches were not liturgically active commented on its "orphaned" state. They only reluctantly frequented the "foreign" (*chuzhoi*) church to which they were assigned, feeling that they had "left behind" their ancestors in their church's cemetery.[120] Peasants from the village of Goretov in the Riazan diocese explained that they had shared the same sacred space as their forefathers; therefore, they were unwilling to leave their own church, which had united generations since "time immemorial."[121] For similar reasons, when parishioners of the Epiphany church (Borisoglebskii district) in the Iaroslavl diocese finally regained their parish's independent status, they considered the event so significant that they vowed to have a Divine Liturgy served annually on that day.[122]

Of course, church officials encouraged laity in their liturgical orientation. Popular devotional literature and sermons supported and prompted liturgical participation through dramatic stories of personal fortune and tragedy. For example, one frequently recounted story, set in Christianity's early centuries, concerned a poor family who, in order to avoid starvation, sold their only son into slavery. During their sorrowful parting, the father offered his son his paternal testament: "Whenever you pass by God's temple and see that a liturgical service is underway, go in and do not leave until the service is completed." This advice eventually saved the boy's life. His unplanned presence at a Divine Liturgy thwarted his owners' plot to have him beheaded because of a fellow servant's false accusations against him.[123]

It is noteworthy that devotional pamphlets did not always discuss Eucharistic participation in the context of the spiritual and worldly benefits of churchgoing. For example, one priest, in encouraging his parishioners to sustain their "temple consciousness" throughout the summer months when they worked in the fields, directed them to imagine creation as a temple. In a series of parallels—between stars and candles, a breeze and the grace that God bestowed on those who pray, the chirping of a bird and sacred hymns—he never explicitly mentioned the Eucharist.[124]

This is not to say that clergy did not consider the Eucharist central to the Christian life or to the churchgoing experience. Churchmen of the time clearly spoke of the Eucharist, along with the Word of God, as the primary forms of spiritual nourishment and sustenance, as well as the means by which believers could enter into communion with God and one another in this life.[125] "The union of the faithful in the sacrament of Communion is the foretaste of that blessed unity" that was believed to await believers in the Kingdom that was to come. A means by which the spiritual illness caused by sin was overcome and death was transformed to life, the Eucharist, as one bishop noted, was freely offered. Why, he wondered, were not churches filled to capacity during the celebration of the Divine Liturgy with those awaiting to partake?[126]

Yet at the same time, Orthodoxy in late imperial Russia followed that tendency in the Christian tradition that applied the language of fear to the consecrated bread and wine that manifested the presence of Christ and, through him, God.[127] The consecrated bread and wine were "holy ground," as was the burning bush in which God had revealed himself to Moses (Exod. 3: 4–6).[128] Because of this, "drawing near" demanded certain preparation. According to A. V. Balov, a civil government official from the Iaroslavl diocese, believers usually attended liturgical services during the entire week before they would partake of the Eucharist. Since most believers partook of the Eucharist during Great Lent, the services they might have attended included the following: Matins, Presanctified Liturgy, and Compline on Wednesday; Matins and Presanctified Liturgy on Friday. Following this last service, the priest would read the preparatory prayers for confession, a rite that sometimes lasted into the evening. While confessions themselves were heard, a Compline service would be read along with prescribed prayers, including canons to Jesus Christ, the Mother of God, and the Guardian Angel. It was considered a sin to eat or drink following confession until reception of the Eucharist during the Liturgy on the following morning. On Saturday morning, those who were to partake of Communion attended Matins, after which prayers for preparation for Communion were read. Only after this was the Divine Liturgy served.[129] With such preparation considered the norm, frequent Communion simply was not feasible, especially for those believers who lived great distances from their parish churches.

Believers also considered a period of time following the partaking of Communion as especially sacred. That particular day, for instance, they refrained from spitting and kissing. It was also not uncommon for believers to continue a lenten dietary pattern for two days following the reception of the Holy Gifts.[130] Others watched over their behavior for six weeks afterward in order not to offend the sanctity of the Sacrament. Since many believers relegated conjugal relations to the category of activities that diminished the

Eucharist's sanctity, it is not surprising that peasant newlyweds tended to avoid confession and Communion during the entire first year of marriage.[131]

It is important, therefore, not necessarily to equate the perceived importance of the Eucharist with the frequency of its reception. Many believers partook of the Eucharist relatively rarely not because they considered it unimportant or insignificant but precisely because of the sense of awe and holiness with which it was associated. Some would even go to confession but abstain from Communion, fearing that they would bring about their condemnation rather than their salvation.[132] Such an attitude was only reinforced by the fact that "proper" piety, as defined by law, called for the Orthodox Christian to go to confession (byt' na dukhu, as peasants said) and to receive Communion only once a year, preferably during Great Lent. Although clergy in their writings and sermons called for believers to partake more frequently, many lay persons did not consider it abnormal to miss a year, two, or even three.[133] According to the reports of correspondents for the Tenishev Bureau, such lapses could be attributed more to fears and dread of the act of confession than to disregard for the Eucharistic ritual itself. A correspondent from the Penza diocese noted that peasants only began looking askance at people as apostates after they had missed confession and Communion for seven years. According to a Synodal directive of September 1858, however, priests were to report those who failed to fulfill this "Christian responsibility" three years in a row.[134] In any case, for all practical purposes, most lay persons associated "liturgical participation" not with the Eucharist as such but with the act of corporate prayer, an act that could find expression in settings other than the church building.

Two developments in parish life during the nineteenth century further promoted churchgoing among lay persons. The first involved the introduction of church choirs. Before the second half of the nineteenth century, a sacristan or reader alone usually chanted Liturgies in rural churches. Consequently, liturgical services were often not as ceremonious as today's stereotypic images of Russian Orthodox services suggest. In the postreform period, during a general campaign to educate peasants, church officials focused on proper church singing as a vital educational resource. Not only did choirs allow for lay participation but they also more effectively engaged believers in the sacred stories that were sung in hymns. As one priest explained, church singing was a "great unifying and inspirational force for parishioners," and therefore any efforts to renew parish life should begin with its proper ordering.[135]

The character of these choirs varied considerably from parish to parish. The Khalezskii parish (Kadnikov district) in the Vologda diocese, for instance, had two choirs that would join in the middle of the church to sing in unison and included some two hundred participants.[136] Others parishes had more modest choirs, some mixed, some strictly male or female. In most rural parishes, however, choirs consisted mostly of children, usually boys, from nearby schools.[137] Clergy recognized the benefits of singing as a key acculturation tool that directly involved children in ecclesial life and that served as a means of catechism. Parish priests frequently noted that in parishes where children's choirs had been organized, parishioners seemed to come to church more readily.[138]

A 1902 petition to the Vologda consistory from the village of Parchegskoe illustrates the attraction children's choirs held for believers. The villagers wanted to construct a church in their locality because they had heard the children's choir in their parish church, which they attended rarely on account of its distance. Now that a school had opened in their village, they hoped that their own children might be able to form such a choir.[139]

Children's choirs not only drew adults to liturgical services but also encouraged them to participate in the singing. Congregational singing marked another significant development in late nineteenth-century liturgical life.[140] Many clergy sought to foster a broader appreciation of the Liturgy as a collective action—"a celebration of the human relationship with God"—that called for the active engagement of all those present.[141] As one priest noted, congregational singing was one means by which to channel and express amorphous religious sentiments, since "music . . . was the language of feelings."[142] Many priests hoped that lay response to this effort would be as encouraging as that voiced by a group of parishioners from the Vologda diocese: "Now is not like before. Before you would go to church and watch; now you go to church once and the next time you go unwittingly because [this singing] draws you in."[143]

Not all clergy or laity, however, were so enthusiastic about this development. Some felt that congregational singing was aesthetically mediocre in comparison to choral singing. Others, especially clergy, became discouraged by the practical complications in organizing congregational singing. Many priests complained that because their congregations were so large and dispersed, any congregational singing had to count on a small core group of regular parishioners. Laity, in turn, were not always receptive. Some viewed it as an "innovation" and found it intrusive or disruptive.[145]

Congregational singing, however, offered a way in which laity could become actively engaged in the Divine Liturgy. Most popular devotional liturgical commentaries at the time directed those present at the Divine Liturgy to concentrate on every ritual movement as a reenactment of key moments in Christ's life and ministry.[146] Many commentaries also included historical details of how particular hymns and rituals originated and thereby incorporated notable past "events" into the present corporate celebration.[147] Commentaries not only assigned meaning to the priest's every movement and gesture with respect to the Jesus story but also guided the believers' responsive private thoughts.[148] They coached believers about what to feel and imagine during the various high points of the service. Some even offered private prayers and gestures with which believers could respond.[149] Advocates and opponents of congregational singing took sides as to whether this form of liturgical participation enriched or detracted from the Liturgy's ritual meaning.

The second development in parish life that nurtured liturgical participation during the late imperial period was the introduction of the so-called periliturgical or extraliturgical discussions (*vnebogosluzhebnye besedy*). In contrast to sermons and catechesis that took place in the liturgical context, these discussions occurred between or following liturgical services. They also differed in format from sermons and formal catechetical talks since they took place in an informal environment and placed less stress on systematic presentation of doctrine. These were a new type of sermon, often accompanied by the use of magic lanterns, that in many parishes served as a form of a popular adult religious education program.[150] Indeed, in many places it provided the only organized forum in which rural women could receive religious education.

While such discussions may have taken place in a minority of parishes in the eighteenth and early nineteenth centuries, rural clergy began introducing them on a widespread scale in the 1860s. By the 1890s they became virtually a standard feature of parish life.[151] Churchmen regularly commented on the popularity of these discussions, with many priests maintaining that they did not have the facilities to seat all of the parishioners who gathered. Attendance varied from parish to parish, depending on the character of the speakers, the size of the parish, and the distances of the villages from the church. Attendance increased during the Lenten season; it was poorer in those parishes where there was a strong influence of Old Believers and in large trading towns. Nevertheless, as many priests noted, it did not matter if all adult members attended. Those who attended returned home and related the discussions to family and friends, and in this way the debates received a wider audience.[152] In some parishes, however, attendance was quite impressive. In the Iuzskii parish (Nikolsk district) in the Vologda diocese, for instance, more than fifteen hundred parishioners attended such gatherings weekly.[153] By the late nineteenth century, many priests attributed more active attendance at church services, as well as more frequent Communion, to the success of these discussions.[154] A priest from the Nikolsk district in the Vologda diocese, for instance, reported that many parents began bringing their children more frequently to Communion on Sundays. He noted that in one of parishes in his deanery, between 150 and 200 children regularly attended in church on Sundays. This was indeed a dramatic change, since because of distance and severe weather conditions it was not customary for children to attend church very frequently. Because confession, even by law, was not required for children before the age of seven, many parents simply did not bring their young children to Communion on any regular basis. Confession and Communion records in most parishes had high absentee rates for children.

Clearly, then, these efforts on the part of the clergy were bearing some fruit in terms of promoting and enriching the temple culture, already established at the grassroots, that was so vital to the devotion and spirituality of many lay people. However, in a broader religious culture that was in many ways shaped by the laity themselves, the influence of the clergy raises the complex and somewhat thorny issue of the management of the temple and its culture. How was temple life, whose liturgical order was hierarchical but whose very raison d'être was communal and "catholic," actually administered, and what were the competing visions of its administration on a local level?

⊷⩪◉⩫⊶

## Managing God's Abode

Without a doubt, the most complicated and tension-ridden aspect of temple culture was the managerial one. The most prominent and pivotal figure in this administrative arena was the parish priest, who, at least in theory, oversaw Russia's temple life. His role in the life of the parish community was not neatly defined, but several generalizations about it can be made.

The parish priest stood as the leader of the ecclesial community in the traditional theological sense: he was the *predstoiatel'*,[155] the spiritual leader of his flock, guiding them in the precepts that would move them closer to the Kingdom of God. The faithful recognized him as such and valued his presence and service. Though peasants were well aware that it was less costly to live without a priest, few rural Orthodox faithful remained content without one. In addition, the faithful usually did not consider sharing a priest with another parish a satisfactory arrangement. Just as they had a strong sense of their own parish church, so they also displayed a desire and need for their own parish priest.

The parish priest stood as an authority in the ecclesial system not only liturgically but educationally as well. Parishioners recognized him as a teacher and preacher, not only in religious and ethical matters but also in regard to more practical concerns. They saw in him a valuable witness and mediator in community disputes.[156] He was often the only person in any proximity with medical or veterinary knowledge, subjects that in some seminaries were regular parts of the curriculum.[157] Peasants also often looked to the priest for suggestions on agricultural methods and, in the northern provinces in the early twentieth century, on setting up cooperatives.[158] The faithful usually respected the priestly title because of such liturgical and educational duties.

Guided by a vision of and desire for the ideal pastor, parishioners rarely tolerated a priest whom they perceived as negligent in the timely administration of sacraments, especially in cases of baptizing sick infants and offering Communion to the dying. For them, such negligence was tantamount to malpractice.[159] Laity took offense when a priest would not show due honor or respect toward the holy. They complained to diocesan officials if priests disrupted liturgical services by giving loud verbal directions to the sacristan, made blatant errors in the order of services, or publicly admonished individuals in the community during a sermon.[160]

Such were the community's expectations of the parish priest in his role as pastor. In his administrative capacity, however, the relationship between priest and community was somewhat different. In the managerial sphere he did not function independently but rather was aided in his efforts by a church elder, a church warden, a parish assembly, a *prosfora* baker, and in many places a parish guardianship.[161] Moreover, even this small group did not function as a self-enclosed management system, as members of the parish community at large regularly took an active interest in their church's affairs. Thus, in acting as administrator, the priest found himself not so much at the top of a hierarchical system as in the middle of a complicated web of relationships. Indeed, the full extent of the complexity of this web becomes apparent when one considers the heterogeneous composition of the parish membership.

Even though rural Russia was not religiously pluralistic in any modern sense of the word and every peasant's Orthodox identity was virtually a legal given, the parish community did not usually consist solely of voluntary, committed believers. Officially, of course, the peasantry was regarded as a religiously homogeneous group, except for a minority that was registered with local church authorities as either "schismatics" (Old Believers) or sectarians.[162] Until the laws of religious toleration in 1905, such a situation made it virtually impossible to distinguish committed believers from nominal believers and nonbelievers in any given rural community. Even following 1905, the stereotypic notion that all Russians were Orthodox until demonstrated otherwise continued to distort the analysis of a religiously more complex situation.

The religious community (parish—*prikhodskoe obshchestvo* or *prikhodskaia obshchina*) and the civil community (village—*sel'skoe obshchestvo* or *sel'skaia obshchina*) overlapped in fundamental ways, although administratively and juridically the two were distinguished.[163] The village assembly, in particular, played an essential role in the local parish system since it was responsible for various collections taken for maintaining the temple.[164] According to civil law, the support of the parish clergy and the maintenance of the parish churches, including the collection of dues for construction and maintenance projects, fell in the purview of village assemblies.[165] Village assemblies also had the authority to oversee such charitable tasks as caring for the elderly and poor. In addition, though not legally within their scope, village assemblies also sometimes discussed such matters as the celebration of village feast days, the construction of chapels, the purchase of special village icons, and dissatisfaction with the clergy.

Given this role of village assemblies, the parish assembly in most regions remained a superfluous entity in the ecclesial system and convened only on specific occasions: during elections of parish guardians; during times of internal parish conflict when a dean or civil authority wished to clarify a certain law or ruling; and when a priest wished to suggest a major new undertaking, such as the construction of a parish school or a new church. Even in these cases, priests often appealed to the local village assembly. Moreover, when the parish priest wanted to initiate new practices or procedures, such as the way a procession was performed, the church elder often insisted that the issue be discussed with the entire village community.[166] If, in turn, the village community had specific desires regarding the collection or spending of church funds, they would negotiate with clergy through the mediation of the church elder or members of the parish guardianship.[167] Despite this prominent role of the village assembly in parish affairs, the major postreform legislation on parish management did not mention it.[168] From the official ecclesiastical standpoint, the village had no role in parish affairs.

The fact that the parish assembly's legal status was poorly defined only further facilitated believers' tendency to rely on the village assembly in the management of the temple.[169] Moreover, the few existing rules that governed the parish assembly differed from those that governed the village assembly—a situation that resulted in confusion about the protocol of the parish meeting. For example, according to the 1864 Rules on Parish Guardianship, a quorum of the parish assembly existed when one-tenth of those who had the right to participate were present.[170] Decisions concerning collections for particular projects were mandatory only for those members of the parish who agreed to the collections. A village assembly, on the other hand, required a quorum of two-thirds of those who had the right to participate. The village assembly's decisions, at least regarding civil matters, technically were mandatory for all members of the community even if they had not been not present at the assembly. Furthermore, local civil authorities did not enforce the decisions of the parish assembly, because by the standards of village assemblies, they were considered "illegally composed." If local civil authorities did not regard decisions taken by parish guardianships or parish assemblies as having legal validity, there was no way to enforce their decisions in the community.[171]

The relationship between parish and village was further complicated by the fact that the village community consisted of all persons residing in a particular region, regardless of religious sentiments or convictions. In theory, persons who had little or no interest in the Orthodox ecclesial world (i.e., Old Believers, various sectarians, nominal Orthodox Christians, and unbelievers) could have formed, if not the majority, at least the decisive voice in the assembly.[172] Significantly, parish clergy noted that the more faithful members of the parish frequently did not attend village assemblies. They avoided the "unpleasantness" often resulting from confrontations with the "loudmouths" (gorlopany or krikuny), a name given to those who dominated village assemblies with their brashness and ability to yell louder than anyone else.[173]

The relationship between the parish and village, therefore, was complex.[174] The parish, far from being a self-standing organizational unit, in many ways functionally depended on people who may not have particularly identified with the religious concerns and interests of the parish as a whole. Since all the members of the parish community were subject to the various dues and donations for the support of church and clergy, the village assembly was, from a secular standpoint, a natural arena for discussion of parish issues. From an ecclesiastical standpoint, however, such an arrangement posed a potential quandary: nonparish issues could influence ecclesial matters, and parish issues became the concerns of a group of people who were not necessarily acting on behalf of the ecclesial community.

The interface between parish and village interests conditioned rural believers' perception of their own role within the ecclesial community in two
critical ways. First, individual believers often found their ecclesial understanding shaped by two cultural worlds and sets of interests: those connected with
their home village and those related to their own church. Frequently no
conflict of interest existed between the two, but there were instances where
the interests of the village community clearly prevailed.

Such instances were especially evident in cases that involved accusations
of extortion (*vymogatel'stvo*) made by parishioners against a priest. Community
contracts with priests routinely listed those fees and goods that parishioners
promised to offer the priest in return for services, such as the performance of
baptisms, weddings, funerals and so on. Few seemed happy with this system.
Usually the religious press focused on the degradation and humiliation the
priest had suffered in being forced to rely on such payments. The secular press,
in turn, tended to portray the priest as little more than a liturgical extortionist
who would not baptize a sick child or give Communion to a dying old
woman until he had his payment in hand.[175]

Cases where numerous members of a village within a parish accused a
parish priest of extortion were in fact relatively frequent. The accusation was
a serious one and carried severe penalties for the priest in the event that he
was found guilty. According to ecclesiastical rulings, a priest found guilty of
extortion for clerical services was removed from his assigned parish and temporarily lowered in rank to a sacristan. If found guilty more than once he was
threatened with defrocking.[176] Certainly there were instances where a priest
was insensitive to his parishioners and to his own position and was found
guilty of trying to force peasants to pay for liturgical services as if he were
bartering and trading goods. Yet even if he was found innocent, a priest was
often demoralized and frequently asked to be transferred to another parish.

A close reading of cases involving accusations of extortion, however,
shows that persons often used the accusation as a device to further some other
interests. Illustrative in this sense is a 1916 complaint filed by twenty-seven
heads of households from the multivillage Old St. George parish in the
Vologda diocese (Nikolsk district). Among other things, the complaint said
that their priest demanded higher-than-customary fees for certain services and
refused to perform such prayer services when parishioners could not pay up
front. Upon interviewing the parishioners in the parish, the dean found that
no one had any complaints against the priest except for the people from one
village. The real issue, it seemed, was not that of extortion but a dispute over
a piece of pasture land.

The dean also found that many of the villagers who had either signed the
petition or had their names signed because they were illiterate claimed to
know nothing about the issue of extortion.[177] Many also claimed not to have
even been present at the village assembly where the decision of filing a
complaint against the priest had been made. Some declared that they did not
know what was even presented in the complaint against the priest. Neverthe-

less, all those whose names appeared on the petition claimed to agree with the complaint submitted by the assembly. As the fifty-seven-year-old peasant Evgenii Gomzikov explained to the dean, "I myself was not present when the complaint was signed, and do not know what is written in it. But I am in full agreement with the warden [*desitaskii*] who had called the assembly and composed the petition against the priest." Another peasant, seventy-eight-year-old Pavlin Kubokov, who also was not present at the assembly, claimed he signed the petition simply because he was asked to do so by members who had been there: "I do not reject [the wishes] of the assembly."

The point here is that even believers may not always have been able to extricate themselves from considering the authority of the peasant community even in purely ecclesial affairs. They were accustomed to the continual process of negotiation over mundane, administrative matters, and they subjected parish affairs to the rules governing their own local "moral economy."[178] It is not unlikely that the same attitudes carried over into matters of a religious nature: ecclesiastical officials were not necessarily the only authority that was to be followed in matters concerning their faith.

A second way that the interface between parish and village interests conditioned rural believers was that believers became accustomed to managing temple affairs from *outside* the ecclesial context, a habit that had direct implications for local ecclesiology. For example, many church officials defined donations as gifts to God that belonged to the parish church as an institution. The bishop and his representative (the parish priest) oversaw this property.[179] The blurring of the distinction between village and parish, however, effectively undermined this official view. Priests complained that lay persons treated church property as their inalienable property; similarly, "laity vehemently protested whenever they believed ecclesiastical officials infringed upon their 'right' to participate in the management of *their* church property."[180]

The parish priest, though officially the director and overseer of the temple's organizational affairs, technically was not allowed to participate in village assemblies.[181] The village context, therefore, empowered laity in a way that the parish context did not. If a village assembly thought it necessary to consult with the parish priest, it directed a representative to him.[182] Conversely, if a priest needed to discuss certain issues with the village assembly, he, too, often did so through a liaison, such as the church elder.[183]

The practical effects of village involvement in parish affairs were most dramatic with respect to financial support of the parish priest. Despite state subsidies to pastors in especially poor areas, local communities continued to support parish priests in rural European Russia up to 1917 and beyond. In many areas clerical support was defined by contracts that enumerated the various features of the priest's "benefits package." Although present in some communities prior to 1861, such contracts became a standard feature of parish life in the postreform period, when ecclesiastical authorities paid particular attention to raising the material welfare of parish clergy.[184]

By encouraging the formation of more formal contracts, ecclesiastical officials hoped in some way to regulate pastor-flock relations. On the one hand, they wanted to provide security for the parish priest by formalizing the flock's obligations toward him. Tithing, after all, was not a customary practice in the Christian East; believers felt that any material support for the church building or the clergy should be offered on purely voluntary terms.[185] On the other hand, they believed the contracts would protect parishioners from clergy who might arbitrarily set fees for liturgical services. The contracts, therefore, were supposed to prevent the uncertainty and instability for both clergy and laity that might result from oral misunderstandings between pastor and flock.[186]

Despite good intentions, these contracts proved ineffectual almost from the beginning. Many priests complained that the agreed-on settlement was rarely upheld.[187] Certain peasant households were too poor to offer anything while others simply habitually evaded supporting parish clergy.[188] Most parishioners were even less forthcoming in their support in those parishes where the treasury supplied the priest with a supplementary income. One problem with these contracts was that they were composed by village rather than parish assemblies. Accordingly, their terms applied equally to all members of the village community, despite personal disposition toward the Orthodox faith. The *collective* fulfillment of the agreement was thus subject to peasants' appreciation of the contract as a legally, or at least morally, binding document. Although church officials considered these agreements binding, many peasants clearly did not, and they distinguished them from obligatory civil agreements.[189]

Both diocesan officials and parish clergy tried various means to give such contracts the air of legality. Diocesan officials, for instance, advised that the promised collections for clergy be gathered by a village-appointed collector, preferably the local tax collector, who would collect the dues along with state and local taxes, and not by the priest himself. They hoped that placing the collection duties on the community would make these parish-related obligations a communal responsibility and not simply a private matter between the priest and each parish member.[190]

Before 1892, parish priests sometimes attempted to have these agreements enforced by seeking civil recourse from authorities overseeing peasant affairs. Such a recourse, however, usually only undermined morale in parish life. By 1892, the number of pastoral complaints reaching the Holy Synod regarding the nonadherence of communities to their written agreements reached significant enough proportions to warrant a statement by the Holy Synod. In that year, the Synod ruled that diocesan bishops should not allow priests to turn to civil courts to resolve the issue but should encourage them to rely solely on their "moral influence" to settle disputes.[191] In those cases where villagers still refused to honor the terms of the agreement, the local bishop was given the authority to transfer the priest to another location, rescind a parish's independent status, and attach it to a neighboring parish church.[192] Therefore, if village or township officials did not enforce the contracts composed at village assemblies, compliance was left up to the goodwill of each individual member.[193] As one frustrated priest asked, "Why is it that agreements [that concern non-church matters] that are notarized by the township administration have legal, binding power . . . but those regarding the church and clergy that are notarized do not enjoy the same legality?"[194]

With such confusion between village and ecclesial communities in matters of parish management, any number of reasons could account for noncompliance with these agreements. Animosity, simple indifference to priest and temple, or a consciously different religious identity (Old Belief) could serve as motivating factors for some villagers in their avoidance of prescribed dues. Parishioners, however, also refused to comply as a means of exercising their self-perceived rights in the realm of managing their temple's affairs. Such "regulation" of their pastor occurred frequently, with no ulterior ideological sentiments determining their behavior.

During 1903 and1904, for example, the priest of the church of the Resurrection (Velsk district) in the Vologda diocese complained that parishioners were defaulting on their contractual obligations. He blamed their actions on the lack of any legal repercussions for those who did not fulfill the contract's terms. As the diocesan investigation into the case progressed, however, it turned out that he and the parishioners were involved in a dispute over the repair of two churches. Parishioners claimed that the priest had unilaterally decided to renovate one church without first completing the project begun on the other, for which parishioners had collected funds and on which they had already begun work. They complained that the priest had never consulted them regarding his plans. When they objected, he had proceeded anyway, using the funds they had donated.[195]

Similarly, in 1909 the priest of the church in the village of Korovaevo in the Vladimir diocese complained to ecclesiastical officials that his parishioners routinely failed to fulfill the terms of their contract. Eventually, diocesan officials decided to rescind the church's independent status, transferred the priest, and assigned the parishioners to a neighboring parish. In a series of petitions, the church elder, Vsevolod Matorin, explained that it was not that parishioners objected in theory to meeting their obligations but that the priest's behavior had been unacceptable to them. By not fulfilling the terms of their agreement, they hoped to force him to seek a position elsewhere and to have a new priest appointed to their parish.[196]

The confusion resulting from the blurring of boundaries between parish and village became most evident during the local pockets of turmoil in 1905–6, in the wake of the so-called liberation movement.[197] During this period peasants in many areas unilaterally changed the terms of their contracts with their parish priest. Yet, again, a uniform reading of these cases is impossible. In some areas local peasant activists influenced by competing modern revolutionary ideas inspired the initiatives. These activists had no pretenses of identifying with the Orthodox faith, and their actions were aimed against the institutional church. In such cases, the fluid boundaries between village and parish enabled them to disrupt ecclesial relations for their own purposes and to intimidate others to follow suit.[198]

For example, in 1907, after composing a new resolution that reduced support for their priest, a village assembly in the Smolensk diocese appointed "witnesses" in each village to see that no one paid the clergy more than the newly established fees. They also directed these "witnesses" to attend liturgical services to monitor what parishioners paid for extra liturgical services.[199] Such tactics often instilled fear in believers. In another case, a group of parishioners from the church of the Nativity of Christ (Solvychegodsk district) in the Vologda diocese sent a counterpetition protesting their village community's refusal to fulfill their obligations toward the clergy. They spoke of the pressures that a minority group within the assembly had exerted over others; they claimed they were fearful of the consequences they might suffer should their names, as supporters of the parish priest, become known. Therefore, they left their petition unsigned.[200]

Not all contractual reformulation or reneging, however, was purely an-tiecclesial in nature. Often it reflected a growing self-awareness among peas-ants as Orthodox *laity*. By such actions, lay people showed themselves as active members of the ecclesial community, who consciously saw it as their right to participate in directing the affairs of their temple. Many believers took the opportunity of the charged environment of 1905–6 to censure the behavior of priests that for years they had found displeasing.[201] In other instances, parish-ioners left the contract with the priest intact but asserted what they saw as their lay rights by refusing to pay general diocesan dues that were used to support such diocese-wide needs as seminary education. In 1906 parishioners of the church of the Meeting of the Lord in the Viatka diocese decided that because of their poor financial state they were going to keep the diocesan dues to renovate their church.[202] Parishioners from the village of Abramovka in the Simbirsk diocese were even more forceful in their refusal to forward these diocesan dues. "[Our] church is a house of God, a house of prayer, and not a commercial establishment. It was constructed on funds procured by the blood of peasants [*muzhikov*], and therefore does not belong to any circulating capital."[203]

In any single case, therefore, it is difficult to label the behavior of "laity" or "villagers" as *either* purely political *or* purely religious.[204] Decisions made by village assemblies were deceptive in that they appeared to be unanimous when frequently they were not.[205] Not only could different peasants renege on a contract for different reasons, but a single person might have mixed reasons for agreeing to support a contractual change. Without access to the details of each local case, determining the intentions of those involved in contractual changes is impossible. In the Vologda diocese, for example, small groups of peasants were frequently behind such movements to annul a contract. As one group of peasants who supported their parish priest wrote, "the person who never paid anything is the one who screams louder than anyone else; it is only him you hear talking about reducing the dues."[206] A priest from a neighboring district similarly noted that peasants who had not contributed anything toward the support of their clergy in the past, and who found their fellow-villagers' support unnerving, pushed to nullify these contracts.[207]

The same complex dynamic between village and parish characterized other aspects of parish management such as land use.[208] According to law, peasants who desired to form a new independent parish had to portion off a certain amount of land that was to belong to the parish church for clerical use. Peasants, however, often did not view this land as inviolable parish church property. Instead, they saw themselves as allowing and offering clergy temporary use of the land, but with the understanding that ultimately the property still belonged to them.[209] Therefore, when the village community, or individual members of it, determined that they needed the land for their own use, they saw nothing improper about demanding it back.

Such principles of peasant justice especially affected parish-related land matters during the unrest surrounding 1905. During those years, many parish communities, especially those with a history of unresolved tensions regarding the use of land, found themselves embroiled in disputes. In 1906 two villages that belonged to a parish in the Vologda diocese informed their parish clergy that they had "the most pressing need for arable, brush, and meadow lands" and therefore had decided "to take into their own use" such lands being used until then by the parish clergy. Their fathers, they maintained, had given the land to the clergy to use as a source of income. They reasoned that since the clergy had begun to receive a state salary, they no longer needed the land and for them to continue using it would be unjust.[210]

When it came to land issues, then, many peasants—especially those who were nominal believers at best—treated the parish priest as a fellow village member and treated parish lands as if they were peasant lands. They did not consider parish church lands in any way sacred territory, nor did they consider clerical property rights as taking precedence over peasants' rights to cultivation. Especially in cases where the post-Emancipation land surveys had failed to distinguish between parish lands and peasant communal holdings, and where the church had no documentation to prove ownership, the parish priest found himself at the mercy of the village assembly. "As the [assembly] decides, so you must abide," one priest was told regarding certain customs regarding working the land.[211] Church property, including the land cultivated by the clergy, was more susceptible to infringement than that of peasants.

Thus the influence of the village assembly in parish affairs directly affected the pastoral role on various levels. Faced with such a system, priests found their attention divided. Instead of focusing on one flock with shared interests and concerns, the pastor often found himself facing subgroups of parishioners who had little to do with one another outside their formal affiliation with the same parish church. Except perhaps for matters that concerned the beautification of the temple, it was often difficult to unite the flock in order to pursue interests such as charity work, given that each village had its own priorities.

Moreover, the rural priest found himself subject simultaneously to the norms and principles of two different spheres of operation. On the one hand, he was the main liturgical celebrant and bishop's representative, with all the expectations and roles, reviewed earlier, that came with such a position. On the other, he also found himself part of a local rural community that had its own order, customs, and unwritten rules for solving disputes and organizing activities. Lay people did not easily exchange their own mores for other ways that might be considered more proper by church officials. Since the maintenance of the temple entered the sphere of the community's interests, the village assembly naturally discussed a broad range of issues, including the worthiness of the priest. But in this village context, peasants treated the priest less as a clergyman than as simply another person in *their* community. Here a priest's educational role and liturgical function receded in importance. More salient in this context were his personal traits: his integrity, honesty, attitude toward money, and ability to work with people.[212]

The church elder and, to some extent, members of the parish guardianship also stood between village and parish. On the one hand, parishioners chose the church elder as *their* representative and considered it their right to do so.[213] On the other, the church elder's immediate superiors were the parish priest, the local dean, and ultimately the diocesan authorities.[214] Not surprisingly, such a situation carried the potential for conflict. Church elders, by virtue of their endorsement by the village assembly, frequently considered themselves the primary managers of parish business affairs. Priests, thinking otherwise, sometimes found it difficult to work with a candidate chosen by the laity and would sometimes attempt to influence the election of an elder.[215] In 1869, for example, a priest from the Saratov diocese, Grigorii Felikosov, complained that his parishioners treated church property as their inalienable property. He believed that the appointment of a different elder might alleviate the growing tension in the parish. The village assembly, in turn, complained to diocesan officials and accused their priest of "self-willed" behavior (*samovolie*), since he insisted on doing everything independently, without consulting the community at large.[216]

Such complaints by laity were common. Laity applied the charge of "self-willed" behavior to clergy, especially in complaints to the diocesan bishop about their priest. Rural parishioners often took offense when their pastors failed to involve parishioners directly in the process of decision making regarding parish projects. In the 1860s, parishioners from a church in the Vologda diocese charged their priest with "self-willed behavior" because he was not "acting properly"—that is, he was acting without the community's approval.[217] These types of complaints directly challenged the clergy's assumption that they held the primary role in the management of the ecclesial community. Interestingly, diocesan consistories generally sided with parishioners in such cases and advised priests against acting unilaterally without consultation with the parish community.

A case in 1905 involving the church of the Resurrection in the Vologda diocese illustrates the delicate position of the church elder between priest and village, both acting from their sense of authority. In that year diocesan authorities directed the parish to purchase the home of their former sacristan in order to have permanent housing for clergy. When the church elder received news of this order, he announced it to the parishioners before allocating church funds. Paying no attention to the directive, parishioners forbade the church elder to purchase the home. For several weeks, the priest attempted to convince the church elder of the importance of the purchase but without success. The church elder continued to insist that he had to take into account parishioners' wishes. Finally, when the church elder succumbed and agreed to allocate the money, word quickly spread within the village community. Peasants gathered into a combined village assembly and decided to reduce greatly their financial support for the priest. Furthermore, they appointed three representatives from the community to scrutinize more closely the church elder's management of church finances.[218]

In effect, then, rural temple culture found itself under dual management: the church elder as the parishioners' elected representative on the one hand and the parish priest as the bishop's representative on the other.[219] Since the elder answered to all legally registered parishioners, he answered in effect to the village assembly as well, and he often acted on their behalf without consulting the parish priest. In turn, the assembly expected him to uphold their interests and desires over and against the parish priest's in situations of conflict. When communities suspected the elder of not upholding their interests, they often protested. In 1902, the assembly of the village of Chernovo in the Riazan diocese complained to diocesan officials that their elected elder, Dimitrii Gubin, along with the parish priest, Nikolai Smirnov, had not reported to the assembly their financial activities regarding the church construction project. To remedy the situation, they elected their own representatives to oversee the remainder of the project.[220]

The problematic relations between village and parish communities were not entirely lost on ecclesiastical officials in the late imperial period. As one bishop noted in 1905, "it is difficult to clarify . . . the difference between a parish assembly . . . on the one hand, and the village assembly, which often consists of persons who have no relationship to the church . . . on the other.[221] Church officials saw peasant self-government as infringing on the realm of strictly *parish* life, a realm of which many believed the priest should be the main overseer and coordinator, in matters financial as well as liturgical and educational.[222] During the post-Emancipation period, both parish priests and diocesan officials made limited and sometimes inconsistent attempts to balance the relationship between village and parish.

First, many clergy wanted to formally extend their influence into the village community by participating in (or even presiding over) village assemblies. In the 1880s several bishops proposed such involvement to the Special Commission on the Affairs of the Orthodox Clergy. The bishop of Viatka, Apollos (Beliaev), for example, opposed the exclusion of clergy from township and village assemblies because they often discussed issues pertaining to parish life. Moreover, parish priests lived in rural communities alongside peasants and, therefore, should participate in the community's decision-making process. Apollos also maintained that pastoral input into this process would raise the moral and ethical standards of the peasant community. Finally, because township elders and village scribes were not always sympathetic to church-related matters, Apollos advocated that parish priests be given the right to confirm the persons whom communities voted into these positions.[223]

Many bishops expressed similar views in 1905 in their replies to the Holy Synod on church reform. Most bishops agreed that clergy in general and parish priests in particular should be allowed to participate directly in civil organizations. The bishop of Kholm, Evlogii (Georgievskii), for instance, maintained that such participation was only natural in a country where church and state were so closely identified.[224] Many bishops considered it necessary, especially because rural (and urban) administrative organs often consisted of persons who openly considered themselves either nominally Orthodox or non-Orthodox and who thus were not concerned with protecting the interests of the parish church. In addition, since village assemblies frequently decided parish-related issues, as well as educational and charity-related issues, the parish priest, they reasoned, should be a regular member of such assemblies.[225]

While aimed at providing more symmetry in the village-parish relationship, the proposed pastoral involvement in village life would have only further enmeshed the structures and functions of the two already overlapping communities. Those bishops who opposed involvement advocated that priests remain in their ecclesial sphere of life and not attempt to "serve two masters." They took this position despite their view that the church should remain the favored religion of the state.[226] Other bishops favored limited participation of clergy in local administrative organs, namely in those instances when they discussed matters concerning church construction, education, or charity work.[227]

Although not directly addressing the issue of the boundary between village and parish, one rural priest, Pavel Runovskii, at least recognized the implications of these boundaries for defining the pastoral role. In an article entitled "Is It Desirable for the Pastor to Participate in Village Assemblies?" he maintained that such participation would only lower the image of the priest in the parishioners' eyes. Runovskii recalled how as a young priest he believed that he would only have to appear at the village assembly and that immediately the authority he enjoyed as a liturgical celebrant and educator would enable him to bring order to the meeting, to limit the role of the "loudmouths," and to regulate and direct the course of the discussion. Now, as an older priest, he realized that such a view was idealistic. The peasant community, in his eyes, had an order of its own. Peasants, even those who generally respected the parish priest, did not consider it the priest's business to get involved in the day-to-day affairs of the village community, even when the community was discussing parish-related matters. By appearing regularly at the assembly as a voting member, the priest would present himself outside the ecclesial context in a sphere where the peasants dictated the order. At best he would enjoy only the respect and the rights for which any other peasant might hope. More likely, peasants would shun him as an outsider.[228]

Ecclesiastical officials also attempted to modify existing village-parish dynamics by limiting the scope of temple-related issues that village assemblies could discuss. In 1887 the Holy Synod issued an ukase regarding the temple-related subjects that village or township assemblies could discuss. Except for those distinctly mentioned in the General Rules governing peasant life (namely, collections for the construction and maintenance of churches, and financial support of clergy), parish issues—especially those concerning the merits or demerits of their parish priest—were not to be discussed at village assemblies.[229] Consequently, the Synod deemed certain petitions and written agreements that village assemblies submitted to diocesan officials an intrusion into ecclesial matters and directed diocesan officials to ignore them.[230] Despite such attempts to delineate the village and parish as operationally separate entities, many communities continued to discuss parish matters at village assemblies, often notwithstanding pressure from local civil authorities not to do so.[231]

Many peasants favored making financial decisions at the village assembly rather than the parish assembly. Not only was the village assembly a more convenient forum but its decisions at least technically enjoyed a semblance of authority, while decisions made by a parish assembly did not. Because of this disparity, clergy also desired to see certain changes in the rules governing parish assemblies. For instance, besides wanting the quorum to be similar to that of village assemblies, they wanted parish assembly resolutions to carry the same legal weight as those of village assemblies. In 1913 the ober-procurator of the Holy Synod, V. K. Sabler, raised these issues with the minister of the interior. It was decided that any action in this regard must await future parish reform.[232]

In the end, the overlap of village and parish communities in administrative matters confused the question of Orthodox identity in rural Russia in two fundamental ways. First, from the perspective of the laity, the village assembly provided an established and familiar base from which to manage the temple culture they so painstakingly supported and maintained. It allowed them to bring ecclesial matters onto home ground and to orchestrate the day-to-day aspects of their religious life in their own way. By operating from within the village assembly, however, the laity separated themselves from an ecclesial context. They placed themselves in a position of continual negotiation not only with parish clergy but also with members of their own community who did not share the same religious worldview. The use of the village assembly as a forum for managing parish affairs became increasingly problematic following 1905, and especially following 1917. During this period, the inroads of modernization resulted in rapid political and religious differentiation in Russia's rural areas and challenged the previously indiscriminate mixing of village and ecclesial affairs.

Second, the blurring between village and parish in temple administrative affairs made it difficult for clergy to identify "the flock." This can be seen in the way diocesan bishops read the process of political and religious differentiation in Russia's countryside in the post-1905 period. Bishops' reports to the Holy Synod during this time reveal mixed observations with respect to the flock's religious leanings and sensibilities. Some bishops commented on a decline in lay religiosity, while others noted a growing self-awareness among peasants of their Orthodox faith.[233] This varied reading is probably best explained in terms not of geographic differences but of a simultaneous process of broad religious alienation combined with an intensification of belief among more conscious adherents that often characterizes modernizing societies.

The difficulty in defining "the flock" reemerged during the 1917–18 All-Russian Church Council, when members found themselves at odds over identifying who precisely constituted "the parish." Were parishioners simply all nominal "Orthodox" people living within a particular radius around a church building? Should parishioners demonstrate their "belonging" in some particular manner? As the layman A. S. Vasiliev noted, it was clear that the parish should be composed only of genuine Christians. Nevertheless, everyone knew that there were atheists who were registered as "Orthodox." The question was how to differentiate among the millions of legally registered Orthodox people in Russia.[234] This was no minor matter, especially when the issue of ownership of church property was raised, since it involved a matter of trust. How were "lay persons" to be trusted if they were not necessarily committed Orthodox believers? [235] The matter would have serious ramifications for the Orthodox Church during the Soviet period.

The temple in the culture of late imperial rural Russia was a semantically complex entity whose multiple and overlapping layers of meaning generally related to one of three overarching functions of the temple in Russian culture at that time. First, the temple stood as an "official" sacerdotal structure whose significance proceeded from a history and context independent of its immediate locality. By its presence in that locality, therefore, the temple impressed meaning on it. The temple, through its assigned clergy and their use of space, ritual, words, and images, established a context that was meant to be *entered*, as opposed to created or defined by its members anew.

At the same time, however, the temple also stood as a narrative repository that actively and creatively engaged those lay persons who were drawn to it as a reference point for both personal and shared religious experiences. Its perceived holiness was tied to multiple factors that included, most saliently, the memory of God and of one's forefathers, the solace and "fullness" of liturgical prayer, and a powerful sense of divine presence that brought order and perspective to their lives. By investing in its material upkeep and participating in its liturgical life, believers channeled various emotions and affections toward the temple; they endowed it with their own meaning, making it theirs. By virtue of its presence in a particular locality, then, the temple was a familial place, enabling believers, both individually and collectively, to find significance in aspects of their lives that otherwise might have remained without coherence.

Finally, standing at the intersection between village and parish life, the temple in late imperial rural Russia was an enduring forum for relational dialectics with respect to both the internal life of the faith community and the world outside it. By managing their temple's affairs from within the village context rather than the strictly ecclesial one, believers found a means by which to exert their sense of responsibility and authority in a world where their place was not always self-evident and often contested or dismissed. In this sense, the temple functioned as a vehicle for lay legitimation.

At the same time, because the worlds of the village and the ecclesial community were so intimately intertwined, the temple also found itself caught in a dialectic between the sacred and the profane or, at times, in a dialectic concerning the very definitions of the sacred and the profane. The stakes of this dialectic greatly increased in the Soviet period. During this time, believers and nonbelievers vied to control temple culture. Where believers held sway, the village provided a secular forum by which they could attempt to preserve and protect their religious heritage. But village involvement in ecclesial affairs also rendered temple culture vulnerable to disruption by nonbelievers and manipulation by revolutionaries for the purposes of imposing their own competing grand narratives on the populace.[236]

# 3

## Chapels

### Symbols of Ecclesial Antinomies

During the debates over church reform, many of Russia's religious intellectuals had turned their attention to the spiritual, theological, and sociopolitical aspects of the parish and its temple culture. If Orthodoxy was to play a vital role in the formation of a new society, they believed it could do so only through the local faith community, the parish. Not everyone, however, agreed with this assessment. The conservative religious activist Lev Tikhomirov, for instance, argued that it was shortsighted to place such a wager on the parish. Although agreeing that it was the "bright ray amid dark disquiet" of the times, he maintained that the parish was not as central to Orthodox identity, especially among laity, as many church intellectuals believed.[1]

A closer look at Russia's religious landscape shows that the temple with its parish community was not the exclusive center of ecclesial identity, especially in rural Russia. Believers expressed their ecclesial solidarity in other settings and ways. Not least among these alternative markers of Orthodox identity were chapels. Indeed, a 1906 devotional leaflet aimed against the "gang of godless" Social Democrats took as its backdrop a chapel instead of a rural parish church or urban cathedral.[2]

Chapels held a unique place in Russia's religious life. On the one hand, worship in them was not entirely a private or personal matter, as it usually was in the confines of one's home; on the other, prayer in chapels was not of the same order as the corporate celebration of the Divine Liturgy in the parish church. Chapels stood between the religious centers of home and church, and their place in Orthodox life revealed another way believers expressed and manifested their corporate Orthodox identity.

Even though relatively little was formally written about chapels, they were ubiquitous in Russia's religious landscape. Remarkably, their number almost doubled in the period between 1861 and 1917.[3] Although in the late nineteenth century lay persons constructed some chapels in urban areas and provincial towns, especially in marketplaces, by far the most chapel construction took place in Russia's rural areas. In part, as with temples, this was because

Russia's large cities and towns already had numerous churches and chapels and church officials were reluctant to add to their numbers.

The growth in the number of chapels during the late nineteenth and early twentieth centuries raises several questions whose answers are critical for understanding the ecclesial world of Russian Orthodox laity. Why did lay believers construct chapels? What functions did they serve in the local faith community? How did local clergy view chapels and the activity associated with them? And finally, from this investigation, what can we conclude regarding the role of laity, especially rural laity, in the broader Church community in the crucial postreform period?

⊷⇒◉⇐⊷

## The History of Chapel Construction in Russia

The Russian word for chapel is *chasovnia*, from the word *chas*, or "hour," signifying that it was primarily a place for the reading of the hours, something that could be performed by laity without the presence of clergy. The Eastern Christian Eucharistic service, the Divine Liturgy, was not usually served in chapels, since, unlike regular churches, they did not traditionally have their own *antimins*.[4] An *antimins* is a silken or linen cloth in which the relics of saints have been sewn; on it is depicted the entombment of Christ and the four Evangelists. According to Eastern Orthodox liturgical practice, the Eucharistic liturgy generally is not to be performed without one. Thus a Liturgy could be served only if a priest brought an *antimins* to the chapel. Similarly, clergy did not as a rule perform the sacraments of matrimony and baptism in chapels, though such services were allowed in extraordinary circumstances and usually required the permission of the diocesan bishop. Although believers considered their chapel construction efforts to be part of the "Orthodox custom of the Christian faith,"[5] there appears to have been no specific liturgical service for the blessing of a chapel. Services for the blessing of a home and the consecration of a church were widely known and used but chapels were usually blessed under the same rubric as that of a home.

Chapels had a long history, not only in Russia but in Christendom in general, with some scholars tracing their origins back to the martyries erected over martyrs' graves in the fourth century.[6] Nineteenth-century Russian churchmen understood Christ's directive to pray privately (Matt. 6:5) as the impetus for the development of the chapel tradition. They saw rooms built both inside and outside of homes for purposes of private prayer, as well as roadside shrines found throughout the Byzantine East, as the predecessors of the contemporary chapel.[7] Chapels in Russia dotted roadsides and riverbanks and provided sacred spaces in public buildings, marketplaces, and even train cars (fig. 3.1). Chapels, however, were not uniformly distributed throughout

3.1  Roadside chapel; in honor of St. Nicholas the Wonderworker, Perm
province, Vetluga Settlement. 1910. Library of Congress, Prints and
Photographs Division, Prokudin-Gorskii Collection.

Russia. From tables 3.1 and 3.2, which list the number of chapels by diocese
in 1860 and then again in 1914, one can see that the largest number of chapels
were located in the provinces of northern European Russia. A sample listing
of chapels in the provinces of the more southern, black earth region shows
that their number was significantly, often even dramatically, lower. In large
part geography and population explain this difference. Parishes in the north
tended to stretch over relatively large expanses (as many as 100 miles and
sometimes more). Because of these distances, in the severe northern weather
peasants could not attend church regularly. Local conditions compounded the
difficulties created by the weather. It was not uncommon for rural believers
to complain that they were unable to make it even to Paschal services because
of impassable roads.[8]

Despite their place in mainstream Orthodoxy, chapels in Russia were not
without a troubled past.[9] Before the seventeenth century, chapel-centered
faith communities, or "chapel-parishes" (*chasovennye prikhody*), formed the
smallest organizational units within the Church.[10] At that time, laity in such
communities held complete jurisdiction over chapel construction. Neither
laity nor hierarchy considered an episcopal blessing or formal permission from

TABLE 3.1    Chapels and Parish Churches in Select Dioceses
of European Russia, 1861[a]

| Diocese | Population | Chapels | Parish churches |
| --- | --- | --- | --- |
| Novgorod | 951,085 | 2,711 | 608 |
| Olonets | 281,093 | 1,130 | 239 |
| Kostroma | 1,069,676 | 1,256 | 948 |
| St. Petersburg[b] | 662,246 | 1,169 | 252 |
| Perm | 1,885,475 | 829 | 602 |
| Pskov | 673,157 | 765 | 382 |
| Tver | 1,455,447 | 697 | 918 |
| Vologda | 927,592 | 596 | 687 |
| Iarolavl[c] | 990,130 | 444 | 844 |
| Viatka | 1,980,211 | 386 | 444 |
| Arkhangelsk | 256,269 | 266 | 229 |
| Moscow[b] | 1,404,956 | 243 | 1,146 |
| Voronezh | 1,818,241 | 21 | 723 |
| Tula | 1,110,997 | 19 | 819 |
| Vladimir | 1,224,064 | 8 | 1,034 |
| Riazan | 1,381,560 | 6 | 833 |
| Orel | 1,433,567 | 4 | 832 |
| Kaluga | 912,883 | 2 | 603 |
| Kursk | 1,683,118 | 0 | 905 |

[a]*Izvlecheniia iz otcheta po vedomostvu dukhovnykh del pravoslavnago ispovedaniia* (St. Petersburg, 1864).
[b]The higher number of chapels for the dioceses of the two capitals might reflect chapels built on the patronage of wealthier peasants-turned-merchants and of the nobility. Also note that many urban public buildings and factories housed chapels.
[c]All figures from Iaroslavl are from 1884.

ecclesiastical or civil authorities necessary to construct a chapel.[11] The chapel also enjoyed complete administrative autonomy from the central parish church. Since laity frequently chose to build chapels with an altar space, it is not surprising that in many places they became substitutes for parish churches. Believers would see nothing unusual about hiring retired clergy or hiero-monks from nearby monasteries to celebrate liturgical services in their villages. As a result, church officials began to worry that laity might come to see their participation in broader parish life as superfluous. Such independent behavior on the part of communities of rural believers, coupled with the Old Believer schism in the Russian Orthodox Church, led local bishops in the seventeenth century to limit the independent status of chapels.[12]

From that time on, both ecclesiastical and civil authorities considered chapels potentially troublesome because clerical supervision of activities in and around them was minimal. Viewing unsupervised chapels as potential gather-

TABLE 3.2   Chapels and Parish Churches in Select Dioceses
of European Russia, 1914[a]

| Diocese | Population | Chapels | Parish churches |
|---|---|---|---|
| Novgorod | 1,517,032 | 3,264 | 753 |
| Olonets | 438,107 | 1,715 | 292 |
| Kostroma | 1,587,018 | 1,735 | 1,033 |
| Petrograd | 1,057,846 | 1,638 | 301 |
| Perm | 1,555,812 | 1,169 | 428 |
| Pskov | 1,263,618 | 997 | 377 |
| Tver | 1,931,457 | 1,031 | 926 |
| Vologda | 1,643,251 | 1,607 | 748 |
| Iaroslavl | 1,168,643 | 790 | 861 |
| Viatka | 3,242,889 | 750 | 667 |
| Arkhangelsk | 441,950 | 452 | 454 |
| Moscow | 1,639,186 | 513 | 1,228 |
| Voronezh | 2,995,542 | 58 | 984 |
| Tula | 1,629,142 | 257 | 836 |
| Vladimir | 1,625,020 | 18 | 1,124 |
| Riazan | 2,051,992 | 56 | 926 |
| Orel | 1,995,989 | 58 | 882 |
| Kaluga | 1,265,696 | 147 | 615 |
| Kursk | 2,421,692 | 18 | 1,053 |

[a] *Vsepoddanneishii otchet oberprokurora Sv. Sinoda po vedomstvu pravoslavnago ispovedaniia* (St. Petersburg, 1915).

ing places for Old Believers, Peter the Great ordered their construction outlawed in November 1707. Later, in April 1722, the newly formed Holy Synod issued an edict saying that all existing chapels should be leveled and no new ones built.[13] In 1734, another ruling tempered the situation by allowing old chapels to remain but reiterated the ban on the construction of new ones.[14] Yet, because of the practical needs chapels served in remote rural areas and because of their continued construction in rural areas despite legal measures against them, ecclesiastical authorities frequently relented and allowed chapel construction.

Thus early in Russia's history the chapel became a focal point for tensions between varying ecclesiological sentiments within the Orthodox Church. The chapel symbolized differing views on such crucial issues as religious authority, the roles of laity and clergy, and the position of the individual vis-à-vis the faith community. Church hierarchy, state officials, parish clergy, and laity all potentially saw chapels as embodying, or not embodying, their various convictions on these issues.

### Constructing a Chapel

By the mid–nineteenth century, legislation concerning chapels had become more lenient. By that time, church officials had become aware that the closure of chapels had had adverse effects on Orthodox believers and their prayer life, especially in areas where the local parish church was located at a considerable distance. Consequently, in 1853 the Holy Synod made allowances for the construction of chapels in areas where there was need of a church but where the financial resources of a parish community did not allow for a larger church structure.[15] In 1865, the Synod turned over decision making concerning chapel construction to local bishops and consistories. From then on, the Holy Synod usually handled only appeals made by individuals and communities who wished to challenge a diocesan rejection of their request to construct a chapel.[16]

In order to construct a chapel, believers generally had to endure a complex application process that often took years and resembled the petition process for building a new church. With chapels, however, petitions usually originated with individuals or with smaller groups of believers, as opposed to entire parish communities.[17] In Russia's provincial towns and in the two major capitals in particular, individual merchants and noblemen petitioned to construct chapels, as did town councils, groups of factory workers, and tradesmen. While individual peasant believers also petitioned for permission to construct chapels, usually rural petitions originated with a single village assembly or a group of several village assemblies. As with other rural community matters, a valid decision required that a majority of the voting members of the village assembly be present. As a 1906 petition to build a chapel in the village of Soliatino in the Vologda diocese said, "one day . . . returning home from church services, we gathered and discussed whether it would not be possible for us to petition for permission to construct a new chapel in our village . . . but because not all peasants were home since some were away working in the city, the decision was delayed until the return of these peasants."[18]

Usually a village, group of villages, or town council appointed one or two members of their community to oversee the construction of the chapel—a role that included corresponding with the diocesan consistory. We know little about these people, except that they were always male and usually literate. Certain histories of chapels suggest that these men tended to be materially better off than the average villager and often provided the initial idea for the project.[19] Sometimes several believers joined together to oversee the chapel construction process, thereby forming a village building committee.

The desires and needs of believers themselves usually prompted the drafting and submission of petitions. Only in isolated cases does evidence suggest that the idea of a chapel originated with the local priest or with the bishop. As a product of the "will of the people,"[20] chapels materially expressed the laity's self-perceived role in organizing their religious life. Laity initiated the process, covered the full cost of construction, and, particularly in Russia's rural areas, provided raw materials and donated their time and energy in the actual construction work. In urban areas, those individuals or groups of believers who initiated a construction project either took responsibility for its upkeep or made arrangements for its maintenance with the church or monastery to which the chapel was assigned.[21] In rural areas, the village or group of villages that constructed a chapel took full responsibility for its maintenance.

According to established procedures, the initial petition to the diocesan consistory had to explain why a chapel was needed or desired. It also had to include a description of the location where the proposed chapel was to be built, an explanation of how its construction was to be financed, and, in cases of rural villages, a statement of how many people were present at the assembly that decided the matter. To these petitions rural believers usually attached the collective agreement that they had composed at the village assembly and that each voting member had signed or marked. On the basis of the petition, the diocesan or synodal administration decided whether or not the proposal presented a "worthy reason" for constructing a chapel. If the consistory decided that the reasons presented were not valid, it rejected the petition.

If the consistory believed the petition merited consideration, the application process proceeded to its next phase. The consistory required an architectural plan for the chapel and also solicited a report from local police officials concerning any grounds for not building the chapel, including any potential zoning problems. In rural areas, the consistory also expected the local police to notify them in cases of any schismatic or sectarian tendencies among the local population that might suggest that peasants were constructing the chapel for reasons other than those formally stated in the petition. Finally, the diocesan administration frequently requested the local parish priest's opinion on the need for this chapel.

Believers' self-imposed sacrifices for the sake of having a chapel in their village or town included more than money and time. Especially in rural areas, when a single believer initiated the idea, the village assembly offered the land on which the chapel was to stand. In 1915, for instance, peasants from the village of Dorki in the Vologda diocese received a plan for a chapel that a woman from their village who then resided in St. Petersburg desired to have built in her home village. They eagerly embraced the idea, promising to set aside the necessary amount of land.[22] In other cases, local inhabitants were even willing to move their home or barns so that chapels could be built in a particular place.[23] Even in towns and cities, the new chapels that were constructed usually depended on lay efforts.[24]

In addition to their material investments, believers expressed their commitment to chapel projects by tirelessly pursuing the ratification process. In case after case where church officials initially denied permission or responded with great delay, laity would follow up with numerous petitions, sometimes over the course of five or even fifteen years.[25] They would not stop with their local bishop but would take the time and energy to petition the provincial governor, the Holy Synod, the metropolitans of the two capitals, even the tsar or the empress—basically anyone who might be able to influence the local bishop's decision.

What laity probably did not suspect was that petitions concerning chapels addressed to the tsar, empress, or another bishop were not decided independently by these persons but forwarded to the Holy Synod. In turn, before making any decision, the Holy Synod reported the petition to the local bishop and requested his opinion on the matter. Hence the appeals simply returned to the desk where the request was originally denied. Even with this system in use, the Synod overruled the local consistory's decision relatively often, citing the zeal and unwavering energy that laity displayed.[26]

⋆⇒◉⇐⋆

## Russia's Chapelscape

Chapels did not stand as testimonies to any single set of emotions or religious sentiments on the part of believers. The chapels constructed in 1867 at the Russian embassy in Nice, in 1876 by the peasants of the village of Liubunino in the Novgorod diocese, in 1888 by the merchant Ippolit Andreev in the provincial town of Rzhev in the Tver diocese, and in 1898 by the baroness Varvara Mengden von Al'tenvog in the Poltava diocese—each of these chapels spoke to different ways of expressing and even constructing religious identity.[27]

Generally speaking, chapels and the sentiments that motivated their construction can be grouped according to whether individuals or communities were petitioning to build them. Many petitions for chapel construction originated with relatively wealthy individuals who sought to memorialize personal sacred experiences or their own personal causes. In 1862, for example, the merchant Ippolit Andreev from the Tver diocese received permission to construct a chapel on the grounds of his parish church in the provincial town of Rzhev in honor of a Tikhvin icon of the Mother of God that was housed in the church and that he specially revered. He hoped the chapel would facilitate the veneration of this icon, since a chapel would remain open twenty-four hours a day, while a church generally remained locked between services.[28] In 1904, the merchant Aleksandr Solodov was moved by "the will of his deceased father" and the blessing of his spiritual father to construct a chapel in his home village.[29]

Individuals also looked to chapels as a means of memorializing their own lives and the lives of their loved ones. In 1898 the Holy Synod granted permission to the baroness Varvara Mengden von Al'tenvog to construct a chapel over the grave of her father, located in the village of Paryshkovo in the Poltava diocese.[30] In addition to constructing chapels on family grave sites, wealthier Russians in particular were sometimes ready to bequeath or donate houses or land to monasteries for the construction of chapels in return for that monastic community's eternal prayers for their departed souls, though such petitions were not readily granted by church officials. For instance, the barrister Fedor Plevako donated his Moscow home and land to the St. Peter monastery in Rostov in the Iaroslavl diocese. Once the monastic community legally owned the land, Plevako requested that its members construct a chapel and perpetually remember during prayer services all those whom he had listed in his will. Although the abbot of the monastery supported the idea, the metropolitan of Moscow discouraged it, claiming that with more than thirty chapels and three hundred churches, Moscow had no need for more houses of prayer.[31]

Poorer peasant believers also individually petitioned for the construction of chapels but usually with different motives. Many rural believers who individually sought to construct a chapel were hermit or monastic types who, in their pursuit of a desert Christian ideal, desired to have a special place for prayer. For example, in 1887 the twenty-four-year-old peasant woman Elizaveta Trepacheva from the village of Lytina in the Iaroslavl diocese petitioned to construct a chapel. Having vowed to "dedicate herself to a God-pleasing life," she "renounced the world" and began the life of a recluse in a community with three other women. According to Trepacheva, she had vowed to the recently deceased "abbess" of their community to pursue the construction of a chapel, which would serve as a "support and comfort to us."[32]

Similarly, in 1891, the middle-aged peasant Elisei Rodin from the village of Lopatino in the Nizhnii Novgorod diocese wanted to rebuild an old village chapel that stood in a state of disrepair at the site of a spring. According to oral tradition, the spring had appeared when a cross had been found on the site decades before. Since then, Rodin claimed, the chapel had not been properly cared for. Having himself been healed from blindness twelve years earlier by waters from this spring, Rodin had made a vow to "leave the world" and live at this site. Rodin built for himself a small hut nearby and began caring for the chapel. Gradually believers from surrounding villages began visiting the location to pray.[33]

Diocesan and synodal authorities generally viewed this type of individual request with suspicion, questioning the motives of not only the petitioner but those people who gathered to pray at such sites. Often suspecting "sectarianism," they worried that these chapels might encourage behavior that was "contrary to the Christian spirit, tempting to others, and not in accord with the characteristics of a God-pleasing faith." Such was the verdict reached by local clergy with respect to a small group of five or six believers who had settled on the site of a former monastery in the Tambov province and who wished to see the chapel that once stood there rebuilt.[34] Similarly, in the case of Rodin, in order to have more control over the activities in and around the chapel and to prevent any "assemblage of sectarians," local clergy decided to lock the chapel.[35]

Generally, however, chapel construction, especially in rural areas, tended to be collective projects rooted in the life of the entire local community.[36] Broadly speaking, the numerous reasons rural laity had for constructing chapels fall into two groups, which could be labeled centralizing and decentralizing. The first set of reasons was more parish focused and reflected a desire to be connected to a perceived broader religious community. The centralizing tendency evident in this group treated chapels as ecclesial outposts or branches of the main organization. The second set of reasons focused more on local concerns that may not have held much meaning for believers from other localities. This decentralizing set of reasons manifested a conservatorial attitude on the part of laity toward the chapel as a testimonial to God's presence in its own right and as a nurturer of the seed of faith disseminated to their locale.

⤞═◎═⤝

## Chapels as Centralizing

R ural communities often desired chapels to serve as substitute parish churches. Frequently such communities would rather have constructed a church but were too small to afford it. Low population density in the northern regions where chapels were most numerous meant that new parishes grew relatively slowly. Chapels, however, proved a relatively inexpensive way to alleviate the problem of distance and to guarantee a place for prayer for the ill and elderly on Sundays and feast days during inclement weather. Church-going was apparently sufficiently important in rural believers' lives that in instances where prolonged absences were forced on them by factors outside their control (weather, local conditions, old age), they sought to replicate the temple environment as close to home as possible.[37] They distinguished between personal, home prayer and public, communal prayer, and the first was not seen as a replacement for the second.

In 1888 believers from the village of Pervaia Korlinskaia in the Vologda diocese wrote that seasonal problems connected with the small river Pocha made it extremely difficult to get to church. Frustrated with this situation, they wrote, "Church law and Holy Scripture demand that an Orthodox Christian does not separate himself from communal prayer."[38] Nevertheless, communal prayer in their view was not necessarily restricted to worship in the parish church. Rural laity felt that a chapel could also "stimulate a prayerful mood in the feeling of the Christian faith."[39]

In 1895 the peasant Nikolai Chumovskii, from the village of Aleshevskoe in the Vologda diocese, explained the function of the village chapel in the following way:

> On feast days and Sundays my trustees as well as those from the neighboring village gather for prayer in this chapel. Seventeen years ago, the local retired deacon . . . led the readings and the chanting. Following his death, a literate person was found who took over his

functions, and a year ago the teacher in the local parish church school located in our village took over these duties. In this way my trustees from the very founding of this chapel came here on Sundays and feast days and spent these days in a religious mood, enjoying the readings from the Holy books (i.e., the psalter and Scripture). Our parish is located eight miles from the parish church and others live still farther than our village, some twenty miles away. If such folk did not go to the chapel, they would be deprived of the pleasure of hearing the Word of God.[40]

Similarly, believers from the village of Iukhnev in the Olonets diocese lived a great distance from their church. On Sundays and feast days, they would gather at the chapel to pray, and a priest would travel to conduct services in the chapel only several times per year.[41] Rural laity used chapels, therefore, to organize liturgical and religious educational activity. As one petition maintained, "some of the literate peasants would read books of a spiritual-ethical content, while others would listen and learn."[42] These two activities clearly paralleled the main functions of parish churches.

Chapels also sometimes served as substitute churches in a more practical way. For instance, some communities desired a chapel as a place to keep the dead prior to their being taken to the church for burial. Distance sometimes made it difficult for peasants to get the dead to church for burial by the third day. In 1862, believers from the village of Redbuzhi in the Novgorod diocese explained that all of the surrounding villages had chapels in which the bodies of the dead could be kept until burial. Although their village, Redbuzhi, was located only two and a half miles from the parish church, they were separated from it by the river Luga. Hence they requested permission to construct a small wooden chapel.[43]

Chapels might serve other functions that were tied to the festal liturgical calendar. Figure 3.2 offers an example of a chapel that was constructed near a river or stream, and used during the rites of the blessing of waters, which were of two general types. The "lesser" or "minor" blessing of waters usually took place inside a church or home on certain feasts and local occasions such as the celebration of parish feast days. It also took place on 1 August—the feast of the Carrying-Forth of the Venerable Wood of the Life-Creating Cross of the Lord—either within the temple or at a live water source. A second type, the "great" blessing of waters, was held on the feast of Theophany, which celebrated Christ's baptism in the Jordan river. It was considered the feast of light and enlightenment since Christ was the "light of the world." On the eve of this feast, the blessing of waters usually took place in the narthex of the church, and on the day of the feast an entire parish might walk in procession to a nearby river or stream, the waters of which would then be blessed during a prayer service. Believers considered the water blessed during this feast as having exceptional healing properties and took it home for periodic consumption throughout the entire next year.

3.2   Chapel for the blessing of water in the village of Deviatiny
(Russian Empire). 1909. Library of Congress, Prints and Photographs Division,
Prokudin-Gorskii Collection.

The idea that believers saw chapels as substitute or miniature temples is reinforced by the fact that, in their chapel construction, they strove to replicate the church environment in terms of architectural style and interior decor. Although some village chapels were indeed nothing more than simple wooden hut-type buildings (fig. 3.3),[44] they were often quite elaborate structures resembling small churches, complete with a bell, a small dome, and a cross on top (fig. 3.4).[45] Inside and more rarely, outside, some were fully adorned with frescoes (fig. 3.5).[46]

But more than anything else, the iconostasis contained in many chapels spoke of believers' desire to reproduce the church environment closer to home.[47] The iconostasis was one of the most characteristic features of Russian Orthodox church architecture. Because many chapels did not have an altar space, believers often erected chapel iconostases in front of the main wall of the chapel (fig. 3.6).[48] Moreover, in churches, the iconostasis traditionally had a rationale to its design: icons were placed in a particular order that had theological significance.[49] In the case of chapels, this theological meaning was linked directly to the life of the local community. Lay believers decided both on the specific icons and on their positioning in the chapel. As a result, iconostases in chapels tended to have their own local logic. Community members chose icons to commemorate events considered sacred in the village's history.[50]

3.3　Wooden chapel. Riazan province, Kasimov
district, village of Bolshie Peksely. Photograph by V. M.
Matechkin, 1910. The Russian Museum of
Ethnography, St. Petersburg.

In one important way, however, chapels could never entirely replace a
parish church: the Divine Liturgy was not routinely served in them. In urban
chapels, clergy often scheduled prayer services during which believers could
come with their own individual needs. Such services usually included the
reading of *akathistoi* hymns, a different one each day of the week.[51] In rural
areas, even though believers might themselves mark a Sunday or feast day by
prayer services in the chapel, such services could never replicate the ceremony
of liturgical worship led by a priest, a feature of liturgical prayer that rural
believers highly cherished. Because of this lack of liturgical ceremony, many
rural believers saw chapels as secondary to the parish church. In fact, some
rural communities viewed chapels as temporary constructions that served as
antecedents of parish formation. Wishing to have a parish church but knowing

3.4    View of chapel. Olonets province, Povenetskii district, village of
Gapselga. 1912. The Russian Museum of Ethnography, St. Petersburg.

that their request would be denied by diocesan officials because of their
financial inability to support a parish church, rural believers sometimes sought
to build a chapel first, believing it would make it easier to convince ecclesiastical authorities to allow them to form their own independent parish at a later
date.[52]

Sometimes the move from chapel to parish church would happen much
more naturally and would seem to suggest a pattern that occurred commonly
and without any conscious planning by believers. In 1906, Ivan Akhat'ev, a
peasant from the village of Nechaevsk in the Riazan diocese, constructed a
chapel in his village with the hope that vesperal services could be held during
times of cold weather. By 1908, the chapel could not hold all the faithful who
wished to worship there. In response, saying that he was moved by a desire to
support the religious sensibilities of factory workers who lived in his area,
Akhat'ev petitioned diocesan authorities to have the chapel enlarged. The
workers' faith, he maintained, "had already begun to weaken under the
influence of new trends." His hope was that three to five times a year local
clergy from the nearby church could serve a Divine Liturgy in the chapel.
Subsequently, he received permission to include a sanctuary area and all the
necessary items to conduct such Liturgies. Akhat'ev termed the resulting
construction a chapel-church, a project that in the end cost him some 25,000
rubles.[53]

3.5 Chapel in honor of the Presentation of the Mother of God into the Temple. St. Petersburg province, Novoladoga district, village of Kulinbor. The Russian Museum of Ethnography, St. Petersburg.

On one level, then, rural believers constructed chapels in order to maintain their connection with the broader Orthodox community. From an official Orthodox perspective, parish communities were supposed to provide that connection. When little more than nominal membership at the nearest parish church was possible, however, rural communities frequently took it upon themselves to manifest their unity with the broader faith community through their chapel. Chapels enabled rural lay people to manifest their membership in that larger community.

Petitions from rural believers also reveal another, different type of centralizing tendency. Believers not infrequently asserted that they sought to build chapels to commemorate a political event or an occurrence in the life of the imperial family.[54] Requests to dedicate chapels to such events came from believers of virtually every socioeconomic background—nobility, merchants, townspeople, workers, and peasants. Given, however, that the majority of chapels were built by rural laity, especially those of peasant background, the prevalence of such dedications in rural areas raises the

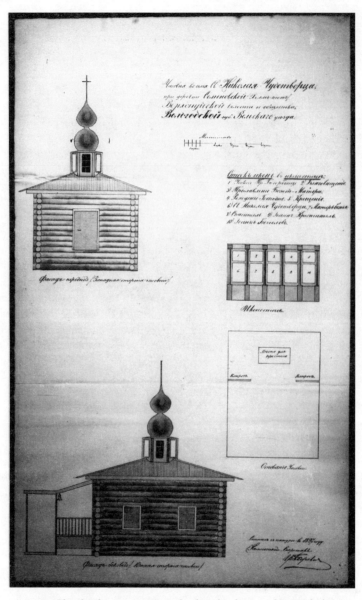

3.6  Plan for the construction of a chapel in honor of St. Nicholas
in the Vologda province, Velsk district, village of Semenovskoe. The
icons that are listed to appear in the iconostasis are the following:
(1) Dormition of the Mother of God; (2) Annunciation; (3) The
Glorification of the Mother of God; (4) The Nativity of Christ;
(5) Epiphany; (6) St. Nicholas the Wonderworker; (7) The Mother
of God; (8) The Savior; (9) John the Baptist; (10) John the
Theologian. Courtesy of the Vologda State Regional Archive.

complex issue of the relationship between religious, political, and national identities of rural laity.

It is difficult to draw definitive conclusions on this issue on the basis of chapel petitions alone. On the one hand, they reveal what some historians have already observed: peasant authors of petitions and letters to both civil and ecclesiastical officials took their addressees into account and attempted to play up to them in order to get what they wanted.[55] For instance, there were occasions when church authorities denied an initial petition to construct a chapel and peasant believers then proceeded to reapply with a new clause affirming their desire to build the chapel in memory of an event in the life of the royal family. Clearly we might question the sincerity of the dedication to the imperial family in such cases.[56] Similarly, we might question the declared motives of those who dedicated a chapel in memory of Alexander III and then neglected to include an icon of his patron saint among those they chose for their chapel.[57] It is reasonable to hypothesize in these cases that believers presumed that such a clause might guarantee the approval of their chapel request. Indeed, church officials sometimes suspected as much. In 1869, church officials from the Orel diocese denied the peasant Ivan Korobochkin permission to fund the construction of a chapel in memory of the thwarting of the assassination attempt on the life of Alexander II. He had the support of his fellow parishioners, especially since their former chapel had come into major disrepair and the icons from it were currently being kept in a private home. Suspecting Old Believer leanings behind his expressions of loyalty for the emperor, the consistory instead suggested that Korobochkin direct his efforts and finances into constructing a new parish church.[58]

On the other hand, it would be incorrect to dismiss all such requests as artificial, manipulative, or insincere. The mention of the tsar and the expression of loyalty to the Romanov dynasty, after all, did not guarantee the approval of a chapel project. There were instances when rural laity requested that a chapel be dedicated to the memory of a tsar and both diocesan and synodal officials denied the request. Believers from the village of Beliaevo in the Kostroma district, for instance, petitioned in 1884 to rebuild a chapel that had been destroyed by a fire some thirty-five years before. They desired to construct the chapel in commemoration of the coronation of Alexander III and his wife the empress Maria Feodorovna. Nevertheless, both diocesan and synodal officials denied their request, claiming that the tsar would be more honored by the opening of a parish church school in their village than by the construction of a chapel.[59] Furthermore, believers commonly made no mention of such a dedication or commemoration, and authorities approved their requests. Clearly, diocesan policy did not explicitly indicate to believers that a chapel would be allowed if they included an imperial dedication in their petition. Even believers from other social groups who desired to dedicate a chapel to an event from the life of the imperial family had their requests denied. In 1905, for instance, the nobleman Stepan Mogilatov from the Kazan diocese petitioned to construct a chapel in honor of the birth of the heir to the throne, Alexei Nikolaevich, only to have his "gift" rejected by church officials.[60] Therefore, it is reasonable to assume that in some instances at least, rural believers genuinely assigned sacred meaning to political events and to events in the life of the imperial family.

Chapels that commemorated national historical events formed a distinct grouping among Russia's chapels. While perhaps rooted in a religious world-view that followed historical events as an unfolding of a divine plan, these chapels were not considered testimonies to the holy in the same way as chapels that were constructed in memory of an immediate hierophany or miracle on that particular site. Instead, such chapels stood at the interface between political and religious cultures in Russia and belonged to the narratives of both.

Lay believers from various social groups chose to honor a wide array of political and imperial events by the construction of a chapel: the emancipation of the serfs, failed assassination attempts on tsars, births of heirs to the throne, imperial marriages and coronations, and major anniversaries in the lives of the imperial family, such as the three hundredth anniversary of the Romanov dynasty in 1913. Chapels in Russia had served as memorials of historical events and national sentiments for centuries. According to oral tradition, a chapel near Pereslavl–Zaleskii was constructed on the site where, in the late sixteenth century, Tsaritsa Anastasiia Romanov gave birth to her son Feodor while on pilgrimage.[61]

The event that appears to have elicited the most response in the second half of the nineteenth century was the 17 October 1888 derailment of the train carrying Alexander III and his family (fig. 3.7).[62] The event officially was deemed a "miracle by the mercy of God" in a manifesto issued by Alexander III on 23 October 1888 and was further popularized in the press and in special prayer services, sermons, and popular devotional pamphlets.[63] The widespread popularization of the event inspired believers to dedicate their chapel-building endeavor to this event. As a 1892 petition from the village of Petretsov in the Vologda diocese recounted, the community had been ready to decide on the construction of a chapel to honor the feast day of the Protection of the Theotokos when some of the elders in the village suggested that as a sign of their "loyal feelings" toward the tsar they should also dedicate their chapel to the 17 October 1888 event and commemorate the event annually.[64] Similar sentiments motivated the nobleman N. Durnovo in 1891 to construct a chapel on his estate in the Novgorod diocese.[65]

A sermon delivered by the priest Vasili Al'bitskii in St. Petersburg on the occasion of the dedication of a chapel in the St. Petersburg navy hospital in honor of this event reflects the complex mixture of memories that chapel-monuments could evoke:

> This holy memorial will remind us of the frightening visitation of God . . . and of the manifestation of God's mercy. . . . It will testify that divine favor rests on all the Russian people; that the almighty

3.7 View of the Sviatogorsk Spasov hermitage and church on the site
where the imperial train derailed near the Borki railroad station on the
Kursk-Kharkov line, 17 October 1888. At the top is a depiction of the
Holy Trinity—Father, Son, and Holy Spirit—surrounded by angels.
Beneath the Trinity is an image of the Protection of the Mother of God.
One each side of her are saints. Chromolithograph. 1904. The Russian
National Library, St. Petersburg.

hand of God . . . directs all the events in their lives toward the good.
. . . It will kindle our faith in that we are God's people. It will
proclaim to all: "For God is with us!"[66]

One apparent difference between petitions from peasant laity and laity of
other social standings that mentioned tsarist dedications is that the former
rarely identified a political or imperial event as the sole event to be commemorated. Usually when peasant believers proposed such a dedication, they
included a dedication to a purely Christian feast day as well and listed other
circumstances that motivated them to construct a chapel. They distinguished
among traditional feast days established by the Church and the so-called tsar's
days—the cycle of feasts commemorating birthdays, name days, and coronation days of tsars and various members of the imperial family—and political
holidays that commemorated a battle victory. Of these days, church feasts
were usually the most important to peasant believers.

-→≡◉⇐-→·

## Chapels as Decentralizing

Laity, especially rural laity, also voiced reasons for chapel construction that were rooted in local community experience, as distinct from the broader centralizing reasons mentioned earlier. For example, they frequently listed the desire to commemorate a natural disaster, be it plague, epidemic, drought, fire, or an especially poor harvest. Believing that God often revealed himself in the crises of human life, they saw natural disasters as divine events, not in an animistic or pantheistic sense but in the sense of signaling a visitation by God. The state peasants of the village Andreevskoe in the Vologda diocese wrote in 1879 that by virtue of the epidemic that had destroyed virtually all their livestock over the past year, "we were made wise by this visitation of God."[67]

Two considerations in particular usually motivated believers to build chapels on the occasions of various calamities: chapels offered a way of atoning for sins committed by the community or of offering thanks that the calamity had passed. Peasant believers often expressed their sense of collective responsibility in the face of natural disasters. "During the past year, we lived through a very difficult summer," wrote the peasants of the village of Eliunikhi in the Vologda diocese in 1915. "It must be that the Lord became angry with us for our sins."[68] This view simply echoed the customary prayers found in the Orthodox Church's *Trebnik*, or Book of Needs, on the occasion of natural disasters. One of the first litanies in such prayer services was a petition to God "to remember not the sins or offenses of Your people and to turn away from us all of Your anger which is justly turning on us."[69]

What types of sins did believers think elicited the wrath of God? These sins included those that were seen as directed against God or his house: stealing money, candles, or other objects from the temple; showing disrespect toward the church or toward the sanctity of feast days; laughing or jeering at objects of religious veneration; and infrequent confession and communion. One peasant from the Totma district in the Vologda diocese reasoned as follows.

> If one does not anger God, then he will never first do anything; but when they, the non-Christians [*ne-khristi*], anger him, well, he just can't leave it like that. So God punishes them, and together with them, we must also endure. Take for example . . . Mikola Khliup, who worked on a feast day; God punished him with hail . . . but all of our crops were destroyed, too.[70]

Even though the sins might have been those of a particular individual or a group of individuals, the entire community suffered and took it upon itself to respond. Rural laity desired to construct a chapel as a response to God's anger, as a collective promise to remember his wrath and his eventual mercy through special prayer services to be held on that day.

Believers also spoke of another incentive to construct a chapel on the occasion of a natural disaster: "thanks to the Almighty."[71] Rural laity wished to memorialize the mercy God had shown in allowing an epidemic, storm, or fire to subside. The theme of thanksgiving in fact appeared more frequently than the theme of God's wrath in petitions for chapel construction. In such cases, peasant believers used the chapel to celebrate annual thanksgiving services.

In either case, chapel construction kept alive the memory of an event in an active and tangible way. In this context, chapels and the communal worship that took place within them had a historical dimension. In a sense, village and provincial town chapels were often local counterparts to those chapels that stood as monuments commemorating national events in Russia's history. Village and town chapels, too, were historical monuments testifying to an event whose memory required preservation for the sake of posterity. Believers in such cases were simply incorporating their own histories into the salvation history of the broader church community. God's signs and wonders were not merely past events recorded in scripture but current events in their lives that served as evidence of God's presence among them. Chapels glorified that presence and testified to it.

The importance of the chapel as a sacred historical monument may also be seen in the fact that rural believers often rebuilt chapels that had come to ruin. Petitions for such reconstruction demonstrate that even as modernization and industrialization began having their effects on remote village life, believers did not see chapels as relics from the past to be discarded. Nor did chapel construction fall into the category of so-called superstitious behaviors that tended to wane as formal schooling made deeper inroads into the countryside. Instead rural laity renovated old chapels or rebuilt ones that had been destroyed by fire, perceiving them as links between their ancestors and their own children. They considered it their responsibility both to remember and to pass on the memory of a sacred event that they had experienced, so that "these events and feasts would not be terminated by their children."[72] Rural believers would sometimes even lament "their ancestors' indifference" in allowing a chapel to come to ruin; their indifference had caused a holy place "to be forgotten and to disappear into oblivion."[73] In such instances, they petitioned to construct a chapel anew in order to revive the holy place. Chapels, in this context, served to reinforce and sanctify familial and communal bonds.

Believers also wanted to construct chapels to fulfill vows they had made to God. The vow was a common feature of Orthodox piety among all social groups in Russia, including clergy, long before the nineteenth century.[74] Alongside the institutionalized, lifelong monastic and marriage vows stood unregulated ones that were usually more temporary in nature. Individuals commonly vowed to do something in God's honor on various occasions: a difficult pregnancy, a sick child, a severe toothache, or being saved from a life-threatening situation such as drowning. A vow typically might have involved a pilgrimage to a monastery to venerate a particular icon or to work at that monastery for a given period of time. But vows could also entail giving more than usual to the poor, offering special attention to beautifying the parish church, carrying icons during feast day processions, adding days or weeks of fasting during the year, or constructing a chapel. In fact, petitions for chapel construction frequently contained references to a personal vow.[75]

Vows were self-imposed acts understood not so much in terms of payments to God for divine favor as acts of love and gratitude testifying to God's presence and activity in believers' lives. They also often were meant to purify the body and senses; this process, it was hoped, would lead to purity of heart. The soul uses vows instead of wings, one churchman wrote, by which it widens its flight to God.[76] Commonly understood as typifying the kinds of acts in which believers might participate as part of a vow was the woman's anointing of Jesus' feet with a pound of costly ointment (John 12:3). Though pleasing to Christ, it was in no way an action put forth as a universal commandment. Orthodox Christians considered the vow to be a practice inherited from ancient Israel, as depicted, for example, in the story of Jacob (Gen. 28:20–22; 31:13). While all virtue might demand effort, such effort was more highly regarded when it was the result of a conscious and willful act not demanded by law. Similarly, while acts involved in a vow could easily be undertaken without the pronouncement of the vow itself, the vow was understood as a disciplinary reminder of one's obligation before God. It fixed a moment in one's mind in which one's relationship with God was understood with a clarity that could not easily fade.

Although the character of vows suggests that they were a feature of personal piety—something between an individual and God—such personal promises often spilled over into the lives of others and became a communal concern, especially when a person chose to construct a chapel to fulfill a vow. In 1898, believers from the Iarensk district petitioned the bishop of Vologda regarding a chapel standing in their village. Years before, a member of their community, Philip Iaranov, had gone to the Solovetsk monastery to pray before the relics of Saints Zosima and Savatii to fulfill a vow he had made while he was ill. On the way back he was caught in a life-threatening storm. This time he made another vow to return home and perform a "task pleasing to God." When Iaranov returned home, he erected a cross near a spring that the local community believed to have healing effects. He built walls around the cross to protect it from bad weather. Over time, people placed icons in the small structure and it took on the character of a chapel. Thousands of faithful from more than a hundred miles away gathered annually at this chapel. In 1898, when the small chapel-like construction fell into disrepair, the entire community to which Iaranov had belonged took on the cost of constructing a new chapel and cared for it as a communal building.[77]

Vows could also be made by a community and in such cases were usually made after natural disasters. These petitions—whether sent by rural or urban communities—had an urgency in their tone that was absent from requests giving other reasons for chapel construction. Believers from the village of

Lebedevskaia in the Vologda diocese justified their need for a chapel on the occasion of their vow by quoting Deuteronomy 23:21–23: "When you make a vow to the Lord your God, you shall not be slack to pay it; for the Lord your God will surely require it of you, and it would be sin in you." Most members of rural communities appeared to have at least tacitly adhered to the communal vow, regardless of their religious beliefs, since no individual wanted to be blamed for any calamities that might follow if the vow were not fulfilled.[78]

The presence of the vow, then, adds yet further texture to Russia's chapelscape. Chapels, in this context, testified to a particular, covenantal relationship between a local community and God, a covenant that was annually reaffirmed with prayer services. Vows that were given for an indefinite period of time, to be carried on by posterity, gave recalling and remembering a featured place in Orthodox religious culture. Just as with ancient Israel, believers thought that lapses in such memory threatened to elicit the wrath of God. Because of the seriousness of the events that prompted the vow—along with the sense of repentance, sacrifice, and hope associated with them—chapels and the worship within them carried an importance in rural believers' lives that was not necessarily enjoyed by the parish church.

Believers also constructed chapels to store locally revered icons or to house icons when they were brought annually to their village. It is well known that rural believers kept icons in their homes; however, what is less well known is that villages collectively owned icons as well. Many villages obtained an icon of the feast on which a given event occurred, or of the saint to whom the villagers had turned for help, as a "tangible reminder of God's mercy."[79] Villages purchased such icons with communal funds, and they remained the property of the entire community. On the anniversary of the event, the local clergy would come from the parish church and serve a prayer service before the icon in the center of the village. During the rest of the year, the icon would be kept in peasant homes, or sometimes in the local parish church.

Believers considered it inappropriate for an icon to be without its own place—an attitude consistent with the Eastern Orthodox Christian tradition of icon veneration. Believers from the village of Zalese in the Vologda diocese, for example, obtained a copy of the Smolensk icon of the Mother of God after an epidemic. At first villagers in this community rotated the icon through their homes during the course of the year, but they soon had their representative write the bishop that "we consider such a place for the icon as not entirely decent and impious."[80] They wanted to construct a chapel in order to create a sacred space within the village proper so their icon would have its own permanent home. In 1878, Lavr Semenov, a peasant and church elder from the village of Pavlovskoe (Tver province), had a dream in which he heard a voice directing him to construct a "proper place" for an icon of the Mother of God named "Life-Bearing Spring." This dream resulted in a decade-long effort to construct a chapel that came to include members of not only his village but surrounding villages as well.[81]

3.8    Chapel in honor of St. Peter. Olonets province,
between the villages of V. Novoe and Kosmozero.
The Russian Museum of Ethnography, St. Petersburg.

In other cases, peasant believers did not so much seek to create a sacred space through the construction of a chapel as to mark one that they believed already existed. Both laity and clergy recognized an entire network of holy places in Russia's religious landscape that had not gained official recognition by ecclesiastical authorities but attracted large numbers of pilgrims. Frequently the location of such places spread by word of mouth, and they seldom remained isolated attractions for the villages near which they were located.

What made a particular place holy? In the cases of wells or springs, rumors of healings by the water would be enough to attract the attention of believers living at considerable distances (fig. 3.8).[82] Usually such waters first caught believers' attention for a particular reason: either someone discovered an icon in or near the spring or well and believed it to have miraculously appeared[83] or someone told of a dream in which a saint directed the person to locate a particular water source.[84] Generally speaking, the appearance of an icon or cross at any location, be it a spring, field, well, or riverbank, designated a place as holy. Believers regarded such icons as owned by the entire village, even when they were found by a single person. While usually these places were already denoted by a makeshift shrine (a covered wooden cross or an icon hanging on a nearby tree), rural believers often wanted a chapel to give the place more prominent recognition and to facilitate prayer services at the site.[85]

Finally, believers considered as holy the sites of former monasteries and churches, in part because of those holy persons who may have visited, prayed, or lived there, and in part because of the specially revered icons that may have been housed at the site. The very recognition of the temple as God's abode, moreover, elicited a respect for particular grounds and, in some believers' minds, called for a chapel to memorialize the remnants of a former community. In a request to construct a chapel on the site of a former monastery, believers from the village of Peregonovki in the Poltava diocese wrote in 1900: "What can serve as a more pious ecclesial memory (*tserkovnoe vospominanie*) of the one-time monastery and the fifty-year sojourn there of the miracle-working icon of the Mother of God?"[86]

The effort of believers to construct chapels, then, reveals a dual orientation in the ecclesial world of rural Orthodox laity. On the one hand, the desire to build a chapel often manifested a centripetal orientation in believers' religious life toward the parish church, and through the parish church to the Orthodox Church at large. Especially in large parishes where the parish community was composed of numerous villages and consisted of over five thousand people, chapels broke down the parish unit into more personal subcommunities. In this regard, these smaller groups might be seen as an Eastern Orthodox counterpart to the "basic ecclesial communities" that in recent times have been said to characterize Catholic Latin America.[87] Rural believers indeed saw no incongruity between owning their own chapel and belonging to the larger parish flock and diocese. Chapels generally expressed a desire to be part of "officially" defined Orthodoxy and not to manifest a resistance to it. And while dedications of chapels to political events and events in the life of the imperial family would not usually be considered parish oriented, they were nevertheless manifestations of a centralizing tendency in rural religious life.

On the other hand, chapel construction also attested to a centrifugal tendency in rural Orthodoxy, away from centralizing institutions. Especially when believers lived relatively close to the parish church, their desire for chapels showed their inclination to experience their faith in the context of the immediate village community. In this sense, chapels may be seen as reflecting the broader lay (and not merely peasant) tendency to make things "their own." The result was, in some cases, that lay ecclesial consciousness, particularly in rural areas, was formed more by chapel experience than by liturgical activity in the nearest parish church. This localizing tendency in piety was facilitated by official church practice, which saw annual participation in the Eucharist as sufficient to be an Orthodox in good standing. Because of the relative lack of identification of liturgy with Eucharistic participation in the popular mindset, the Divine Liturgy, to some degree, was seen as just one among many liturgical services. And though the absence of a priest might have lessened the stature and pomp of a prayer service, "prayer was prayer" for many believers, and thus reading the *obednitsa* or psalms in chapels would be seen as basically equivalent to attending church.[88] The chapel, therefore, historically offered an alternative to churchgoing and helped create an ecclesial arrangement that was even more locally and community based than the parish.

Finally, it should be emphasized that for a given believer or community a chapel could symbolize both of these tendencies simultaneously. A single petition could list reasons for chapel construction that fell into both categories, such as distance from the parish church and the wish to commemorate a natural disaster. Therefore, even when believers built chapels to mark a holy place or to house a miraculous icon, these chapels did not have the dispersing and parochially constricting effects that might be expected. Religious life around these chapels often had a dynamic of its own that was little connected with the religious life of the local parish, except for the chapel's bureaucratic assignment to it. At the same time, such chapels became part of a widespread pilgrimage network that reached beyond the boundaries of the parish. Thus, even in these cases, the rural believer's ecclesial world was not limited to the confines of what they saw as their own. Orthodoxy and the faith community were phenomena that transcended one's own local community and were equally and authentically present elsewhere.

⁘⟚⟛⁘

## Chapel Tensions

Members of the clergy differed in their attitude toward chapels. Many parish priests overwhelmingly supported chapel construction efforts. It was not uncommon for them to turn to the bishop in a community's defense after a petition had been rejected by the diocesan administration. Parish priests commonly saw chapels as "necessary and healthy when taking into account the extent of peasant efforts and the pious zeal displayed in the [chapel construction] endeavor."[89]

In 1888, the clergy of the St. Elijah parish in the Vologda diocese (Totma district) voiced support for a village's chapel project. They asserted that the chapel would inspire the faithful to fulfill their religious responsibilities. On Sundays and feast days those unable to attend church would be able to hold prayer services in the chapel. During the singing of hymns, "the chapel will remind them of their holy [parish] church and they will be able prayerfully to express their feelings and desires as if standing before the face of the Creator Himself."[90]

Priests supported chapel construction efforts because of the chapel's association with the temple, and because it served as a constant "inspiration to religious thought."[91] Moreover, local clergy often used the chapels to serve vigils on the eve of special feast days, so as to ensure that all members of a particular village or community located far from the parish church could attend. This was especially helpful for the women in northern rural areas where the church was located at some distance and where women were known to stay home from church on feast days in order to prepare the festive meals.[92]

In addition, in some regions priests began to support the construction of so-called chapel-schools. A typical design of a chapel-school included separate rooms in the front of the building for a custodian or watchman, a school teacher, a kitchen, and those children who lived too far from the school to spend the night at home. The chapel area proper doubled as a classroom and a place of prayer. When such facilities were located especially far from the parish church, diocesan officials sometimes permitted the addition of a sanctuary with an altar table.[93]

Parish priests supported chapel construction not only when the practical matter of distance from the parish church was an issue or when a communal vow was involved. They also sometimes displayed respect for lay inclinations to mark sacred places. For example, in 1872, a priest from the Viatka diocese petitioned the diocesan bishop on behalf of a group of his parishioners for permission to construct a chapel at the site of what the local population called "the holy spring." A popular pilgrimage point for over fifty years, the spring at that time had begun to attract even more people, with some reporting healings. After an official investigation of the site conducted with the cooperation of local police and a physician revealed no evidence of fraud or superstitious behavior, both the diocesan bishop and the Holy Synod granted permission for the chapel's construction.[94]

As these and numerous other examples show, many clergy saw nothing wrong with peasant believers' desire to build chapels. They exhibited no concern about "superstitious" behavior or potential threats to normal parish life. Seeing the sincere attitude of their parishioners toward the local parish church, many clergy saw chapels simply as extensions of the parish into each and every village. In fact, parish clergy were frequently so supportive of chapel projects that it was not uncommon for lay persons to consider the pastor's approval as sufficient to initiate construction and to bypass the official consent of diocesan authorities.

Nevertheless, other clergy did not so readily embrace chapel construction projects. As already noted, efforts to construct chapels in urban areas, especially in Russia's two capitals, St. Petersburg and Moscow, were usually denied because church authorities felt there were plenty of temples to which believers could turn.[95] In more rural areas, some clergy questioned the motivations behind certain behavior with respect to holy sites or the unexpected appearance of icons. Particularly when associated with specially venerated icons, wells, or springs believed to be holy, the construction of chapels often came under closer scrutiny. According to the *Spiritual Regulation* of Peter the Great, such phenomena—which were not new to Russia and had been part of Eastern Christian culture in general—were potentially associated with "false miracles" and with the broad understanding of "superstition." While the Statute of Diocesan Consistories, adopted in 1841, also directed bishops and parish priests to deter Orthodox Christians from "all sorts of superstitions and superstitious rituals," it did not define the terms themselves.

How was the notion of superstition used by clergymen at this time? The term for superstition in Russian was *sueverie*, which was derived from the words meaning "empty" or "vain" and "faith." As one homiletic encyclopedia noted, it was "faith that was not based in anything."[96] Another reference book defined it as faith in something that either does not exist or that exists but is falsely understood.[97] In many ways, similar to the *Spiritual Regulation* of Peter the Great, such definitions of superstition potentially allowed for the inclusion of a broad spectrum of customs and beliefs to be associated with that term. These included beliefs and customs that were attributed to a pagan past and that were believed to lie outside the bounds of Orthodoxy, such as belief in certain spirits, divination, folk incantations that incorporated parts of traditional Orthodox prayers, and fortune telling. Such practices, pastoral handbooks reminded their readers, had carried strict penalties in early Christianity, including up to five years of non-Communion.[98]

Clergy had varying attitudes toward customs they associated with Russia's pagan past. Pastoral journals such as the *Guide for Rural Clergy* regularly included articles denouncing various beliefs and practices that they traced to pre-Christian pagan roots. Some clergy believed that all "superstitions" were sinful and concealed self-love as well as a lack of faith in God.[99] Other clergy, however, were more discriminate when approaching such folk ways. As one pastoral handbook noted under the heading "superstition," there was "no need for pastors to exaggerate the situation." It explained that many remnants of the pagan past, such as belief in various spirits, were not detrimental and had no harmful moral consequences. Consequently it was not worth the pastor's effort to struggle actively against them.[100] Generally, with respect to chapels, clergy did not express concerns about superstition understood in this way.

The term "superstition," however, in some cases was also used with respect to certain practices associated with traditionally Orthodox phenomena, such as miracle-working icons and healing waters from wells or springs. Here the criteria for determining what was Orthodox were not so clear and were not uniformly agreed upon even by clergy. From the standpoint of many pastors, the spiritual discernment needed in such cases was beyond the abilities of many common lay people. The characteristic sign of superstition, one reference book claimed, "is that it sees a mysterious connection among the most unrelated things and then attributes to them miraculous attributes or actions."[101] The problem was that the actions with which an allegedly superstitious disposition was often associated—the veneration of an icon, the drinking of holy water—were very much a part of Orthodox practice as a whole.

The difference, clergy would maintain, was the attitudes and intention with which such an action was undertaken. One priest suggested that superstition entailed the attribution of miraculous powers "to things as things," and it was the pastor's duty to struggle against such a superficial understanding of Christianity.[102] Apparently sharing this view, the bishop of Kostroma in 1884 declined a request from members of the village of Beliaevo to construct a chapel on which a church had stood more than two hundred years earlier. Because pilgrims would gather here for prayer and frequently take dirt from the site to cure illnesses, he maintained that the location was an object of "superstitious veneration." To allow the construction of a chapel would only encourage this questionable behavior.[103]

These concerns, however, were not the most prominent that clergy adduced in their arguments against the construction of chapels in late nineteenth- and early twentieth-century Russia. Instead, the consideration voiced by one dean from the Vologda diocese in 1874 was much more common:

> I have noticed that whenever a chapel is built in a village, those peasants' enthusiasm toward the parish church weakens, as does their zeal toward church services. . . . The main reason behind the construction of chapels is not so much the peasants' seemingly religious inclination, but some sort of ambition and vanity—to have a chapel as an exclusive part of their village.[104]

The dean voiced the opinion of many church officials who were concerned with believers' potential preference for their village chapel over and above their parish church. It is noteworthy that at no time did the dean question the Orthodoxy of peasant laity. The dean's reference to their ambition and vanity pointed to a more subtle pastoral issue, one that had to do with the *internal* workings of the faith community: the independence of the laity and the potential withdrawal of certain groups from the larger parish community (which was under the direct supervision of a priest) into their own, relatively unsupervised, local village setting. Clergy were sensitive to any displays of "self-willed" or "self-authorized" behavior (*samovol'nost'*, *samochinstvo*), whether in the form of gatherings of lay believers to hear lay preachers who lived near a chapel or in the form of lay construction of chapels without official approval.[105]

The term "self-willed" is found in Russia's prerevolutionary church archives often enough to warrant a brief digression. In the early eighteenth century, the bishop of Rostov (and later saint), Dimitrii, included "self-will" in his general list of sins to consider in preparation for the sacrament of confession. This list continued to be widely distributed in Russia up until the Revolution. As applied to issues in parish life, the charge of being self-willed usually appeared in cases dealing with certain displays of piety among believers. Such activities as chapel construction, the celebration of feasts, and the veneration of icons are clearly longstanding aspects of mainstream Orthodox

Christianity. In prerevolutionary Russia, however, clergy sometimes treated such activities as un-Orthodox when the attitude of those involved appeared to distort or disrupt ecclesial order. For the clergy, self-willed behavior on the part of the laity implied functional autonomy and pointed to a tendency toward self-interest and self-reliance in essentially communal matters.

It is important to recall that the idea of "self-willed" behavior was known in the general religious culture of the time and was not merely a rhetorical tool of any supposed clericalism. As I showed in the last chapter, laity also applied the charge of "self-willed" to members of the clergy, especially in complaints to diocesan bishops about their priests. Parishioners often took offense when their pastors failed to involve parishioners directly in the process of decision making regarding parish projects. Clearly, therefore, self-willed behavior was understood by *both* clergy and laity as having a negative connotation. It implied a deficit in one's sense of communal responsibility and accountability. Since it was also used by the laity, this charge of self-willed behavior was not simply one of disobedience in the monastic sense. It was something more nuanced than that. Indeed, rarely in the archives was this term used in cases when the personal piety of a single individual was in question. Rather the term referred essentially to the individual in relation to the sacred community, a community that was composed of both clergy and laity and that embraced a shared cultural system of symbols and structures, roles and customs.

Returning to the subject of chapels, clergy were also concerned that such undue attention to chapels would lead to financial loss for a parish church since laity would redirect their resources. Money in this case became a symbol of allegiance and unity. If believers were reluctant to extend their financial support to the parish church, this could mean that the parish church was not the ecclesial focus of the village's religious life. From the lay perspective, clerical resistance to an active chapel culture was often read as resentment on the part of the clergy toward the large crowds that chose to gather for prayer there instead of at the parish church.[106]

A vivid case in point concerns the chapel constructed in 1874 in the village of Aleshevskoe in the Vologda diocese. Twenty years after its construction, the clergy of the parish to which this village belonged complained to diocesan authorities that parishioners were not financially supporting their parish church. The villagers, in turn, justified their actions before the bishop by claiming that they had to support their chapel. In choosing to support their chapel over the parish, the clergy maintained, believers isolated their chapel from the parish, its clergy, and its elder. The villagers had chosen their own elder to oversee the chapel. Neither the villagers nor this elder recognized the parish priest's or parish elder's "legal control" (*zakonago kontrolia*). Furthermore, the clergy complained they did not have free access to the chapel. Whenever they came to celebrate a prayer service they would have to wait until someone could be found to let them in. When they tried to resolve the problem on their own, they had no success "due to the peasants' . . . beloved practices of self-government."[107]

Generally, tensions between ecclesiastical representatives and lay persons regarding chapels arose largely from conflicts in perception. What clergy regarded as a display of "self-willed behavior" or "self-governance" on the believers' part lay people saw simply as a sincere expression of religious convictions, a ministry to their spiritual needs, and a protective stance toward what they believed they owned. While not severing ties with the general flock and not rebelling against the unwritten code of behavior that traditionally governed the relationship between the flock and its pastor, believers sought to control those matters that they believed were within their domain.

Although negative reaction to chapels from the local clergy came only sporadically, the concerns and fears they expressed set the tone for official policy toward chapel construction. Both the consistory and the Holy Synod vigilantly searched for signs that lay people might be evading parish responsibilities in favor of supporting their own chapel. The only article devoted to chapels in the journal *Direction for Rural Priests*, "Chapels in Our Villages," spoke of them in a guarded tone, thereby giving the impression that all parish priests looked negatively on chapels. The author, Fr. Nikolai Iustinov, saw chapels as competing communal prayer space, drawing people away from the "proper" liturgical context of the parish church. As Iustinov noted, when parishioners whose villages had chapels were asked by the priest why they had not been in church on a particular Sunday morning, they often remarked: "We were in our chapel; prayer is prayer everywhere." This attitude, claimed Iustinov, had two negative repercussions. First, it led believers to become accustomed to communal prayer without the presence of a priest. Second, it detracted needed income from the parish church.[108]

Such a negative view of chapels had historical roots in Russia's church history, especially in the seventeenth-century Old Believers' Schism, which was one of the reasons Peter the Great looked with suspicion on them. Yet in the late nineteenth century, the fear of Old Believer activity generally no longer contributed to clerical suspicion. By this time, church legislation concerning chapel construction betrayed a suspicion of lay initiative in general. According to existing rules, chapels could be built only "for reasons worthy of attention."[109] In order to avoid conflicts of interest, ecclesiastical authorities usually laid out very specific conditions when granting permission for a chapel. They informed believers in no uncertain terms that the chapel would remain officially under the administrative jurisdiction of the local parish clergy and the church elder. Technically, peasant communities could not appoint elders to oversee the local chapel. They also had to divide received donations equally between the chapel and the parish church.[110] In order to discourage the use of chapels as an alternative to churchgoing, diocesan regulations forbade altar tables in chapels as well as bell-ringing to signal services in them.[111] As the bishop of Kostroma, Alexander (Kul'chitskii), explained, the bells that would call believers to prayer could easily distract parishioners from attending their local parish churches.[112]

Despite all these measures, laity continued to display independent, so-called self-willed behavior with regard to construction and decoration. They did not always seek diocesan permission to build or enlarge a chapel. In many cases, lay believers simply received their parish priest's blessing for such an endeavor. This occurred even with nonpeasant believers.[113] In other cases believers applied for permission and, seeing no reason why it should be denied them, commenced construction before receiving a reply. They continued to attach small bell towers, and they frequently elected a chapel elder to oversee a chapel's maintenance.[114]

Church officials throughout Russia learned about incidents of unauthorized chapel construction only when someone reported them or when for some reason a chapel drew their attention.[115] In 1867, for instance, diocesan authorities learned of a chapel located on the church grounds in the village of Burtsevo in the Moscow diocese only when money had been reported stolen from that chapel. The chapel had apparently been constructed without any official permission and had never been registered in any parish document.[116]

A similar discovery occurred in the Vologda diocese in 1895. During a routine investigation of stolen money from a village chapel, diocesan officials noted that the chapel was not listed in the parish records; no official permission for its construction had ever been sought. This discovery led to yet a further finding. Diocesan officials learned that similar chapel-like structures were located in every surrounding village, although parish records officially listed only one chapel. The local clergy argued that believers constructed these buildings to house icons and maintained them without any financial detriment to the parish church. In the end, the consistory concluded that such structures, unrecorded in parish records, were probably located in other areas of the diocese as well.[117]

Consequently, on 5 September 1895, the Vologda consistory issued a directive to all the deans in the districts to report the existence of such chapel-like constructions.[118] Deans from all but one district in the Vologda province disclosed the existence of unlisted chapels. Memo after memo noted that village communities initiated their construction and maintained them by communal funds. These communities often gave the keys for the building to one of their revered members, chosen by consent of the entire village. He oversaw its maintenance and reported on his activities to the village assembly alone. The village assemblies gave no part of the donations for chapel upkeep over to the parish church.

The reports clearly disturbed the consistory. Not only were rural laity building these small chapels without official permission, and often without prior knowledge of the parish priest, but their activity in them was not "subject to any proper controls."[119] On 10 May 1897 the consistory issued a circular decree spelling out the measures it considered necessary to regulate these unauthorized chapels. All chapels constructed without official permission were to be leveled, and parish clergy were to transfer the icons in these buildings to the local parish church for safekeeping.[120]

The swift response from believers reflects the strong attachment to chapels shared by believers throughout Russia. Learning from parish priests that their chapels were subject to leveling, they sent in petitions declaring why their chapels were necessary and why they should be allowed to remain standing. Many of these petitions calmly outlined the chapel's religious significance for the village community. As the villagers from the fifteen-household village of Semenovskoe wrote, they had constructed their chapel seventeen years before. Though they had not petitioned diocesan officials, they had constructed it with the knowledge of their parish priest. They found the chapel necessary, especially during the summer months when they could not easily go to church. They frequented the chapel on Sundays and feast days and listened to the reading of the psalter by literate members of the community. In addition, their priest visited them twice annually to conduct prayer services in the chapel. They requested that the chapel be allowed to remain standing for "eternal prayer."[121]

Other communities, however, did not respond as calmly or as graciously and voiced their confusion and frustration with the policy. As believers from a village in the Totma district wrote, "we consider leveling chapels a strange thing and a great sin."[122] Another group of villagers warned that "closing and leveling such an honored chapel will lead us into great sadness and regret and will elicit unhappy murmurings from people who live nearby."[123] In another petition, believers voiced their despair over the policy, claiming that it led to their humiliation in front of their Old Believer neighbors. "The schismatics have begun to yell in full voice about the closure of chapels: 'See what is happening with you Nikonians . . . they have begun to close your houses of prayer and that means your faith is untrue.' "[124] In short, the attempt by ecclesiastical authorities to regulate chapel construction only drove a wedge into the ecclesial community and placed the people and the bishop on opposing sides.

Generally parish priests supported their parishioners and notified the consistory that such a policy of leveling chapels, particularly when these chapels contained specially revered icons, could have a negative effect on the people's religious sensibilities. One parish priest wrote to the consistory that if the chapel in question were closed and leveled, the people would become suspicious, saying that their forefathers had never heard of Orthodox chapels being closed and that if they were being closed, "something was not right."[125] In those cases where villages bypassed the consistory and appealed directly to the Holy Synod, the Synod tended to agree with the decision of the local consistory. From the archival sources it is unclear how many chapels diocesan officials actually closed on account of the 1897 directive, but the very fact that they threatened to close them was enough for some peasant believers to question the orthodoxy of the official ecclesiastical authorities.

While it is unclear whether a systematic search for unauthorized chapels ever occurred in other dioceses, diocesan authorities nevertheless were known to have directed that chapels built without the appropriate permission be leveled.[126] In 1886, for instance, members of three neighboring villages in the Kostroma diocese that belonged to different parish churches wrote the ober-procurator of the Holy Synod concerning the fate of their chapel. They had managed to dismantle it safely during a village fire four years before. After having rebuilt the village, they remained "distressed" seeing that "the holy place where the chapel once stood remained empty, without the holy building where we, as our ancestors, offered warm prayers."[127]

The local clergy informed those villagers of the required procedure before they could begin construction. With the payment of a fee, they enlisted the help of a local parish priest in obtaining the proper documentation. In the meantime, the local district police advised them simply to rebuild the chapel from the same material on the place it had stood for over one hundred years, which they proceeded to do. The consistory learned about this from the local dean, deemed such behavior "self-willed," and ordered the chapel leveled. It directed that the wood be used for heating the parish church. Complaining to the Holy Synod that they refused to follow the directive since they considered it a sin, the members of these villages pleaded for the Synod to reverse the decision, which it did.[128]

Not all believers were so lucky. Il'ia Mashechkov from the village of Kulikovo in the Tambov diocese, for instance, constructed a chapel without diocesan permission. Diocesan authorities apparently only learned of this when Mashechkov petitioned to have the local clergy annually conduct two requiem services in memory of the deceased tsar, Alexander II. Instead of receiving permission for these services, Mashechkov learned of the decision to level the chapel. In a last effort to save it he wrote: "to level this chapel would offend my sacred sensibilities. If true Christian duty lies in prayer, then any obstacles to such a sacred activity should not be allowed."[129] Similarly in 1879 the efforts of Lavr Semenov, a parish church elder from the Tver diocese mentioned earlier, were thwarted. Having claimed to have received the direc-tive to construct this chapel in a dream, Semenov received the support of his fellow villagers to build it in honor of a locally revered icon of the Mother of God and in memory of Alexander II. Because the chapel had been built without official permission, however, diocesan officials ordered it leveled and directed the parishioners to express their religious sentiments in the confines of the parish church.[130]

Although the rule to level unauthorized chapels remained in effect until the end of the ancien régime, certain diocesan officials relaxed their policies toward chapels after 1906. In instances where rural believers constructed a chapel without awaiting official permission, consistory officials did not nec-essarily routinely level them. When local officials took severe measures, dio-cesan and synodal officials frequently reversed them. The peasant Pavel Zhgu-tov from the Kostroma diocese, for instance, wrote the Holy Synod regarding his experiences in trying to fulfill a thirty-year-long wish to mark a particular sacred place on the road he frequently traveled from St. Petersburg to his home village. In 1912 he constructed a temporary shrine at the site—"a beacon of Orthodoxy," as he called it—only to learn soon thereafter that it had been leveled. He was horrified to learn that the instigators of this act were "not sacrilegious villains but . . . it is terrifying to say, servants of the Church."[131] The local dean together with the local police had leveled the shrine because its construction was "self-willed" and because it attracted donations that were not under the direct supervision of the local clergy. In the end, the diocesan bishop together with the Holy Synod agreed to allow Zhgutov to rebuild the shrine.

In a similar vein, many diocesan officials after 1906 no longer saw closer proximity of a village to a parish church as an obstacle to chapel construction. Believers received permission to construct chapels even when they provided little or no explanation for their requests. Even individual believers in rural areas, who since the time of Peter the Great had had a more difficult time getting permission for a chapel unless they had community support, were sometimes granted permission to construct chapels for personal vows or simply for the "salvation of one's soul."[132] This reformed attitude toward chapels was part of a general trend among many church officials, who became notably more sensitive to lay religious sensibilities, especially those of peasant laity, in the wake of the events of 1905.

Chapels occupied a unique place in the ecclesial world of Orthodox laity in late imperial Russia. In contrast to churches with their complete liturgical cycles, chapels with their limited liturgical schedules did not embody the full scope of the Christian story. Instead, insofar as lay persons constructed them to mark personal, local, or national events, chapels were more focused in their commemorative function. They stood as snapshots of particular events, as structuralized feast days, so to speak, because a chapel's very presence bore testimony to the particular event daily. By constructing chapels, lay believers, especially in Russia's rural areas, inscribed their sometimes varying personal and local collective memories and sacred feelings onto the broad canvas of images that defined Orthodoxy in prerevolutionary Russia.

Despite their prominence in Russia's religious topography, chapels stood at the "frontiers" of Orthodoxy in Russia, insofar as the Church's institutional structure did not extend strongly into the religious life around chapels. Despite a chapel's assignment to a cathedral, parish church, or monastic community, it was a self-contained ecclesial space where the usual hierarchical ordering of clergy and laity was not a dominant feature. Chapels provided a setting where community in Orthodoxy could be constituted and experienced in a different way. Laity here tended to decide for themselves on the holiness of matters, as well as to organize both the space and the schedule of services and public religious readings. Indeed many members of the All-Russian Church Council of 1917–18 believed that it remained up to parish communities to decide which chapels within their geographic confines—many of which were constructed on personal initiative—to maintain collectively.[133]

For those church officials and priests who equated hierarchical leadership and the bureaucratic center with Christian unity and the "proper" ordering of community life, however, chapel culture was a source of recurrent anxiety and even irritation. They tended to see any "unauthorized" or "self-willed" activity in or around a chapel as potentially harmful insofar as, in their understanding, it undermined the "proper" dynamics of corporate ecclesial life. Chapels in such estimations were "nests" in which various types of "sectarian" religious movements were just waiting to hatch.[134]

While religious dissent may have manifested itself periodically around chapels or other holy sites, a broader examination of chapel culture has revealed that chapels in general seem to have contributed to the cohesion of the Orthodox community at large. Members of the 1917–18 All-Russian Church Council agreed, affirming that while chapels should be constructed only with the permission of diocesan officials, the clause "only for valid reasons" should be eliminated from the consistory regulations. As the church historian S. G. Runkevich noted, the chapel itself justified its own existence, since in the end it "turned a person's gaze toward heaven, toward God."[135] This relative autonomy of chapel life provided an arena in which lay believers could exercise their sense of responsibility for their faith and actively share their identification with that historical faith that they, like the clergy, felt as their own. It is likely that this opportunity to know and live their faith as something other than a colony of clericalism often helped to obviate more widespread, reactive movements within Russian Orthodoxy.

# 4

# Feasts

## The Setting of Sacred Time

On a holy day, the vanities sleep;
A holy day, and our cares sleep.

—Russian folk proverb

The relationship between churches and chapels and the distinct though related ways in which they mobilized individual sensibilities and became expressions of collective belonging found parallels in the celebration of sacred time. The collective marking of sacred time in prerevolutionary Russia was a complex process that involved not only ecclesiastical authorities but lay believers and civil officials as well. As members of a sacred community, believers were bound to a calendar that recalled key events in the life of Christ, Mary, and the saints, as well as particular Marian icons. This annual cycle occurred together with a weekly one that began and culminated with the celebration of the Divine Liturgy—a celebration of Christ's life, death, and resurrection—every Sunday.[1] Russia's civil calendar buttressed the Orthodox one and to a large extent overlapped with it. Holy days and holidays, therefore, for the most part coincided.

The collective keeping of sacred time among believers, however, was not an automatic process in which believers reflexively conformed to an imposed standard calendric rhythm. Lay believers actively contributed to its setting and often assimilated established feasts in a way that made sense in their local worlds. This chapter explores the communal dynamics in the celebration and marking of sacred time in Orthodoxy in late imperial Russia and the tensions that arose with the growing demands of modernity on that time.

## Standard Sacred Time

While no day was a commemorative blank, the Orthodox calendar did not honor each day equally. It distinguished among major, "middle," and lesser feasts, and church services were celebrated accordingly. Easter, the "feasts of feasts," stood in its own class. Next in order of importance were the twelve major feasts: six commemorating events in the life of Christ, four recalling events in the life of Mary, the Exaltation of the Cross, and Pentecost. The calendar also recognized several "great" feasts that it did not count among the major twelve. These included the Protection of the Mother of God, the circumcision of Christ, the birth and beheading of St. John the Baptist, and the feast of Saints Peter and Paul. The "middle" category of feasts included the commemoration of John the Evangelist, St. Nicholas the Wonderworker, the Three Hierarchs, St. George, and St. Sergius of Radonezh, as well as the commemoration of certain Marian icons. Lesser feasts included those of numerous saints and such events as the conception of St. John the Baptist.[2] Moreover, certain times of the year, though not technically feasts, were considered particularly holy: the Thursday, Friday, and Saturday preceding Easter, the week following Easter, and certain commemorative Saturdays.

Sermons and devotional pamphlets frequently addressed not only the meaning of each individual feast but also the significance of feasts in general. Tracing the roots of Christian feasts to the Book of Genesis, in which God is portrayed as "blessing the seventh day" and "resting from all the work he had done in creation" (Gen. 2:3), Orthodox churchmen reminded believers that feasts were not human inventions but divinely established.[3] In one discussion aimed at a lay audience, a well-known writer on issues of spirituality, the priest Georgii D'iachenko, highlighted the nature of feasts. He encouraged believers to see each feast as an earthly manifestation of the heavenly celebration, as a "sign" and "prefeast" of that eternal feast that awaits the chosen in the heavenly kingdom.[4] After all, it was on feast days in particular that believers were invited to the sacramental banquet as a sign of that heavenly banquet of which the chosen will partake in the Kingdom. In order to participate properly in the celebration of feasts, churchmen encouraged believers to follow the divine example and to free themselves on these days from daily chores and activities. Rest from worldly cares, as one author said, was the first condition and characteristic of the feast day.[5]

This view of resting on feasts, however, does not mean that churchmen preached a negative view of work. In their sermons on this issue, they made it clear that work, too, was divinely established and was part of the human vocation, even prior to the Fall. They reminded believers that God placed humans in the Garden of Eden in order to "till and keep it" (Gen. 2:15), an activity that did not hinder but rather furthered them in their blessed condition.[6] By giving this directive, clergy explained, God showed that humans were not created for the purpose of being simply passive onlookers to creation. Instead, God involved them in his acts of wisdom and offered humans a source of pleasure and enjoyment in their labors.[7]

Churchmen emphasized the dramatic shift in the Christian story with respect to work after the Fall. Instead of a source of joy and pleasure, humans now found work a source of suffering. Nevertheless, churchmen taught that work continued to have a salvific character, in terms of both temporal and eternal life. Following the Fall, they explained, God transformed labor into a form of penance through which humans could cleanse themselves and find a means of self-discipline and improvement.[8] They reminded believers that work remained a divinely established condition of human salvation that could not be bypassed, even through prayer.[9]

Despite the sacred meaning they attributed to work, churchmen maintained that it still had to be set aside during Sundays and feasts. They made it clear, however, that abstinence from work alone was not a holy act since work in and of itself was not sinful. Claiming that such an attitude was an Old Testament way of thinking, they reminded believers that Christ offered another example: to serve God by sanctifying time and oneself through worship, meditation, and charity.[10] Churchmen generally maintained that Christ sanctioned only the most essential forms of work on Sundays and feasts—transportation services, for instance—and thus it was not sinful to carry them out on these days. Nevertheless, to the extent that most types of work (especially commercial business) distracted people from service to God on Sundays and feast days, they were discouraged.[11]

Sacred time involved not merely feasting but fasting as well.[12] Most of the significant feast days or feasting periods in the Orthodox calendar were preceded by a period of fasting. The most significant fasting period—Great Lent—was the forty-day period (in addition to Holy Week) preceding the celebration of Easter that mirrored Christ's own forty-day sojourn in the desert. The second fasting period in terms of prescribed austerity was a two-week period before the feast of the Dormition, followed by the Nativity and Apostles' fast. In addition, Wednesdays and Fridays of routine weeks were considered fast days in commemoration of Judas's betrayal and Christ's crucifixion. In all, Orthodoxy claimed about half of the calendric year as fast days.

Fasting was not considered optional in an Orthodox worldview. Preachers often pointed out that abstinence from certain foods was part of the original order before the Fall, as God had commanded Adam not to eat of the tree of the knowledge of good and evil (Gen. 2:16–17). The path of humanity's return to paradise, therefore, necessarily included fasting. Although the body carried the brunt of the fasting effort, the body was not itself the end but a means by which that effort would help to move a person toward the telos of communion with God. Lenten periods were times of healing for both soul and body. It was firmly believed that fasting—usually meaning abstinence from certain foods such as meat, eggs, and dairy products—strengthened the person internally in his or her movement toward God in two ways. First, it enabled a person to discern those aspects of worldly life to which he or she had become excessively attached, for these distracted the believer's attention away from God. Lenten periods were meant to teach believers how to eat and drink for the glory of God. Second, fasting, along with the spirit of repentance that accompanied it, strengthened and freed the will to turn toward God.[13] These positive goals were emphasized in liturgical hymns marking the first

week of Great Lent: "Let us joyfully begin the all-hallowed season of abstinence; and let us shine with the bright radiance of the holy commandments
of Christ our God, with the brightness of love and splendor of prayer, with
the purity of holiness and strength of good courage."[14] Ideally, that which a
person learned in lenten seasons would carry over into nonlenten times and
condition him or her to a lifelong lenten spirituality.

Clergy often stressed that abstinence from certain foods was not the sole,
and perhaps not even the most essential, act involved in fasting. The principle
of abstinence was also to be applied to the senses in general—to the eyes, ears,
mouth, and so forth. They also reminded members of their flock to apply the
notion of fasting to their worldly desires or searchings for fame, power, and
glory. Such physical and spiritual abstinence was also to be accompanied by
particular God-pleasing actions. Not separating the ascetic from the social or
apostolic ideal, one priest noted that while fasting, the most important rule to
remember was that given by Christ: "I was hungry and you gave me food, I
was thirsty and you gave me drink, I was a stranger and you welcomed me,
I was naked and you gave me clothing, I was sick and you took care of me, I
was in prison and you visited me" (Matt. 25:35–36). Only fasting that was
accompanied by this spirit of care and charity fulfilled the Orthodox rule of
fasting. As the well-known archbishop of Kherson, Innocent (Borisov), had
written in the first half of the nineteenth century, it would be better for a
person to eat whatever he or she pleased as long as he or she would simultaneously feed those who border on starvation.[15]

Orthodox believers, especially peasants, took fasting seriously, as docu-
mented especially by correspondents reporting for the Tenishev Bureau. Many
correspondents noted that modernization was affecting the observance of fasts,
especially among migrant workers. This common observation leads to the
question of the religious identity of these migrant workers and to whether
they identified with the Orthodox faith and whether they modified their
understandings of that faith with respect to fasting. In any case, most correspondents noted that women believers of any age group observed fasts with
more strictness than their male believing counterparts. Interestingly, one writer
noted that literate peasant believers tended to take fasting more seriously than
the illiterate.[16]

Among the fasts, believers observed Great Lent and the Dormition fast
most strictly. Church attendance in many localities rose during these periods.
The first meal during Great Lent would often be taken only later in the day,
especially on Wednesdays and Fridays.[17] Nursing women made little exception
for themselves when it came to fasting and usually immediately confessed their
lapses to their parish priest, especially if they had consumed milk.[18] Such strict
practices also applied to children, in some localities from as early as three years
of age.[19] Parish clergy did not as a rule advocate such strict fasting measures,
especially when it came to nursing women, children, and those who were ill.
It was not uncommon for peasant believers to criticize their priests if it became

known that he or members of his family had broken the fast because of illness.[20]

Many rural believers added additional days to their fasting calendar. Believers were inspired to such self-imposed fasting for various reasons. Elderly people and women, for instance, often added Mondays to the usual Wednesday and Friday weekly fasting days. For elderly people, such a fast might have been inspired by the thought of death—"for the salvation of their souls." For younger women, a special fast might have been taken as a vow for the health and well-being of their children.[21]

Others added such days as self-imposed disciplinary acts for their perceived sinful ways. Believers might also fast on the day preceding their saint's day as an expression of their respect for and devotion to that saint, or on the eve of the anniversary of the death of a particularly close loved one as a special offering to God accompanying their prayer for the departed. As already mentioned, believers also routinely fasted for several days before their local parish or village feasts, often citing a vowed commemoration of a visitation by God (in the form of a cattle epidemic or storm, for example) for such a practice.[22] Peasants from the Vytegorsk district in the Orel diocese donated the shortening they had not used during one such fasting period for the maintenance of their local church.[23]

Moreover, in addition to the regular lists of allowed and forbidden lenten foods (*skorom*), believers often created their own rankings. For instance, peasant believers from the Spas district in the Kazan diocese considered bread, *kvas*, water, and garden vegetables the stricter foods and fish (smoked or fresh), vegetable or olive oil, white bread, tea, honey, melons and berries as "lesser" lenten foods.[24] Aware that the spirituality of fasting extended beyond food and body, rural believers also made the collective effort during both prescribed and self-imposed fasts to refrain from public festivities, such as dancing, nonliturgical singing, and ribald discussions such as those frequently encountered in taverns.[25] Curiously, they used the same word (*skoromnyi*) to describe such discussions as they did to describe nonlenten foods such as meat, milk, and eggs.

Believers often took a person's fasting profile into account when interpreting life events. In the village of Arkhangelsk (Orel diocese), believers attributed one man's loss of fortune and subsequent fate as a beggar to his lack of observance of fasts. The school teacher from the village, Maria Mikheeva, recorded their thought in the following way: "So, there it is. Before he consumed milk on Wednesdays and Fridays, and now if only he could gulp some milk on nonfast days. But he has none since his soul was probably besmirched. God became angry with him."[26]

Although fasting was seen as a way to cleanse oneself spiritually and to order one's life properly in the movement toward God, it was not simply an act of individual inspiration and motivation.[27] Rather, individuals understood themselves as participating in an entire rhythm of sacred time and as participating through fasting alongside others involved on the same journey. Hence in rural areas those believers who did not fast were frequently seen as threats to the community's welfare. Persons who were known to ignore or dismiss fasting often lost the respect of fellow villagers and could be referred to pejoratively as *busurmany* (technically Muslims, but frequently used more broadly to refer to infidels in general) or *grekhovodniki* (sin-tempters).[28] In some areas, they would not be allowed to participate in village assemblies.[29]

Orthodox clergymen spoke and wrote about what they felt were two major threats to an Orthodox understanding of fasting. They wrestled with the modern tendency to compare such rules about fasting to the notion of progress and the findings of science, and then to see at best little worth in the practice and at worst a practice that threatened one's health. People thought nothing of becoming vegetarians because of the latest fad, Bishop Nikon (Rozhdestvenskii) noted, but found it troublesome to combine some of these very restrictions with a broader view on the spiritual life.[30] At the other end of the spectrum, churchmen chastised those who insisted on fulfilling the letter of the law to the point of absurdity. One favorite story, or variation thereof, that preachers told was that of a very poor person who had killed a wanderer (*strannik*) in the process of robbing him of his collected coins in order to purchase something to eat. It turned out, however, that the wanderer had no money on him but was carrying only a stick of sausage. When questioned by police as to why, if he had been so hungry, he did not eat the wanderer's stick of sausage, he replied he could not do so since it was Lent. Another recalled a doctor who when called to the bedside of a dying patient declined to offer his services since it was Lent and he was committed to going to church in order to take confession and Communion.[31]

Before 1917, Russia's civil calendar, which designated public holidays, still very much upheld the Orthodox Christian calendar as the standard of sacred time and, in churchmen's eyes, provided the necessary conditions for the proper marking of feasts.[32] In 1905, for instance, public holidays included the twelve major feasts honoring Christ and Mary and several "middle" feasts—two days in honor of St. Nicholas and the days of the Holy Spirit; Saints Peter and Paul; the beheading of St. John the Baptist; St. Alexander Nevskii; St. John the Theologian; the Protection of the Mother of God; and the Kazan icon of the Mother of God. Government and public employees also received several additional holy days, including the three lenten days before Easter and the week following Easter.

Except for the relatively religiously neutral days of New Year's and two days during *maslenitsa* (Shrovetide), the rest of the public holidays in 1905 commemorated various tsar's days: the coronation of Nicholas and Alexandra and the birthdays and name days of Nicholas, Alexandra, the empress dowager, Maria Feodorovna, and the heir to the throne, Alexei.[33] These imperial celebrations were integrated into the liturgical cycle of worship, with Divine Liturgies served on these occasions in many churches. Public holidays for 1905, including Sundays, totaled ninety-three days.

State monitoring of how days off were spent was relatively new in Russia's history. Though a Byzantine inheritance guided medieval Russian clerics in their beliefs and practices regarding holy days, Muscovy's state law codes made no mention of rules concerning work on feasts. Similarly, the *Domostroi*, the sixteenth-century manual governing everyday behavior, did not explicitly forbid work on these days. Such legislation began appearing only in the late sixteenth century and found definitive expression in the mid–seventeenth century during the reign of Alexei Mikhailovich, who attempted to legislate the keeping of Sundays and feast days as sacred times. In a March 1647 directive, Alexei Mikhailovich ordered that no one should work on Sundays or during the feasts of the Lord, a ruling that applied to both "lords and slaves." The directive declared that work should be curtailed on Saturday, between three and five o'clock in the afternoon, depending on the time of the year, and not resumed until the completion of the Divine Liturgy the following morning. But even this directive made an allowance for the sale of animal feed, hay, and oats. This directive, inspired mostly by religious considerations, was soon followed by a more politically motivated ruling: the public celebration of the birthday and name days of the tsar and his family. Bishops, monasteries, and parish priests were notified accordingly, and the ruling eventually entered Russia's law code.[34] An ecclesiastical directive followed in 1667 that charged that no work be done on Sundays and on the feasts of the Lord and of the Birth-Giver of God. Except for food, nothing was to be sold, and, except for that "necessary for the tsar," no administrative work was to be carried out on those days.

During the early part of his reign, Peter the Great for the most part ignored Alexei Mikhailovich's efforts to institutionalize sacred time on a statewide level. He had no qualms about directing certain residents of St. Petersburg, for instance, to practice sailing on Sunday mornings, under penalty of a fine for noncompliance. Only toward the end of his life did Peter take a strict legislative stance on the matter. In 1718, he made churchgoing mandatory on Sundays. He also outlawed trade on Sundays and feasts.[35] Peter was motivated, however, not so much by a pious concern for the keeping of sacred time as by a desire to monitor and limit the activities of Old Believers. Since he also appropriated the church pulpit as his own platform when necessary, this was a good way to ensure the presence of his subjects when his directives were read in churches.[36]

For nearly seventy years following the death of Peter the Great, Russia's emperors and empresses paid relatively little attention to the way Sundays and feasts were marked. Much of the legislation that had been established by their predecessor, Alexei Mikhailovich, was simply ignored or forgotten. Churchgoing that had once been made mandatory was now voluntary. Two events, however, significantly altered the course of the state's position on Sundays and feasts. The first was the French Revolution. In an attempt to minimize its effect, Paul I (1796–1801) hoped to restore a sense of reverence for Sundays and feasts by forbidding theatrical performances during Great Lent and on

Saturday evenings, when services were conducted in most urban churches.[37] A year later, in 1797, he also issued a manifesto forbidding landowners to force peasants to work on Sundays.[38] Finally, he reinstituted previous rulings that forbade the selling of alcoholic beverages during the celebration of the Divine Liturgy in churches.

The second event that affected the process by which the stated monitored the keeping of sacred time was the compilation and systematization of Russia's legislation into the legal code known as the *Svod zakonov* in the 1830s. Before then, legislation had often been printed in an arbitrary manner. It was difficult for state officials, especially on the local level, to know the governing policies on any given issue. Many of the laws that dealt with people's behavior on Sundays and feasts during the second half of the nineteenth century were collected in this law code. For instance, civil legislation asserted that church and civil feasts were to be days dedicated both to resting from work and to the devout honoring of these days. The law advised persons to abstain from their "dissipated ways of life" and to attend church.[39] Although carrying no penalties for noncompliance, this ruling nevertheless set the standard. It did prohibit, under severe penalty, landlords from forcing their serfs to work on Sundays and feasts. Legislation directed that on all feasts, when schools were closed and no state administrative offices were open, no other state work should be performed without official permission.[40] Certain key offices were exempt from these rules, however, including banks, customs officials, and postal and telegraph workers. State laws also attempted to regulate the types of activities that could take place on holy days. For example, the trade of alcoholic beverages was technically forbidden during religious processions and until the Divine Liturgy was completed.[41] Police were to ensure that no games, dancing, singing, theatrical performances, and trading in kiosks began on feasts before midday, when the Divine Liturgy usually ended.[42] Only permanent stores, hotels, and kiosks that sold food and horsefeed were exempt. By law, governors supervised the implementation of these rules on the local level.[43]

On first glance, then, church and state seemed to a large extent unified in their marking of sacred time, and we might think that the keeping of this time was more or less uniform. Indeed, such a Christian calendar remained the standard for the vast majority of Orthodox believers in Russia, that is, the rural peasant population, in a very fundamental way: their calculation of duration. Many peasants did not know the names of months, for instance, and often confused their order. They preferred instead to calculate their birthdays, time of tax collection, and periods of employment according to the *zeitgeber* of the Orthodox Church—the liturgical calendar.[44] As the correspondent for the Tenishev Bureau from the Penza diocese, the deacon N. Liustrov, noted, peasants conceived of duration by church feasts: from Pokrov to Easter designated an approximate six-month period beginning on 1 October.[45] Even with this existing standard, however, the keeping of sacred time proved to be a much more complex matter.

## Local Sacred Time

While church and civic calendars configured holy days according to the universal Christian and national civic feasts, lay believers, though guided by this timetable, also qualified the configuration in terms of their own local circumstances. If rest from labor was any measure of the perceived importance of particular feasts, then it would appear that believers did not everywhere uniformly observe all of the days designated as public holidays. For instance, although the civic calendar applied to educational institutions, the administrators of each institution ultimately decided which days students would be in the classroom. Different schools, therefore, followed variations of the standard sacred calendar.[46]

Believers also did not systematically follow the ecclesiastical ranking of feasts. Correspondents for the Tenishev project often noted that peasants determined the duration of time off for each feast. The Tenishev correspondent V. Antipov from the Novgorod diocese reported that on those feasts that peasants deemed "large" they often received three days off from work, while on "smaller" ones they received only one.[47] In the Dimitro-Shingorskii parish in the Vologda diocese, peasants tended to take time off from work only for twelve of the officially recognized feasts. Believers honored such feasts as the Dormition (15 August), the Beheading of St. John the Baptist (29 August), and the Presentation of the Theotokos in the Temple (21 November) only with the morning off, and even then only in some of the villages of the parish.[48] Except for New Year's day, none of the civil holidays was honored with time off. In some localities, believers even honored days of the week differently. For instance, P. Fomin, a schoolteacher from the Orel diocese, reported that peasants in the village of Ovstuga honored the fasting days of Wednesdays and Fridays more than Sundays in terms of time off from work.[49] To some extent, then, parishes might prioritize holy days in such a way that what was virtually a nonevent in one region might be strictly honored in another.

It is noteworthy that the tsar's days—the cycle of feasts commemorating birthdays, name days, and coronation days of tsars and various members of the imperial family—were not among the days most celebrated in rural areas.[50] Though churchmen urged believers to fulfill their Christian duty as "sons of Russia" by participating in public worship, a Russian proverb countered by noting that "a tsar's feast is not our day, but the sovereign's."[51] Many Tenishev correspondents noted the relative lack of attention to these feasts among the peasant population. A. V. Starshinin, a zemstvo teacher from the Tver diocese, observed that peasants did not consider these days special and continued to work.[52] This did not mean, however, that lay people did not count as sacred any days related to civil and political events. In fact, they often themselves instituted the celebration of such days. They appear to have distinguished what they considered days of more private concern—such as those commemorating birthdays and name days—from those in which they saw immediate relevance for the entire country.

Two phenomena in particular influenced the manner in which sacred time was appropriated and set at the local level—parish and village feast days—both of which deserve close attention as they eventually emerged as the subject of much debate.

⋆⇒◉⇐⋆

## Parish Feasts

Generally, the parish church, in both rural and urban areas, gave rise to various types of feasts, by far the most significant and widespread of which was the parish feast day. A parish feast day commemorated the day of the saint or event in honor of which the altar of the parish church was named (usually corresponding to the name of the church itself). If a parish had only one church with one altar, it would celebrate only one parish feast day. Since parishes in Russia sometimes consisted of at least two church buildings (a summer and a winter church), each of which might have more than one altar, the number of church-related feasts in any parish could be high.

Believers in both provincial towns and rural areas celebrated parish feasts as high points in the liturgical year, often honoring them as much or even more than the major feasts. A Tenishev correspondent from one village in the Kazan diocese noted that in terms of time off from work, the two parish feasts in honor of the Nativity of the Theotokos and the Nativity of Christ were celebrated as festively as Easter.[53] Looking to St. Dimitrii Cherno-Shingorsk parish in the Vologda diocese, we find four parish feasts celebrated: 11 February in honor of the holy martyr Blaise; 3 June in honor of the translation of the relics of the martyr crown prince of Russia, Dimitrii; 21 September in honor of the uncovering of the relics of St. Dimitrii, metropolitan of Rostov; and 1 November in honor of Saints Cosmas and Damian.[54] These feasts, each lasting two or three days, were celebrated with vespers on the eve and the Divine Liturgy on the day of the feast and were often better attended than the standard major holy days. Believers, including clergy and church choirs, often came from neighboring parishes to join in collective worship, accompanied by more solemnity and ceremony than usual. A parish feast day was considered such a central event in local religious life that even Old Believers, who otherwise shunned and criticized the Orthodox Church, were known to have attended the services and to have participated in the festivities.

The specifics of the celebration of parish feasts varied from place to place. In virtually all parishes, however, liturgical celebrations extended beyond the setting of the Divine Liturgy. Usually a procession broadened the liturgical space beyond the confines of the church. In the Transfiguration parish in the Vologda diocese (parish feast 6 August), clergy and parishioners processed around the church, saying a special prayer service before its sanctuaries. Two school-aged boys led the procession carrying lit candles; male members of the parish carried the icons. The procession moved to the nearby Kokshenga River and stopped on a platform that believers had constructed over the water especially for the event. While clergy and believers sang a prayer service for the blessing of the waters, men and women who had made a personal vow to God during a time of misfortune entered the water up to their waist and stood for the duration of prayer. After the service, these believers left their garments on the banks of the river for the poor. Similarly, believers who had made a vow related to the health and well-being of their livestock often brought their horses to stand in the water during the blessing of waters.[55] The parish priest usually did not discourage such practices. Finally, everyone processed back to the church and the communal meal would begin.

The celebration of the parish feast in some regions also moved from the immediate vicinity of the parish church into the villages themselves. During the two or three days of a feast, a village or groups of villages might sponsor the celebration activities for a particular day.[56] For instance, in one parish in the Vologda diocese, when all of the thirty-two villages comprising the parish celebrated a feast, the villages divided themselves into four groups and annually rotated the duties of preparing for the feast.[57]

Besides the parish feast, the local church generated other well-attended, one- or two-day celebrations, such as for the laying of a church foundation, the blessing of a new church, the renovation of an existing one, or the setting up of a new bell. Believers greeted all of these events with enthusiasm, and there was usually not enough room in church to accommodate all the faithful.

In his report to the Tenishev Bureau, V. Antipov from the Novgorod diocese described one church consecration that had taken place in the village of Ulom.[58] Several weeks before the event, parishioners sent out printed announcements to neighboring villages. It was not unusual for parishes to advertise such events in the local diocesan newspaper. Believers in the village of Ulom considered inviting either their diocesan bishop or John of Kronstadt to mark the celebration but decided against both: the bishop cost too much, and they believed John of Kronstadt would be too busy to attend. They eventually arranged to have ten priests come from surrounding parishes, the presence of whom recast the event from a purely local to a regional one.

Believers, many of whom had traveled for several days, began arriving on the eve of the consecration. While many visitors stayed with friends, some also camped out on the church grounds. It was clear from the time the bell ringing marked the start of the vigil that not everyone could fit into the church. About sixty local police were on hand to monitor the gathering pilgrims. Because of the number of believers, the anointing with oil, a common practice in the Orthodox Church during vigil services, took until well past midnight to complete. Believers clearly did not mind waiting, given the popular belief that the cross anointed on the forehead during this ritual remained until the time of the Last Judgment.

The climax of the consecration service that followed the next day was the consecration of the altar, a ritual that in some ways paralleled the baptism of a person.[59] During this ritual, which was understood to grant "spirit and life" to the church building, priests donned protective white garments over their vestments and fastened the altar table top in place. To do so they used four nails, in memory of the four nails with which Christ had been nailed to the cross. They then rubbed a special ointment over these areas as a sign of the mixture of myrrh and aloes with which Christ had been anointed upon his burial. Next, they carefully washed the table with soap and blessed water, then rinsed it with rose water as a sign of the blood and water that had flowed from the side of Christ while on the Cross. Finally, just as a person was sealed with chrism after baptism, as a sign of the Holy Spirit, so in the consecration of the church, a priest sealed the altar table by anointing each side with chrism in the sign of the cross.

It is noteworthy that during this ritual in the village of Ulom, while priests were rinsing the altar table, some believers would toss white handkerchiefs onto the soleas. The church elder and police keeping order would pick these up and take them into the sanctuary, and the priests would use them to wipe down the altar. The elders then returned them to their owners. Believers saved these handkerchiefs until their death, desiring to have them placed in their coffins. In his description of this custom, Antipov noted that it was mostly local intelligentsia who tossed the handkerchiefs. Many "simple folk" would have liked to participate but generally did not own handkerchiefs. Those who did hesitated, saying that they had little hope that their cloths would be honored to touch the altar.

⋆⇒◉⇐⋆

## Village Feasts

Both annual parish feast days and the celebrations that marked momentous occasions in the life of the church building reestablished believers' bonds with the local parish community and highlighted their identity with it. Not all local feasts in rural Russia, however, were temple focused. A significant number of feasts were centered not on the parish church but on the villages, whereby a particular village or group of villages became a focus of religious attention for a day.

Referring to village feasts, as they often did to chapels, as "vowed," "promised," and "cherished" days, local village communities established such feasts entirely on their own initiative.[60] Believers usually held these days in highest esteem, and those living in urban areas often returned for their celebration.[61] Certainly, not every celebration in a village had religious overtones. The festivities during the week before Great Lent (Shrovetide) and the period between Christmas and Epiphany (Christmastide), for instance, had no pretext of being liturgical celebrations, even though they might have taken place around important periods in the Orthodox calendar.[62] The so-called village or local feasts, however, were intimately connected to communal worship and were a prominent feature of liturgical life in rural Orthodoxy. The religious character of these feasts is reflected in the way in which believers often referred to them: *bogomol'e, molenie, molebstvie,* or *mol'ba*.[63] If the general Christian and parish feasts had been in place often for centuries with little or no change, this category of feasts continued to manifest the dynamism of liturgical life in Russia right up to the 1917 revolution.

Following the emancipation of the serfs in 1861, when millions of peasants were left free to organize their time, the number of these feasts in many regions began to grow. At the end of the nineteenth century, Tenishev correspondents frequently reported at least two or three such feasts per village.[64] In addition, in many localities the increase in the number of village feasts seems to have paralleled the popularity of periliturgical discussions. It could be argued that these feasts, at least in certain areas, indicated an increasingly informed Orthodox consciousness on the part of rural believers.

We can see the proliferation of such feasts in the villages that formed St. John the Baptist parish in the Vologda diocese. In 1873, only four out of the nine villages comprising the parish celebrated an annual commemoration day. By 1897, eight of the nine villages celebrated at least two such days.[65] Similarly in one parish in the Iaroslavl diocese, several feasts that had initially been celebrated by one village were appropriated by other villages in the parish, thereby increasing the number of feasts for each.[66]

The reasons behind the establishment of local feasts varied from village to village. While it might be argued that in rural areas such feasts were closely related to the peasants' agricultural calendar, it would be shortsighted to ignore other, more religious motivations for their establishment.[67] After all, similar feasts characterized the urban liturgical landscape as well. As in the case of chapel construction, feasts were established whenever and wherever a community felt a divine intervention in their lives. Often believers established them on the day of a saint whom they considered to have exerted his or her protection over the community during an epidemic, fire, or other natural disaster. Believers hallowed the day the event occurred and celebrated what was commemorated on the general Orthodox calendar on that day as their own special feast.

In 1891, for instance, believers from the village of Davidovo (Novgorod diocese) petitioned to celebrate 20 July annually in commemoration of God's visitation of a serious illness on their cattle. In one day, they reported, three horses and two cows had perished. Although this event might appear mundane, it inspired them to vow to celebrate this day by fasting an entire week and then not working on the day itself in memory of their experiences.[68] Similarly, in 1889, the head of the provincial town of Mosalsk (Kaluga diocese) petitioned for official recognition of a procession to mark the day of a terrible flood that had devastated their town in 1824.[69] In 1910, workers from a factory in the Vladimir diocese petitioned to have an annual prayer service to commemorate a typhoid epidemic from which many of their coworkers had died a decade earlier.[70] Clearly believers established these feasts not only for the immediate present but for the sake of future generations as well, who in remembering God's past visitations "would try to live by divine command-ment."[71]

Individual as much as collective experiences played a role in the establish-ment of local feasts. Villagers from Terebaev in the Vologda diocese, for instance, established one of their feast days in the 1890s in the following manner. One of the peasants of the village, Ivan Zherikhin, had a dream of an elder who said that if the village did not serve a prayer service the following day, a terrible storm would arise and destroy their crops. On the following day, Zherikhin called together his fellow villagers and related his dream. Interpreting the elder's appearance as a messenger of God's will, the residents of Terebaev invited the parish priest on the following day to their village. They requested he hold prayer services not only to Christ and the Mother of God but also in honor of St. Nicholas, since Zherikhin claimed that the elder he saw most resembled this saint. Furthermore, the villagers decided to hold a similar prayer service annually just before the harvest.[72] In the 1880s, in the Orel diocese, a violent hailstorm in the village of Radomil occurred on the day of St. John the Warrior. It so happened that the village elder dreamt of a young boy who directed him to announce that in the future no one should work on this day. A village assembly took the elder's dream seriously and on the next day established an annual feast.[73] In the Novgorod diocese, the illness of one man and his subsequent personal vow led to the establishment of an annual feast for the entire village.[74]

Though village feasts found their individual order and coloring in the unique context of each locality, they shared certain common features. Several days of preparation, for instance, preceded the actual feast day. Just as the more universally recognized major feast days of the Orthodox Church were fre-quently preceded by a lenten period, so believers often fasted for up to a week prior to their village feast.[75] Many regions, therefore, had their own local lenten cycle in addition to the lenten days prescribed by established liturgical order. Believers used such time creatively. In one parish, believers donated the butter that went unconsumed during that period to the parish church.[76] This prefestal week could also include community cleanup efforts, the preparation of special foods, and brewing beer. In some regions a specially chosen peasant (who held a three-year term) oversaw the organization of the festivities.[77]

When villages elected not to have a Divine Liturgy served on the day of the feast, chosen members of the village community would set out for the parish church, summon the priest for a prayer service, and bring select icons back to the village. Otherwise, believers attended Divine Liturgy at the parish church, which they requested the priest to serve. In some areas, liturgical services began very early. A correspondent from the Vladimir diocese noted that in the village Petrokovo, matins for the local feast day began at 3 a.m. and that villagers considered it imperative to attend. Not surprisingly, believers would return home to sleep after the services and would begin the festive celebrations only on the next day.[78] During Liturgies on this day, special petitions were said for the health and well-being of the village. It was also a day for remembering deceased relatives.

Following the Liturgy, if a village was located at a reasonable distance, believers, together with vested clergy, moved back to the village in a procession that included a cross, banners, lanterns, and various icons, including the feast day icon. The process of selecting the people who would carry these items, especially the icons, also varied. Within the Vologda diocese, for instance, in some places volunteers carried the icons,[79] while in others members of the community chose the icon carriers.[80] In some areas women and young girls processed with the icons.[81] In others, the icon-bearers were persons who had a vow to fulfill.[82]

Processions were perhaps the most characteristic feature of local feasts, both in rural and urban areas (fig. 4.1). From a historical perspective, they are also one of the most elusive aspects since, like the construction of chapels, they were often not recorded or registered, even in parish records. In addition to processions prescribed empire-wide for 1 August, 6 January, and Easter,[83] each locality, urban or rural, had its own schedule of processions. Imperial decrees could also establish processions in honor of events that affected the imperial family. For instance, in April 1866, state and church officials directed that an annual procession be held in provincial capitals from cathedrals to town squares with day-long bell ringing to commemorate the saving of Alexander II's life.[84] In addition, there were two other types of processions in rural Russia: those that were performed ex tempore, as, for example, the blessing of the fields or wells during a drought; and those that were performed annually in commemoration of a particular calamity that had once hit the community.

True to the spirit of the Petrine reforms, in the eighteenth century the Holy Synod attempted to regulate the establishment of annual processions. It directed believers to petition "higher ecclesiastical authorities" for permission to establish processions and ordered that those that had been established without permission be curtailed.[85] Synodal and diocesan authorities reiterated such directives in the late nineteenth century.[86] Nevertheless, evidence suggests that believers continued to hold annual processions without written permission from the Holy Synod or the diocesan consistory, relying only on the oral agreement of parish priests.[87] In many cases, believers only sought official ratification when local clergy refused to conduct the ritual until permission was received. No such permission, however, was required in the case of a one-time procession in the event of an immediate calamity.[88]

Records from St. Nicholas Grigorovskii parish in the Vologda diocese offer an insight into the process by which believers established an annual procession. In the late nineteenth and early twentieth century, the villages in this parish had suffered bad harvests several years in a row. Even the wealthier

4.1   Procession 1900. Kaluga Province, Mosalskii district, village Putaogino.
Photograph by K. Bulla. Central State Archive of Cine-, Photo-, and Phono-Documents,
St. Petersburg.

peasants had suffered extreme losses, and the situation was made worse by the
fact that few people had domestic or cottage industries to fall back on. In 1903
the tide turned. "Anyone who knew what hardships had befallen the local
peasants," wrote the parish priest Fr. Arkadii, "and anyone who shared their
concerns and fears can understand that joy which they were now experiencing
in the face of the unexpected harvest."[89] Believers in the parish were convinced that their improved situation was mercy shown to them by God
because of the intercession of St. Nicholas, the parish's patron saint. To demonstrate their gratitude both to God and to St. Nicholas, they petitioned the
consistory for processions from their church to their villages. They desired
that it be held annually on 29 and 30 August "not only by them, but by their
descendants as well," so that God and St. Nicholas would not abandon them.
As a sign of veneration, they vowed to refrain from work on these days. They
asked in addition that the locally revered icon of St. Nicholas join the procession and that they be able to ring the church bell during those two days "so
that the surrounding hills, forests, and groves would respond in echo to our

joy and our prayerful thanks; so to arouse not only rational creation but all of nature surrounding us to the glorification of our Creator together with us."[90] Not all believers were so eloquent, and even this poetic plea did not win official permission for the two days of bell ringing. Nevertheless, the same principles of thanksgiving and memory typified most of the requests for processions throughout rural Russia.[91]

In addition to the technical term "cross procession" (*krestnyi khod*), villagers often referred to a procession as the "raising of icons" (*podniatie ikon*). Once a procession was underway, believers either followed behind or ran ahead. The believers who ran ahead then waited for the procession to approach them, and they would prostrate themselves on the ground so that the procession would be forced to move around them. Those carrying the icons would lift them over these believers' heads. According to certain believers, God sent his grace upon them when the icon was passing over their heads.[92] In some locations, believers would ring the church bells until the procession returned to the church.[93]

When a procession arrived in a village, the entire community usually greeted it. Believers placed the cross and icons either in the village chapel or in a partitioned area with a table in the middle of the village. Here clergy conducted a general service of the blessing of the waters. Then the entire village along with the clergy processed to the blessing of the fields. This ritual could last several hours, since in many locations fields were scattered within a two- or three-mile radius.[94] On each field, clergy would conduct a different prayer service: in honor of the Life-Giving Cross, St. Nicholas, and the Holy Martyrs.[95] Following the blessing of the fields, the villagers and the clergy processed to the common pasture, where peasants drove their cattle and horses past the clergy for a blessing. Everyone then returned to the village, where believers could ask the clergy to conduct personal prayer services in their homes. When the clergy had completed these private services, the villagers again corporately gathered, and the clergy began the common meal. In some villages clergy sat at a table set up for them in the center of the village; in others a wealthier peasant invited them to his home. After the clergy and the icons left guests and relatives began arriving from neighboring villages to join the common meal and festivities.[96]

In their petitions to establish annual processions, lay believers rarely dwelt on their theological meaning. They typically wrote about their desires for memorialization of events or their hopes for God's protection. Sermons, periliturgical discussions, and devotional readings on the subject reinforced these sentiments. One priest, A. Chernyshev from the Viatka diocese, described the value of processions in maintaining the historical memory of events that might otherwise be forgotten: they were "immortal chronicles" that were much more effective than "memorials of marble or metal." He spoke of them as "open books," a phrase that was usually associated with icons, and described them as interactive in nature, involving those in the historical present in the lives of their forefathers. Thus they allowed the past to come forward in "vivid images" and gave believers the opportunity to spiritually connect with those who came before them.[97] Other churchmen, too, emphasized the visual and auditory effects of processions on the believer's disposition.[98] They also recognized the power of processions to elicit certain "holy feelings" conducive to prayers of thanksgiving and forgiveness and thereby helped to satisfy what one author referred to as the human impulse for public worship.[99]

Clergy and authors of popular devotional pamphlets spoke further about the meaning of processions. Most churchmen followed the roots of the ritual back to the Old Testament prototype of the movement of the Israelites behind the Ark of the Covenant and the divine directive to do so.[100] Yet they also grounded their readings of the ritual in the New Testament, with some associating it primarily with Jesus' procession with the cross to Golgotha (John 19:17).[101] Imagining that event, one author recalled Simon of Cyrene carrying the cross, followed by the apostles, Mary, and the myrrh-bearing women. So, too, he continued, the contemporary procession paralleled this event, with the carrying of the cross followed by the banners and icons that represented Jesus' followers.[102]

Most churchmen focused on the cross that was carried at the head of processions. In their minds it was through the power of the cross that air, water, fields, streets, and city squares could be sanctified.[103] More important, however, the presence of the cross gave processions a sense of victory: a victory of both Christ and human faith over evil and death. Elaborating on the theme of victory, churchmen encouraged believers to look at processions as a movement of God's warriors—the faithful. The priest G. Krasnianskii, for instance, spoke of the body of believers moving in procession as warriors "heading for battle," with "the enemy" designated as "the flesh" and "the devil." Believers were urged to come to their own personal victory through prayer, fasting, and a pious life.[104]

Interestingly, churchmen also spoke of processions as "temples outside the temple" (*khram vne khrama*) and "moving temples." Vissarion, the vicar bishop of Moscow, wrote that they allowed believers to imagine themselves inside the church: the cross and gospel reminded them of the altar; the icons reminded them of the iconostasis, and so forth. Because of this, Vissarion spoke of processions as rituals in which God manifested his presence—in which God could "rest" just as he had in the Tabernacle.[105] In this way, the sacred space of the temple building was seen as expanding out into nature, thereby sanctifying all of creation. "The ground upon which we walk and on which we live," wrote one priest, "is blessed by the steps of Christ, Mary, and the saints," who joined the procession in their iconographic representations.[106] Similarly, the song and words of prayer were seen as blessing the air humans breathe; the glow of candle flames as hallowing fire, and the blessing ritual as hallowing water. Given this perceived divine presence, it is not difficult to see how churchmen ascribed healing potential and missionary value to them.[107]

One final aspect of processions in Orthodox thought and practice should be mentioned. Just as in the case of chapels, many requests came from lay believers to establish processions in memory of tsar-related events. Such requests became especially numerous near times of coronation[108] or soon after an event when the emperor or members of his family were believed to have been miraculously saved from physical harm.[109] For instance, in 1897 six residents of the town of Dobryi (Tambov diocese) mustered the support of town officials and clergy to organize a city-wide procession annually on 14 May in honor of the coronation of Nicholas II and Alexandra.[110] The same year, believers from the village of Miatusov in the Olonets diocese requested an annual procession from their parish church to their chapel in honor of St. Nicholas the Wonderworker and St. Alexandra in order to commemorate the coronation. They had had an icon made of these two saints and had placed it in the chapel.[111] Churchmen generally supported such requests since many localities had no monuments commemorating civic events.[112]

Despite the significance of processions in both the private and the collective lives of believers, they were not always automatically approved by church officials. For instance, synodal officials tended to discourage processions in memory of Alexander II, explaining that the procession ritual was tied to joy and thanksgiving rather than to the sorrow that accompanied a requiem service.[113] Church officials also weighed such requests in terms of their religious significance in the lives of believers. In 1865 the head of the city administration in Murom (Vladimir diocese) petitioned synodal authorities to have an annual procession from the cathedral to the chapel that was located over the source of the city's water supply. Popular devotional literature in fact encouraged believers to conduct special prayer services near public water sources, rivers, and lakes in order to "disclose" the healing powers of the waters.[114] Nevertheless, synodal officials denied the request. They claimed that processions were supposed to commemorate a significant event in the lives of Orthodox Christians and that this request did not do so.[115] Given that diocesan authorities in this case had no objections to the procession, it seems that church officials did not always agree on what constituted a "significant event."

Church officials tried to weed out requests for petitions they felt proceeded from questionable or unfounded motives. In 1907 a church elder from the Tver diocese (Rzhevsk district) petitioned for an annual procession from the Kozheozersk monastery in the Arkhangelsk diocese to his parish church. He asked that the monastics bring an icon of the locally revered saint, Nikodim of Kozheozersk. The church elder based his request mainly on two reasons: thanksgiving for not having been affected by revolutionary turmoil and a desire to aid the Kozheozersk monastery financially. Members of his parish had learned about the monastery's financial difficulties from a fellow parishioner, Vasilii Obraztsov, an avid reader of "godly books." After sending a modest donation to this monastery, Obraztsov received a letter of thanks that also lamented the monastery's financial state. He began convincing members of his village, especially its women, to come to the monastery's aid. Although the Tver diocesan consistory had no objections to such a procession, the bishop of Arkhangelsk was not so favorably predisposed. He did not feel any historical or social justification to make the approximately five-hundred-mile journey to commemorate the deliverance of the northern part of the Rzhevsk district, Tver province. He also did not find the argument for financial aid compelling, given that he understood this monastery to be quite well off.[116] The Synod, therefore, denied the request.

Consistory officials were also wary of seeing too many established processions in any one locality. In 1899 a church elder from the city of Elatmy in the Tambov diocese requested a procession in honor of the imperial coronation. Both diocesan and synodal officials denied his request because they believed there were too many annual processions in that locality already.[117] Very much aware that a procession formally marked an event, memory, or locality as sacred, church authorities also hesitated to grant permission if they felt such a marking might be unwarranted.

The celebration of local feasts and the procession rituals that they included played another important role in communities where written local histories were nonexistent. As one correspondent for the Tenishev Bureau, A. V. Balov from the Iaroslavl diocese, noted, these were "historical" feasts,[118] serving as records of events and ceremoniously bonding the living generation with their deceased forefathers. Because of this, communities often felt obliged to commemorate these days, even if the immediate reason for doing so no longer seemed so pressing.

As with the case of chapels, both parish and village feasts had two different effects on the religious life of the laity. On the one hand, they tended to localize people's religious sentiments to such an extent that it might have been difficult to transplant these sentiments onto the foreign soil of another setting, be it urban, provincial, or even rural. Local feast days were symbols of communally experienced events that would have little meaning to outsiders and might quickly lose their unique historical meaning in other settings. On the other hand, the very presence of such feasts in every locality made local sacred time a standard that would be anticipated by believers wherever they lived. Part of making a new locality one's own would mean, in part, becoming familiar with these local festivities and becoming a part of them.

Moreover, because local feast days involved the commemoration of a saint, or an event in the life of Mary or Christ, they were linked to a universally recognized liturgical cycle and church calendar that transcended narrow parochial concerns. They served to incorporate the joys, memories, and concerns of a community into the standard cycle of liturgical time and in this way integrated the life of a community into the life of the Church at large. In this sense, local feasts, just as chapels did, exemplified an integration of Orthodoxy with local histories and cultures, whereby people identified with a broader faith community through particular events in their own lives and in the lives of their kin. Even the Church's major feast days tended to be most celebrated when they corresponded to an event in the life of the local community.

These two tendencies—a locally focused understanding of Orthodoxy characterized by diverse religious practices and a more uniform, universally oriented understanding of the faith community—are two antinomic tendencies that have been present in the history of Christianity to some degree from the beginning, but especially from the fourth century, when Christianity was established as the religion of the Roman Empire. What is interesting, however, is how these tendencies showed themselves in any particular historical moment, and how the tensions created by them affected the faith community at large.

⊷═◉═⊷

## Resetting Sacred Time: Holidays and Drinking

Despite their meaning for the local community, as well as their integration into the liturgical life of the parish church, local feasts were targets of much criticism in the postreform period. Critics focused on two features of village feasts that were tied to broader issues and stereotypes concerning rural life in general and the peasantry in particular in late imperial Russia: the issue of work and the consumption of alcohol.

The increasing demands of labor production, as well as the summons of modernity to progress, led to a heightened confrontation between business interests and religion in Russia. Throughout the second half of the nineteenth and the early twentieth century, various government committees, as well as the secular press, repeatedly addressed the negative effect that Russia's numerous feasts were having on labor patterns and economic production. The discussion spanned the entire postreform period, and despite the fact that certain limited legal measures were taken, the issue was still not resolved on the eve of the 1917 revolutions.

In 1865, A. I. Vasil'chikov, a representative of the St. Petersburg Society of Agricultural Landlords, presented the typical argument against local feast days that would echo through the next decades.[119] Blaming Russia's economic lag behind America and western Europe on the fact that Russians celebrated more feasts, he calculated that the typical Russian worked some fifty fewer days per year than his western European counterpart. The problem was the number of local feast days. If Russia's civil calendar listed some ninety days as officially recognized holidays, the typical rural calendar could boast anywhere from 100 to 150 days off from work. Not only did this situation decrease Russia's ability to compete effectively on the world grain market but it also resulted in significant losses of income for every working, especially rural, Russian household.[120]

Such market-oriented discourse about local feasts was associated with a barrage of criticisms of rural life. Government officials and the secular press portrayed peasants as lacking any strong desire for additional comfort and conveniences, often linking this lack to their alleged predisposition to laziness and apathy. Based on an erroneous understanding of the notion of celebration (*prazdnovanie*), this position argued that "the people" simply used the pretext of local feasts to do nothing. Once "enlightened," peasants would gain a proper understanding of work and would no longer maintain these local feasts.[121] Moreover, secular writers also suggested that peasants promoted a communal servitude of sorts that forced all the members of a community to observe these customs even if they did not wish to do so.[122] These attacks were all the more fierce because urban journalists often regarded local and especially village feast days not as bona fide Orthodox feasts but rather as pagan remnants and reflections of ignorance and superstition.[123] Economic concerns therefore combined with ethical ones in the state's campaign to regulate work and rest for "national well-being" (*narodnoe blagosostoianie*).

Evidence suggests that rural communities could and indeed did regulate work on feast days. Consequently, normative behavior on a feast day varied from community to community.[124] Tenishev correspondents confirm that in most locations, rural communities took some measures to regulate communal work on feasts, although several correspondents noted that the decision to work ultimately was left up to each individual person.[125]

While no community had all of its members abstaining from work, there were local customs and religious beliefs that deterred widespread work on Sundays and feasts. In many localities, the deterrent of choice appears to have been fines. Local village assemblies drew up written decisions (*prigovory*) regulating such fines. A local parish school teacher, F. Kostrin, from the Orel district (Orel diocese), for instance, noted that various levels of fines existed for various types of work performed on feasts. On the eve of a feast, the field watchman made the rounds through the villages, reminding people that no one was to work the following day before noon, or evening, depending on the solemnity of the feast. If a person was caught working, he would be brought before the village assembly. If a person admitted his fault in good conscience, he would be responsible for paying the fine agreed on by the village. If, out of stubbornness, he attempted to defend his practice, the community would fine him doubly or triply.[126] The peasant S. F. Staroverov from the Vologda diocese reported that in cases of violation of communal agreements not to work on Sundays and feasts, some village communities appropriated a part of the culprit's hayfield land and divided it for use among the rest of the villagers for one year.[127]

One correspondent from the Vologda diocese, A. Mertsalov, even claimed that certain villagers insisted on collective agreements not to work in order to restrict the more industrious peasants from working and "getting ahead" while the others took time off.[128] Another correspondent from the Vologda diocese, A. Aristarkhov, made a similar observation. Peasants he knew believed that those who worked on the village feast day "tempted" others by their behavior. As soon as one started working, others quickly followed, only to defend themselves later by saying that they were "tempted" by the behavior of their neighbor.[129]

Collective decisions regulating work on feast days often elicited opposing reactions from religious and civil officials. In 1863, for instance, a group of village elders and *volost'* judges decided that the following feasts should be "preserved and sanctified by us from generation to generation until the end of time": all twelve major feasts, parish feasts, village feasts, 19 February (anniversary of the emancipation of the serfs), 27 August (day of Great Martyr George), 9 March (day of St. Nicholas), 20 July (day of the Prophet Elijah), 26 August (coronation of the tsar and feast of the local wonder-worker Adrian), 30 August (day of St. Alexander Nevskii and name day of the tsar-emancipator, Alexander II). Members of the community who did not adhere to the decision would be subject to reprimand, fines, or arrest, depending on the nature of their nonconformity.

The decision received an immediate response from the local arbitrator (*mirovoi posrednik*), a governor-appointed official from the local nobility. He declared the decision "unfair" and reprimanded one of the village elders for encouraging sloth and drunkenness instead of industriousness and hard work. The Iaroslavl Provincial Bureau backed the arbitrator's judgment, ruling that the decision made by the group of village elders could not be enforced for several reasons. First, it was made at a meeting that was not called according to protocol. More important, such decisions did not lie in their purview. Although Russian law called people to abstain from dissolute behavior and to attend church on many of the days listed by the peasants, it did not address the period of time following church services. After services, people then could do as they wished, including voluntary work for the good of society or their family. Work was only forbidden for certain state and public offices. The Ministry of Internal Affairs in St. Petersburg, to which the case was reported, also agreed, maintaining that the interference of spiritual authorities into civil affairs was "extremely inconvenient," especially when it came to the question of labor on feast days.

Although urged by the Ministry of Internal Affairs to direct the attention of local bishops and pastors to this issue, the ober-procurator of the Holy Synod declined. He maintained that the matter fell under the purview of the Holy Synod and local bishops could not make such decisions unilaterally. Moreover, he reminded civil authorities that the church was directed in its thinking by ancient church canons; deciding the issue of labor on feasts could not be considered the sole prerogative of state officials. If this issue came before the Holy Synod, warned the ober-procurator, church officials could easily come to the conclusion that pastors not only had the right but the responsibility to disagree with civil authorities on this issue. Therefore, he recommended that the matter be put to rest—an approach that would not be possible for long.[130]

In 1895, similar tensions between civil and religious authorities could be detected. That year the bishop of Kazan, Vladimir, informed the ober-procurator of the Holy Synod that several rural communities, under the guidance and influence of their local clergy, had composed collective decisions, which included fines, in order to discourage young people from working on Sundays and feast days. These decisions had been declared illegal by the local official. In addition, in order to enforce his position, the zemstvo official had announced that if all the villagers in question indeed refused to work on feast days, he would fine everyone who signed the collective decision. He only agreed to rescind his decision once the local village assembly promised never again to compose such an agreement concerning work on feast days.

In response, the local diocesan consistory maintained that church-related feasts were divinely established and were not simply human creations. It also asserted that these feasts had a deep educational significance. Their observance did not impoverish a person but on the contrary might be expected to improve his material lot in the long run. Moreover, as far as the consistory knew, such collective decisions had not been considered illegal before. Members of the consistory essentially supported the local priests in their efforts but advised them to discourage their parishioners from taking mandatory fines from persons who did not abide by their rulings regarding Sundays and feasts. Fines could, however, be collected in the form of "voluntary donations." Finally, they decided that the local bishop should consult with the governor about advising zemstvo officials not to impede local communities from making such decisions.

Once again, the matter came to the attention of the Ministry of Internal Affairs and the ober-procurator of the Holy Synod. Again, the two parties came to opposite conclusions. The Ministry of Internal Affairs had maintained that while rural assemblies had the right to discuss various social needs, they had no right to interfere in the private lives of individuals. The ober-procurator, on the other hand, expressed his admiration for the intentions of the village assemblies. He criticized the local zemstvo officials for undermining the authority of parish clergy, who by definition were obligated to care for the religious and moral life of their flocks. In compliance with the local bishop's request, he also asked the governor of Iaroslavl to advise local zemvstvo officials not to impede local communities in their good efforts.[131]

The issue of work on feasts was related to notions of crime and sin. According to Tenishev correspondents, people often associated labor on Sundays and feasts with the latter category.[132] In addition, since many communities established feasts as part of a communal vow, believers viewed working on these days as a violation of a covenant. Therefore, sin became an issue of social welfare as well and became one of those matters with which rural communal assemblies were concerned. A day of thanksgiving was a day of corporate supplication, and when a person neglected such a communal concern, others looked on him or her as irreverent. Such a person threatened the entire community with divine wrath.[133] Therefore, even if a person had no religious predisposition to abstain from work, the threat of social alienation undoubtedly often prevented him or her from doing so anyway.[134]

Tenishev correspondents also pointed out that these feasts were the primary and sometimes the only days when family and friends gathered from other villages and parishes. Villagers were under the watchful eye of their neighbors, many of whom regarded an absence of guests as shameful. Many people scorned those who did not participate in the festivities and judged them to be "not a good person."[135] In other areas they were jeered. Thus even those who could not afford to spend the money did so in order to be part of the festivities.[136] A. Malinin, from St. George Shuborov parish in the Vologda diocese, reported that with the influx of kin and close friends on that day, every household, poor or wealthy, celebrated the feast as best it could. Shying away from such celebrations was considered the "first of dishonors."[137]

Peasants were supported in these views by what they heard in sermons and what they read, or heard read, from popular religious literature. Believers also told stories either about their own experiences or about those of acquaintances that confirmed the imperative to obey the Fourth Commandment.[138] P. Kamanin from the Vladimir diocese recounted one such story he heard from a peasant widow from the Melenkov district. Once she had a dream, in which she found herself in her parish church, listening to a sermon by her priest, Fr. Vasilii. In his unusually long sermon, Fr. Vasilii spoke about how sinful it was to work on feast days. When the woman went home after the liturgy, she saw there was no roof on her house and cried out. She then woke up shaking. In the next couple of weeks, the widow explained, her husband died. Despite her warning, her husband had gone out to work during the feast of Epiphany and had fallen off his cart. God had punished him, she concluded.[139]

A prevalent attitude toward work on feasts was perhaps most dramatically portrayed in a well-known oral story recorded by the Vologda ethnographer N. S. Ivanitskii in his study of the Vologda province. The story, called "The Angel and the Passerby," told of an angel who was walking by a river. On his way, he saw a young girl drowning an infant in the river. He went up to her and said, "God, help her!" and continued on his way. After some time passed, the angel returned along the river bank and came upon the very same spot. This time he saw another woman washing her clothes in the river. He passed by her without stopping or saying anything.

A passerby then met the angel and asked, "Why did you ask God to help the young woman who was drowning her child, but said nothing to the woman who was washing her clothes?" The angel replied, "The first young woman suffered from her parents and her neighbors for her sin; she sincerely repented before God and prayed with all of her soul to the Lord to forgive her for her crime. The Lord heard her prayer and forgave her sin. The second woman, however, was washing clothes on a feast day; she violated the sanctity of the feast and God will not forgive her for this."[140]

The story illustrates the moral and religious reasoning that might have motivated some rural believers to shun those who did any sort of unacceptable labor on Sundays and feast days. As the school teacher I. Shadrin from the Vologda diocese noted, some peasants referred to those who worked on Sundays and feast days as "godless."[141] Peasants from one village in the Kaluga diocese followed suit, claiming such persons were "pure un-Christians" (chisto nekhristi).[142]

What is less clear from the sources is what types of activities constituted "work" in its sinful connotation. As already noted, rural believers rarely came to church on Sundays during the summer months. They often stayed home to attend to domestic chores like sewing, fixing tools, chopping wood, fishing, and picking berries and mushrooms or to participate in collective aid for a fellow village member.[143] A priest from the village of Shchelkanov in the Kaluga diocese even scheduled the Divine Liturgy earlier on Sundays during summer months so his parishioners would have time to work.[144] It is noteworthy that many peasant communities generally did not condemn or censure personal, domestic chores, especially if they were done after the Divine Liturgy.[145]

The picture becomes even more complex when we realize that believers also took people's intentions into account when evaluating work and sin. In his report to the Tenishev Bureau in 1899, P. Gorodetskii from the Vologda diocese noted that frequently by the afternoon of a village feast, merry-making activities began intensifying. In order to avoid them, many peasants in this particular region chose to work in the fields after the completion of the prayer services. While some community members resented this move, other saw it as wise and more pious. In the past several years, Gorodetskii claimed, many others in the village had begun to follow suit.[146]

Gorodetskii's observations raise several key questions when evaluating the dynamics shaping Orthodoxy in the late imperial period. Since religious and social concerns often overlapped, it is difficult to tell where the sets of concerns begin and end. When did believers abstain from work because of fear of social reprisal and when did they do so from genuine religious motivations? When were communal agreements to censor or fine particular behaviors on feast days inspired by the perceived workings of God and when were they manifestations of "communal servitude"? Since believers from all social backgrounds did not hold uniform views on the definition of work and the honoring of sacred time, both the person who worked and the one who abstained could be equally devout or nonobservant in their faith. Gorodetskii's comments suggest that in some instances religious sensibilities and social pressures hung in a precarious balance when it came to festal behavior.

Rural believers also did not view village assemblies and local court sessions, often held on Sundays and feasts, as work. The practice of conducting such administrative matters on Sundays and feasts became institutionalized after the emancipation of the serfs and soon became widespread so that peasants would not lose precious work time.[147] Apparently certain peasants enjoyed attending the proceedings of the local court. According to the 1908 notebook of A. A. Zamaraev, a peasant from the Totma district, he would frequently journey into the town of Totma from his outlying village in order to "attend court" on Sundays in the fall and winter.[148]

More ambiguous was the status of trade and commerce. While some stories related horrible accidents that happened while a person was "working" on a Sunday or feast, such story lines rarely involved the activity of trade or commerce. Both smaller local and larger regional bazaars and trade fairs took place regularly on feasts. In the Spaso-Sengovskii parish in the Vologda diocese, for example, bazaars took place annually on Annunciation, Pentecost, Transfiguration (the parish feast day) and 22 October, the day of the Kazan icon of the Mother of God. Regular weekly trading also took place on Sundays starting with the second week of Great Lent until winter.[149]

We should not conclude from such reports that believers had a uniform understanding of the relationship between trade, work, and the hallowing of time. In the 1860s, not only certain diocesan bishops but various local merchants and many peasant communities petitioned the Holy Synod to move the days on which trade fairs were held. This began what the historian of Sunday in Russia, Dimitrii Smirnov, has called the "rather significant social movement" to end or at least limit trade on Sundays.[150] The Synod also tried to convince the Ministry of Internal Affairs to legislate weekdays as the proper time for such fairs. When held on Sundays, they were seen as a "custom most harmful for morality."[151]

In looking into the matter, the Ministry of Internal Affairs found that even provincial governors were divided on the issue.[152] In 1867 the Ministry decided that the schedule of trade fairs was a civil matter and that provincial governors and city dumas should decide them.[153] In effect this ruling institutionalized diversification in the marking of sacred time as far as trade and commerce were concerned. Despite this decision, the issue did not die and continued to occupy the attention of ecclesiastical authorities up until 1917.[154]

The issue of feasts was not simply a rural one. It also concerned urban areas and persons of all social backgrounds. Russia's stock exchange closed on the officially recognized feasts, as did the post office, banks, and schools; the loading and unloading of goods ceased, forcing their owners to pay for their protection on trains. The issue of feasts became especially poignant at the end of the nineteenth century in Moscow and St. Petersburg, where many of the workers were migrants from rural areas. Before the emancipation of the serfs, laws had prevented landowner exploitation of peasants on Sundays and feasts. Following the emancipation, however, no such law protected sacred time for Russia's common folk. Factory owners and merchants had more or less free rein in making their employees' work schedules. In June 1897 Nicholas II took the advice of the State Council and issued a directive concerning the civic calendar for factory and industrial workers, leading to yet another variation in standard sacred time. A leaner version of the some ninety public holidays listed at the outset of this chapter, the holiday schedule for industrial workers included only sixty-six days.[155] These included Sundays and certain major Orthodox feasts. The feast of the Meeting of the Lord in the Temple—one of the twelve major church feast days—as well as the feast of St. Nicholas were conspicuously absent. In 1898 workers in certain factories displayed their annoyance over this change and boycotted work. For instance, on 2 February, in one St. Petersburg paper factory, only 150 out of 1,262 workers appeared. Workers from the same factory later attempted to negotiate with their employers for a holiday on 9 May. When their employers denied their request, only thirty workers appeared for work.[156] While employers rarely sought legal action against their workers for such behavior, they feared such instances would only multiply if some sort of legal measures were not taken. In 1900 state officials gave in to these pressures and added three more feasts to the industrial holiday roster—the Meeting of the Lord in the Temple, the Exaltation of the Cross, and the Meeting of Theotokos in the Temple—all of which were major feasts in the Orthodox calendar. Interestingly, the new law allowed workers to substitute other, locally revered feasts in their place. It also reminded both employers and workers that the establishment of other holidays rested with the factory administration.[157]

In addition to criticizing people for virtually equating feasting (*prazdnik*) with idleness (*prazdnost'*), government officials and the secular press maintained that the rural population in particular was disposed toward carousing that resulted from "ethical underdevelopment," "ignorance," and "crude instincts."[158] They often accused peasants of fabricating feasts in order to get another drinking day. Indeed, in some areas of Russia the village feasts were sometimes referred to as "beer feasts" because of the custom of brewing beer for the communal meal that followed the prayer services. In the Kokshenga region of the Vologda diocese, for example, the clergy of Transfiguration Savior parish regularly brewed beer on one of the parish feast days as an annual sign of gratitude for their parishioner's support.[159]

Such practices led to the common assumption that believers had distorted the original religious ideas behind the celebration of these feasts. The large quantity of beer at village feasts, along with purchased alcohol, contributed to the stereotypic view of these local feasts as nothing but revelry that ended with drunken clergy staggering home, drunken brawls among the villagers that sometimes resulted in death, and scandalous behavior among the youth. While some individuals might have engaged in such behavior, it is questionable whether this view of feasts was entirely justified. Some Tenishev correspondents went out of their way to point out that widespread excessive drinking was rare on these days. One correspondent from the Novgorod diocese, the school teacher V. I. Ivanov, denied that these feasts involved a "universal, reckless drunkenness." Instead he characterized them as a "school" in which believers shared knowledge and experiences during their small gatherings.[160]

Moreover, especially beginning in the 1890s, many local communities imposed limits on their consumption of alcohol at feasts. People familiar with rural life in Russia at this time noted that rural assemblies began voting to curtail alcohol consumption and more actively monitored the celebration of their village feast. Whether because of tight financial budgets, a rise in educational levels, the urging of clerical or government officials, or the success of periliturgical discussions, such local, self-imposed measures often decreased the drinking excesses.[161]

Even before these trends developed, it appears that many communities organized village feasts so as to keep the sacred and the profane distinct. Believers designated the preparatory days prior to the feast as a lenten period with all the associations that went with such a designation. As mentioned earlier, believers marked the morning and early afternoon with a Liturgy, procession, and prayer services, and in some cases customs of feeding the poor. They also often held the common meal in stages, with the clergy and the poor eating first. Villagers and their guests began eating and drinking after the clergy and icons had left.

Furthermore, not all believers necessarily viewed beer brewing as entirely profane and sinful. From 1887 to 1893 the governor of Vologda province, for instance, carried on a correspondence with the diocesan bishop regarding the custom of the blessing of grain mash that existed in various parishes through-out the diocese, but especially in the Kadnikov district.[162] In investigating the governor's report, the bishop of Vologda, Izrail, learned that variations of this practice could be found in numerous parishes. All of the deans that responded positively to the bishop's inquiry reported that the custom had existed "from time immemorial." Like most paraliturgical rituals, this one was not celebrated in a uniform fashion. Sometimes the blessing took place in the narthex or in a building next to the church. In many parishes, believers did not leave mash (*suslo*) for the clergy; other times it was divided between the clergy, the church's *prosfora* baker, and older, poorer, single people who lived in an almshouse on the parish grounds.[163]

One priest, Fr. Nikolai Bogoslovskii of the Ukhtomsk Dormition church in the Vologda diocese, described in detail certain practices in his deanery. After natural disasters such as droughts, floods, and hailstorms, people turned to God with prayers of thanksgiving, and they collectively vowed to offer a portion of their grain to brew beer. They promised to offer annual prayer services to Christ, the Mother of God, and a particular saint whom they considered their protector and intercessor. As their offering or oblation they brought a part of the grain mash to the church for blessing.

Members from each household who were responsible for brewing the beer that year came on the day before the feast and left their containers with the mash in the narthex of the church. On the next day, after the Divine Liturgy, believers brought their containers and placed them around the festal icon in the center of the church. The troparion and kontakion for the feast day were sung. The priest then read the prayers from the *Book of Needs* that pertained to the blessing of boiled wheat and honey prepared on the occasions of memorials for the dead, and blessed the grain mash with holy water.[164] Afterward, parishioners offered part of the mash to the clergy and distributed the rest to friends, relatives, and everyone present, while asking them to remember their deceased kin in their prayers. In so doing, the members of the community who were present greeted each other with the usual feast-day greeting—"with the feast day" (*s prazdnikom*)—combined with the phrase "with the fulfillment of the vow." When the entire parish, which consisted of more than four hundred households, celebrated a local feast, the number of containers that stood in the church could be quite high.

Priests who described this custom were not disturbed by it. "Given the prayers that exist in the *Book of Needs* for the blessing of this or that item" wrote Fr. Nikolai, "we would be wrong to deny [the parishioners' request to bless the mash]."[165] Moreover, he continued, to disrupt the custom of blessing that had existed for generations, and that was conducted nobly, "would only insult the religious sensibilities of the people." Parishioners saw this as an offering, as a sacrifice to God. Similarly, another priest, Fr. Veniamin Nekliu-dov, wrote that he saw nothing wrong, strange, or contrary to Orthodoxy in this custom and therefore did not believe it should be curtailed.[166]

In making their decision about the custom, members of the diocesan consistory took two issues into account. First, they compared the grain mash to the offering of the first fruits of the harvest, as well as to the boiled wheat that believers customarily offered in memory of the deceased. They also compared it to the practices of bringing cheese, eggs, fruits, and vegetables for blessing on other feasts. Second, local clergy unanimously claimed that to forbid this custom would only "stir up" the people. In view of these two considerations, on 17 December 1887 the Vologda diocesan consistory decided that blessing the grain mash should not be discouraged but simply "left to time."[167]

More interesting than the details of the custom is the fact that it surfaced to become the subject of discussion. While this custom had supposedly existed since "time immemorial," it was only brought to the consistory's attention in 1887, and then by a civil servant, the governor. The parish clergy, who intimately knew the ways and customs of their parishioners, had not thought it worthy of reporting. To them it was just an example of "churching" local customs. For the villagers whose feast day it was, the blessing of the grain mash was essential both as an offering and as a bond to their deceased kin, whose vows they were fulfilling. For them it was so important, as one priest noted, that if they, the parish clergy, did not bless it, the peasants would find someone else to do so.[168] The religious sensibilities of the people, coupled with the local clergy's tolerance and even acceptance of the practice, was obviously enough to convince the consistory not to disturb what had come to be a common custom in various parishes. The governor's judgments regarding what was superstitious and what was not were dismissed.

Members of the intelligentsia were not the only ones to criticize village feasts. In their annual reports to the bishops, especially before the 1890s, parish clergy themselves frequently complained about the way believers spent their feasts. Although certain clergy desired to see a shift in focus away from the local to the universally celebrated Orthodox feast days,[169] most tended, at least publicly, to defend the local feasts. This is not simply because they were paid for their liturgical activities on these days; after all, most priests by this time favored a flat income arrangement. Many rural clergy defended these feasts because they were closely involved in the local life of their parishioners and saw the meaning feasts had in believers' lives and in the local rural communities. Priests fundamentally challenged the notion that they were "pagan" or "superstitious" in nature. As one rural priest wrote:

> Let us say that the celebrations of these saints arise from everyday considerations of the people. But, placing the hand on the heart, who among us would not admit that we ourselves frequently pray about our own everyday welfare and prosperity? And what in this is so blameworthy?[170]

Furthermore, as another priest explained, since the people generally did not know theological and liturgical fine points or the details of church history, there was no reason for them to prioritize feasts in the same way the universal church calendar did. The idea that they as clergy should, or even could, somehow discourage or limit the celebration of local feasts could only be suggested by someone who was not familiar with peasant life. For it was the local communities, not the clergy, who established these days.[171] Proceeding from this framework, the apologetic efforts of the profeast rural clergy focused on two main arguments: the observance of local rural feasts and popular attitudes toward work on these days.

Regarding attacks on the way believers spent their feasts, many rural clergy argued that feasts were not responsible for the abuses that often accompanied them. They thought more energy should be directed toward celebrating feasts properly rather than curtailing their numbers.[172] Defending their flocks, they questioned which social group could in fact claim uniformly to spend any of the major feast days in a "correct manner."[173] One priest even questioned the effects the military's prioritization of tsar's days over major Christian feasts had on young peasant conscripts. Perhaps above all else, however, defenders of local feasts questioned the critics regarding their identification of faith with superstition, and their confusion of the restful honoring of the feast days with the vice of sloth.[174] They took exception to the stereotypical dichotomous thinking of the critics, for whom there were only two possibilities: either a peasant labored in the fields or a peasant was drunk and idle.

In making this point, many clergy were reacting to what they saw as a more fundamental issue: an economically driven mindset for which consumption and production were the main criteria governing human life. Such a mindset, they claimed, was foreign to Christian goals and ethical values.[175] They opposed the idea that religious feasts should be replaced by generic "days off from labor." This concept, they argued, only demonstrated that those who advocated banning local festal celebrations measured human welfare solely in terms of material well-being. They accused their detractors of having no understanding that "the people" might have interests, concerns, and priorities that did not match those set by materialistic agendas.[176]

Regarding the issue of work and feast days, profeast clergy usually argued that the level of industrial, agricultural, and educational development was more important than the amount of time people actually labored. Their detractors would be better off spending their time developing more advanced forms of agricultural techniques and tools than worrying about the amount of time peasants worked.[177] In addition, clergy argued that the celebration of a feast day did not preclude all types of labor. Peasant communities distinguished between various types of work—communal and personal. And while labor that was considered communal might be censured by a community, personal work, which was a central part of the peasant economy, was routinely carried out on local feast days.[178]

It is noteworthy that in their sermons aimed at modifying certain behaviors associated with feasts, clergy routinely tried to shame members of their flocks by comparing them to other ethnic and religious groups, especially the Jewish faithful. In one characteristic story printed in the edifying journal *Healthy Readings for the Soul*, a school teacher, Dimitrii Korsunskii, found himself having to travel to the city of Poltava on the major feast of the Meeting of the Lord in the Temple (2 February). Along the way, at eight o'clock in the morning, he stopped at an inn to warm himself. There he found a group of drunken Orthodox Christians being lectured by the inn's keeper, a Jewish man, on the scandal of their violating the holiness of their feast and their being an affront to God and their Christ.[179] As one priest rhetorically asked about feast days, what must persons of other faiths think about Orthodox Christians who pass their feasts in such un-Christian ways?[180]

Faced with an expanding calendar of feasts, church and state officials debated these issues throughout the late nineteenth and early twentieth centuries. These debates reveal sharply differing priorities and standards by which feast days were evaluated. Both church and state officials felt it was their prerogative to decide these matters. On the local level, government officials sometimes openly expressed their reluctance when faced with the proposal of a new procession, which for them signaled another day off.[181] Concern for Russia's rural economy and agricultural production also led to the subject of local feasts figuring prominently in debates and studies of government commissions, debates in which the Holy Synod participated.

In 1862, at the initiative of the metropolitan of Moscow, Philaret (Drozdov), the Holy Synod discussed various difficulties associated with the celebration of the numerous feasts that constituted the Russian Orthodox calendar. As a result, it petitioned the tsar himself to allow tsar's days of secondary importance to be celebrated on the nearest Sunday and to allow the celebration of various military victories that had lost their meaning to be curtailed. The permission was granted.[182]

In 1867, at the request of civil authorities, the ober-procurator and the Holy Synod discussed the issue of establishing and curtailing feast days; they maintained that the prerogative to do so belonged to ecclesiastical authorities. In June 1868, the ober-procurator of the Holy Synod, Dimitrii Tolstoi, sent a note to the Ministry of Internal Affairs summarizing the Synod's discussion and giving his view of feasts. While insisting that feasts universally celebrated by the Orthodox Church and tsar's days must remain officially recognized public holidays, members of the Synod believed that local feasts were dispensable. It was their position that these feasts for the most part had no special religioethical significance and diverted celebrants' attention from agricultural work and led to drunkenness. The only way they could be effectively eliminated, in the Synod's eyes, would be to limit access to alcohol on these days. The celebration of these days for many people would then lose all value.

The notion that local feasts might have held more religious significance for many communities than the major feast days seems to have escaped both the ober-procurator and members of the Holy Synod. Nevertheless, they recognized that the local feasts had at least some degree of importance to the rural population. They warned that any feast-related policy would have to be enacted with utmost caution to avoid offending "the religious sensibilities of the people" and eliciting popular unrest because of a perceived intrusion into matters of their faith.[183]

In 1873, the Ministry of Internal Affairs' Commission for the Study of Agriculture and Agricultural Production in Russia drew on the ober-procurator's 1868 report when examining the issue of feast days. This commission took two actions. First, it asked the Synod to issue a "confidential invitation" to rural parish priests to use their moral influence to prompt their parishioners to fulfill all religious responsibilities "mandated by the church" yet take fewer days off from work annually. Second, the commission, in conjunction with the Holy Synod, established a special committee to investigate how to lessen the number of nonworking days among the rural population.[184]

The special committee, under the auspices of the commission, agreed with the ober-procurator's 1868 assessment, especially with the idea that any reduction in holidays should come only from the category of local feasts. The major problem with rural local feasts, from both the committee's and the Synod's points of view, was that there were no rules or regulations governing the establishment of these days. Believers needed no formal permission to celebrate a particular day; rural communities decided the matter.

The committee sorted local rural religious feasts into six groups: parish feasts; neighboring parish feasts; days commemorating particular saints not marked for special celebration in the official church calendar; days revered in memory of events—fire, storms, and so on; celebration of a locally revered icon; and days on which villages curtailed work for special prayer services on the occasion of an epidemic, drought, and so on.[185] According to the committee, except for the parish feast days, all other local feasts should be gradually eliminated by means of legal and administrative measures. They thought that rural areas should have a list of feast days approved by both civil and ecclesiastical authorities. These days should include no more than a single parish feast celebrated for one day. They could also include a limited number of exceptional feasts, such as a day set aside for a locally revered icon—for example, the day of the Kursk icon of the Mother of God in the Kursk diocese. Members of the special committee believed that this approved list of local feasts should be posted in churches, schools, and rural administrative buildings, where believers could easily see it. The committee envisioned that, except for the universally recognized church feasts, the tsar's days, and those days appearing on the recognized list, all other days were to be working days.

To reduce the number of additional feasts, the committee advised diocesan authorities to encourage peasants to name their churches in honor of especially revered saints or feasts that were already recognized public holidays.[186] It also recommended that believers limit their parish-related celebrations to the commemoration of the feast in honor of the main altar and that they not celebrate the feasts of side altars. Finally, the committee proposed holding all processions and prayer services on the occasion of drought or epidemic only on Sundays and established public holidays. This idea was ultimately rejected when one of the members of the committee pointed out that the significance of such prayer services lay precisely in their being a response to an immediate, often life-threatening situation. The prayer services would lose their meaning if they were regulated in the manner proposed.

In addition to regulating the frequency of local feast days, the committee discussed the relationship between the parish clergy and the local feasts. Members of the committee felt that parish clergy were not dependable allies in this matter because the large number of feasts was financially beneficial for them. Some members also wanted to see government officials monitoring clerical measures to limit and direct the course of such feasts. The committee, however, eventually dismissed as inappropriate any measures that would make civil administrators watchdogs over ecclesiastical activity. One member felt that such monitoring might interfere with ecclesiastical administrative activities. Other members, however, including the Holy Synod's representative, the priest I. V. Tolmachev, referred to what they were proposing not as interference but as the "friendly aspirations of two branches of administration, each in its own sphere, toward one and the same positive goal."[187]

The Holy Synod, however, concurred with those who preferred to keep the civil and ecclesiastical administrative spheres of influence separate when it came to the regulation of local feasts. While agreeing with the committee's findings on most points, the Synod politely pointed out that it had already considered most of the committee's suggestions regarding pastoral behavior. The Synod's main point of contention was another issue: the procedure for establishing feasts. The special committee had thought it proper that local petitions for the establishment of feast days be addressed to the district zemstvo assemblies, which in turn would petition the governor for final approval. The governor would then contact the local diocesan authorities to clarify whether or not the request had religious significance and merit. Finally, the request would be forwarded to the Ministry of Internal Affairs for final approval.[188]

The Synod found the proposal unacceptable because it would leave ecclesiastical authorities on the periphery of an essentially religious matter.

Because the special committee was ultimately concerned with economic production, its primary goal was to *limit* the number of local feast days. The Holy Synod, however, was not troubled so much by the economics of the matter. Its main concern was with procedure and the arbitrary means by which these feasts were established and celebrated. Therefore, it focused more on *regulating* local feasts. In the end, however, neither the economic concerns of the agricultural committee nor the Holy Synod's preoccupation with procedure brought either body closer to exploring or discussing the spiritual significance of local feasts.

The state never implemented the recommendations set forth by the special committee in the 1870s. Yet the issue of feasts and their celebration did not disappear. In 1904 the state finally took a limited, though decisive, legal step regarding work and feasts. Temporarily laying aside efforts to do away with local feasts—an issue that remained under active discussion—the government instead issued a ruling that sought to clarify the existing laws with respect to *voluntary* work on feast days.

Affirming that it was the government's responsibility to facilitate the dissemination of "sensible views" on the character of feast day celebrations, the 1904 ruling attempted to modify local civil officials' readings of existing legislation regarding work on feasts.[189] Claiming that local authorities had repeatedly misinterpreted the spirit of existing legislation and often had prevented peasants from working even on their own private plots of land, state officials now claimed that the notions of rest and "pious reverence" on feasts and public holidays did not preclude *voluntary* work. In order to prevent further confusion on this matter, state officials also deleted any reference in existing legislation to the prohibition of work on such days. They maintained that existing laws had been previously issued more as "moral advice" than as legal rulings. In its new "clarified" form, the law now stressed that each person could freely work on any day, including Sundays and feasts. No authority, including local village officials, could obstruct the individual in his or her voluntary efforts to do so. Should a person decide to work, he or she would neither be disobeying the Church nor violating the law.[190] In addition, the special committee came to the conclusion that in order to do away with the celebration of local feasts, the help of the Church would be needed. Therefore, turning to the ober-procurator of the Holy Synod, it requested that the Synod help to curtail the celebration of local feasts through educational means.

This ruling was revolutionary from a pastoral standpoint for two reasons. First, it challenged much of the message that clergy had preached throughout the postreform era—that the holiness of Sundays and feasts depended on spending them in a holy way, which by definition did not include attending to daily work that furthered one's material well-being. Sundays and feasts were days for *spiritual* labor and God-pleasing forms of rest and recreation. They should be spent in church, reading and discussing scripture or other religious writings, or performing works of charity, such as feeding the poor and visiting those in prison. While priests made a point of explaining that idleness and drinking were not proper alternatives to work, they did not generally advocate work instead of idleness. In fact, it was not uncommon for priests to include in their sermons or discussions stories that illustrated the tragedies befalling persons who ignored the Fourth Commandment and saw to "worldly matters" on Sundays and feasts.[191] The moral paralleled one found in some of the stories that lay people recounted: "God punishes those who forget him and do not follow his commandments."[192]

Second, the 1904 ruling, perhaps more than any other in pre-1905 Russia, disclosed the parting of ways between Church and state at the beginning of the twentieth century. By taking the initiative of *legislating* the priority of individual conscience in this matter, the state in effect distanced itself from the ecclesial community. Sacred time as kept and celebrated by Orthodoxy now became an optional time, one that each individual could accept or reject. Moreover, even prior to the Stolypin reforms that undermined the collective authority of peasant communes, this ruling neutralized the power the village communities had had in influencing individual behavior on feasts.[193]

The 1904 ruling challenged the widespread religious sensibilities that had kept the notion of "worldly cares" at odds with that of "keeping the feast holy." The new ruling, therefore, was nothing less than the state's attempt to refashion what it considered a faulty work ethic, especially for the rural believer. The Holy Synod attempted to make the best of the situation and, in its own July 1904 ruling, clarified the new law to pastors.[194] Explaining that the law was aimed first and foremost at correcting those "evils" that the arbitrary establishment of local village feasts tended to induce, the Synod encouraged rural priests to clarify for their flocks the "true meaning" of rest on Sundays and feasts. It urged priests to "establish firmly in the consciousness of the people" that work, and especially agricultural work, could never be displeasing to God. People should understand work as "a source of spiritual and physical health." Therefore, they should abstain from it only in those cases when it was necessary to regain strength or in cases when "some other equally holy or pure considerations" motivated them to do so. For many rural believers, a procession in honor of a vow, or a prayer service in thanksgiving for God's mercy, would no doubt qualify as a "holy or pure consideration."

The Synod also refashioned the standard reading of scriptural texts regarding work on Sundays and feasts. It maintained that the Lord's commandment did not have the goal of tearing a person away from daily work, as if work in and of itself were displeasing to God. It also explained that God had not forbidden every type of work on the Sabbath. The only work that was unconditionally forbidden was that motivated by profit or greed, which led a person to forget God. The Synod then reiterated a point that clergy had frequently made in the past: not all types of rest fulfilled God's Fourth Commandment. Only free time spent "sanctifying" the feasts qualified. Since the

Church did not condone empty idleness, Synod officials urged parish priests to explain that, except for Sundays and the twelve major feasts, parishioners should mark the remainder of the feasts, including locally celebrated ones, only with a Divine Liturgy. Following the Liturgy, all those who wished to work should be given the blessing to do so. In order to be pleasing to God, the observance of Sundays and feasts had to be a sacrifice. And by definition a sacrifice had to be voluntary. What was done against one's will was not a sacrifice and would neither please God nor benefit one's soul.

Churchmen had mixed responses to this law. Bishop Nikon (Rozhdest-venskii) of Vologda reported that the new law caused a stir in rural parishes. The new message, going as it did against the age-old axiom that attending to "worldly cares" did not correspond to the God-pleasing pastimes demanded by holy days, only sowed confusion among rural believers.[195] Still other clergy noted the law's positive effect of eliminating the element of coercion in the celebration of feasts. As one clerical publicist noted, the law might indeed reduce the number of persons observing holy days, but such a reduction would have a purifying effect on the ecclesial community. Why, he asked, did the church community need members who did not willfully belong to and identify with it?[196]

Despite such reactions, the 1904 law appears not to have radically altered either clerical or lay attitudes on a widespread scale. Sermons and periliturgical discussions published after 1904 still expressed the pre-1904 view that Sundays and holidays should be days spent in spiritual labor. Therefore, it is not surprising that in 1909 the issue of feasts arose once again, this time under the auspices of a special commission appointed by the State Council.

State officials were still disturbed by widespread views that working on feast days was sinful. They believed such attitudes had a negative moral effect on the population by reinforcing laziness and idleness. They maintained that past efforts to influence people morally through the help of local clergy had been fruitless. They also believed it would be impossible to abolish these feasts simply through legislative fiat. State officials, therefore, changed tactics again and returned to the idea of simply reducing the number of public holidays, from the current ninety-one to sixty-three.[197] In particular, they wanted to eliminate multiple days associated with the celebration of such feasts as Easter and Christmas. Instead of the usual week associated with Easter, the civil calendar would reflect only two days. Similarly, they planned to eliminate days off that corresponded with such Orthodox feasts as the Transfiguration, Ascension, the Nativity and Dormition of the Mother of God, the Elevation of the Cross, and the Kazan icon of the Mother of God. They even considered eliminating Good Friday as a day off, but this idea elicited strong reaction from churchmen.[198]

State officials emphasized that the calendar of days that they set would affect government administrative offices and such state enterprises as railway transportation and schools. Other types of labor would always have their own work schedules because of practical demands, such as seasonal considerations.

But even among state-run functions, complete uniformity was not expected, since areas like customs inspection or railway travel could not stop for feasts. Nevertheless, state officials hoped that a more balanced listing would gradually affect the celebration of rural feasts. Those rural believers who happened to visit a city or provincial town on a feast day, they reasoned, would be struck by the fact that administrative offices and schools still functioned. Knowing that such an arrangement was backed by state authorities, they might reconsider the planning of their own feasts. An even greater educational role would be served by having schools open on certain feasts; children would then be better conditioned to work. In the end, state officials hoped such a measure would not only raise the economic standard of living but also correct one of Russia's national shortcomings: idleness.[199] They defended their proposal by insisting that it was not meant to affect the religious celebration of feasts or the perceived sanctity of such days. State officials instead emphasized the sacred notion of work. They showed that state legislation in Russia forbidding work was in itself a "modern" innovation, dating to the seventeenth century. Before that, no such laws existed. In other words, by returning to Russia's "ancient ways" and by rescinding work-related restrictions on public holidays, state officials hoped to play on and endorse positive Orthodox views of labor as central to the Christian way of life and salvation.

The proposal was greeted with mixed reviews. A commission that was established under the auspices of the State Council to review the proposal did not agree, for instance, with the exclusion of 8 September (Nativity of the Mother of God), 6 December (feast of St. Nicholas), or Good Friday from the roster of days off. Although the commission agreed, in principle, that in limiting the number of days off the state was not interfering in the realm of church affairs since it was not abolishing the feast days from the church calendar, the commission also noted that state officials had to take into account the religious sensibilities of the people when making their changes. Accordingly, members of the commission also thought that for certain other days (e.g., 2 February, Meeting of the Lord in the Temple) it would be best for the work day to begin at noon, following the Divine Liturgy.[200]

Churchmen also had mixed opinions about the proposed legislation. The Holy Synod agreed that a full week of time off for Easter was excessive and could be cut back; it also believed that some of the tsar's days might be moved to the nearest Sunday. However, members of the Synod were adamant about retaining the twelve major church feasts as part of the roster of days off. Individual hierarchs were much more vocal. Bishops Nikon of Vologda and Nikolai of Warsaw, for instance, reacted to what they perceived as state intrusion into religious matters. Comparing Russia's government officials to Egypt's Pharaoh who refused to allow the Israelites to glorify their God (Exod. 5:17–18), Nikon criticized the proposal as potentially enslaving believers to economic interests and violating their freedom of conscience.[201] Nikolai contended that the proposed law directly conflicted with Christian understandings of the meaning of life and attempted to preempt the proper setting of sacred time. This act, Nikolai claimed, lay in the hands of God.[202] Questioning the reception of the new legislation among "the people," Nikon predicted that curtailing public holidays, especially those that corresponded with feasts of Mary, would only undermine state authority in peoples' minds. Finally, both hierarchs questioned the religious sensibilities behind the proposal, with bishop Nikon rhetorically asking "has not our government converted to the faith of the Germans?"[203]

Other ecclesiastical publicists were not so negatively disposed to the new law. V. Pravdin, for instance, writing in the liberal *Church-Social Herald*, thought that fears regarding the negative effect of such legislation on the religious sensibilities of the population at large were unfounded. He observed that industrial and factory workers already had their own schedule of feasts and the peasantry traditionally had never followed the schedule of public holidays. The only persons who would be directly affected by the new "official" list of public holidays would be government bureaucrats and so-called lesser and middle intelligentsia, whose holiday festivities found them more in theaters and cinemas than in churches. The issue at hand, Pravdin maintained, was a purely civil matter. Ecclesiastical holidays and religious sensibilities were not and should not be the state's concern.[204]

The late nineteenth and early twentieth centuries saw several state attempts to redefine prevailing notions of celebration and work and ultimately to disentangle the civil from the church calendar. While very much conscious of the calendar of Orthodox feasts that weighed heavily in the setting of the civil calendar, state officials strove to reset the civil calendar according to an economically based standard that colored their vision of national well-being. Many statesmen believed it was no longer the state's place to designate churchgoing as an activity to pursued on holidays.[205] Despite their attempts, however, local feasts remained a firmly rooted feature of Orthodoxy not only up to 1917 but afterward as well.[206] Strong ancestral ties and the experience of a God who was active in creation and in their daily lives continued to form a powerful sense of community among believers. Often emerging because of personal vows, local feasts not only displayed ubiquitous characteristics of classical Christian worship—commemoration of saving events, offering and sacrifice, thanksgiving and doxology, repentance and supplication—but also integrated universally recognized traits of Orthodox worship, such as processions and veneration of saints and icons, into the fabric of local, especially village, community life.[207] In so doing, such feasts grounded the Orthodox calendar, so that feasts that bore witness to biblical events, saints, or icons of universal or national significance mixed with feasts that testified to similar though chronologically and geographically more immediate events. The God of Abraham, Isaac, and Jacob, who was incarnate for human salvation, had also made himself known among them, in their villages, towns, and cities.

With respect to the celebration of sacred time, Orthodoxy found itself positioned on two fronts: society at large and that of its own communal life.

Faced with a society that found itself in the throes of modernization, ecclesiastical officials attempted to alleviate the tensions between the public celebration of Orthodox feasts and the demands of modernity for economic progress by offering alternative ways of understanding celebration, work, and rest. At the same time, these officials generally resisted any proposed changes in the public holiday schedule and in so doing revealed their inability or unwillingness to separate the spheres of church and state. Moreover, by struggling to maintain the community as a central feature of Orthodox religious life, churchmen generally resisted the state's efforts to make festal observances a purely private concern.

Yet when viewing feasts in general and local feasts in particular from the perspective of the church's internal life, churchmen were much more mixed in their views. Faced with a lack of conscious religious differentiation between certain peasant and faith communities, especially before 1905, churchmen were often themselves skeptical about the intentions of their flock. No less than their state counterparts, they railed against those whose understanding of celebration led to idleness and drinking. Finding it simpler to centralize the celebration of feasts than to disentangle the notions of holy day and holiday at the local level, many ecclesiastical authorities supported the idea of a uniformly celebrated schedule of feasts throughout Russia, with local variations stopping at the level of parish feasts. Such an idea in part grew out of a vision of Orthodoxy in which local aspects of faith were in general subordinated to national and universal ones. Insofar as feasts involved a collective centering in a common recollection of events and persons from sacred history, the consolidation of those recollections almost exclusively around more broadly known Christian feasts and nationally relevant events would have left more local and immediate acts of God outside liturgical purview. For many sincere lay believers, such a resetting would have likely threatened the very mechanism by which their lives were incorporated in that liturgical time.

# 5

⤜⟩⤏

# Icons

## Miracles, Memory, and Sacred History

An icon specially honored by the people—this is the glory and best
adornment of the Church. It is the precious treasure of the people, an
inexhaustible source of spiritual vitality and comfort for all.

—FR. IOANN PARYSHEV, Eniseisk diocese, 1912

In their scholarly pursuit of the meaning of icons in Orthodox Christianity,
art historians and theologians often focus almost exclusively on the visual
characteristics of the icon and on the prototype the image depicts.[1] Accordingly, they base their respective interpretations on the reading of the visual
image and the particular message that it communicates to the faith community.
Historically, however, the meaning of icons for individual believers and for
the faith community at large in Orthodox Christianity stemmed not merely
from the visual image and the narrative it depicts but also from the story
behind a particular icon, from the believers' experiences associated with an
icon, which comprised that icon's history or life and led to its special veneration.[2] Such stories usually involved signs or miracles that led believers to
distinguish particular icons from among the many others in their religious
lives.[3] To a large extent, the entire tradition of icon veneration in the Christian
East rested on these stories, which were officially embraced by the Orthodox
Church during the Seventh Ecumenical Council, when they were adduced to
establish the legitimacy of the practice of icon veneration in general.[4]

Specially revered icons were a prominent feature of the religious landscape
of late nineteenth- and early twentieth-century Russia. Russia at this time
had countless specially revered icons, most of which were of the Mother of
God, with some contemporaries attributing one to every parish or even
village.[5] Furthermore, believers' ongoing experiences with icons resulted in
the appearance of numerous new specially revered icons during this period.
Both men and women from diverse socioeconomic and educational backgrounds not only participated in venerating these icons but were responsible
for initiating their special veneration in the first place. In 1908, for example,

5.1 Miracle-working icon of the Mother of God
named "Kozel'shchanskaia," also known as the
"Kozelshchina" icon. Poltava diocese. Second half of
the nineteenth century. Photograph. The Russian
State Historical Archive, St. Petersburg (f. 835, op. 2,
d. 140, l. 1).

A. Vysotskii countered a stereotypic association between miracle-working icons and the "superstitious" simple folk by pointing out that events leading to the special veneration of one of the most popular and widely publicized icons of the late nineteenth century—the Mother of God named "Kozelsh-china"—involved members of an "enlightened, educated family"[6] (fig. 5.1). Similarly, reports of specially revered icons received by the Holy Synod frequently mentioned the diverse social composition of believers who gathered to venerate them, noting that among such people were not only the "simple folk" but the educated and the "highly respected," as well as members of the military and clergy.[7] On occasion, these icons also led to blurred denominational lines, with Old Believers, Lutherans, and Catholics reportedly participating in their veneration.[8]

The Orthodox Church had no firmly established rules by which particular icons became officially recognized as miracle working, although procedures for investigating reports of such icons had been set in place in the early eighteenth century.[9] Despite the establishment of these procedures, which involved the appointment of a diocesan investigative commission as well as physicians who testified to the veracity of reported healings, icons could and sometimes did become officially revered as miracle-working without any formal proceedings. Several terms were used to describe such icons—miracle-working (*chudotvornye*), locally revered (*mestnochtimye*), and specially revered (*osobochtimye*)—and the criteria for using one term over another were not always clearly defined.[10] While at least some ecclesiastical officials considered it proper to refer to an icon as miracle working only if so sanctioned by the Holy Synod, both clergy and laity regularly used that term in reference to icons not officially sanctioned.[11] Indeed, the very definition of officialdom in prerevolutionary Russian Orthodoxy with respect to the special veneration of icons is highly ambiguous. Out of the numerous specially revered icons of the Mother of God, for example, only some twenty-five had official miracle-working status in the sense that they enjoyed national recognition and were listed in the liturgical Menaion.[12] At the same time, on the local level, diocesan bishops and parish clergy also officially recognized many more icons of Mary as miracle working. Given the lack of formal rules governing the categorization of specially revered icons, the process by which an icon became publicly honored as miracle working offers unique insight into the working dynamics of Orthodox ecclesial life, and especially into the laity's role in that life.

The scope and complexity of ecclesial issues that the special veneration of icons entailed become apparent only with an understanding of the cult of such icons at the grassroots. Therefore, this chapter begins by describing the genesis of an icon's special veneration and the religious dynamics this veneration set in motion at the local level. It looks at the ways an icon initially drew believers' attention and the process by which its veneration moved from an isolated individual's religious experience to a communal celebration. It then situates this grassroots behavior in its broader religious and theological context by considering the devotional teachings on miracle-working icons at the time. The main purpose of these first three sections is to explore the religious means by which such icons linked individuals and local ecclesial communities into a larger body of faithful. Finally, I turn to the pockets of conflict that periodically surfaced within the ecclesial community over these icons and to the tensions within the Church that were exacerbated by such conflicts in the critical years before Russia's 1917 revolutions. What potential challenges might have these icons—so often signs of communal coherence—presented to the believer's experience and conception of church?

## The Birth of a Specially Revered Icon

The life of a specially revered icon usually began with an individual's perceived encounter with the sacred by means of a particular icon. An event would take place in which believers discerned a sign that informed them of a sacred presence. In addition to more dramatic occurrences such as experiencing detailed dreams or hearing voices,[13] other signs commonly associated with such icons included the apparent self-cleaning or renewal (*obnovlenie, ponovlenie*) of an icon[14] or the unusual flickering or self-lighting of a candle or lampada that burned before it.[15]

The most widespread type of specially revered icon, not only during this period but in the history of Russian Orthodoxy as a whole, was the so-called *iavlennaia*, or epiphanic icon.[16] Believers considered such an icon extraordinary, not merely because it was "found" (*obretennaia*) but because they perceived a sign in the unusual manner in which it first appeared to them—in a field, on a riverbank, in a tree, or in a well. They understood its epiphany as providential—God, as well as the saint depicted, intended for the icon to appear at that particular place and time.

As with other perceived signs that initially marked certain icons as special, believers saw these appearances as revelatory and described the perceived signs as resulting from God's grace (*blagodat'*) and mercy (*milost'*) or from the activity of the Holy Spirit.[17] The noblewoman Alexandra Eck, for instance, referred to the self-renewal of her icon as the work of God's "unseen hand" occurring by his "divine consent."[18] Having had such an experience, believers deemed that the only proper response was to bear witness to what they had seen, to give thanks, and to glorify God—and the icon involved.

An example of the process by which an icon gained exceptional attention can be seen in the case of an icon of the Mother of God named "It Is Truly Meet" (*Dostoino Est'*) in the Vladimir diocese (fig. 5.2).[19] In the 1870s, not long after her marriage, Vera Iakovleva, from the village Ivanovo, suffered a physical breakdown. She could no longer carry out the normal household duties expected of a peasant woman. Her husband stayed with her for three years and then, seeing that she was not getting better, left her and went to Astrakhan to develop his trading business.

As an invalid who could not carry out her share of household or community responsibilities, Iakovleva became a burden to her family and a social outcast. Feeling oppressed by her village community, she left for the town of Murom, where she lived hand-to-mouth. When her condition worsened and she could no longer live alone, she tried to live with various family members but was not well received. Eventually, she began praying regularly for her life to end.

One evening in the autumn of 1875, while staying with her sister in the village of Kovardishch, Iakovleva dozed off and dreamt of two elderly monks

**5.2**  An icon of the Mother of God named "It is Truly
Meet" (*Dostoino Est'*). Prior to 1850. From the private
collection of Robin R. Jones, M.D.

who carried with them an icon of the Mother of God. They urged her to pray
before the icon, which she did with abundant tears. The same dream repeated
itself several months later, this time with the monks identifying the iconographic type as *Dostoino Est'*. As a type, the icon of the Mother of God named
"It Is Truly Meet" was not new to Russia. The name of this icon is connected
with a well-known liturgical hymn of the same name in honor of the Theotokos. The icon's story is set on Mount Athos in the late tenth century. An
unknown monk visited a novice while he was praying in his cell. During
prayer, the novice was about to chant the words from the *Magnificat*, when
the guest unexpectedly interrupted and began singing a new hymn, which
began with the words "It Is Truly Meet." Taken aback, the novice requested
that the monk write down the words for him. The latter did so by carving the
words in a stone slab with his finger. The stranger then revealed himself as the
Archangel Gabriel and disappeared.[20]

Having been urged in her dream to pray before this icon, Iakovleva bowed down before it in prayer. As she did so, she heard the Mother of God speak to her, directing her to have the icon made. She had promised help and protection to Iakovleva and "to all Orthodox Christians" who prayed before this icon regularly. On the next day, Iakovleva felt relief from her illness, from which she had by then suffered for more than ten years. Soon she became completely healthy and able to work as usual.[21]

Iakovleva's story, however, did not end here, and the events that followed were just as crucial to the icon's eventual special recognition as the initial dream event itself. First, Iakovleva did not attempt to conceal her religious experiences. Indeed, specially revered icons earned their status primarily because people generally felt compelled to talk about, and in most cases even publicly proclaim, their experiences. Iakovleva, as well as others, appeared to share the belief that such revelatory events were not private affairs but had a direct relevance for the believing public.

Some believers saw the failure to proclaim such an experience as a sin. For example, in telling others about the myrrh streaming from the hand of their family icon of the Mother of God, a hospital supervisor and his wife from the Perm diocese in 1886 claimed that not doing so could lead to grave consequences: "the concealment of something sacred lays a mortal sin on the soul."[22] These sentiments were supported by well-known icon narratives in which the Virgin and saints directed individuals to tell others of the experiences.

In addition to relating her experiences to family members and neighbors, Iakovleva also sought to "church" her experience by relating it to the parish priest. According to a law instituted in the eighteenth century and still active in the late nineteenth, it was considered a statutory crime to spread rumors about false miracles;[23] believers such as Iakovleva, however, obviously did not consider what they were reporting to be false. They routinely notified parish clergy of personal religious experiences and, as a group of parishioners from the Ekaterinoslavl diocese proclaimed, were ready to "suffer the punishment of the law" if their assertions did not prove true.[24]

Believers often explained this notification of the parish priest on the basis of the religious experience itself. Characteristically, in 1879 two shepherd boys from the Simbirsk diocese who had had visions of an icon in a spring had also heard a voice directing them to go to their parish priest. The boys were to tell him and members of the village community to gather immediately for a Divine Liturgy and then to gather for prayer at the place they had seen the icon.[25] Similarly in 1893, while ringing the church bell, a pious fourteen-year-old peasant boy from the Kazan diocese encountered "a maiden clothed in white" who directed him to notify the priest about a particular icon that had been carelessly abandoned in the church's storage area. Although the boy had immediately proclaimed to others what had occurred, he neglected to tell the parish priest. That night he had a dream in which angels reminded him to notify the parish priest of the abandoned icon.[26]

Believers usually considered a priest's participation as part of what it meant to specially honor an icon. This was so even when believers did not immediately donate a specially revered icon to the parish church, as Iakovleva had.[27] At a minimum, they wanted a priest to honor the icon by conducting a prayer service in their homes.[28] Others, however, desired more. In 1870, the peasant widow Matrona from the Moscow diocese requested that the parish priest conduct prayer services whenever unusually large crowds of people gathered to venerate the icon of St. Nicholas and the Virgin Mary in her home; furthermore, she wanted her icon taken in procession to the parish church on feast days.[29]

Priests' reactions to such experiences were mixed, ranging from complete dismissal to active embrace. The participation of priests in the celebration of the icons, however, was frequent enough to preclude this phenomenon from being categorized exclusively in terms of folk religion or lay Orthodoxy. By complying with parishioners' requests to celebrate a particular icon, priests gave the events and experiences associated with that icon an ecclesial (and not merely public) orientation. In writing synodal authorities about a specially revered icon of the Mother of God that had been in her family for more than two hundred years, the townswoman Natal'ia Maslenikova from Kaluga described how local priests had conducted prayer services in her home not only on her request but on the request of others as well.[30] Similarly, in 1879 a priest conducted prayer services on the site where two peasant women from the village of Betino in the Tambov diocese had found an icon of Christ. He also gave his blessing to the parishioners' desires to construct a chapel at the site.[31] In 1894, a priest from the Novgorod diocese spoke publicly in church about an icon that had appeared to one of his female parishioners in a dream and then invited everyone present to venerate the icon.[32] The same year a priest from the Poltava diocese acknowledged the "special" character of an icon by bringing his ill daughter to the home where it had miraculously renewed itself.[33] In another case, in 1900, a priest from the town of Trubchevsk in the Orel diocese carried a "self-renewed" icon from the home of the townswoman Kseniia Pontriagina to the town's cathedral in a formal procession accompanied by bell-ringing from the town's churches.[34]

Once individuals related their extraordinary experiences to others, the veneration of a particular icon shifted from being a matter of private and insular devotion to one of mutual religious concern among believers, even when the icon remained in a private home. While at this point an icon's special veneration was still rooted primarily in the personal concerns of each individual, the act of gathering allowed for the development of a religious dynamic that transcended the individual. In this stage of an icon's special veneration, local believers celebrated the icon in recognition that what had occurred specifically for an individual like Iakovleva had taken place among all of them. In other words, in Iakovleva's case, believers saw the grace granted personally to her as potentially available to all individuals who venerated the icon. Consequently, news of signs associated with icons drew believers not only from the immediate area but from neighboring districts and even from other dioceses. In 1909 the bishop of Penza, Mitrofan, reported to the Holy Synod that in the span of two weeks more than five thousand people, many of whom went to confession and received Communion, had come to venerate an icon of the Mother of God that had been found in the village of Vladyk-ino.[35] Reports of healings usually surfaced as soon as believers began flocking to such icons. In these gatherings, with their reverential affinity and kinship in prayer, a shared veneration emerged from otherwise private devotion. As representatives of the village of Kamennyi Brod wrote with respect to the specially revered icon in their village, "being linked together through prayer with this icon filled with grace serves to strengthen Orthodoxy."[36]

As the story of a specially revered icon unfolded, the icon rarely remained exclusively the subject of personal piety. Individual believers routinely associ-ated such icons not only with their personal lives but also with the fate of their immediate community, the entire region, and sometimes even the Russian nation as a whole. In 1895, parishioners from the church in the village of Nikolo-Zamoshe (Iaroslavl diocese) wrote that God had "blessed their local-ity" through an icon's self-renewal in the home of one their fellow parishion-ers, the peasant Marem'iana Guzanova.[37] In 1909, when believers from St. Timothy parish in the Poltava diocese wrote about an icon of the Three Hierarchs that had inexplicably renewed itself in the home of a widow in their parish, they spoke of the event as a revelation to the entire community: "The Lord God, out of the abundance of His mercy, granted *our parish* His grace in the form of the images of the Three Hierarchs."[38] Similarly, in 1912, believers from St. Nicholas parish in the Eniseisk diocese recognized as epiphanic an icon of the Mother of God named "The Joy of All Who Sorrow." While it had originally "appeared" to a man and his young niece who had gone to a spring on a hot July day in 1911, the details of the lives of the two persons who found this icon soon became secondary. Believers in the community, which for the past four years had experienced poor harvests and drought, sensed that the icon was "a sign of God's benevolence" to them all. God had manifested this sign to them as a suffering community during their "days of sorrow and tribulation." The icon, they claimed, brought "joy and merciful serenity" into their collective lives.[39] Once such an icon remained long enough in a local community, it frequently became an integral part of that community's history and even a symbol of local identity. As a group of residents from the town of Tikhvin in the Novgorod diocese wrote in 1888 regarding a miracle-working icon of the Mother of God housed in the town's monastery, "with this icon our grandfathers and fathers were born, lived, and died. Tikhvin cannot imagine itself without it."[40]

The lives of most specially revered icons were typified by a mixture of individual and communal experiences, in which the fates of sometimes anon-ymous persons designated only by the strands of beads or gifts they left before the icon intertwined with the fate of one or more villages or towns.[41] For instance, the special veneration of the Bogoliubov icon of the Mother of God in the village of Zimarovo in the Riazan diocese reportedly began in the eighteenth century, in the Moscow home of the village's noble landowner, Vasilii Lopukhin. In 1771 an unidentified sick man came to Lopukhin's home and asked to have a prayer service conducted before this icon. The man claimed he had been directed to this particular icon by a revelation in a dream. Lopukhin searched his home for the icon, eventually finding it in the attic among piles of discarded items. After the man was healed, news of the icon spread throughout Moscow. Eventually, in 1780, Lopukhin donated the icon to the parish church on his estate in Zimarovo.

In Zimarovo it enjoyed the favor not only of individual believers but of the entire village, as well as of the neighboring towns of Skopin, Riazhsk, Spasskoe, and Ranenburg. On the occasion of cholera outbreaks in 1831, 1848, 1861, 1871, and 1892, these towns held public processions with this icon and attributed the cessation of the epidemics to the icon's presence. In 1860 believers in the provincial capital of Riazan also attributed their relief from a cholera epidemic to this icon, the veneration of which took place in a complex series of services and processions that involved all of the city's churches.[42]

In some instances, believers associated the special veneration of an icon with the fate of Russia as a whole. During World War I, Nicholas II himself requested that the well-known icon of the Mother of God named "Vladimir" be brought to the General Headquarters at the war front.[43] The life of the icon, which began outside the borders of Russia, was intimately tied to the history of the Russian nation. The icon belonged to that group of Marian images that have been attributed to the brush of the evangelist Luke.[44] According to the Vladimir icon's story, it was brought to Russia in the twelfth century as a gift from the patriarch of Constantinople, Lukas Chrysoberges, to the grand prince of Kiev, Iurii Dokgorukii. It traveled with Iurii's son, Prince Andrei, in the mid–twelfth century to northern Russia and became associated with the establishment of the principality of Moscow as Russia's center. Throughout the following centuries, believers attributed the survival and welfare of the Russian state, especially during times of national crisis, to the protection of the Mother of God through this icon.[45] Now, in the midst of World War I, Nicholas II turned to this icon in distress and hope, as had his forefathers.

Common laity also associated specially revered icons with the nation's welfare. In 1903 a veteran of the Crimean War had a dream of the Mother of God standing on the banks of a sea, holding a linen cloth with the image of Christ (fig. 5.3). She warned him that Russia would soon become involved in a difficult war on the shores of a distant sea and directed him to have an image of her depicted as he saw her in the dream. Many believers subsequently tied this icon, which came to be known as "The Victory of the Blessed Mother of God," to Russia's fate in the Russo-Japanese war. The icon started on a long odyssey to Port Arthur that involved members of the imperial family, statesmen, and church hierarchs along the way through Vladivostok. Many believers attributed Russia's defeat in that war to the fact that the icon never made it

5.3 An image of the Mother of God named "Port Arthur," also known as "The Victory of the Blessed Mother of God." From V. N. Mal'kovskii, comp., *Skazanie ob ikone "Torzhestvo Presviatyia Bogoroditsy" izvestnoi po imenem Port-Arturskoi Bozhiei Materi.* (Tver, 1906).

to Port Arthur.[46] In addition, in 1916 the head chaplain serving Russia's military and naval forces declined a petition from a group of residents from the Perm diocese in which they had asked to send their town's specially revered icon to the war front. The army, he explained, could not accommodate a long line of similar requests.[47]

The celebration of specially revered icons, therefore, was not merely the commemoration of the person or the episode in salvation history that was depicted in the image. This celebration also encompassed the individuals and communities who were honoring these icons in the historical present. It involved the recognition and remembrance of those like Vera Iakovleva who were responsible for the special veneration of an icon in the first place, as well as the individuals who would then gather before the icon in the hopes that their own lives might become woven into the narrative that made the icon special. In this way, the stories behind specially venerated icons often served as keepers of collective memories on both the local and the national level.

‑‑◉◉‑‑

## The Expansion of an Icon's Community

Both laity and clergy helped to expand the geographic parameters in which an icon was known and revered in several ways. Historically in Russia, many locally revered icons remained known through oral accounts and oral histories, as well as local liturgical use and commemoration.[48] In the late nineteenth century, however, knowledge of many icons spread through the increased publication and distribution of icon-related stories, both in diocesan newspapers and separately in the form of edifying devotional pamphlets. The increased printing of such stories contributed in part to making the widespread veneration of these icons a uniquely modern phenomenon.

The impact of the pamphlets can be seen when examining the spread of the story associated with the "Abalak" icon of the Mother of God from the Tobolsk diocese (fig. 5.4). In the summer of 1877, a group of pilgrims or wanderers (*stranniki*) came from central Russia to Siberia in order to venerate its holy sites. During their stay at the monastery where this specially revered icon of the Mother of God was housed, the pilgrims obtained published pamphlets of its life. On their way home, they stopped in the provincial capital of Nizhnii Novgorod and took lodging in the home of Glafira Ivanova, the poor wife of a soldier. In return for her hospitality, they left as a gift a pamphlet describing the story of the icon of the Mother of God named "Abalak." When Glafira finally read the book, she "became consumed with some sort of special zeal" and began to tell everyone she met about the pamphlet she had read. Between 1878 and 1880 the Abalak monastery in the Tobolsk diocese received more than one hundred and fifty orders from Nizhnii Novgorod for the same pamphlet.[49]

Knowledge of an icon's story, however, did not yet mean special devotion toward the icon. Such special devotion or fervor, facilitated by prayer before the image, was greatly fostered by dissemination of copies of that icon. Glafira Ivanovna in Nizhnii Novgorod, for instance, not only told people about the icon's story but encouraged invalids to have a copy of it made and to pray before it. As a result, several recorded healings took place, including, as one devotional pamphlet noted, the "moral" healing of an alcoholic father who witnessed his own son's healing from prayer before a copy of this icon. Between 1878 and 1880 believers from Nizhnii Novgorod had ordered more than six hundred copies of this icon from local iconographers. Such copies were soon found in the city's churches.[50]

Believers did not necessarily wait for episcopal sanction of their icons to distribute copies of them. In 1911 the priest Ioann Paryshev from St. Nicholas church in the Eniseisk diocese allowed lithographic copies of an epiphanic icon of the Mother of God named "The Joy of All Who Sorrow" to be distributed in the parish church just weeks after that type of icon had been discovered by a twelve-year-old girl and her uncle.[51] The very making and

5.4   Miracle-working icon of the Mother of God
named "Abalak." From Prot. A. Sulotskii, *Skazanie ob
ikone Bozhiei Materi imenuemoi Abalatskoiu i o
vazhneishikh kopeia s neia s izobrazheniem ikony Abalatskoi
Bozhiei Materi*, 5th ed. (Omsk, 1877).

distribution of such copies helped to sustain the life of the original and
geographically expanded the boundaries of the community that specially revered it.

Copies of well-known miracle-working icons frequently became specially revered themselves. The speed of this process is evident in the case of
the "Kozelshchina" icon of the Mother of God (fig. 5.1). Its fame began in
1881 when Maria, the daughter of Count Vladimir Ivanovich Kapnist, was
cured in the village of Kozelshchina in the Poltava diocese. People immediately began flocking to the Kapnist estate, with Sundays and feast days drawing
as many as five thousand persons.[52] In 1885 miracles from a copy of this icon
were reported in the Astrakhan diocese and in 1890 in the Tver diocese.[53] By

1894, a copy of this icon was also taken to the homes of Moscow residents for prayer services on request.[54]

Copies of miracle-working icons played an important role in Russia's culture of icon veneration, enabling individuals and communities to identify more closely with a well-known image. While visually associated with the original, copies allowed individuals or entire communities to attach their own stories to the image, thereby making a prototype located at a great distance meaningful for them. In the aforementioned case of Vera Iakovleva, for instance, the icon type ("It Is Truly Meet") originated in Greece. With Vera Iakovleva's experience, however, the life of this iconographic type was updated, and the icon became specifically relevant for this particular community. Indeed, national cults of icons of the Virgin Mary, such as the Kazan icon of the Mother of God, were sustained in large part by the proliferation of specially revered copies of that image, many of which had their own narratives associated with them.

One of the most spectacular illustrations of an icon linking individuals and communities located over a wide geographic expanse can be seen in so-called icon visitations (poseshchenie ikony), which occurred with increasing frequency in the nineteenth and early twentieth centuries (see table 5.1). These visitations involved processions with icons normally kept in urban cathedrals, monasteries, or parish churches. On request, these icons were brought to other communities and into the homes of believers in these communities (fig. 5.5). Technically, icon visitations could be seen as a form of procession. In general processions, however, the focus of the activity was on the act of processing itself. In icon visitations, the focus was on the particular icon being carried. Such visitations were a widespread phenomenon in European Russia before 1917 that found their way into the work of Russia's artists (fig. 5.6). The itinerary for a specially revered icon could include travel to villages within a particular parish, as well as to other districts, or even dioceses.[55] In the 1890s, diocesan bishops reported that many icon visitations had been long-established events, taking place since "time immemorial." In some dioceses, however, a large proportion of visitations began, or at least were officially registered, during the second half of the nineteenth century.[56] Moreover, many icons that had been making visitations for generations found their travel itineraries expanding throughout the postreform period.

The expansion of the itinerary for the specially revered icons from the Dormition Trifonov monastery in the Viatka diocese reflects the persistent, and even growing, popularity of these visitations. At the end of the eighteenth century, two icons from the monastery traveled for two months of the summer to two cities and several villages. By the end of the nineteenth century, this itinerary had grown to include four icons traveling to eight cities, ten factories, and more than two hundred villages during a seven-month period. Moreover, the visitations had initially taken place only once every other year but from 1879 on had been annual.[57]

TABLE 5.1    Number of Icons Making Visitations in 1894
(by Diocese[a])

| Diocese | Number of icons making visitation |
|---|---|
| Moscow | 70 |
| Kostroma | 65 |
| Pskov | 55 |
| Viatka | 49 |
| Vladimir | 40 |
| Orel | 36 |
| Iaroslavl | 35 |
| Kazan | 26 |
| Vologda | 26 |
| Tver | 24 |
| Kursk | 23 |
| Riazan | 20 |
| Novgorod | 20 |
| Chernigov | 19 |
| St. Petersburg | 19 |
| Perm | 18 |
| Kaluga | 16 |
| Tambov | 15 |
| Nizhnii Novgorod | 13 |
| Tobolsk | 13 |
| Smolensk | 12 |
| Tula | 12 |
| Voronezh | 12 |

[a]RGIA, f.796, op. 187, d. 6929. Dioceses not listed had fewer than ten icons making annual visitations. These figures include visitations by specially venerated crosses as well; such visitations were relatively few. Diocesan bishops in their reports did not specify the criteria they used to determine which icons were specially revered. For example, the bishop of Viatka distinguished between specially revered icons and icons that traveled in processions but were not specially revered. Such a distinction can be questioned, however, since parish clergy and believers might have specially venerated an icon they included in a procession. Because of these and other inconsistencies, it is best to take these figures as approximations. Finally, it should be noted that the number of icon visitations does not correspond to the number of specially revered icons found in any given diocese. As the bishop of Olonets noted, although his diocese had only three icons that regularly made visitations, most monasteries and parishes had specially revered icons that did not travel anywhere.

5.5   The Greeting of an icon. Chernigov province, Gorodnianskii district,
village of Khorobishch, 1914–16. The Russian Museum of Ethnography,
St. Petersburg.

An icon's schedule included not only the towns and villages on its itinerary but also the private homes it visited in any given locality; thus these
schedules were often tightly organized. Prior to reforms by the bishop of
Novgorod in the late nineteenth century, for instance, visitations with some
icons in that diocese had taken place day and night. Local clergy and laity
would greet the icon whenever it arrived at its destination. First, the icon
would be taken to the parish church for a general prayer service; then it would
be carried to private homes for private prayer services. Some priests estimated
that two or three hundred private blessings at people's homes could be served
in a twenty-four-hour period.[58]

The laity initiated most visitations.[59] Chosen representatives of village or
parish assemblies as well as town councils would invite an icon by contacting
the monastery, cathedral, or parish church where it was housed.[60] Visitations
varied in the way they were conducted. In 1879, believers from the town of
Aleksandrov Posad in the Pskov diocese offered to send thirty icon bearers
and six horse-drawn carts every year in order to bring two specially revered
icons from the Pskovo-Pechera monastery.[61] For long-distance visitations, a

5.6   Savitskii, K. A. *The Greeting of an Icon*. 1878. Oil on canvas. 141 × 228 cm.
Tretyakov Gallery, Moscow, inv. no. 591.

miracle-working icon was frequently transported in a carriage.[62] At nights
between settlements, believers would take turns guarding the icon.[63] Although
in some places the icon was also carried in procession between destinations,
diocesan officials urged that such processions take place only on approaching
and leaving a town in order to minimize the crowds of believers that would
typically surround the icon.[64]

Believers sometimes anticipated the visitation of an icon with as much
preparation as for Easter. Rural villages arranged for an icon's arrival by
decorating homes and setting special tables to provide bread for those who
accompanied the icon. Dressed in their best attire, believers would often greet
the icon on the outskirts of a village and accompany it to its destination by
singing the refrains "Most holy Theotokos, save us" and "Glory to Thee, Our
God, glory to Thee."[65] When a parish church was located in the village,
believers would ring its bells as part of the icon's greeting. Once in the town
and settled in the parish church, the icon would then visit private homes.

Communities requested visitations because believers desired to have their
villages or homes blessed by the icon's presence. Although believers could
travel to the monastery or church in order to venerate a particular icon, the
experience would be significantly different from a visitation. As believers from

the town of Vyshnii Volochek in the Tver diocese noted in 1884, pilgrimages often were not possible for the maimed, the elderly, the weak, and the poor—those who frequently most desired to venerate such icons.[66] Moreover, individual pilgrimages were to a large extent motivated by private concerns, in contrast to the public, shared concerns that brought about a visitation to an entire community.

In effect, these visitations were pilgrimages in reverse, with the object of veneration journeying to meet the believers. Just as pilgrimages were often made because of a vow related to an event in a person's life, so icon visitations were usually initiated by a communal decision to honor or memorialize an event. These events routinely included such misfortunes in the life of the community as an epidemic, a drought, or a fire.[67] In 1886, for example, believers from the village of Krevy in the Tver diocese who were suffering from an epidemic requested a visitation by a revered icon of the Mother of God named "Smolensk" from their parish church. Subsequently, the epidemic passed, and in 1890, believers requested that this icon visit their community annually in memory of the 1886 event. The day of the icon visitation became their annual village feast day.[68]

Similarly, in 1914 believers from the village of Churiukov (population ten thousand) in the Tambov diocese reported that the year before virtually half of their village had been destroyed by fire. This calamity came on the heels of ten years of poor harvests. In addition, they had not yet recuperated from the collapse of their newly constructed church seven years before, and the subsequent voluntary resignation of their favorite parish priest. "Oppressed by such misfortunes and horrors, the people, though shaken, have not fallen in spirits." Because of these events, the believers "unanimously and with one spirit" desired to invite the Tikhvin icon of the Mother of God from the nearby St. Peter and Paul monastery in the Riazan diocese to visit their village annually.[69]

Icons frequented towns and cities no less than rural areas. In 1876 the residents of the provincial town of Pogara in the Chernigov diocese petitioned the Synod for the visit of a miracle-working icon of St. Nicholas from the Orel diocese. They hoped for the "granting of blessings both temporal and eternal" and the deliverance from "recent epidemics and fires.[70] In 1879, residents of the provincial town of Bogoroditsk in the Tula diocese desired to establish an annual visitation of the Vladimir icon of the Mother of God located in a rural church some twenty miles away. The icon had periodically visited the town since 1860, especially on the occasion of cholera outbreaks. As the head of the town's administration wrote, during such visitations residents became aware that they were "not deprived of the mercy of God and were protected from all types of misfortune and adversities."[71] In the Nizhnii Novgorod diocese merchants annually welcomed the icon of a locally revered saint, Makarii of Zheltovo and Unzha, which was brought from the nearby Holy Trinity convent to the chapel located in the city's trade fair for special prayer services near their trading booths.[72]

Visitations could also be initiated by church officials and carry sociopolitical overtones. In Pskov the memory of Russia's victory over Napoleon was kept alive through annual visitations with icons of the Mother of God, St. Nicholas, the forty martyrs of Sebastea, and St. Barbara from the Pskov-Pechera monastery.[73] In 1889 missionary concerns of the bishop of Stavropol, Vladimir (Petrov), intertwined with broader national interests. In that year he petitioned the ober-procurator of the Holy Synod for an icon of St. Prince Mikhail of Tver to visit Stavropol annually from a nearby monastery. Backed by petitions from the city's Orthodox residents, the bishop hoped such a visitation might "shine forth the light of Christ into the dark souls" of the local Muslim population.[74]

Visitations were a source of income for both clergy and churches. Combined donations and proceeds were usually divided between clergy who traveled with the icon and clergy from the church where the icon stayed. Portions also went for the maintenance of the church where the icon was permanently housed and the church that it visited. In some dioceses, part of the clerical proceeds also went to the diocesan fund for needy clergy. It is noteworthy, however, that believers did not generally complain about donations for these visitations since prayer services with an icon in the home were completely voluntary. This stands in contrast to *treby* fees for baptism, weddings, and funerals, which, for believers, were not voluntary services. Usually the only tensions that existed with respect to icon visitations concerned how the money was divided between the clergy from the icon's home church and the clergy and church where it visited.[75]

Although technically the Holy Synod was supposed to confirm the establishment of all such visitations, they had not always done so. In 1880 Makarii, the metropolitan of Moscow, noted that because of a relative lack of laws governing them, most visitations in the Moscow diocese simply took place on the basis of longstanding custom.[76] To bring order to this practice, in 1893 the Holy Synod issued a directive in which it reminded diocesan bishops that synodal permission was required to carry icons outside the boundaries of a particular parish. The full scope of the visitation phenomenon became clear, however, only at the end of the nineteenth and in the early twentieth century when the Holy Synod solicited reports from diocesan bishops and learned that nearly eight hundred icons made visitations annually, a large proportion of which had been established by the blessing of local bishops, abbots, and parish priests.[77]

Synodal officials were clearly uncomfortable with the lack of centralized management of the visitation phenomenon. In particular, they were concerned with the growing numbers of such visitations, fearing that instead of inspiring people, frequent visitations would only repel them, suggesting that in the realm of the sacred, too, familiarity could breed contempt.[78] They were also concerned about the manner in which icons were carried: careless treatment by certain clergy and laity might damage the icon but, more significantly, might undermine believers' respect for it. Diocesan and synodal officials, consequently, were more comfortable with the traditional pilgrimage. A miracle-working or specially revered icon, they believed, should ideally remain in the monastery, cathedral, or parish church where it was housed so it would be available for pilgrims.[79] Consequently, church officials periodically pushed for the reorganization of visitation itineraries to ensure that an icon would spend most of the year at its home base.[80] They encouraged believers who lived relatively close to such churches to set out on pilgrimage to venerate the icon, claiming that these pilgrimages were more in accordance with the meaning of icons.[81] In 1902 the Holy Synod criticized the lengthy itinerary of the icon of the Mother of God housed in the Valdai monastery in the Novgorod diocese and directed the abbot to establish a new, shorter itinerary.[82] As a result, the itinerary was cut almost in half. Such decreases in visitations, however, frequently elicited an emotional reaction from lay believers, and the visitation itineraries would gradually swell again.[83]

Though the reasons given for icon visitations varied, a recurrent theme that characterized this ritual was the coming together of believers in an expression of corporate identity. When a group of believers rallied in reverence around an icon, they embraced the experiences the icon represented. By inviting the icon, they were establishing their own involvement in the icon's history. It was fitting liturgically to celebrate this perceived shared history through the greeting of the icon and through special prayer services in the homes of town or village residents. Some communities also symbolically expressed this relationship to a particularly revered icon by having an icon from their own village or parish temporarily join in the procession.[84] Finally, the routing of specially revered icons from urban cathedrals and monasteries to rural areas, or from rural churches to factories and urban areas, had the practical effect of incorporating otherwise isolated communities into a broader body of faithful with a shared experience.

Although icon visitations, on one level, were primarily communal events, they sustained their high level of appeal because they allowed for continued personal involvement. In coming to venerate such an icon, one late nineteenth-century author wrote, "each person brings his or her own stream into the wave of human prayer."[85] Individuals would often follow in procession behind the icon as it traveled between towns and villages. Once it reached its destination, believers often invited the icon to their homes for a more personal special blessing following the communal celebration of the icon in the local church.

In 1887, in his short story *Za ikonoi*, the populist writer V. G. Korolenko captured the religious essence of the experience of venerating a specially revered icon, highlighting the interdependence of the personal and communal involvement that icon visitations entailed. Describing a procession with an icon that stopped at a rural roadside chapel, Korolenko wrote:

> It [the icon] was surrounded by the faithful. Suffering, ill, feeble, and mourning people enveloped the icon as in a wave. Not looking at

one another they all focused on the same point. . . . Across all these faces passed an air of vitality that smoothed all of the various shades of suffering, subsuming them under a general expression of tenderness [*umilenie*]. Such a wave of human grief, such a wave of human hope. . . . And what a huge mass of singular spiritual movement cleansing every separate suffering, every person's woe as a drop sinking in an ocean. . . . Perhaps it was here, I thought, in this mighty stream of human hope and faith, that the source of healing power lay.[86]

## Miracle-Working Icons and the Christian Story

Specially revered icons and the stories behind them were not unique to Russia and were not a peripheral phenomenon in Orthodoxy. They were not merely a part of Orthodox folklore. Rather, they were very much embraced by the Orthodox religious tradition, as evidenced in the proceedings of the Seventh Ecumenical Council (787). The participants in the council, for instance, listened to an account from the life of St. Mary of Egypt that recalled the role an icon of the Mother of God played in her conversion experience. According to that story, Mary of Egypt embarked on a journey with a group of pilgrims to Jerusalem for the feast of the Exaltation of the Cross. She was interested not in the pilgrimage but in the prospect of attracting new lovers. On the day of the feast, she followed the crowds to the church but found she could not enter it. With each attempt to enter into the nave, she was held back by an unseen force. Looking up, she saw an icon of Mary, the Mother of God, hanging on the wall of the narthex. At this moment, Mary of Egypt reevaluated her recent life and before this icon admitted to the Mother of God that she knew why she could not enter the sacred space. She vowed that should the Mother of God petition Christ to grant her entrance into the church, she would never again defile her body and would depart from "this world." Following this prayer, Mary felt a "fullness of faith" and with hope she entered the church with no obstacle. Having venerated the cross of Christ, she once again turned to the icon and prayed that the Mother of God would guide her in her new life. At that moment, Mary of Egypt heard a distant voice say, "if you go to the Jordan, there you will find peace."[87]

Following the telling of this account, one of the council's delegates noted, "we have seen this icon in the holy city of Christ our God and have frequently venerated it." The council also recalled the words of Germanus, patriarch of Constantinople (715–30): "Through various icons, God performed miracles which many people desire to proclaim; for example, He healed the sick, which we ourselves have experienced."[88]

Orthodox writers and preachers in late imperial Russia were aware of this tradition and drew on it extensively in their treatises, devotional pamphlets, and sermons on icons. They drew in particular on the well-known treatises on icon veneration by St. John of Damascus, citing both his christological and psychological reasoning. Theologically, depictions of Christ testified to the reality of the Incarnation; devotionally, icons testified to the way humans could enter into communion with God—through both soul and body. Reiterating John of Damascus's thoughts, Russian Orthodox writers argued that it was impossible for humans to relate to God purely spiritually since humans were not purely spiritual beings; rather, they had a need to see and hear in their worship and to express their love of God through some form of material means. Icons, therefore, were part of a broader Orthodox understanding of the centrality of ritual in religious and spiritual life. To insist on the worship of God without ritual and its material aspects, claimed one priest, was to present the believer with an impossible demand.[89] Moreover, Russian Orthodox writers insisted that icons helped to condition the sense of sight so that believers could discern the grace of God.[90]

Within the general literature on icon veneration, reflections on miracle-working icons occupied a special place and were not a routine part of the discussion. Systematic reflection on miracle-working icons arose in part as a response to the challenges posed by Protestantism as well as the rationalism and positivism often associated with the Enlightenment. The first such systematic work, Dimitrii Sosnin's essay *On Holy Miracle-Working Icons in the Christian Church*, appeared in the first half of the nineteenth century. Literature on the subject became more frequent in the decades that followed.

In this literature, miracle-working icons were linked to teachings concerning the Incarnation, revelation, and grace. According to these texts, the perfect self-revelation of God took place once in history, in the person of Jesus Christ, through whom everything was manifested that is needed for the knowledge of God and for salvation. After Jesus' death and resurrection, God's activity and presence in the Christian community had continued through the communication of his Holy Spirit. One way God had manifested his "work" or "mercy" to humans was through miracles performed by the apostles. Such miracles were a sign of God's presence and disclosed truths regarding human salvation; they were part of the mystery of redemption.[91] They were signs of divine guidance as well as of a divine reordering of the disorder of the fallen human condition.[92] Consequently, "a lack of faith in miracles was tantamount to a lack of faith in the power of God and even in God himself."[93]

Once Christ and the apostles departed, the texts explain, the grace that had acted in and through them was now made manifest in and through their images. In order to renew faith in God and Christ, God continued to reveal himself personally through such means as miracles from icons. Icons were a medium chosen by God to show forth the grace of his Spirit; they were left by the Lord as a means by which people could enter more closely into communion with him.[94] God, wrote another nineteenth-century author, "opens and pours forth [through icons] miraculous gifts to his people."[95] God grants His grace through icons, claimed yet another, "so as . . . to enliven and to make the human soul more accepting of [divine] activity."[96] Similarly,

Bishop Sergei (Spasskii) of Mogilev noted in 1887 that contemporary Christians were rarely given the gift of healing others and that this gift was currently being manifested through icons and holy relics.[97] In the 1890s Sergii (Liapidevskii), bishop of Moscow, drew a parallel between a miracle-working icon and the coal from the altar of God that touched the prophet Isaiah's lips (Isa. 6:6–7): just as the coal cleansed the prophet's unclean soul, so the veneration of icons offered the same cleansing grace. He also compared it to the healing power of Christ's touch.[98]

While in theory every icon could become miracle working, the general view was that God found it pleasing to grant only certain icons "the grace and the power of wonder-working for those who gathered before them in faith and hope."[99] In this regard, one author reasoned that the purpose of miracles was to "confound our entire being." Miracles were the "live and active Word of God," preached not in written form but manifested through actions. Only certain icons were rendered miracle working so that believers would not become used to miracles and consider them common occurrences.[100]

Miraculous actions were not seen as working against God's laws; in miracles, Orthodox writers saw a return of nature to its basic laws, which had been disrupted because of the Fall.[101] This understanding of miracles was consistent with the worldview of Orthodox churchmen and laity that generally saw nothing irrational in seeking modern medical care while also praying for healing.[102] Such an attitude was reflected in the fact that the institutional Church had trained seminarians in basic medical skills during the nineteenth century in order to provide medical care in remote rural areas where physicians were still scarce.

Russian Orthodox writers and preachers explained the revelatory nature of miracle-working icons by making use of the same biblical imagery that Orthodox Christians had drawn on for centuries in defense of their icon veneration practices. In particular, Russian Orthodox writers and preachers compared such icons to the Ark of the Covenant. The same presence of God that was once manifested through the Ark now made itself known through specially revered icons.[103] At the same time, treatises on miracle-working icons made it clear that the wonder-working power displayed by a particular icon did not belong to the icon alone but resulted from an encounter between God, the person(s) depicted, and the believer, who came before it in prayer and with faith.[104] As the bishop of Moscow, Filaret Drozdov, had noted, "the prayer of faith is a spiritual force that attracts grace and miracle-working power."[105] Miracles related to icons thus bore testimony to the presence of both divine energy (or grace of the Holy Spirit) and human faith.

Devotional pamphlets also explained the manner by which a copy of a miracle-working icon could share the same healing power as the original. Copies of miracle-working icons were like mirrors. A mirror receiving the rays of the sun could reflect these rays to another mirror, and that mirror in turn to another, and so on to eternity. Each of these mirrors, however, would shine with the light of the same sun. In a similar fashion, copies of miracle-working icons could also reflect the healing light of the original.[106] The late nineteenth-century Russian theologian and priest Pavel Florenskii supported this understanding when he wrote: "The spiritual content of these copies is not something new (when compared to the prototype) nor is it something similar; rather the spiritual content is *exactly the same*." In discourse about miracle-working icons, the terms "original" or "prototype" referred more often to an icon than to the person represented on the image.[107]

Religious experiences associated with specially revered icons were also liturgically confirmed. The Orthodox service for the blessing of icons called for religious experiences associated with miracles and hence implicitly not only sanctioned the stories behind icons but gave them a place in the liturgical life of the Church. In the service for the blessing of icons of Christ, for instance, one of the prayers says:

> Hearken O Lord my God and mercifully send down your holy blessing upon this icon and give it the power of healing every sickness and infirmity, the power of driving off every crafty design of the devil from those who in faith seek refuge with it.[108]

The service for the blessing of icons of the Mother of God even more directly anticipates religious experiences from prayer before the icon: "O Lord, our God, send down the grace of your most Holy Spirit on this icon which your servants have designed in her honor and memory and sanctify it with your heavenly blessing: *and grant to it power and strength of miraculous works*."[109]

It was precisely the combination of the Orthodox theological understanding of icons and miracles along with extensive lay involvement with such icons on the local level that made specially revered icons figure so prominently in the lay ecclesial experience and in the formation of their ecclesial identity. While not sacred texts on the level of scripture or even liturgical hymnody, the stories behind icons were nevertheless very much part of the fabric of Orthodox religious life. Lay believers orally transmitted accounts of events that took place with such icons and read about them in published devotional pamphlets. Priests recounted them during sermons or periliturgical discussions. In this sense they were part of the body of texts and narratives that informed both personal and corporate Russian Orthodox identity.

According to Orthodox teaching, God himself chose to reveal the grace of his Spirit through icons. Therefore, the accounts that set these icons apart—so-called icon narratives—can be seen as appendices to the basic biblical narrative that informs Christian identity. The symbolic linking of the biblical narrative with the narratives behind icons is evident, for example, in the fact that many of these icons had churches built in their honor. According to its narrative, for instance, the icon of the Mother of God named "Hodigitriia of the Holy Mountain" from the Pskov diocese was tied to the religious experiences of a pious fifteen-year-old shepherd boy who was considered a "fool for Christ" in his sixteenth-century community. Following this icon's glorification, a church was constructed in the icon's honor, with the altar table—a symbol of Christ's tomb, the throne of God, and the heavenly banquet table—constructed over the site of this boy's initial experiences with the icon.[110] In late imperial Russia, laity continued in this tradition and petitioned to construct churches or chapels on the site where an icon's life began.[111]

The stories behind specially revered icons, therefore, actively connected the experiences of persons and communities living in the historical present with those episodes or persons from the history of salvation depicted by the icon's visual image. They spoke of the believers' own involvement in a God-directed history. Specially revered icons held meaning not only because they visually testified to and called forth the paradigmatic events told in scripture but also because they bore witness, through the stories of signs and miracles associated with them, to the believers' own perceived participation in the same ongoing sacred story. The glorification of such icons, consequently, was also the celebration, as it were, of every lay person's experience of divine grace gathered up into the collective movement of salvation history.

Indeed, in a world where ecclesiastical matters were managed by priests, male monastics, and bishops, the laity at first glance appear to have counted little when it came to the ongoing life of the Russian Orthodox Church. A woman such as Vera Iakovleva had virtually no voice in the practical or theological matters of church life. And yet, on account of the icon of the Mother of God named "It Is Truly Meet," her life experience took on a sacred meaning that was incorporated into the history of the Orthodoxy community. Her experiences became part of the collective memory that, at least locally, was celebrated liturgically through communal doxology before the icon.

The flourishing of such stories behind specially revered icons was closely related to the mnemonic function of icons themselves. If iconographic depictions served as visual narratives of divine activity in the unfolding of ecclesial life, then the stories behind the icons recalled God's presence and ongoing activity in the lives of the faithful. In this way, icon-related narratives became part of the anamnesis or memory experience that icon veneration itself entailed. The act of venerating and gazing on such an image, one devotional pamphlet maintained, "awakens the memory of God's grace manifested through it."[112] Icon-related narratives remembered God's remembrance of individual persons, local communities, and even an entire nation.[113] The act of remembering the manifestation of God's grace through the icon testified to human faith and thereby could increase the flow of that grace. Forgetting those works of God manifested in the past, in turn, could result in the diminution of an icon's miracle-working ability. Remembering was integral to an icon's efficacy.[114]

The meaning of an icon's veneration, however, was not exhausted by the anamnesis of sacred history that it evoked. Believers also flocked to a specially revered icon as a locus of divine presence, as a possibility of immediate personal encounter with the holy that was in itself beyond history. This relational aspect of icon veneration—which included magnification, identification, and a sense of deference and dependence—provided for a mode of bonding within the faith community that fostered ecclesial cohesion. In their posture of supplication before the image, believers not only tacitly affirmed their shared convictions but also manifestly placed their hope in the same eternal power.

Accordingly, in their liturgical act of relating to the divine through the image, which was both a focus of prayer and the point of convergence of all the stories associated with the icon, believers united their disparate selves into a body of faithful. Thus in the act of veneration the reciprocity of image and narrative—the relational and the anamnestic—synergistically enhanced personal and corporate Orthodox Christian experience and identity. This idea was eloquently expressed in 1908 by a priest from Kazan, Aleksandr Vorontsov, in a sermon he gave on the occasion of the greeting of a specially revered icon of the Mother of God. Speaking of the benefits of such a visitation, he said:

> In seeing it [the icon], our memories are awakened by the many thousands of persons who poured out their souls before it—who poured out comforting tears of joy, quiet tears of tenderness [*umilen-iia*], or bitter tears of grief; the holy icon visibly and invisibly unites us with an entire assembly of our brethren—alive and deceased; our personal spiritual and bodily weakness is fortified by the universal, corporate strength of the Church.[115]

⊷⊜⊷

## Tensions over Specially Revered Icons

The nineteenth and early twentieth centuries continued to see the birth of specially revered icons, some of which went on to become quite well known.[116] We will never know the true numbers of such icons, since many remained local phenomena confined to immediate villages or parish communities. We do know, however, that in certain cases the lives of newly surfaced specially revered icons did not always progress smoothly. As long as believers did not openly ascribe a miracle-working quality to an icon, they were usually able to venerate it without incident. In the 1860s, for example, Vasilii Andrianov from the Vologda diocese, while residing in St. Petersburg, had a series of dreams in which he had been directed to venerate a particular icon of the Christ named "Not-Made-by-Hands." He subsequently attributed the destruction of his belongings by a fire in his home village to not having heeded the directive and vowed to seek out the icon he had seen in his dream. He notified his parish priest in the Vologda diocese about the events, and the priest, together with several parishioners, helped to locate the icon in the church's storage area. They had the icon restored and some thirty years later it continued to be revered in the parish.[117]

Once believers began openly congregating around a particular icon and venerating it as miracle working, however, and once such icons came to the attention of diocesan officials, the life of an icon often entered a new phase.

Questions concerning the authenticity of the signs and the religious experiences associated with these icons usually generated diocesan-led inquiries and investigations that set certain ecclesial dynamics in motion.

Tensions within the ecclesial community with respect to these icons were generated on several levels. First, operating in the Petrine bureaucratic structure that looked with suspicion on the proclamation of the miraculous, synodal and consistory officials often attempted to curb displays of special devotion toward particular icons. They actively resisted, for instance, officially sanctioning an icon as miracle working by discouraging the special prayer services and the ceremony that went along with such recognition.[118] They often allowed a newly revered icon to remain in a local parish church only under certain conditions, such as having it publicly venerated as a common icon (as opposed to a miracle-working one) or, in other cases, kept out of public in the altar area.[119]

Diocesan officials reminded priests that according to ecclesiastical rules, they were to notify their diocesan bishops in a timely manner of any proclaimed miracles.[120] They reprimanded those clergy who conducted prayer services before certain specially revered icons for their "self-willed" actions, for decisions that "lacked common sense," and for fueling rumors and superstitions and sometimes took disciplinary measures against them.[121] For example, in 1879 a priest in the Kishinev diocese, Vasilii Kochubinskii, conducted a prayer service in the home of a parishioner where a special sign from an icon had been perceived and then placed the icon in the church where it could be openly venerated. After he had learned about the incident and communicated with diocesan officials, the dean locked up the icon and passed on a warning to Kochubinskii from diocesan officials for his careless actions.[122]

The priest involved in Vera Iakovleva's case, Aleksei Edemskii, was demoted from first to second priest and then transferred to another parish. Despite his appeal that he did not "consider it his right to deny the faithfuls' request to hold prayer services before a common, although specially revered, icon," the diocesan decision was not reversed.[123] In a similar case, diocesan authorities in 1862 ordered the priest Anatolii Lavrov from the Totma district in the Vologda diocese to serve a two-month penance in the Totma Spasso-Sumorin monastery for having given cause "to the deception and superstition of the people." He was to take this occasion to "clear his conscience" for having blessed an epiphanic icon at the request of the "gullible people" and allowed believers to venerate it openly in the parish church.[124]

In addition to simply discouraging the special veneration of such images, some church officials at this time were guided in their actions by a still standing 1722 law that, in the Tridentine spirit in which it was formulated, tried to safeguard against superstitious practices and profiteering by bringing the veneration of miracle-working icons under centralized control.[125] According to this law, newly surfaced miracle-working icons were to be investigated (in a manner similar to that of Catholic investigations of Marian apparitions) and taken from private homes and placed in provincial cathedrals and monastery churches for safekeeping.[126]

On the basis of this law, diocesan and synodal officials ordered numerous icons removed from private homes during the late nineteenth and early twentieth centuries for purposes of examination and safekeeping. In August 1862, for instance, the civil servant and hospital inspector Dormidont Volochiev and members of his family noticed myrrh streaming from the hands of the Virgin depicted on their Smolensk icon of the Mother of God. Suspecting fraud, the local dean gave the icon to the diocesan bishop, who, following a month of observation, placed the icon in the Perm cathedral's vestry. As the Holy Synod noted in its review of the case, the bishop's actions were justified on the basis of the 1722 law. On the one hand, should the myrrh as witnessed by the Volochievs reappear while the icon was located in the diocesan cathedral, it would be situated in a more appropriate and honorable place than a private home.[127] On the other hand, synodal officials reasoned, if no such further occurrences took place, it was better that the icon be removed from its place of origination in order to prevent further rumors.[128]

Similarly, in 1872, the priest from the village of Kunikovo in the Kostroma diocese reported that in the home of one of his parishioners, the peasant Kuzma Leont'ev, tears had appeared on the Feodorov icon of the Mother of God. The godmother of Leontiev's son had presented the icon as a gift on the occasion of his son's wedding the year before. When the priest, Fr. Dobrovol'skii, offered to have the icon placed in the parish church, both Leont'ev and his son categorically refused. The consistory, in turn, ruled that with the help of local police, the icon should be removed from Leont'ev's home and brought to the diocesan cathedral.[129]

Though the 1722 law was specifically formulated with respect to newly surfaced miracle-working icons located in private homes, ecclesiastical officials at this time also on occasion applied the law's principles to icons located in parish churches, indicating that some officials did not consider the parish setting to be central enough. Significantly, late nineteenth-century pastoral handbooks that offered advice on various practical subjects sometimes presented a slightly modified version of the 22 February 1722 law on perceived miracle-working icons. In addition to drawing attention to icons located in private homes, the handbooks noted that such icons located in private homes *and in other places* should be taken to cathedrals or monasteries.[130] In July 1862, for example, the reader Konstantin Pen'evskii found an icon of the saints Varnava and Tikhon of Zadonsk on the grounds of the Mother of God church in the Vologda diocese. The clergy subsequently publicly blessed the icon and ceremoniously carried it into the church. Parishioners soon began to venerate the icon as miracle working and requested special prayer services before it. They also erected a cross on the site where the icon had been found, and pilgrims began congregating at the site. Learning of these developments, the bishop of Vologda, Khristofor (Emmausskii), directed a priest to remove the icon from the church secretly with the help of local police and to send it to him for storage in the diocesan cathedral.[131] Similarly, in June 1876, the Holy Synod ordered Vera Iakovleva's icon of the Mother of God to be taken from the local parish church to the diocesan cathedral. Heated protest from the parish priest, as well as extreme discontent on the part of parishioners that, according to local church officials, threatened to result in schism, did nothing to change the decision of the Synod and the local consistory.[132] Even though parishioners' pleas for the icon's return could be heard in the Synod some twenty-nine years later, synodal officials were not moved to have the icon returned.[133]

It is difficult to ascertain the variety of believers' reactions when ecclesiastical authorities either questioned or interfered with the special veneration of an icon, since these cases were not always reported to the Holy Synod. In many cases it might have been little more than a quiet resignation on the part of believers that church officials had "proven" their icon not to be miracle working. In 1903, when an icon of the Mother of God named "Life-Giving Source," located in the home of the peasant Sergei Smirnov from the Tula diocese, began drawing believers on account of its apparent self-renewal, things calmed down after the local dean and priest made a concerted effort to explain to the people that the icon was not miracle working.[134] Nevertheless, during the late nineteenth and early twentieth centuries, the Holy Synod received many letters and petitions from laity who, both individually and collectively, defended their special veneration of an icon and questioned the behavior of certain church authorities with respect to it. In their attempts either to secure an icon's return or its special veneration, these petitions reveal a laity who, as witnesses to God's activity in their lives, challenged diocesan and synodal authorities on several fronts.

First, believers were bewildered by ecclesiastical officials' objections to displays of extraordinary devotion toward a particular icon. In 1901, the peasants Evdokim and Anna Grigor'ev from the Vladimir diocese petitioned diocesan authorities for the return of an epiphanic icon of St. Nicholas that had been taken from their parish church some eight years earlier. The icon, which had been found by their father and had attracted believers to their home, had been donated by their parents to the parish church. "Having made inquiries in Vladimir," wrote the Grigor'evs, "we learned that the icon was taken from our church because we too frequently and openly displayed our zeal toward this icon." Accordingly, they concluded, "we simple parish people will have to conceal the fact that a certain icon is specially honored among us."[135]

Believers also attempted to counter the allegations of superstitious behavior. In 1888, for example, Martin Semenov, a peasant from the village of Sobchakovo in the Riazan diocese, found a copy of the Kazan icon of the Mother of God while he was digging a ditch. On hearing the news, believers began specially venerating it. Soon healings were reported. Having learned of the event, the diocesan officials directed local civil authorities to curtail the gatherings of believers at the site where the icon had been found; they also directed the local dean to remove the icon from its central position in the church (where it had been placed by the parish priest), to place it out of sight in the vestry, and to reassure believers that it was simply a common icon. Soon thereafter representatives of the village of Sobchakovo petitioned the consistory to construct a chapel on the site where the icon had been found in hopes of placing the icon in a more suitable place. Both requests were denied. In response, in 1892, as part of their twenty-odd-year campaign to gain the sanction to specially venerate this icon as an uncommon one, representatives of the village Sobchakovo wrote:

> we were saddened that our prayers before the image of the Mother of God were considered unauthentic and superstitious as if we had retreated from our Orthodox faith and begun to venerate someone whom Orthodox Christians should not even think about.[136]

Hoping to "correct" the consistory's impression, they requested that diocesan officials carry out a formal investigation into the matter and again petitioned to construct a chapel on the site where the icon had been found.

In addition, believers were unnerved by the semblance of science that characterized diocesan officials' investigation of reported miracles and by the focus exclusively on what was called the "common" versus "uncommon" nature of the icon, both of which failed to take into account the faith of believers. In 1886, believers from the Kharkov diocese referred to a diocesan decision to remove a specially revered icon from their parish church as "anti-religious." They disagreed in particular with the investigative process that sought to "prove" healings based on "indisputable facts." "We think the best facts are now before our eyes; no others are necessary. The retired soldier Andreevich Kromskii, who had been completely blind, can now see."[137] Similarly, a year later, believers from the Kursk diocese criticized church officials for conducting a scientific analysis of the spring water in which a particular icon had been found and that was now being credited with healing powers. They claimed that they would never attribute the power of healing to the water. That power was to be found in "the deep faith in the miracle-working nature of the icon which drew [believers] from hundreds and thousands of miles for prayer and repentance before it." Instead of respecting that faith, the local police warden complained to the Holy Synod, members of the investigative commission "had tried either to destroy peoples' faith in God's mercy by explaining everything away through rational reasons, or to belittle the significance of their icon."[138] In reaction to a specially revered icon of the Resurrection of Christ being taken from their parish church in 1895, parishioners from the village of Nikolo-Zamosh'e in the Iaroslavl diocese wrote: "Lord! Who would dare to examine your works? Could it be that even today there are persons who doubt miracles?"[139]

In 1907, the head of the Tula city duma pointed out the futility of a policy that would recognize an icon as miracle working only when its effects were experienced directly by members of the consistory. Since that time might never come, he reasoned, those who had experienced the icon's miracle-working power had to judge events on their own.[140] Similarly, in 1912, when consistory officials claimed that the icon specially revered by the parishioners from St. Nicholas church in the Eniseisk diocese was only a "common" one, two trustees for the parishioners responded that such a conclusion could only be reached by those who focused on the icon in and of itself and who failed to take into account what the icon had done for them. "It might be that for some people this icon is ordinary," they wrote, "but we cherish it as a blessing."[141]

Indeed believers sometimes questioned the entire procedure by which events that led to an icon's special veneration had been investigated and the way clergy handled such icons. For example, in 1894 more than four hundred believers from the Chernigov diocese turned to the Holy Synod about "the grief which had confused their spiritual world." Retelling the life of an icon of the martyr Barbara that had renewed itself in the home of one of their fellow parishioners, the townsman Joachim Litvinenko, they complained that the investigation into "the wisdom of God" that had led to the removal of the icon from their parish church was "superfluous and criminal."[142] Consequently they requested that another investigation be carried out. In 1896, parishioners from the village of Mikhailovo in the Tavrida diocese complained to synodal authorities that their parish priest had come after midnight to a private home in order to remove a specially revered icon to the parish church, and he did so without any sort of liturgical service.[143]

In 1901, representatives of several villages from the Novo-Tagmalikov township in the Poltava diocese requested that a Kazan icon of the Mother of God that had been removed from the home of one of their parishioners in 1899, the peasant woman Kharitina Tsybina, be returned to their newly constructed church. The church had been built using the funds of one of their parishioners, the landowner Lev Komenikov, who had been healed by prayers before this icon. Their request was denied. Some fourteen years later, in 1915, the metropolitan of St. Petersburg received another petition regarding this icon, this time ostensibly from an army officer, B. P. Obruchev, who had been wounded at the front and who had heard about the icon from a landowner and an elderly monk whom he had met at the Poltava train station. After having sought out the icon at the Poltava diocesan cathedral and having been healed from war-related wounds from his prayer before it, he took up the cause of petitioning for the icon's return to its original location. He described the consistory's decision to take away the icon from the local church as "wild arbitrariness" and questioned the legality of such a move. "My God, Our Heavenly Father," he rhetorically wrote, "manifest Your great mercy and enlighten the pastors of the city of Poltava!"[144]

Finally, believers protested the policy of removing icons on the basis of their ownership. Diocesan and synodal officials appear to have acted on the principle that once an icon displayed miracle-working activity in a private home, the icon's owners no longer held any rights to it.[145] The donation of an icon to the parish church only reinforced the officials' sense of their prerogatives as overseers, since, as a donation, the icon technically became property of that church. Hence many church officials believed that they had the right to manage the icon as they saw fit.[146] Some of them interpreted lay hesitancy to give up their icons as "stubbornness" that had "no basis."[147]

Laity, on the other hand, remained firm in their claim to such icons, especially when they had been part of a familial heritage that they believed should not be disrupted. For example, in 1896 the elderly peasant Mark Karpov from the Kaluga diocese petitioned the Holy Synod, requesting that a self-renewed icon taken from his home be returned. If the icon could not be returned to him, he hoped that it might be returned to his descendants, since the icon had been in the family for generations.[148] By 1914 his sons had taken over his cause and petitioned not only for the icon's return but also for the construction of a church in its honor.[149]

The noblewoman Aleksandra Eck from the Simbirsk diocese demanded that her icon be returned in 1902 on the basis that it was her only remaining "treasure" and that her mother had blessed her with it before her death.[150] The following year, in 1903, the sixty-six-year-old widow Anna Boguslav from the Chernigov diocese informed the consistory that she would rather lose everything she owned than forsake her self-renewed familial icon. Consistory officials had ruled that the icon should be taken to the nearest monastery, even though she was willing to donate it to the local parish church. Insisting she was too old to journey to the monastery to venerate her own icon, she left town with the icon.[151] In 1904, the peasant Elena Zelenaia refused to allow church officials to move her self-renewed icon of Christ to one of the diocese's monasteries. When police accompanied the local dean to her home in order to take the icon, Zelenaia placed it around her chest, had herself surrounded by family members, and categorically refused to have the icon taken anywhere but to her local parish church.[152]

Even when believers allowed an icon to be placed in the parish church, their sense of ownership did not necessarily cease. In 1909, the peasant Mikhail Sherstobitov wrote to the Synod about a perceived miracle-working icon of the Mother of God that had belonged to his father and had been placed in his parish church at the direction of the local dean several decades earlier. Now, as a "direct heir" to the icon and with the support of the local civil authorities, he was requesting that the icon be transferred to the church of the newly formed parish of which he was a part. Diocesan authorities denied his request also on the basis of ownership. The icon, they claimed, was the "inalienable property" of the church where it was currently housed since it had been donated by Sherstobitov's father.[153]

Not only individuals but entire communities challenged church officials' definition of ownership. In 1890 representatives from the Starosavinsk community in the Kaluga diocese, Adrian Razorenov and Efim Ratnikov, petitioned for the return of an icon of the Mother of God that had been moved five years earlier from a chapel located in their village to the diocesan cathedral and then to another church located in the provincial capital. Their previous request had been denied since, according to diocesan officials, they had not demonstrated their rights to the icon. The peasants claimed that the icon, which had been in their midst for some two hundred years, was housed in a chapel they had built on their own land. Diocesan officials, in turn, argued that both the chapel and the land on which it stood was owned by the provincial church in which the icon in question was currently housed; they therefore denied the peasants' request.[154]

In 1901 parishioners from St. Nicholas church in the Kursk diocese petitioned the Synod for the return of an icon of St. Nicholas and the martyr Barbara that had renewed itself in the home of the peasant Aleksandr Bondarenko and been donated by him to this church. Consequently, they wrote, "this icon became the holy item [sviatynia] of our humble St. Nicholas parish." That year diocesan officials had directed that the icon be removed from the parish church to the diocesan cathedral while they investigated the icon's miracle-working activity. The icon was never returned. Complaining of the humiliation to which their icon had been subjected on account of this ruling, the parishioners wrote: "Would it not be more just to return the icon to our parish church where we, along with other Orthodox Christians, could light candles before it and turn to it in prayer, than to have it lie in a monastery basement?" They admitted being aware of the 1722 law, but they reminded synodal officials that this law concerned miracle-working icons. Since diocesan authorities did not find the icon to be miracle working, it should be returned to them according to the principles of ownership. "Because it was donated to our church, it is our property and not that of the consistory."[155] Despite this argument, the Synod denied their request.

Such diverging understanding of ownership also surfaced with respect to icon visitations. When their request to lengthen an icon's visitation was denied, believers from the Ufa diocese reminded diocesan and synodal officials that the icon was originally "theirs" and that it therefore made no sense to deny them the veneration of their "own" icon.[156] In 1895, a case concerning an icon of the Mother of God named "The Joy of All Who Sorrow" in the Vologda diocese reflected the complexity of the ownership issue. In 1766, diocesan officials had directed that the icon be removed from the Lostenskii parish where it had originated. For some 125 years it remained in the Vologda cathedral, where it, too, had become specially revered. Believers of Vologda, including members of that town's city duma, did not wish to see the icon returned to its original locality, claiming the length of time it had been in Vologda by default gave them rights over it. In the end, diocesan and synodal authorities granted the parishioners of the Lostenskii church permission only to receive the icon for a brief period during an annual visitation.[157] The issue of ownership figured most prominently following 1917, when some local parish communities demanded the return of their long-revered icons.[158]

Letters to the Holy Synod from laity demanding the return of icons became bolder and more numerous beginning in the 1890s, but especially after 1905, when the lay self-awareness that had been growing since the 1880s became even more acute. Undoubtedly influenced by the broader sociopolitical movement, peasant laity in particular began questioning the legal basis for the Synod's and consistories' policies.[159] In 1906 the representatives for the village of Dubishche in the Kaluga diocese, Koz'ma and Daniil Petrov (the latter the village elder), petitioned the Synod for the return of an icon of St. Nicholas that had originally belonged to a fellow villager. Reminding the Synod of the tsar's recent ruling on religious toleration, the Petrovs wrote: "In cases where there are no willing donations, property must be returned to its owner, and personal opinion [i.e., that of diocesan authorities] has no significance or force."[160]

In 1909 parishioners from St. Timothy church in the Poltava diocese wrote the Holy Synod that "even if the consistory does not recognize the miracle-working nature of our icon, it still does not have the right to take it from the parishioners and to deprive them of their spiritual sustenance, and to kill in them their religious sensibilities and faith in everything sacred."[161] The same year another peasant, Vasilii Popov from the Arkhangelsk diocese, threatened to sue the consistory if his icon was not returned to the chapel he had constructed in its honor.[162] The icon had been taken from him a decade before and stored in the local parish church.

The potential for more serious developments stemming from specially revered icons also increased after 1905, when religiously fueled sentiments concerning "truth" and "justice" resonated with broader social and political issues. For example, in July 1906 a church elder from the parish church in the village of Makshina in the Chernigov diocese, the nobleman Petr Borianovskii, informed diocesan officials that their confiscation of a locally venerated icon of Christ from the parish church had made a "dispirited impression" on the community. The peaceful village, he wrote, which until that time had taken no part in agrarian disturbances, now "rebelled," and its residents demanded that the icon remain in their church.[163] In 1907 a dean from the Pavlovsk district in the Voronezh diocese warned the diocesan bishop that taking a recently "renewed" and now specially revered icon from the parish church would lead to "great indignation on the part of parishioners" and ultimately to the "intervention of military forces."[164] Similarly, in 1908, ecclesiastical authorities chose not to follow the 1722 law when they heard the "unimaginable noise and shouts" from parishioners when it was announced that an icon would have to be removed from the site where it had been found and taken to the diocesan cathedral.[165]

Despite repeated attempts to see their icons properly venerated or returned, believers' requests before 1905 were usually turned down on the basis that the return of the icon might "give cause to unfounded speculation among the people."[166] In other words, synodal and diocesan officials did not want believers to interpret an icon's return or an allowance of its special veneration as an official sanction of its miracle-working nature. Moreover, church officials reasoned, if they returned one icon, they would have to fulfill the requests of numerous other believers as well.[167]

Yet, significantly, in 1894, the bishop of Chernigov, Antonii (Sokolov), petitioned the Holy Synod to allow perceived miracle-working icons that surfaced in private homes to be allowed to remain in local parish churches instead of being taken to the provincial cathedral. In recent years his diocese had seen the appearance of numerous self-renewed icons in private homes, and the automatic implementation of the 1722 law had met with great resistance from laity. Moreover, his diocese had also seen the rise of sectarian groups that rejected icon veneration. Such icon confiscations gave these sectarians the opportunity to taunt Orthodox believers with rumors that their own church officials did not support the veneration of icons. Despite these considerations, synodal authorities denied the bishop's request and directed the continued implementation of the 1722 law.[168]

By 1905, however, some church officials, sensitive to the mood of the population, displayed a heightened sense of discretion in relation to the implementation of the 1722 law. In 1908, Ioann, the bishop of Poltava, described the resentment and years of petitioning that would often follow an icon's removal from a private home. He requested, therefore, that the practice of taking such icons for "safekeeping" to diocesan cathedrals be made the exception rather than the rule and that the icons instead be taken to the local parish church. The Synod agreed.[169]

In other cases, especially after 1905, church officials occasionally returned an icon after persistent petitioning by a community of believers. In 1897, a wife of a Cossack, Elizaveta Panchkova, from the Don diocese, appealed to the Holy Synod about a self-renewed icon of the Savior and St. Nicholas that had been in her family for generations and that had been removed by diocesan officials a decade before. Since then, she had petitioned the diocesan consistory four times for the icon's return from the diocesan cathedral to her parish church. This time, diocesan and synodal authorities agreed to her request.[170]

In 1908 diocesan officials ordered an icon, originally belonging to the peasant Ivan Kovalenko in the Chernigov diocese, removed from the parish church to which he had donated it. Diocesan officials were disturbed by what they considered the excessive zeal that believers displayed toward it. A year later the local dean described to the diocesan bishop the dispiriting effect this decision was having not only on Kovalenko and his family but on the entire local population as well. He petitioned that the icon be allowed to remain in the local parish church in order to "facilitate an uplift in [believers'] religious sensibilities." Both the bishop and the Holy Synod complied with the dean's request.[171] Similarly, the same year, synodal and diocesan authorities from the Chernigov diocese decided to meet the request of parishioners for the return of a copy of the Smolensk icon of the Mother of God that had been taken from their parish to a local monastery. As diocesan authorities reasoned, "taking into account the strong faith in God that is displayed by the parishioners with regard to the icon," the return of the icon could uphold their faith in the current irreligious times, while taking it away could anger them.[172]

In 1913 Bishop Arsenii of Novgorod reasoned that if the members of the Itkolsk parish had not forgotten their icon, which had been removed seventeen years before, "then the reasons at the basis of such veneration must be serious." Consequently, he directed the icon be returned.[173] The return of such icons was occasionally even reported in the local newspaper, and believers greeted the news with great elation.[174] In 1912 more than ten thousand people reportedly gathered in the village of Nikolskoe in the Eniseisk diocese to greet the icon of the Mother of God named "The Joy of All Who Sorrow," which diocesan authorities had taken from them the year before.[175]

The set of dynamics and tensions surrounding the special veneration of perceived miracle-working icons, however, was not simply a clash between "official" and "popular" religious cultures.[176] Given the devotional, liturgical, and theological basis for the special veneration of icons on the one hand and a reticence among certain church officials towards miracles proclaimed by common believers on the other, the official position on specially revered icons was often inconsistent, and took various factors into account. Persons whose voices would usually be considered those of official Orthodoxy—synodal officials, diocesan bishops, consistories, and parish priests—were not themselves uniform in their thinking about such cases.

Diocesan and synodal authorities often came to different conclusions regarding the special veneration of an icon. A graphic example occurred in 1899 when the bishop of Kursk, Lavrentii, desired to make 8 March an annual diocese-wide feast celebrating the miraculous preservation of a locally revered icon of the Mother of God "of the Sign" after someone had attempted to destroy it with a bomb the year before. The icon had a long history tied to the Kursk region in particular and to the Russian nation as a whole. On this occasion, believers interpreted the bombing as a sign from God to Russia as a nation. On the one hand, the "evil-minded" culprits who had attempted to blow up the icon exposed "the rotting from within" that was taking place in the "mighty oak" of Russia. On the other hand, the divine preservation of the icon was a sign of hope to the faithful.[177] Despite such religious sentiments, the Synod declined the bishop's request.[178]

Similarly, a Tikhvin icon of the Mother of God belonging to the townsman Nikolai Tolkachev from the town of Mtsensk in the Orel diocese was taken away from his home in 1876. The icon had been recognized by local believers as miracle working for some thirty years. In 1875 that interest was reawakened when Tolkachev's home was spared from a fire that destroyed many neighboring homes, reportedly because he had processed around his house with the icon while flames raged only yards away. The local bishop had initially offered Tolkachev the option of donating the icon to any church in the city that he desired; the Holy Synod, however, directed the bishop to act on the 1722 law and send the icon to the diocesan cathedral. After Tolkachev petitioned the tsar to return the icon to the church in the cemetery where his family was buried, the Holy Synod agreed to make an exception and return the icon, as long as it was kept in the church's vestry.[179]

In addition, when icons were already located in a parish church, diocesan and synodal authorities often opted not to act on the principles of the 1722 law and allowed the icons to remain in place, clearly considering the parish church within the bounds of manageable oversight. In 1862 Matrona Dimitrieva from the Tver diocese approached her parish priest following a liturgical service and asked him to locate a particular icon in the church's storage shed. The peasant woman maintained that she had had several dreams in which the Mother of God requested that this icon be placed in the parish. Finding the icon, the parish priest placed it in a central position in the church and conducted a prayer service before it. Soon, healings were reported, and the icon began to draw more than one thousand believers on a given day. Both diocesan and synodal authorities decided to let the icon remain in its place.[180]

In 1870, the governor of Viatka notified the ober-procurator of the Holy Synod about reported miracles from an icon of the Mother of God named "It Is Truly Meet" located in the village church of Iurevsk. The icon, a copy of the miracle-working original located on Mount Athos, had been donated to the church by the parishioner and peasant Filipp Sadyrov. An investigative committee had found no conclusive evidence supporting the recognition the icon as miracle working, although even the local bishop had maintained that people had been healed "by the strength of their faith and the zeal of their prayer." Diocesan and synodal authorities decided simply to leave the icon where it was.[181]

In 1884 the bishop of Vladimir, Alexei, reported to the Holy Synod an "obvious miracle" that had taken place from an Iveron icon of the Mother of God located in the parish church in the village of Igovo in the Vladimir diocese. The icon, which had also been made and blessed on Mount Athos, was donated to the parish church by a local gentrywoman. Soon after the icon arrived from Mount Athos, the sixty-three-year-old parishioner, Vasilii Makarov, a cripple, was reportedly healed by praying before the icon. Although the bishop claimed that according to the February 1722 law the icon should be taken to the diocesan cathedral, he feared that such an action might offend the gentrywoman who had donated the icon in the first place. Moreover, he noted the pedagogical benefits such an icon could have on existing sectarians in the region who rejected icon veneration and who might be "enlightened" by such a healing. The synod agreed with the bishop's decision and directed that the parish priest record future healings from the icon.[182]

In 1897 diocesan officials directed the dean from the Kazan diocese (Kazan district) to bring an epiphanic icon of St. Nicholas that had been found by two peasants on the bank of a river to the diocesan cathedral while an investigation was carried out. The dean reported it was impossible to do so since the icon was guarded day and night by believers. Eventually the synod agreed not only to allow the icon to remain but also to allow the villagers to construct a church in its honor with the funds that had been collected.[183] Only on rare occasions did both diocesan authorities and members of the Holy Synod confirm the "unnatural" means by which a believer had been healed and direct that the reports of the events be disseminated through the religious press.[184]

Finally, it appears that even specially revered icons in private homes were not always taken away. In 1912 parishioners from the Eniseisk diocese, in hopes of securing the fate of their own icon, wrote the Holy Synod about an epiphanic icon in a neighboring parish in the Tomsk diocese. The icon remained in the home of the peasant who had found it, while a copy of it was made and placed in the local parish church for public veneration.[185]

Given the power of icons to assemble believers, and given the diverging responses among church officials to such newly surfaced icons, the conflicts that arose in the ecclesial community were obviously not simple disagreements over whether an icon could be considered "uncommon" and thereby merit special attention. From sermons and the reports of church officials located in archival cases concerning icons, it is clear that even the most educated of Russia's clergy, including the hierarchy, did not philosophically or theologically doubt the possibility of miracles in and of themselves. In this sense they followed neither classical Protestant teaching espoused by Luther and Calvin that the age of miracles had ended nor the nineteenth-century liberal Protestant view, which, under the influence of rationalism and the Enlightenment, at times questioned the reality of those miracles found even in the New Testament accounts. The issue for Russia's clergy during this period rarely involved the question of the philosophical possibility of a miracle.[186] What some Russian churchmen, especially members of consistory boards and certain bishops, did often question was the ability of lay people to discern or distinguish true miracles—as works of God—from misperceptions. Such questions were supported in part by legitimate concerns about fraud and profiteering, and the concern that the *tremendum* of the sacred might be belittled as a result of an unguarded acceptance of every reported miracle as true. Yet such concerns only partially explain the official response to such icons. Tensions also arose because of several deeper issues that reverberated with the diverging ecclesial visions within Russian Orthodoxy at this time—visions that frequently transcended simple lay-clerical categorization.

First, newly surfaced miracle-working icons begged questions concerning the fundamental principles of ecclesial ordering. By attempting to modulate and direct the veneration of these icons, many church officials acted according to the principle that, as a sign from God, such an icon belonged to the entire ecclesial community of which they were the overseers. The bishop of Kursk, Sergii (Liapidevskii), made this claim in 1876, during a sermon he delivered to a parish from which a specially revered icon had been taken. Everyone, he maintained, knew what types of icons were called miracle working. What was less clear was to whom the judgment in such cases belonged. From his perspective, the answer was unequivocal: to higher ecclesial authorities.[187] In this vein, the thinking of certain church officials seemed to assume a simple alignment of the perceived miraculous with the hierarchical. It is thus not surprising that some officials would attempt unilaterally to direct an icon's life by deciding on its proper location and on the character of its veneration. Many lay believers also acted in accordance with the notion of unconditional hierarchical ordering, judging the status of their icon on the basis of episcopal ruling.

At the same time, many other believers, including clergy as well as laity, did not equate episcopal authority with the sacred authority of a miracle working icon. In 1876, in response to a believer's request to call an icon of the Resurrection of Christ located in his local parish church miracle working, the bishop of Kostroma, Platon (Fiveiskii), claimed that there were no ecclesiastical regulations by which an icon, through formal investigation, could be deemed miracle working. Some icons are called miracle working, he noted, not because of the judgment of authorities but because of a "tradition of faith."[188] This response was not entirely accurate in the sense that historically there had been cases when church officials had formally approved the designation of an icon as miracle working. Nevertheless, Platon's comments expressed a common belief that it was God who established icons as miracle working and that in the icon's life, bishops along with laity were mere witnesses. In 1915 the Holy Synod articulated the same ancient idea: The recognition of particular icons as miracle working was "based not on special resolutions by church officials but on the very reality of miracles that occur by prayers before these icons."[189] This view stood in sharp contrast to the principles according to which the 1722 law was not only originally formulated but also actively implemented in the late imperial period; it also stood in contrast to the apparent protocol of acquiring permission from the Holy Synod to specially venerate an icon officially recognized as miracle working. It understood the sign, the miracle, the wondrous as a hierophany that stood as its own independent directive to the faithful and by virtue of its occurrence commanded recognition.

Laity routinely distinguished hierarchical and hierophanic principles of ecclesial ordering when they insisted that a specially revered or miracle-working icon could not be equated with common church property to which church officials could lay claim. In their estimation, such an icon belonged to that place where it initially revealed its special character. In petitioning for the return of an icon of St. Nicholas that had been removed from their area a century before, for instance, parishioners from the Tver diocese wrote that St. Nicholas, through the appearance of his icon, himself chose the place where the icon was to be housed. By removing the icon from its original locus of appearance, humans placed their will and judgment over the will of God.[190] In 1909, the peasant Mikhail Kon'ki from the Ekaterinoslavl diocese offered to level his home in order to have a chapel and then a church constructed on the site where an icon had reportedly renewed itself.[191] In cases of epiphanic icons, many believers desired to construct a chapel or church on the site where the icon had been found.[192] If the icon could not remain at its original site, then believers chose to have it placed in the church nearest to where it had appeared.[193]

Second, newly surfaced miracle-working icons also begged the question of lay integrity as witnesses and challenged the Orthodox ecclesiastical establishment on two fronts: who would decide such matters, and by what process consensus on such matters could be reached.[194] Generally, cases regarding miracle-working icons show that laity, parish priests, and bishops differed even among themselves over the question of who in the ecclesial community held the authority to discern the reality of signs and miracles. It appears that clergy—parish priests and diocesan bishops—employed the term "superstitious" in various ways. Often it seems to have been used loosely to indicate a lay claim to having witnessed or experienced a miracle. The notion of superstition in such cases therefore often referred more to the perceived status of the believer than to the character of the religious action or belief in and of itself. Such reflexive use of disparaging language by clergy frustrated believers who were growing more aware of their role as lay persons and members of the Church as the Body of Christ. Consequently, the rise in the number of complaints regarding specially revered icons filed by laity with the Holy Synod beginning in the 1890s testifies to a growing crisis in episcopal authority that in part resulted from such clerical attitudes. In 1900, peasants from the village of Sorma in the Kazan diocese heatedly refused to let the local dean take a newly surfaced epiphanic icon of the Nativity of Christ from their parish to the diocesan cathedral. As the bishop of Kazan, Arsenii (Briantsev), reported, the peasants became "firmly entrenched in the idea of not relinquishing their icon, of not obeying legal demands, and even, if need be, suffering for the sake of the icon." Accordingly, the bishop thought that the icon's very presence in the local parish church was "totally undermining the authority of diocesan officials" and was potentially serving as the basis of similar "disorders" in neighboring villages.[195] Indeed, in other similar cases, the issue of ecclesiastical authority was directly raised. As residents from the town of Mozdok (Vladikavkaz diocese) starkly wrote in 1900, "the bishop is subordinate to the icon and not the icon to him."[196] Such confrontations clearly resonated with the theological issues of ecclesial ordering that confronted the Orthodox Church at the beginning of the twentieth century.

Finally, newly surfaced specially revered icons brought competing notions regarding the proper locus of ecclesial gatherings into bold relief. Church officials often responded negatively to the movement and gathering of believers around these icons, especially when they remained in homes or in the localities where they were under no direct clerical supervision. Some church officials clearly felt uncomfortable with such spontaneous acts of gathering, during which the clerical ordering of liturgical celebration could not be ensured. Their unease is comparable in some ways to that of their episcopal Byzantine counterparts, who, as Peter Brown has convincingly shown, had understood the immediate presence of the holy to be found in only a few symbols—the Eucharist, the church building, and the sign of the Cross. The iconoclasm of certain Byzantine bishops was at least in part based on their resistance to the centrifugal pull of both the icon and the holy man as bearers of the holy outside the hierarchically sanctioned sacramental order.[197] So, too, in the late nineteenth century, certain Russian clergy saw such gatherings around icons as setting the stage for potential "sectarian" activity. Consequently, as in the case of chapels, often the official impulse was to prevent the formation of these gatherings, either by completely removing their focal point—the icon itself—or by clerically centering the phenomenon by placing the icon in the parish church and insisting on the icon's common status. For laity, however, the icon itself was a focus of ecclesial centering, with its actual spatial setting—home, chapel, church, or cathedral—taking on a secondary importance.

A series of letters written in 1916 and 1917 by the peasant and police constable Vasilii Konstantinov Novoselov to the Holy Synod graphically depicts the nature of the alienation that often resulted from diverging understandings of religious authority and ecclesial priorities with respect to specially revered icons.[198] Novoselov and a group of fellow villagers from Kichma in the Viatka diocese had purchased a copy of an icon of the Mother of God named "Multiplier of Crops" as a gift for their community (fig. 5.7). Novoselov's correspondence with the ober-procurator, the Holy Synod, and the metropolitan of St. Petersburg began when parish clergy refused to allow the village to honor this icon and "locked it up," pending special permission from the Holy Synod for its veneration.

The icon in question was of relatively recent composition; it was first made in 1890. Its story was intimately tied to Ambrose, the famous elder of the Optina monastery.[199] The problem was that believers throughout Russia began specially venerating the icon prior to any official blessing by the Holy Synod. In fact, the synod attempted to discourage veneration of the icon and in July 1896 prohibited the production of copies.[200] Yet the fact that Ambrose himself had distributed reproductions of the icon and that monasteries had for years been printing copies of it proved blessing enough for such veneration from the believer's perspective.[201]

When the Holy Synod declined his request for the greeting of the icon and prayer services before it, Novoselov became indignant with what he saw as the icon's "humiliation." He charged church officials with creating new policies that were in direct violation of the Seventh Ecumenical Council. He accused them of "playing with holy items as with dolls" and of carrying on a "second iconoclasm." Moreover, he openly spoke of the division he saw in the Church over the issue. Speaking of his local community of believers as a "council of faithful" (sobor veruiushchikh), he claimed they had no choice but to preserve the purity of the faith in the face of such "iconoclastic" treatment of the icon by church officials.[202] Moreover, Novoselov identified this "council of faithful" with "the Orthodox Church," intimating that the centralized institution of the Holy Synod was not the exclusive guardian of the faith. He spoke of the Synod as a department "established by the tsar" neither "to ruin

5.7   Print of the specially revered icon of the Mother of
God named "Multiplier of Crops." The Russian State
Historical Archive (f. 796, op. 173, d. 2670a, l. 4).

the Church" nor "to leave petitions and appeals without action." For Novoselov, ecclesial polarization resulted from unilateral decisions by church officials regarding which icons could be specially revered. Ultimately, therefore,
he was left asking "Who exists for whom? The Holy Church for the Synod,
or the Holy Synod for the Church?"[203] Such questions found themselves a
part of the legacy of the 1917–18 All-Russian Church Council, as Novoselov
did not shy away from letting his concerns regarding the veneration of this
icon be known both to Patriarch Tikhon and to members of the Council.[204]

The culture of specially revered icons in the Christian East expanded the
narrative aspect of iconographic tradition to include not only the narratives associated with the visual image but the stories behind the specially
revered icons as well. In late imperial Russia such stories frequently emerged

from individuals' experiences with icons that were embraced by other believers as testimonies to the manifestation of God's grace in their midst. Believers then identified stories of God's workings in their own lives with the story conveyed through that icon's particular iconographic depictions. The accounts they related about specially revered icons reflected their perception of their ongoing participation in the Christian story and the divine plan that story suggests. To follow the stories behind a specially revered image, then, means to follow the strands by which a certain ecclesial formation around the icon was recurrently taking place, both locally and nationally. Through these icons believers, individually and collectively, tied their present lives not only to a common sacred past but to an ongoing, living community of meaning and common identity that provided hope in both the present and the age to come.

The troubled lives of many newly surfaced specially revered icons bore no less testimony than their more established, widely accepted, and often ancient counterparts to the story of the ecclesial community in Russia on the eve of revolution. On the backdrop of a firmly ingrained and active culture of miracle-working icons, the pockets of conflict that arose in connection with them disclosed underlying tensions in the dynamics of ecclesial life. These tensions involved manifold relationships that in many ways were inherent in the phenomenon called church—relationships between hierarchical and collective ways of thinking, between the national and the local, and the individual and the communal. Such tensions were not new to nineteenth-century Russian Orthodoxy but were demanding increasing attention in a church that was struggling with modernizing culture. In nineteenth-century France, Catholic clergy actively promoted miracles in their struggle against challenges posed by the modern world, as well as in their attempt to create a national community of Catholics.[205] In Russia, ecclesiastical officials exhibited no such systematic acceptance of newly surfaced miracle-working icons and, in fact, often seemed ambiguous in their stance toward them. Certainly there were ordained clergy and monastics who, like their counterparts in France, welcomed reported miracles as signs of religious vitality at a time when a religious way of life was being challenged by the rising number of atheists in Russian society.

Yet other Orthodox churchmen responded to newly proclaimed miracles not as welcome succor in a new and modernizing world but as symptomatic of that world. Indeed, even most of the canonizations of saints that occurred at the end of the nineteenth and beginning of the twentieth century, including Serafim of Sarov—perhaps the most popular among lay believers—took place in an atmosphere where churchmen displayed varied levels of reticence, often based on their perception of the laity. This caution was exercised despite any attraction to the idea of having national spiritual rallying points in the midst of social, political, and philosophical instability.[206] Such rallying points often seemed to have developed despite and not because of any aggressive work by church officials.

Ironically, many newly surfaced specially revered icons in Russia came to represent those challenges to traditional authority structures that moderniza-tion frequently entailed. Because these icons usually originated with the ex-periences of lay men and women from all social backgrounds, they gave lay people an independent means by which to exercise their spiritual discernment and express both their personal and communal involvement in the unfolding of sacred history. Independence with respect to miracle-working icons was nothing new, since lay people had historically demonstrated it throughout Russia's history, despite the Petrine legislation of 1722 that attempted to curb it.[207] In the climate of the growing revolutionary movement in Russia from the 1890s on, however, certain icons that at another time might have crea-tively united the lay and clerical aspects of ecclesial life in a common celebra-tion now only accentuated strains between the two. It is not surprising that the subject of miracle-working icons was raised during the 1917–18 All-Russian Church Council in the context of discussion of the ownership and management of holy items.[208] Indeed, given the social and political develop-ments in Russia toward the end of the ancien régime, the chronicles of events behind such icons often lead the historian to a broader story of reform and renewal in the Russian Orthodox Church at the beginning of the twentieth century.

# 6

⊷⊶⊜⊷⊶

# The Message of Mary

> About her it is said: Source of the Church. . . . She is the exclusive
> center of Church life. . . . She is the Church.
>
> —PAVEL FLORENSKII, *The Pillar and Ground of the Truth*

In the history of the Christian West, believers have experienced Mary's "presence" frequently, if not mostly, through visions and apparitions. In Russia, however, believers have experienced the activity and presence of Mary primarily through the phenomenon of Marian icons. Although often established by virtue of personal experiences, specially revered icons were intimately involved in the shaping and experience of community life. Such icons, most of which were of Mary, generated, sustained, and on certain occasions challenged the sense of community among Russian Orthodox believers from the local to the national level. As early as the mid–seventeenth century, an archdeacon from Antioch, Pavel Aleppo, noted in his well-known account of his travels through Russia that he had not seen one church that did not house a miracle-working icon of the Mother of God.[1] Each of these icons of Mary, or the Birth-Giver of God (*Bogoroditsa*) as she was called in Russia, had its story, and these stories collectively sculpted that Orthodox tradition with which common lay men and women manifestly identified.

In an overview of Marian theology and piety through the past two millennia, the Catholic theologian Elizabeth A. Johnson has referred to Mary as a "collective noun," as a name that calls to mind the "ambiguity and pluralism of the Marian tradition."[2] This chapter pursues the notion of Mary as a "collective noun" but in a somewhat redefined manner. It looks not so much to the diversity in thinking about Mary as to the diverse roles she played, through her icons, in shaping Orthodox communal identity. In doing so, it turns to the scores of stories associated with Marian icons as a manifold chronicle of experiences of Mary that, regardless of their dates of origin, continued to stir religious sensibilities among Orthodox believers in Russia.

Initially born from religious experiences, icon stories typically had been sustained orally; often, though not always, they eventually found their way into printed form. Whether in oral or published form, the sharing of such stories brought these experiences from the private realm into the public sphere, where they conveyed a range of messages. Frequently functioning in a prescriptive capacity, these stories strengthened and influenced people's behavior as well as their vision of community life. They related the workings of the economy of salvation, mainly through accounts of the bestowal of divine grace and retribution, and exemplified righteous and impious values and sentiments.

While manuscripts and published accounts about miracle-working icons existed well before the nineteenth century, it was only during this century that literature about Marian icons, even about those known heretofore only locally, began appearing on a wide scale.[3] Catalogues and lists describing such icons became readily available in print. The second half of the nineteenth century also saw the mass publication of devotional pamphlets concerning the lives of Marian icons for popular consumption.[4] Authors of these narratives or histories of Marian icons based their accounts predominantly on oral histories, though they also routinely consulted parish church and diocesan archives for any relevant records.[5]

The proliferation of published Marian icon narratives could not help but undermine any efforts at constructing an officially directed cult of miracle-working icons. For all practical purposes, these publications made the categorization of such icons into national, local, or simply specially revered subtypes less meaningful. Through their published Lives, icons, whose histories might otherwise have remained unknown beyond a local area, were mainstreamed into a broader ecclesial culture. Compilations of such stories were especially effective in this sense. Usually arranged according to the icons' day of liturgical commemoration, they compressed hundreds of icons that had appeared in Russia over some nine hundred years into a single calendar of Marian events, any instance of which could be annually remembered by any local church community. These collections, however, gave an only apparent order to the otherwise dispersed local celebrations of Marian icons.

Lay people were clearly stirred by miracle-working icon stories. Clergy, too, appreciated their didactic function. The priest A. Speranskii, for instance, claimed that such stories increased believers' love of Mary, supported them in their hope for her intercession before God, and strengthened their faith in her indefatigable protection of Russia.[6] In 1916, Bishop Nikodim reiterated Speranskii's belief that icon stories recalled events that sparked faith and hope. In contrast to Speranskii's emphasis on faith in the collective and national sense, however, Nikodim emphasized the personal effect of these stories. Miracle-working icon stories, he wrote, not only engender "salvific thoughts" but also "draw believers to the grace-filled, celestial heights where eternal love reigns."[7]

Ironically, the stories about Mary recounted by Orthodox clergy in attempting to guide lay believers were in large part themselves molded by lay believers. The role of lay persons in shaping the Marian icon cult can be indirectly gleaned by reviewing the hundreds of stories told about her.

Changes in the profile of the primary protagonists in icon stories began to take place from the fifteenth century onward and were comparable to trends that characterized Marian apparitions in Catholic Europe.[8] Whereas the central characters in more ancient narratives tended to be male monastics, clerics, and princes, by the nineteenth century the overwhelming number of icon stories concerned common laity—peasants, merchants, or townspeople, male and female. Indeed, accounts like the one that stood behind the Tolga icon of the Mother of God in the fourteenth century would have been an anomaly in the nineteenth. In that story, the bishop of Rostov, Prokhor, witnessed light radiating from an icon he discovered in a forest and related his experience "to the people."[9] The process of witnessing to perceived revelations later began to move from the bottom up—from accounts by lay men and women to corporately embraced ecclesial experiences that only subsequently (if ever) received episcopal sanction.

Some nineteenth-century presentations of the story behind one of Russia's most famous icons, the "Kazan" icon of the Mother of God, stressed this feature of icon stories. They pointed out that the Kazan icon, which was responsible for Russia's fate on numerous occasions, had its beginnings not with civil authorities, a bishop, or a wealthy person but with a child from a simple family.[10] In addition, whereas prior to the fifteenth century only a small number of recorded root narratives of specially revered icons related the experiences of women, by the nineteenth century women's experiences reached at least parity with that of men. Taking into account those stories that were known only orally, the numbers may indeed have surpassed those of men. Modern Marian icons, therefore, very much like Marian apparitions in the Catholic West, in the words of Victor Turner, "pointed to the hidden, nonhierarchical domain of the Church."[11]

This increase in the publication of such stories in the nineteenth century also had its effects in the liturgical and periliturgical realm of church life. The incorporation of icon-related stories into the liturgical life of the Church was evident, for example, with the composition and publication of new *akathistos* hymns in honor of various Marian icons, which were based on stories that made the particular icon special. A genre of eastern Christian hymnography that dated to perhaps as early as fifth-century Byzantium, the *akathistos* hymn (*akafist* in Russian) was originally developed as a liturgical expression of devotion towards Mary the Mother of God. By the end of the Byzantine period, it had developed into a broader genre of laudatory hymnody.[12] Before the eighteenth century, the Church in Russia had no officially approved *akathistoi* in honor of specific icons of Mary. By the second half of the nineteenth century, however, seventeen icons of the Mother of God had officially approved *akathistoi* published in their honor.[13] In addition, during the second half of the nineteenth century, published menologions listing the lives of saints also began listing the lives of locally revered icons of the Mother of God in addition to the nationally known types.[14] The inclusion of locally revered icons greatly expanded the list of those nationally recognized icons that usually had been listed in published menologians.[15] Finally, in 1907, a special commission under the aegis of the Moscow Synodal Press published a special addition to the Russian language version of the eighteenth-century Menologion (*Chet'ii Minei*) compiled by Dimitrii, the bishop of Rostov. This addition included the lives of hundreds of specially revered icons of the Mother of God.[16] Through such publications, the stories behind these icons entered into that body of devotional literature that served as material for preaching and teaching.[17]

Second only to the vast body of liturgical hymnody in her honor, Marian icons and their related stories provide one of the richest sources through which we can appreciate Mary's role in the ecclesial world of late imperial Russian Orthodoxy. In order to situate Marian icon stories in a broader context, I first briefly examine the image of Mary herself—without her icon—as a symbol of collective Orthodox experience that emerges from devotional literature. I then describe the special relationship between Mary and her icon and the way icon stories portray Mary making use of her own image. Next, traversing the terrain of ecclesial life set forth in these stories, I search for the values and sentiments that the icon of Mary encouraged, especially with respect to the issues of religious authority, the community, and the individual. What was the example she set and what aspects of collective Orthodox experience did she represent?

## The Marian Persona and the Christian Community

Marian icons were part of a broader Marian-centered culture in Russia that was nurtured primarily by a rich liturgical tradition. Pavel Florenskii estimated that nearly half of the liturgical hymns in Orthodox services were composed in Mary's honor.[18] Sermons, periliturgical discussions, and devotional literature, often drawing on Christian apocryphal literature, especially the *Protevangelium* of James, provided additional avenues by which believers would have heard or read about her. Themselves steeped in and drawing on these sources, Orthodox thinkers frequently identified Mary with the sacred collective, the ecclesial community. This theological association had its roots in ancient Christian liturgical typology that saw Mary symbolically prefigured in the Old Testament Ark of the Covenant, the Tabernacle, and the Jerusalem Temple—the sites of divine manifestation and presence in the midst of Israel. Regularly recalled in liturgical hymnody, especially in the *akathistos* hymns, such associations were based on the view of Mary as the "Birth-Giver of God." Just as the Tent of Meeting and the Temple of Solomon had been filled with the glory of God, so Mary, as *Theotokos*, was a "place hallowed by glory." As such she was a "pillar of fire who guided those existing in darkness," the "fire that enlightened the night of life in this world," directing believers to the way of salvation.[19]

In her role as director and guide, Mary emerges with two distinct profiles in this devotional milieu, which correspond roughly to the periods in her life preceding and following Christ's resurrection. Devotional writers and preachers drew on Mary's life before Christ's resurrection to present her as a standard for emulation. As a young maiden, they portrayed her as having dedicated herself to service to that Temple to which she would later be typologically compared. Devotional texts noted that she spoke little and concentrated more on working, praying, and reading the Word of God. Her bodily movements were modest, and her gait was quiet but firm. Neither poverty nor need pushed her into despair, and she never became embittered by those who offended her. She was respectful of her elders and merciful to the poor.[20]

It was precisely this image of Mary in her early life that commonly served as the representation of the ideal lay person. Makarii (Miroliubov), the bishop of the Don diocese (1887–94), for instance, chose to highlight the attention Mary paid to the Temple as a young girl and encouraged believers to do the same for their own salvation. He claimed that a believer's progress and success in abiding by the laws of God could be judged by his or her zeal toward the temple. "Neither love nor a general disposition toward the law of God can be expected from a person who rarely attends church."[21]

In his presentation of the life of Mary, the priest I. Kassirov also held up Mary's piety as an example for laity to follow. Nothing better demonstrated Mary's humility and meekness, he wrote, than her complete silence during Christ's service to the people, a "wonderful silence" that first revealed itself during the Annunciation. It was not passivity on Mary's part that Kassirov praised but an active self-restraint. Although, as he explained, she was first among believers in terms of her faith and love, and although she understood matters of faith better than anyone else, she was never seen speaking about the divine mysteries or dogmas of faith. "She did not mix her voice with the voice of the apostles."[22] Such an image of Mary seemed to support the views of those such as Makarii Bulgakov who proposed a division in the ecclesial community between the clergy who taught and the laity who were taught.

Even though believers saw Mary as a model for personal emulation, her disposition was not without ambiguities. Devotional writings often interpreted her silence in the New Testament accounts, especially in the Gospel according to Luke, as an act of self-effacement. Yet authors were divided over whether this silence suggested a deference before unfolding events in which Mary quietly "pondered" the saving acts of God or a deference more specifically before Christ, as the embodiment of hierarchical authority.

In addition, devotional literature also portrayed her as a person who had singularly experienced the gamut of emotions that constitute the human condition. Thus churchmen encouraged not only women but all believers, including fellow clergy, to conform their lives to the image of Mary. Unlike Christ, who was considered entirely divine as well as entirely human, Mary was not portrayed "alone of all her sex" or, for that matter, alone of all her creaturely "kind."[23] In the well-known account of a vision experienced by

Serafim of Sarov (1759–1833), Mary appears together with the disciples Peter and John the Theologian and identifies Serafim as "one of *our* kind." By depicting Mary in this fashion, hagiographers acknowledged that while Mary was indeed "special," she was not outside the ranks of human company.[24]

In the Russian Orthodox understanding, Mary, by nature, was no exception among her fellow human creatures. While clergy spoke about her as "the ideal of heavenly perfection"[25] and celebrated her in almost every liturgical service as "more honorable than the cherubim and more glorious than the seraphim," most devotional literature routinely stressed her humanity. Churchmen were cautious in ascribing divine attributes to her and usually tried to depict her as having shared those life experiences that would be familiar to common believers. It was this insistence on Mary's common humanity that came to divide Orthodox thinkers from their Roman Catholic counterparts over the doctrine of the Immaculate Conception promulgated by Pope Pius IX in 1854.[26]

In one sense, then, Mary's success as a guide was contingent on her ever-humanness. Such aspects of Mary's perceived life as virginity and child-bearing, which in the writings of Western scholastics had at times prompted biological speculation, often found more universal application in Russian Orthodox devotional writings and homilies. The future controversial patriarch of Russia Sergius Stragorodskii wrote in the first half of the twentieth century that biological virginity was not the main focus of the theme of Mary's ever-virginity, since even the devil was not subject to the "fall" of the flesh. That fact alone did not and could not make one holy. Rather, in Sergius's estimation, Mary's virginity had much more to do with the integrity (*tselos-nost'*) of her soul: "It had completely attached itself to God to the degree that she did not allow any desire or any attachment to stand between her soul and her beloved Lord."[27] More than a half century earlier, the metropolitan of Moscow, Filaret (Drozdov), had expressed similar ideas when he spoke about the importance of spiritual over biological virginity. By following Mary's spiritual example, he wrote, believers could enter into communion with God. By "gazing upon her as an example of one who seeks communion with God," he said in another sermon, believers could see their own obligations in "the mirror of Mary's perfection."[28]

Mary's humanity also figured into the logic behind trusting Mary as the foundation of human hope. Devotional writers grounded that hope not only in Mary's proximity to God or in her "perfection" but also in the universality of her life's experiences that transcended gender, as well as social, economic, or political standing. "Look at me," Mary is portrayed saying in one pamphlet, "yes, I gave birth to the pre-eternal God . . . but remember what my life was like . . . I witnessed the very depths of suffering."[29]

The meeting between Mary and believers was to take place, therefore, in a relational moment created by compassion and memory. Seeing in her one of their own, believers could ask Mary to "guide the eyes of their hearts toward salvation," as long as they remembered her example and mirrored her love and mercy. "You yourself ask for my maternal blessing for your children," Mary is portrayed as saying. "But have you [remembered to] care for homeless children and unfortunate parents?"[30] Mary, in turn, it was asserted, could respond to and support believers during their own "Golgothas" because she remembered from her own experiences "the great sorrows that could oppress the human heart."[31]

The image of Mary as guide, however, took on a different tenor in devotional writings and sermons concerned with her life after Christ's resurrection. At that point, writers moved her to the center of the Christian community, with the disciples and apostles turning to her for their inspiration. One devotional essay portrayed the apostles as saying: "We were comforted by looking at you, our Lady, as if at our own Lord and Teacher."[32] Another author described how the apostles would leave Jerusalem temporarily to preach, and then return to listen to Mary's "divine words." As a text from the Menologion by Dimitrii of Rostov recounted, God had left Mary on earth so that by her presence, advice, and teachings, the Christian community could establish itself.[33]

Before her death, according to such devotional accounts, Mary summoned the apostles, blessed them, and assured them that she would never abandon them. She promised to use her position at the side of her son's heavenly throne following her death to petition him "face to face" on believers' behalf. She also assured the apostles that she would not leave the world and that she would be present to protect the weak and poor.[34] It is noteworthy that prayers addressed to Mary petitioned her not only for her protection but also for inclusion among *her* flock, which she was guiding to salvation.[35] One of Russia's most celebrated feasts in the prerevolutionary period, the Protecting Veil of the Birth-Giver of God (*Pokrov*), celebrated this pastoral or even episcopal image of Mary as a gatherer of individual believers into a collective "people."[36] Hence Mary was a guide not only in the sense of a model but also in the sense of a gatherer of the community that was to come before the Lord.

While Mary's identification with the ecclesial community depended in part on her special relationship with her son, Orthodox writers in Russia did not hesitate to speak about her as if she had a status that paralleled that of Christ, especially with respect to her role in the ordering of ecclesial life.[37] Fr. Alexander Soloviev, for instance, spoke of both "the Son of God, Savior, and the Mother of God" as the inspirational centers for those in need.[38] Others went further and presented a relationship with Christ as contingent on a prior relationship with Mary. One cannot pay homage to the Son, the monk Sergii reminded his readers, without due respect for his mother. Such a high regard for Mary led Sergii to depict her as a mediator in sacred history, parallel in many ways to Martin Luther's view of Christ. "Covering our bare and shameful lives," he wrote, "she makes us worthy of grace in the eyes of God."[39] Bishop Iustin maintained that only by imitating the "inner image" of Mary could believers "maturely" fulfill Christ's directives.[40] One priest qualified such views by restating that Christ was in all respects the first and foremost image of holiness that his followers were called to emulate. Nevertheless, he maintained, if believers were to follow Christ, the image of Mary was indispensable since she imitated Christ in a perfect way. To imitate Mary was the best way to imitate Christ.[41] In 1918, D. Samarin, in an essay on the Mother of God in Russian Orthodoxy, noted a similar primacy of Mary in the sacred worlds of common Orthodox faithful. In the minds of common lay people, he wrote, Mary had come to displace Christ himself as the central figure in the economy of salvation.[42]

However accurate this assessment may have been, devotional writings about Mary's life after Christ's resurrection presented her as a distinct and active agent in sacred history. At the forefront of the ongoing course of sacred history, she, along with Christ, was continually watching the flow of human history, responding to it according to the measure of human faith and disbelief, and guiding the body of "faithful ones." It is noteworthy that despite the proliferation of literature dedicated to Mary, and despite the conviction on the part of some clergymen that the number of miracles in Russia was on the rise, nineteenth-century devotional literature on Mary did not essentially speak of an "age of Mary" that was dawning as a prelude to the Second Coming of Christ—a theme commonly found in France at the time.[43]

We can follow the practical effects of an ecclesial culture that saw Mary as a central authority figure in a 1907 devotional story about the healing of a twenty-eight-year-old woman, Ekaterina. In that story, Ekaterina had several visions in which Mary directed her to remind the local priest and people to honor Sundays and feast days properly, a directive common in the Marian cult in both Western and Eastern Christianity. When the priest failed to take her experiences seriously, Ekaterina had another vision, this time during the Sunday Eucharistic liturgy. During the singing of the Cherubic hymn, Mary came out of the sanctuary and directed Ekaterina to approach the priest again. When Ekaterina did so, the priest replied that it was not her place to teach the people in the church but his. Ekaterina later directly confronted the priest, asking him whether he believed her account, and the priest admitted he did not. The Virgin then healed Ekaterina, primarily for the correction and edification of the priest.[44]

Mary indeed signified "ecclesia" and was intimately tied to the notion of ecclesiality, both because she was believed to have given birth to God and because through the diversity of her own life's experiences she could identify with and facilitate solidarity among different types of individual believers. A devotional pamphlet entitled "A Zealous Protectress of All" summarized the assorted ways of experiencing Mary. Virgins and monastics, for instance, sought her protection since she herself had been a virgin and had fulfilled the vows associated with the monastic vocation: chastity, humility, and poverty. Women who were pregnant sought her since she had given birth. Parents sought her aid because she had experienced the concerns of parenthood, especially the sufferings associated with illness and separation, since she had temporarily lost her own son when he was twelve. Widows and widowers found comfort with her since she, too, was left as a widow when her guardian, Joseph, died.[45] She was the defender of orphans since her parents had died soon after she had turned three. She was the caretaker of the poor because she had experienced extreme poverty. Yet she did not deny the wealthy her protection, as she remembered the service of the rich man, Joseph of Arimathea, who had comforted her by burying her son. Artists and workers called on her since she had practiced the art of needlework and because her son had been a simple worker. Prisoners and exiles called out to her since she had found herself in exile in the land of Egypt.

Interestingly, however, the "elites"—tsars, clergy (including bishops, priests, and deacons), military personnel, teachers, and students—were linked to Mary through authoritative titles that often had a christocentric focus. Tsars were called to identify with Mary as "the Queen of Heaven." Clergy sought her as the Mother of the High Priest. She was the advocate of warriors since she was liturgically praised as a "victorious leader" who helped the Byzantine emperors in their military battles on numerous occasions. She could identify with teachers and students in their search for wisdom since she had given birth to Christ, the Wisdom of God.[46] Embracing and uniting all believers into one community through her person, Mary did so through a diverse array of experiential and historical associations. The ecclesial experience of Mary, consequently, remained as multifaceted as the woman who stood at its center.

⋆⟞◉⟝⋆

## Mary and Her Image

Specially revered Marian icons were not merely a part of Russia's broader Marian-centered religious culture but its mainstay. Visually, such Marian icons tended to involve believers mostly with the preresurrectional Mary by portraying the face of an exemplary life. Yet through their stories, specially revered Marian icons also involved believers with the postresurrectional Mary who openly and authoritatively took her place at the helm of the economy of salvation. The ancient and well-known story that recounted the origin of Marian icons described their place in this part of Mary's story. According to this story, as told in Russian Orthodox devotional literature, following the death, resurrection, and ascension of Christ, believers desired to see the woman at the center of the burgeoning apostolic community. In order to satisfy this desire, the evangelist Luke painted several images of Mary and the infant Christ. He then showed these to Mary, who in seeing them rejoiced. She did so, explained devotional pamphlets, not because she felt that these images in any way glorified her but because she desired to remain with the ecclesial community for all time in order to help it. As if to ensure this, Mary then blessed these depictions by saying "May the grace of the One born from me and my own blessing be with these images."[47]

This story illustrates an interesting feature of the relationship between

Mary and her icon. By blessing Luke's depiction, Mary was portrayed not only as accepting the accuracy of Luke's rendering or "iconizing" of her but also as determined and ready to work with it. In other words, the person of Mary remains beyond her image, through which she at the same time has consented to remain present. Accordingly, Orthodox devotional literature did not portray Mary's life within the Christian community as ending with her death or dormition. A well-known story in late nineteenth-century Russia, based on the "Life" of St. Andrew, a fool for Christ, illustrates this notion of Mary's ongoing involvement. Andrew, the slave of a Byzantine nobleman, had a vision in which he was "lifted to heaven." When he asked whether he could gaze on Mary, the angel accompanying him told him that she was not there. She had left for the "suffering world," he explained, in order to help people and to comfort those who mourn.[48]

Notably, versions of Mary's "Life" often included lists of miracle-working icons as documentation of her continued life within the community of believers. After her own death, Mary was portrayed as having manifested and pledged her ongoing relationship with the ecclesial community by having left behind these icons. As the priest Vladimir Sokolov noted in an 1892 homily, "these material memorials testify to each believer that the Heavenly Queen never ceased and does not now cease to be involved with this world."[49] Mary left these icons as gifts, the priest Alexander Vorontsov claimed in 1908, as a sign of her love toward the faithful.[50] She established a personal relationship with particular icons for the purpose of relating to the faithful in the historical present.[51]

The phenomenon of miracle-working icons of Mary pointed, therefore, not only to the community's memory of Mary but also to the community's perception of Mary's ongoing presence within it. During visitations of a Marian icon to parishes or villages, believers commonly spoke of it as a "most precious" or "extraordinary" guest. When the icon traveled, believers spoke of Mary traveling.[52] Having become the Mother of all believers, one devotional pamphlet maintained, Mary "is continually present among us . . . in her miracle-working icons."[53] She "comes nearer to us" and "appears to us" through the "wondrous signs from her icons.[54]

Stories behind specially revered Marian icons routinely conveyed the notion of this unique relationship between the icons and Mary, their prototype. In the 1880s, a peasant from the Vladimir diocese, Ivan Demidov, became troubled by a leg ailment and found himself facing its amputation. One of his friends told him about a miracle-working icon of the Mother of God of the Sign located in the Serafimo-Ponetaevskii monastery in the Nizhnii Novgorod diocese (fig. 6.1). Demidov could not make the journey but decided to pray before it *in absentia*. One night, during a light sleep, he heard a voice say to him, "Why are you sleeping? Our Lady has come to you!" He then saw not Mary but this icon of her.[55] In another case earlier in the nineteenth century, a pious elderly woman from the Borisov hermitage in the Kursk diocese, whose task it was to light the lampada before a miracle-

6.1 Miracle-working
icon of the Mother
of God (of the Sign)
named "Serafimo-
Ponetaevskaia." From
*Chudotvornaia ikona
Znameniia Presviatyia
Bogoroditsy i Serafimo-
Ponetaevskii zhenskii
monastyr'*. (Nizhnii
Novgorod, 1886).

working Tikhvin icon of the Mother of God, had a similar experience. One day while walking toward the monastery she met a majestic woman of unusual beauty dressed in white. Instinctively, the elderly woman reverently greeted this figure and asked where she was from. The figure responded that she resided in the monastery. Bewildered, the woman asked whether she had been there long since she had never seen her. "I always live there," Mary replied. "You light the lampada and place candles before me."[56]

It is noteworthy that in such stories Mary is often depicted as making her icons known to believers through dreams. Clergy did not automatically dismiss dreams as superstitious. Orthodox thinkers at the time held firmly to the importance of dreams, though not without discrimination. Navigating through the Scylla of modern science and the Charybdis of a popular dream culture, Orthodox writers legitimized certain unusual dream experiences as religious and revelatory.[57] They generally warned believers that it was fruitless and absurd to guide one's life by dreams. At the same time, as one author noted, dreams should not be dismissed as having no significance whatsoever. Not only could certain dreams provide a means to self-knowledge but, historically, some have also been shown to provide insight into divine will.[58] One devotional pamphlet explained that dreams that followed a period of repentance and fasting, acts of kindness, and experiences of self-denial tended to be more conducive to divine illumination.[59]

Dream accounts associated with icon stories clearly differed from the

majority of commonplace dreams that involved "daily residues"—the lingering impressions that a person experienced during his or her waking hours.[60]
They spoke of believers as having seen or as having had a "vision" in their
dreams or as having experienced a "discovery" or "revelation" during their
sleep. While it was often unclear whether the person in question was awake
or asleep during such experiences, the stories usually emphasized the clarity
with which the person saw a particular icon of Mary and through it experienced the "presence" of Mary herself. Even though in many cases the person
experiencing the dream was ill, the dream state, as it was described in the
story, could hardly be confused with delirium.

In addition, dreams in icon stories were closely related to a person's own
prayer life. In the story of the Iaroslav-Pechersk icon of the Mother of God
located in the provincial town of Iaroslavl, the dream that directed the townswoman Alexandra Dimitriev Dobychkina to locate this icon occurred after
seventeen years of fervent prayer to the Mother of God on account of her
physical ailments and depression.[61] In this way, Mary's post-Dormition presence with the Christian community was depicted as making itself known
through individual prayer and personal revelation.

The perceived close association between Mary and her icon, though, did
not mean that for every different icon of Mary there was a different Mary, as
has been suggested by some contemporary Russian ethnographers.[62] Both
icon stories and popular devotional literature consistently dispelled, or at least
attempted to dispel, such a notion. They always presented a single voice and
person behind the variety of iconographic expressions of Mary. Devotional
pamphlets also discussed the relationship between Mary and the numerous
icons of her. One anonymous author expressed this relationship in this way:
"How many times I remember the many faces of the Lady of our world that I
have met all throughout Russia and that are honored by the Russian people.
All of them form a single wondrous image."[64] Pavel Florenskii gave theological shape to such pious intuition. Every miracle-working icon of Mary, he
claimed, "is an imprint of only one of her aspects, a luminous spot on the
earth from only one ray of the Virgin, full of grace, only one of her iconographic names . . . whence the seeking to venerate different icons."[64]

Just as the numerous icons of Mary were not considered depictions of
separate Marys, so the stories behind these images were not seen as separate
and unrelated chronicles. They were a single chronicle of Mary's "wondrous
works." Since Mary's personal blessing accounted for their miracle-working
abilities, the countless stories stood as a single history of Mary's pledge to the
faith community.[65] In this sense the history of Marian icons was simply another
chapter in the continued Life of Mary in the ecclesial community.

By linking the presence of Mary with her icon, stories established such
icons as a recurrent identifying marker of Orthodoxy in Russia in the postreform period (and earlier). One hymn in honor of the well-known Kozelshchina icon of the Mother of God from the nineteenth century read, "As a
brightly shining star amidst your holy icons, O Virgin, your image of Kozelsh-

china leads people toward salvation."[66] Insofar as believers thought of Mary as acting through her icon, they very much pictured Mary's icons along with Mary herself as establishing and maintaining the ecclesial community. I now turn to these icon stories to see the various ways they did so.

⊶≡◎⊜⊷

## Mary, Her Icon, and the Making of the Body Sacred

In a late nineteenth-century sermon in honor of the Tikhvin icon of the Mother of God, one churchman typically called on the Mother of God to unite those present—"wealthy and poor, the exalted and the oppressed"—in "a union of brotherly love," just as the apostles of her Son had been united in one spirit among themselves.[67] His petition thematically resonated with the image of believers congregating in prayer around an icon of Mary, an image frequently reflected in liturgical hymns honoring Marian icons. Such hymns spoke of the angels along with bishops, monastics, and common people assembled around an icon of Mary, praising God for the joy the icon had brought.[68] They occasionally even drew on Eucharistic imagery to convey the quality of this type of veneration. The late nineteenth-century service in honor of the Kozelshchina icon of the Mother of God, for instance, referred to this icon as "the cup of love, flowing over with gifts of the Holy Spirit." When it called believers to "taste and see" the greatness of Mary's mercy, it was using language that was associated with the lenten Presanctified Liturgy.

Icon stories spoke of several types of events that brought a Marian icon to the center of community life. Stories that described accounts of divine light radiating from icons, for instance, were especially effective in conveying the message of their spiritual potency. The story of a Smolensk icon in the ancient southern town of Belgorod in the Kursk diocese demonstrates this. In the late seventeenth century, a pious resident of Belgorod named Semizorov fulfilled a vow by placing a Smolensk icon of the Mother of God on the town's gates. In 1703, the town's sentry, Mefodii Ivanov, reported witnessing a bright light radiating from it. Many doubted Ivanov's account; however, the healing of a paralytic woman who had heard of the event and who came to pray before the icon soon resulted in that icon's special veneration. By 1705, a church was built in its honor.[69]

A story about an icon of the Virgin with the Christ child in the Kievan Caves monastery directly linked the light radiating from the icon with the light of the Holy Spirit. In that story, while painting the main church, a group of iconographers witnessed an icon of the Mother of God miraculously appearing on the walls of the sanctuary. They then saw a dove fly from the lips of the Virgin to an icon of Christ and then around the church. When the dove flew once again from the Virgin into the lips of Christ and out again, light enveloped the icons.[70]

One late nineteenth-century poetic account of the Tolga icon of the

Mother of God conveyed the dynamics of assembly that began once believers learned about that icon in the fourteenth century. It began with a bishop witnessing light radiating from the icon in the fourteenth century.

> News about the miracle with the bishop in Iaroslavl
> Quickly spread to the ends of the city,
> And roused the hearts of all its inhabitants
> With joy about God's great mercy.
> Desiring to cling to the icon with their hearts,
> Many that moment set off in journey.
> People of all ages, gender, and standing,
> In health and in sickness they went. . . .
> Elders and monastics, men and women,
> The poor behind the noble trudged.
> Clergy and laity—with the appearance of the icon
> In joy, all people merged.[71]

Frequently, such stories of illumined icons included accounts of an icon's movement from place to place, as if seeking a place to establish a new worshiping community. In the sixteenth-century story concerning an icon of the Dormition of the Mother of God in the village of Ryshkov (Moscow diocese), a "simple man," Feofan, could not reach an icon that he had found radiating light, as it was perched on a tree. The local parish priest organized a procession and brought the icon back to the parish church. After three days in the church, however, the icon reappeared in its original location. When the parish priest and believers gathered at the site to pray to the Mother of God, they heard a voice from the icon announce that it was "pleasing to the Mother of God for the icon to remain here." Believers constructed a chapel in its honor at the site. Later the icon was moved to Moscow's Dormition Cathedral. Yet despite this apparent honor the icon, the story claims, miraculously found its way back to its original place of appearance.[72]

Such stories of miraculously moving icons reinforced the position of Marian icons as independent foci of ecclesial gathering that commanded the attention of believers. More than one story depicted believers asking in prayer for Mary to bring about an icon's placement among them.[73] These stories also helped to support the view that an icon belonged to the place where it first revealed itself as miracle working, even if that meant founding a new community or moving an already existing one. In one icon story that takes place in the sixteenth century outside Moscow, an icon of the Mother of God disappeared from a parish church and reappeared some six miles away. After consultation with his parishioners (a not insignificant point), the parish priest journeyed to Moscow to inform the patriarch of the event and to receive permission to move the parish church to the place the icon had "chosen."[74] These stories also described how persons who willfully removed icons from their chosen homes suffered divine retribution for doing so.[75] The association of icons with the establishing of worshiping communities is further shown in the histories of numerous churches in Russia whose founding was related to newly surfaced miracle-working Marian icons. Believers constructed not only entire churches in honor of such icons but countless side altars and chapels as well. In the early nineteenth century, a former landowner from the Volhynia diocese became ill and, after exhausting all medical options, began praying before an icon of Mary that he owned. Soon thereafter, Mary appeared to him in a dream and promised to heal him if he would construct a small church or chapel in her honor.[76] In such ways, Mary and her icon became part of the sacred narrative symbolized by the church building and celebrated by its worshiping community.

Monastic communities also often traced their founding to icons of Mary. For instance, in the mid-fourteenth century, a monk named Abraham set out to pursue an eremitical way of life in a remote area in the Kostroma diocese. Subsequently, in praying to the Virgin, he thanked the Lord for having been enlightened by the "ineffable light" and glory of God that shined on him through the icon. In response to the directions he received from a voice coming from the icon, he abandoned his reclusive intentions and established a monastic community.[77] The story of the establishment of the Igritsk monastery (Kostroma diocese) in the seventeenth century tells of believers who settled at the site where they had found an icon of the Mother of God because they desired to "dedicate their entire life to service" to her.[78]

Marian icons were also directly tied to the very process of church construction, as the Life of the "Vladimir icon of the Black Mountain" so vividly illustrates. According to its story, believers faced problems with the construction of a church on the site where this icon had appeared. The Mother of God facilitated the completion of the church when she appeared to a terminally ill carpenter and directed him to the site in order to receive healing. In this way, the story reads, "the Mother of God Herself chose the builder for her church."[79]

Finally, many stories associated Marian icons with critical events in local histories, both rural and urban, such as destructive fires, epidemics, and unusually fierce storms. In 1822, for example, several fires had been deliberately set in the town of Slaviansk in the Kharkov diocese, but the residents could not identify the arsonist. A pious old woman in the town had a dream in which it was revealed that the fires would end if an icon of the Mother of God named "The Burning Bush" were painted and prayer services were said before it. On the day she had this dream, another fire was set, but this time local authorities apprehended the arsonist at the scene of the crime. In thanksgiving, believers constructed a special case for the icon and wrote on the back of the icon, "in memory of the town's salvation from fire in 1822."[80] In a similar vein, in 1831, during a cholera epidemic, believers discovered an ancient fresco of the Smolensk icon of the Mother of God under a piece of cracked plaster in the Church of the Transfiguration in Novgorod. Interpreting this discovery as a sign of God's mercy, believers began streaming to the church to pray before the image. The epidemic soon passed, and after that time the icon was referred to as the "Cholera" icon of the Mother of God.[81]

In their structure as well as effects, icon stories such as these were not ordered according to the modern distinctions between natural and faith communities and, thus, also between natural and sacred history proper. It is interesting to note that when, in the early nineteenth century, Metropolitan Evgenii Bolkhovitinov wanted to include a specially venerated icon of the Virgin in his history of Pskov, Count N. P. Rumianstev challenged Bolkhovitinov's definition of history by questioning whether icons could in fact be understood as lying within its domain.[82] Icon stories indeed begged the question of the modern definition of history and the interpretation of historical "facts." Yet insofar as they served a central role in organizing and transmitting historical and social memories, they placed Mary at the mnemonic center of ecclesial life. Not only did these stories closely associate Mary with the sacred collective, they also provided its members with a common ideational base that gave cohesion and purpose to that assembly in the present.

⤞≡◎⊂≡⤝

## From Private Worlds to Ecclesial Culture

By this point, it is evident that the majority of Marian icon stories began with individual believers and not with communities of believers as such. As noted, miracle-working and specially revered icons of Mary were associated with the prayers and dreams of individuals, often involving a transformation in the form of healing or enlightenment in these persons' lives. Marian icon culture thus created a context within Orthodoxy where many found their religious needs fulfilled.

Even the most intimate encounters with Mary, however, had a social or communal dimension. This communal dimension is evident in one of the better known miracle-working icons of Mary in prerevolutionary Russia, the icon of the "Life-Bearing Spring" (*Zhivonosnyi istochnik;* fig. 6.2). This icon depicts Mary with the Christ child seated in a fount from which water flows into a pool below. People are depicted approaching and drinking from the life-giving water. The Life of this icon begins in Byzantine times and is associated with Emperor Leo I (d. 478), who was known for his devotion to the Virgin Mary. While still a soldier, Leo met a blind man in a small grove in Constantinople that had long been associated with Mary. Seeing that the man was lost, Leo guided him back to the road and then, suggesting he rest, offered to find him some water. While searching for a water source, Leo suddenly heard a voice say, "Leo, don't search far for water. There is some close by." Startled by the mysterious voice, Leo looked around but could see nothing. He then heard the same voice again, directing him to a water source. After telling Leo to give the blind man drink and to rub the mud from the source on his eyes, the voice said: "Then you will recognize who I am, who have

6.2   An icon of the Mother of God named "Life-Bearing
Spring" (*Zhivonosnyi istochnik*). 1841. From the private
collection of Robin R. Jones, M.D.

long sanctified this locality. I will help you to construct a church here in my
honor, and the prayers of every one who comes here and calls upon my name
in faith will be heard and will receive healing from their ailments."[83]

Once he became emperor, Leo I remembered his encounter with Mary
and the blind man and constructed a church over the site of the water source.
A century later, as the icon's story relates, the emperor Justinian I (d. 565)
suffered from a severe case of edema that caused him much agony. Once, in
the middle of the night, he heard a voice telling him that he could not become
well until he drank "from my spring." That message, however, only pushed
Justinian further into despair since he did not know to which spring the voice
was referring. Then the Virgin appeared to him during the day and directed
him to drink from the water source. After his healing, Justinian constructed a
new and larger church next to the one that had been constructed by Leo I.

Both the visual representation and the story associated with the icon of the Life-Bearing Spring convey themes about Mary that were frequently encountered in liturgical hymns, sermons, and devotional pamphlets. Churchmen referred to Mary and her icon as a "river of God," or the "river of life," to which individual believers journeyed to quench their thirst.[84] One of the well-known supporters of the Marian cult in Russia, the seventeenth-century bishop of Rostov, Dimitrii (d. 1709), wrote the following about a miracle-working icon of the Mother of God:

> The person oppressed by grief journeys and drinks joy; the ill person comes and drinks health; the weak person journeys and drinks strength; the sinful person comes and drinks salvation; . . . those with no hope come and drink hope; the ignorant person comes and drinks wisdom . . . and all those who journey to the miracle-working icon . . . drink their fill of grace.[85]

The collective moment in this image of Mary as "salvific water"[86] or as a "river of God" is found in the gathering of individuals at this source. Certain common sensibilities brought these persons to the icon in the first place, just as certain common experiences united them in the process of their consolation and healing. The author of one devotional pamphlet went so far as to write that Mary stood not at the periphery but at the center of the world, and the world itself could be characterized as one great infirmary in which everyone was ailing.[87]

The notions of both ailment and healing, in this context, must be understood broadly. In these stories people struggled not only with a wide array of physical ailments but with mental illnesses as well. Furthermore, healing, as it was portrayed in icon stories, was not usually an instantaneous and purely gratuitous act from above but a process that involved a long, arduous effort requiring persistence and searching on the part of believers. The story of the peasant woman Irina Petrova from the village of Kostiushin in the Moscow diocese was typical in this respect. Suffering from an unspecified internal illness for seven years, she had found no solace from physicians. When all seemed hopeless, her mother advised her to turn to prayer and to go to the nearby village of Ivanovskoe where an old church was being dismantled, there to request one of the icons of the Mother of God. Petrova learned, however, that all of the icons from the church had already been distributed. At that point, she decided to have an icon of the Mother of God made for herself.

Before she could order the icon, Petrova had a dream in which a person from the village of Ivanovskoe was taking collections. An ancient icon that had become darkened with age lay on his plate. When the collector asked Petrova why she did not request an icon from a nearby church that was being dismantled, she replied that she had heard that all of them already were distributed. The collector then explained that if she went to the church and asked for an icon of the Mother of God named "The Joy of All Who Sorrow" and prayed before this image, she would be healed. Following this dream, Petrova prayed before this type of icon of the Mother of God in her own

parish church but did not yet seek it from the church that was being dismantled.

She then had another dream in which a woman appeared to her (implied
in the story to be the Mother of God) and strongly urged her to find this
particular icon, assuring her that she would be healed. If she did not locate this
icon, her sufferings would increase. Although Petrova on this occasion went
to Ivanovskoe and asked about the icons from the old church, the parish priest
told her they had all been given away, offering her an icon from the old
iconostasis instead. Disappointed, Petrova returned home empty-handed. After one final dream, in which her deceased brother-in-law chastised her for
her negligence and showed her the image she was to search out, Petrova went
back to Ivanovskoe and pleaded for the parish elder to help her find it.
Unexpectedly, they located the icon and, following a special prayer service
before it, Petrova was healed.[88]

As this story and many others like it show, healing was not a matter that
involved only the person healed or even that individual together with Mary
and God. While Petrova's illness was presented as her private ordeal, and her
healing ultimately depended on her discernment and actions, the active involvement of others—her mother, the local parish priest and the elder, a
deceased relative, and an unidentified figure in a dream—suggests that the
success of Mary's own involvement through her icon depended also on the
faith, discernment, and collective efforts of others. In the story of the Kazan
icon of the Mother of God from the village of Pavlovsk (Moscow diocese),
for instance, Mary is portrayed speaking to one peasant in the village about
the illness of another, clearly making the fate of the latter dependent on his
fellow villager.[90]

The power of Mary's work also depended on the well-being of the icon
itself. As a rule, the discovery and restoration of a forgotten or discarded icon
led not only to a person's recovery or renewed wholeness, whether emotional
or physical, but to a revitalized corporate worship as well. In 1823 an ailing
woman, Alexandra Tolbuzina, from the village of Bogorodskoe in the Iaroslavl
diocese, decided to go on a pilgrimage to holy sites in the provincial town in
hopes of being healed from her various diseases. One night, however, she
heard a voice in a dream that warned her that she did not have the strength to
make such a journey. Instead the voice directed her to find a copy of the
Pechera icon of the Mother of God in her local parish church and to venerate
it.[91] Similarly, in 1894 an ailing merchant from Petersburg had a dream in
which Mary told him to go to the Alekseev monastery in Iaroslavl, to locate
an icon of her that was locked away in a storage closet, and to pray before this
image in order to be healed.[92]

The main obstacles in such quests for healing were usually internal and
included lack of faith and carelessness. In one story that takes place in the
1840s, a peasant, Feodosia Vasilievna, had a dream in which she heard the
voice of the Mother of God speak to her through an icon, directing her to
find this icon and have it restored. "Restore me," the voice said. "I will then

be a help to Christians. How many years I have lain around and no one wanted to find me and restore me." When Feodosia, who suffered from what seemed to have been pseudocyesis, asked how she was to find this particular icon, she received a cryptic response: "When you will go, you will find it." After that, still in this same dream, a young boy appeared and showed her the icon she was to find.

When Feodosia found the icon in a neighboring parish church and saw its poor condition, she was determined to have it restored immediately. When she got home, however, she had what was described as a seizure, during which she heard a voice speaking to her from within: "Why have you begun to concern yourself with this icon? It has lain around for a hundred years; let it do so for two hundred more." Though she struggled with waves of doubt, she remained firm in her intention and collected the money necessary to have the icon restored. Yet Feodosia soon ran into another obstacle: the elder on whom she depended for the icon's restoration did not at first heed her request (and then experienced divine wrath for not doing so). Feodosia nevertheless remained unwavering through several more such difficulties before finally being healed by prayer before the icon.[93]

What can be said of the individuals themselves who so tirelessly searched for healing? As noted earlier, the social profile of the main characters in icon root narratives shifted over the centuries. Common lay people, both men and women, frequently found a place in these stories from the fifteenth century onward, and especially from the seventeenth through the nineteenth centuries. It is likely, however, that the time when a particular icon story took place or when an icon was painted was of secondary importance to a believer; some icon narratives, in fact, were not even situated in any particular time period, suggesting that they were compiled from oral histories that did not place much emphasis on date.[94] For believers, the dating of an image—a primarily modern concern of art historians—held little practical importance.[95] More significant considerations from the believer's standpoint were probably the nature of the initial miracle worked by the icon and whether or not other miracles were thought to have continued to result from prayers before it.

Setting aside the date, then, we can note that root narratives about healings involved all ages and social groups: princes,[96] peasants,[97] children,[98] townspeople,[99] clergy,[100] and so on. Indeed, icons of the Mother of God added social and gender diversity to an otherwise highly male monastic profile of Russian Orthodoxy. The stories concerning women deserve special attention not only because their published numbers were growing but also because by means of such stories the experiences of women entered into the annals of Russian Church history. They allow us to see Mary working among those who at the time had little voice in the Church's establishment and whose experiences and thoughts are thereby harder to unearth. Marian icons, perhaps more than any other arena of ecclesial life, have provided testimony to women's religious experiences within Orthodoxy.[101]

The conditions that brought women to the foreground as protagonists in icon narratives were varied, but all were characteristic of those experiences that typified the lives of women. For example, the gentrywoman responsible for the special veneration of the icon of the Mother of God named "Fertile Mountain" in the Tula diocese began to think of suicide because of the emotional stress she experienced as a newlywed bride in her in-laws' home.[102] A "distinguished woman" from Moscow fell into despair after she had suffered three major setbacks: her husband had been falsely accused and sent into exile, the state treasury had confiscated her estate, and her son had been taken as a prisoner of war.[103] A coachman had assaulted a single woman, the nun Mirona Dankova, who then feared being killed by him during the trip from Moscow to the Ascension Monastery in the Tambov province.[104] Specially revered icons were born from the experiences of women who had a difficult time conceiving or giving birth or who agonized over their ailing children.[105] They were also associated with the distress of women who suffered from various forms of mental illness, usually described in terms of possession (besnovanie), or klikushestvo ("shrieking").[106] According to Dostoevsky's description of such women in his novel The Brothers Karamazov, this condition "testified to the unhappy lot of village women, an illness caused by debilitating work undertaken too soon after difficult, complicated and medically unsupervised labor, and further aggravated by hopeless misery, beatings, and so on."[107]

Many of these stories offered a mixed message. On the one hand, they portrayed women who generally tolerated, or at least attempted to tolerate, their situations. They recounted the fates of women who had made every effort to do what many clergy would have considered to be the "right thing." In a devotional pamphlet addressed to a wife with an alcoholic husband, for instance, the woman's grief and tears were not discouraged. On the contrary, they were encouraged as a way of easing her plight, but with the understanding that she not complain publicly, since such open protest would only "rub salt" in her emotional wounds. The pamphlet reminded women that they were "of one flesh" with their spouses. "He is your head," asserted the pamphlet. "And when your head aches, do you remove it from your body?"[108]

On the other hand, while women may have often followed the way of long-suffering, they were memorable and memorialized in icon stories not so much for this virtue but for the wholeness and justice they eventually attained with the help of Mary. In matters of physical or emotional illness, Mary often sought to contain the disruption and anguish that such illnesses caused. Usually this meant a woman's recovery or, in cases of mothers grieving over the condition of a child, the health and safety of that child.

In cases where the behavior of a spouse threatened a women's well-being, however, Mary did not always seek to reconcile husband and wife. Certainly there were well-known stories in which Mary went to great efforts to enlighten and spiritually reorient the offending spouse. In one story known in Russia from its Greek original, for instance, a husband who had become bored with his pious wife was tempted by a "clever-looking man" (who we learn later was the devil) to exchange his wife for a large sum of money. A series of financial misfortunes had further provoked the husband to agree to this settlement. He agreed to bring his wife at dusk to a deserted area where the "clever-looking man" would then hand him the agreed sum in exchange. Along the way to the arranged meeting place, the unknowing wife saw a church and asked her husband whether they could stop so she could go in to pray. While the husband refused to go in, he did not deny his wife's request. She went in and, unbeknownst to the husband, fell asleep while in a prayerful prostration before an icon of Mary. In the meantime, a woman resembling her came out of the church with her head covered. She accompanied the husband, who gradually began having doubts about his action. The horror he experienced when following through with his planned act and witnessing the disclosure of identities and the confrontation between the devil and the woman, Mary, resulted in the husband's "enlightenment" and changed perception of his wife.[109] Such a story supported the image of the Mother of God as dispensing "pure and wondrous water that cleanses the heart of sludge."[110]

A woman's prayer for Mary's involvement, however, did not magically lead to a person's enlightenment. Much depended on the character of the antagonist as well. In another story, a merchant's pious daughter, Anna, married an abusive man who forbade her both to visit her parents and to attend church. Having become unfaithful and having managed to squander the dowry, he eventually abandoned her and their five-year-old daughter. Anna, however, being "completely innocent and having always only carried out the will of her husband as an obedient and meek wife," shared her misery with no one except the Mother of God during her prayer before her icon. When she privately sought the husband out for child support payments and thereby exposed his identity to his new wife and family, he became enraged and, seeking revenge, brought legal charges against her. He claimed, among other things, that she had stolen money from him. While Anna remained hopeful and refused to lose confidence and self-control during her trial, the husband became frenzied and hung himself. Such is the power of faith and hope, the story concludes, in the guidance of the Mother of God.[111]

Hailed as a "quiet refuge," Mary was the person most commonly associated with believers' efforts to find meaning in their lives and to explain events gone awry. She was the face of hope to which believers would turn to find their own "faces" when their identity was critically threatened by the ravages of physical or emotional ailments. The believers described in such stories did not simply blend into a faceless mass, as might be inferred from the description by the populist writer V. G. Korolenko in the previous chapter. While they assembled around a Marian icon, believers did so as distinct persons, and they remained as unique persons before the image, each with his or her own unrepeatable fate. The corporate prayer into which their cries may have blended still preserved the distinct voice of every person present. The power of healing, as the lives of Marian icons testify, consequently remained rooted in the faith and hope of the person. Yet, at the same time, the perceived healing or enlightenment of any individual reconfirmed and reestablished Mary's presence and, by association, God's presence among them all.

⊷⊜⊶

## The Ordering of Community

Some of the stories behind specially revered Marian icons spoke not only about the "calling forth" of believers but about the internal ordering of the sacred community as well. In these stories, Mary and her icon seemed not to discriminate between people on the basis of their rank or place in the hierarchical structure of church life. Especially addressing the themes of doubt and disbelief, these stories often depicted dramatic reversals in the relational world of church life and portrayed inversions of roles and authority, thereby challenging what constituted the normative in this world.

To a large extent such reversals stemmed from the theme of obedience, or *poslushanie*, as it was addressed in icon stories involving dreams and visions. Obedience was a common feature not only of Russian Orthodox spirituality in particular but of Eastern Orthodox spirituality in general. Having developed primarily in the desert monastic culture of the third and fourth centuries, the practice of obedience belonged to a culture in which it was assumed that not everyone could equally discern the workings of the Holy Spirit.[112] While Orthodox teachings commonly held that a spiritual life was characterized by submission or obedience as compared to the insubordination and disobedience of a "fleshly life," this posture was for the most part spoken of with reference to God and not to other human beings. The key was a heart that was "obedient to and in conformity with the will of God."[113]

The idea that not everyone had developed the ability to discern the workings of the Holy Spirit in their lives, however, accounted for the prominent role of the spiritual elder, or *starets*, in Russia's Orthodox culture. Interestingly, while such elders frequently appeared in icon stories, they usually did so in the context of a dream or vision. Icon stories in this respect often pulled the dynamics of religious experience back to the inner world of the individual and demanded an independent exercise of will and discernment.

The story of the Abalak icon of the Mother of God is typical in many ways. In that story, which takes place in the seventeenth century, a pious widow, Maria, dreamt of an icon of the Mother of God in which St. Nicholas and St. Mary of Egypt were depicted on each side (fig. 5.4). She heard a voice speak to her from the icon directing her to tell "the people" to construct a church in honor of the icon of the Mother of God of the sign with two side altars—one in honor of St. Nicholas and the other in honor of St. Mary of Egypt. In a second vision that soon followed, Maria heard the voice of St. Nicholas reminding her to make the necessary announcement, since the prosperity and fate of the local faith community depended on it. "If they [the people] do not listen," he warned her, "they will incite the wrath of God, and not only will the priest perish but all of the best parishioners as well." Even at this point, Maria hesitated to tell anyone about her revelation since she feared public ridicule. Only after a third vision in which St. Nicholas threatened her with God's wrath for her doubts did Maria gather the courage to approach her father confessor about her experience and request that he announce it publicly. He, too, however, had doubts, and Maria's revelation remained undisclosed.

In her fourth and final vision, St. Nicholas appeared once more, chastising Maria for her procrastination. Should she delay any longer, he warned her, she would suffer paralysis. He also reassured her not to concern herself with public reaction. "If you announce this and people do not listen, they will suffer, not you." Following this vision, Maria sought an audience with the diocesan bishop, told him about her experiences, and then proceeded to speak about them to the public. Believers, including the bishop, found Maria's account credible and commenced the construction of a church.[114]

This account has several noteworthy features. First, the story implies that every member of the ecclesial community was potentially a bearer of revelation and, accordingly, deserved to be heard. Second, such stories placed certain limits on the virtue of silence. Although the Virgin Mary might have been portrayed as "pondering things in her heart" during her own life, icon stories emphasized her voice. She was depicted as urging believers of all social and ecclesiastical standings to move beyond the posture of silence when necessary to witness to immediate revelations. Personal revelations, according to these accounts, brought knowledge and insights that should be proclaimed for the welfare of the entire community. In order to help individuals overcome their self-doubts or fears of public ridicule, the Virgin or a saintly messenger would often severely admonish believers for their timidity and threaten punishment for remaining silent.[115]

The sixteenth-century story about a Kazan icon of the Mother of God located in Tobolsk recounted the lessons learned by the sexton Ioanikii about unbelief and indecision. In a series of dreams, Mary directed him through "a prelate resembling John Chrysostom" to exhort the community to construct a church in honor of the Mother of God and to place her icon named Kazan in that church. In this dream, the prelate also instructed Ioanikii about the annual celebration of the icon. When, out of fear of ridicule, Ioanikii failed to tell anyone about his experience, the prelate continued to reappear in his dreams, each time more severely chastising him for not acting, and threatening not only him but the entire city with divine retribution.

Finally, one day, when Ioanikii was publicly reading the story of the icon of the Kazan Mother of God in the monastery church on the occasion of the icon's feast, he suddenly fell to the ground and lost consciousness. He later recounted that he had seen the same prelate from his dreams enter the church while he was reading. When he had reached the point in the story's plot where the bishop of Kazan had publicly repented for having initially doubted Matrona's story, the prelate approached Ioanikii and rebuked him for not having himself believed in what he was reading. He then struck Ioanikii with his staff, saying: "From now on be incapacitated [*driakh*] until the divine work is completed." Out of fear, Ioanikii fell to the ground unconscious. When he came to, he began that work by telling his story.[116]

While icon stories often included accounts of clerical skepticism, this does not mean that these stories were necessarily anticlerical in tone. Instead, by showing unbelief and misgivings as conditions that potentially affected all members of the ecclesial community, clergy and laity alike, such stories offered a prophylaxis against clericalism by deemphasizing the hierarchical difference between clergy and laity in the face of the holy. These stories never identified church and truth exclusively with the clerical establishment. Furthermore, these stories emphasized the role of the institutionally faceless believer in maintaining the integrity and well-being of the ecclesial community.

In numerous stories, as in that of the Abalak icon, clergy were in fact portrayed as embracing the personal experiences of common lay men and women. In the nineteenth-century story of an icon of the Mother of God named "The Joy of All Who Sorrow," the very remembrance of this icon, which was located in his parish church in the Siberian city of Tobolsk, saved a merchant's life. His experience led to the icon's public commemoration by the clergy every Sunday following the Divine Liturgy. The merchant also requested the bishop's blessing to have the icon celebrated annually on its established feast of 24 October; the bishop agreed.[117] Similarly, in the nineteenth-century story of the Chernigov icon of the Mother of God located in the Gethsemane skete in the Moscow diocese, the metropolitan of Moscow, Innocent, asked to meet the peasant woman whose healing was responsible for the special veneration of that icon.[118] Therefore, while the sequelae of newly surfaced miracle-working icons paralleled those intra-ecclesial dynamics unleashed by Marian apparitions in Catholic Europe, I would describe their effect not so much in terms of turning the hierarchical world of the institutional church upside-down as pointing to the basic tenuousness of that world to begin with.[119]

At the same time, icon stories also warned laity of the temptations brought about by that proximity to the sacred center. The fifteenth-century story of the Koloch icon of the Mother of God in the Moscow diocese recounted the fate of a poor peasant, Luke, who had discovered an epiphanic icon nestled in a tree near his home. When a longtime cripple was healed following prayer before the icon, news spread. "Obeying a sacred sign from on high," Luke began traveling with the icon to different localities, including Moscow. Far from encountering skepticism, Luke enjoyed the attention of clergy, dignitaries, and throngs of simple laity wherever he went. In Moscow, even the metropolitan, Photius, greeted him and the icon. In thanksgiving for the numerous healings that took place, believers generously donated money to Luke for the construction of a church in the icon's honor. Although Luke eventually returned to his home village of Koloch and constructed a church in honor of the icon, he also used much of the money to further his own material comfort. Among other things, he built a new mansion and hired servants to manage it. Moreover, he became arrogant with respect to traditional authority figures, who tolerated him only because they believed Mary had found him worthy to reveal a miracle-working icon through him. Only an encounter with a bear that almost killed him "enlightened" Luke and brought him to repentance. He subsequently donated all his belongings toward the construction of a monastic community, into which he himself was tonsured.[120]

Again, such humbling reminders were not only associated with lay people who had somehow strayed; Russia's corpus of Marian-related stories also spoke of her saving clergy from the trappings of their positions of power. One story of a Vladimir icon of the Mother of God, for instance, described the taming of a cleric's episcopal ambitions.[121] Similarly, the story of Theophilus, a highly esteemed Byzantine monastic, was known in nineteenth-century Russia. It is found in the Menologion by the bishop of Rostov, Dimitrii, and tells of Mary's humbling of ecclesiastical careerists. On sincerely pious grounds, Feofil had turned down an offer to be consecrated bishop after his own episcopal mentor died. His "fall" came when, finding himself lacking a position of power once a new bishop had been appointed, he succumbed not only to intrigue and deceit but also to a written denial of Christ and the Mother of God in order to regain his former position of power and influence.[122] Only after some forty days in prayer and repentance before an icon of her did Mary appear to Theophilus and forgive him his action against her. She also agreed to petition the Lord on his behalf. Only through prayer before the icon and Mary's subsequent intervention did Theophilus mysteriously receive back his original signed pact with the devil as a sign of his divine forgiveness.

The stories associated with specially revered Marian icons, therefore, introduce us into an ecclesial world where distinctions between laity and clergy played a secondary role. The lines of demarcation that Metropolitan Makarii Bulgakov drew so sharply between a "subordinate" laity and a "divinely directed" hierarchy were repeatedly confounded in the world of miracle-working icons of the Mother of God. As ecclesial centers in their own right, such icons produced stories that, while not undermining the institutional ecclesial order, also did not necessarily align with centralized hierarchical thinking. Stories of Mary and her icon pointed to another kind of ecclesial understanding that coexisted with the purely hierarchical one.

⊶≡◐≡⊷

## Defining Communal Boundaries

In 1748 two young servant girls on the estate of Vasilii Khitrov in the Kaluga diocese were busy cleaning out the nobleman's attic. One of the girls, who was pious, found what she thought was a portrait of a nun reading a book and showed it to her more insolent friend, Evdokia. Evdokia spat at the portrait,

6.3 Miracle-working icon of the Mother of God named "Kaluzhka." Nineteenth century. On display at the St. Anne Shrine Icon Museum, Sturbridge, MA.

saying "This is how much I fear your abbess." According to the story, as soon as she had uttered these words, she lost her sight, fell mute, and began to convulse. Her family, as well as the nobleman Khitrov, presumed death would soon follow. That night, however, both of Evdokia's parents had a dream in which Mary appeared and explained that with her brazen behavior their daughter Evdokia had offended not an abbess but Mary herself. "For she vilified my image," said Mary, through which "by the will of my Son and my God, I will intercede for your city." She then directed Evdokia's parents to notify the local parish priest about these events. She advised them collectively to hold a prayer service and to bless the ailing girl with holy water. By following Mary's directives, Evdokia was eventually healed, and the icon, which came to be known as the "Kaluzhka" icon of the Mother of God (fig. 6.3), soon became involved in other healings, including Khitrov's own daughter.

The pattern of events in this story found similar expression in numerous other icon-related stories. The author of one devotional pamphlet, Vasilii Doronikin, commented on Mary's demeanor in such stories by noting that while she was benevolent toward the faithful, she also "turned her face in anger from those who did not wish to honor her icon with love."[123] Marian anger was not unique to Orthodox Russia. In his reading of the "dark side of holiness" with respect to Marian apparitions in Catholic Italy, the sociologist Michael P. Carroll has juxtaposed the Mary of such stories with the Mary "favored by the Universal Church." The latter, he claims, portrays Mary as a symbol of warmth and nurturance and, in its liberal interpretation, as the feminine face of a loving God. The Mary of certain apparition stories, however, shows herself as a "powerful goddess, who demands worship and who is willing to use her immense power over nature to coerce human beings into honoring her."[124]

While I hesitate to comment on the image of Mary in the Roman Catholic tradition, I would argue that such an interpretation for the Russian experience of Mary would be misleading. From what we know about miracles and icons, and from what has been noted so far about Mary and community life, it is clear that believers in Russia did not envision Mary as a lone, vengeful goddess in the heavens whose primary concern was self-adulation. At the least, such stories can be interpreted in the same iconodulic spirit that inspired defenders of icon veneration in Byzantium when they recounted similar stories in support of the use of icons in the "right worship" that the very term "Orthodoxy" implied. In this sense, stories that follow the pattern of the Kaluzhka icon reinforced what was liturgically sung, for instance, during the feast in honor of the Kazan icon of the Mother of God: "Whosoever does not honor the Most Holy Birth-Giver of God and does not venerate her icon, anathema to them."[125]

These stories spoke not only about Mary and her icon but also about the individuals and community to which they were intimately tied. They repeatedly depicted Mary standing at various boundaries of that life, defending, sometimes by extreme means, its integrity. The story about the Kaluzhka icon of the Mother of God recounted earlier, for instance, portrays Mary explaining her severe action against the initially impious Evdokia in terms of what that image was destined to do for the *community*. Indeed, as its Life eventually showed, the Kaluzhka icon became closely connected, not only with the provincial capital of Kaluga, but with the fate of Russia as a whole.[126] What initially seemed to be only a personal act on Evdokia's part actually had potentially long-term ramifications on many others, as its intent was to denigrate a holy image that would later prove necessary for the entire community.

Other episodes portrayed Mary reacting against iconoclastic behavior in similar ways. Stories that told of Mary's harsh response to thieves robbing churches, especially the jeweled decorations or precious metal encasings from icons, for instance, spoke to Mary's guarding the memories that believers invested in these decorations. Plundering such objects was not only a sacrilege but, just as important, a violation against those members of the community who honored Mary. Violence against an icon of Mary was also an act of disregard for the hopes and fears of those who had identified with her.

We can see the same dynamic at work in stories where Mary threatened those who did not fulfill her directives. In the mid–seventeenth century, a woman from the Novgorod diocese who ostensibly had become possessed soon after her marriage and had remained so for some seven years had fallen into such despair that she had contemplated suicide on numerous occasions. Praying to the Mother of God to alleviate her suffering, she vowed to enter a monastery should she be healed. Although she was healed, she soon forgot about her vow and continued in her married life and proceeded to have a family.

One day, when she remembered the vow she had violated, she again became ill. According to the story, Mary visited her on this occasion and reminded her of her negligence. She then directed the woman to announce to others her vision and to tell the people to abstain from anger, envy, and drunkenness and to live with unassuming love toward one another and to respect Sundays and feast days. When the ailing woman did not fulfill this directive, Mary appeared two more times and, after the third visit with no response, punished the woman with stroke-like symptoms—a crooked carriage of the head, a disfigured mouth, and a weakened body. Then Mary offered the woman a final directive, which included locating and decorating a particular icon of her. Only when she fulfilled this admonition was the woman healed.[127]

Two features of this story are noteworthy. First, the woman's troubles began when she failed to fulfill a vow she had made. The vow was a prominent feature of both private and public Orthodox life. Both individuals and communities staked their welfare on such covenant-type relationships with God. It is not surprising, therefore, that these stories portrayed severe penalties for an infraction of the rules. The breaching of such an agreement implied a spiritual forgetfulness that could potentially have ruinous effects on both the individual directly involved and those surrounding him or her. In such cases, Mary and her icon stood at the border of remembering and forgetting; she helped individuals and communities remain centered by guiding their individual and social attention and memory. Second, and related, Mary's directives had even broader implications than restoring an ailing woman's personal integrity. Again, though seemingly a private arrangement between herself and God, the woman's vow and her subsequent breach of it had potential communal repercussions. By not entering the monastic community, she had denied the world the prayer that life was believed to entail. Furthermore, by ignoring the second directive of keeping Sunday holy, she failed to help to preserve the integrity of the community. She finally did help to support the ecclesial community by bringing a new specially revered icon to the fore. Mary and her icon, in this sense, helped keep the individual and the communal elements of ecclesial life well integrated.

The tenor of the message shifted somewhat when the stories involved persons affiliated with other faith traditions. In the seventeenth century, the peasant Lev Shapok from the Minsk diocese found an icon of the Mother of God in an isolated spot in the middle of a forest. Interpreting this icon's appearance as the manifestation of God's grace, Shapok and his fellow villagers began constructing a church on the site without first requesting permission from the estate's owners, the aristocratic Radzivilli family. The estate's overseer, Iakov Pakosha, who according to the story happened to be a Calvinist, heard about Shapok's activity and ordered the construction workers to disband. As the story reads, however, "Providence punished him." Pakosha's horse crushed him to death while he was on his way to the site where the epiphanic icon had appeared. In memory of the "awe-inspiring punishment" of this steward who attempted to infringe on the construction of a church, believers erected a cross at the site and eventually built a chapel there as well.[128]

While those who were portrayed as Orthodox believers also suffered divine retribution in icon-related stories, Pakosha's fate takes on added meaning on account of his religious identity. The severity of his punishment undoubtedly stemmed from his being identified with the Protestant tradition that many Russian Orthodox believers associated with iconoclastic tendencies. In a similar fashion, the Life of the well-known Pochaev icon of the Mother of God tells of a Lutheran who in the seventeenth century had inherited the land on which the monastery that housed the icon was located. He had taken the icon from the monastery to his home and one evening involved it in jesting against the Orthodox faith. His wife played the role of a priest during the charade and became ill with frequent convulsions. She was cured only when the icon was returned to the monastery.[129] Finally, the story of the Kazan icon from the village of Tabynskoe (Ufa diocese) described the iconoclastic behavior of several Turkish Bashkirs, an indigenous ethnic group who were Muslims. All of them were blinded for their profanation of the icon.[130]

These and similar stories showed Mary situated on the boundary between the Orthodox community and other faiths. They pictured her using her icons to show the truth and power of Orthodoxy.[131] As its defender and sustainer,[132] Mary was responsible for the conversion of others. Several stories, such as the one concerning the Bashkirs, included incidents of Mary blinding persons until they were "illumined" by a ray of faith and converted. Only then did they receive their "sight," the power to see Orthodoxy's truth.

It is important to note, however, that icon stories did not uniformly portray persons of different confessions as hostile to Marian icons. Some stories indeed highlighted non-Orthodox faith affiliation for pedagogical and political reasons when describing iconoclastic behavior. Yet stories that showed non-Orthodox persons honoring such icons also held up the religious Other as a source of inspiration and edification. For example, the Dormition icon of the Mother of God that was associated with the famous Piukhtitsy Orthodox convent in Estonia began its life thanks to the benevolence of a group of Lutheran shepherds.[133] The special veneration of a copy of the Vladimir icon in the Vitebsk diocese began with the healing of a Jewish man, and reportedly not only Orthodox Christians but Jews and Catholics revered it.[134] In a similar vein, the story of a specially revered icon of the Mother of God from the

Ekaterinoslavl diocese described a Muslim Crimean khan who had turned to the icon in prayer before he set out for battles.[135] Such accounts portrayed Mary's presence and activity extending beyond those boundaries that separated different confessions of faith, "edifying us," as one devotional pamphlet noted, "and uniting all into a single flock."[136]

⋯⊷⊜⊶⋯

## The Chosen Nation

In a sermon on the national feast of the Kazan icon of the Mother of God—probably the most honored image in Russia at the time—a priest from the Astrakhan diocese, Peter Il'inskii, recalled that icon's history and its role in the fate of Russia. In doing so, he highlighted the power of national unity when a people was faced with the threat of foreign domination. During the Time of Troubles, he noted, "all of Russia" collectively had united in prayer and fasting and had "stood up for its defense as one person." The spiritual celebration that marked the icon's feast was, therefore, a "great national feast for every truly Russian person."[137]

More than Christ himself or any one saint, Mary as present in several of her icons stood at the interface between religious and national identity in Russia. Already Russia's medieval *Primary Chronicle*, which tells the story of Rus' history from its origins to the early twelfth century, spoke of Mary as a defender of Rus' against its enemies and hence identified her with the course of Russia's national history.[138] The tradition of tracking Russia's history through the behavior of Mary, and in particular though the lives of her icons, continued throughout the late nineteenth and early twentieth century, with clergy frequently using the occasions of feasts of nationally known miracle-working Marian icons to reiterate age-old themes: Russia was Mary's "home" and "principality"; her numerous miracle-working icons were one means by which Mary designated Russia's divine election.[139] "The story of our fatherland," the bishop of Mozhaisk said in 1915, "is at the same time a portrayal of the miracles performed on its behalf by the Mother of God."[140] "No other people," claimed the priest Serafim Vvedenskii from the Simbirsk diocese, "has received so many signs and miracles from icons as we Russians have."[141]

The stories of many Marian icons indeed drew little distinction between Russia's national, political history and the sacred history of human salvation and encouraged believers to link the two in their minds. The priest Ioann Vostorgov, for instance, took the occasion of the feast of the Kazan icon in 1907 to remind believers of Russia's messianic world mission. He suggested that Russia had a unique position in time and geography among all the Christian peoples. Although admitting that western Europe had been Christian longer than Russia, Vostorgov pointed to a gradual eclipsing of Christianity in the West. At the same time, in his view, Christianity in the East fell victim to its struggles with "fanatic Mohammedanism." At this late hour in history, Vostorgov claimed, "the Lord put forward a new luminary of faith . . . in the Russian people."

> Divine Providence, calling us Russian Slavs of central Europe into the bosom of the Church of Christ, in the very geographic placement of our country on the border between Europe and Asia, East and West, showed us a great mission: to carry the treasure of Christ and true faith that we received to the little-known eastern and northern Europe and further into . . . Asia, and to struggle with the darkness of paganism . . . and to enlighten the wild tribes of aliens [inorodtsy] and to have them join in participating in the kingdom of God and in the life of enlightened humanity.[142]

Devotional literature frequently stressed that throughout its history Russia had enjoyed the love and good will of Mary. Times of both glory and calamity were tied to her and could be traced in the glorification of her most venerated icons.[143] Also speaking on the feast of the Kazan icon of the Mother of God, the priest F. Vasiutinskii from the Chernigov diocese rhetorically asked his parishioners: "Who else delivered Russia from her numerous calamities and sorrows? Who preserved the spirit of national patriotism? Who preserved the Russian people from subjection to a foreign power?"[144]

The majority of specially revered icons in prerevolutionary Russia remained known only locally. Nevertheless, the stories behind the prototypes for many of these locally known images—the various Vladimir, Kazan, Smolensk, Bogoliubov, Feodorov, and "the Sign" icons—involved the private and public lives of Russia's rulers. By virtue of their association with the political interests and personal destinies of members of the royal family, these icons were propelled into the national limelight, and the momentum by which an icon's special veneration was maintained tended to shift. For example, the well-known Kazan icon of the Mother of God began its life with the dreams of the nine-year-old daughter of a musketeer, Matrona, and the healing of a blind man. Once it became known to and accepted by Tsar Ivan IV, however, its narrative changed direction and left Matrona behind, turning instead to the theme of the domestication of conquered territory. One nineteenth-century devotional pamphlet characteristically interpreted the initial miracle from this icon, which involved healing from physical blindness, as a sign that the icon appeared by God's grace "mainly for the spiritual enlightenment of many faithless persons who until then had been blinded by the false teachings of Mohammed."[145] The icon's life became further entwined in Russia's political fate when, during Russia's tumultuous period of internecine struggles in the seventeenth century (the so-called Time of Troubles), a copy of the icon was credited with liberating Moscow from Polish domination on 22 October 1612. Furthermore, the icon's feast day, 22 October, was initially a local Moscow event, established by the first ruler of the Romanov dynasty, Mikhail

Fedorovich. His son, Tsar Alexei Mikhailovich, then decreed it a national feast in 1649, partly in thanksgiving for the birth of his son, Dimitrii, which took place on 22 October.

The association between particular icons and the lives of members of the imperial family continued in the late nineteenth century. When Alexander III and his family escaped from harm during the derailment of their train on 17 October 1888, for instance, two relatively little-known icons of the Mother of God drew more widespread acclaim simply because their celebration fell on that day. First, the icon of the Mother of God named "Deliverer" had initially been tied to the life of a schemamonk from the Russian Panteleimon monastery on Mount Athos. Because the icon had been delivered on the first anniversary of the derailment, 17 October 1889, to Russia's "New Athos" in the Caucasus, it came to be associated with the commemoration of that event.[146] Second, the history of the obscure though specially revered icon of the Mother of God named "Ever-Virgin" from the St. Nicholas-Pesnosh monastery in the Moscow diocese had been celebrated locally on 17 October. It began its life in 1827 with the professional misfortunes of a captain of an infantry unit, Platon Shabashev. Following a cholera epidemic in 1848, it became more widely known. A service was composed in its honor, and it began to be celebrated locally each year on 17 October. The number of copies of this icon that believers requested grew considerably after the 1888 derailment.[147]

Icon stories that told of Mary's special protection of Russia from "hostile forces" on both the eastern and western frontiers took place during some of that country's most trying historical periods: the struggle against the traditionally Muslim Mongols and Tatars, especially from the thirteenth through the fifteenth centuries; the social and political turmoil during the Time of Troubles, the seventeenth-century war with the Swedes; the 1812 war with Napoleon. Showing another side of spiritual enlightenment and of the maternal, these stories advanced the ancient Byzantine portrayal of Mary as a "victorious leader of triumphant hosts"; in the story of the Fedorov icon of the Mother of God, for instance, blinding rays of light emitted by the icon dispelled Tatar forces attacking Kostroma in the mid–thirteenth century.[148]

Such stories of Marian intervention in battles on Russia's behalf were not simply tales held over from a medieval past. Virtually every major war in which Russians fought up to the 1917 revolution (and even beyond) found its way into a Marian icon story. Prior to the 1812 battle with Napoleon's troops at Borodino, for instance, the commander of the Russian troops, Prince Mikhail Kutuzov, directed his troops to conduct prayer services in front of the Smolensk icon of the Mother of God.[149] In a letter written to his wife following the decisive battle against the French troops, Kutuzov described the return of the Smolensk icon to its "home" in Smolensk. In doing so, he recounted the Gospel reading for that day that told of the meeting between two expecting women, Elizabeth and Mary. Noting that the reading ended with the phrase "And Mary remained with her about three months, and returned to her home" (Luke 1:56), Kutuzov reflected on the fact that the

**6.4**  A painting of the miraculous appearance of the Mother of
God to Russian troops near the East Prussian city of Augustow.
Oil on canvas. Courtesy of the Russian State Historical Archive
(f. 796, op. 199, 6 ot., 3 st., d. 277a, l. 24).

icon had remained with his troops for exactly three months as well. He then
spoke of Mary's "child-bearing assistance" to the Russian troops and compared the icon's experience in battle with Mary's experiences in her final three
months of pregnancy. Just as her icon has shared with his army all of the
difficulties and stresses of his troops, so Mary had spent her final months
sharing in Elizabeth's difficult "old-age" pregnancy.[150]

During World War I, in September 1914, Russian newspapers reported
that a division of troops retreating from eastern Prussia had collectively experienced a vision of Mary holding the Christ child and pointing with one hand
to the West (fig. 6.4). According to the accounts, a unit of transports had
inadvertently become separated from the group and had stopped to spend the
night. Notified of approaching German troops, they fell into despair. Know-

ing that they would be no match for the enemy and fearing for their lives, some of the soldiers began to pray. At eleven o'clock at night, in this forlorn atmosphere, both the officer and the soldiers claimed they saw the image of Mary in the clear night sky, blessing them, to which they attributed their ultimate safe return.[151] Iconographic depictions of this event soon found their way into print and, undoubtedly inspiring hope, found themselves in popular demand up to 1917.

In the late nineteenth century, clergy in their sermons not only recalled stories of Mary's role in Russia's historical past but also interpreted the significance of the past for the historical present, in both their personal and their collective lives. In 1902, while remembering the involvement of the Kazan icon in rallying Russians against Polish domination in the seventeenth century, a priest from the Samara diocese called on his parishioners to apply the image of Mary as liberator of Russia from foreign domination to their own personal spiritual lives. Every person is a warrior, he maintained, on the field of his or her soul, on which only a continual self-examination and daily confession can arm a person for victory. Just as warriors have turned to Mary on the fields of military battle, so he urged the faithful to turn to her for help in their own spiritual warfare.[152] In this way, believers could transform stories of military and political victory into personally relevant accounts that had meaning for their own daily struggles.

Past accounts of the military feats of Marian icons gained special significance during the Russo–Japanese War in 1905. Clergy turned to the history of such icons in order to inspire laity to "stand as one person" as their forefathers had in the stories related to such icons. Icon stories recall memories of the past, one bishop maintained, "and imperatively demand entrance to the soul" in order to teach persons how to pray in the present in hope of victory over the enemy.[153] Similarly, believers interpreted the June 1904 theft of the Kazan icon of the Mother of God from the Kazan Devich'i convent as an omen that God had rescinded his protection of Russia in the east.[154]

The "enemy" from which Mary protected the Russian nation, however, was not always necessarily a foreign or "alien" one. In 1891, the priest S.A.S. warned of the possible repercussions of the current social and political trends in Russia by recounting the story of the icon of the Mother of God named "the Sign" from the Novgorod diocese. He noted the icon's entanglement in the internecine strife that had plagued medieval Russia when the appanage system had threatened political unity. According to the story of the Novgorod icon of the Sign, in 1170 the prince of Suzdal had united with several other princes in order collectively to defeat Novgorod. Finding themselves surrounded and faced with imminent defeat, the Novgorodians gathered in collective prayer before this particular image of the Mother of God, which they then placed on the gates to the city. At that moment, Mary turned her gaze from the attackers toward the Novgorodians, as a sign of mercy toward them. Subsequently the aggressors were blinded by her image and badly defeated. Does not such a sign, the priest S.A.S. rhetorically asked, "warn us that internecine strife and enmity toward one another will turn the face of the Birth-Giver of God away from us?" He cautioned against the strong dominating the weak and the wealthy tyrannizing the poor, since the oppressed historically had Mary on their side and could always call for her in their defense and protection.[155]

In 1903 the priest Constantine Iakimovich spoke of the alarming times that had befallen Russia, drawing particular attention to the economic dimension of Russia's current spiritual crisis. "Our adversaries are plundering us," he wrote, "tempting us with modern teachings, agitating souls." Most significantly, he claimed the danger came from an ancient temptation: wealth.

> To our great shame and disgrace there have appeared among us those who have been corrupted and, along with the enemy, denounce us, repudiate our Orthodox faith and our holy sites . . . we are all sinking from the expense of life. . . . Neighboring countries are enriching themselves at our expense.[156]

During the late nineteenth century, Catholic Europe looked to Mary as a bulwark in its struggle with modernity. Similarly Russian clergy during this time found parallels between Mary's past defense of the Russian nation and the current struggle with the "enemy" of unbelief born from the "spirit of modernity."[157] In one devotional pamphlet published in 1912, the author reminded believers that the growth and prosperity of the Russian nation was directly associated with Mary's protection. However, he warned that her protection and defense was conditional. Very much in the spirit of the covenant between the ancient Israelites and God as told in the Old Testament, Russia's strength depended on the collective faith of its people. That collective faith, however, was being eroded by the growing numbers of sectarians, socialists, revolutionaries, and "all such servants of the antichrist." Believers, by their exposure to the teachings of such persons, therefore, not only "poisoned" themselves but also threatened the well-being and integrity of the entire nation.[158] A priest from the Saratov diocese noted that those who "shout about freedom" only advocate "enslavement to arbitrariness" and a "reign of passions."[159] The priest Arsenii Pokrovskii from the Tver diocese noted that divisions had arisen not only in secular matters but in matters concerning faith as well.[160]

Some clergy interpreted the times cataclysmically, pointing to such events as Russia's defeat in the Russo-Japanese War and revolutionary uprisings as signs that Mary was turning away her countenance from them as a nation.[161] The politically conservative priest Ioann Vostorgov claimed that Russia was failing in its messianic mission. The light of Christianity was fading among the Russian people, as demonstrated by the fact that the theft of the Kazan icon of the Mother of God in 1904 did not lead to a "nationwide outcry." Russia, predicted Vostorgov, would face numerous afflictions before it could regain its strength of spirit and former dignity. Such afflictions, in his observation, could already be witnessed in the form of the so-called liberation movement that had swept across Russia and that signified the victory of unbelief and the profanation of authority.[162]

Other devotional pamphlets were not nearly so reactionary or apocalyptic in their message. Instead they pointed with hope to the continued signs of Mary's presence in Russia. In 1903, the author of one pamphlet about the Chernigov icon wrote that despite the fact that even believers often displayed "modern" ways of thinking, God did not desire the death of sinners. Instead of turning away, God responded to this lack of faith and manifested his power by granting healing to those who petitioned Mary. In so doing, God strengthened humans in faith and piety.[163] Similarly, another author spoke of God and Mary as themselves entering into the current battle against unbelief by granting the appearance of new miracle-working Marian icons in order to spark and renew faith.[164]

Such was the message that devotional pamphlets generally attributed to the well-known icon of the Mother of God named "The Joy of All Who Sorrow, with Pennies" (fig. 6.5). The icon, located outside of St. Petersburg in the village of Klochki, became widely known in July 1888, when "heavenly fire"—a lightning bolt—struck the chapel in which this icon was housed. Although lightning had burned the interior of the chapel and had singed other icons, this particular icon of Mary remained unharmed. Two "signs" accompanied the miraculous preservation of the icon. First, time and soot had earlier led to its darkening; now it had miraculously lightened. Second, the collection box for donations that had been standing nearby the icon had been broken by its fall. In the process, twelve half-kopeck pieces had somehow become fastened to the icon. News of the icon's miraculous preservation spread quickly, and believers began streaming by the thousands to venerate it. The first reported miracle from the icon took place in 1890, with the healing of a fourteen-year-old boy, Nikolai Grachev.[165]

One devotional pamphlet claimed that these events took place against a backdrop of vacillation in commitments to faith that had plagued Russia since the 1860s.[166] Most pamphlets focused in particular on the meaning of the half-kopeck pieces that had become stuck to the icon. The Mother of God had chosen to decorate herself with these symbols of the poor, which in her eyes were more valuable than the gold or gemstones with which many of her icons were decorated.[167] These pennies were a sign or, rather, a summons for all to move against the contemporary trend of "living for wealth and earthly pleasure" and to lead a modest lifestyle characterized by hard work and freedom from vanity and luxury.[168] In addition to the streams of believers who came to the prayer services that were conducted before the icon daily from eight in the morning to six at night, the icon also attracted imperial patronage. Tsar Alexander III and his wife Maria Feodorovna visited the chapel in 1893 and donated land on which a church was later built in honor of this icon.

Given the associations that believers quickly made between icons and significant events taking place around them, it is not surprising that the end of the ancien régime and the beginning of a new era in Russia's history quickly

6.5   Miracle-working icon of the Mother of God named
"Joy of All Who Sorrow, with Pennies." Housed in the
chapel in honor of the Mother of God named "Joy of All
Who Sorrow." 1913. Central State Archive of Cine-,
Photo-, and Phono-Documents, St. Petersburg.

became associated with a particular image of the Mother of God. The circumstances of the emergence of this image were typical. On 19 October 1917, just
several days before the Bolsheviks stormed the Winter Palace, the Holy Synod
received a report from the metropolitan of Moscow and Kolomenskoe (and
future patriarch), Tikhon, about a peasant woman, Evdokia Andrianova, who
had had a series of dreams alerting her to an icon of the Mother of God in a
local parish church.[169] When it was found with the help of the parish priest,
believers began flocking to pray before it. Soon they were requesting that the
icon be brought to their homes, churches, factories, and monastic communities for special services and blessings.[170] As in numerous cases in the past,
members of the Holy Synod took no action on the case. Since the finding of

**6.6** Copy of the icon of the Mother of God named "She Who Reigneth" (*Derzhavnaia*). After 1917. 31 × 27 cm. From the Collection of the Kolomenskoe State Museum-Preserve, inv. no. 1555. Purchased in 1972. Origin unknown.

the icon occurred on 2 March 1917, the day on which Nicholas II had abdicated the throne, believers eventually took the occasion of Evdokia's revelation to make religious sense of events that were happening around them. Significantly, the icon was named "She Who Reigneth" (*Derzhavnaia*) because of the way the Mother of God was portrayed on the icon (fig. 6.6), alluding to the hope that now Mary would be at the helm and rule Russia.

In the end we can only speculate about the effect that stories behind nationally known prototypes of Marian icons had on common believers and local community life. How might the proliferation of these stories have affected the ritual act and experience of venerating Mary? For instance, in figure 6.7 we see a traditional depiction of the Kazan icon of the Mother of

**6.7**  Icon of the Mother of God named "Kazan."
Second half of the ninteenth century. From the private
collection of Gary Hollingsworth,
Hollingsworth Fine Arts, Orlando, FL.

God, a generally recognized symbol of Russian national identity. Yet, in the
shadows of the Christ-child, we also see the tiny figure of the third-century
St. Kirik, a boy of three who reportedly witnessed the torture of his mother
and who came to her defense and the defense of the Christian faith and who
subsequently was also martyred. The size of the image was more typical of
one that was kept in a home. Why would a family have had Kirik included in
the icon of the Mother of God named "Kazan"? Was he associated with the
memory of a deceased child or one who had been miraculously healed from
an illness? In what way would believers have synchronized the stories of Kirik
and the Kazan image and their own personal ones?

A similar series of questions arises when we look to the village of Novosele
in the Olonets diocese. Here we find that believers suffered hardships for

several years before 1916 because of a recurring cattle plague. As a result, they decided to establish a village feast on 23 June in honor of the Vladimir icon of the Mother of God. On that day, a procession came to their village from the local parish church. The hymns that would have been sung in their village in honor of the icon, however, would have commemorated another event. The 23 June feast of the Vladimir icon of the Mother of God, established at the end of the fifteenth century, commemorated this icon's role in the final lifting of the Tatar Yoke over Russia in 1480. Prayers said on this day in the village of Novosele, therefore, would have contextualized the local festivities in a national setting. They would have reminded the faithful of the broader community to which they belonged. The troparion hymn that would have been sung for the feast, for instance, proclaimed: "Today the splendid city of Moscow vividly shines, having received your miracle-working icon, O Lady, like a ray of sunlight."[171] A lengthier prayer for that feast was chanted in the first person plural, incorporating all those present into the collective *we*, "the Russian people."[172] But while believers in Novosel'e might have been summoned liturgically to join Moscow and "the Russian people" during their special veneration of this icon, the question remains: to what extent did the local celebration facilitate each believer's identification not only with the broader ecclesial community but also with the collective, national "we"?

We will never know the complete extent to which Marian icon stories affected common believers in their experiences and sensibilities. We can only guess what went through any individual believer's mind when he or she approached an icon of Mary and whether or not an icon's story in any way shaped these thoughts. Yet when we move from the inner world of subjective experience to the terrain of an ecclesial culture and communal identity, we can say something about the relationship between Mary, her icon, and believers' life experiences.

That relationship can perhaps best be pictured visually, by means of an iconographic depiction of what I have discussed. One relevant depiction is that of the annual Menaion or liturgical calendar, which often included Marian icons within the frame of the menaion icon itself (fig. 6.8). In the late nineteenth century it was not uncommon to find icons of icons, especially icons depicting numerous icons of Mary.[173] Such iconographic representations apparently appeared in Russia in the eighteenth century and were initially composed by iconographers as a sort of manual of the different types of Marian icons (fig. 6.9).[174] From that time on, the inclusion of numerous icons of Mary became more common.

The icon of the annual Menaion was a visual collective memory bank of sorts, calling to mind many of the events and persons in sacred history that marked the annual cycle of sacred time. In the image depicted here, we see a body of saints and fifty miracle-working icons of Mary grouped around the central image of the "feasts of feasts," the Resurrection of Christ. On initial glance, this icon might be thought of as representing the inner circle or elect

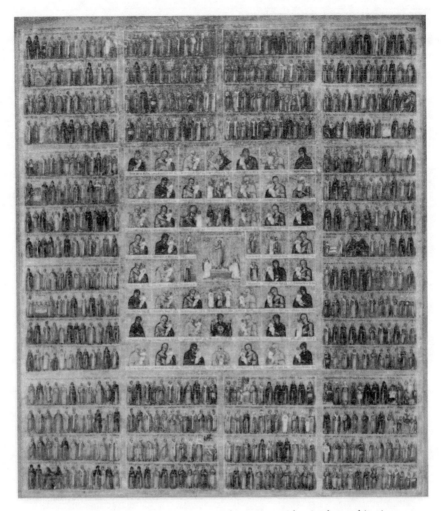

6.8    The Resurrection of Christ. Annual menaion with miracle-working icons
of the Mother of God. Second half of the ninteenth century 36 × 31 cm.
Tretyakov Gallery, Moscow, inv. no. P 65002.

of the "People of God," Mary along with the saints, God's friends.[175] In this
view, one might see the ecclesiastical establishment—predominantly males
and monastics accompanied by a towering figure of Mary—as the primary
lineaments of the eternal sacred body in God's Kingdom.

Yet such a view is shortsighted precisely because of the presence of Marian
icons and their placement in it. The saints in the icon remain the saints—
those selected being mostly monastic and mostly male—holy places in their

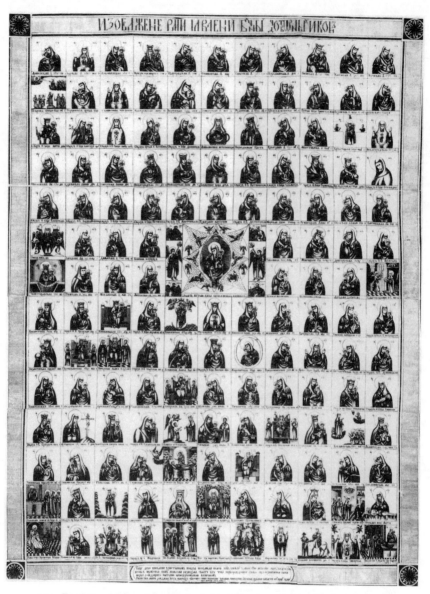

6.9 Depiction of drawings of miracle-working icons of the Mother of God. Eighteenth century. The Russian State Historical Archive (f. 835, op. 4, d. 26, l. 1).

own right, canonized by their earthly colleagues as dwellings where God abides.[176] The icons of Mary, however, rarely had such canonical recognition. Their very placement within the annual Menaion, therefore, bears testimony to the complexities of the dynamics of spiritual power, ecclesial recognition, and religious authority. Moreover, they bring to mind not only Mary but also all those persons whom she, through her icons, managed to remember and thereby enabled to envision their own lives moving within sacred history. While the central focus of the icon is the Resurrection of Christ—the celebration of which stands at the center of Orthodoxy—the centering of the *community* that has consolidated on account of that event is represented by Mary and her icons. If Mary's icons here push the multitude of saints toward the periphery, so to say, it is to make room for the memories of Mary's involvement with common believers, both individually and collectively, that her icons bear. In so doing, Mary, through her icons, includes common believers as well in the fold of witnesses to the manifestations of God's salvific actions.

# Conclusion

On the eve of one of the most cataclysmic events in Russia's history, Orthodox Christianity in that country faced a genuine *krisis* in corporate self-understanding. Not only was Orthodoxy being vehemently challenged from without by Marxist revolutionaries, an "enlightened" atheistic worldview, and an openly religiously diverse society but, perhaps more significantly, also from within. Sensing these various challenges and hoping to fortify the ecclesial body in the wake of this new period in Russia's history, Orthodox churchmen and theologians sought renewal of the communal spirit of the Orthodox faith. Yet, even though it was at the forefront of many believers' minds, the notion of "church" remained seemingly beyond the grasp of consensus. Many aspects of ecclesial life—hierarchy and community, religious authority, parish and patriarch, the local, national, and universal—elicited mixed sentiments and evaluations. The fact that a group of highly educated churchmen could reach no agreement on the meaning and significance of such a basic phenomenon as the parish, let alone the more complex idea of *sobornost',* suggests that Orthodox ecclesial thinking faced a major impasse.

Debates over the character and nature of the Church and how that sacred body worked revealed several critical fault lines, two of which seemed to surface frequently. One concerned the laity and their role and place in the ecclesial body; it was a subject that in many ways seemed to lie at the root of the crisis. The writings of two priests that occurred only five years apart vividly illustrate the dilemma. In 1912 the priest Ioann Paryshev from the Eniseisk diocese defended the special veneration of an icon in his parish in part by referring to an old proverb: "The voice of the people is the voice of God."[1] In contrast, in 1917 in an article discussing issues of church reform, the priest S. Kozubovskii claimed that granting the right of pastoral election to the "dark masses" would be like "putting a knife in the hands of a lunatic."[2] The presence of such radically different views of "the people" with respect to the body called "church" pointed to a sacred community that was still coming to terms with the profound political and social shifts that were taking place in their midst, the effects of which it could not escape. Anticipating a separation of church and state, for instance, some churchmen began reminding themselves and others that the church was a "nonnational" union of believers.[3]

Such a view posed a challenge to those who tended to think of their flock in terms of "the Russian people"—be they a "dark mass" or a divinely chosen lot. The political and social realities, however, were only part of the problem. Radically different views of the laity also stemmed from different readings of the past, especially the Byzantine past. Different historical interpretations, in turn, often stemmed from differing theological understandings of how the Church as a sacred community should be ordered and managed in a modernizing world. Practically speaking, how could the scriptural notion of the equality of all baptized believers as children of God and heirs "according to the promise" (Gal. 3:25–4:7) be harmonized with the equally ancient principle of hierarchical ecclesial ordering, manifested through the sacrament of ordination? These were not new questions but old ones that had to be addressed again in a new age.

A second prominent fault was related to the question of who or what constituted the organizational or administrative center of church life. Should churchmen concentrate their efforts toward church renewal in the parish or in the position of the patriarch? Disagreements on this front arose from differing emphases that clergy and lay theologians placed on the local, the regional, and the national in their own definitions of "church." Moreover, it was not clear how the various layers of the ecclesial community were or should be linked, practically or theologically speaking. Differences were made more pronounced by the fact that the various visions of what was considered authentically Orthodox with respect to understandings of church did not neatly correspond to a person's position in the body sacred. As groups, bishops, parish priests, monastics, and lay people did not consistently hold uniform views on any single issue.

While in the intellectual world of Russia's theologians and in the world of Russian ecclesiastical legislation the concept of "the laity" was having a difficult time getting established, in practice, believers were quite actively shaping communal life in Russian Orthodoxy. This study has focused on five arenas in which the dynamics of sacred community building and its associated tensions were played out. Taken together, they prompt us to think about church and the church experience in Russian Orthodoxy in different ways.

In addition to involving polity and governance, church as sacred community also involves the notion of belonging and is inseparably tied to particular understandings of reality and history. Moreover, as this study has indicated, church can be spoken about as something lived and experienced. Temples, chapels, the celebration of feasts, and the veneration of icons, especially those of the Mother of God, have offered occasions to observe the contours of this experience in prerevolutionary Russia and to examine some of the ways a church consciousness and a sense of belonging were fostered and sustained.

One means of sustaining a sense of ecclesial community involved stories—the telling and retelling of accounts of individual and collective encounters with the holy. There was a narrative quality to ecclesial life, which consisted of multiple strands. Among these, scripture was foundational. Accounts taken from scripture formed the basis of the liturgical life of the Church, as evidenced in hymnography, iconography, and ritual. But there were other types of ancient stories as well: the lives of saints, well-known accounts of Mary's intercession for the sake of individuals and entire communities, and well-known stories of healings and miracles attributed to faith and prayer. Some of these stories could be found in liturgical texts on the occasions of particular feasts; others were conveyed visually through icons; and still others could have been recounted in sermons and periliturgical discussions. They also could also have been read by literate believers and recounted orally in family or informal gatherings.

In addition to recalling established accounts of what once was in ancient times and faraway places, however, common believers themselves told stories of their own encounters, both personal and collective, as well as of the encounters of their forefathers with the holy—with Mary and the saints, for instance. In nineteenth- and twentieth-century Russia that voice could be heard in part through the stories that were told about signs and healings. These stories were more tenuous and transient in the narrative fabric of ecclesial life than the scriptural ones or the ones that had already entered the annals of liturgical texts or established lives of saints. Personal or local experiences could remain in the recesses of a single believer's heart and perish when he or she died. When recounted to a small circle of believers or family, they could easily be forgotten or dismissed by hearers as superstitious or not credible. Some of these stories, however, were more widely embraced and withstood the test of time. Often the more enduring ones depended not only on oral communication for their transmission; their permanence was reinforced by their association with the construction of certain churches and chapels, the celebration of village and sometimes parish feasts, and the veneration of icons, especially those of the Mother of God.

The relationships between the various narrative strands that informed the local, regional, national, and even more universal understandings of ecclesial life were highly complex. Believers' stories about the workings of God in their or their forefathers' worlds (or even the world of Russia) were often associated with scriptural accounts, as communicated through icons of Christ, Mary, and the saints or as celebrated in conjunction with well-established feasts. At other times these accounts became associated with architectural monuments—temples and chapels—in which liturgical services of one form or another were conducted. Consequently, with regard to their memory and their celebration, it was not easy to untangle the scriptural from the nonscriptural narratives or to separate them neatly into "great" and "little" strands without altering the quality and character of the church experience.[4] Since sacred history was understood to be still evolving, the numerous narrative strands collectively spoke of a sense of continuity and of perceived blessings, mercy, and grace, and the presence of the divine.

Modernization had a mixed effect on the narrative fabric of ecclesial life and on the power of these narratives to bond believers. On the one hand, "enlightened thinking" and the doubt and suspicions that accompanied it challenged the veracity of all Orthodox Christian sacred narratives—including the fundamental ones found in the New Testament. The increase in educational opportunities that accompanied modernization inevitably brought exposure to these radical critiques of Christianity, which were often difficult to ignore. In addition, "modern" ways of being Christian that had evolved and were still evolving in the West challenged the very telling of certain stories. Stories of miracles, healings, divinely inspired dreams, and divinely guided events, along with the rituals they inspired, only seemed to some people to crowd out what they would accept as belonging to the essence of Christianity.

On the other hand, modernization also frequently helped to strengthen and reinforce the various narrative strands. Growth in the means of communication, including the railroad, and the rise in the number of publications of devotional stories gave many such accounts a larger forum and a greater chance at longevity. Broader access to local accounts of God's works helped blur the boundaries between the local, the regional, and the national ecclesial community and made it easier to accept each as one's own. The development of educational opportunities also offered believers more chances to learn about, think through, and even defend their beliefs.

The fabric of ecclesial life, however, was not without its internal strains. An ancient and hegemonic principle of prerevolutionary Orthodox thinking, espoused by Irenaeus of Lyons in the late second century, designated bishops as the main "keepers of the story" in the Christian community. According to the principle of apostolic succession, bishops were to guard the "deposit of faith" and to preserve the apostolic tradition and "the preaching of the truth."[5] Interpreted in accord with the Petrine injunction that bishops should investigate the stories people told in order to establish their veracity, this teaching seemed to provide bishops with the authority to pass judgment on the authenticity of proclaimed miracles, healings, and divine signs in order to keep "the rule of truth in the Church."[6] The extent to which claims to episcopal authority in this area were accepted by the faithful—be they bishops themselves, parish priests, monastics, or lay people—is impossible to establish. Given the evidence presented, however, it appears that when it came to experiences of the holy, the bishop was not universally acknowledged as the sole authority. The ubiquitous image of Mary, the Mother of God, is instructive in this regard. Closely associated with prayer and the spiritual life of many individual believers, her image often accompanied stories that related the exercise of independent will and discernment by lay men and women. In this context, her image represented not so much a symbolic balance to the male figure of Christ as a religious balance to a hierarchical ordering of ecclesial life. The history of her image suggests that in terms of the *experience* of church, hierarchical ordering was less salient than histories of the ecclesiastical institution might suggest.

The tensions that arose in Orthodox ecclesial life over the construction of certain churches and chapels, the celebration of certain feasts, and the veneration of certain icons, and the tensions that surfaced in intellectual debates over how the Church should be ordered were related, and they stemmed from common origins. Operative in these sets of tensions were two powerful yet often diverging understandings of religious authority. One was focused on the bishop; the other on the perceived workings of the Holy Spirit and the responsibility of all believers to bear witness to that Spirit. Tensions were also aggravated by the manifestation of two different tendencies in ecclesial ordering: a centralizing one and a decentralizing, localizing one. Neither of these tendencies would fully yield to the other, and for some believers they were viewed as intertwined. In their attempts to renew and strengthen Orthodox collective identity, Orthodox clergy and theologians expressed differing understandings of both the principles of religious authority and the ordering of the ecclesial body. Berdnikov's vision, for instance, seemed to ignore the fact that in many ways lay persons already approached their parish church and community as "their own" and in their efforts to participate in that community attempted to manage it accordingly. Papkov's views, on the other hand, focused almost exclusively on the parish. His ideals seemed to be formulated without due consideration of the fact that with respect to Orthodox identity formation, the parish church with its parish community was only one of several types of sacred centers of Orthodox life, and for many Orthodox believers at that time not necessarily the most significant.

Nearly a century has passed since the revolutions that took place in Russia in 1905 and 1917. Decades of often violent and relentless assault by an atheistic regime and the vast destruction of Orthodoxy's old narrative repositories—its chapels, churches, icons, and established feasts—might be said to have altered the ecclesial terrain in Russia forever. Yet a Moscow conference held in 1994 entitled "The Parish in the Orthodox Church" suggests that old issues have resurfaced in another new context. Both clergy and lay participants—conferring just six years after a meeting between Mikhail Gorbachev and the patriarch of Moscow, Pimen, had signaled a new period in Russian church history—referred repeatedly to a current "crisis in ecclesial understanding." They paid particular attention to the low "status" of lay people in the church and spoke of the writings and ideas of A. A. Papkov. Reflecting on their own times and the thinking of their own bishops on church matters, they referred to the seemingly radical views of Russia's hierarchs on the eve of the 1917 Bolshevik revolution.[7] In the following year, 1995, the *New York Times Magazine* ran a story on the photographs of Vladimir Syomin, that year's winner of photojournalism's top prize. Among Syomin's photographs was that of a provincial pilgrimage in Russia to a site where an icon of St. Nicholas had been discovered in 1383. Near the site stands a makeshift altar where a priest conducted a Divine Liturgy or prayer service. In this photograph, a woman makes her way on all fours under the hollow beneath a tree where the icon supposedly had appeared. The caption of the photograph reads: "The pilgrimage has taken place annually since [1383]: in 1551, when the villagers skipped it, snow fell in midsummer."[8] One can only wonder when, how, and if these distinct strands of ecclesial life—the institutional, the theological, and the lived—will fully meet in the story of Russian Orthodoxy.

# NOTES

## INTRODUCTION

1. Georges Florovsky, "The Church: Her Nature and Task," in *Bible, Church, Tradition*, 59.

2. Yves Congar, *L'Ecclésiologie du Haut Moyen-âge* (Paris, 1968), 324–25; quoted in Eric G. Jay, *The Church*, 1:147–48.

3. Jaroslav Pelikan, *Christian Doctrine and Modern Culture (Since 1700)*, vol. 5 of *The Christian Tradition: A History of the Development of Doctrine* (Chicago: University of Chicago Press, 1989), 280–82.

4. For the notion of the priesthood of all believers in the New Testament, see 1 Peter 2:9. Peter Meinhold, "Modern Europe, 1800–1962," in *The Layman in Christian History*, ed. Stephen Charles Neill and Hans-Reudi Weber (Philadelphia: Westminster Press, 1963), 170; Martin Luther, "An Appeal to the Ruling Class of German Nationality as to the Amelioration of the State of Christendom," in *Martin Luther: Selections from His Writings*, ed. and trans. John Dillenberger (New York: Doubleday, 1962), 407–10.

5. Pelikan, *Christian Doctrine*, 289.

6. GA RF, f. 3431, op. 1, d. 294, l. 557.

7. David B. Barrett, ed., *World Christian Encyclopedia* (Oxford: Oxford University Press, 1982), 9.

8. See comment by the professor of canon law A. I. Pokrovskii in *Deiianiia Sviashchennogo Sobora Pravoslavnoi Rossiiskoi Tserkvi 1917–1918* (Petrograd, 1918), 5:232.

9. Several studies of peasant book holdings conducted in the mid and late nineteenth century show that in the late nineteenth century religious and moral books still constituted a significant portion of peasant book collections. Even those who remained illiterate could easily have had access to devotional literature, since oral readings by literate neighbors or family members, especially during the winter months and on Sundays, continued to be a popular form of socializing in rural areas. See S. A. An-skii, *Ocherki narodnoi literatury* (St. Petersburg, 1894), 137; An. Tarutin, "Chto chitaiut krestiane Udimskoi volosti i kak oni otnosiatsia k shkole i knige," *Russkaia shkola*, 1 (January 1892): 139–40; Krestianin Ivan Ivin, "O narodnoi lubochnoi literature," *Russkoe obozrenie* 9 (1893), 256. Also see the findings of the Tenishev Bureau in REM, f. 7, op. 1; the Prugavin and Rubakin studies can be found in the Manuscript Division of the Russian State Library, f. 358. Churchmen were well aware of the dramatic increase in secular titles during the second half of the nineteenth century. See N. G. Petrushevskii, "O religiozno-nravstvennoi knige dlia narodnago i detskago chteniia," *RSP* no. 13 (1907): 327–28. For a study of popular secular commercial publications, see Brooks, *When Russia Learned to Read*.

10. Claudia Carlen, comp., *The Papal Encyclicals*, vol. 1, 381–86; vol. 3, 71–98 (Ann Arbor, MI: Perlan Press, 1900).

11. These figures are drawn from *Rossiia: Entsiklopedicheskii slovar'* (Leningrad, Lenizdat, 1991), 76, 86; *Vsepoddaneishii otchet ober-prokurora sviateishago sinoda po vedomstvu pravoslavnago ispovedaniia za 1899* (St. Petersburg, 1902), vedomost' 5.

12. Wilhelm Pauck, "The Idea of the Church in Christian History," *Church History* 21 (1952): 193.

13. Lewis W. Spitz, "History: Sacred and Secular," *Church History* 47 (March 1978): 10; C. W. Monnich, "Church History in the Context of the Human Sciences," in *Church History in Future Perspective*, ed. Roger Aubert (New York: Herder and Herder, 1970), 45.

14. Yves Congar, "Church History as a Branch of Theology," in Aubert, *Church History in Future Perspective*, 85.

15. For examples of the traditional style of histories of the Orthodox Church in Russia, see A. V. Kartashev, *Ocherki po istorii Russkoi tserkvi*, 2 vols. (Paris: YMCA Press, 1959); D. Pospielovsky, *The Orthodox Church in the History of Russia* (Crestwood, NY: St. Vladimir's Orthodox Seminary Press, 1998); I. K. Smolitsch, *Istoriia Russkoi tserkvi, 1700–*

*1917*, trans. B. B. Vik, F. K. Kon'kov, A. V. Nazarenko, Prot. Vladislav Tsypin (Moscow: Spaso-Preobrazhenskii Valaamskii Monastyr', 1996–1997); N. D. Tal'berg, *Istoriia Russkoi tserkvi* (Jordanville, NY: Holy Trinity Monastery, 1959); Prot. Vladislav Tsypin, *Istoriia Russkoi Tserkvi, 1917–1997*, vol. 9 of *Istoriia Russkoi Tserkvi* (Moscow: Spaso-Preobrazhenskii Valaamskii monastyr', 1994–97).

16. Paul Evdokimov, *Ages of the Spiritual Life*, orig. trans. Sister Gertrude; rev. trans. Michael Plekon and Alexis Vinogradov (Crestwood, NY: St. Vladimir's Orthodox Seminary Press, 1988), 227–43; Pelikan, *Christian Doctrine*, 13–14.

17. The "insider/outsider" dichotomy in the study of church history relates to broader issues in the study of religion. See Russell T. McCutcheon, *The Insider/Outsider Problem in the Study of Religion* (New York: Cassell, 1999).

18. As examples, see Freeze, *Parish Clergy*; Robert P. Geraci, *Windows on the East: National and Imperial Identities in Late Tsarist Russia* (Ithaca, NY: Cornell University Press, 2001); Laurie Manchester, "The Secularization of the Search for Salvation: The Self-Fashioning of Orthodox Clergymen's Sons in Late Imperial Russia," *Slavic Review* 57, no. 1 (spring 1998): 50–76.

19. For the late nineteenth century in Russia, see the pivotal study by the protopresbyter and doctor of theology E. P. Akvilonov (1862–1911), *Tserkov'*, and the highly influential essay by A. S. Khomiakov (1804–60), *Tserkov' odna* (reprint, Moscow: Gosudarstvennaia publichnaia istoricheskaia biblioteka, 1991).

20. The study of Russian Orthodox ecclesiology has been woefully neglected. Except for fragments in Florovsky's study, *The Ways of Russian Theology*, and several theses from Orthodox theological schools, it is a subject that has not received its due attention from cultural or intellectual historians. Alexander Garklavs, "Ecclesiology in Russian Theology, 1840–1917" (M.Div. thesis, St. Vladimir's Orthodox Theological Seminary, 1982); Vladimir, Metropolitan of Kiev and All Ukraine, "Ekkleziologiia v otechestvennom bogoslovii" (Magistersakaia dissertatsiia, Kiev, 1987).

21. See discussion of this point in Shevzov, "Letting 'the People' into 'Church'." For examples from the historiography on western Europe, see Blackbourn, *Marpingen*, 48, 51; Jean Delumeau, *Catholicism between Luther and Voltaire: A New View of the Counter-Reformation* (Philadelphia: Westminster Press, 1977), 175–231; Obelkevich, *Religion and the People*, 4–5; Keith Thomas, *Religion and the Decline of Magic* (New York: Scribner, 1971); Eugen Weber, *Peasants into Frenchmen* (Stanford: Stanford University Press, 1976), 357–74. For a discussion of the problems with "the popular," see Peter Burke, *Popular Culture in Early Modern Europe*, rev. ed. (Cambridge, UK: Scolar Press, 1994), xiv–xxii. For examples from the historiography on Russia, see Chulos, "Peasant Religion," especially the figure on p. 443; Freeze, "Institutionalizing Piety"; Moshe Lewin, "Popular Religion in Twentieth-Century Russia," in Ecklof and Frank, *The World of the Russian Peasant*, 155–68; Worobec, *Possessed*, 20–86.

22. G. A. Nosova, "Opyt etnograficheskogo izucheniia bytovogo pravoslaviia," 151–63; Nosova, *Iazychestvo v pravoslavii*, Nosova, *Russkie: istoriko-etnograficheskie ocherki* (Moscow: Rossiiskaia akademiia nauk, In-t etnologii i antropologii im. N. N. Miklukoho-Maklaia, 1997). L. A. Tul'tseva, "Religioznye verovaniia i obriady russkikh krest'ian na rubezhe XIX i XX vekov," 31–46. In post-Soviet times, the study of "popular Orthodoxy" shed much of its Marxist-Leninist framework, but the study of Orthodoxy among the peasantry still occasionally seemed separate from the history of "the Church" and the religious lives of believers from other social groups. Gromyko, *Mir russkoi derevni*; Panchenko, *Narodnoe pravosalvie*. More recent scholarship emerging from Russia does not leave such an impression, although the approach sometimes seems even less historically

critical. As an example, see Gromyko and Buganov, *O vozzreniiakh russkogo naroda*. For a more critical analysis of current trends among Russian scholars, see T. A. Bernshtam, *Molodost' v simvolizme perekhodnykh obriadov vostochnykh slavian*, 72–73.

23. I addressed the problems with the three usual approaches to the study of church culture models in Shevzov, "Popular Orthodoxy," 1–3; 10–23. Since then, the problem of approach and method in the study of Orthodoxy and the Russian Orthodox Church have been actively discussed and debated by Russian historians. See the study that resulted from a 1999 workshop at the University of Michigan on "Orthodoxy and the Russian Historical Experience": Valerie A. Kivelson and Robert H. Greene, eds., *Orthodox Russia: Studies in Belief and Practice, 1492–1936* (University Park: Pennsylvania State University Press, 2003). Influenced by the study of lived religion as pursued in the study of religion in America—see Hall, *Lived Religion*—the search for a more inclusive understanding of Orthodoxy has since been seen in Kizenko, *Prodigal Saint*, 4–5. For an example of differing approaches, compare Chulos, "Peasant Religion," and his later "Orthodox Identity at Russian Holy Places," in *The Fall of an Empire, the Birth of a Nation: National Identities in Russia*, ed. Chris J. Chulos and Timo Piirainen (Aldershot, UK: Ashgate, 2000), 28–50.

24. Reginald E. Zelnik, "To the Unaccustomed Eye: Religion and Irreligion in the Experience of St. Petersburg Workers in the 1870s," *Russian History* 16, nos. 2–4 (1989): 302.

25. For parallel discussions regarding the notion of "nation," see the recent studies by Alon Confino, *The Nation as a Local Metaphor;* Peter van der Veer and Hartmut Lehmann, *Nation and Religion: Perspectives on Europe and Asia* (Princeton: Princeton University Press, 1999).

26. Sergei Bychkov, "The Synod against a Council," *Moskovskii komsomolets*, 19 August 2000, reported and trans. Paul Steeves; available online at: www.stetson.edu/~psteeves/relnews; "Zalozhen khram vo imia Derzhavnoi ikony Bozhiei Materi," *Radonezh*, no. 1 (85) (January 1999): 4; "V den' godovshchiny avarii na chernobyl'skoi ZES osviashchen zakladnoi kamen' budushchei chasovni," *Radonezh* no. 8 (73) (April 1998): 2; "Vazhnost' soversheniia krestnykh khodov, *Sobornaia vest'*, no. 16 (1999): 6; "V Ivanovo mirotochat bolee tysiachi ikon," *Radonezh*, no. 4 (88) (March 1999); L. Alekseeva, "Zemlia Bozhiei Materi," *Pravoslavnyi Sankt-Peterburg*, no. 4 (82) (1999): 2.

27. This term is borrowed from Louis Bouyer, *The Church of God: The Body of Christ and the Temple of the Spirit,* trans. Charles Underhill Quinn (Chicago: Franciscan Herald Press, 1970), 279.

## CHAPTER I

1. *Zhurnaly i protokoly*, 3:277–78, 352.

2. *Zhurnaly i protokoly*, 1:295–359; Troitskii, *Otnoshenie gosudarstva k tserkvi*, 186–98; Aggeev, *Istoricheskii grekh;* Antonov, *Vozrozhdenie tserkovno-prikhodskoi zhizni*; Pisiotis, "Orthodoxy versus Autocracy."

3. Sv. V. Il'inskii, "Sviashchennik k dukhovenstvu," *Rus'*, 35 (21 February/6 March 1906): 3. Also see A. Chiretskii, "O tserkovnoi revorme," *BV* 7 (July 1906): 492.

4. Bishop Evdokim, "Na zare novoi tserkovnoi zhizni," *BV* 5 (May 1905): 155. See also comments by the professor at the University of Kharkov, M. A. Ostroumov, in *Zhurnaly i protokoly*, 3:359. For a discussion of the new focus on the "self" and the consequences for religious life, see Kartashev, *Reforma, reformatsiia i ispolnenie tserkvi*, 19.

5. Vasilii, arkhimandrit, *O Tserkvi: Rech' v torzhestvennom sobranii Kievskago pravoslav-*

*nago religiozno-prosvetitel'nago obshchestva, 17 oktiabria, 1913* (Kiev, 1913), 5. See also Sadov-skii, *Tserkovnyi soiuz;* Troitskii, *Khristianstvo ili tserkov'*.

6. A. Chiretskii, "O tserkovnoi reforme," *BV* (July 1906): 476.

7. Sv. D. Silin, "Dukh i organizatsiia," *BV* (May 1909): 73.

8. See, for example, the remarks by N. D. Kuznetsov in *Zhurnaly i protokoly*, 3:274–75; Sadovskii, *Tserkovnyi soiuz*, 4; Troitskii, *Khristianstvo ili tserkov'*.

9. Quoted in Preobrazhenskii, *Tserkovnaia reforma*, vii.

10. "Pis'mo pravoslavnago episkopa," in Preobrazhenskii, *Tserkovnaia reforma*, 34–37. See also comments by Sadovskii, *Tserkovnyi soiuz*, 10.

11. "Zapiski Religiozno-Filosofskikh sobranii v S. Peterburge," *Novyi put'* 1 (January 1903): 36.

12. Compare, for instance, the views of Andrei, the bishop of Ufa, in *O narodnom golose v delakh tserkovnykh*, with those of Lev Tikhomirov in *Sovremennoe polozhenie prikhod-skago voprosa*. This period in Russian Orthodox Church history confounds the usual stereotype that Orthodoxy was neatly divided into three "camps"—black clergy, white clergy, and laity. See Roslof, "The Renovationist Movement," 24–28.

13. Antonii, Metropolitan of Volhynia, in *Otzyvy eparkhial'nykh arkhiereev*, 1:114–15.

14. See, for example, Aggeev, *Istoricheskii grekh*, 10.

15. Quoted in Preobrazhenskii, *Periodicheskaia pechat'*, 4.

16. Preobrazhenskii, *Periodicheskaia pechat'*, 77; *Dokladnaia zapiska*, 7.

17. An example of a negative evaluation of the Church reforms of Peter the Great can be found in Tikhomirov, *Zaprosy zhizni*. Also see the overview of the literature in Ver-khovskoi, *Unchrezhdenie*, vol. 1, CLXIV–CLXVI.

18. Verkhovskoi, *Uchrezhdenie*, 633.

19. For a translation of this text and a historical introduction, see Muller, *Spiritual Regulation*. See also Cracraft, *Church Reform*.

20. The character of Peter's own religious sensibilities is a complex subject. See, for instance, Cracraft, *Church Reform*, 23–27; Verkhovskoi, *Uchrezhdenie*, 1:46–95; Reinhard Wittram, *Peter I, Czar und Kaiser: Zur Geschichte Peters des Grossen in seiner Zeit* (Gottingen: Vandenhoeck and Ruprecht, 1964), 2:170–218.

21. Muller, *Spiritual Regulation*, 10.

22. Freeze, "Handmaiden," 89.

23. John Meyendorff, "Russian Bishops and Church Reform in 1905," in Nichols and Stavrou, *Russian Orthodoxy under the Old Regime*, 170.

24. *PSZ*, ser. 1, vol. 19, 1774, no. 14231.

25. *PSZ*, ser. 1, vol. 17, 1765, no. 12483.

26. Muller, *Spiritual Regulation*, 45, 52.

27. Muller, *Spiritual Regulation*, 46.

28. Muller, *Spiritual Regulation*, 47.

29. *The Encyclopedia of Religion*, ed. Mircea Eliade, vol. 14, s.v. "superstition."

30. Muller, *Spiritual Regulation*, 13.

31. *PSPR*, ser. 1, vol. 2, 1722 (St. Petersburg, 1872), 243.

32. The celebration of twelve "Fridays" during the course of the year by certain peasants, especially women, usually occurred before major church feasts. These Fridays were linked with the name of St. Paraskeva and were marked by fasting. For a description of this phenomenon, see Ivanits, *Russian Folk Belief*, 33–35. The Church in Russia had long struggled with what it saw as pagan holdovers. See as an example D. E., Kozhanchi-kov, ed., *Stoglav* (1863; reprint, Letchworth, England: Bradda Books, 1971), 140–42.

33. The *akathistos* hymn belonged to a genre of eastern Christian hymnography that

dated to perhaps as early as fifth-century Byzantium. It originally developed as a liturgical expression of devotion to Mary, the Mother of God. By the end of the Byzantine period, it had developed into a broader genre of laudatory hymnody. The phenomena mentioned here were associated not only with the peasantry; the *Regulation* called for bishops and priests to be examined as to whether they were superstitious prior to their consecration or ordination, respectively.

34. Robert Muchembled, quoted in Kselman, *Miracles and Prophecies*, 191. These concerns were not new to Russia and had precedents from the mid–seventeenth century onward. See Bushkovitch, *Religion and Society*, 100–127.

35. Not all ecclesiastical officials may have understood superstition in the same way as Russia's "enlightened" rulers. In 1744, for instance, the Holy Synod rescinded a 1722 law that had prohibited icons from being taken from churches to private homes for special prayer services. Members of the Synod noted in particular that many ancient church histories "showed that those who came to holy icons with faith in God . . . attained victory over the devil and healing from illness." For this reason, members of the Holy Synod directed that the practice of going to homes with icons be allowed once more, but with the provision that clergy abstain from discussing the subject of miracles during these visits. *PSPR*, ser. 2, vol. 2, 1744–45 (St. Petersburg, 1907), 56.

36. See discussion in Freeze, *Russian Levites*, 77. For a discussion of central and diocesan administrative organs and their relationship to Russia's civil administrative organs, see Freeze, *Russian Levites*, 51–54.

37. The history of these processes are described in detail in Freeze, "Disintegration of Traditional Communities," and in *Russian Levites*, 147–83.

38. See, for example, Kniaz' V. Cherkasskii, "Nekotorye cherty budushchego sel'skago upravleniia," *Sel'skoe blagoustroistvo* 9 (1858): 225–70. For a similar view, see "Ob ustroistve krest'ian Sapozhskogo uezda," *Zhurnal zemlevladel'tsev* 10 (1858): 25–57. Cited in Papkov, *Tserkovno-obshchestvennye voprosy*, 70.

39. For a review of the discussions about the parish during this period, see Ivanov, *Reforma prikhoda*, 1–23; Papkov, *Nachalo vozrozhdeniia*; Papkov, *Tserkovno-obshchestvennye voprosy*; Titlinov, *Vopros o prikhodskoi reforme*.

40. Danilov, *Polozheniia o sel'skom sostoianii*. Part I, "Obshchee Polozhenie o krest'ianakh, vyshedshikh iz krepostnoi zavisimosti," par. 44.

41. Polunov, *Pod vlast'iu ober-prokurora*, 91.

42. "Opredeleniia Sviateishago Sinoda ot 18 iulia–8 avgusta 1884 po povodu khodataistva moskovskago gubernskago zemskago sobraniia ob izmeneniiakh v ustroistve gorodskikh i sel'skikh prikhodov," *Spravka po voprosu o preobrazovanii pravoslavnago prikhoda*, 98–107.

43. See, for example, Freeze, *Parish Clergy*; Oswalt, *Kirchliche Gemeinde und Bauernbefreiung*; Papkov, *Tserkovno-obshchestvennye voprosy*.

44. This pertains even to such reforms as the 1859 establishment of parish councils in the Amur region, which appeared to be concerned with the role of laity. See Vostorgov, *K voprosu o prikhode*, 29–30.

45. Aivazov, *Tserkovnye voprosy*; Freeze, *Parish Clergy*; Papkov, *Tserkovno-obshchestvennye voprosy*; Runovskii, *Tserkovno-grazhdanskiia zakonopolozheniia*.

46. For a review of the 1869 parish reforms, see Freeze, *Parish Clergy*, 315–19; 363–83. The reform effort was a complete failure on account of the lay uproar it caused, and by 1885 it was revoked.

47. "Pravoslavnyi prikhod," *PTsVed* 36 (September 1907): 1530.

48. Blochlinger, *The Modern Parish Community*, 21–27.

49. Much of the discussion that follows is based on the observations made by Zaozerskii, *Chto est' pravoslavnyi prikhod*.

50. Palibin, *Ustav dukhovnoi konsistorii s dopolneniiami*, especially pars. 92–101. For a detailed presentation of this observation, see Zaozerskii, *Chto est' pravoslavnyi prikhod*, 5–8, 13–14.

51. "Zakony o sostoianiiakh," *Svod zakonov*, vol. 9, (1899), par. 448.

52. Kur'ianov, *Ob upravlenii; Ustav dukhovnoi konsistorii*, pars. 130–49; *Instruktsiia tserkovnym starostam*, par. 1 (1890).

53. "Zakony o sostoianiiakh," pars. 443, 449. See also Sv. V. Shingarev, "K voprosu o vozrozhdenii tserkovnago prikhoda," in *Spravka po voprosu o preobrazovanii pravoslavnago prikhoda*, 1031–32.

54. *Ustav dukhovnoi konsistorii*, par. 134.

55. Kur'ianov, *Ob upravlenii*, 12–15. Kur'ianov also speaks of the church as sole owner and manager of property, but discusses the "rights" of laity as juxtaposed to those of "the church."

56. Malevinskii, *Instruktsiia tserkovnym starostam*, pars. 8–18.

57. For the official role of the elder, see Malevinskii, *Instruktsiia tserkovnym starostam*, par. 54, 167–68. The only benefit the church elder enjoyed was freedom from other community responsibilities during his tenure of service. For a history of the position of church elder in Russia, see K. I., *Chto takoe tserkovnyi starosta*.

58. By law, the church elder had to be at least twenty-five years old, preferably literate, and known in the community for his piety and his dedication to the parish. Those who did not annually receive confession and Communion; those who were under investigation for a crime; as well as those who held the position of township elder or who were township scribes were not eligible for the church elder position. See Malevinskii, *Instruktsiia tserkovnym starostam*, par. 7, 13–15.

59. Malevinskii, *Instruktsiia tserkovnym starostam*, see pars. 24, 42.

60. *PTsVed* 13 (1908): 585; Papkov, *Upadok pravoslavnago prikhoda*, 79.

61. Titlinov, *Vopros o prikhodskoi reforme*, 8. For the legislation concerning the parish *popechitel'stva*, see *Polozhenie o prikhodskikh popechitel'stvakh*. For a review of the history of the *popechitel'stva*, see Kudriavtsev, *Istoricheskii ocherk;* Malyshevskii, *O tserkovno-prikhodskikh popechitel'stvakh;* Nikol'skii, *Ob obshchestvennoi blagotvoritel'nosti;* Papkov, *Nachalo vozrozhdeniia;* Young, "Into Church Matters," 367–84.

62. Malevinskii, *Instruktsiia tserkovnym starostam*, 18–19. See also the comments by Ognev, *Chem dolzhen byt' pravoslavnyi prikhod?* 2.

63. *Polozhenie o prikhodskikh popechitel'stvakh*, par. 8; par. 2.

64. For further discussion, see Zaozerskii, *Chto est' pravoslavnyi prikhod*, 36–37.

65. Papkov, *Tserkovno-obshchestvennye voprosy*, 170–74.

66. I. S. Aksakov, *Sochineniia*, vol. 4 (Moscow, 1886), 134.

67. Aksakov, *Sochineniia*. 4:13–24, 142–50.

68. Papkov, *Tserkovno-obshchestvennye voprosy*, 134. It should be noted, however, that even this relatively empathic attitude toward "the people" did not lack paternalistic and condescending overtones. See, for example, A. V. Gumilevskii, "Zametki sel'skago sviashchennika: Temnye liudi," *Strannik 1*, otdel V "Smes' " (January 1860): 1–6; A. Svirelin, "O tserkovnoi propovedi," *DKh* (December 1861): 309. For a discussion of the emergence of a more socially minded clergy, see Manchester, "Secular Ascetics," and Hedda, "Good Shepherds."

69. "Vospominaniia protoiereia I. I. Bazarova," *Russkaia starina* 107 (July 1901): 83–85.

70. Runkevich, *Prikhodskaia blagotvoritel'nost'*, 1; Benzin, *Prikhodskaia blagotvoritel'-nost'*, 9.

71. "Vospominaniia protoiereia I. I. Bazarova," 84. For more on Gumilevskii, see Lindenmeyr, *Poverty Is Not a Vice*, 132–34.

72. When clergy found themselves divided along urban-rural lines, Gumilevskii usually sided with the village clergy. Skrobotov, *Prikhodskoi sviashchennik A. V. Gumilevskii*, 320.

73. Freeze, *Parish Clergy*, 398–449.

74. B. B. Glinskii, "Konstantin Petrovich Pobedonostsev: Materialy dlia biografii," *Istoricheskii vestnik* 4 (1907): 247–74; Preobrazhenskii, *Konstantin Petrovich Pobedonostsev;* Byrnes, *Pobedonostsev.*

75. Kuznetsov, *Preobrazovaniia v Russkoi tserkvi*, 39.

76. See the commentary on this mentality by V. M. Myshtsyn, "Obshchestvenno-osvoboditel'noe dvizhenie i interesy tserkvi," *BV* (May 1905): 200.

77. See, for example, his essay "Tserkov'," in K. P. Pobedonostsev, *Sochineniia* (St. Petersburg: Nauka, 1996), especially 396–406.

78. Makarii Bulgakov taught dogmatic theology at the St. Petersburg Theological Academy and was subsequently bishop of Tambov, Kharkov, and Latvia before becoming metropolitan of Moscow; he was an active advocate of reform of Russia's ecclesiastical schools. In 1854 he was chosen as a member of Russia's Academy of Sciences, to which he donated all the proceeds from the sale of his books in order to fund academic prizes. G. I. Titov, *Makarii, Mitropolit Moskovskii i Kolomenskii*, vols. 1–2 (Kiev, 1895–1903).

79. Bulgakov, *Pravoslavno-dogmaticheskoe bogoslovie*, 148.

80. What follows is a summary of Makarii's thought as presented in his *Pravoslavno-dogmaticheskoe bogoslovie*, 162–80.

81. Indeed, many historians of Russia tend to think first of German Romanticism when considering Khomiakov's intellectual development and forget that he was well versed in patristic writings; it was these, as well as his own experiences, that lay at the base of his ecclesiological sensibilities. Khomiakov's own writings on the Church can be found in the second volume of his collected works, *Polnoe sobranie sochinenii Alekseia Stepanovicha Khomiakova. Sochineniia bogoslovskiia.* Khomiakov and his ecclesial vision have enjoyed extensive academic attention. See, as examples, Nicholas V. Riasanovsky, "Khomiakov on *Sobornost'*," in Simmons, *Continuity and Change*, 183–96; Christoff, *Introduction to Nineteenth-Century Russian Slavophilism.*

82. Jakim and Bird, introduction to *On Spiritual Unity*, 7.

83. Khomiakov, "The Church Is One," in Jakim and Bird, *On Spiritual Unity*, 31.

84. In this respect, Makarii's and Khomiakov's might be seen as two different approaches to the study of the ecclesial community. For a description of the two approaches, see A. Katanskii, "O nauchno-bogoslovskikh opredeleniiakh tserkvi," *TsVes* 42 (1894): 657.

85. Khomiakov, "Tserkov' odna," in *Polnoe sobranie sochinenii*, 2:41.

86. Khomiakov, "Po povodu broshiury g-na Loransi," in *Polnoe sobranie sochinenii*, 2:78.

87. Khomiakov, "Tserkov' odna," 41–42.

88. Khomiakov, "Some Remarks by an Orthodox Christian Concerning the Western Communions on the Occasion of a Brochure by Mr. Laurentie," in Jakim and Bird, *On Spiritual Unity*, 59.

89. Khomiakov, "Po povodu broshiury g-na Loransi," in *Polnoe sobranie sochinenii*, 2:91.

90. Christoff, *Introduction to Nineteenth-Century Russian Slavophilism*, 152.

91. Pain, "Sobornost'," 93–94; Jakim and Bird, introduction to *On Spiritual Unity*, 8.

92. George L. Kline, "The Religious Roots of S. L. Frank's Ethics and Social Philosophy," in Kornblatt and Gustafson, *Russian Religious Thought*, 226.

93. Khomiakov, "O znachenii slov 'kafolicheskii' i 'sobornyi,' " in *Polnoe sobranie sochinenii*, 2: 279.

94. Pevnitskii, "Pravoslavnomu obozreniiu," *TKDA* 1 (1870): 729. See also criticism by P. Florenskii, *Okolo Khomiakova*.

95. Khomiakov, "Tserkov' odna," 49–50. Later, amid polemics concerning the notion of *sobornost'*, some churchmen would assert that historically the word for "Catholic" in the Slavonic Creed was not *sobornyi*, as Khomiakov had claimed, but *kafolicheskaia*. See Episkop Feodosii, "Chto znachit' 'sobornaia' (sobstvenno kafolicheskaia) Tserkov' simvola very?" *PTsVed*, 2 (1906): 50–55.

96. Khomiakov, "Tserkov' odna," 48.

97. Khomiakov, "Neskol'ko slov pravoslavnogo khristianina o zapadnykh veroispovedaniiakh," in *Polnoe sobranie sochinenii*, 2:140, 142.

98. Indeed, one of the latter readings of *sobornost'* was in terms of "popular," or *narodnoe*. See, for example, "Upravlenie i samoupravlenie v dukhovnom mire," *Novoe vremia*, 21 March 1905.

99. Khomiakov, "Po povodu broshiury g-na Loransi," in *Polnoe sobranie sochinenii*, 2:84.

100. "Zamechaniia A. V. Gorskago na bogoslovskiia sochineniia A. S. Khomiakova," *BV* (November 1900): 518–20. For Linitskii's evaluation, see P. Linitskii, "Po povodu zashchity Slavianofil'stva v *Pravoslavnom Obzrenii*," *TKDA* 1 (1884): 88–90.

101. See Georges Florovsky, *Ways of Russian Theology*, part 2, 329, n. 161.

102. Pavlov, *Ob uchastii mirian v delakh tserkvi*. For another example of a churchman whose ecclesial sensibilities reverberated with those of Khomiakov, see Prot. A. M. Ivantsov-Platonov's series of articles that appeared in 1882 and was later published as *O Russkom tserkovnom upravlenii* (St. Petersburg, 1898).

103. See, for example, P. Smirnov, *O tserkvi*, in which, in discussing the creed's four "marks" of the Church—unity, holiness, catholicity, and apostolicity—he skips over the topic of catholicity, or *sobornost'*, altogether. Usually, most treatises on the Church continued to discuss the term *sobornyi* in terms of simple geographic universality and to limit the active role in ecclesial affairs to the hierarchy. See, for example, Svetlakov, *Izlozhenie ucheniia*; Malevanskii, *Opyt dogmaticheskago bogosloviia*, 4:224–26, 251–53. Also note the 1915 observation of Iu. A. Kolemin, former secretary of the Russian Embassy in Madrid and secretary of the chancellery of the Ministry of Foreign Affairs, who laments that Khomiakov's teaching of the Church was not a standard part of the Orthodox catechesis for students. See his *Avtoritet v voprosakh very* (Sergiev Posad, 1915), 14.

104. Malevanskii, *Opyt pravoslavnago dogmaticheskago bogosloviia*, 4:232.

105. Malinovskii, *Pravoslavnoe dogmaticheskoe bogoslovie*, 3: 524, 549–50.

106. For example, see Akvilonov, *Tserkov'*, in which he argued against speaking about the Church as "society" but exclusively in terms of "body" and "organism." See also the section on the clergy and laity in Ostroumov, *Pis'ma*, 125–36. From the 1860s on, the journal *Pravoslavnoe obozrenie* promoted an ecclesial worldview that was similar in many ways to Khomiakov's. For examples, see the lively debate that took place between F. Smirnov and P. Linitskii regarding Khomiakov's understanding of the Church, its hierar-

chy, and the laity in P. Linitskii, "Po povodu zashchity slavianofil'stva," 77–94; F. Smirnov, *Vopros o Protestantstve v vozzrenii Khomiakova*," *PO* (March 1884): 533–52.

107. Aksakov, *Dukha ne ugashaite.*

108. *Zhurnaly i protokoly*, 1:142. See also the comments by the church historian A. I. Brilliantov in *Zhurnaly i protokoly*, 1:161; Chiretskii, "O tserkovnoi reforme," 448; A. Lebedev, "Za chem nam nuzhen patriarkh?" *BV* (January 1907): 12; V. Sokolov, "Predstoiashchii vserossiiskii tserkovnyi sobor, ego sostav i zadachi," *BV* (May 1906): 50.

109. Florovsky, *Puti russkogo bogosloviia*, 220–23.

110. It is noteworthy that it was in this context that Khomiakov contemplated the notion of "catholic." In attempting to define the essence of Protestantism, Khomiakov denied that it lies either in protest, reform, or freedom of investigation—features he said were present in the history of Christianity as a whole. Protestantism, he claimed, lies in a negation of the spirit of catholicity whereby the individual or community acts without any regard for the ecclesial body as a whole. In this respect, Khomiakov traced Protestantism's roots not to sixteenth-century reforms but to the Roman papacy and its inclusion of the *filioque* in the Nicene-Constantinopolitan creed. He denied any essential difference between Roman Catholicism and Protestantism, seeing them as two sides of the same coin. See his essay "Po povodu broshiury g-na Loransi," in *Sobranie sochinenii*, 2:67–105.

111. For the history of the Preconciliar Commission and a review of its main tasks and conclusions, see Cunningham, *A Vanquished Hope*; for a critical assessment of its composition, see Ognev, *Tserkovnyi sobor*, 9–10.

112. See I. S. Berdnikov, "Osoboe mnenie professora Kazanskoi dukhovnoi akademii Il'i Berdnikova," in *Zhurnaly i protokoly*, 1:115. Also compare comments in *Zhurnaly i protokoly*, vol. 1, by N. D. Kuznetsov, 140, and A. Almazov, 144; in *Zhurnaly i protokoly*, vol. 3, by the priest T. I. Butkevich, 73–74, and N. D. Kuznetsov, 89. Also compare Antonii, the metropolitan of Volhynia, "Pervaia otvetnaia dokladnaia zapiska Sviateishemu Pravitel'stvuiushchemu Sinodu," *BV* (December 1905): 698–710, with V. N. Myshtsyn, "Naskol'ko obiazatelen avtoritet tserkovnykh kanonov," *BV* (December 1905): 819, and Chiretskii, "O tserkovnoi reforme," 460.

113. Compare, for example, comments in *Zhurnaly i protokoly*, vol. 1, by F. D. Samarin, 90–91, by the archbishop of Kherson, Dimitrii, 137–39, and by A. Almazov, 429.

114. These two tendencies had already surfaced in public debates and are discussed in Boldovskii, *Vozrozhdenie*; Gorain, *Papkovskaia teoriia prikhoda*; Ivanov, *Reforma prikhoda*; Nikol'skii, *Novaia literaturnaia popytka*; Popov, *O vozrozhdenii tserkovno-prikhodskoi obshchiny*; Preobrazhenskii, *Periodicheskaia pechat'*; M. Sviderskii, "Vopros o tserkovnom prikhode v Predsobornom Prisutstvii i v russkoi literature do XX veka," *RSP* 19 (1913): 18–23; Tikhomirov, *Sovremennoe polozhenie*; Titov, *Kritiko-bibliograficheskii obzor*.

115. Papkov was one of the main historians of the Russian parish at the end of the nineteenth and beginning of the twentieth centuries. His works include "Drevne-russkii prikhod," *BV* (February 1897): 251–84; (March 1897): 373–95; (April 1897): 42–67; *Pogosty v znachenii pravitel'stvennykh okrugov*; *Upadok pravoslavnago prikhoda v XVIII–XIX vekakh*; *Nachalo vozrozhdeniia tserkovno-prikhodskoi zhizni v Rossii*; *Neobkhodimost' obnovleniia*; *Vozzvanie k sviashchennikam*; *O blagoustroistve*; *Besedy o pravoslavnom prikhode*. To a large extent, Papkov's views prevailed in the draft of a parish statute, the so-called *Proekt normal'nago ustava*, developed by the fourth section of the Preconciliar Commission. See *Zhurnaly i protokoly*, 2:83–105. At the same time, he believed certain of his ideas were not well presented in this draft, and therefore he composed his own. During the Preconciliar Commission, those who usually voted along with Papkov on parish-related issues included A. Aksakov, N. Kuznetsov, and N. Zaozerskii.

116. Papkov, *Vozzvanie k sviashchennikam*, 4.

117. Papkov, *Besedy o pravoslavnom prikhode*, 8.

118. Papkov, *Vozzvanie k sviashchennikam*, 5–6.

119. Papkov, *Besedy o pravoslavnom prikhode*, 55.

120. Ibid., 56.

121. For example, in his "Mystagogy" St. Maximus the Confessor writes: "For numerous and of almost infinite number are the men, women, and children who are distinct from one another and vastly different. . . . All are born into the Church and through it are reborn and recreated in the Spirit. To all in equal measure it gives and bestows one divine form and designation, to be Christ's and to carry his name. . . . [Through the Church] everyone converges with all the rest and joins together with them by the one, simple, and indivisible grace and power of faith." Berthold, trans., *Maximus Confessor*, 187. He then cites Galatians 3:28.

122. Papkov, *Vozzvanie k sviashchennikam*, 5. This idea is compatible with the teaching of St. Maximus regarding the unity of the Church—specifically, the unity of the sanctuary and the nave (or the priests and the faithful): "By their relationship to the unity it frees these parts from the difference arising from their names. It shows to each other that they are both the same thing, and reveals that one is to the other in turn what each one is for itself." "Mystagogy," 188.

123. Papkov, *Vozzvanie k sviashchennikam*, 11; *Besedy o pravoslavnom prikhode*, 7–8.

124. Papkov, *Vozzvanie k sviashchennikam*, 4–7.

125. See comments of Stefan, bishop of Mogilev, in *Zhurnaly i protokoly*, 3:352. See also Zaozerskii, *Chto est' pravoslavnyi prikhod*, 14–17.

126. Shingarev, "K voprosu o vozrozhdenii tserkovnago prikhoda," in *Spravka po voprosu o preobrazovanii pravoslavnago prikhoda*, 1027.

127. See comments of N. D. Kuznetsov, *Zhurnaly i protokoly*, 3: 319. See also M. I. Benemanskii, "Otkliki pechati. Nadezhdy i razocharovaniia," *BV* (January 1907): 199–205.

128. See, for example, Kuznetsov, *Tserkov', dukhovenstvo i obshchestvo*, 57; Rufimskii, *Tserkovnyi prikhod*, 4.

129. Papkov, *Proekt normal'nago ustava*, pars. 10–12. This parish statute also explicitly mentioned the role of deaconesses in parish life.

130. For this view, see M. M. Tareev, "Tserkovnost' kak printsip nravstvennago bogosloviia," *BV* (September 1909): 81–83.

131. For a review of the anticipated activities of the parish assemblies and councils, see Papkov, *O blagoustroistve*, 19–42; Shingarev, "K voprosu o vozrozhdenii tserkovnago prikhoda," 1038–39.

132. Papkov, *Proekt normal'nago ustava*, pars. 58–60.

133. *Proekt normal'nago ustava*, par. 41. Papkov advocated the organization of "fraternal courts" (*bratskie sudy*) in parishes in order to mediate intraparish disagreements both among laity and between laity and clergy. Papkov, *O blagoustroistve*, 24–25.

134. The only exceptions Papkov made were with regard to persons who were convicted criminals or had been accused of some crime that resulted in their being denied civil or ecclesial rights. Papkov, *O blagoustroistve*, 20–21. For a variation of Papkov's views but with even less emphasis on the parish priest, see Tsvetkov, *O prikhode*, 18–19.

135. Papkov, *O blagoustroistve*, 35–37.

136. *Zhurnaly i protokoly*, 3:318. See the similar criticism by Zaozerskii, *Chto est' pravoslavnyi prikhod*, 36.

137. Zaozerskii, *Chto est' pravoslavnyi prikhod*, 56.

138. Zaozerskii, *Chto est' pravoslavnyi prikhod,* 37. It is noteworthy that more hierarchically minded members of the ecclesiastical establishment also did not look favorably on the Synod's 18 November 1905 parish reform effort. As one bishop noted with hindsight, many bishops became convinced it was dangerous when "enemies of the Church and clergy" entered the ranks of church councils. "They grabbed all affairs into their own hands and alienated pastors from their leadership roles." RGIA, f. 833, op. 1, d. 6, l. 68 (*Deianiia i protokoly Sviashchennogo Sobora,* nos. 82–89).

139. Papkov, *Proekt normal'nago ustava,* par. 7.

140. *Zhurnaly i protokoly,* 4:10.

141. Papkov, *Proekt normal'nago ustava,* par. 2.

142. Papkov, *O blagoustroistve,* 10–14.

143. V. K-V, *Svet* 197 (1 August 1906):1. Quoted in Preobrazhenskii, *Periodicheskaia pechat',* 31.

144. P. D. Gorodtsev, *Religiozno-tserkovnye voprosy* (St. Petersburg, 1911), 87.

145. *Zhurnaly i protokoly,* 3:346–47.

146. Berdnikov's views can be found in his following essays: *Separativnyi proekt polozheniia o pravoslavnom russkom prikhode; Chto nuzhno dlia obnovleniia pravoslavnago russkago prikhoda?; Kommentarii g. Papkova i K. na suzhdeniia Predsobornago Prisutstviia po voprosu o reforme pravoslavnago prikhoda;* "O protestantskom i pravoslavnom prikhode v Finlandii," *TsVed* 48 (1907); no. 4 (1908). Members of the Preconciliar Commission who consistently voiced views similar to those of Berdnikov were L. Tikhomirov, A. Almazov, and A. Dmitrievskii.

147. See Ignatius of Antioch's letter "To the Smyrnaeans," trans. Cyril C. Richardson, ed., *Early Christian Fathers* (New York: Macmillan, 1970), 15.

148. Ivanov, *Reforma prikhoda,* 60.

149. Berdnikov, "Separativnyi proekt polozheniia o pravoslavnom russkom prikhode," *Zhurnaly i protokoly,* 3:387.

150. Khomiakov, *Sobornoe zavershenie;* reprinted in 1917 as *Sobornost', prikhod i pastyr'.*

151. *Zhurnaly i protokoly,* 3:288–89.

152. Ivanov, *Reforma prikhoda,* 29–30; *Zhurnaly i protokoly,* 3:290–91.

153. *Zhurnaly i protokoly,* 3:388–89.

154. Berdnikov, *Separativnyi proekt,* 19; Tikhomirov, *Sovremennoe polozhenie,* 12.

155. Berdnikov, *Separativnyi proekt,* 46.

156. Papov, *Zametki prikhodskago sviashchennika,* 48.

157. *Zhurnaly i protokoly,* 4:9–11.

158. See comments by the priest T. I. Butkevich, *Zhurnaly i protokoly,* 3:321.

159. *Zhurnaly i protokoly,* 3:335; 390. For similar criticism of the guardians, see Fudel', *Osnovy tserkovno-prikhodskoi zhizni,* 10–15.

160. *Zhurnaly i protokoly,* 3:381.

161. Berdnikov, "Osoboe mnenie," *Zhurnaly i protokoly,* 1:116.

162. *Zhurnaly i protokoly,* 1:124. Berdnikov was referring here to imagery in the letter of Ignatius of Antioch to the Ephesian church. Richardson, *Early Christian Fathers,* 89.

163. See, for example, the comments by A. Almazov, *Zhurnaly i protokoly,* 2:427–28.

164. *Zhurnaly i protokoly,* 1:124, 168–70.

165. For a discussion of similar issues and trends with respect to the idea of a council, see Paul R. Valliere, "The Idea of a Council in Russian Orthodoxy," in Nichols and Stavrou, *Russian Orthodoxy under the Old Regime,* 183–201. For ecclesiological trends

among Russia's religious intelligentsia, see Paul Valliere, *Modern Russian Theology—Bukharev, Soloviev, Bulgakov: Orthodox Theology in a New Key* (Edinburgh: Clark, 2000).

166. Tsvetkov, *O prikhode*, 4–5.

167. A representative example of this pastoral-centered ecclesial vision can be found in Gruppa Peterburgskikh sviashchennikov, *K tserkovnomu soboru*. See also the comments of the priests from the Griazovets district in the Vologda diocese, in GAVO, f. 496, op. 1, d. 19925, l. 270b.

168. Ognev, *Chem dolzhen byt' pravoslavnyi prikhod*? 1.

169. N. Smirnov, "O tsentralizatsii v tserkovnom upravlenii," *Sever* (3 July 1907):2.

170. Ognev, *Chem dolzhen byt' pravoslavnyi prikhod*? 7–8.

171. For an example of the extensive collections taken in parishes in 1912, see Malevinskii, *Instruktsiia tserkovnym starostam,* 141–42. The numerous collections included the following: aid to poor and ailing clergy and their families; the Orthodox Missionary Society; the construction of churches in communities of migrants to Siberia and the Far East; the maintenance of Russian Orthodox properties in the Holy Land; the Russian chapter of the Red Cross; the construction of a church on the field of Kulikovo; and the construction of a church in memory of sailors who perished in the Russo-Japanese war. Many clergy held these numerous collections responsible for the lack of parish charity work, especially in Russia's poorer isolated regions. This point was raised in the discussions on parish reform held in the Third Duma. *Spravka po voprosu o preobrazovanii pravoslavnago prikhoda*, 128–31.

172. Ognev, *Chem dolzhen byt' pravoslavnyi prikhod*? 22–23. For a summary of a scathing address to the Church's bishops regarding their self-imposed alienation from the rest of the ecclesial body, which was published in various newspapers in 1917, including the financial *Birzhevye vedomosti*, see "Svetskaia pechat' o blizhaishikh tserkovnykh reformakh," *RSP*, 10 (1917): 325–32.

173. Ternovets, *Mysli mirianina*, 7.

174. Sv. A. Derzhavin, "Polozhitel'nyia storony prikhodskoi reformy," *Prikhodskaia zhizn'* 9 (1916): 519–20.

175. One priest said that granting the right of pastoral election to the "dark masses" would be like "placing a knife in the hands of a lunatic." Sv. S. Kozubovskii, "Po voprosam prikhodskoi reformy," *Prikhodskaia zhizn'* 3 (1917): 134.

176. Kozubovskii, *Prikhodskaia zhizn'* 4/5 (1917): 204–14.

177. Ognev, *Chem dolzhen byt' pravoslavnyi prikhod?*, 9–10.

178. For examples of discussion of the parish as a small zemstvo unit, see Kropotkin, *Prizyv k ozhivleniiu prikhoda*; Kupchinov, *Prikhod kak melkaia zemskaia edinitsa*; Rovinskii, *Melkaia zemskaia edinitsa*.

179. A. G. Shcherbatov, *Prikhod: Tverdynia russkoi narodnosti*, 3–5. See also his *Prikhod i ego znachenie v sovremennom gosudarstvennom stroe*.

180. M. Sviderskii, "Vopros o tserkovnom prikhode v Predsobornom Prisutstvii i v russkoi literature do XX veka," *RSP*, no. 19 (1913): 5–8; Shcherbatov, *Prikhod: Tverdynia russkoi narodnosti*, 6–14.

181. V. I., "Prestupnost' i prikhod," *TsVes* 59 (1906): 1631–35.

182. A notable exception is the essay by the priest Nikolai Antonov, *Vozrozhdenie tserkovno-prikhodskoi zhizni v Rossii*.

183. Papov, *Zametki prikhodskago sviashchennika*, 10.

184. A. Papkov, "Vorpros o pravoslavnom prikhode v epokhu osvobozhdeniia krest'ian," *Prikhodskoi sviashchennik* 7 (19 February 1911): 10–12.

185. *Zhurnaly i protokoly*, 3:388; Ep. Antonii (Kamenskii) *Kanonicheskii prikhod;* Tikhomirov, *Sovremennoe polozhenie.*

186. Antonii (Khrapovitskii), *Vosstanovlenie prikhoda*, 2; comments by Almazov in *Zhurnaly i protokoly*, 3:369. See also comments by clergy from the Kiev diocese to this effect in RGIA, f. 796, op. 445, d. 223, l. 7.

187. Preobrazhenskii, *Periodicheskaia pechat'*, 75.

188. Antonii, *Vosstanovlenie prikhoda*, 6. For a similar analogy, see A. A. Almazov's comments in *Zhurnaly i protokoly*, 2: 427–28.

189. *Zhurnaly i protokoly*, 3:286.

190. *Zhurnaly i protokoly*, 3:304–5; Preobrazhenskii, *Periodicheskaia pechat'*, 31.

191. Note the revealing (but theologically nonsensical) comment by M. A. Ostroumov in *Zhurnaly i protokoly*, 3:303, where he claims that in Papkov's opinion the subject of ownership is the parish, while in the opposition's view it is the church.

192. *Zhurnaly i protokoly*, 3:84.

193. Papkov, *O blagoustroistve.*

194. See, for example, Zaozerskii, *Chto est' pravoslavnyi prikhod*, 43.

195. Kuznetsov, *Tserkov', dukhovenstvo i obshchestvo*, 57–58.

196. *Zhurnaly i protokoly*, 3:107, 303.

197. Sv. S. Broiakovskii, "Tserkovno-prikhodskaia zhizn' na novykh nachalakh," *Zvonar'*, nos. 5–6 (1906): 237–49.

198. *Zhurnaly i protokoly*, 3:297.

199. N., "Chem podmeneno sobornoe nachalo v sovremennom tserkovnom stroe," *Tserkovno-obshchestvennaia zhizn'*, no. 24 (1907): 716.

200. Ognev, *Tserkovnyi sobor*, 22, 31.

201. Soborianin, "Prikhodskaia konstitutsiia," *TsOV* 14 (4 October 1912): 5.

202. Proceedings of this special commission were published in a series of articles with the title "Pravoslavnyi Prikhod" in *PTsVed*, 36–40, 42, 49 (1907); 1, 3–9, 17 (1908). Both Berdnikov and Papkov actively participated in this commission. The Synod approved a version of its own proposal for the organization of parish life in May 1908.

203. *PTsVed*, no. 37 (1907): 1351.

204. For a brief review of this history, see RGIA, f. 797, op. 84, d. 396, ll. 16 ob.–27.

205. RGIA, f. 797, op. 84, d. 396, l. 39 ob.

206. "K reforme prikhoda: Tolki pechati," *OKh* 1, razdel "Tserkovnoe obozrenie" (January 1912): 165–73.

207. RGIA, f. 796, op. 202, 2 ot., 2 st., d. 66a, l. 6.

208. RGIA, f. 796, op. 445, d. 223.

209. *Vremennoe polozhenie o pravoslavnom prikhode* (Petrograd, 1917), 3–4.

210. RGIA, f. 796, op. 445, d. 223, l. 12.

211. Maksimov, *Peredacha tserkovnykh zemel, domov i kapitalov.*

212. *Kaluzhskii tserkovno-obshchestvennyi vestnik* 28–29 (1916), 3.

213. RGIA, f. 796, op. 445, d. 223, ll. 39–40; 43. For another graphic example of divisions along these lines, see P., "Priznaki razdeleniia v dukhovenstve," *RSP* 13/14 (1917): 403–7.

214. RGIA, f. 833, op. 1, d. 6, l. 6 (*Deianiia i protokoly Sviashchennogo Sobora*, nos. 82–89).

215. Sviashchennyi Sobor Pravoslavnoi Rossiiskoi tserkvi, *Deianiia*, kniga 10, vyp. 1, Deianie 117, 34.

216. Ibid., 33.

217. Ibid., 41.

218. GA RF, f. 3431, op. 1, d. 274, ll. 22–50.

219. RGIA, f. 833, op. 1., d. 38, l. 139; A. V. Vasil'ev, "Patriarshestvo i sobornost'," *Deianiia Sviashchennogo sobora,* vol. 3, (Deianie 31), 28–37.

220. RGIA, f. 833, op. 1., d. 38, l. 156, 140.

221. Sv. A. Beliaev, "Tserkovnaia sobornost' i gosudarstvennaia demokratichnost'," *Kaluzhskii tserkovno-obshchestvennyi vestnik* 20 (10 July 1917): 1–2.

222. RGIA, f. 833 op. 1, d. 38, l. 144.

223. "Veruiu . . . v sobornuiu i apostol'skuiu tsekrov'," *Tserkovnyi golos* 3 (20 January 1906): 65–67.

224. "Sobornyi stroi," *TsOV* 9 (1913): 6.

225. "Veruiu . . . v sobornuiu i apostol'skuiu tserkov'," 65–67.

226. B. Titlinov, "Istoki sobornosti," *Russkoe slovo* 201 (2/15 September 1917): 2.

227. RGIA, f. 833, op. 1, d. 9, ll. 51–52, 57.

228. Himes, *Ongoing Incarnation,* 1–42.

229. *Zhurnaly i protokoly,* 3:284–86. Papkov himself commented on the irreconcilability of these two tendencies.

230. For the parish statute voted on by the members of the 1917 All-Russian Council, see Sviashchennyi sobor Pravoslavnoi Rossiiskoi tserkvi, *Sobranie opredelenii i postanovlenii,* vyp. 3 (Moscow, 1918), 1–41.

231. Valliere, "The Idea of a Council," 199.

232. "Dukhovenstvo i obshchestvo v ikh otnoshenii k voprosu o vozrozhdenii i ozhivlenii tserkovno-prikhodskoi zhizni," *Kaluzhskii tserkovno-obshchestvennyi vestnik* 28–29 (1916): 3.

## CHAPTER 2

1. Quoted in P. K., "Iz zametok o khrame," *RSP* 45 (1901): 225.

2. REM, d. 1307, l. 41. In their annual reports to the Holy Synod, bishops during the period 1861–1914 tended to note that relatively few rural churches were neglected. The annual bishops' report to the Holy Synod can be found in RGIA, f. 796, op. 442. In addition, correspondents to the Tenishev Bureau also consistently maintained that rural inhabitants actively and "zealously" donated funds for the beautification of their parish churches. See, for example, REM, d. 63 (Vladimir); d. 416 (Viatka); d. 533 (Kaluga); d. 676 (Novgorod). This does not mean, however, that the standards on which such statements were based were always uniform or necessarily very high.

3. RGIA, f. 796, op. 186, d. 2087, l. 3 (1905). For believers' view of the temple as the house of God, see REM, d. 536, l. 4 (Kaluga); op. 2, d. 1120, l. 4 (Orel).

4. GAVO, f. 496, op. 1, d. 19366, l. 97 ob.

5. See the following cases, respectively: RGIA, f. 796, op. 142, d. 2136; op. 133, d. 1296, l. 7; op. 146, d. 1255, ll. 13–14; op. 198, 2 ot., 2 st., d. 493.

6. RGIA, f. 796, op. 159, d. 1211 (Tambov, 1878); op. 188, 2 ot., 2 st., d. 2222 (Tver, 1907); op. 198, 2 ot., 2 st., d. 604 (Viatka, 1914); op. 185, 2 ot., 2 st., d. 2106 (Novgorod, 1904).

7. RGIA, f. 796, op. 153, d. 1628, l. 1.

8. *Ustav dukhovnoi konsistorii,* par. 45.

9. For standard land allotments for clergy and peasant reimbursement for its use, see Ivanovskii, *Obozrenie,* 97.

10. *Ustav dukhovnoi konsistorii,* par. 46.

11. For cases where such doubts were raised, see GAVO, f. 496, op. 1, d. 13939 (1865); d. 17187, l. 10 (1897). RGIA, f. 796, op. 141, d. 691 (Voronezh, 1861); op. 145, d. 1247 (Riazan 1864); op. 171, d. 900 (Viatka, 1890); op. 173, d. 1074 (Voronezh, 1892); op. 185, d. 2117, l. 1 (Kursk, 1904); op. 186, d. 2078 (Novgorod, 1905); op. 191, d. 642 (Voronezh, 1910). See also Malevinskii, *Instruktsiia nastoiateliam,* 70.

12. RGIA, f. 796, op. 144, d. 1296 (Viatka, 1863); op. 145, d. 1247 (Riazan 1864); op. 180, d. 1599 (Tambov, 1899); op. 185, d. 2389, l. 7 (Kaluga, 1904).

13. RGIA, f. 796, op. 188, 2 ot., 2 st., d. 2222, l. 2. For other examples of diocesan concern about communal support, see op. 173, d. 1110 (Voronezh, 1892); op. 176, d. 1428, l. 3 (Viatka, 1895); op. 180, d. 2455, l. 8 (Viatka, 1899); op. 188, 2 ot., 2 st., d. 2386, l. 14 (Viatka, 1907).

14. See, for example, Stefanovskii, *Prikhodskaia letopis';* Klevezal', *Prava i obiazannosti,* 2. Parishioner participation in these committees varied, depending in part on the primary source of funding. If, for example, a church was to be constructed primarily using funds raised by the parish guardianship, the building committee included parish trustees. If funding came directly from the village community, then the building committee usually included the village elder along with members chosen from the community at large. See *Spravochnaia kniga,* 384–85.

15. By the end of the nineteenth century, most dioceses had their own architect who oversaw the planning and construction of churches. Regarding diocesan architects, see Kalashnikov, *Alfavitnyi ukazatel',* 23, 26. For information regarding building codes, see *Ustav dukhovnoi konsistorii,* par. 48. Churches, for example, could not be located near especially noisy places such as taverns or trading grounds. Ivanovskii, *Obozrenie,* 87; for the role of provincial civil officials in the ratification of the architectural plan and the construction of a church, see 87–88.

16. REM, d. 1143, l. 30 (Riazan).

17. "Istoricheskaia zapiska po ustroistvu Nikolaevskago Filisovskago khrama, nakhodiashchegosia v Vologodskoi gubernii," *VEV* 3 (1909): 44. See also *Molomskaia Mikhailo-Arkhangel'skaia tserkov' Nikol'skago uezda Vologodskoi gubernii* (St. Petersburg, 1904), 11.

18. For examples of such communal efforts, see GAVO, f. 496, op. 1, d. 16631, ll. 33–46 (1894); d. 18753 (1909); d. 19376, l. 144 ob. (1913); RGIA, f. 796, op. 185, 2 ot., 2 st., d. 2106 (Novgorod, 1904); REM, d. 274, l. 19 (Vologda); d. 1307, l. 47 (Penza); Molchanov, *Tserkovnaia letopis',* 155–59; "Mestnochtimye ikony Tverskoi eparkhii," *TvEV* 10 (1890): 303.

19. For examples in the Vologda diocese, see GAVO, f. 496, op. 1, d. 16502, ll. 306–15 (1893); d. 16634 (1894); d. 17187, l. 48 (1897); d. 17475, l. 56 (1899); d. 18372, l. 9 (1906). RGIA, f. 796, op. 176, d. 1176 (Pskov, 1895).

20. Malevinskii, *Instruktsiia nastoiateliam,* 70; Kalashnikov, *Alfavitnyi ukazatel',* 334. For examples of village assembly decisions regarding these matters, see REM, d. 326 (Vologda); d. 572, l. 12 (Kostroma); d. 1369, l. 4 (Penza); RGIA, f. 796, op. 155, d. 1263 (Tambov, 1874); op. 178, d. 1808 (Novgorod, 1897); op. 183, d. 1830 (Samara, 1902); op. 185, 2 ot., 2 st., d. 2106 (Novgorod, 1904); op. 188, 2 ot., 2 st., d. 2222, l. 2 (Tver, 1907).

21. For sentiments about the sinfulness of not donating for the parish church, see REM, d. 583, l. 3 (Kostroma); for land rentals, see GAVO, f. 1063, op. 85, kor. 225, d. 22, l. 40; REM, d. 630, l. 15 (Kursk); d. 1369, l. 4 (Penza); RGIA, f. 796, op. 173, d. 1110 (Voronezh, 1892); op. 183, d. 1671, l. 4 (Voronezh, 1902); for rentals of booths, see GAVO, f. 1063, op. 93, d. 26, l. 15 ob.; d. 23, l. 57; f. 496, op. 1, d. 17807, l. 23; RGIA, op. 188, d. 2386, l. 2 (Viatka, 1907). Lin'kov, *Opisanie Tiksnenskoi Preobrazhenskoi tserkvi,*

20. For donation of livestock, see REM, d. 345, ll. 14–15. For a description of a similar auction, see d. 385, l. 8. Other correspondents described parishes where peasants donated goods to sell for the support of church maintenance projects. Such community donations and parish sales of goods were especially common when a particular church construction project was underway.

22. REM, d. 540, l. 2 (Kaluga). For an example of a pledge drive, see GAVO, f. 496, op. 1, d. 13807, ll. 163–64. For other types of donations, see the comment in Rozanov, *Voskresenskaia tserkov'*, 51; "Strelitskaia Preobrazhenskaia tserkov' Totemskago uezda Vologodskoi gubernii," *VEV* (chast' neoffitsial'naia) 6 (1902): 155–57; (1902) 7/8 (1902): 230. Generally many authors who published histories of parishes noted that most items in rural churches were donated by parishioners.

23. REM, d. 385, l. 8 (Vologda); d. 540, l. 2 (Kaluga). GAVO, f. 496, op. 1, d. 19367, l. 219 ob.; f. 1063, op. 85, kor. 255, d. 22, l. 39.

24. For examples of willed donations, see RGIA, f. 797, op. 53, 3 ot., 4 st., d. 48, l. 16 ob.; REM, d. 326, l. 14 (Vologda). For other examples of peasants leaving land or money to their parish church, see GAVO, f. 496, op. 1, d. 14975; 16463, l. 124 ob.; d. 18156; d. 18592; Rozanov, *Voskresenskaia tserkov'*, 60; "Opisanie tserkvi Voskreseniia Khristova, chto v Raslove, Griazovetskago uezda Vologodskoi gubernii," *VEV* (chast' neoffitsial'naia) 1 (1897): 143. For rules and laws governing a church's acceptance of willed gifts, see Malevinskii, *Instruktsiia nastoiateliam*, 77.

25. REM, d. 262, l. 6; RGIA, f. 797, op. 53, 3 ot., 4 st., d. 48, l. 16 ob.

26. See, for example, GAVO, f. 496, op. 1, d. 15950 (1887); d. 16297, l. 9 (1891); d. 18605, l. 91 (1908). See also f. 1063, op. 102, d. 13, l. 26. RGIA, f. 796, op. 198, 2 ot., 2 st., d. 908 (Vladimir, 1914); op. 442, d. 2629, l. 30 ob. Molchanov, *Tserkovnaia letopis'*, 155. It should also be noted that parish priests and their spouses sometimes willed their savings to the parish church where they served.

27. Once the need for such a grant was justified, the consistory would contact the provincial office of the Administration of State Domains. See, for example, GAVO, f. 496, op. 1, d. 17187 (1897); d. 18153 (1904); RGIA, f. 796, op. 442, d. 1549, l. 9.

28. Itinerant collectors were known by various names: *sborshchiki, proshaki, zaproshchiki, kubraki*. See Maksimov, "Proshaki i zaproshchiki," in *Brodiachaia Rus'*, 4. For an example of the admiration they often evoked from other believers, see *Agapii Maksimovich. Sborshchik na tserkov'*.

29. Maksimov, "Proshaki i zaproshchiki," 4.

30. Smirnov, *Alfavitnyi sbornik*, 387–88; GAVO, f. 496, op. 1, d. 17818, ll. 11–12 (1901).

31. GAVO, f. 496, op. 1, d. 15429 (1881). Maksimov notes that nuns in particular could be found among the collectors. Collectors came mostly from the peasantry, but townspeople and retired soldiers were also among them. Maksimov, "Proshaki i zaproshchiki," 4.

32. RGIA, f. 796, op. 190, 2. ot., 2 st., d. 362 (Kaluga, 1909).

33. GAVO, f. 496, op. 1, d. 17818, l. 14.

34. See, for example, GAVO, f. 496, op. 1, d. 14180, l. 214 (1867); d. 18153, l. 231 (1904); RGIA, f. 796, op. 149, d. 1334 (Kaluga, 1868). See also the 1908 report of the bishop of Tula, who noted he routinely gave permission to collectors to travel to other dioceses, f. 796, op. 442, d. 2306, ll. 16–16 ob.

35. Malevinskii, *Instruktsiia blagochinnomu*, 51; *TsVed* 37 (1903): 345. GAVO, f. 496, op. 1, d. 14848 (1874).

36. RGIA, f. 796, op. 161, d. 934, l. 11. For a similar figure, see Maksimov, "Proshaki i zaproshchiki," 4.

37. RGIA, f. 796, op. 442, d. 1743, l. 8 ob.

38. RGIA, f. 796, op. 199, 6 ot., 3 st., ll. 1–1 ob. For an account of a female collector from the Vologda province, see "Tserkov' Uspeniia Presviatyia Bogoroditsy, chto na Pesochnom, Vologodskago uezda," *VEV* (chast' neoffitsial'naia) 17 (1897): 337–38. In this account, the peasant woman Nataliia Andreevna Riabinina, who suffered from a serious illness, decided to dedicate her life to collecting money to donate to needy churches for beautification purposes. One priest from the Vologda district claimed that over the years Riabinina had been responsible for about 10,000 rubles of donations of items for his church alone.

39. GAVO, f. 496, op. 1, d. 17210 (1897). For other examples from the Vologda diocese of priests or trustees authorizing collectors without diocesan approval, see d. 14970, ll. 11 ob.–12; d. 15429 (1881); d. 15374, l. 2; 15713, ll. 20 ob.–21 (1885); 15841 (1886); d. 16297, l. 6; 18130, ll. 27–38 (1904).

40. GAVO, f. 496, op. 1, d. 15374, l. 3 (1880).

41. GAVO, f. 496, op. 1, d. 14970 (1875).

42. GAVO, f. 496, op. 1, d. 16297, ll. 1–2 (1891).

43. "Ustav blagochiniia i bezopasnosti," *Svod zakonov*, vol. 14, (1914), par. 77. See also the Synod ukase of 31 October 1865 in Mavritskii, *Tserkovnoe blagoustroistvo*, 300.

44. Mavritskii, *Tserkovnoe blagoustroistvo*, 298–99.

45. M. E. Saltykov-Shchedrin, "Poshekhonskaia starina," in *Polnoe sobranie sochinenii* (St. Petersburg, 1906), 12:346–55. For another literary depiction of the collector, see S. V. Maksimov, "Proshaki i zaproshchiki," 18–33. For more devotional accounts, see Novgorodskii, *Narodnyi sobesednik*, 327–30; Nikol'skii, *Khram Bozhii*, 30–31.

46. Saltykov-Shchedrin, "Poshekhonskaia starina," 349.

47. For rules governing such announcements, see Mavritskii, *Tserkovnoe blagoustroistvo*, 302–3; For examples, see GAVO, f. 496, op. 1, d. 16075 (1888); see also RGIA, f. 796, op. 176, d. 1176 (Pskov, 1895); REM, d. 135, l. 2 (Orel).

48. RGIA, f. 796, op. 198, 2 ot., 2 st., d. 133. For other types of requests, see op. 176, d. 1176; GAVO, f. 496, op. 1, d. 16502, l. 354 (1893); d. 17197, l. 272 (1897); d. 17789 (1901); d. 18153 (1904); d. 19415 (1913). While the Holy Synod had a special budget to aid with construction and renovation projects, it was not limitless, and not all petitioners had their requests met. For examples of such requests, see RGIA, f. 796, op. 173, d. 1335 (Tambov, 1892); op. 176, d. 1352 (Tambov, 1895); op. 198, 2 ot., 2 st., d. 237.

49. For examples of donations to rural construction efforts by Tsar Nicholas II, see RGIA, f. 796, op. 442, d. 2262, ll. 16–16 ob.; d. 2379, l. 20.; for an appeal to the empress, see RGIA, f. 796, op. 147, d. 1501 (Samara, 1866). For appeals to John of Kronstadt, see GAVO, f. 1063, op. 85, kor. 255, d. 22, l. 44; RGIA, f. 796, op. 442, d. 1768, l. 22 ob. For a recent biography that discusses John of Kronstadt's material assistance to others, see Kizenko, *A Prodigal Saint*.

50. For examples of such donations to parish churches from parishioners who were working and residing in St. Petersburg or Moscow, see REM, d. 336, l. 44 (Vologda); RGIA, f. 796, op. 191, 2 ot., 2 st., d. 51, l. 3 (Kaluga, 1910); GAVO, f. 496, op. 1, d. 14760, l. 1 ob.; d. 16629, l. 47 ob.; d. 18137, ll. 98, 110 ob.; f. 1063, op. 85, kor. 255, d. 22, l. 38 ob. See also "Chem dolzhen byt' prikhod?" *RSP* 13 (1906): 336, and Maksimov's observations in "Proshaki i zaproshchiki," 36.

51. For examples of rural believers speaking with pride about such efforts, see RGIA,

f. 796, op. 148, d. 527, l. 1 (Kaluga, 1867); op. 185, d. 2389, l. 2 (Kaluga, 1904); op. 196, 2 ot., 2 st., d. 40 (Tver, 1913); f. 797, op. 57, 3 ot., 5 st., d. 28 (Nizhnii Novgorod, 1887).

52. REM, d. 63 (Vladimir); d. 540, l. 2 (Kaluga).

53. REM, d. 343, l. 3 (Vologda); d. 416, l. 17 (Viatka); d. 536, l. 6 (Kaluga); d. 676, l. 9 (Novgorod); d. 1293 (Penza); d. 1307, l. 42 (Penza).

54. See, for example, Bogoroditskii, *Golos sel'skago pastyria*, 193–99; Kal'nev, *O sviatosti i pochitanii;* Troitskii, *Pouchenie o khozhdenii v khram.*

55. Ornatskii, *O znachenii sviatago khrama*, 5. See 2 Chron. 7:19–20 for the biblical passage frequently quoted in this respect.

56. Preachers often told stories from lives of saints that testified to this divine presence within temples. See, for example, E. Poselianin, "Khram kak dom Bozhii," *Prikhodskoe chtenie* 3 (June 1910): 72–74.

57. Svetlov, *O znachenii khrama*, 4.

58. Sermons on the occasion of Pentecost might not even mention the "church experience" but speak only of the Holy Spirit. See, as an example, the sermon "Chto pouchitel'nago v istorii prazdnika Soshestviia Sviatago Dukha na Apostolov?" in Shumov, *Sbornik obshchedostupnykh pouchenii na vse voskresnye i prazdnichnye dni*, 109–13.

59. *Obiazannosti khristianina*, 3; Nikol'skii, *Khram Bozhii*, 7, 34. An exception to this bypassing of the early Christian period is A. N. Pavlov, *Khram Bozhii* (Moscow, 1892).

60. *Chto takoe khram Bozhii*, 8.

61. Here Makarii was referring to the biblical passage in 2 Chron. 7:16. See his sermon *O znachenii pozhertvovanii na sv. khramy.*

62. See the extensive use of this gospel passage in Kal'nev, *O sviatosti i pochitanii.* For similar arguments, see Zubarev, *O sviatykh khramakh*, 2.

63. Svetlov, *O znachenii khrama*, 6.

64. Bulgakovskii, *Khram Bozhii*, 19.

65. *Chto takoe khram Bozhii*, 5.

66. Bulgakovskii, *Khram Bozhii*, 20; Pustoshkin, *Khram Bozhii*, 7–8.

67. *O sviatom khrame: Po rukovodstvu o. Ioanna Kronshtadtskago* (Moscow, 1896), 10.

68. Ivanov, *O znachenii khrama*, 25; Pavlov, *Khram Bozhii*, 5. For an example of the power of the temple in the formation of childhood memories, see V. Maksimov, *Sel'skaia tserkov'* (St. Petersburg, 1897).

69. Pavlov, *Khram Bozhii*, 6; *Poidem v tserkov'* (Moscow, 1886), 6; Svetlov, *O znachenii khrama* 6.

70. *O sviatom khrame: Po rukovodstvu o. Ioanna Kronshtadskago*, 8–9.

71. Such sentiments are poignantly expressed by a Christian woman on the occasion of the blessing of a parish church in *Sovershilos'. Iz dnevnika khristianki* (Saratov, 1910). See also Usinin, *Neskol'ko slov ob obiazannostiakh*, 2; *Obiazannosti khristianina*, 3; *Obiazannosti prikhozhan.*

72. See, for example, 1 Cor. 3.16; 2 Cor. 6.16; 1 Pet. 2.5.

73. Ep. Feofan (Govorov), *Nashi otnosheniia*, 63.

74. Svetlov, *O znachenii khrama*, 3; Feofan (Govorov), *Nashi otnosheniia*, 26.

75. Demkin, *O liubvi k khramu*, 14–15. For similar comparisons between the individual as a spiritual temple and the church building, see Bogoroditskii, *Golos sel'skago pastyria*, 196; Svetlov, *O znachenii khrama*, 3; Levashev, *Poucheniia sel'skago sviashchennika*, 3–5; Shumov, "Kak khristianinu sdelat'sia khramom Bozhiim," in *Sbornik obshchesdostupnykh pouchenii*, 150–54.

76. In this particular sermon delivered in 1866 on the occasion of the blessing of a

church in the Vladimir diocese, Theophanes typologically compared the parts of the Tabernacle with aspects of the human soul. Feofan (Govorov), *Nashi otnosheniia*, 68.

77. Demkin, *O liubvi k khramu*, 2; Bogoroditskii, *Golos sel'skago pastyria*, 268–71; 279–83. *Pastyr' propovednik*, 165–67; Levashev, *Poucheniia sel'skago sviashchennika*, 123–24; "Posle podniatiia kolokola," *Troitskie listki* 35 (1900); Nikol'skii, *Khram Bozhii*, 4.

78. Feofan (Govorov), *Nashi otnosheniia*, 17.

79. Amfiteatrov, *Besedy*, 23, 27, 32, 79; Bogoroditskii, *Golos sel'skago pastyria*, 195; 283–85; "Mir Bozhii—khram Bozhii," *Troitskie listki*, 182 (1883); *O sviatom khrame: Po rukovodstvu o. Ioanna Kronshtadtskago*, 11; Pavlov, *Khram Bozhii*, 15. In speaking about the Church as mother, the early nineteenth-century professor of homiletics Ia. K. Amfiteatrov, whose writings continued to be widely distributed in the later imperial period, drew attention to Christ's relationship with his disciples during his tribulations in the garden of Gethsemane (Matt. 26:39–44). Just as Christ came three times to his disciples in the garden and chose not to disturb their peace and to pray alone, he wrote, so the Church as mother watches over believers while they "sleep," and though periodically attempting to awaken them nevertheless continues her ceaseless prayer for them if they choose to remain asleep. See his *Besedy*, 71–79.

80. RGIA, f. 796, op. 145, d. 1247, l. 4. For another use of maternal imagery with respect to the church building, see op. 164, d. 1035, l. 2 (Riazan, 1883); op. 184, d. 2170, l. 4 (Pskov, 1903).

81. Demkin, *O liubvi k khramu*, 4; *Chto takoe khram Bozhii*; Pavlov, *Khram Bozhii*, 4, 6; Levashev, *Poucheniia sel'skago pastyria*, 123; Feofan (Govorov), *Nashi otnosheniia*, 65.

82. O. Diakonov, *O khrame Bozhiem* (Saratov, 1915), 1; *Obiazannosti khristianina*, 4; Ep. Makarii, *O znachenii pozhertvovanii na sv. khramy* (Kharkov, 1862), 2–3; Bogoroditskii, *Golos sel'skago pastyria*, 209.

83. *Nebesnaia pomoshch' v stroenii khramov* (Kiev, 1913), 1–4; Bulgakovskii, *Khram Bozhii*, 1–4.

84. GAVO, f. 496, op. 1, d. 18371, l. 10. Correspondents to the Tenishev Bureau frequently noted that peasants considered donations for purposes of church beautification to be among the highest sacrifices to God a person could make. See also Lindenmeyr, *Poverty Is Not a Vice*, 160–61. M. Molchanov, "O khrame, ego proiskhozhdenii i znachenii dlia khristian, i ob obshchestvennoi molitve v nem," *RSP* 43 (1894): 189–99.

85. GAVO, f. 496, op. 1, d. 16463, l. 92; d. 19925, l. 64 ob.

86. RGIA, f. 796, op. 442, d. 2323, l. 64 ob.

87. See, for example, discussions in P. Malinin, "K voprosu o nishchenstve," *RSP* 47 (1903): 339–41; E. P., "Prikhodskaia blagotvoritel'nost'," *RSP* 6 (1906): 161–69. For a popular rendering of this new emphasis on the parish as a Christian social unit, see the published periliturgical discussion *Tserkovno-prikhodskaia obshchina*.

88. Kudriavtsev, *Nishchenstvo kak predmet popecheniia*, 82.

89. A. Gumilevskii, "Sovremennoe obozrenie," *DKh* 3 (1862): 274; Il'inskii, "Blagotvoritel'nost' v Rossii," Nikol'skii, *Ob obshchestvennoi blagotvoritel'nosti*; Pryzhov, *Nishchie na sviatoi Rusi*. For details of this debate in the broader press, see Lindenmeyr, *Poverty Is Not a Vice*, 136–41.

90. For popular devotional literature describing the spiritual benefits of such private penny giving, see *Khristianskaia milostynia*; "Milostynia," *Novo-Afonskie listki* 13 (1894); *Nastavlenie po Prologu o milostyne*; *O blagotvorenii po rukovodstvu o. Ioanna Kronshtadtskago*; "Pouchenie o liubvi k nishchim," in Mavritskii, *Seiatel'*, 346–52.

91. Pavlov, *Khram Bozhii*, 10; Makarii, *O znachenii pozhertvovanii na sv. khramy*, 4.

92. Papkov, *Besedy*, 8.

93. Feofan (Govorov), *Nashi otnosheniia*, 27.

94. *Obiazannosti khristianina*, 5.

95. *Chto takoe khram Bozhii*, 8; Demkin, *O liubvi k khramu*, 11–12.

96. Muriel Heppell, trans., *The Paterik of the Kievan Caves* (Cambridge, MA: Harvard University Press, 1989), 137–38. For the story as recounted in devotional literature and sermons, see Bulgakovskii, *Khram Bozhii*, 7; "Liubiashchim blagolepie doma Bozhiia," *Troitskie listki* 784 (1895); "Osviashchenie khrama Preosviashchenneishim Mitrofanom, Ep. Penzenskim i Saranskim v sele Troitskom, Maksimovka tozh, Chembarskago uezda," *PEV* (chast' neoffitsial'naia) 22 (15 November 1892): 939–40.

97. N. K., "Vopros o tserkovno-prikhodskikh popechitel'stvakh," *Beseda* 23 (1872): 246. Cited by Freeze in *Parish Clergy*, 294. Similarly, the success of guardianships in late imperial Russia is perhaps best measured not merely in political terms of "defiance of perceived clerical privilege in power" or defiance of the state but also in religious terms, in their definition and pursuit of "good works." For the political reading of peasant behavior, see Young, "Into Church Matters," 367–84.

98. Pseudo-Dionysius the Areopagite, "The Divine Names," in *Pseudo-Dionysius: The Complete Works*, trans. by Kolm Luibheid (New York: Paulist Press, 1987), 76–79; Basil, Bishop of Caesarea, *Gateway to Paradise*, ed. Oliver Davies, trans. Tim Witherow (New York: New City Press, 1991), 75–76.

99. Note that vigils only became a regular feature in rural parish life in the early twentieth century. See GAVO, f. 496, op. 1, d. 17993. The number of services also depended in large part on the number of priests assigned to a parish church. See Bulgakov, *Nastol'naia Kniga*, 732–33.

100. RGIA, f. 796, op. 442, d. 87, l. 26 ob.

101. Bulgakov, *Nastol'naia Kniga*, 734; *Vsepoddanneishii otchet oberprokurora . . . za 1886* (St. Petersburg, 1887), 63.

102. For recommended times for Divine services, see Bulgakov, *Nastol'naia Kniga*, 735.

103. REM, d. 345 (Vologda).

104. REM, d. 441, l. 2 (Viatka).

105. REM, d. 540, l. 1 (Kaluga); d. 938, l. 9 (Orel).

106. See, for example, REM, d. 1307, ll. 38–39. Note the popular devotional story of St. Juliana, which was told to offset this notion. Nikol'skii, *Khram Bozhii*, 10–11.

107. REM, d. 1307, l. 37 (Penza); RGIA, f. 796, op. 442, d. 1659, l. 21 (Vologda). A. Popov, *Vospominaniia*, 210; 216–17.

108. For the diverse responses to the question of church attendance with respect to men and women, see REM, d. 63, l. 1 ob. (Vladimir); d. 433, l. 17 (Viatka); d. 443, l. 15 (Viatka); d. 536 l. 4 (Kaluga); d. 603, l. 1 (Kostroma); d. 676 (Novgorod).

109. Attached churches tended to be more numerous in the northern, less densely populated dioceses of Russia, such as Arkhangelsk and Olonets. In 1909, for example, Arkhangelsk had 445 independent parish churches and 133 attached ones. Olonets had 323 independent parishes and 179 attached ones. Kostroma, on the other hand, had 1,015 independent parishes and only 9 attached ones; Tambov had 1,143 independent parishes and 48 attached ones. *Vsepoddaneishii otchet ober-prokurora Sv. Sinoda po vedomstru pravoslavnago ispovedaniia za 1908–1909 gg.* (St. Petersburg, 1911), app. 4.

110. For a review of the 1869 parish reform and its effects on parish life, see Freeze, *Parish Clergy*, 315–19; 363–83. This reform effort was made null and void in 1885, when a new attempt at parish configuration no longer encouraged such attachments.

111. RGIA, f. 796, op. 159, d. 1211 (Tambov, 1878); op. 178, d. 1503 (Viatka, 1897); op. 178, d. 1665 (Tambov, 1897); op. 202, 2 ot., 2 st., d. 30 (Tambov, 1916).

112. GAVO, f. 496, op. 1, d. 14858, l. 311.

113. GAVO, f. 496, op. 1, d. 14760, l. 146 (1873); d. 13807, ll. 232–33 (1864); d. 14858, ll. 21, 74 (1874); RGIA, f. 796, op. 148, d. 527 (Kaluga, 1867), l. 2; op. 190, 2 ot., 2 st., d. 841 (Vladimir, 1909).

114. RGIA, f. 796, op. 190, 2 ot., 2 st., d. 841, l. 7 (Vladimir, 1909).

115. RGIA, f. 796, op. 178, d. 2199.

116. GAVO, f. 496, op. 1, d. 18376, l. 2 (1906). See also the comments of P. Shamshin, a nobleman from the Kaluga diocese, who in 1909 supported a peasant community's decades-long campaign to gain independent status for their church, in RGIA, f. 796, op. 190, 2 ot., 2 st., d. 362, ll. 11–12.

117. RGIA, f. 796, op. 178, d. 1665, l. 3 (Tambov, 1897).

118. GAVO, f. 496, op. 1, d. 14858, l. 76 (1874). Note that while a Divine Liturgy could not be served by a deacon alone, a deacon could lead a congregation in corporate worship in the form of a readers' service, or *obednitsa*. See also d. 14760, ll. 97, 116 (1873), and RGIA, f. op. 186, d. 2405 (Kaluga, 1905), in which peasants claimed they would hire a priest themselves.

119. For the notion of church as spiritual haven, see the comments of the parishioners of the village of Marmyzhei in the Kaluga diocese in RGIA, f. 796, op. 148, d. 527, l. 2 (1867); for peasant appeal to their ancestral ties to their churches in their petitions to rescind their attached status, see GAVO, f. 496, op. 1, d. 14877, ll. 8–9 (1877); RGIA, f. 796, op. 148, d. 1271, l. 2 (Chernigov, 1867); op. 150, d. 1509 (Tver, 1869); op. 445, d. 250, l. 35 (Tambov, 1917); f. 797, op. 54, 3 ot., 5 st., d. 84 (Iaroslavl, 1884).

120. Believers often chose not to attend on any regular basis the parish to which they were assigned but simply waited for those occasions on which a Liturgy would be served in their own church. RGIA, f. 796, op. 148, d. 527, l. 1 (Kaluga, 1867).

121. RGIA, f. 796, op. 178, d. 1757, l. 1.

122. RGIA, f. 796, op. 153, d. 331, l. 1.

123. Bogoroditskii, *Golos sel'skago pastyria*, 199; Nikol'skii, *Khram Bozhii*, 12–13.

124. Note, however, that he did mention the sacrament of baptism. "Mir Bozhii, khram Bozhii," *Troitskie listki* 182 (1883).

125. Bulgakovskii, *Khram Bozhii*, 28; Pavlov, *Khram Bozhii*, 6; Ostroumov, *Pis'ma*, 97.

126. Makarii, episkop Tomskago, "Beseda o sviatom prichashchenii: Telo i krov' Khristova, kak vsesil'noe sredstvo ot boleznei i smerti," *PTsVed* 14 (1897): 515–18.

127. Dix, *Shape of the Liturgy*, 480.

128. D'iachenko, *Propovednicheskaia entsiklopediia*, 551.

129. REM, d. 1826, ll. 17–18.

130. REM, d. 467, l. 30.

131. A. B-skii, "Velikii post v derevne," *RSP* 12 (1866): 405–7.

132. REM, d. 1501, l. 20 (Saratov).

133. GAVO, f. 496, op. 1, d. 16137, l. 59 ob. See also comments in REM, d. 153, l. 8 (Vologda); RGIA, f. 796, op. 442, d. 1120, l. 18 ob.; d. 1608, l. 52.

134. P. Z., "O nepravil'nom vedenii ispovednykh rospisei," *RSP* 50 (1882): 419. Children under the age of seven were not subject to the confession-before-Communion rule. *Svod zakonov*, 3d ed. (St. Petersburg, 1902) vol. 14, "Svod ustavov o preduprezhdenii i presechenii prestuplenii," par. 19. It should be noted that priests did not routinely submit to diocesan authorities the names of parishioners who did not receive confession for three years in a row.

135. For a detailed discussion of rural church choirs in the late imperial period, see Shevzov, "Popular Orthodoxy," 137–44.

136. GAVO, f. 496, op. 1, d. 16353, l. 151 ob.

137. REM, d. 938, l. 9 (Orel).

138. RGIA, f. 796, op. 442, d. 1768, l. 26 ob. (Vologda); GAVO, f. 496, op. 1, d. 19367, l. 145 ob.; f. 1063, op. 85, kor. 255, d. 22, l. 40; REM, d. 938 (Orel).

139. GAVO, f. 496, op. 1, d. 17919, ll. 42–58.

140. For discussion of congregational singing, see "Uspekhi po delu vvedeniia obshchenarodnago peniia v tserkvakh," *RSP* 20 (1886): 85; "Obshchee penie, kak zhelatel'naia prinadlezhnost' khristianskago pravoslavnago bogosluzheniia, i vozmozhnyi sposob ego vvedeniia," *RSP* 43 (1894): 206–10; Sv. Klavdii Bulygin, "Mechty i deistvitel'nost'," *VEV* (chast' neoffitsial'naia) 7/8 (1916): 129. For a popular account of the process by which adults learned to sing from their children, see "O tom, kak povelos' v odnom sel'skom prikhode obshchee tserkovnoe penie," *Troitskie listki* 185 (1903).

141. Nechaev, *Tolkovanie na Bozhestvennuiu Liturgiiu*, 100. While supported by many clergy, congregational singing also had its opponents among the clergy. It was looked on unfavorably especially by those who valued the aesthetics of choral singing. See the comments in N., "Komu ne nravitsia vsenarodnoe penie v tserkvi," *RSP* 25 (1886): 241–43; N. Urbskii, "Vragi i supostaty obshchego peniia pri sovershenii bogosluzheniia," *RSP* 51 (1887): 473–82.

142. V. P-skii, "Ob uluchshenii tserkovnago peniia v sel'skikh prikhodakh," *RSP* 38 (1901): 57–62.

143. *Otchet o deiatel'nosti Vologodskago Pravoslavnago Bratstva za 1891–1892* (Vologda, 1893), 18.

144. N., "Komu ne nravitsia vsenarodnoe penie v tserkvi," *RSP* 25 (1886): 241–43.

145. See comment in "Uspekhi po delu vvedeniia obshchenarodnago peniia," *RSP* 20 (1886): 82; RGIA, f. 797, op. 57, 3 ot., 5 st., d. 28, ll. 13–24 (Nizhnii Novgorod, 1887).

146. A notable exception to this form of commentary was Nechaev, *Tolkovanie na Bozhestvennuiu Liturgiiu*, who disagreed with the notion of viewing the Liturgy as a chronological reenactment of Christ's life and thought more in terms of hearing the Liturgy as one long homily.

147. For example, many commentaries traced the origin of the Trisagion to the reign of Theodosius I in the fourth century, when the people of Constantinople fled into a field for corporate prayer after an earthquake. According to the story, a boy who was present "was carried away to the heavens" and in that state heard the angels singing the Trisagion hymn before the throne of God. When he testified to this before the people, they, too, all began to sing this hymn. Stratilatov, *Katekhizicheskiia besedy*, 115.

148. The following observations are taken from these commentaries: Antonov, *Ob'iasnenie bozhestvennoi Liturgii;* M. Molchanov, "O khrame, ego proiskhozhdenii i znachenii dlia khristian i ob obshchestvennoi molitve v nem," *RSP* 49, 50, 51, 52 (1894); Stratilatov, *Kratkoe pouchenie;* Stratilatov, *Katekhizicheskiia besedy; Iz'iasnenie vecherni, utreni i liturgii.*

149. For example, some commentaries encouraged believers to say Psalm 50 quietly while the priest opened the Holy Doors at the beginning of the Cherubic Hymn. *Iz'iasnenie vecherni*, 27.

150. *Voskresnyia i prazdnichnyia vnebogosluzhebnyia sobesedovaniia*, 15.

151. For comments regarding the use of this format by priests prior to the mid–nineteenth century, see A. Popov, *Vospominaniia*, 14–16. By this time most diocesan bish-

ops mentioned these discussions as a standard feature of parish life in their annual reports to the Holy Synod.

152. Scholars in the past have underestimated the influence of these talks in the religious lives of believers. See, for instance, Young, *Power and the Sacred*, 18. Young's own conclusions seem to be based in large part on the study by Chulos, "Peasant Religion."

153. *Otchet o deiatel'nosti Vologodskago Bratstva za 1890–1891* (Vologda, 1892), 10.

154. For details about when these discussions were held, the types of topics discussed, and so on, see Shevzov, "Popular Orthodoxy," 144–55.

155. From the Greek *proistamenos*. See Rom. 12.8; 1 Thess. 5.12; 1 Tim. 3.4–5; 5.17.

156. REM, d. 150, l. 5; d. 151, ll. 1–1 ob. (Vologda).

157. REM, d. 327, l.5 (Vologda); d. 1400, l. 30 (Penza). Note that rural priests frequently were the only ones available in rural areas to help treat epidemic outbreaks such as cholera. See, for example, "Deiatel'nost' dukhovenstva Penzenskoi eparkhii po prekrashcheniiu kholernoi epidemii," *PEV* (chast' neoffitsial'naia) 23 (1892): 991–93. For discussion of a priest's seminary training, see Freeze, *The Parish Clergy*, 443–37; Manchester, "Secular Ascetics," chap. 6.

158. See comments on these in GAVO, f. 496, op. 1, d. 19367, ll. 266–67; d. 18137, l. 88 ob; "Mechty v deistvitel'nost'," *VEV* (chast neoffitsial'naia) 21 (1916): 416–22; Sv. Z. K., "Zametka o pol'ze kooperatsii dlia prikhoda," VEV 22 (1916): 434–38.

159. For examples, see RGIA, f. 797, op. 186, 3 ot., 5 st., d. 116, l. 7 (Novgorod, 1886); op. 153, d. 331 (Iaroslavl, 1872); op. 154, d. 1469 (Voronezh, 1873); op. 154, d. 1514 (Riazan, 1873); op. 155, d. 1749 (Simbirsk, 1874). When a priest was found guilty of such behavior by diocesan authorities, he was either removed from his place of service and lowered in rank from a priest to a sacristan for an indefinite period of time or he was sent to a monastery for a period of repentance. *Ustav dukhovnoi konsistorii*, par. 183.

160. For examples of clerical affronts to lay liturgical sensibilities, see GAVO, f. 496, op. 1, d. 13197; d. 16019, ll. 113–33; d. 18719; RGIA, f. 797, op. 53, 3 ot., 5 st., d. 48 (Kostroma, 1883).

161. A *prosfora* baker was the person, usually an elderly woman or widow, who baked the bread used for the Eucharist. For a detailed description of the prescribed tasks of each of these, see Shevzov, "Popular Orthodoxy," 107–28.

162. For the perceived distinctions between the two, see D. Gratsianskii, "Chto takoe 'sekta' voobshche i 'ratsionalisticheskaia' i 'misticheskaia' v chastnosti," *MO* 5 (May 1904): 971.

163. Historically in Russia, village and parish communities (*sel'skaia i prikhodskaia obshchina*) had been considered synonymous. See "Sel'skaia obshchina i ee znachenie v tserkovno-prikhodskoi zhizni," *RSP* 37 (1905): 32–33. For a concise overview of the differentiation of these two during the course of the eighteenth century, see Freeze, "Disintegration of Traditional Communities," 32–50. For a discussion of this type of phenomenon in connection with modernization and secularization, see Cassanova, *Public Religions*, 45–48.

164. See the discussion in "Sel'skaia obshchina i ee znachenie," 34–36.

165. Danilov, *Polozheniia o sel'skom sostoianii*. Part I, "Obshchee Polozhenie o krest'ianakh, vyshedshikh iz krepostnoi zavisimosti," par. 178. Also see pars. 51, 78. For the paragraphs with clarifications as they appeared in subsequent legislation, see Volkov, *Sbornik polozhenii o sel'skom sostoianii*, Part I, "Obshchee polozhenie o krest'ianakh," par. 360.

166. "Dni obshchestvennykh bogomolenii na poliakh," *RSP* 14 (1892): 413.

167. For instance, when a group of villages wished to form an independent parish community, matters concerning financial support for the future parish clergy, land allotments, and financial and organizational issues regarding the construction of a new church were all discussed at collective village assemblies. The church elder, however, usually carried on the correspondence with diocesan authorities.

168. For examples of this, see the *Instruktsiia tserkovnym starostam* and *Polozhenie o prikhodskikh popechitel'stvakh.*

169. See the comments from the Ministry of Internal Affairs and the Ministry of Justice in RGIA, f. 796, op. 196, d. 141, ll. 4, 8.

170. *Polozhenie o prikhodskikh popechitel'stvakh,* par. 12.

171. Sv. S. Broiakovskii, "O prikhodskikh popechitel'stvakh," *RSP* 23 (1908): 136–37. For more discussion regarding local officials not paying serious attention to decisions made by the parish assembly, see RGIA, f. 796, op. 196, 2 ot., 2 st., d. 141.

172. S. K., "Bezporiadki krest'ianskago samoupravleniia, prepiatstvuiushchie uspeshnomu khodu bor'by Pravoslavnoi Tserkvi s raskolom i sektantstvom," *RSP* 35 (1891): 470–73.

173. "Bezporiadki krest'ianskago samoupravleniia," 472; GAVO, f. 496, op. 1, d. 19925, l. 28. Many of the Tenishev correspondents from various provinces also noted the dominant role that such peasants played at the village assemblies. REM, d. 346, ll. 5–6 (Vologda); d. 1401 (Penza).

174. For an example of the ambiguity in this relationship, see *Polnyi pravoslavnyi,* 2: 1910–11.

175. See, for example, Ruminskii, *Dukhovenstvo i narod,* 33–34; S. "Po povodu narekanii na pobory dukhovenstva," *RSP* 41 (1872).

176. *Ustav dukhovnoi konsistorii,* par. 184. In the pre-1885 version of the *Ustav,* see par. 194.

177. The priest Feodor Ivoninskii claimed that such a complaint was ludicrous to begin with since he had purposefully avoided taking any payments from the villagers of Kovrigino because he did not want to aggravate the tensions that already existed with that village because of the land issue. GAVO, f. 496, op. 1, d. 19981, l. 23 ob. For another example of peasants signing a petition simply on the basis of community allegiance without having read it themselves or having had read to them the contents of the petition, see d. 18654, ll. 77–83; d. 18383.

178. For the use of this term with respect to peasant cultures, see Scott, *Moral Economy.* For the operation of a moral economy in late imperial Russian peasant culture, see, for example, Kingston-Mann and Mixter, eds., *Peasant Economy.*

179. Berdnikov, *Kommentarii g. Papkova,* 34–36.

180. RGIA, f. 796, op. 150, d. 244 (Saratov, 1869).

181. Malevinskii, *Instruktsiia nastoiateliam,* par. 31. According to existing legislation in the postreform period, outsiders were not allowed to participate in village or township assemblies. A priest, apparently, from the point of view of civil administrators, such as the governor of Vologda, was considered an outsider. GAVO, f. 496, op. 1, d. 18480.

182. "Neskol'ko slov po voprosu ob ustroenii tserkovno-prikhodskoi zhizni i uchrezhdenii prikhodskikh sovetov i sobranii," *Otkliki sel'skikh pastyrei* 3 (1906): 127–30; GAVO, f. 496, op. 1, d. 18480.

183. For example, see GAVO, f. 496, op. 1, d. 18476, ll. 50–59. It should be pointed out that although priests, technically speaking, were not allowed to participate in the village assemblies, there is evidence, at least from the Vologda diocese, that there were

priests who regularly did so. See, for instance, GAVO, f. 496, op. 1, d. 17289; d. 18480; REM, d. 327, ll. 327, 6; d. 367, ll. 5–5 ob. (Vologda). Very probably, such participation depended to a large extent on local custom and on the personality of the priest.

184. Note that not only newly formed parishes were required to produce such written resolutions. In the 1860s, ecclesiastical officials frequently requested that local communities, whose financial support of clergy until that time had been based on oral agreement and voluntary collections, provide such written agreements. GAVO, f. 496, op. 1, d. 13621, ll. 36–39; d. 18151, ll. 11–12. According to post-Emancipation legislation, former serf peasants were directed to establish community-wide collections for the support of their parish churches and clergy. See Danilov, *Polozheniia o sel'skom sostoiani*, Part I, par. 178; Volkov, *Sbornik polozhenii*, Part I, par. 360. Diocesan officials extended this practice to include state and crown peasants as well. For the best English-language treatment of the attempts to improve the clergy's material condition, see Freeze, *Parish Clergy*. For relevant directives on the matter, see Konstantin Lotsos, ed., *Soderzhanie dukhovenstva: Ukazatel' uzakonenii, rasporiazhenii i raz'iasnenii po raskhodovaniiu summ, assignuemykh iz kazni po smete Sv. sinoda na soderzhanie pravoslavnago dukhovenstva* (Petrograd, 1914).

185. This view was not restricted to the peasantry; see, for example, the comments of I. S. Aksakov, *Sochineniia* (Moscow, 1886), 4:137. For its Byzantine roots, see John Meyendorff, *Imperial Unity and Christian Divisions* (Crestwood, NY: St. Vladimir's Seminary Press 1989), 48.

186. The minimum amounts of land for clergy were set in 1829, *Svod zakonov*, vol. 10 (1914), pt. 2, par. 349, in app. 1. It is impossible to determine the number of parishes that had actually drawn up some sort of contract during the postreform period. Moreover, in and of itself it is a secondary issue. The point is that the contract was consistently a problematic variable that placed certain strains on pastor-flock relations and therefore on the ecclesial community as a whole. Contractual disputes offer an insight into the dynamics within the parish unit while it was in a conflictual situation as well as into prevailing notions among peasants regarding their role in the parish system.

187. In his annual report to the Holy Synod, the bishop of Vologda began mentioning this fact already in the late 1870s. See, for example, RGIA, f. 796, op. 442, d. 921, l. 16. By 1885, the bishop of Vologda, Izrail, noted in his annual report to the Synod that many parish priests had begun to initiate complaints about pressing their parishioners to fulfill their responsibilities. Similarly, the consistory of the Viatka diocese noted in 1864 that many village priests did not receive even half of what they were promised by the terms of the written agreements. RGIA, f. 796, op. 144, d. 1296, ll. 7–9; op. 176 d. 1497 (Tambov, 1895). See also Freeze, *Parish Clergy*, 370–71, 376, 423, 430.

188. See, for example, GAVO, f. 496, op. 1, d. 15719; d. 18476, l. 90. Generally, priests took it for granted that the poor would contribute little, if anything, toward the clergy. For example, see REM, d. 127, l. 5 (Vologda); RGIA, f. 796, op. 176, d. 1267 (Kaluga, 1895).

189. See the discussion of this point in P. Runovskii, "K voprosu ob uluchshenii material'nago byta pravoslavnago dukhovenstva," *RSP* 18 (1879): 24–25; *Polnyi pravoslavnyi*, 2, 1910.

The complexity of the situation was reflected in civil rulings. For instance, a 1904 ruling recognized that Old Believers and adherents to other faiths should not be held accountable for dues collected in support of a local parish church and parish clergy, even if the decision for such dues was made by the required two-thirds of the voting members of a village assembly. At the same time, another ruling urged that careful measures be taken to determine whether a person who declared himself of the Old Belief in order to avoid the payment of parish-related dues was truly of this faith. Volkov, *Sbornik polozhenii,* Part I, par. 360, pts. 8–9.

190. As an example see, RGIA, f. 797, op. 36, 2 ot., 3 st., d. 300.

191. When priests defied this directive and out of despair turned to civil authorities, they were reprimanded by their superiors. See, as an example, RGIA, f. 796, op. 178, d. 1783 (Nizhnii Novgorod, 1897).

192. For the synodal directive of 18 December 1892, see *Obzor deiatel'nosti,* 468–69.

193. Also note that peasant communities exerted no communal pressure to fulfill obligations toward the support of their parish priest, as they did with respect to various state taxes. It appears that rural communities considered collections for the parish clergy to be a private matter rather than a matter for the "collective" to regulate.

194. GAVO, f. 496, op. 1, d. 14903, l. 26. Tenishev correspondents noted a similar nonbinding attitude among peasants toward trade and business contracts. See, for example, REM, d. 212, l. 8; d. 163, l. 41.

195. GAVO, f. 496, op. 1, d. 18185, ll. 35–36; for a similar case see d. 16522.

196. RGIA, f. 796, op. 190, 2 ot., 2 st., d. 841.

197. For discussions of the nature of peasant activity in the wake of 1905, see Scott Seregny, "A Different Type of Peasant Movement: The Peasant Unions in the Russian Revolution of 1905," *Slavic Review* 47, no. 2 (spring 1988): 51–67; Matthew Schneer, "The Markovo Republic: A Peasant Community during Russia's First Revolution, 1905–1906," *Slavic Review* 53, no. 1 (spring 1994): 51–67; Verner, "Discursive Strategies in the 1905 Revolution, 65–90.

198. See, for example, RGIA, f. 796, op. 442, d. 2200, ll. 18–22; d. 2262, l. 23 ob.; GAVO, f. 496, op. 1, d. 18185, ll. 14–14 ob.; d. 18384, l. 100. See also the comments by the bishop of Chernigov quoted in Emeliakh, *Antiklerikal'noe dvizhenie,* 109.

199. Emeliakh, *Antiklerikal'noe dvizhenie,* 86.

200. GAVO, f. 496, op. 1, d. 18476, l. 57. For fear of reprisals, peasants frequently expressed apprehension and reluctance when it came to opposing persons in the community who had reputations for being troublemakers. For the Vologda diocese, see A. Popov, *Vospominaniia,* 182. GAVO, f. 496, op. 1, d. 13469, l. 28; d. 14903, l. 36 ob.; d. 18476, ll. 50–59. For a discussion of the internal factions that characterized village assemblies, see Gaudin, "Governing the Village," 102–50; See also Verner, "Discursive Strategies in the 1905 Revolution."

201. As the bishop of the Ekaterinburg diocese reported, such contractual disputes arose in parishes where clergy placed undue emphasis on their material well-being and parishioners reacted in the spirit that "grace was not for sale." See Emeliakh, *Antiklerikal'noe dvizhenie,* 140.

202. RGIA, f. 796, op. 187, ch. 1, d. 781; also see op. 187, ch. 1, d. 721 (Pskov, 1906).

203. Quoted in Emeliakh, *Antiklerikal'noe dvizhenie,* 94.

204. This confusion is seen in contemporary historical presentations of this period when the terms "parishioner," "laity," "believer," and "villager" are used interchangeably with little attention to the question of differentiation in religious identity among Russia's peasantry.

205. For graphic examples of such internal divisions within the village communities in the Vologda diocese, see GAVO, f. 496, op. 1, d. 18476, l. 13; d. 18476, ll. 52–53; ll. 70–71; ll. 102–3 ob.; d. 18384; d. 19981, ll. 74, 83. Indeed, it is important to distinguish between peasants who simply did not want anything to do with the support of the parish priest and those who continued to want a parish priest and who recognized an obligation toward him but simply desired to alter the form that support took. Such a distinction between the

peasant who was hostile toward the priest and the interests of the parish and those who simply wanted to manage and direct parish affairs as they saw fit, without interference from diocesan or other outsiders, became especially clear in the 1917–18 period. During this period there were cases in which groups of peasants from within a parish would take possession of church properties and would refuse to offer the clergy any financial support. But such occurrences for the most part involved a minority of peasants and went directly against decisions made by parish councils or committees. More often than not, the parish councils themselves stood helpless in the face of such actions, with some even expressing fear of repercussion should they publicly denounce such behavior. See, for example, GAVO, f. 496, op. 1, d. 20191, ll. 75, 89, 109.

206. GAVO, f. 496, op. 1, d. 18316, l. 155; also see d. 18654, l. 99.

207. GAVO, f. 496, op. 1, d. 18475, l. 90 ob.

208. For a detailed discussion of village-parish relations in other aspects of parish management, see Shevzov, "Popular Orthodoxy," 237–74. The clergy's cultivation of land as a source of financial support was a subject debated by the secular and religious press alike in the postreform period. An overview of the issue is presented in a debate conducted on the local level in the Vologda diocesan newspaper in 1909–11. Sel'skii sviashchennik, "Nuzhna li zemlia dukhovenstvu?" *VEV* (chast' neoffitsial'naia) 20 (1909): 492–94; Sv. Alexei Sovetov, "K voprosu o tserkovno-prichtovoi zemle," 22 (1909): 548–51; Sv. V. Illarionov, "V zashchitu pravoslavnago sel'skago dukhovenstva, nadelennago tserkovno-prichtovoi zemlei," 23 (1909): 285–88; Sv. Dimitrii Kuz'bozhev, "Zemlia tserkovnaia—kormilitsa dukhovenstva," 4 (1910): 50–53; Sv. P. M., "Nuzhna li dukhovenstvu zemlia," 21 (1910): 373–76; Sv. Leonid Grigorov, "Nuzhna li zemlia dukhovenstvu," 7 (1911): 198–203. For the laws on parish church lands and the use of land by clergy, see Ivanovskii, *Obozrenie*, 97–101.

209. For a general procedure of portioning off land for clergy in a newly forming parish, see *Svod zakonov*, vol. 9. (1876), appendix to par. 441; *Svod zakonov,* vol 9. (1899), par. 446, 447; GAVO, f. 496, op. 1, d. 14848, l. 111; d. 17789, l. 142; d. 18671, ll. 40–49. See also the way land was spoken about in RGIA, f. 796, op. 155, d. 1350, l. 3 (Kursk, 1874).

210. GAVO, f. 496, op. 1, d. 18476, l. 4. Rural believers frequently argued against supporting their clergy once the clergy received a state subsidy.

211. GAVO, f. 496, op. 1, d. 18151, ll. 2 ob.–3.

212. Note that this dual approach to clergy was pointed out by many of the Tenishev correspondents reporting from Vologda. See, for example, REM, 240, l. 67; d. 262, ll. 7 ob.–8. See also GAVO, f. 4389, d. 371, tetrad' 2. ("Tetradi sv. Nikolaia Soboleva," 1907–8). Peasants addressed their priests in the familiar *ty*, which facilitated treating them as simply another member of the community.

213. Parishioners frequently complained to both diocesan and synodal authorities when they felt that their right to choose an elder had been violated either by a priest or diocesan authorities. RGIA, f. 796, op. 154, d. 1469 (Voronezh, 1873); op. 158, d. 1221 (Pskov, 1877); op. 186, 1 ot., 2 st., d. 684 (Kostroma, 1905); f. 797, op. 54, 3 ot., 5 st., d. 47 (Orel, 1884); op. 57, 3 ot., 5 st., d. 28 (Nizhnii Novgorod, 1887). Peasants were not the only ones to complain of such clerical pressure. See the 1871 petition of the landowner and church elder from the Tver diocese, RGIA, f. 796, op. 152, d. 328.

214. Malevinskii, *Instruktsiia nastoiateliam*, par. 31; Ivanovskii, *Obozrenie*, 317–28, par. 43; Kalashnikov, *Alfavitnyi ukazatel'*, 456. Note that in the 1808 "Instruction on Church Elders" (*Instruktsiia tserkovnym starostam*), the stated financial managerial role of the church elder was phrased in such a way that his function appeared to be more independent of the

clergy. In the subsequently revised 1890 "Instructions," however, the idea of cooperation with parish clergy was stressed.

215. RGIA, f. 796, op. 151, d. 1691 (Viatka, 1870).

216. RGIA, f. 796, op. 150, d. 244 (Saratov, 1869); For other examples of parishioners accusing their priest of "self-willed" behavior, see op. 151, d. 1691 (Viatka, 1870); op. 152, d. 328 (Tver, 1871); f. 797, op. 186, 3 ot., 5 st., d. 116 (Novgorod, 1886).

217. GAVO, f. 496, op. 1, d. d. 13197. For other cases, see d. 13469 (1862); d. 16024 (1887); d. 18383 (1905); d. 18723 (1909); d. 19589 (1913). Peasants appear to have been particularly sensitive to a priest's "self-willed" and independent behavior when a church construction project was underway. See GAVO, f. 496, op. 1, d. 18383; RGIA, f. 796, op. 159. d. 1450 (Viatka, 1878).

218. GAVO, f. 496, op. 1, d. 18316, ll. 117–18.

219. For a historical discussion of the dual management of priest and church elder, see *Chto takoe tserkovnyi starosta*, 12–14.

220. Gosudarstvennyi Arkhiv Riazanskoi Oblasti, f. 627, op. 145, d. 13.

221. *Zhurnaly i protokoly*, 3:339. Interestingly, the confusion was not lost on some local village communities as well. In 1905, a "peoples' assembly" (*narodnyi s'ezd*) in the Samara diocese also voted to have all church-related affairs decided by the parishioners of particular churches and not at village assemblies. See Emeliakh, *Antiklerikal'noe dvizhenie*, 98.

222. "Nenormal'nosti v prikhodskoi zhizni i passivnoe otnoshenie k nim sviashchennika," *RSP* 19 (1885): 27–31.

223. *Prisutstvie po delam pravoslavnago dukhovenstva. O sluzhbe pravoslavnago belago dukhovenstva* (St. Petersburg, 1880), 77–78.

224. *Otzyvy eparkhial'nykh arkhiereev*, 2:489.

225. Ibid., 3:12–13.

226. Ibid., 3:42.

227. See, for example, the responses of the bishop of Voronezh in *Otzyvy eparkhial'nykh arkhiereev*, 1:135; the bishop of Novgorod, 2:203; the bishop of Kazan, 3:436.

228. Pavel Runovskii, "Zhelatel'no li uchastie pastyria v mirskikh skhodakh," *RSP* 28 (1887): 353–66. Other priests felt that pastors' main social functions were liturgical and educational in nature and that debates over their participation in local government were superfluous. "K voprosu ob obshchestvennoi deiatel'nosti prikhodskago sviashchennika," *RSP*, 50 (1887): 335–45; 52 (1887): 323–32. For a priest's view on pastoral participation in village assemblies, see also N. Kudriavtsev, "V oblasti tserkovno-prikhodskoi zhizni," *RSP* 18 (1905): 5–29; S. Sotin, "Ob uchastii dukhovenstva v obshchestvennoi zhizni naroda," *RSP* 24 (1905): 183.

229. *Obzor deiatel'nosti*, 467. Note that during the postreform period, diocesan bishops, in reviewing various petitions from village assemblies (especially those where either choice or censure of the parish priest was involved) would sometimes note the impropriety of their addressing such topics at their assemblies. See, for example, RGIA, f. 797, op. 186, 3 ot., 5 st., d. 116, l. 11.

230. RGIA, f. 796, op. 168, d. 2014. A number of diocesan bishops, including those of Viatka, Iaroslavl, Astrakhan, and Saratov, had independently issued similar directives years before the Synod ukase. See Mavritskii, *Tserkovnoe blagoustroistvo*, 18–20. A discussion of this issue can also be found in N. P., "O prigovorakh volostnykh pravlenii krest'ian po obidam, prichiniaemym dukhovnymi litsami," *RSP* 45 (1888): 237–45. For a more positive view of the potential role of local peasant government in parish affairs, see the article by the priest Gavriil Krasnianskii, "O sodeistvii volostnykh pravlenii sel'skim pastyriam v delakh tserkovnykh," *RSP* 5 (1863): 144–60.

231. See, for example, GAVO, f. 496, op. 1, d. 18628, ll. 1–2; d. 18476, l. 15; d. 18654; d. 20163. RGIA, f. 796, op. 154, d. 1469, l. 10; (Voronezh, 1873); op. 196, d. 141 (Viatka, 1913).

232. GAVO, f. 496, op. 1, d. 16463, ll. 9, 21. RGIA, f. 796, op. 196, 2 ot., 2 st., d. 141; f. 797, op. 83, d. 336.

233. Emeliakh, *Antiklerikal'noe dvizhenie*, 128.

234. RGIA, f. 833, op. 1, d. 9, ll. 93–136.

235. RGIA, f. 833, op. 1, d. 15, ll. 61–90.

236. For a continuation of this story, see Young, *Power and the Sacred;* Husband, *Godless Communists.*

CHAPTER 3

1. Tikhomirov, *Sovremennoe polozhenie*, 7; 14.

2. *Zamechatel'nyi sluchai v chasovne Nechaiannoi Radosti* (St. Petersburg, 1906).

3. In 1861, there were 12,186 chapels; in 1914, there were 23,593. See *Izvlecheniia iz otcheta po vedomstvu dukhovnykh del pravoslavnago ispovedaniia za 1861* (St. Petersburg, 1864), vedomost' no. 4, 14–17; *Vsepoddanneishii otchet oberprokurora Sv. Sinoda po vedomstvu pravoslavnago ispovedaniia* (St. Petersburg, 1916), vedomost' no. 3, 6–7.

4. On the *antimins* see Peter D. Day, ed., *The Liturgical Dictionary of Eastern Christianity* (Collegeville, MN: Liturgical Press, 1993), 17. For legislation regarding the serving of the Divine Liturgy in chapels, see *PSZ*, ser. 1, vol. 19, no. 14231, no. 11.

5. RGIA, f. 796, op. 180, d. 1563, l. 1 (Tver, 1899).

6. Josef A. Jungmann, *The Early Liturgy* (Notre Dame, IN: University of Notre Dame Press, 1959), 175–87; also see Andre Grabar, *Martyrium: recherches sur le culte des reliques et l'art Chrétien antique* (London: Variorum Reprints, 1972).

7. For a brief review of the history of chapels and legislation concerning them in Byzantium as well as in Russia until the mid–nineteenth century, see Nikol'skii, *O chasovniakh.*

8. GAVO, f. 496, op. 1, d. 16767, l. 72 ob. (1895); also see "The History of the Leushino Convent," in *Abbess Thaisia: An Autobiography of a Spiritual Daughter of St. John of Kronstadt* (Platina, CA: St. Herman of Alaska Brotherhood, 1989), 210–11.

9. Note that the early *martyria* were also a source of tension within the early Egyptian Christian community. See Jungmann, *Early Liturgy*, 186–87.

10. Iushkov, *Ocherki*, 52.

11. Nineteenth-century Russian church historians present conflicting views on the issue of episcopal blessings of chapel construction projects. Iushkov, in his work on parish life in Russia's northern regions from the fifteenth to the seventeenth centuries, writes that "the construction of chapels did not require any formalities; it did not demand a deed of consent [blagoslovennaia gramota]. It was a private activity on the part of the chapel faithful." Iushkov, *Ocherki*, 56. On the other hand, Nikol'skii maintains that in medieval Russia chapels were built with the bishop's permission. "Their construction without his will was considered illegal and incorrect." Nikol'skii, *O chasovniakh*, 7.

12. Iushkov, *Ocherki*, 63–64.

13. *PSZ*, ser. 1 vol. 40, no. 3.924a. See also GAVO, f. 496, op. 1, d. 19411, l. 3 (1913).

14. *PSZ*, ser. 1, vol. 9, no. 6592.

15. Nikol'skii, *O chasovniakh*, 18.

16. *PSZ*, ser. 2, vol. 40, no. 42349. The exception to this rule concerned chapels

constructed in Russia's two capitals, which needed the tsar's ratification as well. *Ustav dukhovnoi konsistorii* (St. Petersburg, 1898), par. 58.

17. There were, however, chapels that were built on the initiative of entire rural or urban parish communities. Frequently such chapels stood near or on the actual grounds of the church itself. See, for example, RGIA, f. 796, op. 157, d. 285 (Orel, 1876); op. 178, 2 ot., 2 st., d. 1782 (St. Petersburg, 1897); GAVO, f. 496, op. 1, d. 19424 (1912); 19419 (1913). Some chapels were constructed as part of the fortress-type wall surrounding a church that was located on a well-traveled road. These types of parish chapels served as resting points for pilgrims and travelers.

18. GAVO, f. 496, op. 1, d. 18215, l. 4 (1905–8).

19. A. M., "Osviashchenie chasovni-shkoly," *VEV* (chast' neoffitsial'naia) 11 (1898): 263–66; Platov, *Opisanie o sooruzhenii chasovni*.

20. Until the 1917 revolutions, priests often noted in their reports that a particular chapel was being built solely on believers' initiative. See GAVO, f. 496, op. 1, d. 19576, ll. 93–104 (1914). See also d. 16127, l. 8 ob. (1889–1904).

21. If such arrangements were not made ahead of time, individuals might have difficulty getting the chapel they had financed blessed. See, for example, RGIA, op. 193, 6 ot., 3 st., d. 1769 (Orel, 1911).

22. GAVO, f. 496, op. 1, d. 19776 (1915). For other examples, see d. 15327, l. 14 ob. (1879); d. 16934 (1896); d. 19777 (1915); RGIA, f. 796, op. 165, d. 1319 (Tver, 1884); op. 177, 2 ot., 2 st., d. 1674 (Tambov, 1896); op. 187, d. 7006 (Smolensk, 1906).

23. GAVO, f. 496, op. 1, d. 16767, l. 2 (1895); RGIA, f. 796, op. 185, 2 ot., 2 st., d. 2372 (Kostroma, 1904).

24. *Opisanie Krasnogorskoi Bol'she-Okhtenskoi chasovni;* V. F. Berdnikov, *Chasovnia sv. Blagovernago kniazia Aleksandra Nevskago,* RGIA, f. 796, op. 153, d. 1626 (St. Petersburg, 1872); op. 190, 2 ot., 2 st., d. 134 (St. Petersburg, 1909).

25. GAVO, f. 496, op. 1, d. 17190 (1807); d. 16127 (1889).

26. GAVO, f. 496, op. 1, d. 17190 (1889); RGIA, op. 169, d. 1370 (Orel, 1888); op. 178, 2 ot., 6 st., d. 4266 (Poltava, 1898); op. 177, 2 ot., 2 st., d. 1629 (Chernigov, 1896); op. 187, d. 6919 (Arkhangelsk, 1906); op. 190, 2 ot., 2 st., d. 479 (Riazan, 1909).

27. For the respective cases just mentioned, see *Osviashchenie chasovni v Nitstse;* RGIA, f. 796, 2 ot., 1 st., d. 1097; op. 168, d. 1465; op. 178, 6 ot., 2 st., d. 4266.

28. RGIA, f. 796, op. 168, d. 1465.

29. RGIA, f. 796, op. 185, 2 ot., 2 st., d. 2372.

30. RGIA, f. 796, op. 178, 6 ot., 2 st., d. 4266.

31. RGIA, f. 796, op. 177, 2 ot., 2 st., d. 1780 (1896); op. 178, 2 ot., 2 st., d. 1930 (Don region, 1897). See also *Opisanie Krasnogorskoi Bol'she-Okhtenskoi chasovni*.

32. RGIA, op. 168, d. 1360. See also a similar request of the peasant woman Maria Zubkova, who, according to diocesan authorities, "portrayed herself as an abbess" in RGIA, op. 174, d. 1019 (Orel, 1892). For studies on the phenomenon of women ascetics in Russia, see L. A. Tul'tseva, "Chernichki," in *Nauka i religiia* 11 (1970): 80–82; Brenda Meehan-Waters, "Popular Piety, Local Initiative and the Founding of Women's Religious Communities in Russia, 1764–1917," *SVTQ* 25 (1986): 117–42.

33. RGIA, f. 796, op. 172, d. 1364. For similar examples, see op. 155, d. 623 (Simferopol, 1874); op. 161, d. 944 (Smolensk, 1880); op. 179, 2 ot., 2 st., d. 2107 (Simbirsk, 1898); op. 181, 2 ot., 2 st., d. 2022 (Chernigov, 1906); op. 188, d. 2405 (Viatka, 1907).

34. RGIA, f. 796, op. 177, 2 ot., 2 st., d 1674, l. 14 (Tambov, 1896).

35. RGIA, f. 796, op. 172, d. 1364, ll. 1, 5–6.

36. I. Snegirev, "Chasovni v russkom mire," *DCh* 11 (November 1862): 242–43.

37. Note that the desire to use chapels as substitute churches seems to refer to a different perspective on chapels than that of the Russian churchmen who understood chapels as having developed in response to Christ's directive to pray in private (Matt. 6:5). For descriptions of the chapel as a reminder of the church, see GAVO, 496, op. 1, d. 19421, l. 4 (1913); RGIA, f. 796, op. 168, d. 1360, l. 1 (Iaroslavl, 1887). For the distance factor with respect to chapels and monastic communities, see op. 178, 2 ot., 2 st., d 1538 (Saratov, 1897). Owners of factories and their workers supported the construction of chapels for similar reasons. Since migrant workers frequently had no ties to the local population, some worker believers found it less alienating to belong to a chapel community than to try to assimilate into large urban parish communities. See, for example, *Osviashchenie chasovni na farforovo-faiansovoi fabrike.*

38. GAVO, f. 496, op. 1, d. 16075, l. 7 ob. (1888).

39. GAVO, f. 496, op. 1, d. 18745, l. 8 ob. (1909).

40. GAVO, f. 496. op. 1, d. 16767, ll. 48–54 (1895); see also d. 17800, l. 200 ob. (1901); d. 19421, l. 4 (1913); RGIA, f. 796, op. 167, d. 1103 (Tver, 1886); op. 1329 (Viatka, 1892).

41. RGIA, f. 796, op. 172, d. 1621.

42. GAVO, f. 496, op. 1, d. 14848, ll. 136–37 (1874).

43. RGIA, f. 796, op. 143, d. 1027; op. 160, d. 968 (Mogilev, 1879); op. 171, d. 1017 (Tver, 1890). GAVO, f. 496, op. 1, d. 16934, l. 22 (1896).

44. In some places these hut-type chapels were referred to as *ambarchiki*. Technically speaking, an *ambar* was a hut-type building traditionally used for grain storage. However, as N. D. Zol'nikova shows in her study—*Sibirskaia prikhodskaia obshchina*—peasants began building so-called *ambarchiki* during the eighteenth century when the construction of chapels was outlawed.

45. See, for example, GAVO, f. 496, op. 1, d. 18043, ll. 50–50 ob. (1903); Nikolai Sokolov, "Opisanie Pokrovskoi Ugletskoi tserkvi, Griazovetskago uezda, Vologodskoi gubernii," *VEV* (chast' neoffitsial'naia) 19 (1904): 515.

46. GAVO, f. 496, op. 1, d. 16934, l. 73 (1896); d. 16767, 1. 48 (1895–99).

47. A recently published work on the wooden architecture of Russia inaccurately indicates that chapels had no iconostases. See Alexander Opolovnikov and Yelena Opolovnikova, *The Wooden Architecture of Russia: Houses, Fortifications, Churches* (New York: Abrams, 1989), 157.

48. For examples of chapels with an iconostasis, see RGIA, f. 796, op. 168, d. 1465, l. 5 (Tver, 1887); op. 185, 2 ot., 2 st., d. 2372 (Kostroma, 1904); op. 187, d. 6919, l. 26 (Arkhangelsk, 1906); op. 188, 2 ot. 2 st., d. 2386, l. 2 (Viatka, 1907). Occasionally rural believers chose to construct their chapels with an altar space that remained empty, without an altar table or antimins.

49. Leonide Ouspensky, "The Problem of the Iconostasis," *SVSQ 8*, no. 4 (1964): 200–208. For a history of the iconostasis, see A. M. Lidov, ed., *Ikonostas: proiskhozhdenie, razvitie, simvolika* (Moscow: Progress-Traditsiia, 2000).

50. See, for example, GAVO, f. 496, op. 1, d. 16934, l. 73 ob. (1896). Platov, *Opisanie o sooruzhenii chasovni, 1–6.*

51. E. M., *Kratkoe istoricheskoe opisanie chasovni i ikon, 26.*

52. GAVO, f. 496, op. 1, d. 16941, l. 2 (1896); d. 18371 (1906); RGIA, f. 796, op. 152, d. 1599 (Vladimir, 1871).

53. RGIA, f. 796, op. 190, 2 ot., 2 st., d. 479.

54. It should be noted that not only chapels were used to honor an imperial or

political event. In his annual report, the ober-procurator of the Holy Synod frequently listed events in the life of the Russian nation or the imperial family in honor of which laity constructed churches, donated icons and liturgical vessels, held processions, and so forth.

55. Ostrovskaia, "Prosheniia v konsistoriiu," 170. For discussion of peasant petitions and appeals to the tsar in general, see Verner, "Discursive Strategies in the 1905 Revolution," 69–70.

56. For example, see GAVO, f. 496, op. 1, d. 18044 (1903); d. 18752 (1909); RGIA, f. 796, op. 178, d. 1822, l. 4 ob. (1897).

57. GAVO, f. 496, op. 1, d. 16934, l. 83 ob. (1896).

58. RGIA, f. 796, op. 150, d. 135 (Olonets, 1869).

59. RGIA, f. 796, op. 165, d. 1411. See also op. 150, d. 135 (Olonets, 1869); op. 163, d. 1712 (Simbirsk, 1882); GAVO, f. 496, op. 1, d. 16934, ll. 1–8 (1896).

60. RGIA, f. 796, op. 186, d. 2165. For other examples, see op. 153, d. 1657 (Moscow, 1872); op. 177, 2 ot., 2 st., d. 1780 (Moscow, 1896); op. 178, 2 ot., 2 st., d. 1930 (Don region, 1897).

61. Snegirev, "Chasovni v russkom mire," 251–52.

62. Regarding chapel construction and the 1888 event, see I. Preobrazhenskii, *Otechestvennaia tserkov'*, 27. This event was marked not only with chapel construction but with the construction of churches, bell towers, the restoration of iconostases, and the purchase of icons, bells, and other items for liturgical use.

63. RGIA, f. 796, op. 169, d. 182 (1888). For an example of the presentation of the event in popular devotional literature, see A. Agronomov, *Velikoe chudo milosti Bozhiei 17 oktiabria, 1888* (St. Petersburg, 1897). Believers also widely honored the 1888 event by purchasing bells for their parish churches and obtaining an icon to commemorate the event. The icon featured all of the patron saints of the members of the royal family involved in the derailment.

64. GAVO, f. 496, op. 1, d. 16934, ll. 98–99 (1892); RGIA, f. 796, op. 171, d. 1017 (Tver, 1890); op. 175, d. 1279 (Viatka, 1894); op. 177, 2 ot., 2 st., d. 1629 (Chernigov, 1896); op. 181, 2 ot., 2 st., d. 1775 (Iaroslavl, 1900).

65. RGIA, f. 796, op. 172, d. 1289.

66. *Slovo na osviashchenie chasovni.*

67. GAVO, f. 496, op. 1, d. 15327 (1879). See also d. 17919, l. 73 (1902); d. 18743 (1909); RGIA, f. 796, 2 ot., 1 st., d. 1097 (Novgorod, 1896). Note that clergy also routinely referred to natural disasters in these terms.

68. GAVO, f. 496, op. 1, d. 19978 (1915).

69. *Dopolnitel'nyi trebnik* (Moscow, 1895). See also Tikhomirov, *Na prikhode*, 1:44. Also note the ruling issued in July 1834 regarding prayers during times of drought and other natural disasters, *PSZ*, ser. 2, vol. 9, no. 6603. A similar attitude toward natural disasters was also often found in popular religious literature and sermons. See, for example, Ia. K. Amfiteatrov, "Besdozhdie i zasukha," reprinted in the popular leaflet series *Troitskie listki* no. 527 (1890); "Otchego zasukhi i nepogody?" *Troitskie listki* no. 673 (1893); "Bog zovet nas k pokaianiiu groznymi iavleniiami v prirode," *Troitskie listki* no. 318 (1911). The Russian Orthodox Church's *Trebnik* came under severe criticism from some of Russia's intellectuals. Lev Tolstoy, for instance, considered the collection of prayers contained in this book as nothing more than "various devices of sorcery adapted to all possible circumstances of life." For a summary of Tolstoy's views and a defense of the *Trebnik* see the article by the well-known liturgical scholar A. Dmitrievskii, "Kniga 'Trebnik' i eia znachenie v zhizni pravoslavnago khristianina. Po povodu noveishikh vozrenii na etu knigu,"

*RSP* 10 (1902): 289–95; 12 (1902): 327–38; 13 (1890): 374–82; 17 (495–500). Also see F. A., "Spravedlivo li mnenie o knige Trebnik, kak o sobranii sueverii?" *Donskiia eparkhial'nyia vedomosti* 18 (1903): 465–70.

70. REM, f. 7, op. 1, d. 379, l. 17 ob.

71. RGIA, f. 796, op. 173, d. 1140 (Moscow, 1892).

72. GAVO, f. 496, op. 1, d. 15578, ll. 32, 36–37 (1884). For similar reconstruction efforts, see d. 15327 (1879); RGIA, f. 796, op. 167, d. 1281 (Kostroma, 1886); op. 171, d. 1017 (Tver, 1890); op. 187, d. 6919 (Arkhangelsk, 1906).

73. GAVO, f. 496, op. 1, d. 18153, l. 188 (1903).

74. I. A. Kremleva, "Obet v religioznoi zhizni russkogo naroda," *Pravoslavie i russkaia narodnaia kul'tura*, kniga 2 (Moscow: Koordinatsionno-metodicheskii tsentr Prikladnoi etnografii Instituta etnologii i antropologii RAN, 1993), 127–57. The vow continues to be a central feature not only in Eastern Orthodox Christian but also in Catholic piety. See, for example, Jill Dubisch, "Pilgrimage and Popular Religion at a Greek Holy Shrine," in Badone, *Religious Orthodoxy and Popular Faith*, 113–36; Christian, *Person and God*, 119, 166.

75. For examples, see RGIA, f. 796, op. 159, d. 1856 (Pskov, 1878); op. 172, d. 1364 (Nizhnii Novgorod, 1891).

76. "O proizvol'nykh obetakh," in *Pribavleniia k izdaniiu tvorenii sviatykh otsev v russkom perevode*, vol. 17 (Moscow, 1858), 110.

77. GAVO, f. 496, op. 1, d. 17227 (1897).

78. See comments in REM, d. 357, l. 114 (Vologda). For other examples of communal vows made with respect to chapel construction, see RGIA, f. 796, op. 143, d. 2127 (Vladimir, 1862); op. 170, d. 1459 (Tver, 1889).

79. RGIA, f. 796, op. 187, d. 6919 (Arkhangelsk, 1906).

80. GAVO, f. 496, op. 1, d. 13331, l. 26 (1861). For other examples, see RGIA, f. 796, op. 142, d. 546 (Kostroma, 1861); op. 150, d. 135 (Olonets, 1869); op. 181, 2 ot., 2 st., d. 1775 (Iaroslavl, 1900); op. 191, 6 ot., 3 st., d. 234 (Viatka, 1910); op. 203, 6 ot., 3 st., d. 155, l. 5 (Viatka, 1916).

81. RGIA, f. 796, op. 165, d. 1319 (Tver, 1884).

82. For examples of such holy wells and springs, see RGIA, f. 796, op. 153, d. 692, (Tambov, 1872); op. 155, d. 677 (Viatka, 1874); op. 190, 6 ot., 3 st., d. 277 (Samara, 1909).

83. See, for example, RGIA, f. 796, d. 1941, op. 145 (Vologda, 1864); op. 155, d. 677 (Viatka, 1874); op. 159, d. 1856 (Pskov, 1878); op. 168, d. 1439 (Kursk, 1887); op. 167, d. 1452 (Samara, 1886); op. 175, d. 1279 (Viatka, 1894).

84. For example, see the following accounts: RGIA, f. 796, op. 153, d. 685 (Vologda, 1872); op. 155, d. 654 (Samara, 1874). In 1892, a peasant from the Voronezh diocese came home late at night and met an old man whom he took to be holy. The old man told him to bring his neighbors to a particular place the next day and to dig a well there. The water, he claimed, would serve the community well. Later an icon appeared on this site. RGIA, op. 153, d. 728 (1872).

85. See the observations of the priest Nikolai Sobolev in GAVO, f. 4839, op. 1, tetrad' 1, d. 371, l. 6 ob. (1907–8); RGIA, op. 169, d. 1513 (Orel, 1888).

86. RGIA, f. 796, op. 181, 2 ot., 2 st., d. 1871; op. 165, d. 1411 (Kostroma, 1884); op. 194, d. 2070 (Tula, 1912).

87. For a description of the basic ecclesial community, see Hebblethwaite, *Basic Is Beautiful*, 19–51; Bruneau, "Basic Christian Communities in Latin America: Their Nature and Significance (Especially in Brazil)," in Levine, *Churches and Politics in Latin America*,

225–37. There is an extensive bibliography on the subject of basic ecclesial communities in Latin America. For an introduction to this subject, see Boff, *Ecclesiogenesis*.

88. The *obednitsa* is a liturgical service, usually translated as "reader's service," that can be performed without the presence of clergy; it is said in place of the Divine Liturgy under certain conditions. K. Nikol'skii, *Posobie k izucheniiu ustava bogosluzheniia pravoslavnoi tserkvi* (St. Petersburg, 1907).

89. GAVO, f. 496, op. 1, d. 18215, l. 4 (1905).

90. GAVO, f. 496, op. 1, d. 16075, l. 15. (1888).

91. Aleksei Beliaev, "Iz tserkovno-prikhodskoi zhizni Velskago uezda," *VEV* (chàst' neoffitsial'naia) 5 (1900): 130.

92. REM, d. 240, l. 54 (Vologda); d. 345, ll. 5–5 ob. (Vologda); d. 720, ll. 11–12 (Novgorod); RGIA, f. 796, op. 163, d. 1768 (Kostroma, 1882).

93. RGIA, f. 796, op. 173, d. 1329 (Viatka, 1892); op. 175, d. 1279 (Viatka, 1894); GAVO, f. 496, op. 1, d. 16629, l. 41 (1894); d. 17468 (1899).

94. RGIA, f. 796, op. 155, d. 677. See a similar case in op. 177, 2 ot., 2 st., d. 1629 (Chernigov, 1896).

95. See as examples, RGIA, f. 796, op. 153, d. 1657 (Moscow, 1872); op. 161, d. 934 (St. Petersburg, 1880).

96. D'iachenko, *Propovednicheskaia entsiklopediia*, 685–86.

97. *Polnyi pravoslavnyi bogoslovskii entsiklopedicheskii slovar'*, 2: 2129–31.

98. Malevinskii, *Instruktsiia nastoiateliam*, 98.

99. Uspenskii, *Grekhi sueveriia*, 73.

100. *Polnyi pravoslavnyi*, 2:2129; Tikhomirov, *Na prikhode*, 2: 202.

101. *Polnyi pravoslavnyi*, 2: 2129.

102. Tikhomirov, *Na prikhode*, 2: 202.

103. RGIA, f. 796, op. 165, d. 1411. Clerical concerns regarding superstitious behavior were not new to post-Petrine Russian Orthodoxy. Orthodoxy's canonical tradition warned about the construction by lay people of prayer houses in the name of martyrs that were inspired by "visions or vain revelations they had in their sleep." A local council held in Carthage in the early fifth century had encouraged bishops to try to dismantle such chapels. If this could not be done because of popular outcry, then they were directed to instruct members of their flock not to gather reverently at such sites or "to entertain any superstitious awe or delusion under they impression that they were built as a result of divine revelation." *The Rudder of the Orthodox Catholic Church: The Compilation of the Holy Canons*, trans. D. Cummings (1957, reprinted New York: Luna Printing Corp., 1983), 657–58.

104. GAVO, f. 496, op. 1, d. 14848, l. 188 (1874).

105. RGIA, f. 796, op. 165, d. 1319, l. 16 (Tver, 1884); op. 171, d. 1472, l. 8 (Kaluga, 1890).

106. RGIA, f. 796, op. 172, d. 1364 (Nizhnii Novgorod, 1891).

107. GAVO, f. 496, op. 1, d. 16767, ll. 46–47.

108. Nikolai Iustinov, "Chasovni v nashikh selakh i derevniakh," *RSP* 3 (1899): 273–78.

109. *Ustav dukhovnoi konsistorii*, par. 58.

110. It is important to note that these donations were used solely for the financial support of the parish church and were not used to support the parish clergy.

111. See GAVO, f. 496, op. 1, d. 13807, ll. 50–50 ob. (1864). Apparently church officials did not disturb altars in chapels that were constructed before 1842.

112. RGIA, f. 796, op. 163, d. 1768, l. 7 (Kostroma, 1882).

113. RGIA, f. 796, op. 169, d. 1370 (Orel, 1888); op. 190, 2 ot., 2 st., d. 134 (St. Petersburg, 1909).

114. For examples of such activities concerning chapels, see GAVO, f. 496, op. 1, d. 13469, l. 18 ob. (1862); d. 19777, l. 5 (1915). RGIA, f. 796, op. 155, d. 1268 (Smolensk, 1874); op. 159, d. 1808 (Tver, 1878); op. 179, 2 ot., 2 st., d. 2107 (Simbirsk, 1898); op. 183, d. 2508, l. 25 (Kostroma, 1902). Lin'kov, *Opisanie*, 28–29; Rozanov, *Voskresenskaia tserkov'*, 105; Beliaev, "Iz tserkovno-prikhodskoi zhizni," 129–32.

115. The number of existing chapels in many places, therefore, was actually higher than what was officially recorded in diocesan records.

116. RGIA, f. 796, op. 144, d. 1937.

117. GAVO, f. 496, op. 1, d. 16742.

118. Ibid., l. 2.

119. Ibid., l. 1.

120. Ibid., l. 78.

121. Ibid., l. 87.

122. Ibid., l. 108.

123. GAVO, f. 496, op. 1, d. 17800, l. 5 ob. (1901).

124. Ibid., l. 1 ob.

125. GAVO, f. 496, op. 1, d. 17899, l. 8 (1902).

126. *Ustav dukhovnoi konsistorii*, par. 60.

127. RGIA, f. 796, op. 167, d. 1281.

128. For a similar case where the Synod reversed a consistory decision to level a chapel, see RGIA, f. 796, op. 169, d. 1370 (Orel, 1888). In other cases the Synod supported the local consistory's ruling. See op. 155, d. 654 (Samara, 1874); op. 159, d. 1856 (Pskov, 1878); op. 163, d. 1762 (Tambov, 1882); op. 165, d. 1319 (Tver, 1884); op. 177, 2 ot., 2 st., d. 1674 (Tambov, 1896).

129. RGIA, f. 796, op. 163, d. 1762 (Tambov, 1882).

130. RGIA, f. 796, op. 165, d. 1319.

131. RGIA, f. 796, op. 199, 6 ot., 3 st., d. 337. For a similar case, see f. 796, op. 191, 6 ot., 3 st., d. 234 (Viatka, 1910).

132. For example, see GAVO, f. 496, op. 1, d. 18406 (1907); d. 19756 (1914).

133. RGIA, f. 833, op. 1, d. 7, ll. 176–78.

134. See the comment by a dean from the Viatka diocese in 1907 in RGIA, f. 796, op. 188, d. 2405, l. 6.

135. RGIA, f. 833, op. 1, d. 7, l. 176.


CHAPTER 4

1. While monastic communities practiced a daily cycle of liturgical prayer, for most lay believers this cycle was a private, domestic matter.

2. For a detailed description of the Russian Orthodox calendar, see Debol'skii, *Dni Bogosluzheniia*, 1:3–7.

3. "Beseda o neobkhodimosti i spasitel'nosti pochitaniia prazdnikov pravoslavnoi tserkvi," in D'iachenko, *Obshchedostupnyia besedy*, 646–50; Sergii, Arkhiepiskop Kishinevskii, "O pochitanii tserkovnykh prazdnikov. Slovo v den' Sreteniia Gospodnia," *DCh* 3 (1883): 352–54; Nikolai, Arkhiepiskop Varshavskii, "K zakonoproektu 35-ti chlenov Go-

sudarstvennago Soveta o sokrashchenii prazdnikov i neprisutstvennykh dnei," *GTs* 5–6 (1912): 207–12.

4. "O tainstvennom znachenii khristianskikh prazdnikov," in D'iachenko, *Obshche-dostupnyia besedy*, 655.

5. "Beseda o prazdnikakh voobshche," in D'iachenko, *Obshchedostupnyia besedy*, 652. Also see the sermon given by the priest Vasilii Preobrazhenskii to his parishioners in "Iz dnevnika sel'skago sviashchennika," *VEV* (chast' neoffitsial'naia) 14 (1906): 392–93.

6. Sv. I. Ptp—skii, "O trude: Chtenie dlia naroda," *DCh* 10 (1883): 170; Prot. V. Nechaev, "Trudoliubie i prazdnost': Pouchenie v nedeliu desiatuiu," *DCh* 9 (1884): 78.

7. Prot. I. Rozhdestvenskii, "O trude," *DCh* 3 (1860): 251; N. K., "Trud i vremia ego prodolzhitel'nosti po ucheniiu Slova Bozhiia i Sviatoi Tserkvi," *MTsV* 14 (1905): 160.

8. Nechaev, "Trudoliubie i prazdnost'," 78; N. K., "Trud i vremia ego prodolzhi-tel'nosti," *MTsV*, no. 21 (1905): 235; Rozhdestvenskii, "O trude," 255–56.

9. Sv. I. Ptp—skii, "O trude," 177; Rozhdestvenskii, "O trude," 265; D. Bogoliu-bov, "O telesnom trude," *Voskresnyi blagovest*, 11 (1904): 24–27.

10. Sv. Levashev, "Pouchenie o pochitanii prazdnikov," *VorEV* (chast' neoffitsial'naia), 22 (1904): 897–900; M. Nikol'skii, "O khristianskom provozhdenii prazdnichnykh dnei," in *Pastyrskoe nazidanie: Sbornik statei*, vol. 1; N. Rykunov, "Pouchenie o khristianskom preprovozhdenii prazdnikov," *IaEV* (chast' neoffitsial'naia), 11 (1889): 170–74.

11. Sv. I Nabivach, "Chti voskresnyi den'," *VorEV* (chast' neoffitsial'naia), 32 (1914): 859–60.

12. For a useful summary of fasting in prerevolutionary Russia, though one told in the usual "high / low" culture paradigm, see Leonid Heretz, "The Practice and Significance of Fasting in Russian Peasant Culture at the Turn of the Century," in *Food in Russian History and Culture*, 67–80.

13. G. Orlov, comp., *V chem sostoit istinnyi post?* (Moscow, 1900); *Post i pokaianie: Velikopostnyi sbornik* (St. Petersburg, 1900).

14. Quoted from *The Lenten Triodion*, trans. Mother Mary and Archimandrite Kallistos Ware (Boston: Faber and Faber, 1978), 190.

15. D'iachenko, *Obshchedostupnyia besedy*, 858.

16. A. B-skii, "Velikii post v derevne," *RSP* 9 (1866): 302–14.

17. REM, f. 7, d. 22.

18. REM, f. 7, d. 1620, l. 15 (Smolensk).

19. REM, f. 7, d. 1166, l. 23 (Orel).

20. REM, f. 7, d. 1171, l. 18.

21. REM, f. 7, d. 549, l. 4 ob. (Kaluga); d. 1517, l. 83.

22. REM, f. 7, d. 467, l. 30 (Kazan); d. 1693, l. 38 (Smolensk).

23. REM, f. 7, d. 883, l. 8.

24. REM, f. 7, d. 433, l. 20 (Viatka); d. 467, l. 31 (Kazan).

25. REM, f. 7, d. 1175, l. 18 (Orel); d. 1620, l. 14 (Smolensk).

26. REM, f. 7, d. 1161, l. 8.

27. Heretz, "The Practice and Significance of Fasting," 74.

28. As an example, see REM, f. 7, op. 1, d. 821, l. 32 (Novgorod).

29. B-skii, "Velikii post v derevne," 311.

30. Nikon (Rozhdestvenskii), "V zashchitu sviatago posta." *Troitskii tsvetok*, 92 (1913); Orlov, *V chem sostoit istinnyi post*.

31. *Izvrashchenie posta* (Moscow, 1905).

32. See comment by Debol'skii in *Dni Bogosluzheniia*, 1:6.

33. "Neprisutstvennye dni v 1905," *PZh* (Attached to 1905 volume). Such lists of public holidays were published annually in newspapers and journals. Also see *Svod zakonov*, vol. 14 (3rd ed., 1902), par. 24.

34. RGIA, f. 797, op. 98, d. 230, ll. 46 ob.–47.

35. For a summary of imperial legislation concerning work on Sundays and feast days, see RGIA, f. 797, op. 96, d. 230, ll. 46–48. Also see the more detailed study by Smirnov, *Prazdnovanie voskresnago dnia*, 162–247; PSZ, Ser. 1, vol. 5, number 3169.

36. Smirnov, *Prazdnovanie voskresnago dnia*, 218.

37. *PSZ*, Ser. 1, vol. 24, number 17674.

38. *PSZ*, Ser. 1, vol. 24, number 17909.

39. "Ustav o preduprezhdenii i presechenii prestuplenii," *Svod zakonov*, vol. 14 (1890), par. 23.

40. Ibid., par. 24. This ruling eventually caused some controversy, since the word for "state work" was *publichnye raboty*, or "public works," sometimes interpreted as any work taking place in the open. See RGIA, f. 797, op. 96, d. 203, ll. 52–52 ob.

41. "Ustav ob Aktsiznykh sborakh," *Svod zakonov*, vol. 5 (1901), par. 622.

42. Ibid., par. 14. It is noteworthy that the law code preserved Emperor Paul's law forbidding theatrical performances during Great Lent and Bright Week but conspicuously left out the clause regarding such performances on Saturdays. Alexander III further qualified this law in 1881. See *PSZ*, Ser. 3, vol. 1, number 401.

43. "O gubernatorakh," *Svod zakonov*, vol. 2 (1892), par. 300.

44. See, for example, REM, d. 62, l. 6 (Vladimir); d. 251, ll. 13–14 (Vologda); d. 973, l. 24 (Orel); d. 1495, l. 8 (Saratov); d. 1813, ll. 5–6 (Iaroslavl).

45. REM, d. 1317, l. 32.

46. Prot. V. Zhmakin, "K voprosu o prazdnikakh v razlichnykh uchebnykh zavedeniiakh," *PTsV*, 42 (1901): 1534–37.

47. REM, d. 796, ll. 13–14.

48. REM, d. 211, ll. 147–48. Also see d. 1807, l. 2 (Iaroslavl).

49. REM, d. 976, ll. 17–18.

50. REM, d. 211, l. 138; d. 326, ll. 12–13; d. 376, ll. 1–4; GAVO, f. 1063, op. 86, d. 26, l. 21 ob.

51. *Poslovitsy russkogo naroda: Sbornik V. Dalia* (Moscow: Khudozhestvennaia literatura, 1984), 2: 263.

52. REM, d. 1725, l. 7; d. 326, ll. 12–13 (Vologda); d. 1807, l. 3 (Iaroslavl).

53. REM, d. 467, l. 38; d. 1345, l. 28 (Penza). Also see N. Slednikov, "Iz dnevnika Vologodskago eparkhial'nago missionera za 1905," *VEV* (chast' neoffitsial'naia), 20 (1905): 294–95.

54. REM, d. 213.

55. REM, d. 345, ll. 15–17.

56. REM, d. 240, ll. 74–75 (Vologda); d. 563 (Kostroma).

57. REM, d. 335, ll. 143–45.

58. REM, d. 803, l. 1–3 ob. For other examples, see d. 812 (Novgorod); d. 935 (Orel); d. 1820 (Iaroslavl).

59. "Beseda ob osviashchenii khrama," in D'iachenko, *Obshchedostupnyia besedy*, 1134–37.

60. REM, d. 63, l. 7 (Vladimir); d. 318, l. 7 (Vologda); d. 699, l. 29 (Novgorod); d. 1293, l. 40 (Penza); d. 1757, l. 11 (Iaroslavl).

61. REM, d. 1730, l. 2 (Tver).

62. For a description of such nonreligious feasts and celebrations, see, for example, Vladimir Propp, *Russkie agrarnye prazdniki* (Leningrad, 1963).

63. These terms find their root in the verb *molit'*, which means "to humbly petition" or "to pray."

64. For comments on the proliferation of these feasts, see GAVO, f. 1063, op. 53, d. 10, l. 15 ob. See discussion in RGIA, f. 796, op. 155, d. 82a, ll 2–6.

65. GAVO, f. 1063, op. 53, d. 10, l. 15 ob. Such observations about the growth of local feast days were frequently made. See, for example, F. Malevinskii, "Strelitskaia Preobrazhenskaia tserkov' Totemskago uezda Vologodskoi guberni, *VEV* (chast' neoffitsial'naia) 16 (1902): 474.

66. REM, d. 1807, l. 1 ob.

67. See V. I. Chicherov, *Zimnii period russkogo zemledel'cheskogo kalendaria XVI–XIX vekov* (Moscow: Izdatel'stvo Akademii nauk SSSR, 1957).

68. RGIA, f. 796, op. 172, d. 1595.

69. RGIA, f. 796, op. 170, d. 1536.

70. RGIA, f. 796, op. 191, 6 ot., 3 st., d. 90.

71. RGIA, f. 796, op. 179, 3 ot., 2 st., d. 2952 (Arkhangelsk, 1898).

72. REM, d. 292, l. 3.

73. REM, d. 917, l. 4.

74. REM, d. 685, l. 10. For other examples of the establishment of feasts, see d. 357, l. 114 (Vologda); d. 685 (Novgorod). Iv. Pr—skii, "Sel'skii prazdnik," *Sovremennik*, 106 (February 1865): 409–43.

75. REM, d. 240, ll. 64–65 (Vologda); d. 315, l. 14 (Vologda); RGIA, f. 796, op. 172, d. 1595 (Novgorod, 1891); op. 177, 3 ot., 2 st., d. 2448 (Pskov, 1896).

76. See, for example, V. Preobrazhenskii, "Iz dnevnika sel'skago sviashchennika," 396.

77. REM, d. 310, l. 2 (Vologda).

78. REM, d. 63, l. 7.

79. GAVO, f. 652, op. 1, d. 69.

80. REM, d. 284, l. 19 (Vologda).

81. REM, d. 327, ll. 18–19.

82. REM, d. 108, l. 16; d. 345, l. 6.

83. For the feasts of the Procession of the Precious and Life-Giving Cross of the Lord and Epiphany.

84. RGIA, f. 796, op. 162, d. 1685.

85. Law of 20 December 1777. See GAVO, f. 496, op. 1, d. 14533.

86. RGIA, f. 796, op. 171, d. 1449; op. 177, 3 ot., 2 st., d. 2448.

87. See RGIA, f. 796, op. 171, d. 1449.

88. Nikol'skii and Izvol'skii, *Sistematicheskii sbornik*, 111.

89. GAVO, f. 496, op. 1, d. 17995.

90. Ibid.

91. See, for example, RGIA, f. 796, op. 144, d. 1672 (Perm, 1863); op. 153, d. 697 (Tambov, 1872); op. 167, d. 1554 (Tver, 1886); op. 177, 3 ot., 2 st., d. 1230 (Olonets, 1896); op. 177, 3 ot., 2 st., d. 1896 (St. Petersburg, 1886).

92. REM d. 1411, l. 32 (Pskov); d. 1746, ll. 27–28 (Iaroslavl).

93. REM, d. 1747, ll. 27–28.

94. REM, d. 292, l. 6 (Vologda).

95. GAVO, f. 1063, op. 104, d. 10, l. 1 ob. In general, the prayer services that occurred during village feast days came from the *Trebnik* or *Book of Needs*. Moreover, the

order of prayer services was left up to the local clergy, and occasionally priests would compose services themselves for whatever unique occasions might arise. The arbitrariness and lack of standardization of the prayer services during the local feasts was one of the features that irritated some ecclesiastical authorities. See "Vazhnyi vopros tserkovnoi-bogosluzhebnoi praktiki," *RSP* 18 (1907): 1–6.

96. The description of the village feast day given here is a composite drawn from descriptions for the Vologda diocese in the following sources: REM, d. 127, ll. 1–4; d. 130, ll. 30–33; d. 240, ll. 76–77; d. 292, ll. 6–10; d. 315, ll. 9–10. GAVO, f. 652, op. 1, d. 69.

97. Chernyshev, *Krestnye khody Viatskoi eparkhii*, 3–4.

98. Broiakovskii, "Krestnye khody i ikh znachenie," in *Pouchieniia i rechi*, 164–66.

99. Anichkov-Platonov, *Razsuzhdenie o krestnykh khodakh*, 7; *Znachenie krestnykh khodov*.

100. For example, see Num. 10:11–14; 1 Chron. 15:25. See discussion in Krasnianskii, *O zhachenii krestnykh khodov*, 3; Broiakovskii, "Krestnye khody i ikh znachenie"; *O krest-nykh khodakh*.

101. Broiakovskii, "Krestnye khody i ikh znachenie"; *O krestnykh khodakh*.

102. *O krestnykh khodakh*.

103. Krasnianskii, *O znachenii krestnykh khodov*, 4; D'iachenko, *Obshchedostupnyia besedy*, 1121.

104. Krasnianskii, *O znachenii krestnykh khodov*, 6.

105. Ep. Vissarion, "O krestnom khode," *VorEV*, 15 (1892): 563–67; Anichkov-Platonov, *Razsuzhdenie o krestnykh khodakh*, 66.

106. D'iachenko, *Obshchedostupnyia besedy*, 149.

107. Broiakovskii, "Krestnye khody i ikh znachenie"; RGIA, f. 796, op. 203, 6 ot., 3 st., d. 49 (Kostroma, 1916); op. 165, d. 1694 (Perm, 1884); op. 148, d. 665 (Orenburg, 1867).

108. RGIA, f. 796, op. 177, 3 ot., 2 st., d. 2441 (Tula, 1896); op. 178, 3 ot., 2 st., d. 2560 (St. Petersburg, 1897); op. 178, 3 ot., 2 st., d. 2605 (Tambov, 1897); op. 179, 3 ot., 2 st., d. 2893 (Nizhnii Novgorod, 1898); op. 179, 3 ot., 2 st., d. 2971 (Pskov, 1897).

109. See, for instance, processions established to commemorate the 1888 train accident: RGIA, f. 796, op. 170, d. 1403 (Orel, 1889); op. 170, d. 1412 (Chernigov, 1889); op. 177, d. 2402 (Olonets, 1896); op. 184, 3 ot., 2 st., d. 3041 (Pskov, 1903).

110. RGIA, f. 796, op. 178, 3 ot., 2 st., d. 2605.

111. RGIA, f. 796, op. 178, 3 ot., 2 st., d. 2661.

112. RGIA, f. 796, op. 144, d. 1672. It remains unclear, however, whether these more civic processions were usually accompanied by time off from work.

113. RGIA, f. 796, op. 165, d. 1591 (Perm, 1884).

114. Krasnianskii, *O znachenii krestnykh khodov*, 8–9.

115. RGIA, f. 796, op. 146, d. 1424.

116. RGIA, f. 796, op. 188, 6 ot., 3 st., d. 7627.

117. RGIA, f. 796, op. 180, d. 3107.

118. REM, f. 7, op. 1, d. 1789, l. 4.

119. Prince A. I. Vasil'chikov (1818–81) was a publicist and liberal public activist. Born in the province of Tambov, Vasil'chikov was actively involved in local zemstvo activities in the Novgorod province. He also was greatly interested in the peasant agricultural question. His two major publications included *On Self-Government* and *Landholding and Agriculture in Russia and Other European States*. For biographical details, see Nathan Smith,

"Vasil'chikov, Aleksandr Illarionovich," in *Modern Encyclopedia of Russian and Soviet History*, ed. Joseph L. Wieczynskin (Gulf Breeze, FL: Academic International Press, 1976).

120. "Ot chego beden nash russkii narod, i chem pomoch' etomu?" *PO* 1 (1865): 93–108.

121. RGIA, f. 796, op. 155, d. 82a, ll. 32–49.

122. "Vzgliad literatury na vopros o sokrashchenii prazdnichnykh dnei v narode," *RSP* 14 (1877): 424, 426; for a similar view, see S. K., "Kak dolzhno smotret' na obilie prazdnichnykh dnei u russkago naroda," *RSP* 27 (1891): 260–66.

123. I. A. Nikiforov, "O vazhnom znachenii sobliudeniia i osviashcheniia prazdnichnykh dnei," *PO* 3 (1882): 529.

124. GAVO, f. 496, op. 1, d. 19366, l. 324.

125. REM, 1, d. 603, l. 24 (Kostroma).

126. REM, d. 1101, l. 1. For other reports of collection of fines, see d. 467, l. 38 (Kazan); d. 1322, l. 33 (Penza); d. 1807, l. 1 ob. (Iaroslavl). Fines that were collected from these sorts of violations were also used for different ends in different localities, from purchasing vodka to donations to the parish church.

127. REM, d. 221, l. 4.

128. REM, d. 262, l. 9. At the same time, Mertsalov noted that this custom of forbidding individuals to work was falling out of practice in the area in which he was writing.

129. REM, d. 121, l. 14.

130. RGIA, f. 797, op. 33, 2 ot., 2 st., d. 318.

131. RGIA, f. 797, op. 65, 2 ot., 3 st., d. 100.

132. The peasant correspondent for the Tenishev bureau, S. F. Staroverov, also commented on this in his report to the Russian Geographical Society in 1902 on the popular legal customs. See his "Material'nye svedeniia o narodnykh iuridicheskikh obychaiakh," Arkhiv Geograficheskogo Obshchestva, f. P-7, d. 86-VIIIl, l. 5; Also see REM, d. 346, l. 9 (Vologda); d. 821 (Novgorod).

133. REM, d. 433, l. 6 (Viatka).

134. REM, d. 64, l. 7; d. 310. ll. 1–2 (Vologda).

135. REM, d. 343, l. 4.

136. REM, d. 213, ll. 14–17 (Vologda). Because of the expense of these festivities, one priest from the Riazan province noted that sons who had migrated to urban areas would send money home to help their families cover the cost. "Dni obshchestvennykh bogomolenii na poliakh," *RSP* 14 (1892): 409.

137. REM, d. 251, l. 4.

138. This is according to the Eastern Orthodox numbering of the Decalogue, not shared by the Roman Catholic or Lutheran Churches.

139. REM, d. 31, ll. 109–12.

140. N. A. Ivanitskii, "Materialy po etnografii Vologodskoi gubernii," *Izvestiia Imperatorskago obshchestva liubitelei estestvoznaniia, antropologii i etnografii*, vol. 64, Trudy etnograficheskago otdela, vol. 11, vyp. 1 (Moscow, 1890), 215.

141. REM, d. 274, l. 28.

142. REM, d. 547, l. 1.

143. REM, d. 63, l. 1 (Vladimir); d. 251, l. 11 (Vologda); d. 441, l. 2 (Viatka); d. 1101, l. 1 (Orel).

144. REM, d. 546, l. 36.

145. REM, d. 562, l. 7 (Kostroma).

146. REM, d. 130, l. 7.

147. Volkov, *Sbornik polozhenii o sel'skom sostoianii,* Part I, "Obshchee polozhenie o kresti'ianakh," pars. 60, 106, 118. Also see "Zametki," *RSP* 6 (1863): 414–15; "Tsikuliar Vologodskago gubernatora gg. zemskikh nachal'nikam i chinovnikam po kret'ianskim delam ot 20 marta 1896," *VEV* 9 (1896): 117–18.

148. Totemskii kraevedcheskii muzei, P-35, "Dnevnikovye zapisi A. A. Zamaraeva."

149. REM, d. 220, ll. 11–12 (Vologda).

150. Smirnov, *Prazdnovanie voskresnago dnia,* 234.

151. *PO* 10 (1867): 133.

152. RGIA, f. 796, op. 155, d. 82a, ll. 267–89. Those provincial governors who came out for abolishing bazaars on Sundays included the governors of Ekaterinoslavl, Iaroslavl, Kaluga, Kazan, Kharkov, Kursk, Olonets, Nizhnii Novgorod, Riazan, Samara, Simbirsk, Tula, Tver, Ufa, Vitebsk, and Vologda; those against included the governors of Arkhangelsk, Chernigov, Kostroma, Kherson, Minsk, Poltava, Pskov, Saratov, Smolensk, St. Petersburg, Tambov, Vilno, and Voronezh.

153. "Iz otcheta oberprokurora sv. Sinoda," *PO* 2 (1870): 395–416.

154. "Khronika," *PTsV* 24 (1914): 1096–98.

155. *Pravitel'stvennyi vestnik* 129 (14/26 June 1897): 1. It is noteworthy that two years earlier the gold and platinum industry had settled on a holiday schedule of fifty-six days.

156. RGIA, f. 20, op. 13-a, d. 251, ll. 1, 4.

157. "Deistviia pravitel'stva," *Pravitel'stvennyi vestnik* 2–3 (29 January/10 February 1900): 1

158. RGIA, f. 796, op. 155, d. 82a, l. 11.

159. REM, d. 343, l. 30 (Vologda).

160. REM, d. 684, ll. 14–16; also see d. 216, ll. 119–20 (Vologda); d. 803 (Novgorod).

161. For examples of villages collectively voting to curtail alcohol consumption at local feasts or promising to spend feasts "in a Christian manner," see GAVO, f. 496, op. 1, dd. 18360, 18745, 18747, d. 18748; f. 1063, op. 85, kor. 255, d. 22, l. 41 ob. Nikolai Sokolov, "Opisanie Pokrovskoi Ugletskoi tserkvi, Griazovetskago uezda, Vologodskoi gubernii," *VEV* (chast' neofitsial'naia) 18 (1904): 435, 501. "Strelitskaia Preobrazhenskaia tserkov', Totemskago uezda, Vologodskoi gubernii," *VEV* (chast' neofitsial'naia) 18 (1902): 536; A. Il'inskii, "Nikol'shchiny i bratchiny," 372. RGIA, f. 796, op. 442, d. 1712, ll. 25–26. REM, d. 221, l. 4; d. 345, ll. 14, 25; d. 379, l. 35.

162. GAVO, f. 496, op. 1, d. 15904, l. 1.

163. GAVO, f. 496, op. 1, d. 15904, l. 6.

164. *Kut'ia* or *kolivo* is a mixture of cooked kernels of grain, such as wheat or rice, mixed with honey. It is prepared for requiem services that are conducted either in church or in the home. The kernels traditionally signified that just as a kernel of grain that was buried in the ground would sprout to produce new life, so the dead, buried in the earth, would arise in a new life (see 1 Cor. 15:36–38 and John 12:24). The honey signified the sweetness of the life to come.

165. GAVO, f. 496, op. 1, d. 15904, ll. 7–8.

166. Ibid., l. 11.

167. Ibid., l. 22 ob.

168. Ibid., l. 8.

169. Sel'skii ierei O-skoi eparkhii, "Odna iz prichin oskorbitel'nago otnosheniia sel'skikh prikhozhan k sviatosti velikikh prazdnikov," *RSP* 43 (1888): 209–12.

170. M. V., "Eshche neskol'ko slov po povodu stat'i: 'Odna iz prichin oskorbitel'nago otnosheniia sel'skikh prikhozhan k sviatosti velikikh prazdnikov," *RSP* 11 (1889): 336–37.

171. "K voprosu ob obilii narodnykh prazdnikov," *RSP* 28 (1891): 287–28.

172. "Po voprosu ob umenshenii prazdnichnykh dnei v narode," *PO* 4 (1875): 700.

173. M. V., "Eshche neskol'ko slov," 334–39.

174. Nikiforov, "O vazhnom znachenii," 529–33.

175. S. K., "Kak dolzhno smotret'," 263.

176. "Nravstvenno-vospitaiushchee vliianie prazdnikov na cheloveka," *RSP* 38 (1899): 49–57.

177. "Po voprosu ob umen'shenii prazdnichnykh dnei v narode," 699–706.

178. M. E., "Neskol'ko osnovatel'nykh suzhdenii svetskikh liudei o vrede prichiniae-mom blagosostoianiiu krest'ian mnogoprazdniem nashei tserkvi," *RSP* 26 (1891): 244–50; "K voprosu ob obilii narodnykh prazdnikov," 290.

179. Dimitrii Korsunskii, "Evrei-uchitel' pochitaniia prazdnikov," *DCh*, "Izvestiia i zametki," 1 (1870): 49–51. For other examples of such comparisons, see E. P., "Zabytyi obychai," *DCh* 5 (1889): 17.

180. "O khristianskom provozhdenii prazdnichnykh dnei: Iz vnebogosluzhebnykh so-besedovanii," in *Pastyrskoe nazidanie*, 1:431.

181. RGIA, f. 796, op. 153, d. 697 (Tambov); op. 148, d. 778 (Pskov, 1867); d. 1417 (Pskov, 1867).

182. RGIA, f. 797, op. 96, d. 230, l. 10 ob., 93.

183. RGIA, f. 796, op. 155, d. 82a, l. 78 ob., 83; f. 797, op. 96, d. 230, ll. 60–62.

184. RGIA, f. 796, op. 155, d. 82a, l. 6.

185. In addition to the categories listed here, the committee also mentioned certain days on which peasants did not generally work but that were not marked by prayer and thus had no religious significance.

186. RGIA, f. 796, op. 155, d. 82a, ll. 96 ob.–103.

187. Ibid., l. 157 ob.

188. Ibid., ll. 107–9.

189. *PSZ*, ser. 3, vol. 24 (1904), ot. 1, no. 24468.

190. The 10 May 1904 ruling also deleted a clause in the existing law that forbade "public labor" on Sundays and feast days. According to the State Council, this clause was usually interpreted by local authorities as forbidding any type of work done openly, for everyone to see, such as work in the fields, and not merely work by state offices.

191. See, for example, Sv. N. Sergeev, "Nakazanie Bozhie za neposeshchenie tserkvi v prazdnichnyi den'," in Novgorodskii, *Narodnyi sobesednik*, 27–31; Stratilatov, *Katekhizi-cheskie besedy*, 288–92.

192. Sergeev, "Nakazanie Bozhie," in Novgorodskii, *Narodnyi sobesednik*, 27.

193. A. Troitskii, "Po povodu raz'iasneniia uzakonenii kasaiushchikhsia proizvodstva rabot v prazdnichnyia dni," *RSP* 41 (1904): 123–30.

194. "Ukaz Sviashchennago Sinoda ot 14 iiulia, 1904." *VEV* 17 (1904): 394–97.

195. Ep. Nikon, "V zashchitu prazdnikov," *PTs Ved* 9 (1909): 410.

196. P. Kudriavtsev, "Po povodu novago zakona o prazdnichnykh dniakh," *RSP* 10 (1905): 243–51.

197. RGIA, f. 797, op. 96, d. 230, l. 8.

198. RGIA, f. 797, op. 96, d. 230, l. 9.

199. RGIA, f. 797, op. 96, d. 230, l. 20.

200. RGIA, f. 797, op. 96, d. 230, l. 14 ob.

201. Nikon, "V zashchitu prazdnikov," 406–12.

202. Nikolai, Arkhiepiskop Varshavskii, "K zakonoproektu 35-ti chlenov Gosudar-stvennago Soveta o sokrashchenii prazdnikov i neprisutstvennykh dnei," *GTs* 2–6 (1912): 207–21.

203. Nikon, "V zashchitu prazdnikov," 411.

204. V. Pravdin, "Zakonoproekt o sokrashchenii prazdnikov," *TsOV* 49 (1913): 3–5.

205. RGIA, f. 797, op. 96, d. 230, l. 52.

206. Antireligious writers during the Soviet period often noted that the village and parish feasts were the most persistently celebrated and the most difficult to weed out. Rumiantsev, *O prestol'nykh prazdnikah*, 3.

207. For commentary on some of these aspects of the local feasts, see A. Volnin, "Narodnyia vozzreniia na sviatykh i na tserkonye prazdniki s tochki zreniia khristianskago ucheniia o pochitanii sviatykh i prazdnikov," *RSP* 18 (1904): 2–14.

## CHAPTER 5

1. See as examples Paul Evdokimov, *The Art of the Icon: A Theology of Beauty* (Redondo Beach, CA: Oakwood, 1993); Leonid Ouspensky, *The Meaning of Icons* (Crestwood, NY: St. Vladimir's Seminary Press, 1982); Egon Sendler, *The Icon: Elements of Theology, Aesthetics and Technique* (Redondo Beach, CA: Oakwood, 1993); Boris Uspensky, *The Semiotics of the Russian Icon* (Lisse, Belgium: Peter de Ridder Press, 1976).

2. In Russia, these icon stories were referred to as *skazaniia*. For a description of this narrative genre for icons of the Mother of God, see Ebbinghaus, *Die altrussischen Marienikonen-Legenden*. For a discussion of such icons in modern Greece, see Dubisch, *In a Different Place*.

3. One of the best-known examples of such an icon story in the Orthodox tradition is the sixth- or seventh-century account of the healing of King Abgar by an image of Christ "Not-Made-by-Hands." See Averil Cameron, "The History of the Image of Edessa: The Telling of a Story," in *Okeanos: Essays Presented to Ihor Ševčenko,* ed. C. Mango and Omeljan Pritsak (Cambridge, MA: Ukrainian Research Institute, Harvard University, 1983), 80–94; Herbert L. Kessler and Gerhard Wolf, eds., *The Holy Face and the Paradox of Representation* (Bologna: Nuovo Alfa, 1998).

4. Accounts of specially revered icons were presented for the most part during the fourth and fifth sessions of the Seventh Ecumenical Council. *Deianiia Vselenskikh Soborov,* vol. 7 (Kazan, 1873). For the history of the Seventh Ecumenical Council, see the introduction in Sahas, *Icon and Logos;* Abrosios Giakalis, *Images of the Divine: The Theology of the Seventh Ecumenical Council* (New York: Brill, 1994); Dumeige Gervais, *Nicée II* (Paris: Éditions de l'Orante, 1978).

5. Smirnov, *Chudesa,* 15; Ieromonakh Vasilii, *Pouchenie pri poseshchenii ikony Belychinskoi Bozhiei Materi Orshanskago Bogoiavlenskago monastyria* (Mogilev, 1911), 2; Paozerskii, *Chudotvornye ikony,* 91. See also the comment by the bishop of Tver in RGIA, op. 187, chast' 2, d. 6987 (1906).

6. Vysotskii, *Beseda,* 10.

7. For clerical observations on the diverse social composition of believers who came to venerate such icons, see RGIA, f. 796, op. 157, d. 157 (Vladimir, 1876); op. 167, d. 1452 (Samara, 1886); op. 168, d. 1489, l. 13 (Kursk, 1887); op. 169, d. 1399 (Novgorod, 1888); op. 175, d. 1824 (Chernigov, 1894); op. 175, d. 1896, l. 8 (Kishinev, 1894); op. 190, 6 ot., 3 st., l. 1 (Penza, 1909); op. 193, d. 1895, l. 17 (Novgorod, 1913).

8. See, for example, *Chudesnoe istselenie docheri kollezhskago sovetnika;* Narkevich, *Chudotvornaia ikona,* 16. For examples of Lutherans and Catholics venerating such icons, see RGIA, f. 796, op. 175, d. 1824 (Chernigov, 1894), l. 2. For reports of Old Believers venerating such icons, see RGIA, f. 796, op. 155, d. 412, l. 10 (Orenburg, 1875); op. 157, d. 157, l. 8 (Vladimir, 1876); op. 174, d. 1714 (Perm, 1893). In 1887, one townsman from

the Tver diocese even expressed his hopes that a specially revered icon of the Mother of God named "Tikhvin" would be one means by which Old Believers might be drawn to the official Orthodox Church. RGIA, f. 796, op. 188, d. 1465, l. 15.

9. The directive for such investigations were given in the *Spiritual Regulation*. See Muller, *The Spiritual Regulation*, 29, 52. See also comments in 1872 by Platon (Fiveiskii), the bishop of Kostroma, in RGIA, f. 796, op. 156, d. 632.

10. For descriptions of the various types of miracle-working icons, see Sergii (Spasskii), *Russkaia literatura*, 39–40; *Kaluzhskaia Kazanskaia ikona*, 3–4.

11. See the comment by Iuvenalii (Kariukov), bishop of Orel, in RGIA, f. 796, op. 157, d. 225, l. 13. In the late nineteenth and early twentieth centuries, descriptions of locally revered icons began to be published as part of a growing interest in local histories.

12. Sergii (Spasskii), *Russkaia literatura*, 40. The liturgical services and hymns in honor of these icons can be found in *Miniia*, 12 vols. (St. Petersburg, 1885); *Dopolnitel'naia Mineia* (St. Petersburg, 1894). For a list of these icons, see the menologion published by the Holy Synod: *Khristianskii Mesiatseslov*. It should be noted that monastic communities on the local level also composed services or at least special hymns (*troparia* and *kontakia*) in honor of locally revered icons of the Mother of God. The multivolume menologion published by the Russian Orthodox Church in the twentieth century (1978–88) has incorporated some of these locally composed services and hymns.

13. For cases involving dreams see RGIA, f. 796, op. 143, d. 1859 (Voronezh, 1862); op. 156, d. 458 (Orel, 1875); op. 175, d. 1994 (St. Petersburg, 1894); op. 182, 3 ot., 2 st., d. 2564 (Orenburg, 1901); op. 185, d. 2968 (Kiev, 1904); op. 190, 6 ot., 3 st., d. 119 (Riazan, 1909). For cases involving reports of streaming myrrh, see RGIA, f. 796, op. 143, d. 2239 (Perm, 1862); op. 185, 3 ot., 2 st. d. 3043 (Nizhnii Novogord, 1904). For cases involving the hearing of voices, see RGIA. f. 796, op. 160, d. 1764 (Simbirsk, 1879); op. 175, d. 1994 (St. Petersburg, 1894); op. 190, 6 ot., 3 st., d. 119 (Riazan, 1909); op. 203, 6 ot., 3 st., d. 8 (Irkutsk, 1916).

14. This phenomenon involved icons whose image had become darkened and obscured, sometimes to the point of being indiscernible. Inexplicably, these icons would sometimes lighten. RGIA, f. 796, op. 155, d. 671 (Tavrida, 1874); op. 167, d. 1492 (Kostroma, 1886); op. 181, d. 2558 (Orel, 1900); op. 190, 6 ot., 3. st., d. 102 (Vladimir, 1909). Following the *iavlennye* (epiphanic) icons, to be described hereafter, this phenomenon most frequently triggered the special veneration of an icon during the second half of the nineteenth century. By the early twentieth century in some locations it seems to have surpassed the epiphanic type of "sign" in reported numbers. In 1904, Iustin (Okhotin), the bishop of Kherson and Odessa, noted how in that diocese the self-renewal of icons had reached epidemic proportions. RGIA, f. 796, op. 185, d. 3034, l. 10. For testimony concerning the supposedly large numbers of icon renewals in the immediate postrevolutionary period, see Arkhiepiskop Mefodii, *O znamenii obnovleniia sviatykh ikon* (Kharbin, 1925).

15. Cases involving the unusual flickering or self-lighting of a candle were less frequent; they seem to have occurred more often in a convent setting. RGIA, f. 796, op. 166, d. 1526 (Tobolsk, 1885); op. 174, d. 1692 (Viatka, 1893); op. 180, d. 2938 (Voronezh, 1899); op. 185, 3 ot., 2 st., d. 3043 (Nizhnii Novgorod, 1904); op. 193, d. 1800 (Olonets, 1911).

16. RGIA, f. 796, op. 145, d. 1941 (Vologda, 1864); op. 151, d. 662 (Kursk, 1870); op. 160, d. 1754 (Tambov, 1879); op. 167, d. 1452 (Samara, 1886); op. 169, d. 1513 (Riazan, 1888); op. 190, 6 ot., 3 st., d. 310 (Penza, 1909); op. 191, 6 ot., 3 st., d. 234 (Viatka, 1910); op. 195, d. 1547 (Vladimir, 1912).

17. For examples where laity spoke of the revelatory nature of their icons, see RGIA, op. 151, d. 710, l. 3 (Moscow, 1870); op. 175, d. 1994, l. 1 (St. Petersburg, 1894); for the language of grace and mercy, and the work of the Holy Spirit, see op. 168, d. 1466, l. 12 (Poltava, 1887); op. 176, d. 2137, l. 2 (Iaroslavl, 1895); op. 177, 3 ot., 2 st., d. 2423, l. 1 (Kaluga, 1896); op. 185, d. 3034, l. 2 (Kherson, 1904); op. 187, chast' 2, d. 6961, ll. 2-3 (Ufa, 1906).

18. RGIA, f. 796, op. 183, d. 2580, l. 1 (Simbirsk, 1902).

19. RGIA, f. 796, op. 157, d. 157. This iconographic type is also often referred to as "*Miluiushchaia*" or "the Merciful One." The appearance of a specially revered icon set into motion an ecclesial dynamic similar to that set into motion by apparitions in the Catholic West. See Blackbourn, *Marpingen*, 17-28.

20. *Skazanie ob ikone, imenuemoi Dostoino Est'.*

21. Some twenty years later, the story was retold to synodal authorities with some added details. In an account provided by townsman Ivan Zasukhin from Murom, the Mother of God had also reassured Iakovleva that her illness was for the "glory of God." Moreover, in Zakhunin's account, Iakovleva was fully healed only after the icon had been blessed in the church.

22. RGIA, f. 796, op. 167, d. 1490, l. 2. Also see Fedorov, *Chudotvornaia ikona*, 36-37.

23. "Svod ustavov o preduprezhdenii i presechenii prestuplenii," in *Svod zakonov*, vol. 14 (Petrograd, 1916), par. 26. For examples of cases where rumors connected with icons were investigated by regional civil courts, see RGIA, op. 155, d. 671 (Tavrida, 1874); op. 167, d. 1445 (Ekaterinoslavl, 1886). Priests could also be reported to the civil court for facilitating rumors concerning miracles, see RGIA, op. 154, d. 553 (Tavrida, 1873).

24. RGIA, f. 796, op. 167, d. 1445, l. 2.

25. RGIA, f. 796, op. 160, d. 1764; similarly, see the account of a captain's widow, Ekaterina Nikolaevna Popova, and her experiences with an icon of St. Tikhon of Zadonsk, RGIA, op. 143, d. 1859, l. 3 (Voronezh, 1862).

26. RGIA, op. 174, d. 1780.

27. Donations of icons associated with an individual's personal religious experience to either churches or chapels were not infrequent, in part because private homes could not accommodate all those persons wishing to venerate such an icon. See RGIA, f. 796, op. 185, d. 2968 (Kiev, 1904); op. 185, d. 3031 (Chernigov, 1904); op. 190, 6 ot., 3 st., d. 119 (Riazan, 1909); op. 190, 6 ot., 3 st., d. 145 (Poltava, 1909). At the same time, there were also cases, especially with icons that had been in a family for generations, where people resisted having the icon moved to another location. This had to do with understandings of personal property (*sobstvennost'*) and "belonging" (*prinadlezhnost'*) with respect to an icon.

28. For examples where believers without hesitation notified their parish priest about their experiences connected with icons, see RGIA, f. 796, op. 143, d. 2239 (Perm, 1862); op. 144, d. 187 (Tver, 1863); op. 151, d. 662 (Kursk, 1870); op. 160, d. 1764 (Simbirsk, 1879); op. 160, d. 1753 (Tambov, 1879); op. 174, d. 1780 (Kazan, 1893); op. 177, 3 ot., 2 st., d. 2423 (Kaluga, 1896); op. 185, d. 3031, l. 4 (Chernigov, 1904); op. 186, d. 3036 (Tavrida, 1905).

29. RGIA, f. 796, op. 151, d. 710.

30. RGIA, f. 796, op. 145, d. 1998.

31. RGIA, f. 796, op. 160, d. 1753.

32. RGIA, f. 796, op. 193, d. 1895.

33. RGIA, f. 796, op. 175, d. 1939, l. 7.

34. RGIA, f. 796, op. 181, d. 2558. For other examples of priests' participation, see op. 143, d. 2239 (Perm, 1862); op. 144, d. 187 (Tver, 1863); op. 153, d. 661 (Kostroma,

1872); op. 153, d. 728 (Voronezh, 1872); op. 166, d. 1468 (Kharkov, 1886); op. 174, d. 1780 (Kazan, 1893); op. 175, d. 1896, l. 8 (Kishinev, 1894); op. 190, 6 ot., 3 st., d. 119 (Riazan, 1909); op. 195, d. 1547 (Vladimir, 1912). For an example where a priest grudgingly conducted prayer services before an icon after feeling threatened by his parishioners, see op. 183, d. 2473 (Podolsk, 1902).

35. RGIA, f. 796, op. 190, 6 ot., 3 st., d. 310, l. 1. The rise in the number of communicants was noted in other reports of specially revered icons. See RGIA, op. 183, d. 2435 (Orenburg, 1902).

36. RGIA, f. 796. op. 185, d. 2968, l. 3.

37. RGIA, f. 796, op. 176, d. 2137, ll. 1 ob.–2.

38. RGIA, f. 796, op. 190, d. 145, l. 3 ob. (emphasis added). For a similar collective response to an individual's experience, see op. 183, d. 2593 (Simbirsk, 1902); op. 190, 6 ot., 3 st., d. 251 (Chernigov, 1909).

39. RGIA, f. 796, op. 195, d. 1436, l. 5.

40. RGIA, f. 796, op. 169, d. 1399, l. 13.

41. Usually associated with Roman Catholic votives, amulets in the shape of arms, legs, etc. were also left on icons in prerevolutionary Russia, and not only in those areas with a strong Catholic presence. *Skitovskaia ikona Bozhiei Materi* (Mogilev, 1890), 8; Solov'ev, *Sviataia ikona*, 24.

42. For the story of the icon's life, see *Skazanie o chudotvornoi Bogoliubskoi ikone; Skazanie o chudotvornoi Bogoliubskoi ikone Bozhiei Materi, chto v sele Zimarove.*

43. RGIA, f. 796, op. 203, 6 ot., 3 st., d. 117.

44. Belting, *Likeness and Presence*, 47–77.

45. L. A. Shchennikova, "Chudotvornaia ikona 'Bogomater' Vladimirskaia' kak 'Odigitriia Evangelista Luki'," in Lidov, *Chudotvornaia ikona*, 252–81.

46. On this icon, see A. M., "Prebyvanie ikony Torzhestvo Presviatyia Bogoroditsy v gorode Vladivostoke i otpravlenie eia v Port Artur," *Vladivostokskie eparkhial'nye vedomosti* 2 (1905): 31–36; 3 (1905): 64–67; 4 (1905): 88–92; 5 (1905): 112–13; V. N. Mal'kovskii, *Skazanie ob ikone;* A. Andersin-Lebedeva, *Skazanie ob ikone Port Arturskoi;* RGIA, f. 796, op. 201, 6 ot. 3 st., d. 298.

47. RGIA, f. 796, 6 ot., 3 st., d. 70.

48. See, for example, the comment by peasants from the Minsk diocese regarding how knowledge of their locally revered icon was transmitted from generation to generation; RGIA, f. 796, op. 170, d. 1507.

49. *Skazanie ob ikone Bozhiei Materi, imenuemoi Abalatskoiu*, 50. The publication of such stories, however, was not always strictly censored. See the 1916 case involving the publication of an icon-related story in the religious-theological journal *Dushepoleznyi sobesednik*, in RGIA, op. 203, 6 ot., 3 st., d. 1888. For an example of the influence such pamphlets had on common believers, see RGIA, op. 178, 3 ot., 2 st., d. 2615, l. 1; *Chudesa v nahsi dni* (St. Petersburg, 1897), 115; *Skazanie o chudotvornoi ikone Bogomateri imenuemoi Chernigovskaia*, 67–68; *Skazanie ob ikone Tabynskoi*, 29–30. Such devotional pamphlets were commonly found in the possession of peasants. See REM, d. 756, l. 102 (Novgorod); d. 801, l. 9 ob.; 20–21 (Novgorod); d. 948, ll. 6–7 (Orel).

50. *Skazanie ob ikone Bozhiei Materi imenuemoi Abalatskoiu*, 40–50.

51. RGIA, f. 796, op. 195, d. 1436.

52. RGIA, f. 796, op. 162, d. 1721.

53. "Chudesnoe istselenie devitsy Very Gitsevich ot ikony Bogomateri imenuemoi Kozel'shchinskoi," *AsEV* chast' neoffitsial'naia, 13 (1885): 477–80. RGIA, f. 796, op. 171, d. 1586.

54. RGIA, f. 796, op. 187, d. 6929, l. 140.

55. See, for example, the icon of John the Baptist that was housed in the village of Bogorodskoe in the Kazan diocese but that traveled to the Ufa and Samara dioceses (RGIA, f. 796, op. 187, chast' 2, d. 6961, l. 4); the icon of St. Nicholas that traveled from the Orel to the Chernigov diocese (op. 157, d. 225); and the "Sedmiozernoe" icon of the Mother of God that traveled from Kazan to Viatka (op. 191, 6 st., 3 ot., d. 179).

56. RGIA, f. 796, op. 187, d. 6929. In this file see, for example, the reports of the bishops of Novgorod, ll. 47–54; Tver, ll. 193–97; Vladimir, ll. 276–84; Kaluga, ll. 285–95.

57. RGIA, f. 796, op. 187, d. 6929, ll. 155–56.

58. RGIA, f. 796, op. 187, d. 6929, ll. 68–70. Despite reform attempts, such nighttime visitations appear to have come back into practice in the Novgorod diocese by 1907 on account of the growth in population and diocesan authorities' efforts to scale back the duration that an icon was away from its home. See RGIA, op. 190, 6 ot., 3 st., d. 79, ll. 1–3. For other examples of a full schedule, see the description of the visitation schedule of the icon of the Smolensk Mother of God in the Iaroslavl district, RGIA, op. 187, d. 6929, l. 234 ob., and the visitations with icons of the Mother of God, Christ, and St. Nicholas to the city of Tomsk in RGIA, op. 189, d. 8150.

59. Although part of the visitation ritual included private prayer services in people's homes, requests for visitations usually had to come from an entire parish, village, or urban community in order to be honored by church officials. See, for example, RGIA, f. 796, op. 156, d. 451 (Orel, 1875); op. 165, d. 1651, (Orel, 1884); op. 188, d. 1734, l. 4 (Viatka, 1907); op. 193, d. 1747 (Omsk, 1912).

60. In 1910, for example, the abbot from the Pokrov monastery in the Omsk diocese petitioned the Holy Synod to allow visitations with an icon of St. Nicholas to neighboring villages in order to raise funds to support the monastic community. His request, however, was denied since he could show no requests for a visitation from parish and village communities. RGIA, f. 796, op. 193, d. 1747. For other cases where a lack of support from local believers resulted in a diocesan officials' failure to grant permission for such visitations, see RGIA, op. 203, 6 ot., 3 st., d. 242 (Viatka, 1914). Similarly, it appears that if a priest petitioned for the visitation of an icon without support of the parish, the request also could be denied; RGIA, op. 187, chast' 2, d. 7253 (Poltava, 1906).

61. RGIA, f. 796, op. 160, d. 1757.

62. See RGIA, f. 796, op. 167, d. 1444 (Kherson, 1886).

63. *Opisanie chudotvornoi ikony Starorusskoi*, 30.

64. RGIA, f. 796, op. 188, 6 ot., 7. st., d. 7571.

65. Solov'ev, *Sviataia ikona Bozhiei Materi imenuemaia Abalatskoiu*, 27–32; *Opisanie chudotvornoi ikony Starorusskoi*, 52–59. Rituals tied to the greeting of an icon varied from locality to locality. For examples of other prayers sung during the greeting of an icon of the Mother of God, see *Poriadok vstrechi v Kazani i provodov sv. chudotvornoi Smolenskoi Sedmiozerskoi ikony Bozhiei Materi* (Kazan, 1890).

66. RGIA, op. 165, d. 1639, l. 5.

67. RGIA, f. 796, op. 157, d. 136 (Moscow, 1876); op. 158, d. 157 (Tobolsk, 1877); op. 164, d. 1353 (Vologda, 1883); op. 170, d. 1538 (Pskov, 1889); op. 171, d. 1436 (Tver, 1890); op. 187, chast' 2, d. 6961 (Ufa, 1906).

68. RGIA, f. 796, op. 171, d. 1436.

69. RGIA, f. 796, op. 199, 6 ot., 3 st., d. 129. Also see op. 165, d. 1694, l. 9 (Perm, 1884); op. 166, d. 1529 (Iaroslavl, 1885); op. 203, 6 ot., 3 st., d. 172 (Olonets, 1916).

70. RGIA, f. 796, op. 157, d. 225.

71. RGIA, f. 796, op. 160, d. 1752.

72. RGIA, f. 796, op. 187, d. 6929, l. 23. Saint Makarii had been the founder of the Holy Trinity monastery in the fifteenth century. After a complex history, the monastery was transformed into a women's convent only in 1882. For other examples of visitations to towns and cities, see RGIA, op. 145, d. 2350 (Vologda, 1864); op. 153, d. 697 (Tambov, 1872); op. 155, d. 605 (Tver, 1874); op. 185, 3 ot., 2 st., d. 2950 (Nizhnii Novgorod, 1903); op. 188, d. 1734 (Viatka, 1907).

73. RGIA, f. 796, op. 187, d. 6929, ll. 101–2.

74. RGIA, f. 796, op. 170, d. 1401, l. 3.

75. See, as an example, RGIA, f. 796, op. 180, 1 ot., 6 st., d. 7666, l. 57 (Kharkov, 1907). Such visitations were not necessarily lucrative for local priests because a large portion of incoming donations went to the church or monastery from where the icon came. RGIA, op. 156 d. 451 (Orel, 1875); op. 171, d. 1436 (Tver, 1890).

76. RGIA, f. 796, op. 161, d. 1478.

77. RGIA, f. 796, op. 187, d. 6929, ll. 1–4.

78. RGIA, f. 796, op. 191, 6 ot., 3 st., d. 179 (Viatka, 1910).

79. RGIA, f. 796, op. 188, d. 7571 (Voronezh, 1907).

80. RGIA, f. 796, op. 167, d. 1444 (1886); op. 190, 6 ot., 3 st., d. 79.

81. RGIA, f. 796, op. 146, d. 867 (Perm, 1865); op. 157, d. 225 (Chernigov, 1876); op. 165, d. 1639 (Tver, 1884).

82. RGIA, f. 796, op. 190, 6 ot., 3 st., d. 79.

83. RGIA, f. 796, op. 190, 6 ot., 3 st., d. 158 (Voronezh, 1909); op. 190, 6 ot., 3 st., d. 79 (Novgorod, 1909); op. 190, 6 ot., 3 st., d. 64 (Ufa, 1909); op. 203, 6 ot., 3 st., d. 68 (Kostroma, 1916). An increase in population also often led to increased demands for an icon.

84. See the schedule for the icon of the Transfiguration from the village of Verkhov-skoe in the Viatka diocese in RGIA, f. 796, op. 187, d. 6929, ll. 163–64; op. 203, 6 ot., 3 st., d. 1 (Orel, 1916).

85. *Kaluzhskaia Kazanskaia ikona Bozhiei Materi*, 5.

86. V. G. Korolenko, "Za ikonoi," in *Izbrannoe* (Moscow: "Khudozh. Lit.," 1973), 291–92.

87. *Deianiia Vselenskikh Soborov*, 7:312–14; for a translation of the life of St. Mary of Egypt, see Benedicta Ward, *Harlots of the Desert* (Kalamazoo: Cistercian, 1987), 35–56. Russian Orthodox writers often recalled this story in their reflections on the veneration of icons.

88. *Deianiia Vselenskikh Soborov*, 7:257, 350.

89. A. Orlov, "Znachenie ikonopochitaniia i ego neobkhodimost' s psikhologicheskoi tochki zreniia," *PEV* 6 (15 March 1893): 229.

90. Sadovskii, *Sviatye ikony*, 6.

91. Smirnov, *Chudesa*, 1–5.

92. D'iachenko, *Dukhovnyi mir*, 212–13.

93. *O chudesakh i znameniiakh* (St. Petersburg, 1890).

94. Sosnin, *O sviatykh i chudotvornykh ikonakh*, 4–5, 16; *Chudesnoe istselenie ikonoiu Bozhiei Materi Vsekh Skorbiashchikh Radosti* (St. Petersburg, 1896), 10; Romanskii, *O chudotvornykh ikonakh*, 4; Vysotskii, *Beseda*, 2; Sv. Vasilii Dobrovol'skii, "Sv. ikony," *Prikhod-skaia zhizn'* 2 (1917): 99.

95. Sosnin, *O sviatykh i chudotvornykh ikonakh*, 54.

96. *Kaluzhskaia Kazanskaia ikona Bozhiei Materi*, 4–5.

97. Sergii Arkhiepiskop (Spasskii), *Pravoslavnoe uchenie*, 94. According to one author, however, relics were more pleasing to God since, during their lives, saints were living

temples of the Holy Spirit in a way that icons were not. Hence more miracles historically had taken place from prayers before relics than before icons. Romanskii, *O chudotvornykh ikonakh*, 10.

98. *Pastyr' propovednik*, 192; Romanskii, *O chudotvornykh ikonakh*, 2.

99. Vysotskii, *Beseda*, 2; Komarov, *Slovo v den' Preobrazheniia*, 5–6. Romanskii, *O chudotvornykh ikonakh*, 5. For an explanation of why it would be detrimental if all icons were miracle working, see Vorontsov, *Pouchenie na 26-e iiunia, 1908*, 4–5.

100. Sosnin, *O sviatykh ikonakh*, 64–65; Vorontsov, *Pouchenie na 26-e iiunia, 1908*, 4–5.

101. *Polnyi pravoslavnyi* 2: 2370–2375.

102. See similar observations in Kizenko, *A Prodigal Saint*, 109–10.

103. Sosnin, *O sviatykh chudotvornykh ikonakh*, 65, 73; Uspenskii, *O sviatykh ikonakh*, 9; Vysotskii, *Beseda*, 3. For this analogy in a classical Orthodox treatise on icons, see John of Damascus, *On the Divine Images*, trans. David Anderson (Crestwood: St. Vladimir's Seminary Press, 1980), 61, 96.

104. Sosnin, *O sviatykh chudotvornykh ikonakh*, 67, 71; Romanskii, *O chudotvornykh ikonakh*, 2. Lavrskii, "Slovo v den' otbytiia Oranskoi ikony Bozhiei Materi," in *Poucheniia gorodskago prikhodskago sviashchennika*. Lay believers also stressed the importance of faith and prayer when speaking about healings with respect to icons. See, for example, RGIA, f. 796, op. 190, 6 ot., 3 st., d. 145, l. 3 ob. This was an idea expressed by John of Damascus when he said, "Matter is filled with divine grace through prayer addressed to those portrayed in images." *On the Divine Images*, 36.

105. Speranskii, *Skazanie o chudotvornoi Tikhvinskoi ikone*, 4.

106. Sidonskii, *Chudotvornaia ikona Bozhiei Materi Odigitrii*, 2. Note a similar analogy in Speranskii, *Skazanie o chudotvornoi Tikhvinskoi ikone*, 5.

107. Pavel Florenskii, *Iconostasis*, trans. Donald Sheehan and Olga Andrejev (Crestwood: St. Vladimir's Seminary Press, 1996), 74. For a description of the copy phenomenon in Byzantium, see Gary Vikan, "Ruminations on Edible Icons: Originals and Copies in the Art of Byzantium," in *Retaining the Original: Multiple Originals, Copies, and Reproductions*, ed. K. Preciado, Studies in the History of Art 20 (Washington, D.C.: National Gallery of Art, 1989): 47–59.

108. "Chin blagosloveniia i osviashcheniia ikony Khristovy, prazdnikov gospodskikh, edinyia ili mnogiikh," in *Trebnik*, part 2 (Moscow, 1906). This translation of the text was taken from *The Blessing of Ikons*, trans. Mother Mary (Toronto, 1993). Similar prayers characterized the blessing of icons of the Mother of God and saints as well.

109. Emphasis added. "Chin blagosloveniia i osviashcheniia ikony Presviatoi Bogoroditsy," in *Trebnik*, 57. This translation taken from *The Blessing of Ikons*, 13.

110. For the symbolism of the altar table, see "O sviatom altare," *RSP* 30 (1861): 327–28. For the story of this icon, see *Slava Bogomateri*, 526–27.

111. As examples, see RGIA, f. 796, op. 159, d. 1856 (Pskov, 1878); op. 175, d. 1279 (Viatka, 1894); op. 177, 2 ot., 2 st., d. 1629 (Chernigov, 1896); op. 187, d. 7006 (Smolensk, 1906). Such constructions were also made without any formal permission. See RGIA, op. 150, d. 1377 (Nizhnii Novgorod, 1869); op. 183, d. 1539 (Simbirsk, 1902); op. 189, d. 7370 (Ufa, 1908).

112. *Kaluzhskaia Kazanskaia ikona Bozhiei Materi*, 5.

113. "Anamnesis" is a Greek word meaning "recalling to mind." It expresses the Semitic idea (*Kahor*) by which an act of God "in being recalled comes to life in a certain way." See Michael O'Carroll, *Corpus Christi: An Encyclopedia of the Eucharist* (Collegeville, MN: Liturgical Press, 1988), 12–14. For the Semitic roots of this notion, see Brevard S. Childs, *Memory and Tradition in Israel* (London: SCM Press, 1962). For historians' adapta-

tion of this concept with respect to "memory" and "history," see, for example, Iwona Irwin-Zarecka, *Frames of Remembrance: The Dynamics of Collective Memory* (New Brunswick, NJ: Transaction Publishers, 1994). Christian use of this concept with respect to the Eucharist is the subject of numerous studies. For overviews, see F. Chenderlin, *Do This as My Memorial*, Analecta Biblica 99 (Rome: Biblical Institute Press, 1982); Richard J. Ginn, *The Present and the Past: A Study of Anamnesis*, Princeton Theological Monograph Series 20 (Allison Park, PA: Pickwick, 1989); Max Thurian, *The Eucharistic Memorial*, 2 vols. (Richmond, VA: John Knox Press, 1960–1961). In a certain sense, liturgical rituals connected with specially revered icons can be compared to those rituals involved in the eucharistic Liturgy, insofar as the former also call to remembrance key events in sacred history and play a major role in forming personal and corporate religious identity.

114. Lavrskii, "Slovo v den' otbytiia Oranskoi ikony Bozhiei Materi," in *Poucheniia* 377.

115. Vorontsov, *Pouchenie na 26-e iiunia*, 5.

116. Some of the better known specially revered icons of the Mother of God during this period include the Kozelshchina icon of the Mother of God mentioned earlier; the icon of the Mother of God named "the Sign" located in the St. Serafim Ponetaev convent in the Nizhnii Novgorod diocese; the Port Arthur icon of the Mother of God; the icon of the Mother of God named "Joy of All Who Sorrow" in St. Petersburg; the Mother of God named "She Who Reigns"; and the Mother of God named "Multiplier of Grains."

117. "Opisanie tserkvi Voskreseniia Khristova," *VEV* (chast' neoffitsial'naia) 7 (1897): 127–28.

118. Believers frequently desired such a sanction in order to offer their icon what they considered to be due honor. It seems that members of the Holy Synod preferred that processions and special ceremonies in honor of icons be carried out only for those icons that manifested a miracle-working power. RGIA, f. 796, op. 156, d. 425 (Nizhnii Novgorod, 1875); op. 187, chast' 2, d. 6985 (Kharkov, 1906).

119. For examples of ecclesiastical officials directing that an icon remain in the altar area of a parish church, see RGIA, op. 169, d. 1513 (Riazan, 1888); op. 171, d. 1473 (Kaluga, 1890); op. 203, 6 ot., 3 st., d. 86 (Tavrida, 1916). GAVO, f. 1063, op. 102, d. 13, ll. 10–12 ob.

120. RGIA, f. 796, op. 157, d. 146, l. 4 (Kostroma, 1876); op. 160, d. 1764 (Simbirsk, 1879).

121. RGIA, f. 796, op. 160, d. 1764, l. 13 (Simbirsk, 1874). According to Peter the Great's *Spiritual Regulation*, priests, deacons, and other clergy were not to perform prayer services at places reputed to be miracle working that had not been officially recognized as such. See Malevinskii, *Instruktsiia blagochinnomu*, 181–82.

122. RGIA, f. 796, op. 160, d. 1766.

123. RGIA, f. 796, op. 157, d. 157, l. 18.

124. RGIA, f. 796, op. 143, d. 1288. For other examples of higher church officials reprimanding or transferring parish priests for similar reasons, see op. 154, d. 554 (Tavrida, 1873); op. 155, d. 635 (Tula, 1874); op. 160, d. 1764 (Simbirsk, 1879); op. 174, d. 1692 (Viatka, 1893); op. 181, d. 2558 (Orel, 1900); op. 187, chast' 2, d. 6944 (Kursk, 1906); op. 195, d. 1436 (Eniseisk, 1912).

125. For insights into some of these processes for an earlier period but with a somewhat different interpretation, see Freeze, "Institutionalizing Piety." Regarding attitudes toward the special veneration of icons as superstitious, see RGIA, f. 796, op. 160, d. 1764 (Simbirsk, 1879); op. 161, d. 1467 (Kostroma, 1880); op. 169, d. 1513, l. 7 (Riazan, 1888); op. 174, d. 1692, l. 19 ob. (Viatka, 1893); op. 187, chast' 2, d. 6944, l. 13 (Kursk, 1906). For

examples of cases where ecclesiastical officials suspected profiteering, see RGIA, op. 167, d. 1444, l. 7 (Kherson, 1886); op. 177, d. 2423, l. 1 (Kaluga, 1896); op. 187, chast' 2, d. 7389, l. 2 (Vologda, 1906); op. 190, 6 ot., 3 st., d. 102 (Vladimir, 1909). Diocesan officials suspected and charged not only laity but parish clergy as well with having financial motives for keeping such icons. See, for example, RGIA, op. 154, d. 553 (Tavrida, 1873); op. 174, d. 1714, l. 11 (Perm, 1893); op. 186, chast' 2, d. 6944 (Kursk, 1906); op. 190, 6 ot., 3 st., d. 145, l. 11 (Poltava, 1909).

126. *PSPR*, ser. 1, vol. 2, 1722, no. 423 (St. Petersburg, 1879), 65. Malevinskii, *Instruktsiia blagochinnomu*, 10. For a description of the legislation, see Cracraft, *The Church Reform*, 211–31; 291.

127. This argument was common among clergy who removed reportedly miracle-working icons from private homes to parish churches. RGIA, f. 796, op. 145, d. 604, l. 1 (Vladimir, 1864).

128. RGIA, f. 796, op. 143, d. 2239. For a continuation of this case some twenty years later, see RGIA, op. 167, d. 1490.

129. RGIA, op. 153, d. 661. For other examples where diocesan or synodal authorities directed icons to be removed from private homes, see RGIA, op. 151, d. 710 (Moscow, 1870); op. 156, d. 458 (Orel, 1875); op. 161, d. 1467 (Kostroma, 1880); op. 174, d. 1714 (Perm, 1893); op. 181, d. 2581 (Orel, 1900); op. 183. d. 2580 (Simbirsk, 1902); op. 190, 6 ot., 3 st., d. 102 (Vladimir, 1909).

130. Kalashnikov, *Alfavitnyi ukazatel'*, 166; Malevinskii, *Instruktsiia nastoiateliam*, 98.

131. RGIA, f. 796, op. 143, d. 1288.

132. RGIA, f. 796, op. 157, d. 157, ll. 9–31. For other examples where diocesan or synodal authorities issued directives to remove icons from parish churches, see RGIA, op. 151, d. 662 (Kursk, 1870); op. 157, d. 146 (Kostroma, 1876); op. 159, d. 1786 (Moscow, 1878); op. 160, d. 1753 (Tambov, 1879); op. 168, d. 1439 (Kursk, 1887); op. 181, d. 2558 (Orel, 1900); op. 175, d. 1939 (Poltava, 1894); op. 187, chast' 2, d. 7469 (Chernigov, 1906); f. 797, op. 80, 2 ot., 3 st., d. 200 (Perm, 1910).

133. RGIA, f. 796, op. 180, d. 2972, l. 20.

134. RGIA, f. 796, op. 185, d. 2917. Similarly, in 1894, when their icon of St. Barbara was taken away from their parish church, believers from the village of Igny in the Chernigov diocese claimed that by this action, "in the eyes of the people" the icon was seen as not genuinely miracle working. RGIA, op. 175, d. 1824, l. 2.

135. RGIA, f. 796, op. 182, d. 2513, l. 2.

136. RGIA, f. 796, op. 169, d. 1513, l. 7; op. 187, chast' 2, d. 6944 (Kursk, 1906).

137. RGIA, f. 796, op. 166, d. 1468.

138. RGIA, f. 796, op. 168, d. 1439, l. 13 ob.; 156.

139. RGIA, f. 796, op. 176, d. 2137.

140. RGIA, f. 796, op. 188, d. 7630.

141. RGIA, f. 796, op. 195, d. 1436, l. 17. Also see the 1907 comments by the members of the Tula city duma when their special veneration of an icon was questioned by consistory officials. RGIA, op. 188, d. 7630, l. 5.

142. RGIA, f. 796, op. 175, d. 1824 (Chernigov, 1894).

143. RGIA, f. 796, op. 177, d. 2357, l. 1.

144. Diocesan officals dismissed the letter since police could locate no such person living in the city. RGIA, f. 796, op. 201, 6 ot., 3 st., d. 87, l. 3 (Poltava, 1915). For examples of bitter complaints about procedural issues, see RGIA, op. 151, d. 662 (Kursk, 1870); op. 168, d. 1439, l. 144 ob. (Kursk, 1887); p. 169, d. 1512 (Volhynia, 1888); op.

175, d. 1824, l. 42 (Chernigov, 1894); op. 183, d. 2580, l. 2 (Simbirsk, 1902); op. 190, 6 ot., 3 st., d. 102 (Vladimir, 1909).

145. See, for example, RGIA, f. 796, op. 143, d. 2239, l. 21 (Perm, 1862).

146. See the comments by the metropolitan of Kiev, Flavian, in 1909 in RGIA, f. 796, op. 190, 6 ot., 3 st., d. 312, l. 5, as well as by the protopresbyter Popov in op. 143, d. 2239, l. 21 (Perm, 1862).

147. RGIA, f. 796, op. 143, d. 2239, l. 39 (Perm, 1862); op. 171, d. 1586, l. 20 (Tver, 1890); op. 174, d. 1692, l. 19 ob. (Viatka, 1893).

148. RGIA, f. 796. op. 177, d. 2423.

149. RGIA. f. 796, op. 199, d. 175. It was common for the descendants of the person from whom an icon was taken to continue petitioning for its return. See, for example, RGIA, op. 161, d. 1467 (Kostroma, 1880); op. 182, d. 2513 (Vladimir, 1901).

150. RGIA, f. 796, op. 183, d. 2580.

151. RGIA, f. 796, op. 185, 3 ot., 2 st., d. 2925.

152. RGIA, f. 796, op. 185, d. 3031.

153. RGIA, f. 796, op. 190, 6 ot., 3 st., d. 72.

154. RGIA, f. 796, op. 171, d. 1473.

155. RGIA, f. 796, op. 187, chast' 2, d. 6944, l. 13 (Kursk, 1906). For other cases when believers used this argument to request the return of an icon, see RGIA, op. 141, d. 25 (Kiev, 1860); op. 167, d. 1490 (Perm, 1886); op. 185, 3 ot., 2 st., d. 3043 (Nizhnii Novgorod, 1904).

156. RGIA, f. 796, op. 190, 6 ot., 3 st., d. 64 (Ufa, 1909); for a similar case, see RGIA, op. 188, 6 ot., 1 st., ll. 7–8 (Kharkov, 1907).

157. RGIA, f. 796, op. 176, d. 2220.

158. RGIA, f. 831, op. 1, d. 78. It is important to note that varying understandings of ownership with respect to specially venerated icons led to tensions not only between laity and ecclesiastical officials but also between local communities. Icons in such cases often divided rather than unified local parish communities. See, as examples, RGIA, f. 796, op. 144, d. 1962 (Vladimir, 1863); op. 155, d. 624 (Vladimir, 1874); op. 157, d. 147 (Kazan, 1876); op. 166, d. 1439 (Penza, 1885); op. 190, 6 ot., 3 st., d, 72 (Perm, 1909).

159. Such legal questioning of diocesan and synodal policies with regard to icon confiscation was characteristic of petitions involving more educated believers even prior to 1905.

160. RGIA, f. 796, op. 187, chast' 2, d. 7390, ll. 1–1 ob.

161. RGIA, f. 796, op. 190, 6 ot., 3 st., d. 145, l. 4.

162. RGIA, f. 796, op. 190, 6 ot., 3 st., d. 230. Such threats did occur earlier. In 1890, peasants from the Kaluga diocese threatened to take diocesan officials to civil court to decide the issue of an icon's "ownership." RGIA, op. 171, d. 1473, ll. 8–9.

163. RGIA, f. 796, op. 187, chast' 2, d. 7469.

164. RGIA, f. 796, op. 188, 6 ot., 3 st., d. 7713, l. 1.

165. RGIA, f. 796, op. 189, d. 7370, l. 3.

166. See, for example, RGIA, f. 796, op. 141, d. 1240, l. 5 (Smolensk, 1860); op. 169, d. 1512, l. 7 (Poltava, 1888); op. 182, d. 2513, l. 7 (Vladimir, 1901); op. 184, d. 2917, l. 2 (Kherson, 1903).

167. See, for example, f. 796, op. 184, d. 2917 (Kherson, 1903). Believers were aware of the fate of other specially venerated icons. op. 167, d. 1490, l. 4 (Perm, 1886); op. 168, d. 1466, l. 7 (Poltava, 1887).

168. RGIA, f. 796, op. 175, d. 2002. Similarly, in 1895, the bishop of Tavrida also

noted that reportedly self-renewed icons were commonplace in his diocese. RGIA, f. 796, op. 177, d. 2357, l. 16.

169. RGIA, f. 796, op. 189, 6 ot., 1 st., d. 8148. For similar sentiments expressed by the Holy Synod in 1904, see RGIA, op. 185, d. 3034, l. 23.

170. RGIA, f. 796, op. 178, d. 2677.

171. RGIA, f. 796, op. 190, 6 ot., 3 st., d. 69.

172. RGIA, f. 796, op. 190, 6 ot., 3 st., d. 251.

173. RGIA, f. 796, op. 193, d. 1895, l. 17.

174. For an example of such a report in a newspaper, see RGIA, f. 796, op. 167, d. 1490, l. 5 (Perm, 1886).

175. RGIA, f. 796, op. 195, d. 1436, l. 172. Also see op. 203, 6 ot., 3 st., d. 157 (Penza, 1916) where an icon was returned after more than fifty years.

176. This is a common reading of similar dynamics in western European countries. See, for example, Tackett, *Priest and Parish*, 209–15.

177. *Mysli i chuvstva*, 4. Also see *Chudesnoe spasenie ikony*; Denisov, *Chudo 8 marta*.

178. RGIA, f. 796, op. 180, 2 st., 3 ot., d. 2943. See similar dynamics in the case regarding the Kaluzka icon of the Mother of God in RGIA, op. 178, d. 2718.

179. RGIA, f. 796, op. 156, d. 458. Only in 1918, after tirelessly petitioning the diocesan bishop, parishioners from this church won the right to move the icon into the church's vestibule, to conduct prayer services before it, and to carry it to peoples' homes for blessings. When petitioning to have their icon placed in the church's nave, the parishioners from this cemetery church noted that since the icon was located in the vestry, men could venerate it but women could not. RGIA, f. 831, op. 1, d. 78, ll. ll–13. For another example of such divisions between local diocesan and synodal officials, see RGIA, f.796, op. 160, d. 1796 (Novgorod, 1879).

180. RGIA, f. 796, op. 144, d. 187. For similar examples, see op. 165, d. 1633 (Vladimir, 1884); op. 169, d. 1410 (Tambov, 1888); op. 169, d. 1513 (Riazan, 1888); op. 174, d. 1692 (Viatka, 1893); op. 174, d. 1780 (Kazan, 1893); op. 175, d. 1904 (Kursk, 1894); op. 180, d. 2938 (Voronezh, 1899); op. 187, chast' 2, d. 6971 (Smolensk, 1906); op. 190, 6 ot., 3 st., d. 310 (Penza, 1909). In some cases, an icon was allowed to remain in a parish as long as the icon was kept out of sight and the priest did not honor the icon as if it were miracle working.

181. RGIA, f. 796, op. 151, d. 609.

182. RGIA, f. 796, op. 165, d. 1633.

183. RGIA, f. 796, op. 178, d. 2671.

184. RGIA, f. 796, op. 142, d. 1151 (Novgorod, 1861); op. 146, d. 1159 (Orenburg, 1865).

185. RGIA, f. 796, op. 195, d. 1436, l. 5.

186. For a somewhat different evaluation, see Worobec, *Possessed*, 55.

187. Sergii, episkop Kurskii, "Po povodu popytok k proslavleniiu ikony," *DCh* 10 (October 1876): 219–22.

188. RGIA, f. 796, op. 143, d. 632.

189. RGIA, f. 796, op. 201, 6 ot., 3 st., d. 298, l. 14.

190. RGIA, f. 796, op. 187, chast' 2, d. 7007, ll. 7–8 (Tver, 1906). For similar accounts, see op. 185, d. 3034, l. 2 (Kherson, 1902); op. 190, 6 ot., 3 st., d. 291 (Vologda, 1909). For a lengthy discussion of this point by a group of believers from the Kharkov diocese, see RGIA, op. 188, 6 ot., 1 st., d. 7666.

191. RGIA, f. 796, op. 190, 6 ot., 3 st., d. 91.

192. RGIA, f. 796, op. 160, d. 1796 (Novgorod, 1879); op. 168, d. 1466 (Poltava,

1887); op. 169, d. 1513, (Riazan, 1888); op. 171, d. 1473 (Kaluga, 1890); op. 171, d. 1586 (Tver, 1890); op. 182, d. 2513 (Vladimir, 1901); op. 187, chast' 2 d. 7390 (Kaluga, 1906); op. 190, 6 ot., 3 st., d. 201 (Vologda, 1909); op. 195, d. 1547 (Vladimir, 1912). Note that icons housed in monastery and cathedral churches routinely visited the place where they originally had appeared at the demand of the believers who lived in that locality.

193. RGIA, f. 796, op. 187, chast' 2, d. 7007, l. 8 (Tver, 1906). While cases that involved self-renewed icons in private homes were complicated by the issues of personal property mentioned earlier, believers in these cases were also influenced by the notion that an icon should remain in the place where it had revealed its special signs. For example, in 1911 the peasant woman Martha Vorsina and her two sons from the Olonets diocese objected to their icon being taken from their home to the local parish church. They petitioned the Holy Synod for the icon to remain in their home because they did not "desire to disturb the holy icon from the place where it manifested its miracle-working activity," though they were willing to construct a chapel in its honor in their village. RGIA, op. 193, d. 1800.

194. It is noteworthy that even in 1918 some persons held the view that miracles could only be assumed when they were so recognized by the hierarchs of the Orthodox Church. See, for example, *Polnoe opisanie tainstvennykh iavlenii u Nikol'skikh vorot* (Moscow, 1918).

195. RGIA, f. 796, op. 181, d. 2504.

196. RGIA, f. 796, op. 181, d. 2580.

197. Peter Brown, "The Rise and Function of the Holy Man in Late Roman Society," *Journal of Roman Studies* 71 (1971): 80–101.

198. The following is a summary of the case that appears in RGIA, f. 796, op. 203, d. 155.

199. Poselianin, *Bogomater'*, 667–68.

200. RGIA, f. 796, op. 203, d. 155, l. 6; "Opredelenie Sv. Sinoda ot 17–21 iiulia 1896," *TsVed* 30 (1896): 308. This case reflects the ambiguity of the term "official" when applied to specially revered icons. This icon was included in the catalogue of "miracle-working" and "locally revered" icons of the Mother of God published by the Holy Synod in 1907. See *Slava Bogomateri*, 112. At the same time, as late as 1918, the abbess of the women's monastic community founded by Ambrose near Optina Pustyn' was still petitioning the Holy Synod for permission to make copies of this icon and to openly celebrate it on 15 October. RGIA, f. 831, op. 1, d. 78, l. 109.

201. RGIA, f. 796, op. 203, d. 155, l. 11. Although the subject matter of the icon made it especially popular among peasants, who saw in this icon the Mother of God as a helper to and protectress of those whose livelihood depended on agricultural labor, it was also known among educated circles. Note Pavel Florenskii's reference to this image in *Iconostasis*, 87–88.

202. RGIA, f. 796, op. 203, d. 155, l. 4. Very probably, Novoselov had either heard or read about the movement to call a general church council at the time and had heard the term *sobornost'* used along the way. Novoselov, however, appeared to use the term *sobor veruiushchikh* to refer solely to a group of lay believers, as opposed to a group of early bishops and other clergy, which a traditional council included.

203. RGIA, f. 796, op. 203, d. 155, ll. 10–11.

204. GARF, f. 3431, d. 288, ll. 29–30.

205. Kselman, *Miracles and Prophecies*, 190–200.

206. Freeze, "Subversive Piety," 317–18, 329–30.

207. See the evidence found in Freeze, "Institutionalizing Piety," 228–30.

208. RGIA, f. 833, op. 1, d. 15, ll. 87–89.

## CHAPTER 6

1. *Skazaniia o zemnoi zhizni presviatoi Bogoroditsy*, 253.

2. For the idea of "Mary" as a collective noun, see Elizabeth A. Johnson, "Toward a Theology of Mary: Past, Present, Future," 7, 14, in Eigo, *All Generations*.

3. Sergii (Spasskii), *Russkaia literatura*. For a discussion of miracle-working icons of Mary prior to the eighteenth century, see Ebbinghaus, *Die altrussischen Marienikonen-Legenden*.

4. For examples of such nineteenth-century collections of stories of icons of the Mother of God, see Grigorii Sveshnikov, *Opisanie iavlenii chudotvornykh ikon Presviatyia Bogoroditsy s pokazaniem vremeni, kogda onyia sluchilis', i mest, gde sii sviatyia ikony nakhodiat-sia, v kakiia chisla byvaet prazdnestvo im, i po kakomu sluchaiu onoe ustanovleno* (Moscow, 1838); P. Kazanskii, *Velichie Presviatoi Bogoroditsy i Prisnodevy Marii* (Moscow, 1845); *Slava Presviatyia Vladychetsy nasheia Bogoroditsy i Prisnodevy Marii* (Moscow, 1853); Snessoreva, *Zemnaia zhizn'; Blagodeianiia Bogomateri*; Poselianin, *Bogomater'*.

5. For examples of the important role played by oral histories in compiling these lives, see Legatov, *Istoricheskii ocherk*, 8–9; Sofiiskii, *Istoriia chudotvornoi ikony; O chudotvornoi ikone Bogoliubskoi*; Zagorskii, *Pogost Liubiatovo*, 8; *Skazanie ob ikone Tabynskoi*, 16; *Sviataia ikona Vladimirskoi*, 2, 28. For authors' accounts of the wide variety of sources they used to compose an icon's history or "life," see Arkhimandrit Nestor, *Skazanie o chudotvornoi Domnitskoi ikone Bogomateri*, 15; *Skazanie o iavlenii i chudesakh ikony Bozhiei Materi Kaluzh-enskoi*.

6. Speranskii, *Skazanie o chudotvornoi Tikhvinskoi ikone*, 4.

7. Nikodim, *Kaluzhskaia Kazanskaia ikona*, 6, 37.

8. For a brief profile of apparitions of the Virgin Mary in Catholic Europe, see Blackbourn, *Marpingen*, 17–18.

9. *Skazanie o iavlenii chudotvornoi ikony Presviatyia Bogoroditsy imenuemoi Tolgskoiu*.

10. "A. I.," *Blagodatnaia mater'*, 8. It should be pointed out, however, that even in the nineteenth century, children were not more favored than adults in Russia's icon stories.

11. Turner and Turner, *Image and Pilgrimage*, 213.

12. Limberis, *Divine Heiress*, 89–90. Also see Shevzov, "Poeticizing Piety." It is note-worthy that except for a single *akathistos* in honor of the icon of Christ "Not-Made-By-Hands," only icons of Mary had *akathistoi* written in their honor. All other *akathistoi*, including those to St. Nicholas, were written in honor of the saint.

13. Popov, *Pravoslavnye russkie akafisty*. *Akathistoi* in honor of more than twenty other iconographic types had been composed and submitted to the Holy Synod but were not approved. Approved *akathistoi* were submitted for publication not only by abbots and abbesses of monastic communities but by priests, deacons, and civil servants. Many of these texts were written by Andrei Feodorovich Kovalevskii (d. 1901), the author of more than twenty published *akathistoi*. Kovalevskii was a landowner from the Kharkov diocese who had established a monastic community on his estate. See Graf G. Miloradovich, "Slagatel' akafistov. A. F. Kovalevskii," *Russkii arkhiv* 4 (1902): 740–41.

14. See, for example, Dimitrii, *Mesiatseslov sviatykh*.

15. *Khristianskii Mesiatseslov*, 450–51.

16. *Slava Bogomateri*.

17. The liturgical Menaion published by the Holy Synod at the end of the nineteenth century and beginning of the twentieth century contained services and hymns to only eight icons of the Mother of God. Services for many other icons existed on the local level,

especially in monastic communities where such icons were housed. The multivolume liturgical Menaion published by the Russian Orthodox Church in the twentieth century (1978–88) incorporated some of these locally composed services and hymns. It lists services or hymns for over seventy icons of the Mother of God.

18. Florenskii, *The Pillar and Ground of the Truth*, 265.

19. *Uchenie Pravoslavnoi tserkvi*, 21–23; Sergii, *Pokhvala Presviatoi Deve Bogoroditse*, 86; 5.

20. For descriptions of Mary's outer appearance and "interior image," see Iustin, *Poucheniia*, 80–86; Mikhailovskii, *Privetstvie presviatoi deve Marii*.

21. "Slovo v den' prazdnestva chudotvornoi ikone Vladimirskoi Bozhiei Materi," in *S tserkovnago amvona*, 605–8.

22. Kassirov, *Plach*, 20, 60.

23. Warner, *Alone of All Her Sex*.

24. *Chudesnoe iavlenie Bozhiei Materi; Zhitie startsa Serafima*, 25.

25. *Mysli i chuvstva*, 4.

26. Lebedev, *Raznosti tserkvei*.

27. Metropolitan Sergii (Stragorodskii), "Pouchenie Bozhiei Materi po razumu Sviatoi Pravoslavnoi tserkvi," in Chuliukina and Rauch, *Tysiacheletie pochitaniia*, 1–6.

28. Filaret (Drozdov), *Slava Bogomateri*, 98; 110. A vivid exception to the spiritual reading of virginity was the essay by Ignatii Brianchaninov, *Izlozhenie ucheniia pravoslavnoi tserkvi o Bozhiei Materi* (Iaroslavl, 1869).

29. Poselianin, *V pokhvalu Bogoroditse*, 48.

30. Rudnev, *Skazanie o sv. ikone*, 14; "Bud' milostiv sam chtoby poluchit' milost' Bozhiiu," in *Mater' miloserdiia*, 35–37.

31. Arsenii (Chagovets), *O pochitanii Bozhiei Materi*, 6.

32. "Povestvovanie o polednikh dniakh zhitiia i ob uspenii Presviatoi Vladychitsy nashei Bogoroditsy i Prisnodevy Marii," in *Vo slavu Bozhiei Materi*, 9.

33. Poselianin, *V pokhvalu Bogoroditse*, 6; *Vo slavu Bozhiei Materi*, 6–10.

34. Glinka, *Zhizn' Presviatoi Devy Bogoroditsy*, 137–38.

35. As an example, see the service in honor of the Kozelshchina icon of the Mother of God in *Mineia: fevral'* (Moscow: Izdanie Moskovskoi Patriarkhii, 1981), 648, 654.

36. For the story of the feast of the Pokrov, celebrated on 1 October, see Bulgakov, *Nastol'naia Kniga*, 492–93. For the main prayers for this feast, see *Polnyi sbornik molitv*, 58–59.

37. Authors periodically stressed that although it was "meet and right" to give Mary her due honor, it was important to remember that the honor believers give to Mary relates to God himself, since all of the gifts and graces from "above" come from the "Father of Lights" and that all of Mary's glory is only a reflection of the glory of her divine Son. See *Beseda o Presviatoi Bogoroditse* (St. Petersburg, 1901), 9.

38. Solov'ev, *Sviataia ikona Bozhiei Materi*, 3–4.

39. Sergii, *Pokhvala Presviatoi Deve Bogoroditse*, 47, 53.

40. Iustin, *Poucheniia*, 90.

41. *Beseda o Presviatoi Bogoroditse*, 16.

42. D. Samarin, "Bogoroditsa v russkom narodnom pravoslavii," *Russkaia mysl'*, 3–4 (1918): 1–38. For similar sentiments, see N. Berdiaev, *Dusha Rossii* (1915; reprint, Leningrad: Skaz, 1990), 10.

43. Kselman, *Miracles and Prophecies*, 90–94.

44. *Se stoiu u dveri i stuchu*.

45. Note that Joseph was frequently portrayed not as Mary's husband but as her guardian since her youth.

46. *Userdnaia za vsekh zastupnitsa* (St. Petersburg, 1886); Sergii, *Pokhvala Presviatoi Bogoroditse*, 4; *Mater' miloserdiia*, 10.

47. Numerous icons of Mary in both Eastern and Western Christianity were attributed to the brush of the evangelist Luke, in part because the gospel text attributed to him provided the most detailed description of Mary. For discussion of this tradition, see Belting, *Likeness and Presence*, 47–59. One such image in Russia was the Vladimir icon of the Mother of God, which is the reason this story is liturgically remembered during its celebration. For examples of other devotional pamphlets relating to this story, see Sidonskii, *Chudotvornaia ikona; Skazanie ob ikone Iugskoi Bozhiei Materi (Odigitrii)* (St. Petersburg, 1905). This event was also recounted liturgically during services in honor of certain icons of the Mother of God. As examples, see the service in honor of the "Meeting of the Miracle-Working Icon of the Mother of God named 'Vladimir' " celebrated on 21 May, *Miniia: mesiats mai* (1893; reprint, Moscow: "Pravilo very," 1996), 344, and the service in honor of the Kazan icon of the Mother of God on 8 July, *Miniia: mesiats iiul'* (1893; reprint, Moscow: "Pravilo very," 1996), 155.

48. Korobovskii, *Skazanie o sv. ikone*, 31; Poselianin, *V pokhvalu Bogoroditse*, 28–30.

49. Sv. V. Sokolov, *Slovo v den' sreteniia Smolenskoi ikony Bozhiei Materi* (Kazan, 1892), 4.

50. Vorontsov, *Pouchenie na 26-e iiunia 1908*, 4.

51. Doronikin, *O Tikhvinskoi chudotvornoi ikone*, 1; Sidonskii, *Chudotvornaia ikona*, 1.

52. GAVO, f. 1063, op. 57, d. 32, l. 22 ob. (Vologda, Letopis' Nikolaevskoi Valushinskoi tserkvi); RGIA, op. 190, 6 ot., 3 st., d. 158, l. 12. Sermons on the occasion of icon visitations frequently referred to the specially venerated icon as a "guest." See, for example, "Pouchenie po sluchaiu prineseniia Oranskoi chudotvornoi ikony Bozhiei Materi," in Bogoroditskii, *Golos sel'skago pastyria 12*; Komarov, *Slovo v den' Preobrazheniia*, 1; *Skazanie ob ikone Tabynskoi*, 19.

53. *Vo slavu Bozhiei Materi*, 20.

54. *Novoproslavlennaia chudotvornaia ikona*, 13.

55. Ibid., 40.

56. *Slava Bogomateri*, 437–38.

57. As examples, see the discussion in Svetlov, *Prorocheskie ili veshchie sny*, 144–51; Kurdinovskii, *O snovideniiakh*.

58. Kurdinovskii, *O snovideniiakh*, 4–9, 28–30; *Veshchie sny* (St. Petersburg, 1897).

59. "Mozhno li verit' vsiakomu snu?" *Troitskie listki*, 87 (1888).

60. "Mozhno li verit' vsiakomu snu?"; "Snovideniia," in D'iachenko, *Propovednicheskaia entsiklopediia*, 646–47.

61. Izrailev, *Chudotvornaia Pecherskaia ikona; Skazanie o chudesnykh istseleniiakh*. Also see the story of the Chernigov-Il'inskaia icon of the Mother of God housed in the Smolnyi cathedral in St. Petersburg in Nikiforovskii, *Chernigovskaia Il'inskaia ikona*.

62. Tul'tseva, *Traditsionnye verovaniia*, 13. Note that scholars have also spoken about the Marian phenomenon in the West in similar terms. See Carroll, *Madonnas that Maim*, 59.

63. *Tsaritsa stradaniia* (St. Petersburg, 1913).

64. Florensky, *The Pillar and Ground of the Truth*, 267.

65. Solov'ev, *Sviataia ikona Bozhiei Materi imenuemaia Abalatskoiu*, 11.

66. *Mineia: fevral'* (Moscow: Izdanie Moskovskoi Patriarkhii, 1981), 644.

67. Arkhimandrit Antonii, "Slovo v den' iavleniia Tikhvinskoi ikony Presviatoi Bogoroditsy," in *S tserkovnago amvona*, 609–16.

68. For example, see the service in honor of the Kozelshchina icon of the Mother of God, *Mineia: fevral'* (Moscow: Izdanie Moskovskoi Patriankhii, 1981), 650; Service in

honor of the Kazan icon of the Mother of God, *Miniia: mesiats iiul'* (1893; reprint, Moscow: "Pravilo very," 1996), 155.

69. *Slava Bogomateri*, 541.

70. *The Paterik of the Kievan Caves Monastery*, trans. Muriel Heppell (Cambridge, MA: Harvard University Press, 1989), 192–93.

71. Nefed'ev, *Sviashchennaia byl'*, 27, 32.

72. Bogoslovskii, *Skazanie o iavlennoi i chudotvornoi ikone Uspenie.*

73. *Skazanie o iavlenii ikony Presviatyia Bogoroditsy, imenuemyia Feodorovskaia, nakho-diashcheisia v Syzranskom, Voznesenskom muzhskom monastyre* (Moscow, 1871), 3.

74. *Slava Bogomateri*, 38–40. Stromilov, "*Rozhdestvo presviatoi Bogoroditsy.*"

75. As an example, see the story of the Vladimir icon of the Mother of God in the Ordyn pustyn' in the Smolensk diocese. *Slava Bogomateri*, 392–93.

76. Dashkevich, *Kratkoe opisanie.*

77. Ramenskii, *Skazanie o iavlennoi i chudotvornoi sv. Ikone Pokrova.*

78. *Iavlenie i chudesa Smolenskoi ikony Bozhiei Materi nazyvaemoi Igritskoi* (Kostroma, 1892). The role of Mary in the founding of monastic communities can be seen in iconic representations found in Kostsova and Pobedinskaia, *Russkie ikony.*

79. *Slava Bogomateri*, 388–89.

80. *Slava Bogomateri*, 15. For a similar linking of an icon with the capture of an arsonist, see the nineteenth-century story of a Tikhvin icon of the Mother of God in the town of Dankov in the Riazan diocese in *Slava Bogomateri*, 439–40.

81. *Slava Bogomateri*, 472.

82. V. S. Ikonnikov, *Opyt russkoi istoriografii*, vol. 1, book 1 (Kiev, 1891), 212.

83. *Slava Bogomateri*, 344–48.

84. See, for example, hymns in honor of the Kozelshchina icon of the Mother of God, *Mineia: fevral'* (Moscow: Izdanie Moskovskoi Patriarkhii, 1981), 646; the icon of the Mother of God named "Life-Giving Source," *Mineia: aprel'*, pt. 2, (Moscow: Izdanie Moskovskoi Patriarkhii, 1985), 315.

85. Quoted in *Opisanie chudotvornoi ikony Starorusskoi*, 40.

86. See the kontakion in honor of the icon of the Mother of God named "Life-Giving Source" in *Mineia: aprel'* (Moscow: Izdanie Moskovskoi Patriarkhii, 1985), 315.

87. *Mater' miloserdiia*, 40.

88. *Slava Bogomateri*, 127–28; Tokmakov, *Istoricheskiia svedeniia*, 13–14.

89. For examples of similar healing stories, see the "Three-Handed" icon of the Mother of God in the church of St. Vladimir in the Tula diocese in *Slava Bogomateri*, 454–55; the Kazan icon of the Mother of God in the Simonov monastery in Moscow, *O Kazanskoi chudotvornoi ikone Bozhiei Materi v Moskovskom Simonovskom monastyre* (Moscow, 1887); Rozanov, *Svedeniia ob ikone.*

90. *Slava Bogomateri*, 505.

91. *Slava Bogomateri*, 372.

92. *Slava Bogomateri*, 423–24.

93. Rozanov, *Svedeniia ob ikone.*

94. See, for example, the story of the icon of the Mother of God named "The Joy of All Who Sorrow" located in the village of Ivanovo in the Moscow diocese mentioned earlier. *Slava Bogomateri*, 127–28.

95. For a similar observation for the Byzantine experience, see Robin Cormack, "Reading Icons," *Valor: Konstvetenskaplig Studier* 4 (1991): 13–14.

96. See the "Patriarchal" icon of the Mother of God from the Pustyn' monastery in the Mogilev diocese in *Slava Bogomateri*, 578.

97. *Skazanie ob ikone Bozhiei Materi 'Vzyskanie pogibshikh'; Skazanie o chudotvornoi ikone Bogomateri, imenuemoi Chernigovskaia.*

98. *Skazanie o iavlenii i chudesakh ikony Bozhiei Materi Kaluzhenskoi.* Also see the story of the Cyprus icon of the Mother of God in the village of Stromyn' (Moscow diocese), *Slava Bogomateri,* 361–63.

99. Poselianin, *Bogomater',* 261.

100. *Istoriia iavleniia Akhtyrskoi chudotvornoi ikony; Skazanie o Kaplunovskoi chudotvornoi ikone.*

101. I hesitate to conclude that the gradual rise in the number of icon stories having to do with women from the fifteenth century on represents a "feminization" of modern Orthodox Christianity. First, it would be unjustified to draw such a conclusion, given that it is difficult to determine the extent to which Orthodoxy was rooted in the population of Russia before that time. It would be more accurate to judge this situation against the Marian cult in Byzantium, the origins of which already point to a strong feminine presence, albeit in the imperial court. See the study by Limberis, *Divine Heiress.*

102. *Ikona Bozhiei Materi 'Tuchnaia Gora'* (Tver, 1888). Note that the title "Fertile Mountain" has biblical origins and can be found in Ps. 67:14. The ethnographer N. Matorin, who conducted his work in the early Soviet period, maintained that the name of the icon had little to do with prayers but was associated with a hill in Tver to which, according to legend, people would bring their belongings during times of flood. Matorin, *Zhenskoe bozhestvo,* 31.

103. *Ikona Bozhiei Materi 'Trekh Radostei'* (Moscow, 1907).

104. Benediktov, *Chudotvornaia ikona Kazanskoi Bozhiei Materi.*

105. V. Nikol'skii, *Korsunskaia ikona.* It is important to point out, however, that in terms of ailing children, the prayers of fathers were equally stressed and rewarded in "lives" of Marian icons. See, as examples, *Novoe miloserdie Tsaritsy Nebesnoi v g. Rostove Velikom* (Sergiev Posad, 1911); *Skazanie o novoproslavlennoi ikone;* Speranskii, *Skazanie o chudotvornoi Tikhvinskoi ikone,* 27.

106. See, for example, the icon of the Mother of God named "Quick to Hear" located in a chapel dedicated to St. Panteleimon in Moscow. *Slava Bogomateri,* 139. For a thorough study of the phenomenon of "shriekers" in Russia, see the study by Worobec, *Possessed.*

107. Fyodor Dostoevsky, *The Karamazov Brothers,* trans. Ignat Avsey (New York, 1994), 59–60.

108. "Dobroe slovo zhene, u kotoroi muzh pianitsa," in *Mater' miloserdiia* 56–62.

109. Denisov, *Skazanie o zastuplenii;* Maksimov, *Zastupnitsa userdnaia.*

110. See the troparion in honor of the icon of the Mother of God named "Life-Giving Source," in *Mineia: aprel'* (Moscow: Izdanie Moskovskoi Patriarkhii, 1985), 315.

111. *Zastuplenie Bozhiei Materi: Istinnaia povest'* (Moscow, 1847).

112. Špidlík, *Spirituality of the Christian East,* 284–86.

113. A typical discussion of this theme can be found in the well-known treatise of the eighteenth-century saint Tikhon of Zadonsk, entitled *Journey to Heaven: Counsels on the Particular Duties of Every Christian,* trans. George D. Lardas (Jordanville, NY: Holy Trinity Monastery, 1991), 54, 59.

114. *Skazanie ob ikone Bozhiei Materi, imenuemoi Abalatskoiu.*

115. Tarnavich, *Sukho-Kaligorskii chudotvornyi obraz,* 6.

116. *Skazanie o iavlennoi Kazanskoi ikone,* 29–32.

117. Sulotskii, *Ikona Bozhiei Materi Vsekh Skorbiashchikh Radosti.*

118. *Skazanie o chudotvornoi ikone Bogomateri, imenuemoi Chernigovskaia.*

119. Blackbourn, *Marpingen*, 27–28.

120. Varzhanevskii, *Skazanie o iavlenii chudotvornyia ikony*.

121. Evgenov, *Krestnyi khod*.

122. "Povest' o Pokaianii Feofila," *Zhitiia sviatykh, na russkom iazyke izlozhennyia po rukovodstvu Chet'ikh-Minei sv. Dimitriia Rostovskago*, vol. 10, June (1913; reprint, Kaluga: Izdanie Sviato-Vvedenskogo monastyria Optinoi Pustyni, 1997), 500–515.

123. Doronikin, *O Tikhvinskoi chudotvornoi ikone*.

124. Carroll, *Madonnas that Maim*, 68.

125. Service in honor of Kazan Mother of God on 8 July, *Miniia: mesiats iiul'*, 166.

126. *Skazanie o iavlenii i chudesakh ikony Bozhiei Materi Kaluzhenskoi*.

127. *Slava Bogomateri*, 554–56.

128. See the story of the Starchitskaya icon of the Mother of God in *Slava Bogomateri*, 456–57.

129. *Chudotvornaia ikona Pochaevskoi Bozhiei Materi* (Pochaev, 1897).

130. Modestov, *Selo Tabynskoe; Skazanie ob ikone Tabynskoi; Skazanie ob ikone Kazanskiia Bozhiia Materi, nakhodiashcheisia v Voznesenskoi tserkvi*.

131. *Skazanie ob ikone Tabynskoi Bozhiei Materi*, 36.

132. Il'inskii, *Slovo v den' Kazanskoi ikony*, 2.

133. *Skazanie o pochitaemoi chudotvornoi ikone Piukhtitskoi Bozhiei Materi* (St. Petersburg, 1903).

134. *Slava Bogomateri*, 394.

135. *Slava Bogomateri*, 579–81.

136. *Skazanie ob ikone Tabynskoi Bozhiei Materi*, 36.

137. Il'inskii, *Slovo v den' Kazanskoi ikony*.

138. For an English translation, see *The Russian Primary Chronicle: Laurentian Text*, trans. and ed. Samuel H. Cross and Olgerd P. Sherbowitz-Wetzor (Cambridge, MA: Mediaeval Academy of America, 1953).

139. Examples of these themes can be found in Archbishop Makarii, "Slovo v den' prazdnestva chudotvornoi ikone Vladimirskoi Bozhiei Materi," in *S tserkovnago amvona*, 6; Sokolov, *Slovo v den' sreteniia Smolenskoi ikony Bozhiei Materi*, 5; Prot. F. Vasiutinskii, *Slovo v prazdnik Kazanskoi ikony Presviatyia Bogoroditsy* (Chernigov, 1910).

140. Dimitrii, episkop Mozhaiskii, *Vladimirskaia chudotvornaia ikona*, 11.

141. Prot. Serafim Vvedenskii, *Pouchenie v den' prineseniia v gorod Simbirsk chudotvornoi Kazanskoi ikony Bozhiei Materi iz Zhadovskoi pustyni* (Simbirsk, 1914), 2.

142. Prot. Ioann Vostorgov, *Rech' v den' prazdnovaniia Kazanskoi ikony Bozhiei Materi, 8 iiulia 1907* (Moscow, 1909), 4–6.

143. Staropol'skii, *Ikona Presviatoi Bogoroditsy*, 25; *Userdnaia zastupnitsa Russkoi zemli* (St. Petersburg, 1912), 4.

144. Vasiutinskii, *Slovo v prazdnik Kazanskoi ikony*, 2.

145. *Skazanie o iavlennoi Kazanskoi ikone Bozhiei Materi*, 11.

146. Bukharev, *Chudotvornye ikony*, 181–82; Staropol'skii, *Ikona Presviatoi Bogoroditsy*, 20.

147. Rudnev, *Skazanie o sv. ikone*.

148. I. Ia., *Russkim pravoslavnym khristianam. Povestvovanie o chudotvornoi ikone Presviatoi Bogoroditsy Fedorovskoi-Kostromskoi* (St. Petersburg, 1869). "Victorious leader of triumphant hosts" is a phrase from the well-known hymn sung in honor of Mary, the Mother of God, on the feast of the Annunciation; the same hymn is also routinely chanted after the service of the First Hour.

149. The story of the Smolensk icon told of Mary's protection of Russia in its battles against the Tatars centuries before. For the story of the Smolensk icon of the Mother of God, see *Skazanie o chudotvornoi ikone Bozhiei Materi-Putevoditel'nitsy* (Vyborg, 1909).

150. Archimandrit Damian, *Smolenskaia ikona Bogomateri i 1812 g.* (St. Petersburg, 1912).

151. See "Chudo," *Birzhevye vedomosti*, 25 September 1914; *Petrogradskaia gazeta*, 26 September 1914; I. Stratonovich, "Znamenie Bogomateri i Eia pomoshch' Russkomu Khristoliubivomu voenstvu," *Vestnik voennago i morskago dukhovenstva* 21 (1914): 730; *Skazanie o chudotvornoi ikone Bozhiei Materi, imenuemoi Samarskoi* (Moscow, 1916), 21–24; *Iavlenie Bogomateri na pole brani voiskam* (Moscow, 1915). For the synodal investigation of this case, see RGIA, f. 796, op. 199, 6 ot., 3 st., d. 277a. Note that even before the Holy Synod could formally investigate the case, iconographic prints of the event began to be sold.

152. Lavrskii, "Slovo v den' prazdnovaniia Presviatyia Vladychitsy nashei Bogoroditsy i Prisnodevy Marii," in *Poucheniia gorodskago prikhodskago sviashchennika*, 348–56.

153. Dimitrii, episkop Mozhaiskii, *Vladimirskaia chudotvornaia ikona*, 8.

154. *O pokhishchenii Kazanskoi ikony; Pokrovskii, Pechal'naia godovshchina.*

155. S. A. S., *Pouchenie v den' znameniia presviatyia Bogoroditsy skazannoe 27 noiabria 1890 v Troitskom khrame sela Karabanova* (Moscow, 1891), 6–7.

156. Prot. Konstantin Iakimovich, *Pouchenie v den' prazdnovaniia chudotvornago obraza Odigitrii Bozhiei Materi* (Chernigov, 1907), 2–3.

157. Pokrovskii, *Narodnaia sviatynia*, 30. For a description of trends in the Catholic West, see Barbara Corrado Pope, "Immaculate and Powerful: The Marian Revival in the Nineteenth Century," in Atkinson, Buchanan, and Miles, *Immaculate and Powerful*, 183.

158. *Userdnaia zastupnitsa*, 4. Also see *Mysli i chuvstva*, 5.

159. *Blagodatnaia mater' naroda Russkago.*

160. Pokrovskii, *Narodnaia sviatynia*, 30.

161. *Userdnaia zastupnitsa*, 4.

162. Vostorgov, *Rech' v den' prazdnovaniia Kazanskoi ikony*, 11.

163. *Skazanie o chudotvornoi ikone Bozhiei Materi, imenuemoi Chernigovskaia.*

164. Il'inskii, *Slovo v den' Kazanskoi ikony*, 8. *Znamenie milosti Bozhiei*, 5.

165. Narkevitch, *Chudotvornaia ikona.*

166. *Znamenie milosti Bozhiei*, 14.

167. "Mater Bozhiia—Blagodatnaia Mater' Naroda Russkago," *Troitskii tsvetok* 46 (1902), 9.

168. *Blagodatnaia mater' naroda Russkago*, 5–6.

169. RGIA, f. 796, op. 445, d. 348.

170. "Skazanie o iavlenii ikony Bozhiei Materi pri Voznesenskoi v sele Kolomenskom tserkvi, Moskovskago uezda," *Dushepoleznyi sobesednik* 9 (1917): 314–16. See the discussion about the icon's popularity in Matorin, *Zhenskoe bozhestvo*, 6–8.

171. *Miniia: mesiats iiun'* (1893; reprint Moscow: "Prvilo very," 1996), 283.

172. Bulgakov, *Nastol'naia kniga*, vol. 1, 197–98.

173. For some discussion of iconographic representations of icons in Russia, see Tarasov, *Ikona i blagochestie*, 63–69.

174. Sergii (Spasskii), *Russkaia literatura*, 14; I. A. Kochetkov, "Svod chudotvornykh ikon Bogomateri na ikonakh i graviurakh XVIII–XIX vekov," in Lidov, *Chudotvornaia ikona*, 404–17; Tarasov, *Ikona i blagochestie*, 395–96.

175. Orthodox Christians frequently referred to saints in this manner, looking to John 15:15.

176. John of Damascus, *On the Divine Images*, trans. David Anderson (Crestwood, NY: St. Vladimir's Seminary Press, 1980), 84.

## CONCLUSION

1. RGIA, f. 796, d. 1436, l. 114

2. S. Kozubovskii, "Po voprosam prikhodskoi reformy," *Prikhodskaia zhizn'* 3 (1917): 134; see also chapter 1, n. 175.

3. For an example, see N. Zaozerskii, "Proekt-organizatsii tserkovnago ustroistva na nachalakh patriarshe-sobornoi," *BV* (January 1906): 124.

4. For a classic presentation of the notions of "great tradition" and "little tradition," see Robert Redfield, "Peasant Society and Culture" in *The Little Community and Peasant Society and Culture* (Chicago: University of Chicago Press, 1960), 41–42.

5. "Selections from the Work *Against Heresies* by Irenaeus, Bishop of Lyons: The Refutation and Overthrow of the Knowledge Falsely So Called," trans. and ed. Edward Rochie Hardy, in *Early Christian Fathers*, ed. Cyril C. Richardson (New York: Macmillan, 1970): 370–76.

6. Ibid., 378.

7. *Materialy mezhdunarodnoi bogoslovskoi konferentsii: Prikhod v Pravoslavnoi Tserkvi. Moskva, oktiabt' 1994* (Moscow: Sviato-Filaretovskoi Moskovskoi Vysshei Pravosalvno-Khristianskoi Shkoly, 2000), 36–39; 43.

8. Pepe Karmel, "Russian Secrets," *New York Times Magazine*, (26 November 1995), 54–55.

# BIBLIOGRAPHY

ARCHIVAL SOURCES

Arkhiv Russkogo geograficheskogo obshchestva
  P-7       Ethnographic materials from the Vologda province
Gosudarstvennyi arkhiv Rossiiskoi Federatsii (GA RF)
  Fond P-3431    Vserossiiskii Tserkovnyi Pomestnyi Sobor
Gosudarstvennyi arkhiv Vologodskoi oblasti (GAVO)
  Fond 179     Vologodskii okruzhnoi sud
  Fond 496     Vologodskaia dukhovnaia konsistoriia
  Fond 652     Vologodskoe obshchestvo po izucheniiu severnogo
           kraia, 1903–17
  Fond 883     Kraeved I. Suvorov
  Fond 1083    Opisanie tserkvei
  Fond 4389    Vologodskoe obshchestvo po izucheniiu severnogo
           kraia, 1918–30
Rossiiskii gosudarstvennyi istoricheskii arkhiv (RGIA)
  Fond 796     Kantseliariia Sv. Sinoda
  Fond 797     Kantseliariia Ober-prokurora
  Fond 804     Osoboe prisutstvie po delam pravoslavnago dukhoven-
           stva
  Fond 1022    Petrovy
Rossiiskii etnograficheskii muzei (REM)
  Fond 7      Tenishev Collection
Totemskii kraevedcheskii muzei
  P-35–P-47    Dnevniki A. A. Zamaraeva


JOURNALS AND NEWSPAPERS

*Arkhangelskiia eparkhial'nyia vedomosti*
*Astrakhanskiia eparkhial'nyia vedomosti*
*Bogoslovskii vestnik*
*Dukh khristianina*
*Dukhovnaia beseda*
*Dushepoleznoe chtenie*
*Dushepoleznyi sobesednik*

*Etnograficheskoe obozrenie*

*Golos svobodnoi tserkvi*

*Golos tserkvi*

*Iaroslavskiia eparkhial'nyia vedomosti*

*Izvestiia Viatskago eparkhial'nago pastyrsko-mirianskago s'ezda*

*Izvestiia Vologodskago obshchestva izucheniia severnago kraia*

*Izvestiia Vserossiiskago soveta prikhodskikh obshchin*

*Kaluzhskiia eparkhial'nyia vedomosti*

*Kaluzhskii tserkovno-obshchestvennyi vestnik*

*Khristianskoe chtenie*

*Kostromskoi tserkovno-obshchestvennyi vestnik*

*Kurskiia eparkhial'nyia vedomosti*

*Moskovskiia tserkovnyia vedomosti*

*Novyi put'*

*Orlovskiia eparkhial'nyia vedomosti*

*Otdykh khristianina*

*Otkliki na zhizn'*

*Otkliki sel'skikh pastyrei*

*Permskiia eparkhial'nyia vedomosti*

*Pravoslavnoe obozrenie*

*Pravoslavnyi sobesednik*

*Prikhodskaia zhizn'*

*Prikhodskoe chtenie*

*Pskovskiia eparkhial'nyia vedomosti*

*Rukovodstvo dlia sel'skikh pastyrei*

*Russkaia mysl'*

*Russkii palomnik*

*Saratovskiia eparkhial'nyia vedomosti*

*Sel'skii sviashchennik*

*Sever*

*Severnyi krai*

*Strannik*

*Tambovskiia eparkhial'nyia vedomosti*

*Troitskie listki*

*Trudy Vologodskago obshchestva izucheniia severnago kraia*

*Tserkovnoe obnovlenie*

*Tserkovno-obshchestvennyi vestnik*

*Tserkovnost'*

*Tserkovnyia vedomosti*

*Tserkovnyi golos*

*Tserkovnyi vestnik*

*Tverskiia eparkhial'nyia vedomosti*

*Vera i razum*

*Vera i tserkov'*

*Vestnik tserkovno-obshchestvennoi zhizni*

*Vladivostokskiia eparkhial'nyia vedomosti*

*Vologodskiia eparkhial'nyia vedomosti*

*Vologodskiia gubernskiia vedomosti*

*Voronezhskiia eparkhial'nyia vedomosti*

*Voskresnyi blagovest*
*Zhivaia starina*
*Zvonar'*


PUBLISHED SOURCES

"A. I." *Blagodatnaia mater' russkago naroda.* Moscow, 1899.
*Agapii Maksimovich: Sborshchik na tserkov'.* St. Petersburg, 1867.
Aggeev, K. *Istoricheskii grekh.* St. Petersburg, 1907.
Aivazov, I. G. *Tserkovnye voprosy v tsarstvovanie Imperatora Aleksandra III.* Moscow, 1914.
———. *Zakonodatel'stvo po tserkovnym delam v tsarstvovanie Imp. Aleksandra III.* Moscow, 1913.
Aksakov, N. P. *Dukha ne ugashaite.* St. Petersburg, 1894.
Akvilonov, Evgenii. *Tserkov': Nauchnyia opredeleniia tserkvi i apostol'skoe uchenie o nei kak o tele Khristovom.* St. Petersburg, 1894.
Amfiteatrov, Ia. K. *Besedy ob otnoshenii tserkvi k khristianam.* St. Petersburg, 1910.
Amosov, A. A. *Pamiatniki pis'mennosti v muzeiakh Vologodskoi oblasti.* Parts 1–5. Vologda, 1982–88.
"An . . . skii," S. A. *Narod i kniga.* Moscow, 1913.
———. *Ocherki narodnoi literatury.* St. Petersburg, 1894.
Anatolii, Ep. (Kamenskii). *Kanonicheskii prikhod ili prikhod obshchina.* Tomsk, 1916.
Andersin-Lebedeva, A. *Skazanie ob ikone Port Arturskoi Bogomateri.* Odessa, 1916.
Andrei (Ukhtomskii). *O narodnom golose v delakh tserkovnykh.* Vladimir, 1916.
Anichkov-Platonov, I. N. *Razsuzhdenie o krestnykh khodakh Pravoslavnoi tserkvi.* Moscow, 1842.
Antonii, Ep. (Khrapovitskii). *Vosstanovlenie prikhoda. Sem' let nazad i teper'.* Kharkov, 1906.
Antonov, Nikolai. *Vozrozhdenie tserkovno-prikhodskoi zhizni v Rossii.* St. Petersburg, 1906.
Antonov, V. G. *Ob'iasnenie bozhestvennoi Liturgii.* Kiev, 1898.
Anur'ev, Ioann. *K otkrytiiu dukhovnykh sobesedovanii vne tserkovnykh bogosluzhenii.* Moscow, 1883.
Arsenii (Chagovets). *O pochitanii Bozhiei Materi: K dniu Uspeniia.* Kharkov, 1911.
Atkinson, Clarissa W., Constance H. Buchanan, and Margaret R. Miles, eds. *Immaculate and Powerful: The Female in Sacred Image and Social Reality.* Cambridge, MA: Harvard University Press, 1985.
Badone, Ellen, ed. *Religious Orthodoxy and Popular Faith in European Society.* Princeton: Princeton University Press, 1990.
Barsov, N. *Vopros o religioznosti russkago naroda v nashei sovremennoi pechati.* St. Petersburg, 1881.
Barsov, S. T. *Sbornik deistvuiushchikh i rukovodstvennykh tserkovno-grazhdanskikh postanovlenii po vedomstvu pravoslavnago ispovedaniia.* St. Petersburg, 1885.
Batalden, Stephen K. *Seeking God: The Recovery of Religious Identity in Orthodox Russia, Ukraine, and Georgia.* DeKalb: Northern Illinois University Press, 1993.
Beliaevskii, F. *Ocherki po prikhodskomu voprosu.* Petrograd, 1917.
Belliustin, I. S. *Description of the Clergy in Rural Russia.* Trans. Gregory L. Freeze. Ithaca: Cornell University Press, 1985.
Belting, Hans. *Likeness and Presence: A History of the Image Before the Era of Art.* Trans. Edmund Jephecott. Chicago: Chicago University Press, 1996.

Benediktov, P. I. *Chudotvornaia ikona Kazanskoi Bozhiei Materi v Vyshenskoi pustyni, Shatskago uezda, Tambovskoi gubernii.* Tambov, 1886.

Benzin, V. M. *Tserkovno-prikhodskaia blagotvoritel'nost' na Rusi.* St. Petersburg, 1907.

Berdnikov, I. S. *Chto nuzhno dlia obnovleniia pravoslavnago russkago prikhoda?* St. Petersburg, 1897.

———. *Kommentarii g. Papkova i K. na suzhdeniia predsobornago prisutstviia po voprosu o reforme pravoslavnago prikhoda.* Kazan', 1907.

———. *Separativnyi proekt polozheniia o pravoslavnom prikhode.* St. Petersburg, 1906.

Berdnikov, V. F. *Chasovnia sv. Blagovernago kniazia Aleksandra Nevskago, postroennaia v pamiat' 25-ti letiia tsarstvovaniia Imperatora Aleksandra II i prazdnovaniia dnia 8-ogo marta v Votkinskom zavode.* Sarapul, 1898.

Bernshtam, T. A. *Molodost' v simvolizme perekhodnykh obriadov vostochnykh slavian: uchenie i opyt Tserkvi v narodnom khristianstve.* St. Petersburg: Peterburgskoe Vostokovedenie, 2000.

*Beseda o pochitanii sv. ikon.* Samara, 1902.

*Beseda s prikhozhanami o pol'ze 'prikhodskago soveta' dlia prikhodskoi zhizni.* Moscow, 1908.

Bezsonov, V. *Ob obshchestvennoi blagotvoritel'nosti i eia organakh—prikhodskikh popechitel'stvakh.* Moscow, 1876.

Blackbourn, David. *Marpingen: Apparitions of the Virgin Mary in Bismarckian Germany.* New York: Oxford University Press, 1993.

*Blagodatnaia mater' naroda Russkago.* Saratov, 1911.

*Blagodeianiia Bogomateri rodu khristiaskomu chrez Eia sviatyia ikony.* Moscow, 1891.

Blagorazumov, V. N. *K voprosu o vozrozhdenii pravoslavnago prikhoda.* Moscow, 1904.

Blinov, N. N. *Batiushka v sele.* Moscow, 1916.

Blochlinger, Alex. *The Modern Parish Community.* New York: Kennedy, 1965.

Bock, E. Wilbur. "Symbols in Conflict: Official versus Folk Religion." *Journal for the Scientific Study of Religion* 5 (spring 1966): 204–12.

Boff, Leonardo. *Ecclesiogenesis: The Base Communities Reinvent the Church.* Trans. Robert R. Barr. Maryknoll, NY: Orbis, 1986.

*Bog v prirode.* Moscow, 1882.

Bogoliubov, D. I. *O pochitanii sviatykh ikon.* Kharkov, 1902.

Bogoroditskii, F. *Golos sel'skago pastyria.* 3rd ed. St. Petersburg, 1912.

Bogoslovskii, M. M. *Zemskoe upravlenie na russkom severe v XVII v.* 2 vols. Moscow, 1912.

Bogoslovskii, Nikolai. *Il'inskaia Kubenskaia tserkov' Vologodskago uezda Vologodskoi gubernii.* Vologda, 1900.

Bogoslovskii, P. *Skazanie o iavlennoi i chudotvornoi ikone Uspenie Bozhiei Materi nakhodiashcheisia v khrame s. Ryshkova, Borovskago uezda.* Kaluga, 1910.

Boldovskii, A. G. *Vozrozhdenie tserkovnago prikhoda. Obzor mnenii pechati.* St. Petersburg, 1903.

Bouyer, Louis. *Rite and Man: Natural Sacredness and Christian Liturgy.* Notre Dame, IN: University of Notre Dame Press, 1963.

Broiakovskii, S. *Poucheniia i rechi na vsevozmozhnye sluchai iz pastyrskoi praktiki.* St. Petersburg, 1904.

Brooks, Jeffrey. "Competing Modes of Popular Discourse: Individualism and Class Consciousness in the Russian Print Media, 1880–1928." In *Culture et révolution,* ed. M. Ferro and S. Fitzpatrick. Paris: Ecole des hautes études en sciences sociales, 1989.

———. *When Russia Learned to Read: Literacy and Popular Literature, 1861–1917.* Princeton: Princeton University Press, 1985.

Bruce, Steve. *Religion in the Modern World: From Cathedrals to Cults*. New York: Oxford University Press, 1996.

Bukharev, I. *Dobroe chtenie v khristianskoi sem'e i na vnebogosluzhebnykh sobesedovaniiakh*. Moscow, 1906.

———. *Neskol'ko slov o nishchikh*. Moscow, 1902.

———. *Ob uveseleniiakh pod voskresenye i prazdnichnye dni*. Moscow, 1901.

———, comp. *Chudotvornye ikony Presviatoi Bogoroditsy: Istoriia ikh i izobrazheniia*. Moscow, 1901.

Bulgakov, Makarii. *Pravoslavno-dogmaticheskoe bogoslovie*. St. Petersburg, 1857.

Bulgakov, S. V. *Nastol'naia Kniga dlia sviashchenno-tserkovno sluzhitelei. Sbornik svedenii, kasaiushchikhsia preimushchestvenno prakticheskoi deiatel'nosti otechestvennago dukhovenstva*. 2 vols. 1913. Reprint, Moscow: Izdatel'skii otdel Moskovskogo Patriarkhata, 1993.

Bulgakovskii, D. *Raskaianie pri vstuplenii v obshchestvo trezvosti*. St. Petersburg, 1910.

———. *Khram Bozhii i ego sviashchennaia vazhnost' dlia khristian*. St. Petersburg, 1914.

Burke, Peter. *Popular Culture in Early Modern Europe*. New York: New York University Press, 1978.

Burtsev, Evgenii. *Spas na Kokshenge Totemskago uezda Vologodskoi gubernii*. Vologda, 1912.

Bushkovitch, Paul. *Religion and Society in Russia: The Sixteenth and Seventeenth Centuries*. New York: Oxford University Press, 1992.

Byrnes, Robert F. *Pobedonostsev: His Life and Thought*. Bloomington: University of Indiana Press, 1968.

Carrier, Herve, S. J. *The Sociology of Religious Belonging*. New York: Herder and Herder, 1965.

Carroll, Michael P. *Madonnas that Maim: Popular Catholicism in Italy since the Fifteenth Century*. Baltimore: Johns Hopkins University Press, 1992.

———. *Veiled Threats: The Logic of Popular Catholicism in Italy*. Baltimore: Johns Hopkins University Press, 1996.

Cassanova, Jose. *Public Religions in the Modern World*. Chicago: University of Chicago Press, 1994.

Chartier, Roger. *Cultural History: Between Practices and Representations*. Trans. Lydia G. Cochrane. Cambridge, UK: Cambridge University Press, 1988.

*Chasovnia v pamiat' 100-letiia Fridrikhsgamskago mirnago dogovora 1809 mezhdu Rossiei i Shvetsiei*. Finland: Helsingfors, 1913.

Chel'tsov, M. P. *O prikhode i o registratsii prikhozhan*. St. Petersburg, 1905.

Chernyshev, A. *Krestnye khody Viatskoi eparkhii*. Viatka, 1903.

Christian, William. "Holy People in Peasant Europe." *Comparative Studies in Society and History* 15(1973): 106–14.

———. *Local Religion in Sixteenth-Century Spain*. Princeton: Princeton University Press, 1981.

———. *Person and God in a Spanish Valley*. New York: Seminar Press, 1972.

Christoff, Peter K. *An Introduction to Nineteenth-Century Russian Slavophilism. A Study in Ideas*, vol. 1. The Hague: Mouton, 1961.

*Chto takoe khram Bozhii dlia pravoslavnago russkago cheloveka*. St. Petersburg, 1908.

*Chudesnoe iavlenie Bozhiei Materi v sonme sviatykh ugodnits Bozhiikh prepodobnomu Serafimu*. Odessa, 1905.

*Chudesnoe istselenie docheri kollezhskago sovetnika devitsy Ekateriny Levestam Protestantskago ispovedaniia pri ikone Tikhvinskoi Bozhiei Materi v Isaakievskom sobore*. St. Petersburg, 1862.

*Chudesnoe spasenie ikony Znameniie Presviatyia Bogoroditsy ot vzryva.* Odessa, 1898.

*Chudesnyia istseleniia pred ikonoiu Bozhiei Materi "Vsekh Skorbiashchikh Radost'," chto v Akhtyrskom Sviato-Troitskom monastyre, s predvaritel'nym skazaniem ob etoi ikone.* 3rd ed. Kharkov, 1881.

*Chudotvornyia i osobenno mestnochitmyia ikony i krestnye khody v Kazanskoi eparkhii.* Kazan, 1872.

Chuliukina, A., and Albert Rauch, eds. *Tysiacheletie pochitaniia presviatoi Bogoroditsy na Rusi i v Germanii.* Munich–Zurich: Shnell and Shtainer, 1990.

Chulos, Chris. "Peasant Religion in Post-Emancipation Russia: Voronezh Province, 1880–1917." Ph.D. diss., University of Chicago, 1995.

Chuprov, V. I. *Krest'ianskoe dvizhenie na severe v gody pervoi russkoi burzhuazno-demokraticheskoi revoliutsii, 1905–1907.* Syktyvkar: Komi filial AN SSSR, 1982.

———. *Sotsial'no-politicheskaia zhizn' severnoi derevni, 1895-fevral' 1917.* Moscow: Nauka, 1991.

*Chuvstva sleptsa Shiriaeva pred ikonoiu Presviatyia Bogoroditsy.* St. Petersburg, 1862.

Cohen, A. P. *The Symbolic Construction of Community.* New York: Tavistock, 1985.

Confino, Alon. *The Nation as a Local Metaphor: Württemberg, Imperial Germany, and National Memory, 1871–1918.* Chapel Hill: University of North Carolina Press, 1997.

Connerton, Paul. *How Societies Remember.* Cambridge, UK: Cambridge University Press, 1989.

Cracraft, James A. *The Church Reform of Peter the Great.* Stanford: Stanford University Press, 1971.

Crummey, Robert O. "Old Belief as Popular Religion: New Approaches." *Slavic Review* 52, no. 4 (winter 1993): 700–712.

Cumpsty, John S. *Religion as Belonging: A General Theory of Religion.* Lanham, MD: University Press of America, 1991.

Cunningham, James W. *A Vanquished Hope: The Movement for Renewal in Russia, 1905–1906.* Crestwood, NY: St. Vladimir's Seminary Press, 1981.

Curtiss, John L. *Church and State in Imperial Russia.* New York: Columbia University Press, 1948.

Dashkevich, A. *Kratkoe opisanie blagodatnoi ikony presviatoi Bogoroditsy, nakhodiashcheisia v chasovne sela Onyshkovets, Dubenskago uezda, Volynskoi gubernii.* Volyn, 1897.

Davie, Grace. *Religion in Modern Europe: A Memory Mutates.* New York: Oxford University Press, 2000.

Davis, Natalie Zemon. "From Popular Religion to Popular Cultures." In *Reformation Europe: A Guide to Research,* ed. Stephen Ozment. St. Louis, MO: Center for Reformation Research, 1982.

———. "Some Tasks and Themes in the Study of Popular Religion." In *The Pursuit of Holiness in Late Medieval and Renaissance Religion,* ed. Charles Trinkhaus. Leiden: Brill, 1974.

De Sherbinin, Julie W. *Chekhov and Russian Religious Culture: The Poetics of the Marian Paradigm.* Evanston, IL: Northwestern University Press, 1997.

Debol'skii, G. S. *Dni bogosluzheniia Pravoslavnoi kafolicheskoi Vostochnoi tserkvi.* 1901. Reprint, Moscow: Otchii Dom, 1996.

*Deianiia Sviashchennogo sobora Pravoslavnoi Rossiiskoi tserkvi.* 1918. Reprint, Moscow: Novospasskii monastyr', 1994–2000.

Demkin, I. *O liubvi k khramu Bozhiiu.* St. Petersburg, 1900.

Denisov, L. *Chudo 8 marta.* Moscow, 1989.

———. *Razmyshleniia o vnutrennem sostoianii serdtsa chelovecheskago.* Moscow, 1903.

————, comp. *Skazanie o zastuplenii Presviatoi Bogoroditsy za obizhennuiu muzhem zhenu.* Moscow, 1914.

D'iachenko, G. *Obshchedostupnyia besedy o bogosluzhenii Pravoslavnoi tserkvi.* Moscow, 1898.

————. *Propovednicheskaia entsiklopediia: Sputnik pastyria-propovednika.* Moscow, 1903.

————, comp. *Dukhovnyi mir: razskazy i razmyshleniia, privodiashchie k priznaniiu bytiia dukhovnago mira.* Moscow, 1900.

Dimitrii, Ep. Mozhaiskii. *Vladimirskaia chudotvornaia ikona Bogomateri: blagodatnyi istochnik utesheniia vo dni ispytanii Russkoi zemli.* Moscow, 1915.

Dimitrii, Preosviashchennyi. *Mesiatseslov sviatykh, vseiu russkoiu tserkoviu ili mestno chtimykh i ukazatel' prazdnestv v chest' ikon Bozhiei Materi i sv. Ugodnikov Bozhiikh v nashem otechestve.* Moscow, 1893–99.

Dix, Dom Gregory. *The Shape of the Liturgy.* New York: Seabury Press, 1982.

*Dokladnaia zapiska o neobkhodimosti vozstanovleniia prikhoda v kachestve tserkovno-obshchestnnoi edinitsy.* St. Petersburg, 1905.

Doronikin, V. V. *O Tikhvinskoi chudotvornoi ikone Bozhiei Materi, nakhodiashcheisia v Ranenburgskoi Petropavlovskoi Pustyni, Riazanskoi eparkhii.* Kasimov, 1911.

Dubisch, Jill. *In a Different Place: Pilgrimage, Gender, and Politics at a Greek Island Shrine.* Princeton: Princeton Unviersity Press, 1995.

Duffy, Eamon. *The Stripping of the Altars: Traditional Religion in England c. 1400–1580.* New Haven: Yale University Press, 1992.

Dulles, Avery, and Patrick Granfield. *The Theology of the Church. A Bibliography.* New York: Paulist Press, 1999.

Durnovo, M. *Kak dolzhen byt' ustroen prikhod?* Moscow, 1906.

Durylin, S. N. *Prikhod: Ego zadachi i organizatsiia.* Moscow, 1917.

"E. M." *Kratkoe istoricheskoe opisanie chasovni i ikon v nei nakhodiashchikhsia: Tsaritsy nebesnoi "Nechaiannaia Radost' " i sviatitelia Nikolaia Mirlikiiskago chudotvortsa, chto u Serpukhovskikh vorot v g. Moskve.* Moscow, 1909.

Ebbinghaus, Andreas. *Die altrussischen Marienikonen-Legenden.* Wiesbaden: Harrassowitz, 1990.

Eigo, Francis A., ed. *All Generations Shall Call Me Blessed.* Villanova, PA: Villanova University Press, 1994.

Eklof, Ben, and Stephen Frank, eds. *The World of the Russian Peasant: Post-Emancipation Culture and Society.* Boston: Unwin Hyman, 1990.

Elagin, N. *Nishchie v tserkvi.* St. Petersburg, 1886.

Eliade, Mircea. *The Sacred and the Profane.* Trans. Willard R. Trask. New York: Harcourt Brace Jovanovich, 1959.

Emeliakh, L. I. *Antiklerikal'noe dvizhenie krest'ian v period pervoi russkoi revoliutsii.* Moscow: Nauka, 1965.

————. *Istoricheskie predposylki preodoleniia religii v sovetskoi derevne nakanune Velikogo Oktiabria.* Leningrad: Gos. Muzei istorii religii i ateizma Ministerstva kul'tury RSFSR, 1975.

————. *Krest'iane i tserkov' nakanune Oktiabria.* Leningrad: Nauka, 1976.

*Encyclical Epistle of the One Holy Catholic and Apostolic Church to the Faithful Everywhere.* South Canaan, PA: Orthodox Book Center, 1958.

Engelstein, Laura. *Castration and the Heavenly Kingdom: A Russian Folktale.* Ithaca, NY: Cornell University Press, 1999.

————. "Holy Russia in Modern Times: An Essay on Orthodoxy and Cultural Change." *Past and Present* 173 (November 2001): 129–56.

————. "Print Culture and the Transformation of Imperial Russia. A Review Article." *Comparative Study of Society and History* 31 (1989): 784–90.

Evgenov, P. P. *Krestnyi khod k zolotym vorotam i chudotvornaia ikona Bozhiei Materi Vladimir-skaia.* Vladimir, 1912.

Evtukhov, Catherine. *The Cross and the Sickle: Sergei Bulgakov and the Fate of Russian Religious Philosophy.* Ithaca, NY: Cornell University Press, 1997.

Fedorov, Egor. *Chudotvornaia ikona Presviatyia Bogoroditsy, Vsekh Skorbiashchikh Radost' (s monetami).* St. Petersburg, 1907.

Fedotov, G. *Stikhi dukhovnye.* Paris, 1935.

Feofan, Ep. (Govorov). *Nashi otnosheniia k khramam.* Moscow, 1900.

Filaret, Ep. (Drozdov). *Slava Bogomateri.* Moscow, 1890.

Florenskii, Pavel. *Okolo Khomiakova: Kriticheskie zametki.* Sergiev-Posad, 1916.

————. *The Pillar and Ground of the Truth.* Trans. Boris Jakim. Princeton: Princeton University Press, 1997.

Florovsky, Georges. *The Collected Works of Georges Florovsky.* Vol. 1, *Bible, Church, Tradition: An Eastern Orthodox View.* Belmont, MA: Nordland, 1972.

————. *Puti russkogo bogosloviia.* Paris: YMCA Press, 1937.

————. *Ways of Russian Theology.* Translated by Robert L. Nicholas. Belmont, MA: Nordland, 1979.

Freeze, Gregory L. "All Power to the Parish? The Problems and Politics of Church Reform in Late Imperial Russia." In *Social Identities in Revolutionary Russia,* ed. M. D. Palat. Houndmills, NY: Palgrave, 2001.

————. "A Case of Stunted Anticlericalism: Clergy and Society in Imperial Russia." *European Studies Review* 13 (1983): 177–200.

————. "Church, State and Society in Catherinean Russia: The Synodal Instruction to the Legislative Commission." In *—aus der anmuthigen Gelehrsamkeit: Tübinger Studien zum 18. Jahrhundert: Dietrich Geyer zum 60. Geburtstag,* ed. Dietrich Geyer and Eberhard Müller. Tübingen: Attempto, 1988.

————. "Counter-Reformation in Russian Orthodoxy: Popular Response to Religious Innovation." *Slavic Review* 54 (summer 1995): 305–39.

————. "The Disintegration of Traditional Communities: The Parish in Eighteenth-Century Russia." *Journal of Modern History* 48 (March 1976): 32–50.

————. "Going to the Intelligentsia: The Church and Its Urban Mission in Post-Reform Russia." In *Between Tsar and People: Educated Society and the Quest for Public Identity in Late Imperial Russia,* ed. Edith Clowes, Samuel D. Kassow, and James L. West. Princeton: Princeton University Press, 1991.

————. "Handmaiden of the State? The Church in Imperial Russia Reconsidered." *Journal of Ecclesiastical History* 30, no. 1 (January 1985): 82–102.

————. "Institutionalizing Piety: The Church and Popular Religion, 1750–1850." In *Imperial Russia: New Histories for the Empire,* ed. Jane Burbank and David L. Ransel. Bloomington: Indiana University Press, 1998.

————. *The Parish Clergy in Nineteenth-Century Russia: Crisis, Reform, Counter-Reform.* Princeton: Princeton University Press, 1983.

————. "The Rechristianization of Russia: The Church and Popular Religion, 1750–1850." *Studia Slavica Finlandensia* 7. Helsinki, 1990: 101–36.

————. *Russian Levites: Parish Clergy in the Eighteenth Century.* Cambridge, MA: Harvard University Press, 1977.

————. "Subversive Piety: Religion and the Political Crisis in Late Imperial Russia." *Journal of Modern History* 68 (June 1996): 308–50.

Frierson, Cathy A. *Peasant Icons: Representations of Rural People in Late Nineteenth-Century Russia.* New York: Oxford University Press, 1993.

Fudel, I. *Osnovy tserkovno-prikhodskoi zhizni.* Moscow, 1894.

Gaudin, Corinne. "Governing the Village: Peasant Culture and the Problem of Social Transformation in Russia, 1906–1914." Ph.D. diss., University of Michigan, 1993.

Gavril'kov, S. *Kozel'shchanskii obraz Bozhiei Materi.* Poltava, 1913.

Geertz, Clifford. *The Interpretation of Cultures.* New York: Basic Books, 1973.

———. *Local Knowledge: Further Essays in Interpretive Anthropology.* New York: Basic Books, 1983.

George, C. Berthold, trans. *Maximus the Confessor: Selected Writings.* New York: Paulist Press, 1985.

Gibson, Ralph. *A Social History of French Catholicism, 1789–1914.* New York: Routledge, 1989.

Ginzburg, Carlo. *The Cheese and the Worms: The Cosmos of a Sixteenth-Century Miller.* Trans. John and Anne Tedeschi. Baltimore: Johns Hopkins University Press, 1980.

Glinka, Avdot'ia. *Zhizn' Presviatoi Devy Bogoroditsy: po knigam Chet'i-Mineiam.* 15th ed. Moscow, 1911.

Glinka, S. D. *K voprosu o preobrazovanii tserkovnago prikhoda.* Kazan, 1912.

Gorain, A. *Papkovskaia teoriia prikhoda.* Chernigov, 1906.

Grekulov, E. F. "Raskhody, sviazannye s religiei, v biudzhete krest'ian tsarskoi Rossii." *Voprosy istorii religii i ateizma* 12 (1964): 124–49.

Gromyko, M. M. "Mesto sel'skoi (territorial'noi, sosedskoi) obshchiny v sotsial'nom mekhanizme formirovaniia, khraneniia i izmeneniia traditsii." *Sovetskaia etnografiia* 5 (1984): 70–82.

———. *Mir russkoi derevni.* Moscow: Molodaia Gvardia, 1991.

Gromyko, M. M., and A. V. Buganov, eds. *O vozzreniiakh russkogo naroda.* Moscow: Palomnik, 2000.

Gromyko, M. M., V. A. Aleksandrov, and V. K. Sokolova. *Traditsionnye normy povedeniia i formy obshcheniia russkikh krest'ian XIX veka.* Moscow: Nauka, 1986.

Gruppa Peterburgskikh Sviashchennikov. *K tserkovnomu soboru.* St. Petersburg, 1906.

Gumilevskii, Filaret. *Pravoslavnoe dogmaticheskoe bogoslovie.* chast' 2. Chernigov, 1864.

Halbwachs, Maurice. *On Collective Memory.* Trans. and ed. Lewis A. Coser. Chicago: University of Chicago Press, 1992.

Hall, David, ed. *Lived Religion in America: Towards A History of Practice.* Princeton: Princeton University Press, 1997.

Harris, Ruth. *Lourdes: Body and Spirit in the Secular Age.* New York: Penguin Books, 1999.

Hebblethwaite, Margaret. *Basic is Beautiful: Basic Ecclesial Communities from Third World to First World.* London: Fount, 1993.

Hedda, Jennifer Elaine. "Good Shepherds: The St. Petersburg Pastorate and the Emergence of Social Activism in the Russian Orthodox Church, 1855–1917." Ph.D. diss., Harvard University, 1998.

Herlihy, Patricia. *The Alcoholic Empire: Vodka and Politics in Late Imperial Russia.* New York: Oxford University Press, 2002.

Herlinger, Page. "The Religious Identity of Workers and Peasant Migrants in St. Petersburg, 1880–1917." Ph.D. diss., University of California, Berkeley, 1995.

Himes, Michael H. *Ongoing Incarnation: Johann Adam Möhler and the Beginnings of Modern Ecclesiology.* New York: Crossroads, 1997.

Hinchman, Lewis P., and Sandra K. Linchman, eds. *Memory, Identity, Community: The Idea of Narrative in the Human Sciences.* Albany: State University of New York Press, 1997.

Husband, William B. *Godless Communists: Atheism and Society in Soviet Russia, 1917–1932.* DeKalb: University of Northern Illinois Press, 2000.

Hutchison, William R., and Harmut Lehmann. *Many Are Chosen: Divine Election and Western Nationalism.* Minneapolis: Fortress Press, 1994.

"I. Ia." *Russkim pravoslavnym khristianam. Povestvovanie o chudotvornoi ikone Presviatoi Bogoroditsy Fedorovskoi Kostromskoi.* St. Petersburg, 1905.

Il'inskii, Petr. *Slovo v den' Kazanskoi ikony Bozhiei Materi v gradskoi Kazanskoi tserkvi.* Astrakhan, 1899.

Il'inskii, Vl. 'Blagotvoritel'nost' v Rossii." *Biblioteka tserkovnago reformatora* 1. St. Petersburg, 1908.

*Instruktsiia tserkovnym starostam. Vysochaishe utverzdennaia 17 aprelia 1808 g.* Moscow, 1878.

*Instruktsiia tserkovnym starostam. Vysochaishe utverzhdennaia 12 iiunia 1890 g.* St. Petersburg, 1916.

*Istoriia iavleniia Akhtyrskoi chudotvornoi ikony Bozhiei Materi i sobornago Pokrovskago khrama, gde ona nyne nakhoditsia.* St. Petersburg, 1879.

Iushkov, S. V. *Ocherki iz istorii prikhodskoi zhizni na severe Rossii v XV–XVII vv.* St. Petersburg, 1913.

Iustin, Ep. *Poucheniia v chest' i slavu Presviatyia Bogoroditsy.* Moscow, 1900.

Ivanits, Linda J. *Russian Folk Belief.* Armonk, NY: Sharpe, 1989.

Ivanov, I. *O znachenii khrama i obriadakh v oblasti very i religii Khristovoi.* Voronezh, 1894.

Ivanov, P. A. *Kakiia prava mogut prinadlezhat' mirianam v stroenii tserkovno-prikhodskoi zhizni.* Tomsk, 1916.

———. *Reforma prikhoda: Istoriko-kanonicheskoe issledovanie o pravoslavnom russkom tserkovnom prikhode.* St. Petersburg, 1907.

Ivanovskii, Ia. *Obozrenie tserkovno-grazhdanskikh uzakonenii po dukhonomu vedomstvu.* St. Petersburg, 1883.

Ivin, Ivan. "O narodno-lubochnoi literature." *Russkoe obozrenie* 9 (1893): 242–60; 10 (1893): 768–85.

*Iz'iasnenie vecherni, utreni i liturgii.* Moscow, 1896.

Izrailev, A. A. *Chudotvornaia Pecherskaia ikona Bozhiei Materi v Iaroslavskom Spaso-Preobrazhenskom monastyre.* Moscow, 1896.

Izvekov, M. C. *O pochitanii i proslavlenii sv. ikon.* Kaluga, 1891.

*Izvlecheniia iz otcheta po vedomstvu dukhovnykh del pravoslavnago ispovedaniia.* St. Petersburg, 1837–1863. Series title for 1866–1884: *Izvlecheniia iz vsepoddanneishego otcheta ober-prokurora Sv. Sinoda po vedomstvu pravoslavnago ispovedaniia.* Series title for 1886–1915: *Vsepoddanneishii otchet ober-prokurora Sv. Sinoda po vedomstvu pravoslavnago ispovedaniia.*

Jakim, Boris, and Robert Bird, eds. and trans. *On Spiritual Unity: A Slavophile Reader.* Hudson, NY: Lindisfarne Books, 1998.

James, Wendy, and Douglas H. Johnson, eds. *Vernacular Christianity: Essays in the Social Anthropology of Religion Presented to Godfrey Lienhardt.* New York: Lilian Barber Press, 1988.

Jay, Eric. *The Church: Its Changing Image through Twenty Centuries.* 2 vols. London: SPCK, 1977.

Jockwig, Franz. *Der Weg der Laien auf des Landeskonzil der Russischen Orthodoxen Kirche, Moskau 1917/18.* Würzburg: Augustinus-Verlag, 1971.

"K. I." *Chto takoe tserkovnyi starosta. Opyt istoriko-kriticheskago izsledovaniia o proiskhozhdenii i razvitii instituta tserkovnykh starost v Rossii.* St. Petersburg, 1902.

Kaidanov, O. "Nasha deshevaia literatura." *Obrazovanie* 5 (1905): 139–70.

Kalashnikov, S. V. *Alfavitnyi ukazatel' deistvuiushchikh i rukovodstvennykh kanonicheskikh postanovlenii, ukazov, opredelenii i rasporiazhenii Sv. Prav. Sinoda, 1721–1901.* 3rd ed. St. Petersburg, 1902.

Kal'nev, M. *O sviatosti i pochitanii khramov Bozhiikh.* Odessa, 1911.

*Kaluzhskaia Kazanskaia ikona Bozhiei Materi i pamiatniki eia proslavleniia.* Kharkov, 1916.

Kamkin, A. V. *Pravoslavnaia tserkov' na severe Rossii: Ocherki istorii do 1917 goda.* Vologda: Vologodskii gosudarstvennyi pedagogicheskii institut, 1992.

Kaplan, Steven, ed. *Understanding Popular Culture.* New York: Mouton, 1984.

Kartashev, A. V. *Reforma, reformatsiia i ispolnenie tserkvi.* Petrograd, 1916.

Kassirov, I., comp. *Plach Bozhiei Materi s prisoedineniem kratkago eia zhizneopisaniia.* Moscow, 1897.

Khomiakov, A. S. *Polnoe sobranie sochinenii Alekseia Stepanovicha Khomiakova. Sochineniia Bogoslovskiia.* 1907. Reprint, St. Petersburg, 1995.

Khomiakov, D. A. *Sobornoe zavershenie i prikhodskaia osnova tserkovnago stroia.* Moscow, 1906.

*Khram Bozhii i ego sviashchennaia vazhnost' dlia khristian.* Moscow, 1887.

*Khrista radi iurodivye.* Moscow, 1903.

*Khristianskaia milostynia.* Moscow, 1890.

*Khristianskii Mesiatseslov s kratkimi istoricheskimi skazaniami o vsekh sviatykh, proslavliaemykh pravoslavnoiu tserkoviu, i s ob'iasneniem sovershaemykh v onoi prazdnestv.* Moscow, 1900.

Kingston-Mann, Esther, and Timothy Mixter, eds. *Peasant Economy, Culture, and Politics of European Russia, 1800–1921.* Princeton: Princeton University Press, 1991.

Kizenko, Nadieszda. *A Prodigal Saint: Father John of Kronstadt and the Russian People.* University Park: Pennsylvania State University Press, 2000.

Klevezal', V. P. *Prava i obiazannosti. K voprosu o prikhodskoi samodeiatel'nosti.* Kazan, 1907.

Kolosov, N. A. *Tipy pravoslavnago dukhovenstva v russkoi svetskoi literature.* Moscow, 1902.

Komarov, P. *Slovo v den' Preobrazheniia Gospoda 6 avgusta, 1916: o pochitanii ikon.* Tomsk, 1916.

Kornblatt, Judith Deutsch, and Richard F. Gustafson, eds. *Russian Religious Thought.* Madison: University of Wisconsin Press, 1996.

Korobovskii, K. F. *Skazanie o sv. ikone Bogomateri imenuemoi Troeruchitsa i o predstatel'stve i blagodeiianii rodu khristianskomu, okazannyia chrez sv. ikony Bozhiei Materi.* Kiev, 1915.

Kosar, George. "Russian Orthodoxy in Crisis and Revolution: The Church Council 1912–1918." Ph.D. diss., Brandeis University, 2003.

Kostsova, A. S., and A. G. Pobedinskaia. *Russkie ikony XVI-nachala XX veka s izobrazheniem monastyrei i ikh osnovatelei.* St. Petersburg: Gos. Ermitazh, 1996.

Krasnianskii, G. *O znachenii krestnykh khodov i osviashchenii vody.* Moscow, 1892.

Kropotkin, Kniaz' A. *Prizyv k ozhivleniiu prikhoda.* Saratov, 1904.

Kselman, Thomas A. *Miracles and Prophecies in Nineteenth-Century France.* New Brunswick, NJ: Rutgers University Press, 1983.

Kudriavtsev, A. N. *Istoricheskii ocherk khristianskoi blagotvoritel'nosti.* Odessa, 1883.

———. *Nishchenstvo kak predmet popecheniia tserkvi, obshchestva i gosudarstva.* Odessa, 1885.

Kupchinov, I. P. *Prikhod kak melkaia zemskaia edinitsa*. Moscow, 1905.

Kurdinovskii, V. *O snovideniiakh kak proiavleniiakh dukhovnoi zhizni*. Kishinev, 1914.

Kur'ianov, I. *Ob upravlenii tserkovnym imushchestvom. Obshchiia rukovodiashchiia poniatiia*. Kostroma, 1880.

Kuznetsov, N. D. *Preobrazovaniia v Russkoi tserkvi*. Moscow, 1906.

———. *Tserkov', dukhovenstvo i obshchestvo*. Moscow, 1905.

Lavrskii, V. *Poucheniia gorodskago prikhodskago sviashchennika, 1862–1902*. Samara, 1902.

Lebedev, A. *Raznosti tserkvei Vostochnoi i Zapadnoi v uchenii o Presviatoi Deve Marii Bogorod-itse*. Warsaw, 1881.

Lebedev, I. *Tserkovno-prikhodskiia popechitel'stva*. Chernigov, 1902.

Legatov, Il'ia. *Istoricheskii ocherk Liavlenskago prikhoda Arkhangel'skoi eparkhii*. St. Petersburg, 1879.

Levashev, Arkadii. *Poucheniia sel'skago sviashchennika*. Vyp. 1, chast' 1. Kostroma, 1889.

Levin, Eve. "*Dvoeverie* and Popular Religion." In *Seeking God: The Recovery of Religious Identity in Orthodox Russia, Ukraine, and Georgia*, ed. Stephen K. Batalden. DeKalb: Northern Illinois University Press, 1993.

Levine, Daniel H., ed. *Churches and Politics in Latin America*. Beverly Hills, CA: Sage, 1980.

Levitov, M. *Narod i dukhovenstvo*. Kazan, 1907.

Lidov, A. M., ed. *Chudotvornaia ikona v Vizantii i drevnei Rusi*. Moscow, 1996.

Limberis, Vasiliki. *Divine Heiress: The Virgin Mary and the Creation of Christian Constantino-ple*. New York: Routledge, 1994.

Lindenmeyr, Adele. *Poverty Is Not a Vice: Charity, Society, and the State in Imperial Russia*. Princeton: Princeton University Press, 1996.

Lin'kov, A. *Opisanie Tiksnenskoi Preobrazhenskoi Tserkvi Totemskago uezda Vologodskoi guber-nii*. Vologda, 1900.

Listova, T. A., S. V. Kuznetsov, and Kh. V. Poplavskaia. *Pravoslavnaia zhizn' russkikh krest'ian XIX–XX vekov: Itogi etnograficheskikh issledovanii*. Moscow: Nauka, 2001.

Losev, L. *Zemnaia zhizn' presviatoi Bogoroditsy i Prisno Devy Marii*. 2nd ed. Moscow, 1892.

Lotman, Ju. M., and B. A. Uspensky. *The Semiotics of Russian Culture*. Ann Arbor: University of Michigan Press, 1984.

Loya, Joseph A. "Theological Clarifications of Lay Status in the Russian Church Pertaining to the Moscow Reform Council of 1917–1918." Ph.D. diss., Fordham University, 1986.

Maksimov, K. *Peredacha tserkovnykh zemel', domov i kapitalov v rasporiazhenie i pol'zovanie prikhozhan—soglasno li eto so slovom Bozhiim, s pravilami Tserkvi, s zakonami grazh-danskimi i polezno li dlia Tserkvi i dlia pravoslavnago russkago naroda?* Moscow, 1917.

Maksimov, S. V. *Brodiacheia Rus' Khrista radi*. St. Petersburg, 1877.

———. *Nechistaia, nevedomaia i krestnaia sila*. St. Petersburg, 1903.

Maksimov, V. *Zastupnitsa userdnaia roda khristianskago*. St. Petersburg, 1903.

Malevanskii, Sylvester. *Opyt pravoslavnago dogmaticheskago bogosloviia*. 4 vols. Kiev, 1889.

Malevinskii, A. *Instruktsiia blagochinnomu prikhodskikh tserkvei, iz'iasnennaia ukazami Sv. Sinoda, rasporiazheniiami Eparkhial'nago Nachal'stva, Svodom zakonov i tserkovnoi praktikoi*. St. Petersburg, 1910.

———. *Instruktsiia nastoiateliam tserkvei, iz'iasnennaia ukazami Sv. Sinoda, pravilami Sv. Otets, Svodom zakonov i tserkovnoi praktikoi*. St. Petersburg, 1912.

———. *Instruktsiia tserkovnym starostam, iz'iasnennaia ukazami Sv. Sinoda, Svodom zakonov, rasporiazheniiami Eparkhial'nago Nachal'stva i tserkovnoi praktikoi*. St. Petersburg, 1912.

Malinovskii, N. *Pravoslavnoe dogmaticheskoe bogoslovie*. 3 vols. Sergiev Posad, 1909.

Mal'kovskii, V. N. *Skazanie ob ikone Torzhestvo Presviatyia Bogoroditsy, izvestnoi pod imenem Port Arturskoi ikony Bozhiei Materi*. Tver, 1906.

Malyshevskii, I. I. *O tserkovno-prikhodskikh popechitel'stvakh*. Kiev, 1878.

Manchester, Laurie. "Secular Ascetics: The Mentality of Orthodox Clergymen's Sons in Late Imperial Russia." Ph.D. diss., Columbia University, 1995.

Marrus, Michael. "Cultures on the Move: Pilgrims and Pilgrimages in Nineteenth-Century France." *French Review* 1 (1977): 205–20.

*Mater' miloserdiia. Sbornik religiozno-nazidatel'nykh statei na prazdnichnye dni v chest' Presviatoi Bogoroditsy*. St. Petersburg, 1906.

Matorin, N. M. *Pravoslavnyi kul't i proizvodstvo*. Moscow, 1931.

———. *Zhenskoe Bozhestvo v pravoslavnom kul'te. Piatnitsa-bogoroditsa: ocherk sravnitel'noi mifologii*. Moscow: Moskovskii rabochii, 1931.

Mavritskii, V. A. *Tserkovnoe blagoustroistvo*. Moscow, 1883.

———, ed. *Seiatel'. Sbornik propovedei prisposoblennykh k zhizni i ponimaniiu prostago naroda*. 31st ed. Moscow, 1906.

McCrossen, Alexis. *Holy Day, Holiday: The American Sunday*. Ithaca, NY: Cornell University Press, 2000.

Meehan, Brenda. *Holy Women of Russia: The Lives of Five Orthodox Women Offer Spiritual Guidance for Today*. San Francisco: HarperSanFrancisco, 1992.

———. "Popular Piety, Local Initiative and the Founding of Women's Religious Communities in Russia, 1764–1907." *SVTQ* 30, no. 2 (1986): 117–42.

Melikov, F. E. *Bluzhdaiushchee bogoslovie: Obzor veroucheniia gospodstvuiushchei tserkvi*. Moscow: 1911.

Mellor, Philip A., and Christ Shilling, eds. *Re-Forming the Body: Religion, Community and Modernity*. London: Sage, 1997.

Mikhail (Semenov, P. V.). *Malen'kaia tserkov'*. Moscow, 1904.

Mikhailovskii, prot. Vasilii. *Privetstvie presviatoi deve Marii: Raz'iasnenie bogorodichnago evangeliia*. St. Petersburg, 1892.

Mironov, Boris N. "The Russian Peasant Commune after the Reforms of the 1860s." *Slavic Review* 44 (fall 1985): 438–67.

*Mneniia preosviashchennykh eparkhial'nykh arkhiereev otnositel'no proekta preobrazovaniia dukhovno-sudebnoi chasti*. 2 vols. St. Petersburg, 1874–76.

Modestov, N. N. *Selo Tabynskoe i Voznesenskaia pustyn': Tabynskaia ikona Bozhiei Materi i krestnyi khod iz sela Tabynskago*. Orenburg, 1914.

Molchanov, Prot. I. *Tserkovnaia letopis' prikhoda Uspenskoi tserkvi sela Gorodkovich, Spasskago uezda, Riazanskoi eparkhii*. Riazan, 1898.

Morgan, David. *Visual Piety: A History and Theory of Popular Religious Images*. Berkeley: University of California Press, 1998.

Muller, Alexander V., ed. and trans. *The Spiritual Regulation of Peter the Great*. Seattle: University of Washington Press, 1972.

Muratov, M. V. *Neizvestnaia Rossiia. O narodnoi vere i narodnom podvizhnichestve*. Moscow, 1919.

*Mysli i chuvsta po povodu ikony "Znamenie" v Kurske 8 marta. Iz dnevnika pravoslavnago khristianina*. Moscow, 1898.

"N. V." "O derevenskom chitatele i o knige dlia nego." *Russkii nachal'nyi uchitel'* 1 (1894): 1–15.

Narkevich, S. S. *Chudotvornaia ikona Presviatyia Bogoroditsy, Vsekh Skorbiashchikh Radosti (s monetami), nakhodiashchaiasia v chasovne Skorbiashchei Bozhiei Materi v g. S.-Peterburge.* St. Petersburg, 1907.

*Nastavlenie po prologu o milostyne.* Moscow, 1898.

Nechaev, Vasilii. *Tolkovanie na Bozhestvennuiu Liturgiiu po chinu sv. Ioanna Zlatoustago i sv. Vasiliia Velikago.* Moscow, 1873.

Nefed'ev, N., comp., *Sviashchennaia byl' na Volge. Skazanie o iavlenii Tolgskoi ikony Bozhiei Materi preosviashchennomu Prokhoru v skhime Trifonu, episkopu Rostovskomu.* St. Petersburg, 1914.

Nestor, Archimandrit. *Skazanie o chudotvornoi Domnitskoi ikone Bogomateri.* Chernigov, 1913.

Nichols, Robert L., and Theofanis Stavrou, eds. *Russian Orthodoxy under the Old Regime.* Minneapolis: University of Minnesota Press, 1978.

Nikanor (Brovkovitch, A. I.). *Nasha svetskaia i dukhovnaia pechat' o dukhovenstve.* St. Petersburg, 1884.

Nikiforovskii, E. N. *Chernigovskaia Il'inskaia ikona Bozhiei Materi v Smol'nom Voskresenskom Sobore.* St. Petersburg, 1914.

Nikodim, Ep. *Kaluzhskaia Kazanskaia ikona Bozhiei Materi i pamiatniki eia proslavleniia.* Kharkov, 1916.

Nikolaev, A. A. "Kniga v sovremennoi russkoi derevne." *Vestnik znaniia* 8 (1904): 166–77.

Nikol'skii, K. *O chasovniakh.* St. Petersburg, 1889.

Nikol'skii, N. *Ob obshchestvennoi blagotvoritel'nosti i ee organakh v prikhodskoi praktike.* Moscow, 1876.

Nikol'skii, N., and M. Izvol'skii. *Sistematicheskii sbornik nedoumennykh voprosov i otvetov na nikh vstrechaiushchikhsia v tserkovno-prikhodskoi praktike.* St. Petersburg, 1896.

Nikol'skii, Pavel. *Khram Bozhii.* Tambov, 1914.

Nikol'skii, S. *Novaia literaturnaia popytka k pereustroistvu russkago pravoslavnago prikhoda.* St. Petersburg, 1902.

Nikol'skii, V. I. *Korsunskaia ikona Bozhiei Materi v sobornom khrame Bogoiavleniia Gospodnia v g. Usmani, Tambovskoi gubernii.* Kazan, 1907.

Nikol'skii, V. *Skazanie o chudotvornoi ikone Bozhiei Materi–Putevoditel'nitsy.* Vyborg, 1909.

Nosova, G. A. *Iazychestvo v pravoslavii.* Moscow, 1979.

———. "Opyt etnograficheskogo izucheniia bytovogo pravoslaviia (na materialakh Vladimirskoi oblasti)." *Voprosy nauchnogo ateizma* 3 (1967): 151–63.

Novgorodskii, P. F. *Narodnyi sobesednik: sbornik statei dlia chteniia pri vnebogosluzhebnykh sobesedovaniiakh s prostym narodom.* Vladimir, 1893.

*Novoproslavlennaia chudotvornaia ikona Znameniia Bogoroditsy, Serafimo-Ponetaevskii monastyr' Nizhegorodskoi eparkhii Arzamasskago uezda.* St. Petersburg, 1888.

*O blagoustroenii prikhoda. Svod mnenii eparkhial'nykh preosviashchennykh.* St. Petersburg, 1906.

*O chudotvornoi ikone Bogoliubskoi Bozhiei Materi, nakhodiashcheisia v sele Iur'evskom, Borovskago uezda.* Kaluga, 1898.

*O chudotvornykh i mestnochtimykh sviatykh ikonakh Tambovskago kraia.* Tambov, 1902.

*O krestnykh khodakh i khorugviakh.* St. Petersburg, 1889.

*O pochitanii sviatykh ikon.* Kazan, 1911.

*O pochitanii sviatykh ikon.* Stavropol, 1897.

*O pokhishchenii Kazanskoi ikony Bozhiei Materi.* Kazan, 1905.

Obelkovitch, James, ed. *Religion and the People, 800–1700.* Chapel Hill: University of North Carolina Press, 1979.

*Obiazannosti khristianina po otnosheniiu k prikhodskomu khramu.* Moscow, 1896.

*Obiazannosti prikhozhan i starosty tserkovnago k svoemu prikhodskomu khramu.* Moscow, 1911.

*Obzor deiatel'nosti vedomstva pravoslavnago ispovedaniia za vremia tsarstvovaniia Imperatora Aleksandra III.* St. Petersburg, 1901.

Ognev, N. *Chem dolzhen byt' pravoslavnyi prikhod?* St. Petersburg, 1908.

———. *Tserkovnyi sobor i religioznyia zaprosy obshchestva.* St. Petersburg, 1908.

*Opisanie chudotvornoi ikony Starorusskoi Bozhiei Materi i pereneseniia eia iz goroda Tikhvina v gorod Staruiu Russu.* Novgorod, 1896.

*Opisanie Krasnogorskoi Bolshe-Okhtenskoi chasovni, chto po Georgievskoi ulitse, vo imia chudot-vornykh ikon Bozhiei Materi Vladimirskoi i Gruzinskoi.* St. Petersburg, 1880.

Opotskii, N. *Ideal'naia obshchina i put' k ee vosstanovleniiu.* St. Petersburg, 1914.

Ornatskii, F. *O znachenii sviatago khrama v zhizni khristian.* St. Petersburg, 1892.

Orsi, Robert. *The Madonna of 115th Street: Faith and Community in Italian Harlem, 1880–1950.* New Haven: Yale University Press, 1985.

———. *Thank You, Saint Jude: Women's Devotion to the Patron Saint of Hopeless Causes.* New Haven: Yale University Press, 1996.

Ostroumov, Stefan. *Pis'ma o pravoslavnom blagochestii.* Moscow, 1896.

Ostrovskaia, L. V. "Istochniki dlia izucheniia otnosheniia sibirskikh krest'ian k ispovedi (1861–1904)." In *Issledovaniia po istorii obshchestvennogo soznaniia epokhi feodalizma v Rossii,* ed. N. N. Pokrovskii. Novosibirsk: Nauka, Sibirskoe otd-nie, 1984.

———. "Khristianstvo v ponimanii russkikh krest'ian poreformennoi Sibiri." In *Ob-shchestvennyi byt i kul'tura russkogo naseleniia Sibiri, XVIII-nachala XX veka,* ed. F. F. Bolonov and N. A. Minenko. Novosibirsk: Nauka, Sibirskoe otd-nie, 1983.

———. "Nekotorye zamechaniia o kharaktere krest'ianskoi religioznosti." In *Krest'ianstvo Sibiri XVIII-nachala XX v.: Klassovaia bor'ba, obshchestvennoe soznanie i kul'tura,* ed. L. M. Goriushkin. Novosibirsk: Nauka, Sibirskoe otd-nie, 1975.

———. "Prosheniia v konsistoriiu i Sinod kak istochnik po sotsial'noi psikhologii krest'ianstva poreformennoi Sibiri." In *Istochniki po kul'ture i klassovoi bor'be feo-dal'nogo perioda,* ed. N. N. Pokrovskii and E. K. Romodanovskaia. Novosibirsk: Nauka, Sibirskoe otd-nie, 1982.

*Osviashchenie chasovni na farfrovo-faiansovoi fabrike Kuznetsova v Novgorodskom uezde.* Novgo-rod, 1888.

*Osviashchenie chasovni v Nitstse v pamiat' pokoinago tsarevicha Nikolaia Aleksandrovicha i vos-pominanie o nem.* St. Petersburg, 1888.

Oswalt, Julia. *Kirchliche Gemeinde und Bauernbefreiung: soziales Reformdenken in d. orthodoxen Gemeindegeistlichkeit Russlands in d. Ära Alexanders II.* Göttingen: Vandenhoeck und Ruprecht, 1975.

*Otchet po postroike chasovni v pamiat' 17 oktiabria 1888 g. i 29 aprelia 1891 g., sooruzhennoi pri tserkvi sv. Troitsy S-Peterburga.* St. Petersburg, 1896.

Otto, Robert. *Publishing for the People: The Firm Posrednik, 1885–1905.* New York: Garland, 1987.

*Otzyvy eparkhial'nykh arkhiereev po voprosu o tserkovnoi reforme.* 3 vols. St. Petersburg, 1906.

*O znachenii pozhertvovanii na sv. khramy. Slovo preosviashchennago Makariia, Arkhiepiskopa Kharkovskago i Akhtyrskago, po osviashchenii khrama, ustroennago, Akhtyrskago uezda v sele Riasnom, pomeschikom Konstantinom Dmitrievichem Khrushchovym, skazannoe 16 sentiabria 1862 g.*

Pain, J. H. "Sobornost': A Study in Modern Orthodox Theology." Ph.D. diss., Oxford University, 1967.

Palibin, M. N., comp. *Ustav dukhovnoi konsistorii s dopolneniiami i raz'iasneniiami Sv. Sinoda i Prav. Senata.* 2nd ed. St. Petersburg, 1912.

Panchenko, A. A. *Narodnoe pravoslavie. Issledovaniia v oblasti narodnogo pravoslaviia. Dereven-skie sviatyni severo-zapada Rossii.* St. Petersburg, 1998.

Paozerskii, M. F. *Chudotvornye ikony.* Moscow, 1923.

Papkov, A. A. *Besedy o pravoslavnom prikhode.* St. Petersburg, 1912.

————. *Nachalo vozrozhdeniia tserkovno-prikhodskoi zhizni v Rossii.* Moscow, 1900.

————. *Neobkhodimost' obnovleniia pravoslavnago tserkovno-obshchestvennago stroia.* St. Petersburg, 1902.

————. *O blagoustroistve pravoslavnago prikhoda.* St. Petersburg, 1907.

————. *Pogosty v znachenii pravitel'stvennykh okrugov i sel'skikh prikhodov v severnoi Rossii.* Moscow, 1898.

————. *Proekt normal'nago ustava pravoslavnykh prikhodov v Rossii. Sostavlen IV otdelom Vysochaishe uchrezhdennago Predsobornago Prisutstviia pri Sviateishem Sinode.* Iaroslavl, 1906.

————. *Tserkovno-obshchestvennye voprosy v epokhu Tsaria-Osvoboditelia (1855–1870).* 1902. Reprint, Farnborough, UK: Gregg International, 1972.

————. *Upadok pravoslavnago prikhoda XVIII–XIX v.* Moscow, 1899.

————. *Vozzvanie k sviashchennikam i prikhozhanam.* Moscow, 1905.

Papov, D. *Zametki prikhodskago sviashchennika o vozrozhdenii tserkognago prikhoda.* Kharkov, 1904.

Pascal, Pierre. *The Religion of the Russian People.* Crestwood, NY: St. Vladimir's Seminary Press, 1986.

*Pastyr' propovednik: Sbornik luchshikh propovedei sovremennykh arkhipastyrei i pastyrei na voskresnye i prazdnichnye dni.* Moscow, 1904.

*Pastyrskoe nazidanie. Sbornik statei dlia chteniia pri vnebogosluzhebnykh sobesedovaniiakh.* Moscow, 1891.

Pavlov, A. M. *Khram Bozhii.* Moscow, 1892.

Pavlov, A. *Ob uchastii mirian v delakh tserkvi, s tochki zreniia pravoslavnago kanonicheskago prava.* Kazan, 1866.

Petrov, G. *O pochitanii sviatykh ikon.* Kazan, 1911.

Pisiotis, A. K. "Orthodoxy vs. Autocracy: The Orthodox Church and Clerical Dissent in Late Imperial Russia, 1905–1914." Ph.D. diss., Georgetown University, 2000.

Platov, N. D. *Opisanie o sooruzhenii chasovni vremenno-obiazannymi krest'ianami Griazovetskago uezda Vologodskoi gubernii.* St. Petersburg, 1872.

*Pokhvala Presviatoi Deve Bogoroditse. Izbrannyia dushespasitel'nyia poucheniia, stikhotvoreniia, povesti i primery iz zhizni i tvorenii sviatykh otets.* Novgorod, 1905.

Pokrovskii, Arsenii. *Narodnaia sviatynia v gorode Vyshnem Volochke, Tverskoi gubernii.* Sergiev Posad, 1900.

Pokrovskii, I. *Pechal'naia godovshchina so dnia pokhishcheniia iavlennoi chudotvornoi Kazanskoi ikony Bozhiei Materi v Kazani.* Kazan, 1906.

Pokrovskii, N. *Ob ikonopochitanii.* Nizhnii Novgorod, 1910.

*Polnoe sobranie postanovlenii i rasporiazhenii po viedomstvu pravoslavnago ispovedaniia Rossiiskoi Imperii.* Series 1–5. St. Petersburg, 1869–1915.

*Polnoe sobranie zakonov Rossiiskoi Imperii.* 1st ser. 45 vols. St. Petersburg, 1830. 2nd ser. 55 vols. St. Petersburg, 1830–84. 3rd ser. 28 vols. St. Petersburg, 1911.

*Polnyi pravoslavnyi bogoslovskii entsiklopedicheskii slovar'.* 2 vols. 1913. Reprint, London: Variorum Reprints, 1971.

*Polnyi sbornik molitv Spasiteliu, Presviatoi Troitse, Bozhiei Materi, Sviatym ugodnikam Bozhiim i Bezplotnym silam, chitaemykh pred sviatymi ikonami, na molebnakh i vsenoshchnykh bdeniiakh.* St. Petersburg, 1914.

*Polozhenie o prikhodskikh popechitel'stvakh pri pravoslavnykh tserkvakh*. St. Petersburg, 1879.

Polunov, A. Iu. *Pod vlast'iu ober-prokurora: gosudarstvo i tserkov' v epokhu Aleksandra III*. Moscow, 1996.

Popov, A. *Pravoslavnye russkie akafisty*. Kazan, 1903.

Popov, A. *Vospominaniia prichetnicheskago syna: Iz zhizni dukhovenstva Vologodskoi eparkhii*. Vologda, 1913.

Popov, D. *O vozrozhdenii tserkovno-prikhodskoi obshchiny*. Kharkov, 1906.

Poselianin, E. *Bogomater'. Polnoe illiustrirovannoe opisanie eia zemnoi zhizni i posviashchennykh eia imeni chudotvornykh ikon*. St. Petersburg, 1911.

———. *V pokhvalu Bogoroditse*. St. Petersburg, 1903.

Potylitsyn, A. I. *Krest'ianskoe revoliutsionnoe dvizhenie na severe v 1905–1907*. Arkhangelsk, 1930.

*Pravoslavie i russkaia narodnaia kul'tura*. Vols. 1–6. Moscow: Biblioteka Rossiiskogo Etnografa, 1993–96.

*Prazdniki v chest' chudotvornykh ikon Presviatoi Bogoroditsy*. Moscow, 1905.

Predtechenskii, A. *V zashchitu russkago pravoslavnago dukhovenstva ot sovremennykh obvinenii i narekanii*. St. Petersburg, 1863.

Preobrazhenskii, I. V. *Konstantin Petrovich Pobedonostsev, ego zhizn' i deiatel'nost' v predstavlenii sovremennikov ego konchiny*. St. Petersburg, 1912.

———. *Otechestvennaia tserkov' po statisticheskim dannym, 1840–1 po 1890–1 gg*. 2nd ed. St. Petersburg, 1901.

———. *Periodicheskaia pechat' po voprosu o prikhodskoi reforme*. St. Petersburg, 1908.

———. *Tserkovnaia reforma. Sbornik statei dukhovnoi i svetskoi periodicheskoi pechati po voprosu o reforme*. St. Petersburg, 1905.

*Prikhodskoi vopros v chetvertoi Gosudarstvennoi Dume*. St. Petersburg, 1914.

Prugavin, A. S. "Izdanie i rasprostranenie narodnykh knizhek." *Russkaia mysl'* 9 (September 1887): 66–89.

———. "K voprosu o tom, chto i kak chitaet narod?" *Russkaia mysl'* 11 (November 1887): 1–30.

Pryzhov, I. *Nishchie na sviatoi Rusi: Materialy dlia obshchestvennago i narodnago byta v Rossii*. Kazan, 1913.

Pustoshkin, V. F. *Khram Bozhii—sputnik khristianina*. St. Petersburg, 1914.

Ramenskii, I. *Skazanie o iavlennoi i chudotvornoi sv. Ikone Pokrova Presviatyia Bogoroditsy, prinadlezhashchei Uglichskomu Pokrovskomu monastyriu*. Iaroslavl, 1899.

Robson, Roy R. "Liturgy and Community among Old Believers, 1905–1907." *Slavic Review* 52, no. 4 (winter 1993): 713–24.

Rodionov, I. A. *Nashi prestupleniia*. St. Petersburg, 1910.

Romanskii, N. *O chudotvornykh ikonakh i sviatykh moshchakh*. Moscow, 1911.

Romanskii, N. A. *Gde nakhoditsia podlinnaia chudotvornaia ikona Kazanskoi Bogomateri*. Moscow, 1905.

Roslof, Edward Eldon. "The Renovationist Movement in the Russian Church, 1922–1946." Ph.D. diss., University of North Carolina at Chapel Hill, 1994.

Rovinskii, K. *Melkaia zemskaia edinitsa. Ocherki i opyty*. St. Petersburg, 1903.

Rowe, William, and Vivian Schelling. *Memory and Modernity: Popular Culture in Latin America*. New York: Verso, 1991.

Rozanov, A. *Voskresenskaia tserkov' v sele Ust'e Kadnikovskago uezda Vologodskoi gubernii*. Vologda, 1903.

Rozanov, A. I. *Zapiski sel'skago sviashchennika*. St. Petersburg, 1882.

Rozanov, N. P. *Svedeniia ob ikone Bozhiei Materi Tikhvinskoi, Zvenigorodskago uezda, v Bla-*

*goveshchenskoi, sela Pavlovskago, tserkvi, izvlechennyia iz konsistorskikh del*. Moscow, 1872.

Rubakin, N. "Knizhnyi potok." *Russkaia mysl'* 3 (March 1903): 1–22; 12 (December 1903): 161–80; 4 (April 1904): 155–79.

———. "Novyia vremena—novyia veianiia." *Russkaia mysl'* 7 (July 1905): 111–37.

Rudnev, Vasilii. *Skazanie o sv. ikone Bogomateri: Prezhde rozhdestva i po rozhdestve Deva*. Moscow, 1911.

Rufimskii, P. M. *Tserkovnyi prikhod i osnovnyia nachala ego razvitiia i zhiznedeiatel'nosti*. Kazan, 1906.

Rumiantsev, N. V. *O prestol'nykh prazdnikakh*. Moscow, 1940.

Ruminskii, V. *Dukhovenstvo i narod*. St. Petersburg, 1906.

Runkevich, S. G. *Novyi opyt ozhivleniia prikhodskoi samodeiatel'nosti*. St. Petersburg, 1914.

———. *Prikhodskaia blagotvoritel'nost' v Peterburge. K voprosu o prikhode*. St. Petersburg, 1914.

Runovskii, N. P. *Tserkovno-grazhdanskiia zakonopolozheniia otnositel'no pravoslavnago dukhovenstva v tsarstvovanie Imp. Aleksandra II*. Kazan, 1898.

Rusanov, N. *Pravoslavnomu prostoliudinu o pravoslavoi vere*. St. Petersburg, 1897.

Russkii, A—s'. *O vozrozhdenii pravoslavnago prikhoda*. Moscow, 1916.

*S tserkovnago amvona. Sbornik obraztsovykh propovedei, govorennykh darovitymi i talantlivymi nashimi arkhipastyriami i pastyriami*. Moscow, 1890.

Sadovskii, D. *Tserkovnyi soiuz, ego neobkhodimost' i znachenie*. St. Petersburg, 1913.

Sadovskii, Sv. V. *Sviatyia ikony: Neobkhodimyia dlia liudei sviashchennyia napominaniia o Boge i sviatykh ego ugodnikakh*. Simbirsk, 1915.

Sahas, Daniel, trans. *Icon and Logos: Sources in Eighth-Century Iconoclasm*. Toronto: University of Toronto Press, 1986.

Sakharov, P. *Prikhod i prikhodskoi pastyr'*. Moscow, 1915.

Scott, James. *Moral Economy of the Peasant*. New Haven: Yale University Press, 1976.

Scott, Jamie, and Paul Simpson-Housley. *Sacred Places and Profane Spaces: Essays in the Geographics of Judaism, Christianity, and Islam*. New York: Greenwood Press, 1991.

Scribner, Robert W. *Popular Culture and Popular Movements in Reformation Germany*. London: Roncerverte, 1987.

*Se stoiu u dveri i stuchu. Razskaz o chudesnom istselenii devitsy Ekateriny i ob izpolnivshemsia predskazanii Bozhiei Materi*. Sergiev Posad, 1907.

Sennikov, D. *Sviatost' podviga spaseniia utopaiushchikh*. St. Petersburg, 1875.

Serafim, Arkhiepiskop Tverskii. *O vozrozhdenii prikhodskoi zhizni*. Petrograd, 1916.

Serebriakov, V. *Tserkovnyi starosta, ego prava i obiazannosti*. St. Petersburg, 1912.

Sergii, Arkhiepiskop (Spasskii). *Pravoslavnoe uchenie o pochitanii sviatykh ikon i drugiia soprikosnovennyia s nim istiny pravoslavnoi very*. Mogilev, 1887.

———. *Russkaia literatura ob ikonakh Presviatoi Bogoroditsy v XIX v.* St. Petersburg, 1900.

Sergii, Igumen, comp. *Pokhvala Presviatoi Deve Bogoroditse*. Novgorod, 1905.

Shalamov, P. *Tserkovno-istoricheskoe opisanie Votchinskago prikhoda, Ust'sysol'skago uezda Vologodskoi gubernii*. Ustsysolsk, 1911.

Shcherbatov, A. G. *Pravoslavnyi prikhod—tverdynia russkoi narodnosti*. Moscow, 1909.

———. *Prikhod i ego znachenie v sovremennom gosudarstvennom stroe*. Moscow, 1905.

Shevzov, Vera. "Chapels and the Ecclesial World of Prerevolutionary Russian Peasants." *Slavic Review* 55, no. 3 (fall 1996): 585–613.

———. "Icons, Laity, and Authority in the Russian Orthodox Church, 1861–1917." *Russian Review* 58: (January 1999): 26–48.

―――. "Icons, Miracles, and Orthodox Communal Identity in Late Imperial Russia." *Church History* 69, no. 3 (September 2000): 610–31.

―――. "Letting 'the People' into 'Church': Reflections on Orthodoxy and Community in Late Imperial Russia." In *Orthodox Russia: Studies in Belief and Practice, 1492–1936*, ed. Valerie A. Kievelson and Robert H. Greene. University Park: Pennsylvania State University Press, 2003.

―――. "Poeticizing Piety: Mary and Her Icon in Russian *Akathistoi* Hymns." *St. Vladimir's Theological Quarterly* 44, nos. 3–4 (2000): 343–73.

―――. "Popular Orthodoxy in Imperial Rural Russia." Ph.D. diss., Yale University, 1994.

Shumov, P. S. *Dlia chteniia v khrame, v sem'e, v shkole. Uroki iz zhizni sviatykh.* Vyp. 3–4. Moscow, 1905–7.

―――. *Sbornik obshchedostupnykh pouchenii na vse voskresnye i prazdnichnye dni.* Vyp. 5. Moscow, 1912.

Sidonskii, A. *Chudotvornaia ikona Bozhiei Materi Odigitrii, chto v sele Bogorodskom bliz goroda Tomska.* Tomsk, 1892.

Simmons, E. J., ed. *Continuity and Change in Russian and Soviet Thought.* Cambridge, MA: Harvard University Press, 1955.

Sirota, Ioann B. *Die Ikonographie der Gottesmutter in der Russischen Orthodoxen Kirche: Versuch einer Systematisierung.* Würzburg: Augustinus–Verlag, 1992.

*Skazanie ob ikone Bozhiei Materi imenuemoi Abalatskoiu s opisaniem vazhneishikh kopii s neia i o nachale pochitaniia onoi v Nizhnem Novgorode.* Nizhnii Novgorod, 1887.

*Skazanie ob ikone Bozhiei Materi "Vzyskanie pogibshikh" chto v sele Bor, Kaluzhskoi gubernii.* Moscow, 1892.

*Skazanie ob ikone, imenuemoi Dostoino Est.'* Moscow, 1895.

*Skazanie ob ikone Kazanskiia Bozhiia Materi, nakhodiashcheisia v Voznesenskoi tserkvi, Ufimskoi gubernii, Sterlitamakskago uezda, sela Tabynskago.* Ufa, 1909.

*Skazanie ob ikone Tabynskoi Bozhiei Materi, nakhodiashcheisia v Voznesenskoi tserkvi, Ufimskoi eparkhii.* Moscow, 1906.

*Skazanie o chudesnom istselenii Tikhvinskago meshchanina Aleksandra Borovskago pred Tikhvinskoiu Bozhiei Materi.* Tikhvin, 1915.

*Skazanie o chudesnykh istseleniiakh ot Pecherskoi ikony Bogomateri.* Iaroslavl, 1887.

*Skazanie o chudotvornoi Bogoliubskoi ikone Bozhiei Materi.* St. Petersburg, 1869.

*Skazanie o chudotvornoi Bogoliubskoi ikone Bozhiei Materi, chto v sele Zimarove, Riazanskoi gubernii.* Riazan, 1916.

*Skazanie o chudotvornoi ikone Bogomateri, imenuemoi Cherigovskaia, nakhodiashcheisia v Pecherskom khrame, Gefsimanskago skita.* Sergiev Posad, 1896.

*Skazanie o chudotvornoi ikone Bozhiei Materi, imenuemoi Chernigovskaia.* Sergiev Posad, 1903.

*Skazanie o iavlenii chudotvornoi ikony Presviatyia Bogoroditsy, imenuemoi Tolgskoiu, i chudesakh ot neia byvshikh.* Moscow, 1883.

*Skazanie o iavlenii i chudesakh ikony Bozhiei Materi Kaluzhenskoi. Sostavleno po rukopisi prot. sela Boianovich Arseniia Ioannova.* Kaluga, 1888.

*Skazanie o iavlennoi Kazanskoi ikone Bozhiei Materi.* Moscow, 1907.

*Skazanie o Kaplunovskoi chudotvornoi ikone.* St. Petersburg, 1909.

*Skazanie o novoproslavlennoi ikone Bozhiei Materi "Umilenie," nakhodiashcheisia v Blagoveshchenskoi tserkvi g. Rostova, Iaroslavskoi gubernii.* Kazan, 1914.

*Skazaniia o zemnoi zhizni presviatoi Bogoroditsy s izlozheniem prorochestv i proobraznovanii, otnosiashchikhsia k nei, ucheniia tserkvi o nei, chudes i chudotvornykh ikon eia.* Moscow, 1904.

Skrobotov, N. A. *Prikhodskoi sviashchennik A. V. Gumilevskii: Podrobnyi biograficheskii ocherk.* St. Petersburg, 1871.

Skvoznikov, A. *O sviatykh ikonakh. Polemiko-missionerskii ocherk.* St. Petersburg, 1913.

*Slava Bogomateri. Svendeniia o chudotvornykh i mestno chtimykh ikonakh Bogomateri.* Moscow, 1907.

*Slovo na osviashchenie chasovni, sooruzhennoi pri tserkvi S.-Peterburgskago Morskago Gospitalia, v pamiat' chudesnago spaseniia Gosudaria Imperatora Aleksandra III s ego Avgusteishim semeistvom 17-go oktiabria 1888 goda.* St. Petersburg, 1892.

Smirnov, A. "Chto chitaiut v derevne." *Russkaia mysl'* 4 (April 1903): 107–16.

———. "Kniga v derevne." *Russkaia mysl'* 3 (March 1905): 103–20.

Smirnov, Dimitrii. *Prazdnovanie voskresnago dnia: ego istoriia i znachenie.* Kiev, 1893.

Smirnov, P. *Chudesa v prezhnee i nashe vremia.* Moscow, 1895.

———. *O tserkvi: Chtenie v obshchem sobranii S. Peterburgskago Pravoslavnago Bratstva vo imia Presviatyia Bogoroditsy 22 marta, 1887.* St. Petersburg, 1887.

Smirnov, Stefan. *Alfavitnyi sbornik rasporiazhenii neobkhodimykh dlia kazhdago chlena prichta.* St. Petersburg, 1898.

Smith, Jonathan Z. *To Take Place: Toward Theory in Ritual.* Chicago: University of Chicago Press, 1987.

Snessoreva, Sofiia. *Zemnaia zhizn' Presviatoi Bogoroditsy i opisanie sviatykh chudotvornykh Eia ikon.* Moscow, 1891.

Sofiiskii, Nikolai. *Istoriia chudotvornoi ikony Bozhiei Materi Zhivonosnago Istochnika i chasovni, chto na Baranovom kliuche v prikhode sela Borisovskago.* Nizhnii Novgorod, 1917.

Solov'ev, Aleksandr. *Sviataia ikona Bozhiei Materi, imenuemaia Abalatskoiu: eia spisok, nakhodiashchiisia v Semipalatinskom Znamenskom Sobore.* Sergiev Posad, 1909.

Sosnin, D. *O sviatykh i chudotvornykh ikonakh.* St. Petersburg, 1833.

Speranskii, A. *Skazanie o chudotvornoi Tikhvinskoi ikone Bozhiei Materi, nakhodiashcheisia v Isaakievskom Kafedral'nom Sobore.* St. Petersburg, 1898.

Špidlík, Tomaš. *The Spirituality of the Christian East.* Cistercian Studies Series, no. 79. Kalamazoo, MI: Cistercian Press, 1986.

Spitsyn, P. *Temy dlia derevenskikh russkikh pravoslavnykh besed.* St. Petersburg, 1909.

*Spravka po voprosu preobrazovanii pravoslavnago prikhoda.* Petrograd, 1915.

*Spravochnaia kniga. Rasporiazheniia i raz'iasneniia po voprosam tserkovnoi praktiki.* Moscow, 1897.

Staropol'skii, A. P. *Ikona Presviatoi Bogoroditsy Izbavitel'nitsy v tserkvi S. Peterburgskago Morskago Voennago gospitalia.* St. Petersburg, 1905.

Stefanovich, P. S. *Prikhod i prikhodskoe dukhovenstvo v Rossii v XVI–XVII vekah.* Moscow: Indrik, 2002.

Stefanovskii, Trifon. *Prikhodskaia letopis' o prikhode i tserkvi derevni Kolesnikov, Nezhinskago uezda.* Chernigov, 1891.

Stratilatov, A. *Katekhizicheskie besedy s sel'skimi prikhozhanami.* 5th ed. St. Petersburg, 1893.

———. *Kratkoe pouchenie o Bozhestvennoi Liturgii dlia prostago naroda.* St. Petersburg, 1872.

Stromilov, N. S. "*Rozhdestvo presviatoi Bogoroditsy,*" iavlennaia ikona v Lukianovoi pustyni. Vladimir, 1893.

Sulotskii, A. *Ikona Bozhiei Materi Vsekh Skorbiashchikh Radosti v Tobol'skoi Zakhar'evskoi tserkvi.* St. Petersburg, 1866.

Svetlakov, A. *Izlozhenie ucheniia pravoslavnoi tserkvi o Tserkvi, tserkovnoi ierarkhii, blagodati i tainstvakh.* Nizhnii Novgorod, 1878.

Svetlov, P. *O znachenii khrama v dukhovnoi khristianskoi zhizni.* Moscow, 1894.

Svetlov, P. *Prorocheskie ili veshchie sny: Apologicheskoe izsledovanie v oblasti Bibleiskoi psikhologii.* Kiev, 1892.

Sviashchennyi Sobor Pravoslavnoi Rossiiskoi Tserkvi. *Deianiia.* Moscow: Izdanie Sobornogo Soveta, 1917–1918.

Sviashchennyi Sobor Pravoslavnoi Rossiiskoi Tserkvi. *Sobranie opredelenii i postanovlenii,* vyp. 3. Moscow: 1918.

*Sviataia ikona Vladimirskoi Bozhiei Materi v sele Nerekhotskom, Kaliazinskago uezda.* Kaliazin, 1910.

*Svod ukazanii i zametok po voprosam po pastyrskoi praktike.* St. Petersburg, 1875.

Tackett, Timothy. *Priest and Parish in Eighteenth-Century France: A Social and Political Study of the Curés of Dauphiné, 1750–1791.* Princeton: Princeton University Press, 1977.

————. *Religion, Revolution, and Regional Culture in Eighteenth-Century France: The Ecclesiastical Oath of 1791.* Princeton: Princeton University Press, 1986.

Tarasov, O. Iu. *Ikona i Blagochestie: Ocherki ikonnogo dela v imperatorskoi Rossii.* Moscow: Progress-Kultura, 1995.

Tarnavich, Ivan. *Sukho-Kaligorskii chudotvornyi obraz Bozhiei Materi.* Kiev, 1909.

Tarutin, A. "Chto chitaiut krest'iane Udimskoi volosti i kak oni otnosiatsia k shkole i knige." *Russkaia shkola* 1 (1892): 136–47.

Tenishev, V. N. *Programma etnograficheskikh svedenii o krest'ianskoi tsentral'noi Rossii.* Smolensk, 1897.

Terebikhin, N. M. *Sakral'naia geografiia russkogo severa.* Arkhangelsk: Pomorskii mezhdunarodnyi pedagogicheskii universitet, 1993.

Ternovets, N. M. *Mysli mirianina o reformakh v russkoi tserkvi.* Moscow, 1916.

Tikhomirov, L. A. *Sovremennoe polozhenie prikhodskago voprosa.* Moscow, 1907.

————. *Zaprosy zhizni i nashe tserkovnoe upravlenie.* Moscow, 1903.

Tikhomirov, T. *Na prikhode. Sviashchennicheskaia entsiklopediia po vsem storonam pastyrskoi deiatel'nosti s vvodnymi stat'iami teoreticheskago kharaktera.* 2 vols. Moscow, 1915–16.

Titlinov, B. V. *Vopros o prikhodskoi reforme v tsarstvovanie Imp. Aleksandra II.* Petrograd, 1917.

Titov, F. I. *Kritiko-bibliograficheskii obzor noveishikh trudov po istorii russkoi tserkvi.* Kiev, 1904.

Tokmakov, I. F. *Istoricheskiia svedeniia o chudotvornoi ikone Bogomateri 'Vsekh Skorbiashchikh Radosti', proslavivsheisia v Moskve v 1688, i o prochikh spiskakh s neia v Rossii.* Moscow, 1890.

Troinitskii, A. *The Serf Population in Russia According to the Tenth National Census.* Trans. Elaine Herman. Newtonville, MA: Oriental Research Partners, 1982.

Troitskii, N. K. *Pouchenie o khozhdenii v khram Bozhii.* Staritsa, 1915.

Troitskii, P. S. *Otnoshenie gosudarstva k tserkvi po vozzreniiam naibolee vidnykh nashikh pisatelei i obshchestvennykh deiateli.* Moscow, 1909.

Troitskii, V. *Khistianstvo ili tserkov'.* Sergiev Posad, 1912.

Tsekhanskaia, K. V. *Ikona v zhizni russkogo naroda.* St. Petersburg, 1998.

*Tserkovno-prikhodskaia obshchina i religiozno-nravstvennyia obiazannosti eia chlenov po otnosheniiu drug k drugu.* Moscow, 1892.

*Tserkovnyia obshchestva trezvosti i podobnye im tserkovnye uchrezhdeniia.* St. Petersburg, 1911.

Tsvetkov, N. V. *O prikhode.* St. Petersburg, 1907.

Tul'tseva, L. A. "Religioznye verovaniia i obriady russkikh krest'ian na rubezhe XIX i XX vekov." *Sovetskaia etnografiia* 3 (1978): 31–46.

————. *Traditsionnye verovaniia, prazdniki i obriady russkikh krest'ain.* Moscow: Znanie, 1990.

Tulupov, N. "Knizhnye sklady v Rossii." *Russkaia mysl'* 2 (February 1891): 15–43.

———. "Narodnye chteniia v gorodakh i selakh." *Russkaia mysl'* 3 (March 1902): 154–19; 4 (April 1902): 1–18.

Turner, Victor. *The Ritual Process: Structure and Anti-Structure.* Ithaca: Cornell University Press, 1977.

Turner, Victor, and Edith L. B. Turner. *Image and Pilgrimage in Christian Culture: Anthropological Perspectives.* New York: Columbia University Press, 1978.

*Uchenie Pravoslavnoi tserkvi o Presviatoi Bogoroditse.* Moscow, 1888.

*Uchilishche blagochestiia.* Pochaev, 1904.

Usinin, A. A. *Neskol'ko slov ob obiazannostiakh prikhozhan k svoemu prikhodskomu khramu.* Staraia Russa, 1897.

Uspenskii, N. *O sviatykh ikonakh i o pochitanii sv. Khristovykh tain.* St. Petersburg, 1894.

Uspenskii, N. I. *Grekhi sueveriia russkago naroda.* St. Petersburg, 1892.

Uspenskii, V. P. *Chasovnia Bozhiei Materi "Troeruchitsy" Krovotynskago prikhoda Ostashskago uezda.* Tver, 1891.

*Ustav dukhovnoi konsistorii.* St. Petersburg, 1898.

*Ustav dukhovnoi konsistorii iz'iasnennyi s prilozheniem.* St. Petersburg, 1871.

Varzhanevskii, K. A. *Skazanie o iavlenii chudotvornyia ikony Presviatyia Bogoroditsy, imenuemyia Kolochskiia i o nachale monastyria eia Kolochskago.* Moscow, 1872.

Verkhovskoi, P. V. *Uchrezhdenie Dukhovnoi kollegii i Dukhovnyi Reglament. K voprosu ob otnoshenii tserkvi i gosudarstva v Rossii.* 2 vols. 1916. Reprint, Farnborough, UK: Gregg International, 1972.

———. "Znachenie bogoslovskikh trudov A. S. Khomiakova dlia tserkovnoi zhizni i prava." *Pravoslavno-russkoe slovo* 7 (1905): 589–98.

Verner, Andrew. "Discursive Strategies in the 1905 Revolution: Peasant Petitions from Vladimir Province." *Russian Review* 54 (January 1995): 65–90.

Vlasova, I. V., M. M. Gromyko, and T. A. Listova, eds. *Russkie: semeinyi i obshchestvennyi byt.* Moscow: Nauka, 1989.

Voitkov, A. *K voprosu o vozrozhdenii tserkovnago prikhoda. Istoricheskii ocherk.* Kamenets-Podolsk, 1904.

Von Gruyerz, Kaspar, ed. *Religion and Society in Early Modern Europe.* Boston: Allen and Unwin, 1984.

Vorontsov, Aleksander, sv. *Pouchenie na 26-e iiunia 1908. Vstrecha Smolenskoi ikony Presviatoi Bogoroditsy iz Sedmiozernoi pustyni.* Kazan, 1908.

*Voskresenskiia i prazdnichnyia vnebogosluzhebnyia sobesedovaniia kak osobyi vid tserkovnoi narodnoi propovedi.* Voronezh, 1880.

*Vo slavu Bozhiei Materi: Sbornik dlia dukhovno-nravstvennago chteniia.* Odessa, 1899.

Vostokov, Vladimir. *Iz sel'skoi zhizni.* Moscow, 1904.

Vostorgov, I. *Gosudarstvennaia duma i pravoslavnaia russkaia tserkov'.* Moscow, 1906.

———. *K voprosu o prikhode.* Moscow, 1906.

*Vremennoe polozhenie o pravoslavnom prikhode.* Petrograd, 1917.

Vysotskii, A. *Beseda o chudotvornykh ikonakh kak ochevidnom dokazatel'stve istinnosti i bogougodnosti ikonopochitaniia.* Simferopol, 1908.

Ward, Keith. *Religion and Community.* Oxford: Clarendon Press, 2000.

Warner, Marina. *Alone of All Her Sex: The Myth and Cult of the Virgin Mary.* New York: Knopf, 1976.

Worobec, Christine D. *Peasant Russia. Family and Community in the Post-Emancipation Period.* Princeton: Princeton University Press, 1991.

———. *Possessed: Women, Witches, and Demons in Imperial Russia.* DeKalb: Northern Illinois University Press, 2001.

Young, Glennys. " 'Into Church Matters': Lay Identity, Rurual Parish Life, and Popular Politics in Late Imperial and Early Soviet Russia, 1864–1928." *Russian History* 23, nos. 1–4 (1996): 167–84.

———. *Power and the Sacred in Revolutionary Russia.* University Park: Pennsylvania State University Press, 1997.

Zabelin, A. P. *Chto mogut sdelat' prikhodskie blagotvoritel'nye obshchestva?* St. Petersburg, 1880.

Zagorskii, Feodor. *Pogost Liubiatovo, nakhodiashchiisia v Voznesenskoi tserkvi, Ufimskoi eparkhii, Sterlitamakskago uezda, s. Tabynskoe.* Moscow, 1906.

*Zamechatel'noe sobytie v chasovne bliz stekliannago zavoda 23 iiulia 1888 goda s ikonoiu Bozhiei Materi Vsekh Skorbiashchikh Radosti.* St. Petersburg, 1888.

Zaozerskii, N. *Chto est' pravoslavnyi prikhod i chem on dolzhen byt'?* Sergiev Posad, 1912.

Zav'ialov, A. *Tsirkuliarnye ukazy Sv. Prav. Sinoda, 1867–1900 gg.* 2nd ed. St. Petersburg, 1901.

Zenkovskii, V. *Rossiia i Pravoslavie.* Kiev, 1916.

———, ed. *Pravoslavie i kul'tura.* Berlin, 1923.

*Zhitie startsa Serafima, Sarovskoi obiteli ieromonakha, pustynnozhitelia i zatvornika.* St. Petersburg, 1863.

*Zhitiia sviatykh, na russkom iazyke izlozhennyia po rukovodstvu Chet'ikh-Minei sv. Dimitriia Rostovskago.* 13 vols. 1905. Reprint, Kozelsk: Vvedenskaia Optina Pustyn', 1993.

*Zhurnaly i protokoly zasedanii Vysochaishe uchrezhdennago Predsobornago prisutstviia.* 4 vols. St. Petersburg, 1906.

*Znachenie krestnykh khodov.* Perm, 1908.

*Znamenie milosti Bozhiei: chudesnyia istseleniia ikonoiu Bozhiei Materi "Vsekh Skorbiashchikh Radosti."* St. Petersburg, 1896.

Zol'nikova, N. D. *Sibirskaia prikhodskaia obshchina v XVIII veke.* Novosibirsk, 1990.

Zosimovskii, Z. V. *Est' li u russkikh religiia?* St. Petersburg, 1911.

Zubarev, E. *O sviatykh khramakh.* Kostroma, 1914.

# INDEX